YOWAMUSHI PEDAL

WATARU WATANABE

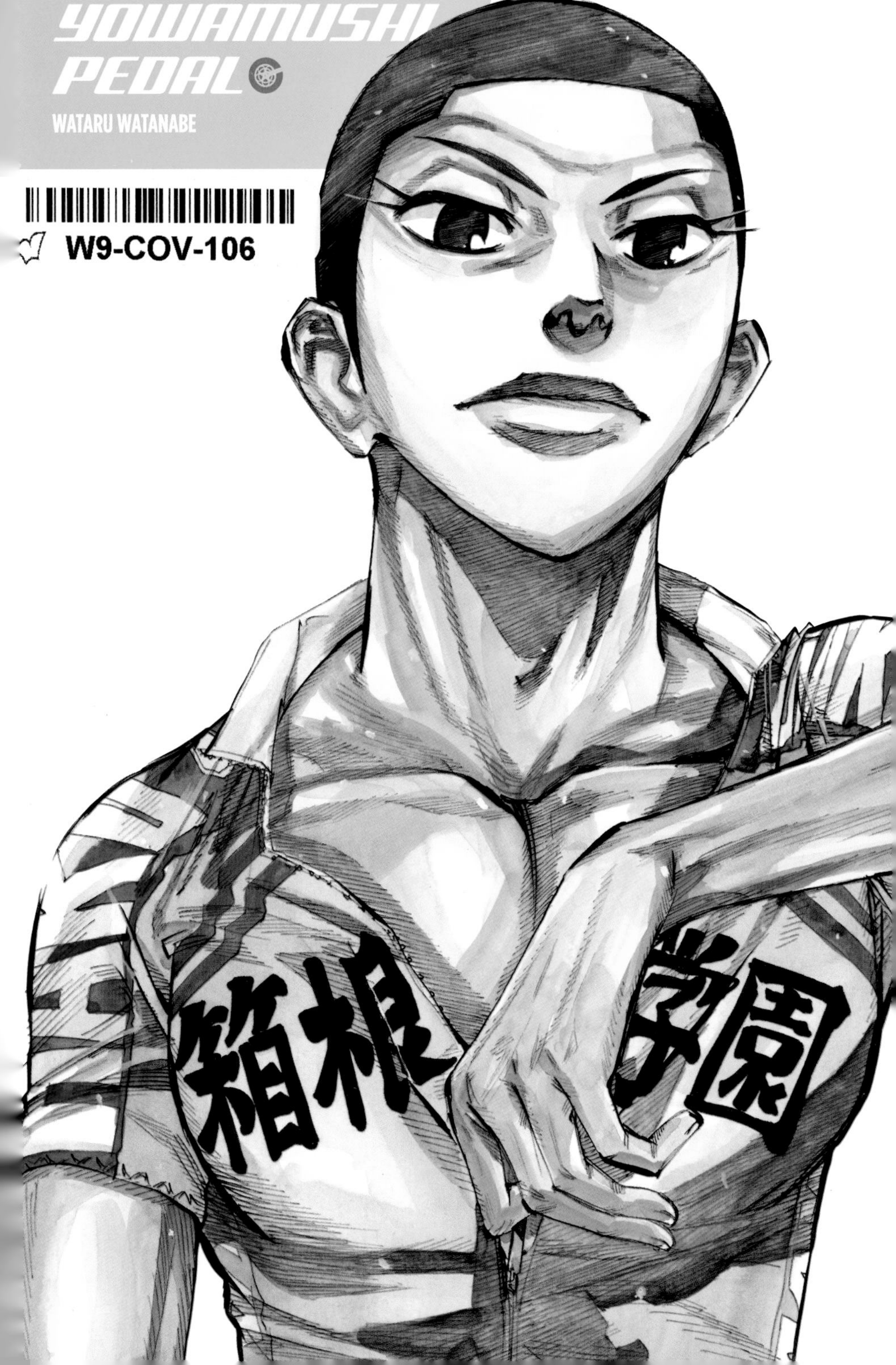
箱根学園

YOWAMUSHI PEDAL

5

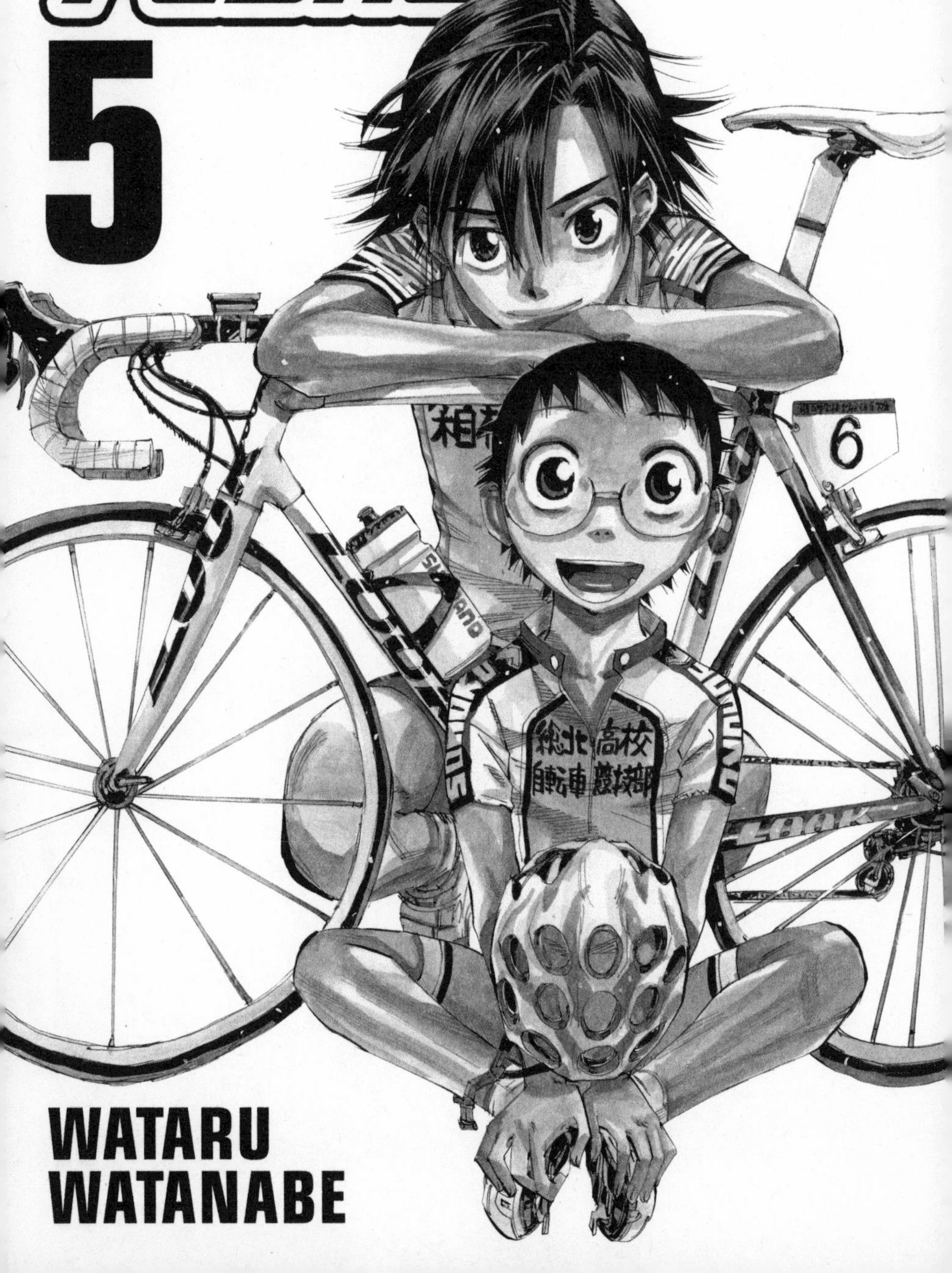
6
総北高校
自転車競技部
LOOK

WATARU WATANABE

YOWAMUSHI PEDAL

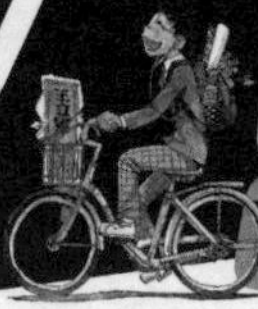

STORY & CHARACTER INTRODUCTION

The 1,000-kilometer training camp ride to determine the members of Sohoku's Inter-High team has ended. Despite completing the course, Sakamichi had given up hope of competing in the Inter-High due to his lack of bicycling experience, technical skill, and general know-how compared to the other members. However, team captain Kinjou judges Sakamichi's "ability to accomplish the unexpected" as a worthy trait to bring to the race and officially makes him a member of the Sohoku Inter-High team. The pressure of living up to the team jersey seems to be too much for Sakamichi at first, but Kinjou explains to him that what truly makes an "ultimate team" is its members' ability to support one another. This reminds Sakamichi of what he is capable of doing for his team, thus reassuring him. With a unified front, Sohoku looks toward the Inter-High, ready to compete!!

As they make their preparations, Kinjou thinks back to the previous summer's Inter-High, when he had battled one-on-one against Fukutomi of Hakone Academy. The fateful incident that occurred between them that day is finally coming to light...

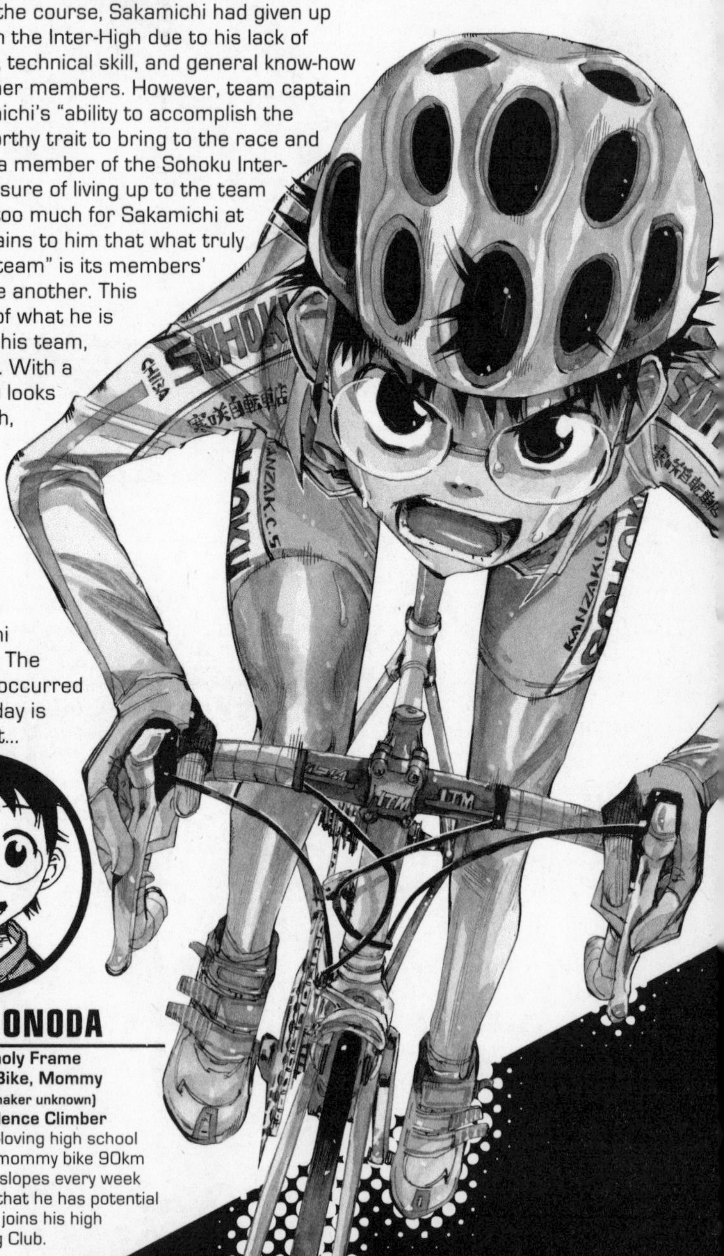

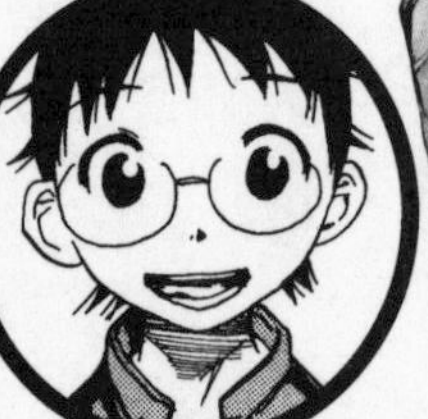

SAKAMICHI ONODA

Preferred Bike: **Chromoly Frame Road Bike, Mommy Bike** (maker unknown)

Cycling Style: **High Cadence Climber**

Sakamichi is an anime-loving high school student who rides his mommy bike 90km round trip up extreme slopes every week to visit Akiba. Hearing that he has potential as a cyclist, Sakamichi joins his high school's Bicycle Racing Club.

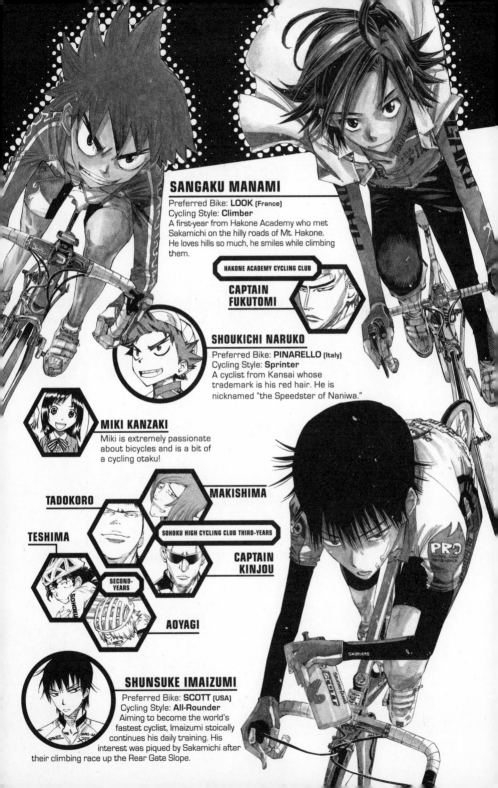

SANGAKU MANAMI

Preferred Bike: **LOOK** (France)
Cycling Style: **Climber**
A first-year from Hakone Academy who met
Sakamichi on the hilly roads of Mt. Hakone.
He loves hills so much, he smiles while climbing
them.

HAKONE ACADEMY CYCLING CLUB

CAPTAIN FUKUTOMI

SHOUKICHI NARUKO

Preferred Bike: **PINARELLO** (Italy)
Cycling Style: **Sprinter**
A cyclist from Kansai whose
trademark is his red hair. He is
nicknamed "the Speedster of Naniwa."

MIKI KANZAKI

Miki is extremely passionate
about bicycles and is a bit of
a cycling otaku!

TADOKORO

MAKISHIMA

TESHIMA

SOHOKU HIGH CYCLING CLUB THIRD-YEARS

SECOND-YEARS

CAPTAIN KINJOU

AOYAGI

SHUNSUKE IMAIZUMI

Preferred Bike: **SCOTT** (USA)
Cycling Style: **All-Rounder**
Aiming to become the world's
fastest cyclist, Imaizumi stoically
continues his daily training. His
interest was piqued by Sakamichi after
their climbing race up the Rear Gate Slope.

VOL.5 YOWAMUSHI PEDAL CONTENTS

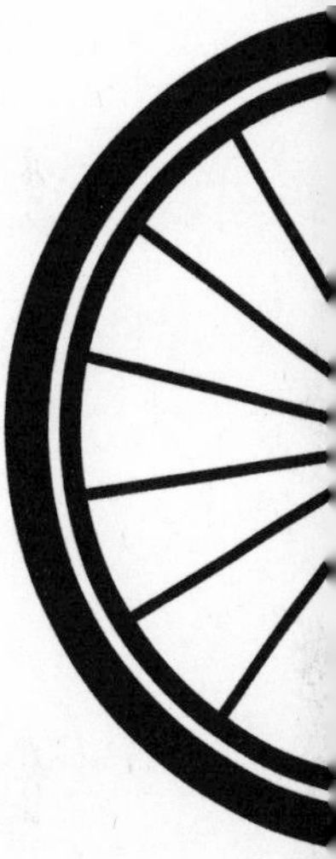

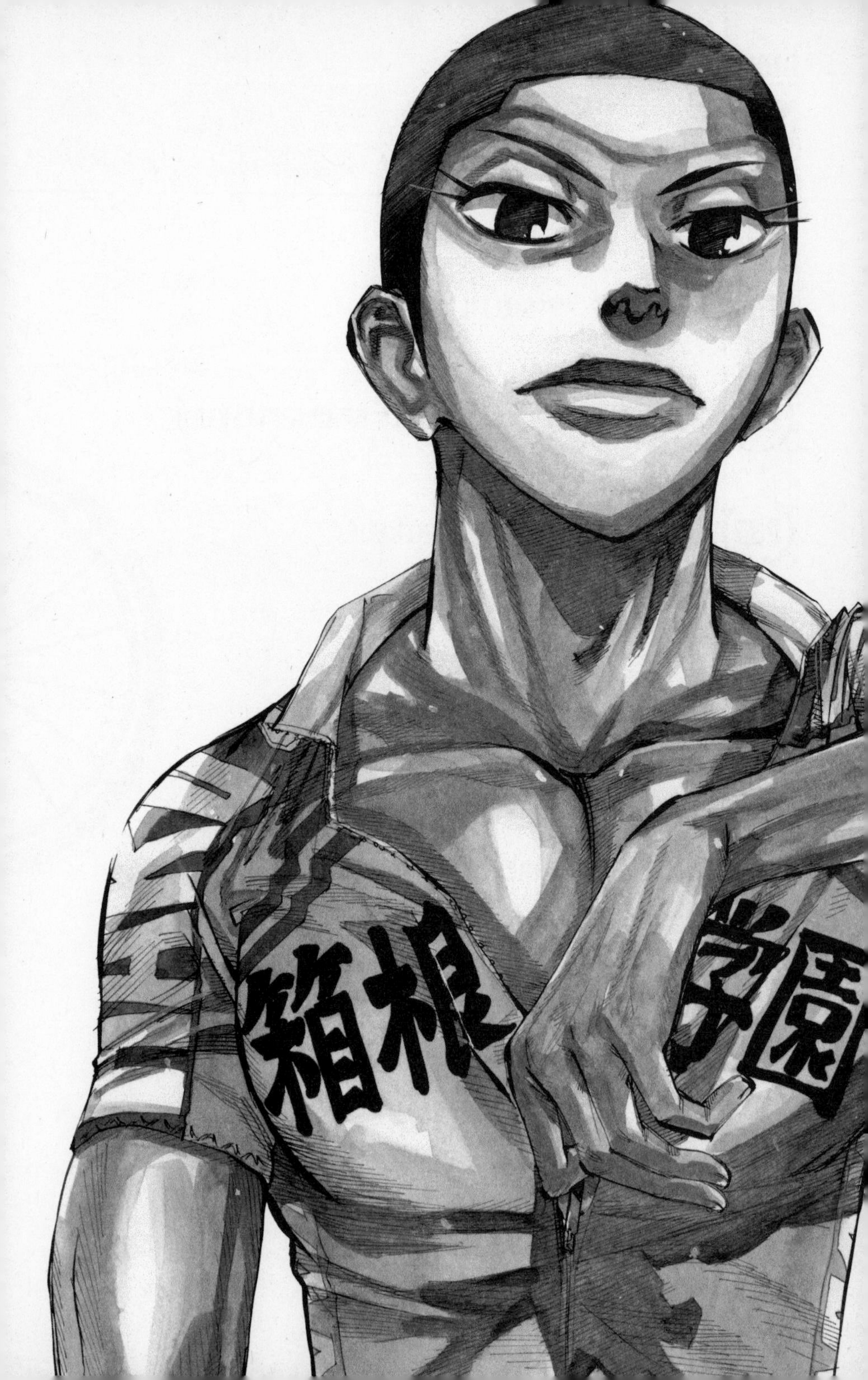
箱根学園

RIDE.70 CRUSHING DEFEAT

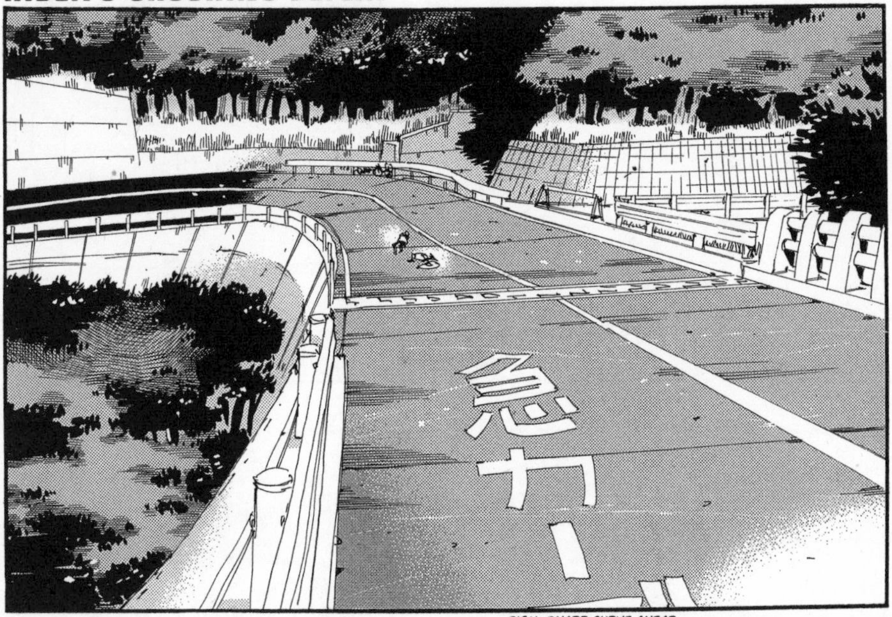

SIGN: SHARP CURVE AHEAD

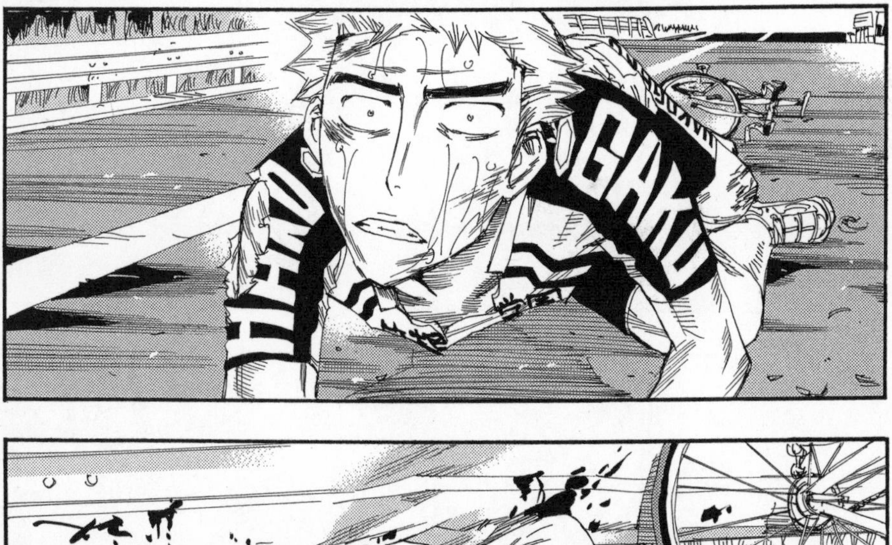

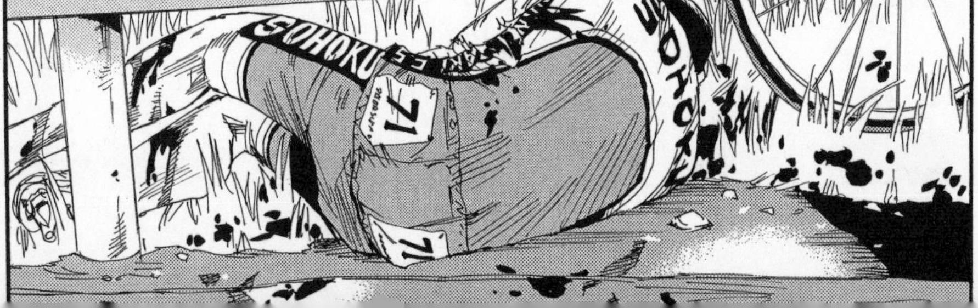

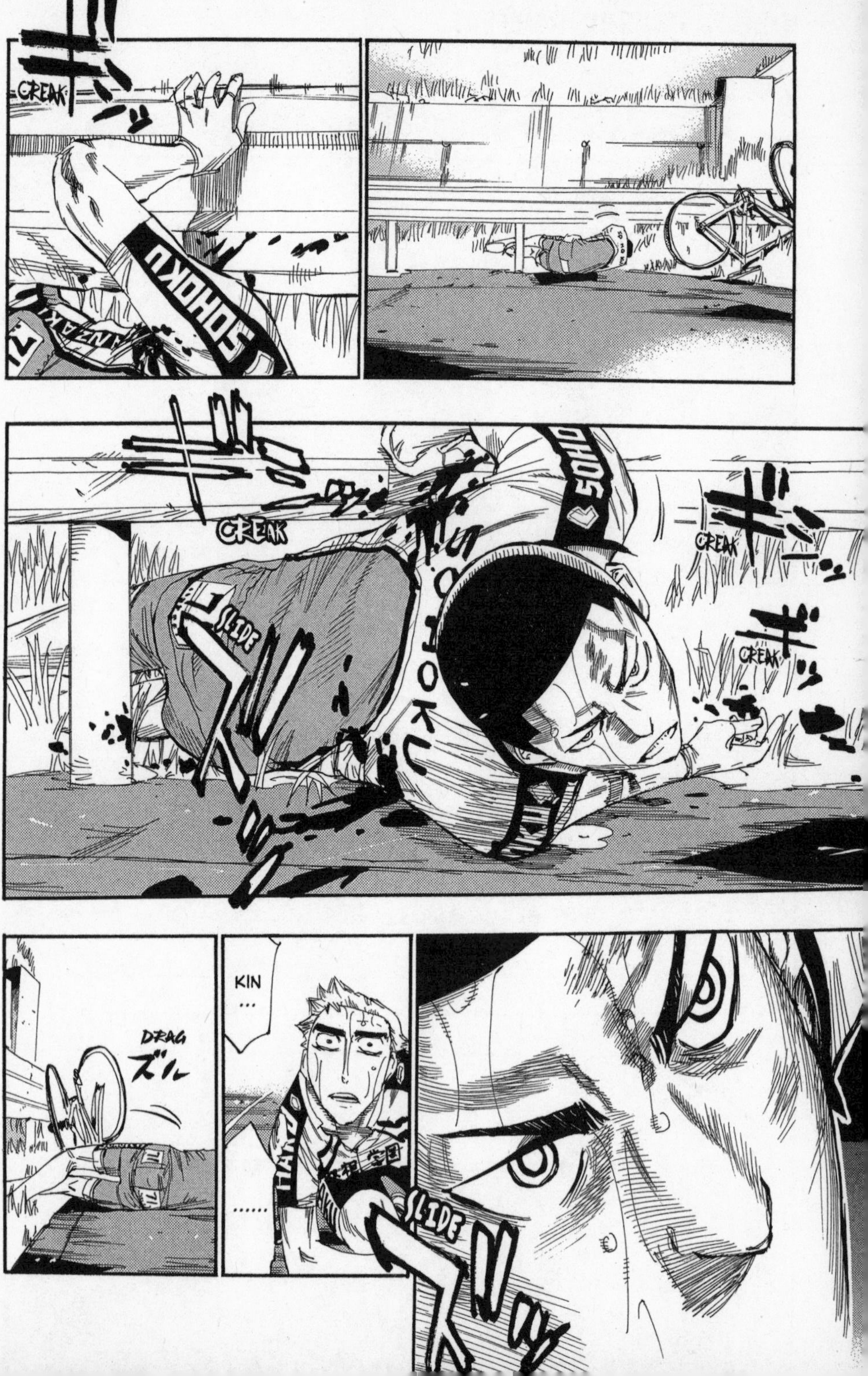

CREAK
CREAK
CREAK
CREAK
SLIDE
SLIDE
KIN
...
......
DRAG
ズル

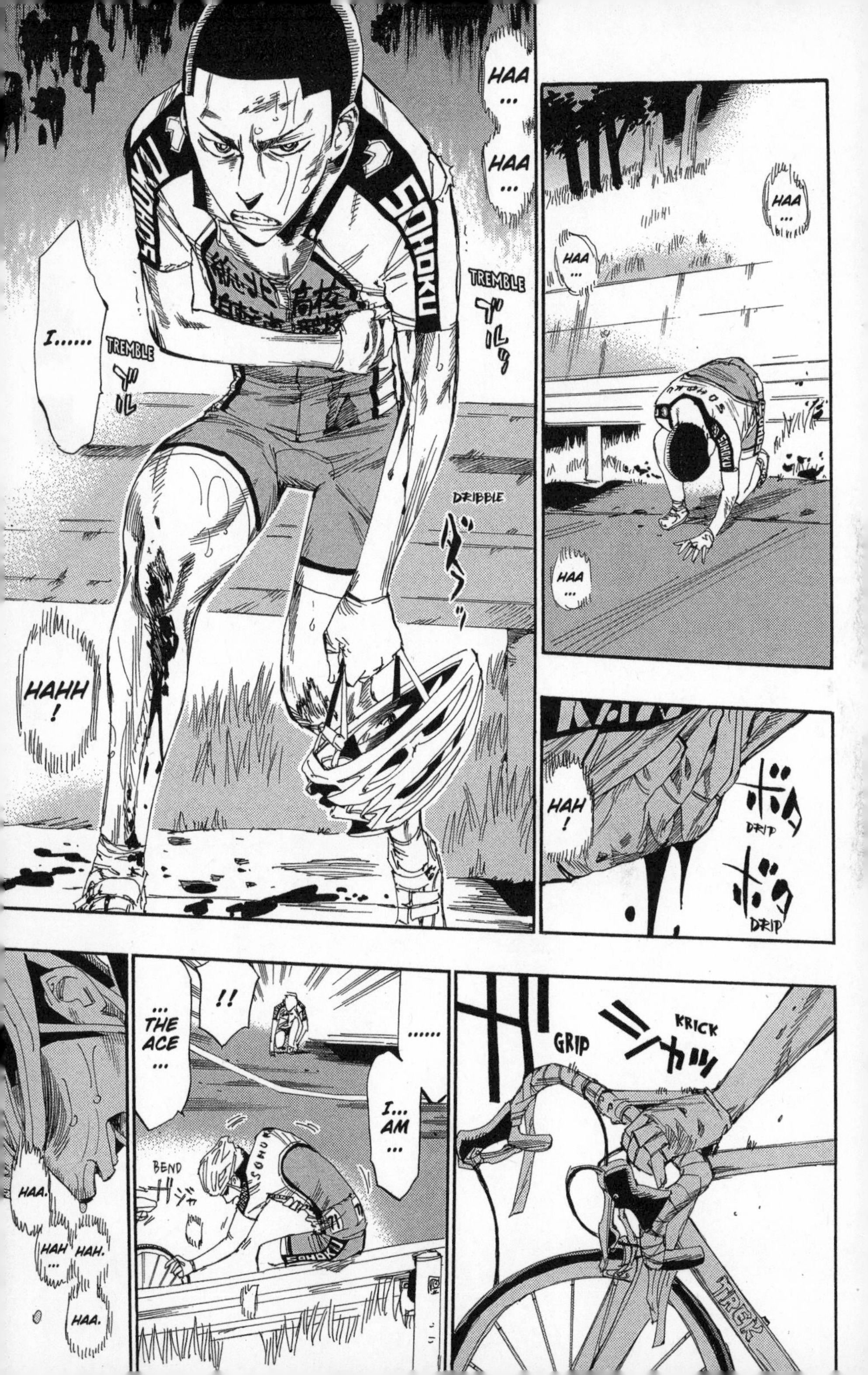
HAA ...
HAA ...
HAA ...
HAH !
DRIP
DRIP
HAA ...
HAA ...
TREMBLE
TREMBLE
I......
DRIBBLE
HAHH !
KRICK
GRIP
!!
......
I... AM ...
... THE ACE ...
BEND
HAA.
HAH ...
HAH.
HAA.

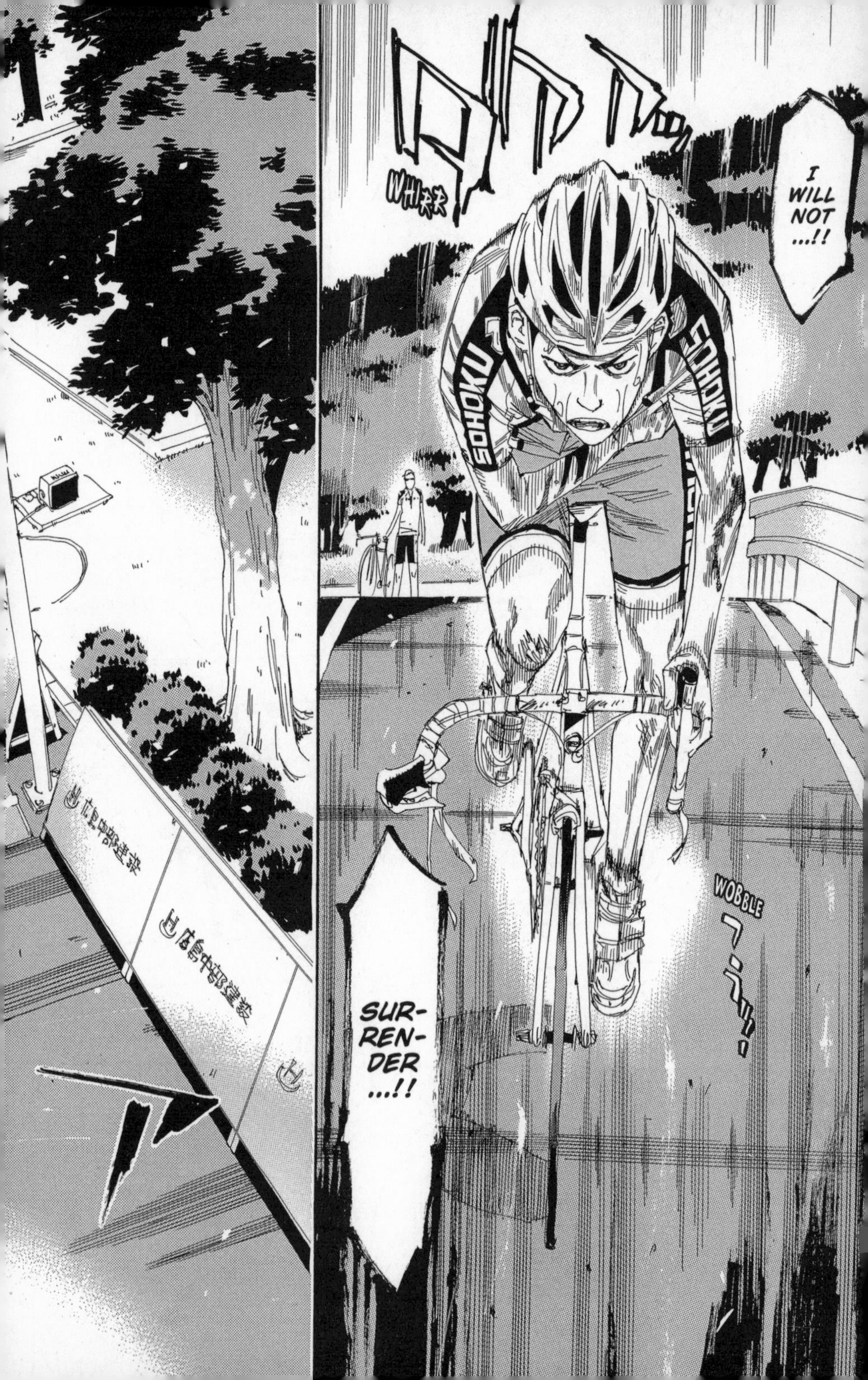
I WILL NOT ...!!
WHIRR
WOBBLE
SUR-REN-DER ...!!

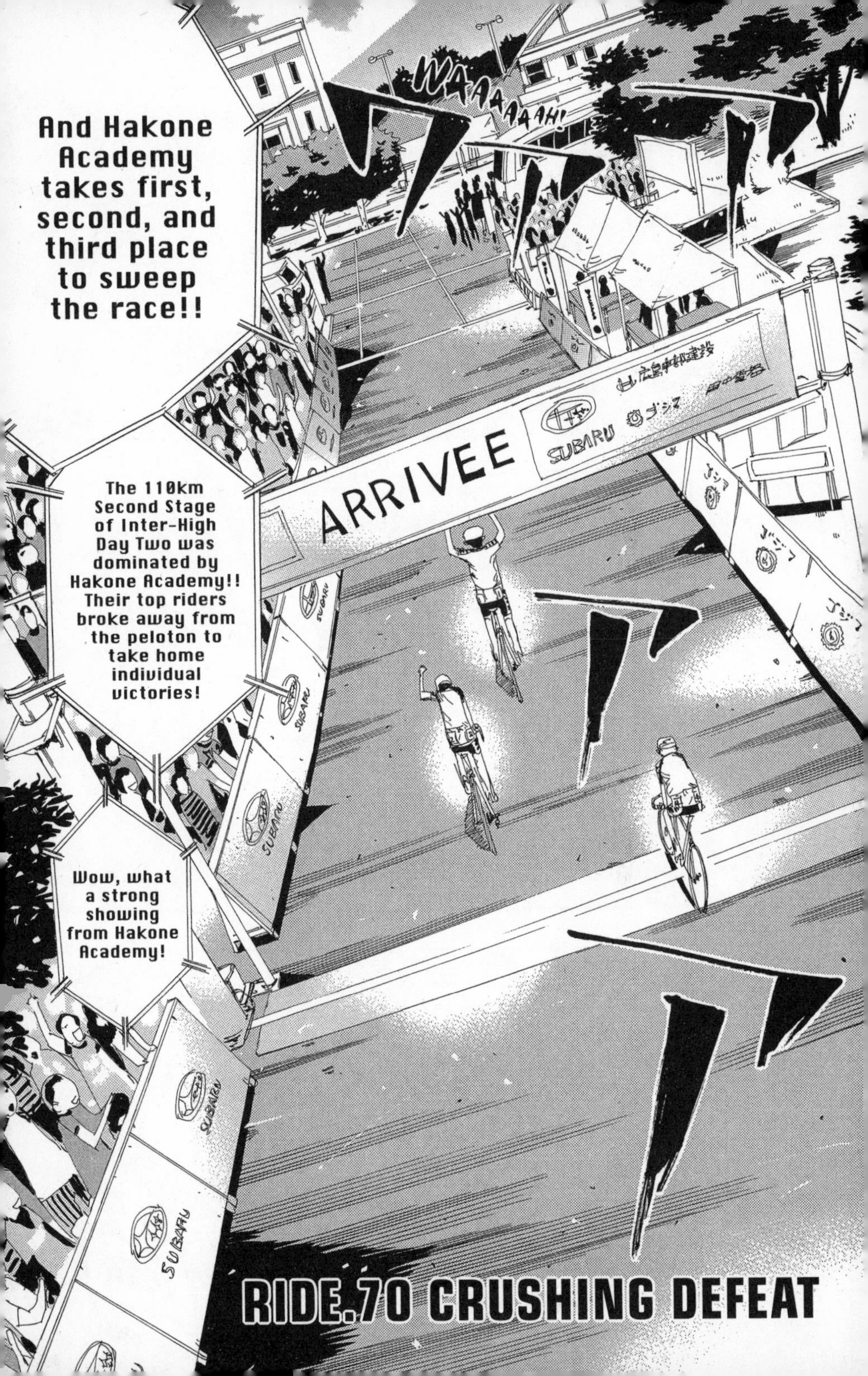
WAAAAAAAH!
And Hakone Academy takes first, second, and third place to sweep the race!!
The 110km Second Stage of Inter-High Day Two was dominated by Hakone Academy!! Their top riders broke away from the peloton to take home individual victories!
Wow, what a strong showing from Hakone Academy!
ARRIVEE
SUBARU
RIDE.70 CRUSHING DEFEAT

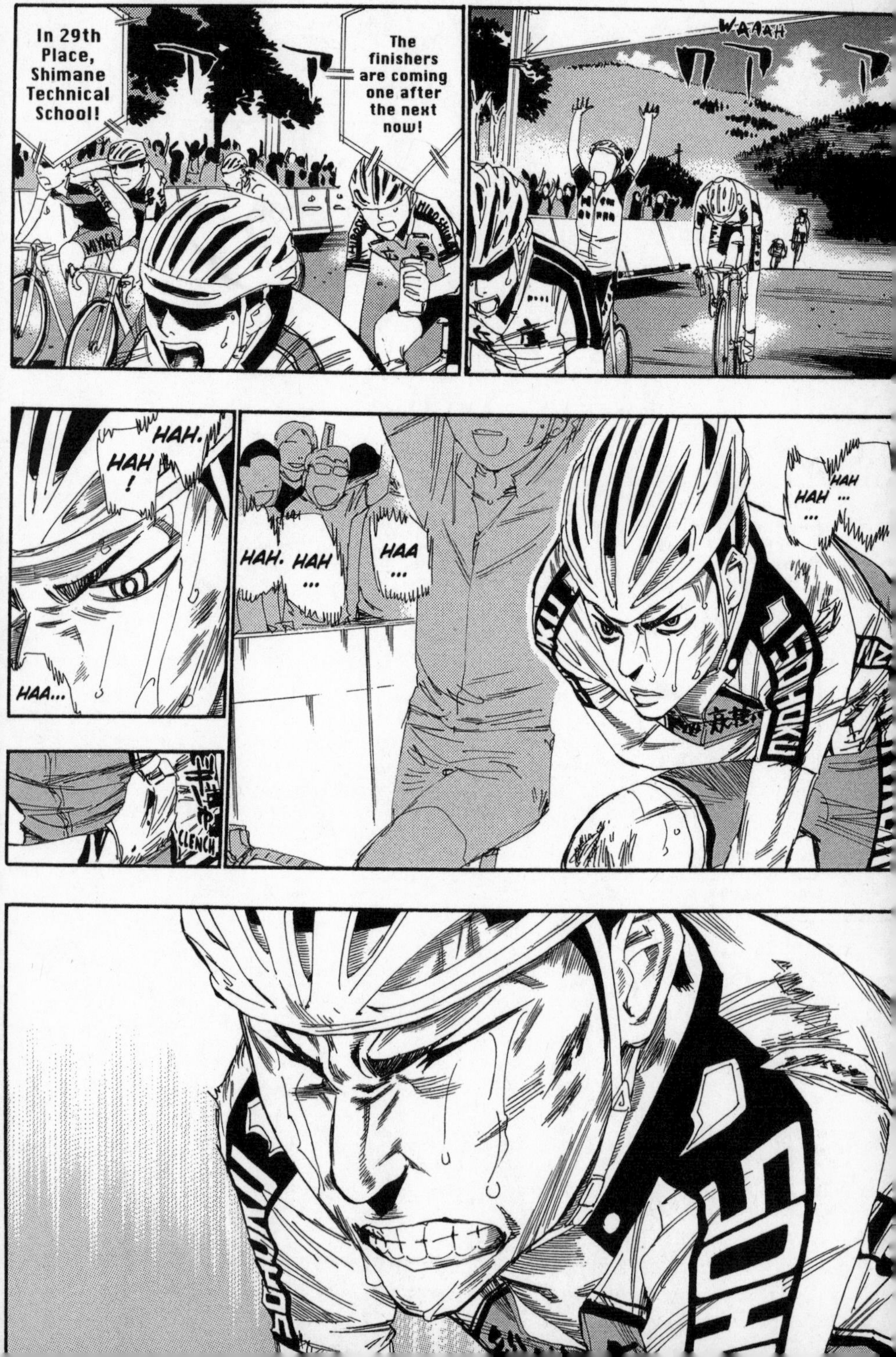
WAAAH
The finishers are coming one after the next now!
In 29th Place, Shimane Technical School!
HAH HAH ... ...
HAA ...
HAH. HAH ...
HAH. HAH!
HAA...
CLENCH

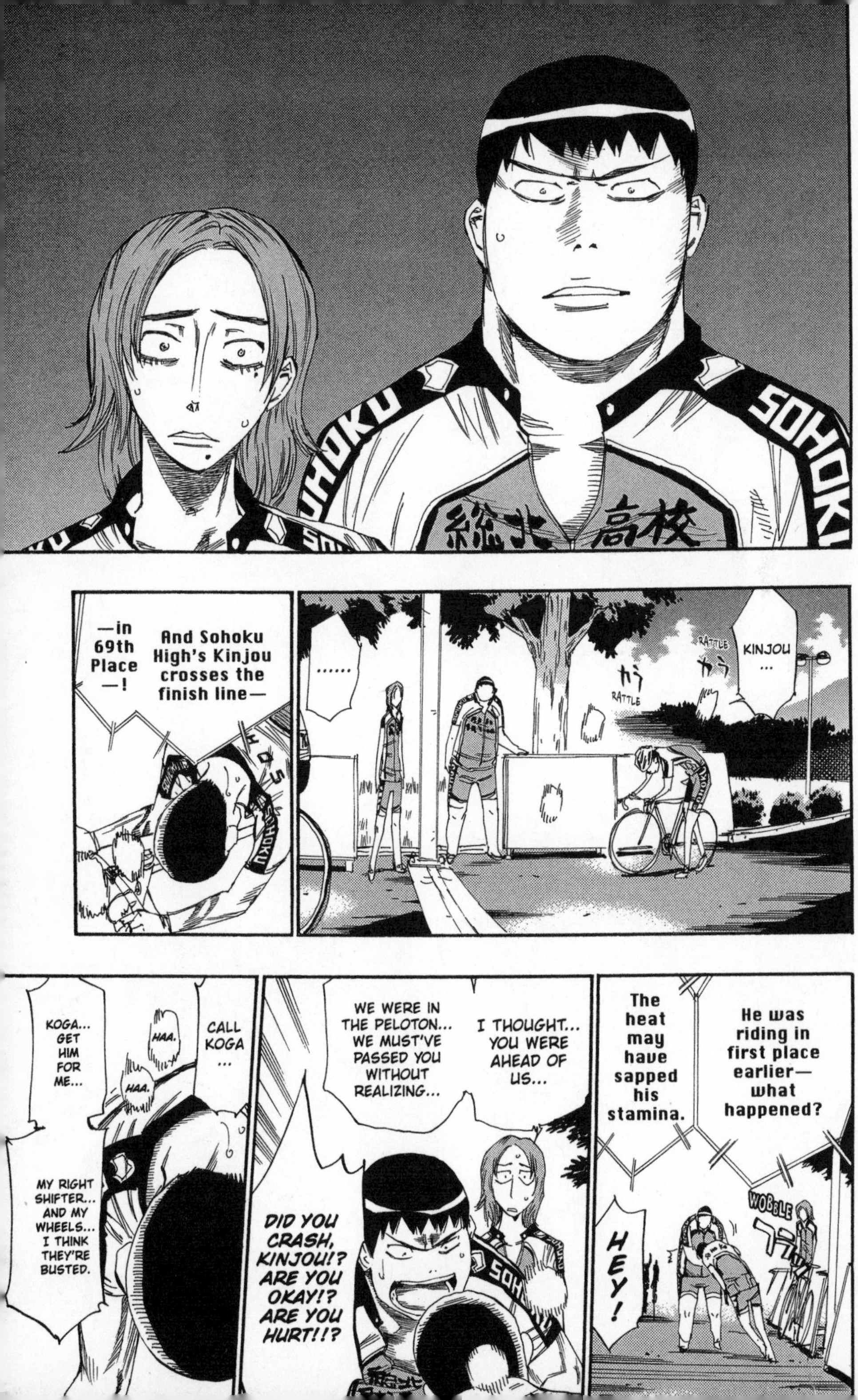
SOHOKU
総北高校
KINJOU ...
RATTLE
カラ
カラ
RATTLE
......
And Sohoku High's Kinjou crosses the finish line—
—in 69th Place—!
He was riding in first place earlier—what happened?
The heat may have sapped his stamina.
HEY!
WOBBLE
I THOUGHT... YOU WERE AHEAD OF US...
WE WERE IN THE PELOTON... WE MUST'VE PASSED YOU WITHOUT REALIZING...
DID YOU CRASH, KINJOU!? ARE YOU OKAY!? ARE YOU HURT!!?
CALL KOGA ...
HAA.
KOGA... GET HIM FOR ME...
HAA.
MY RIGHT SHIFTER... AND MY WHEELS... I THINK THEY'RE BUSTED.

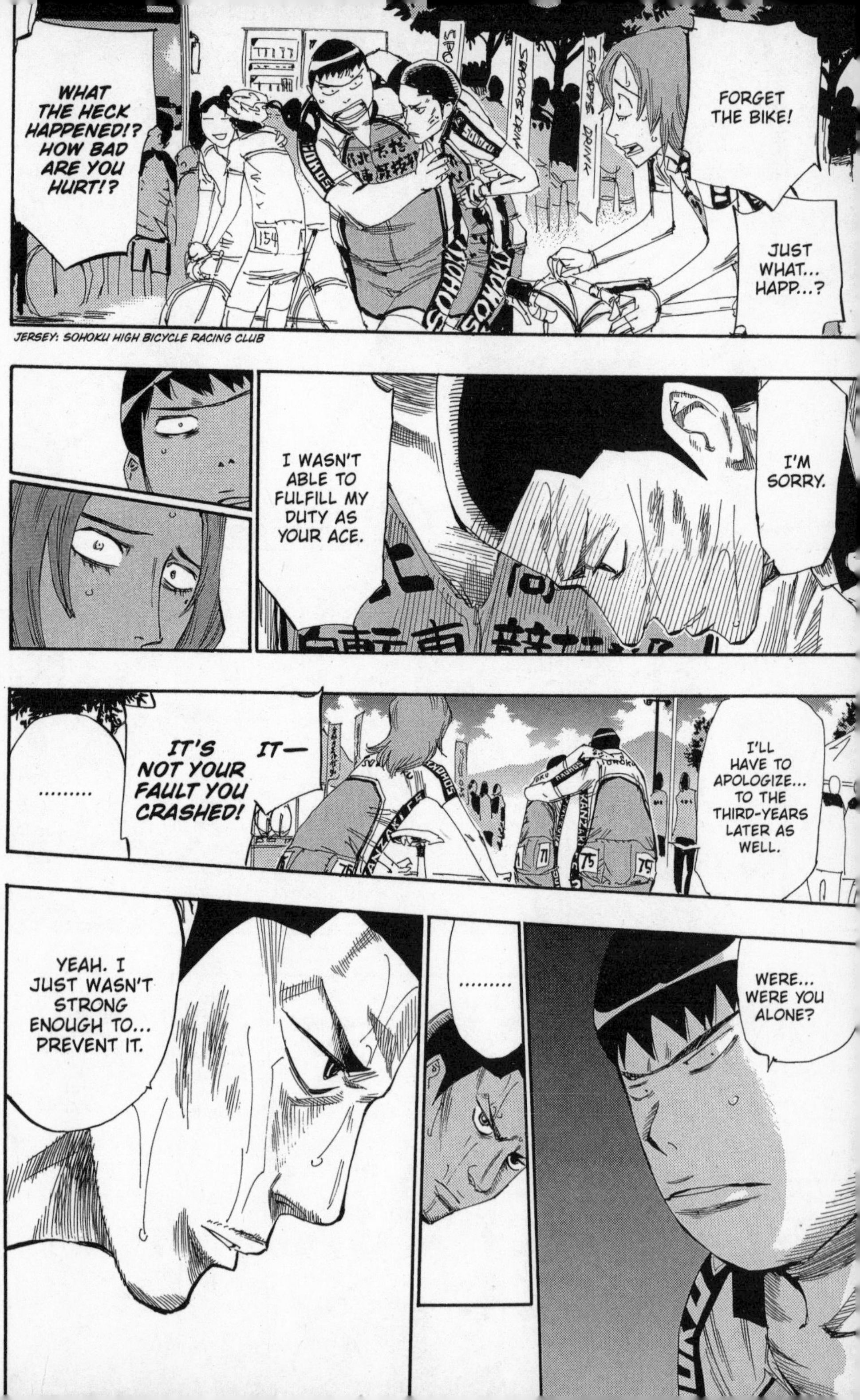
FORGET THE BIKE!
JUST WHAT... HAPP...?
WHAT THE HECK HAPPENED!? HOW BAD ARE YOU HURT!?
JERSEY: SOHOKU HIGH BICYCLE RACING CLUB
I'M SORRY.
I WASN'T ABLE TO FULFILL MY DUTY AS YOUR ACE.
I'LL HAVE TO APOLOGIZE... TO THE THIRD-YEARS LATER AS WELL.
IT— IT'S NOT YOUR FAULT YOU CRASHED!
....
WERE... WERE YOU ALONE?
....
YEAH. I JUST WASN'T STRONG ENOUGH TO... PREVENT IT.

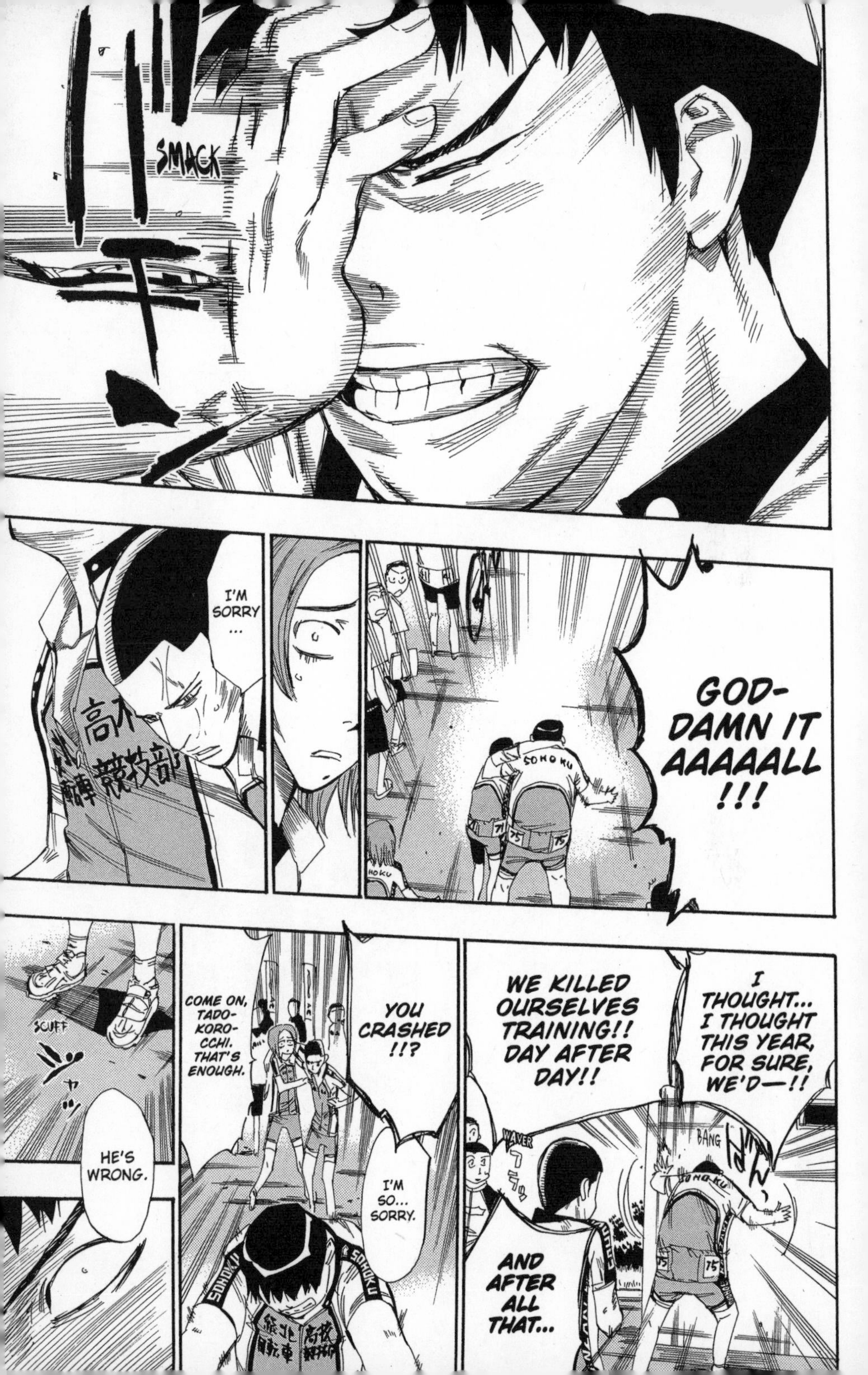
SMACK
GOD-DAMN IT AAAAALL!!!
I'M SORRY...
I THOUGHT... I THOUGHT THIS YEAR, FOR SURE, WE'D—!!
BANG
WE KILLED OURSELVES TRAINING!! DAY AFTER DAY!!
WAVER
AND AFTER ALL THAT...
YOU CRASHED!!?
COME ON, TADO-KORO-CCHI. THAT'S ENOUGH.
I'M SO... SORRY.
SCUFF
HE'S WRONG.

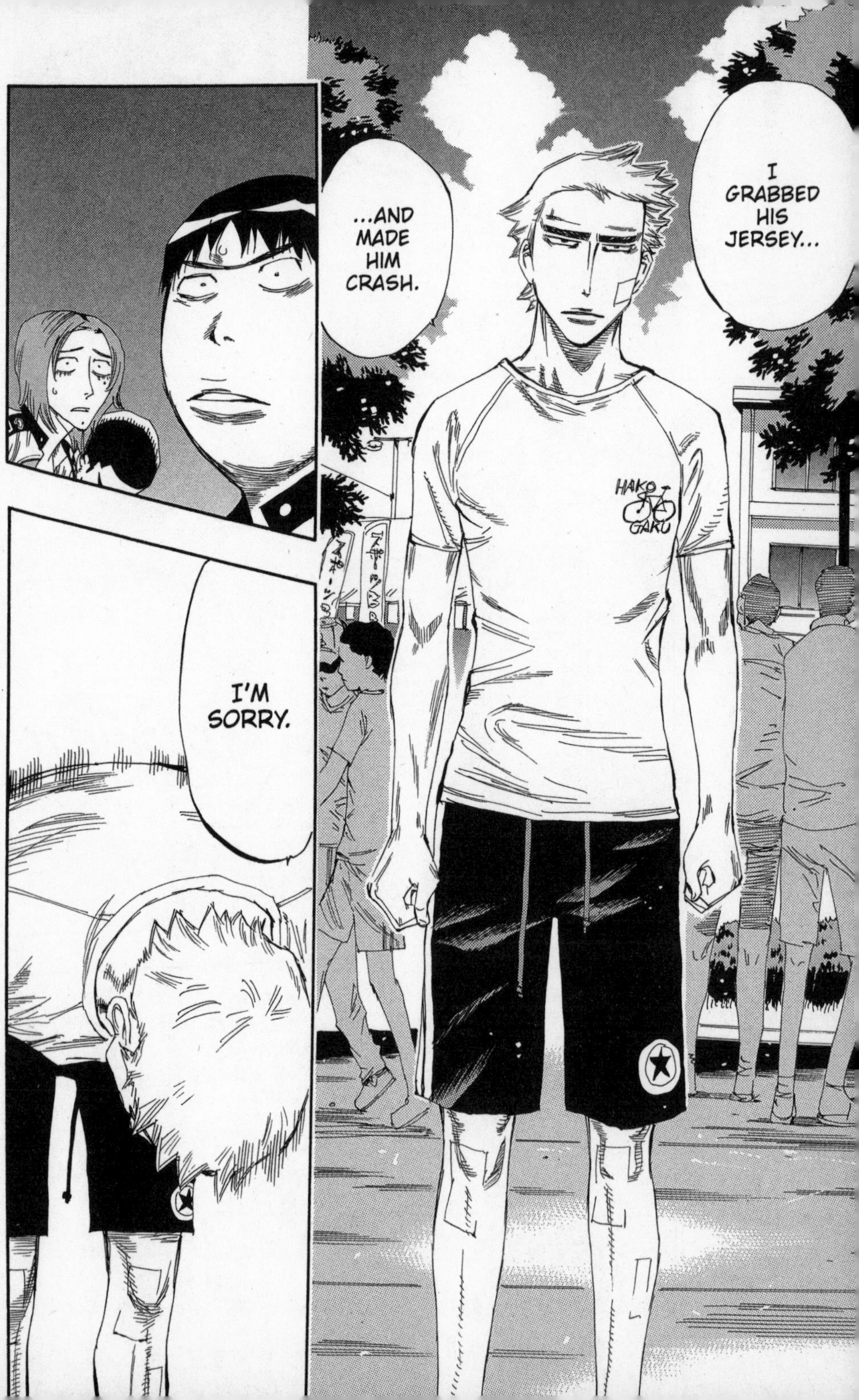
I GRABBED HIS JERSEY...
...AND MADE HIM CRASH.
HAKO GAKU
I'M SORRY.

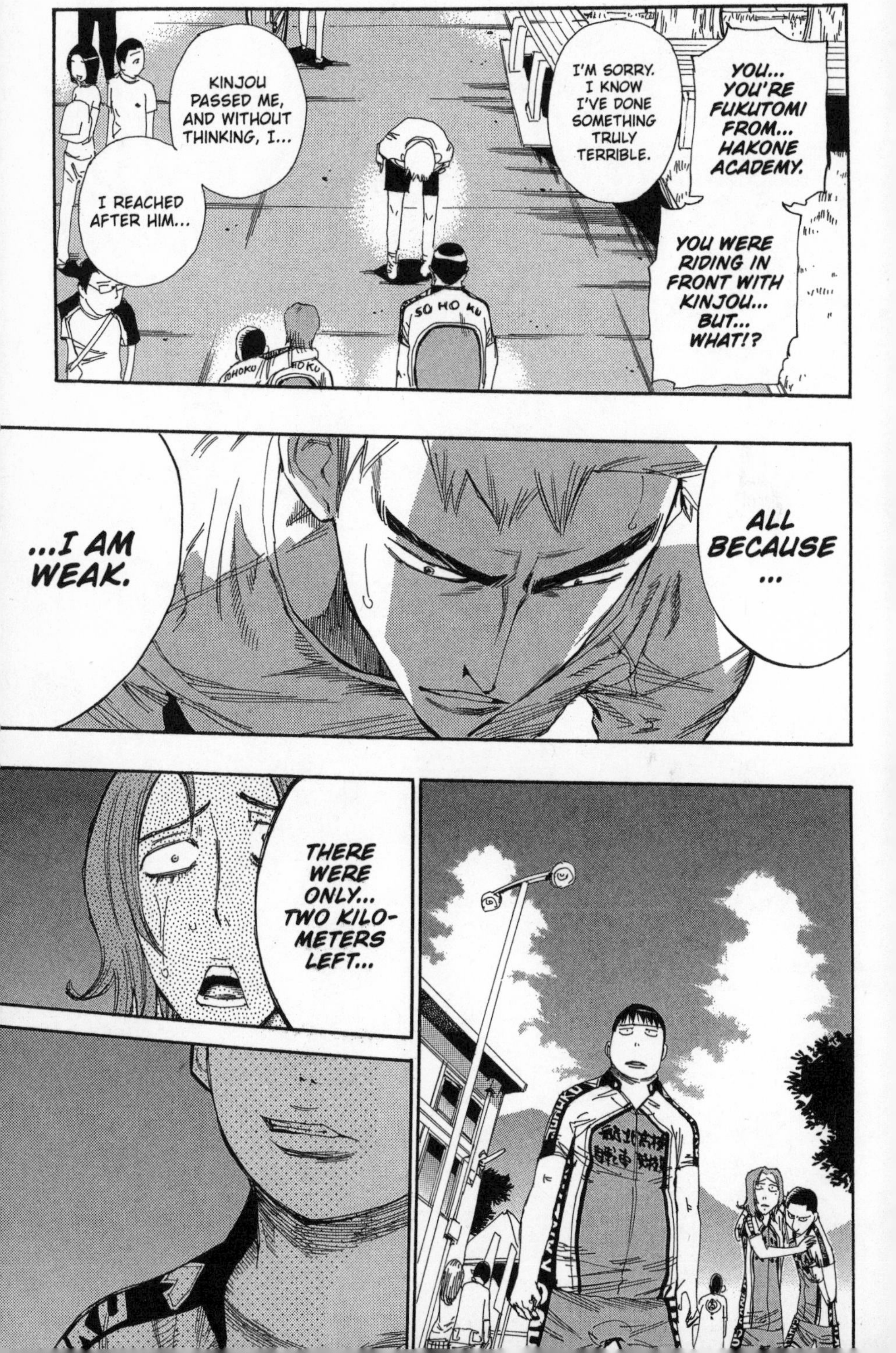
YOU... YOU'RE FUKUTOMI FROM... HAKONE ACADEMY.
YOU WERE RIDING IN FRONT WITH KINJOU... BUT... WHAT!?
I'M SORRY. I KNOW I'VE DONE SOMETHING TRULY TERRIBLE.
KINJOU PASSED ME, AND WITHOUT THINKING, I...
I REACHED AFTER HIM...
ALL BECAUSE ...
...I AM WEAK.
THERE WERE ONLY... TWO KILO-METERS LEFT...

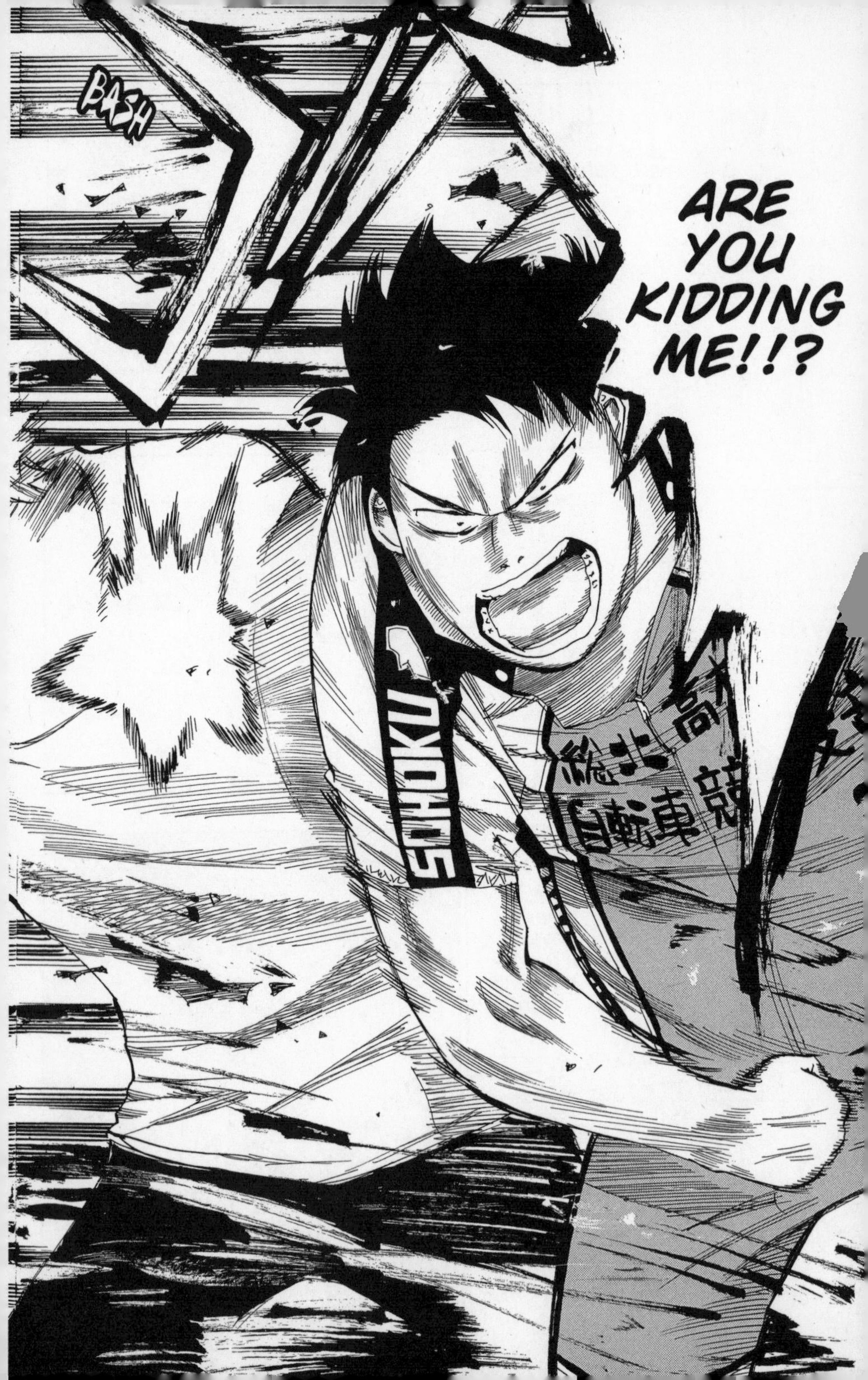
ARE YOU KIDDING ME!!?
BASH
SOHOKU
総北高
自転車競

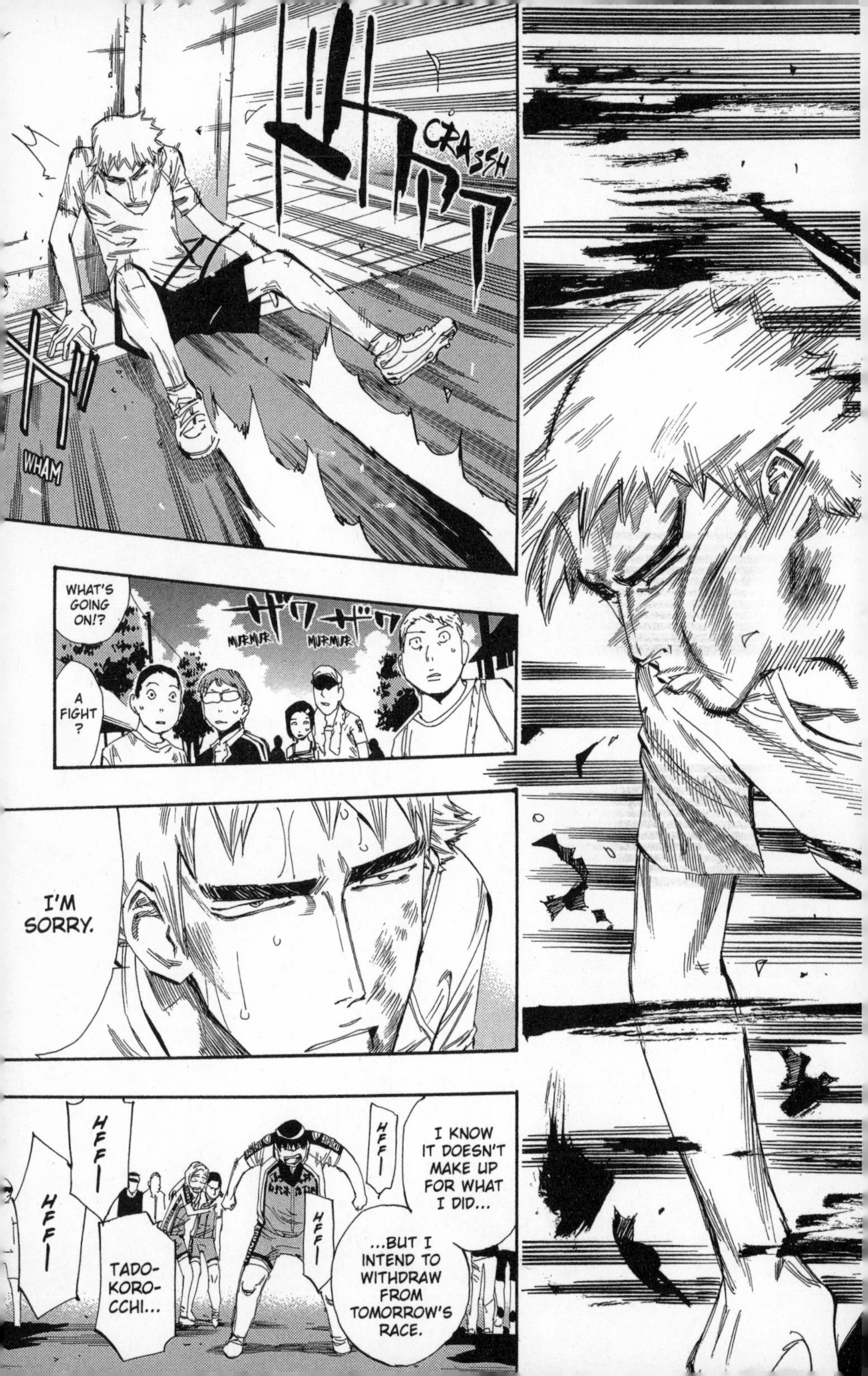

CRASSH
WHAM
MURMUR
MURMUR
WHAT'S GOING ON!?
A FIGHT?
I'M SORRY.
I KNOW IT DOESN'T MAKE UP FOR WHAT I DID...
HFF
...BUT I INTEND TO WITHDRAW FROM TOMORROW'S RACE.
HFF
HFF
HFF
TADO-KORO-CCHI...

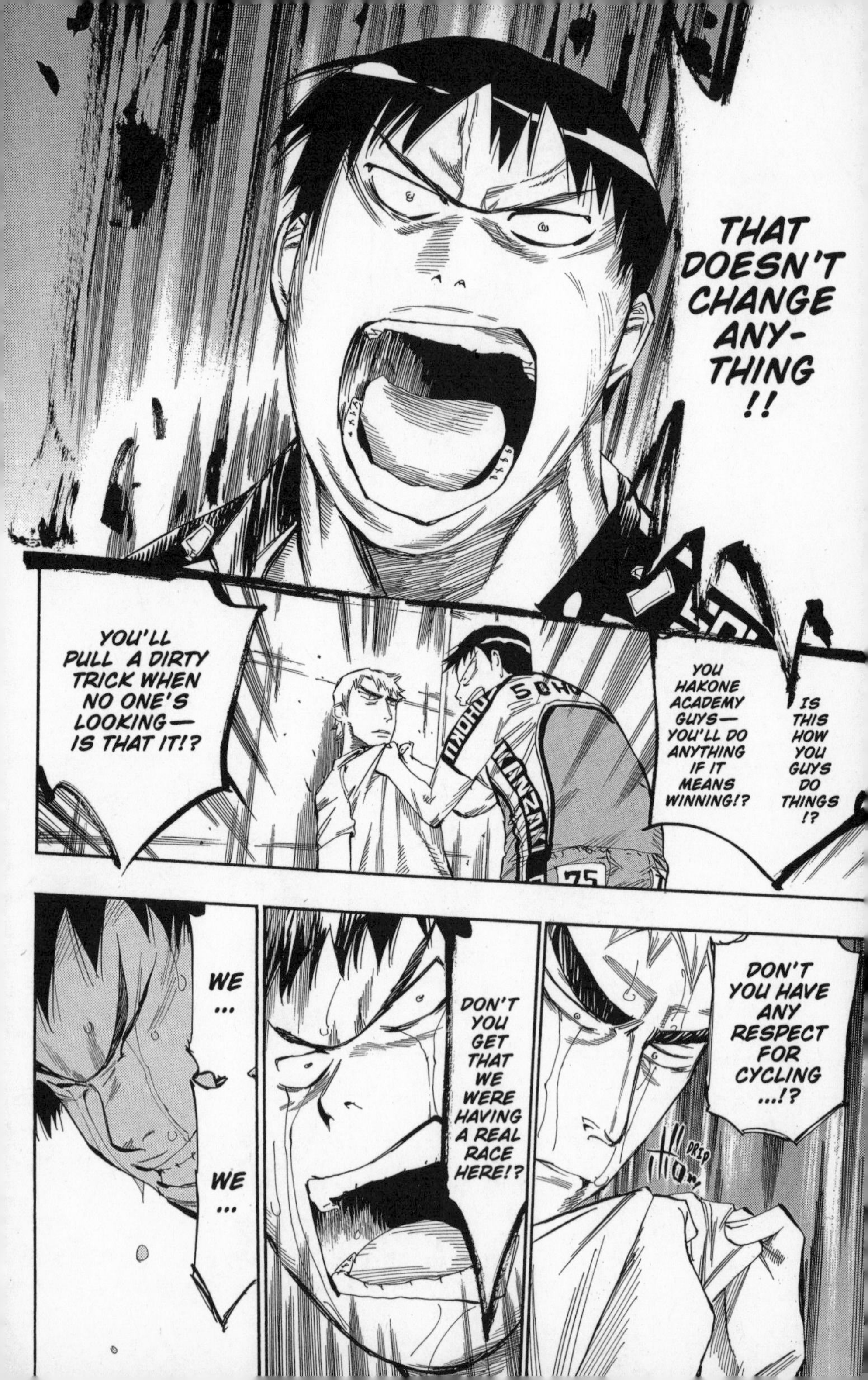
THAT DOESN'T CHANGE ANYTHING!!
IS THIS HOW YOU GUYS DO THINGS!?
YOU HAKONE ACADEMY GUYS—YOU'LL DO ANYTHING IF IT MEANS WINNING!?
YOU'LL PULL A DIRTY TRICK WHEN NO ONE'S LOOKING—IS THAT IT!?
DON'T YOU HAVE ANY RESPECT FOR CYCLING ...!?
DRIP
DON'T YOU GET THAT WE WERE HAVING A REAL RACE HERE!?
WE ...
WE ...

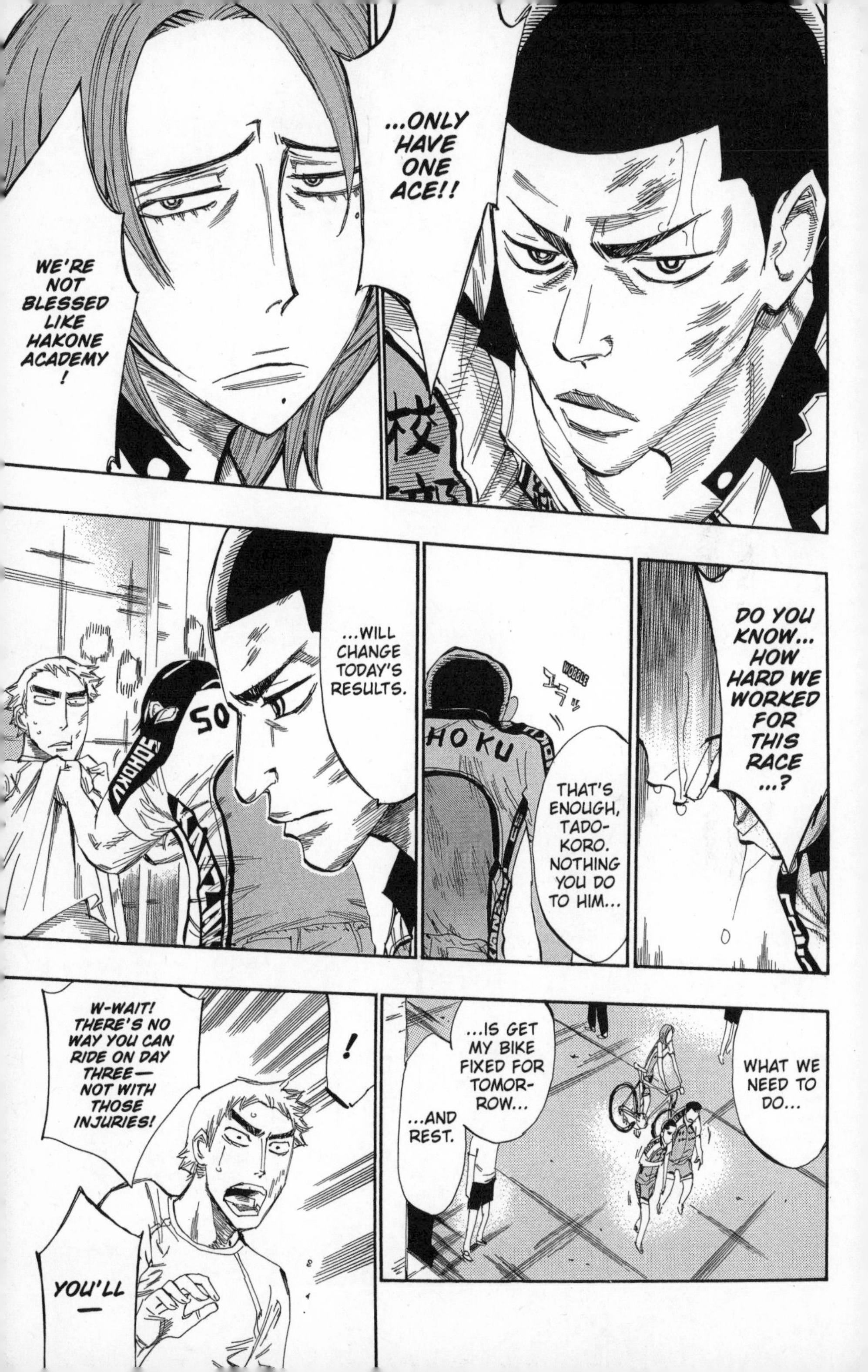
...ONLY HAVE ONE ACE!!
WE'RE NOT BLESSED LIKE HAKONE ACADEMY!
DO YOU KNOW... HOW HARD WE WORKED FOR THIS RACE...?
WOBBLE
THAT'S ENOUGH, TADOKORO. NOTHING YOU DO TO HIM...
...WILL CHANGE TODAY'S RESULTS.
WHAT WE NEED TO DO...
...IS GET MY BIKE FIXED FOR TOMORROW...
...AND REST.
!
W-WAIT! THERE'S NO WAY YOU CAN RIDE ON DAY THREE—NOT WITH THOSE INJURIES!
YOU'LL—

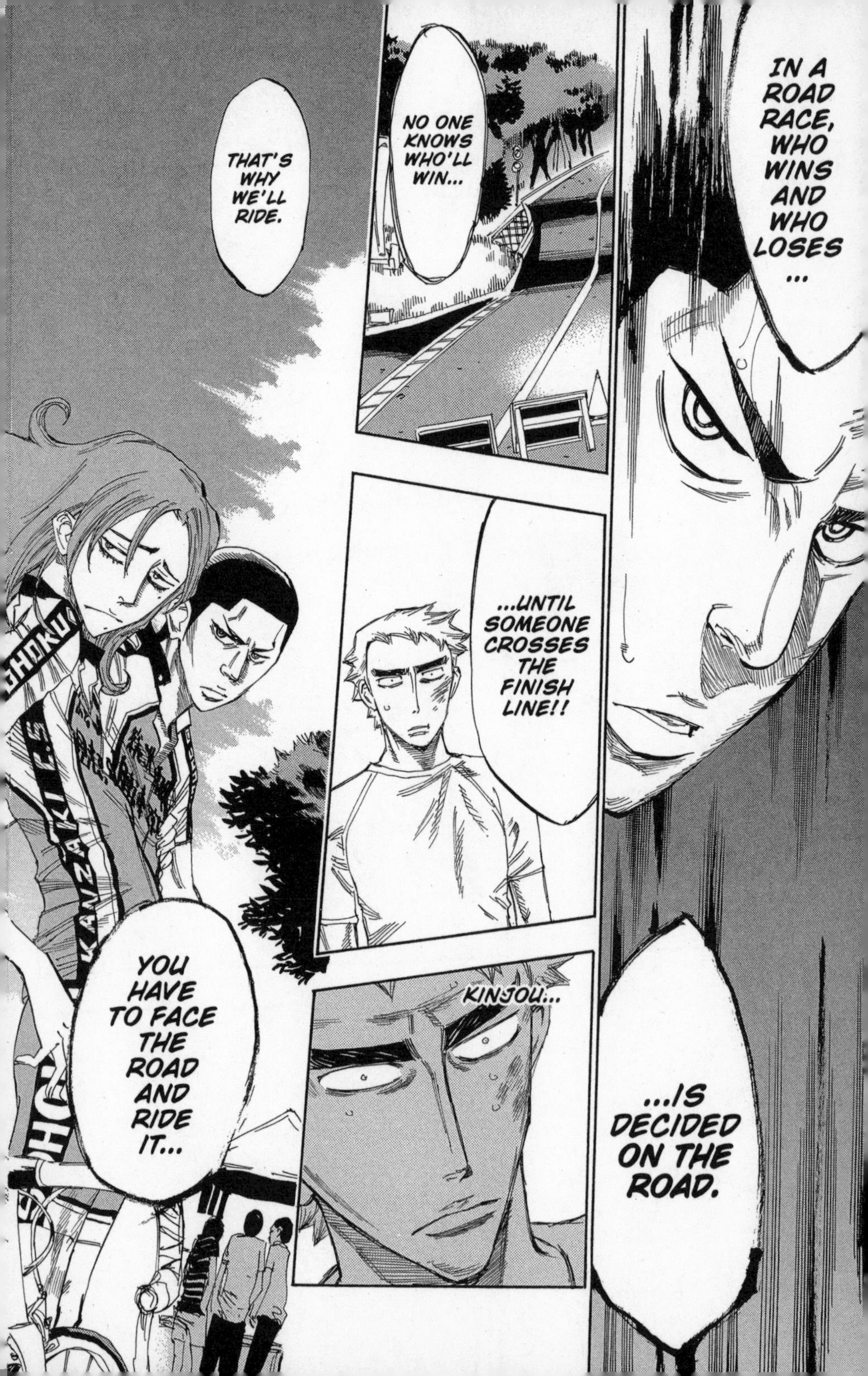
IN A ROAD RACE, WHO WINS AND WHO LOSES ...
...IS DECIDED ON THE ROAD.
NO ONE KNOWS WHO'LL WIN...
...UNTIL SOMEONE CROSSES THE FINISH LINE!!
KINJOU...
THAT'S WHY WE'LL RIDE.
YOU HAVE TO FACE THE ROAD AND RIDE IT...

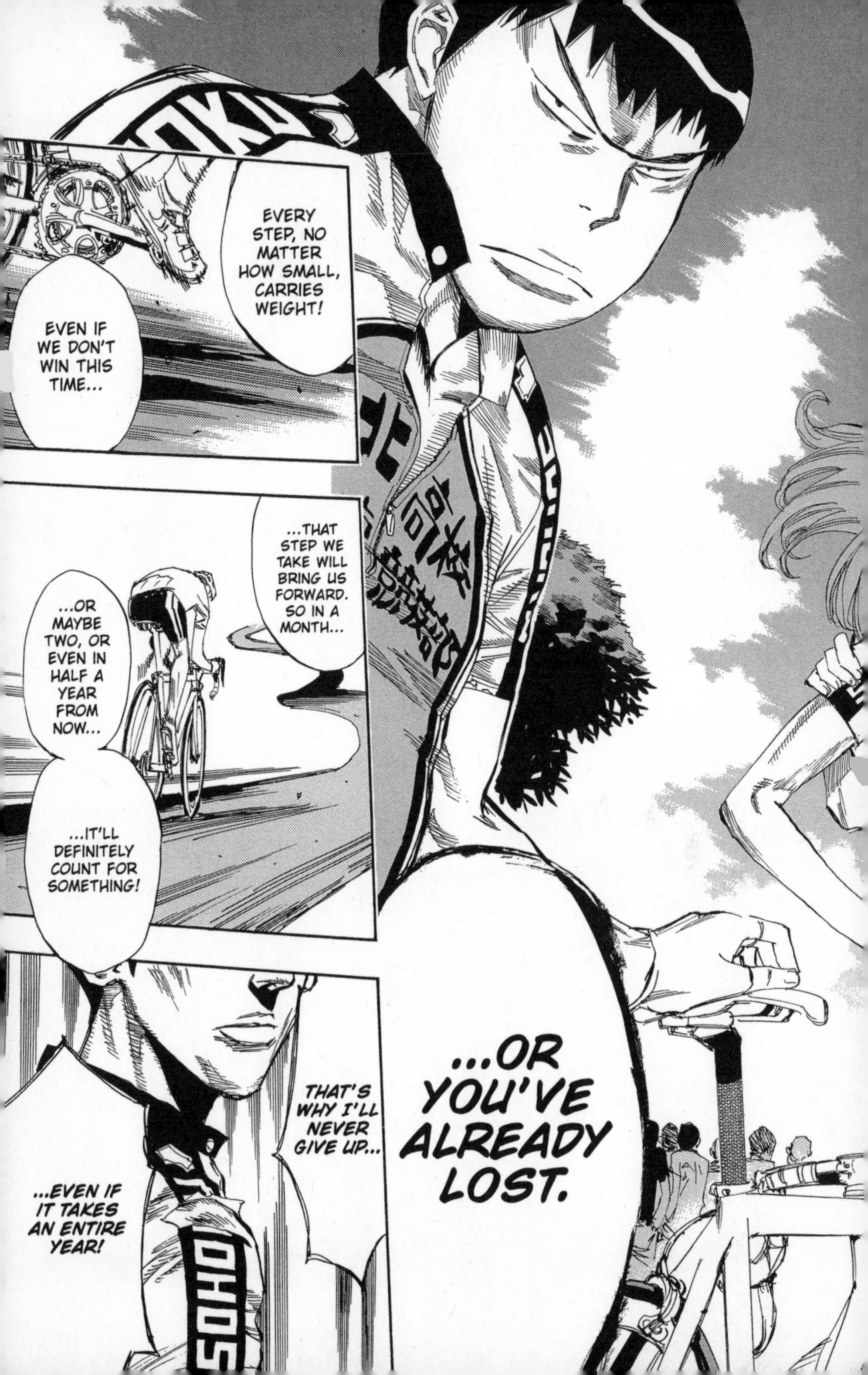
EVERY STEP, NO MATTER HOW SMALL, CARRIES WEIGHT!
EVEN IF WE DON'T WIN THIS TIME...
...THAT STEP WE TAKE WILL BRING US FORWARD. SO IN A MONTH...
...OR MAYBE TWO, OR EVEN IN HALF A YEAR FROM NOW...
...IT'LL DEFINITELY COUNT FOR SOMETHING!
THAT'S WHY I'LL NEVER GIVE UP...
...EVEN IF IT TAKES AN ENTIRE YEAR!
...OR YOU'VE ALREADY LOST.

...TO VICTORY!!

I INTEND TO LEAD SOHOKU...

HIS WILL TO WIN, AS THEIR ACE...!

THOOM

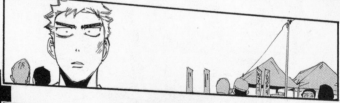

...HIS WILL ....!!

THAT PRESSURE I FELT IN THAT MOMENT...

IT WAS...

HE...IS STRONG...

26

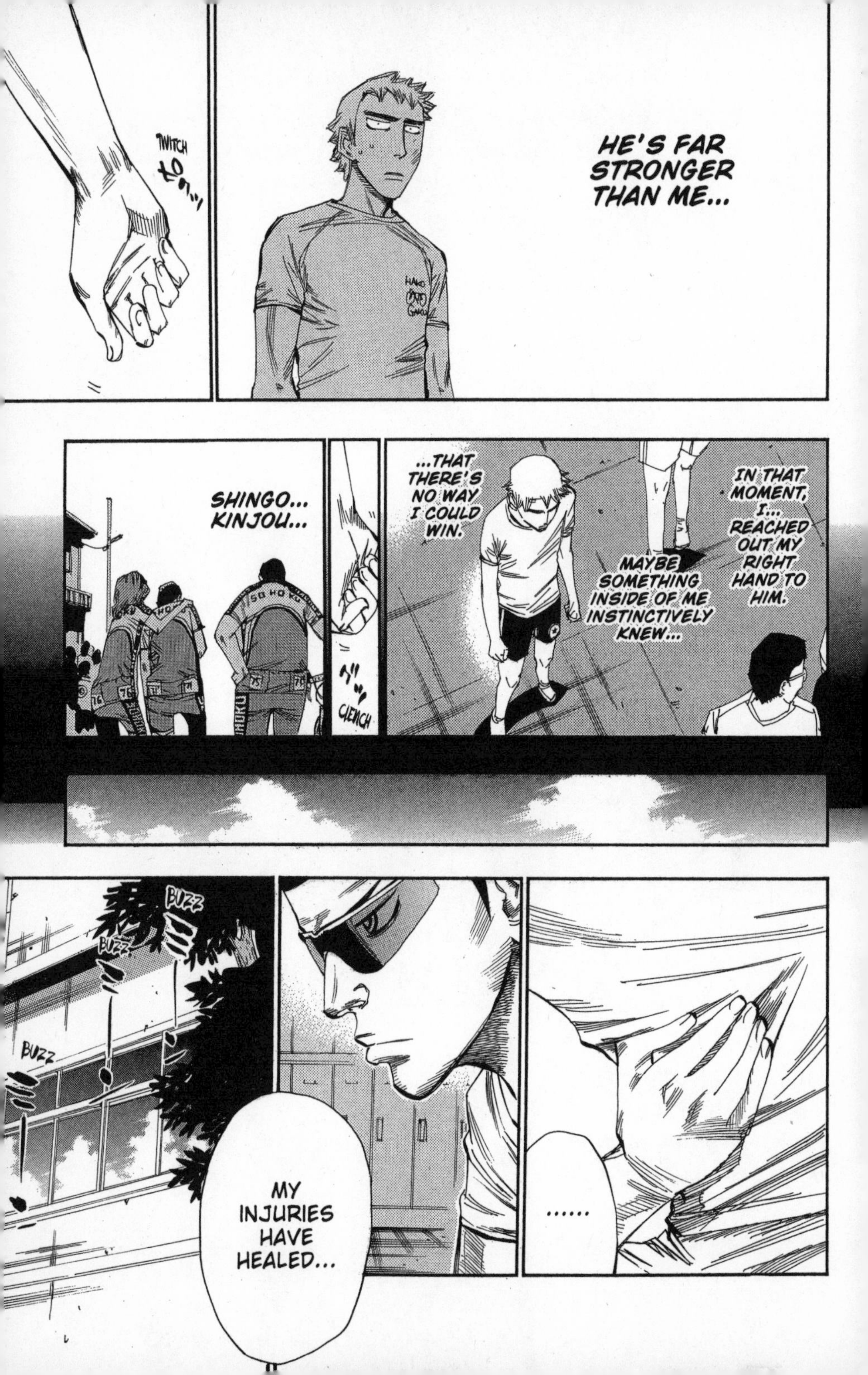
HE'S FAR STRONGER THAN ME...
TWITCH
IN THAT MOMENT, I... REACHED OUT MY RIGHT HAND TO HIM.
MAYBE SOMETHING INSIDE OF ME INSTINCTIVELY KNEW...
...THAT THERE'S NO WAY I COULD WIN.
CLENCH
SHINGO... KINJOU...
......
MY INJURIES HAVE HEALED...
BUZZ
BUZZ
BUZZ

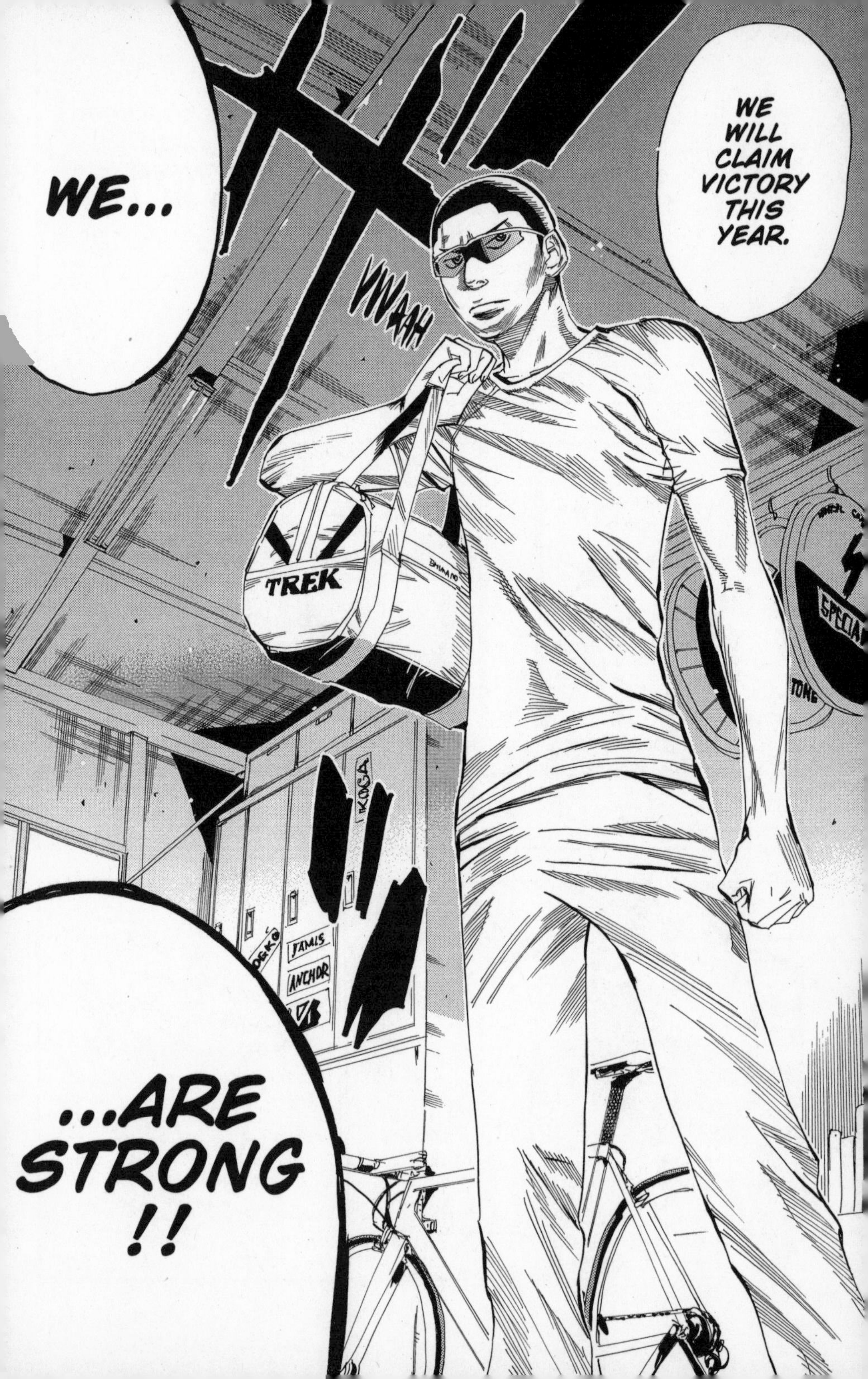
WE WILL CLAIM VICTORY THIS YEAR.
WE...
VWAAH
TREK
KOGA
JAMIS
ANCHOR
...ARE STRONG!!

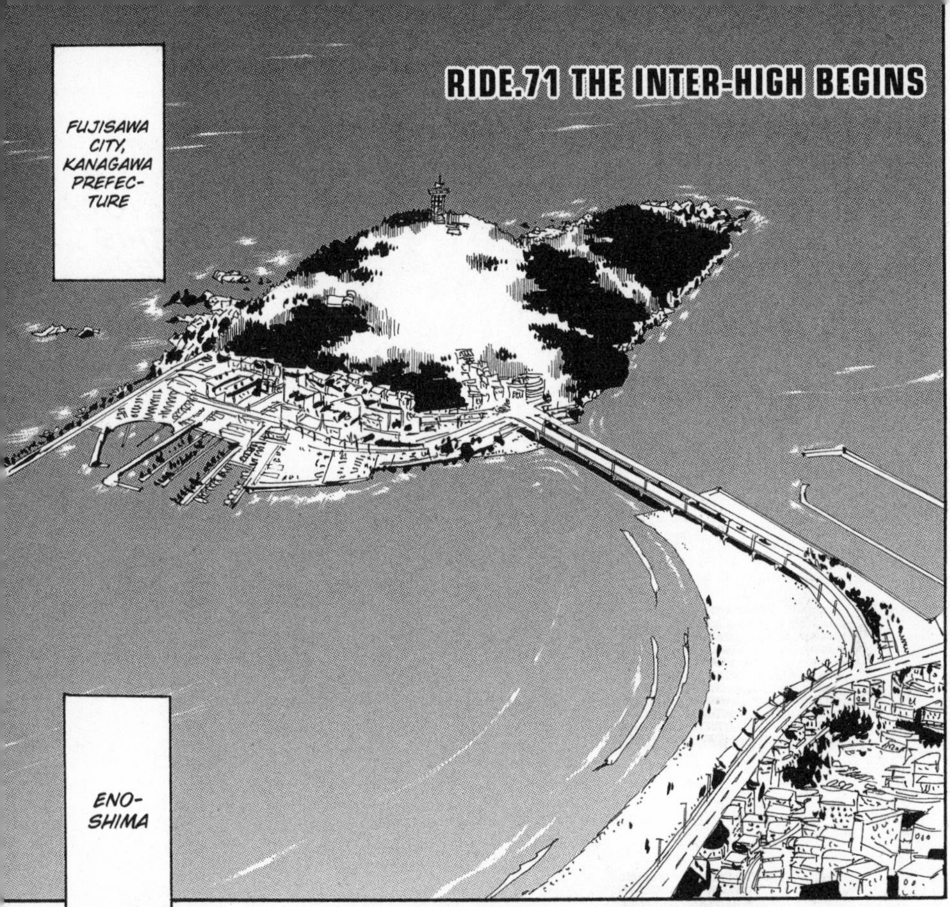
RIDE.71 THE INTER-HIGH BEGINS
FUJISAWA CITY, KANAGAWA PREFECTURE
ENO-SHIMA

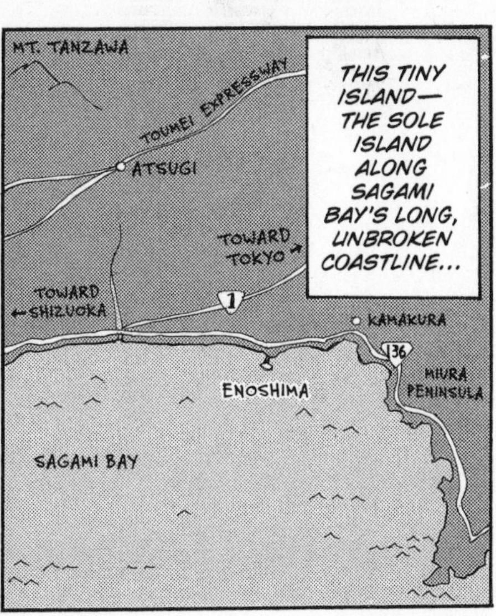
THIS TINY ISLAND—THE SOLE ISLAND ALONG SAGAMI BAY'S LONG, UNBROKEN COASTLINE...
MT. TANZAWA
TOUMEI EXPRESSWAY
ATSUGI
TOWARD TOKYO
TOWARD SHIZUOKA
1
KAMAKURA
136
MIURA PENINSULA
ENOSHIMA
SAGAMI BAY

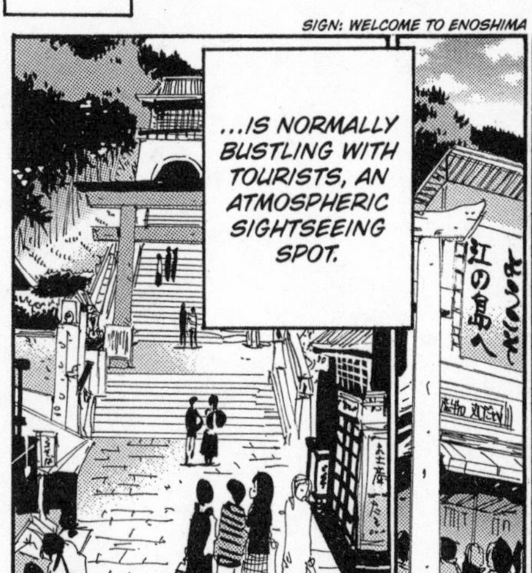
SIGN: WELCOME TO ENOSHIMA
...IS NORMALLY BUSTLING WITH TOURISTS, AN ATMOSPHERIC SIGHTSEEING SPOT.

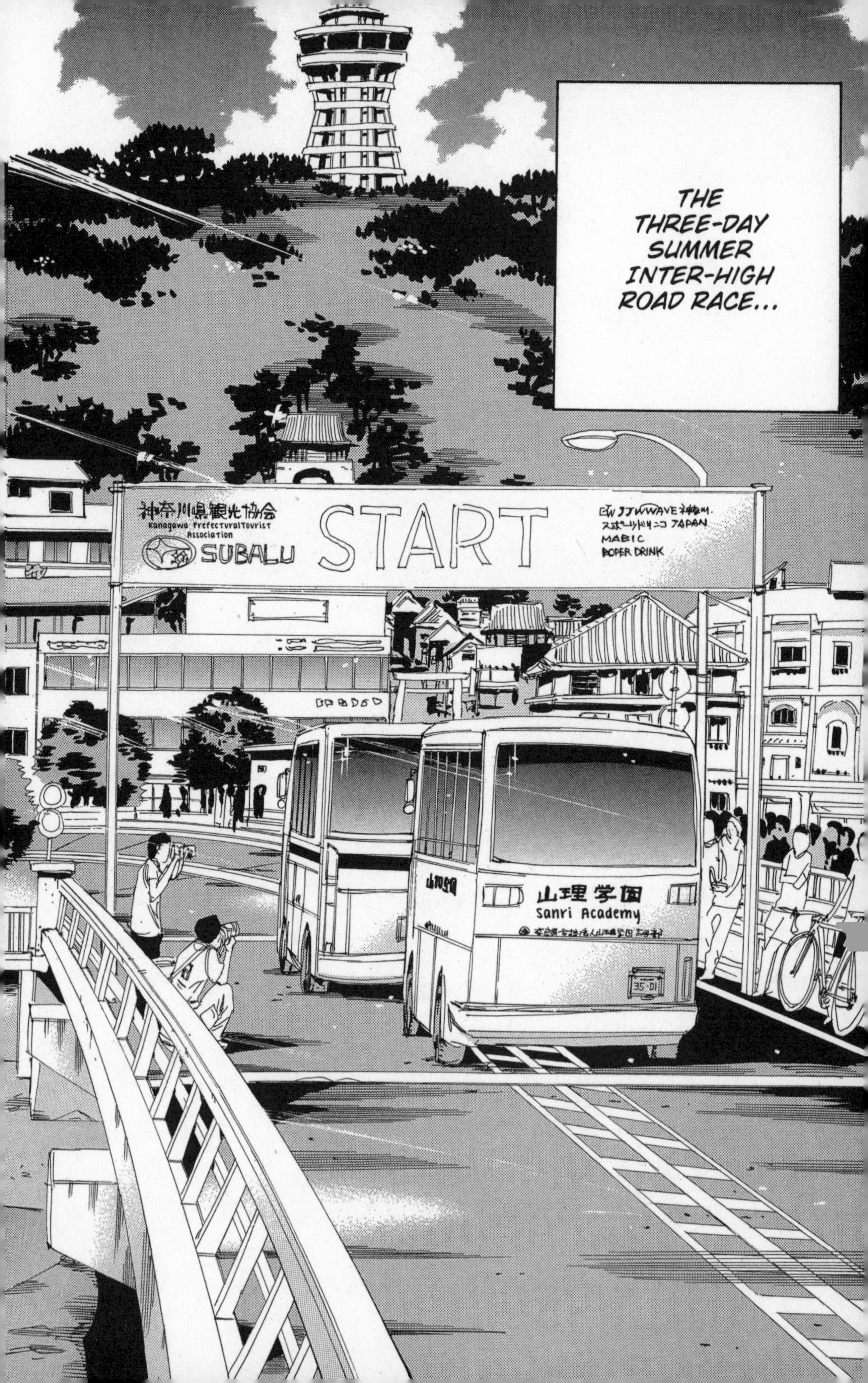
THE THREE-DAY SUMMER INTER-HIGH ROAD RACE...
神奈川県観光協会
Kanagawa PrefecturalTourist Association
SUBALU
START
MABIC
山理学園
Sanri Academy

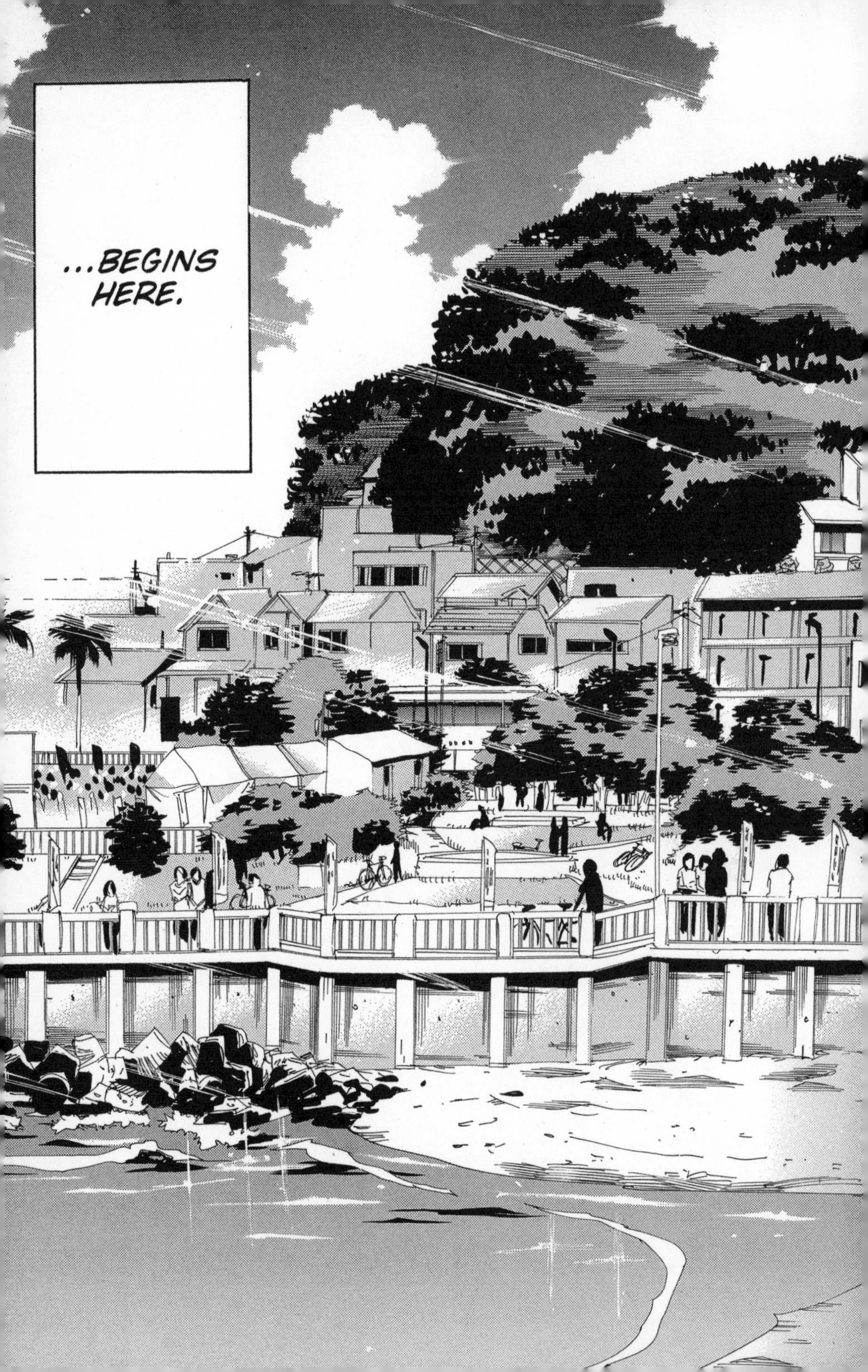
...BEGINS HERE.

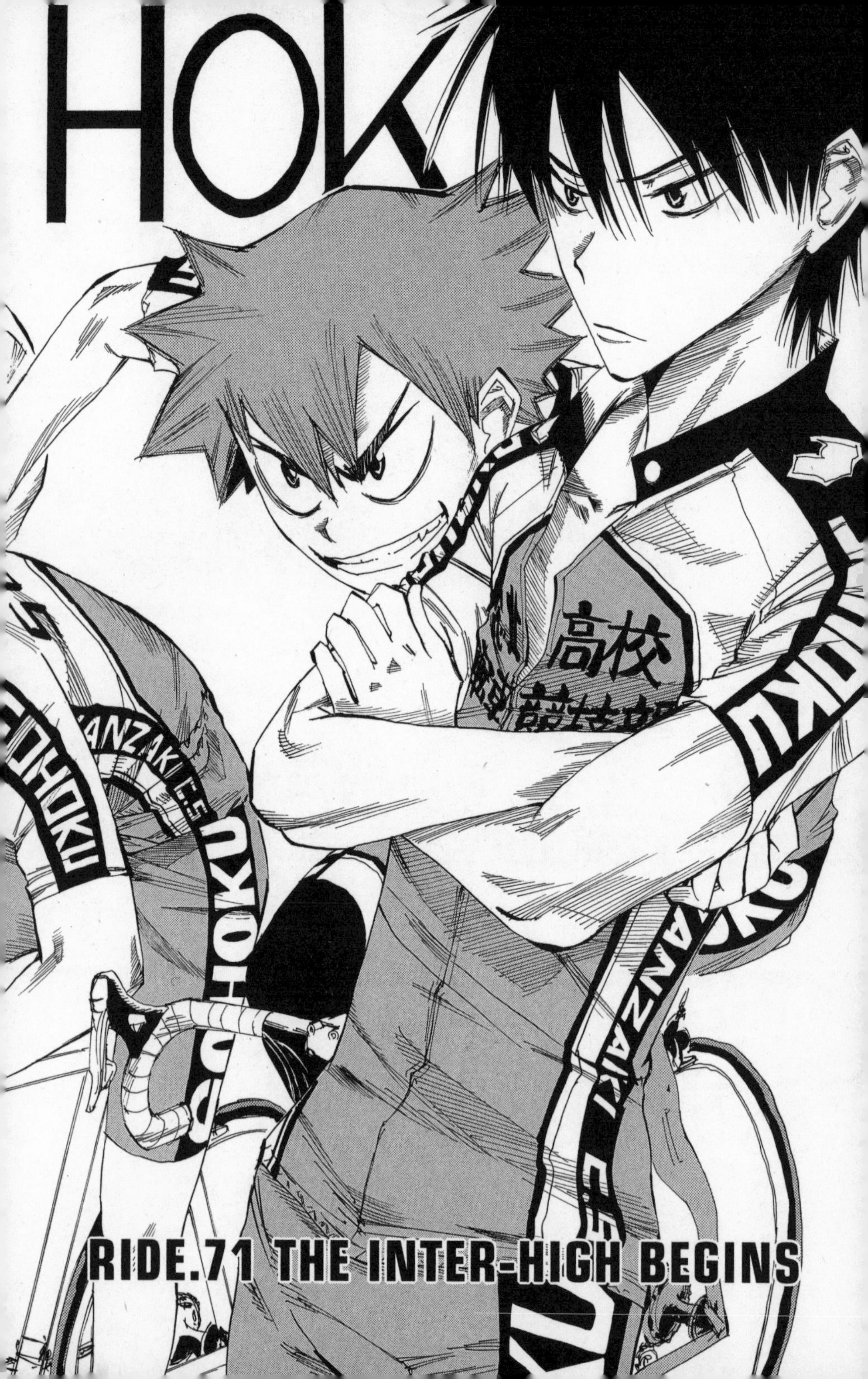
HOK
RIDE.71 THE INTER-HIGH BEGINS

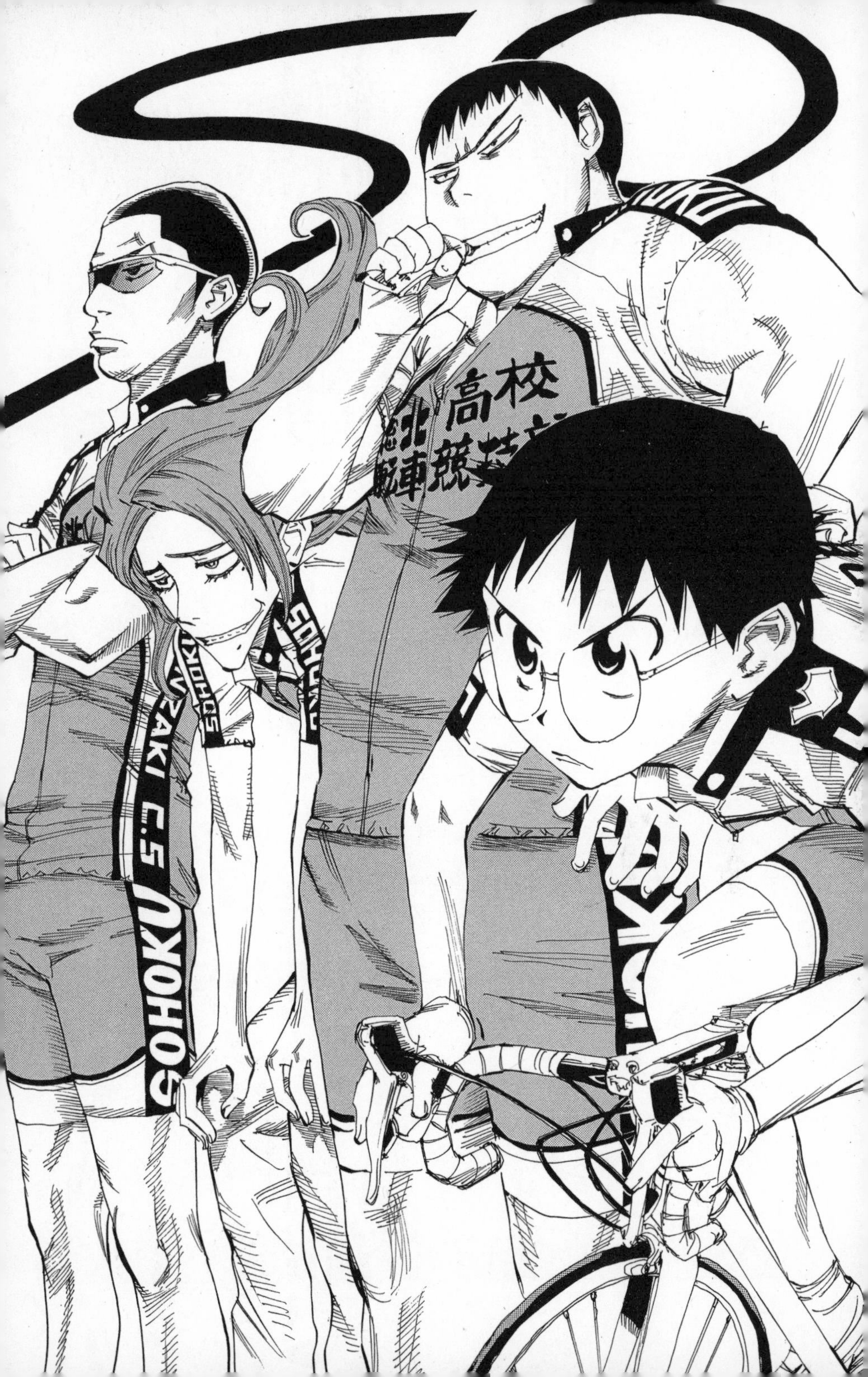

総北高校
SOHOKU C.S

JERSEYS: MIYAZAKI EAST

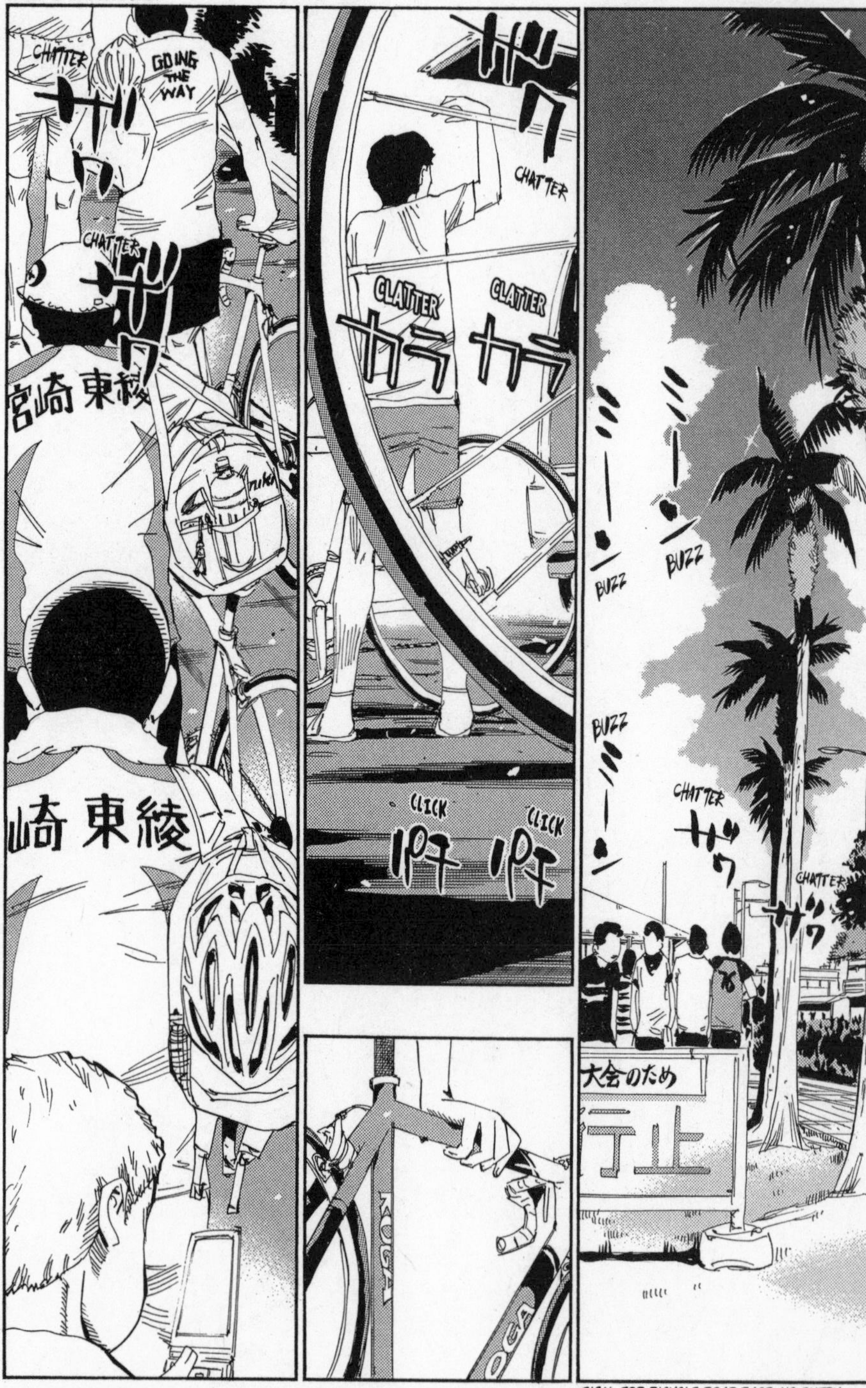
ミーーン
BUZZ
ミーーン
BUZZ
BUZZ
ミーン
CHATTER
ザワ
CHATTER
ザワ
大会のため
行止
ザワ
CHATTER
CLATTER
カラ
CLATTER
カラ
CLICK
パチ
CLICK
パチ
CHATTER
ザワ
GOING THE WAY
CHATTER
ザワ
宮崎東綾
崎東綾

SIGN: FOR BICYCLE ROAD RACE, NO ENTRY

SIGNS: ICE CREAM, SHAVED ICE, LOCAL SPECIALTY; BOXES: MOUNTAIN SPRING WATER

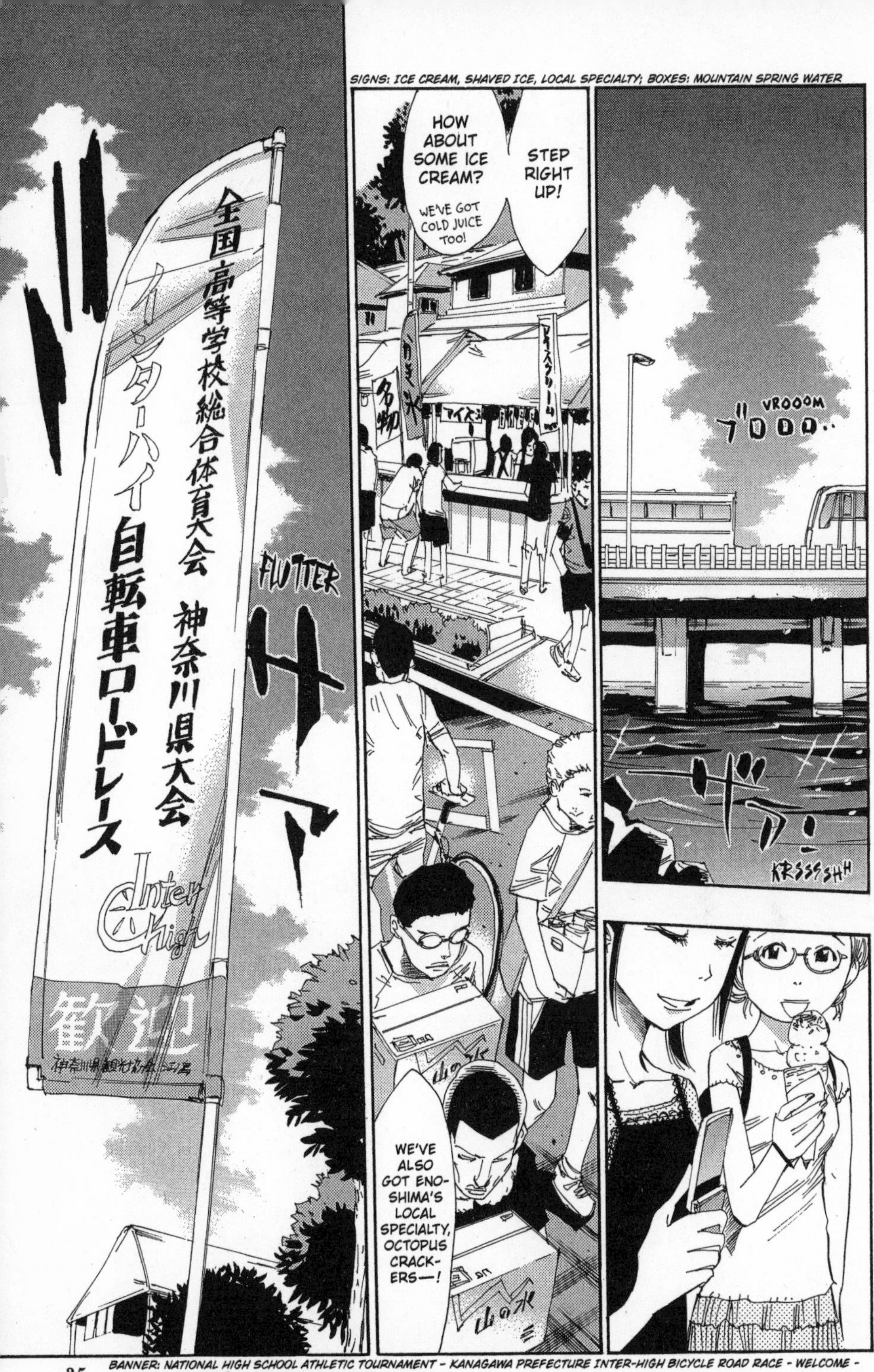
ブロロロ..
VROOOM
ザア!
KRSSSSHH
STEP RIGHT UP!
HOW ABOUT SOME ICE CREAM?
WE'VE GOT COLD JUICE TOO!
山の水
WE'VE ALSO GOT ENOSHIMA'S LOCAL SPECIALTY, OCTOPUS CRACK-ERS—!
山の水
サァ
FLUTTER
全国高等学校総合体育大会 神奈川県大会
インターハイ自転車ロードレース
Inter High
歓迎

BANNER: NATIONAL HIGH SCHOOL ATHLETIC TOURNAMENT - KANAGAWA PREFECTURE INTER-HIGH BICYCLE ROAD RACE - WELCOME - KANAGAWA PREFECTURAL TOURIST ASSOCIATION, ENOSHIMA

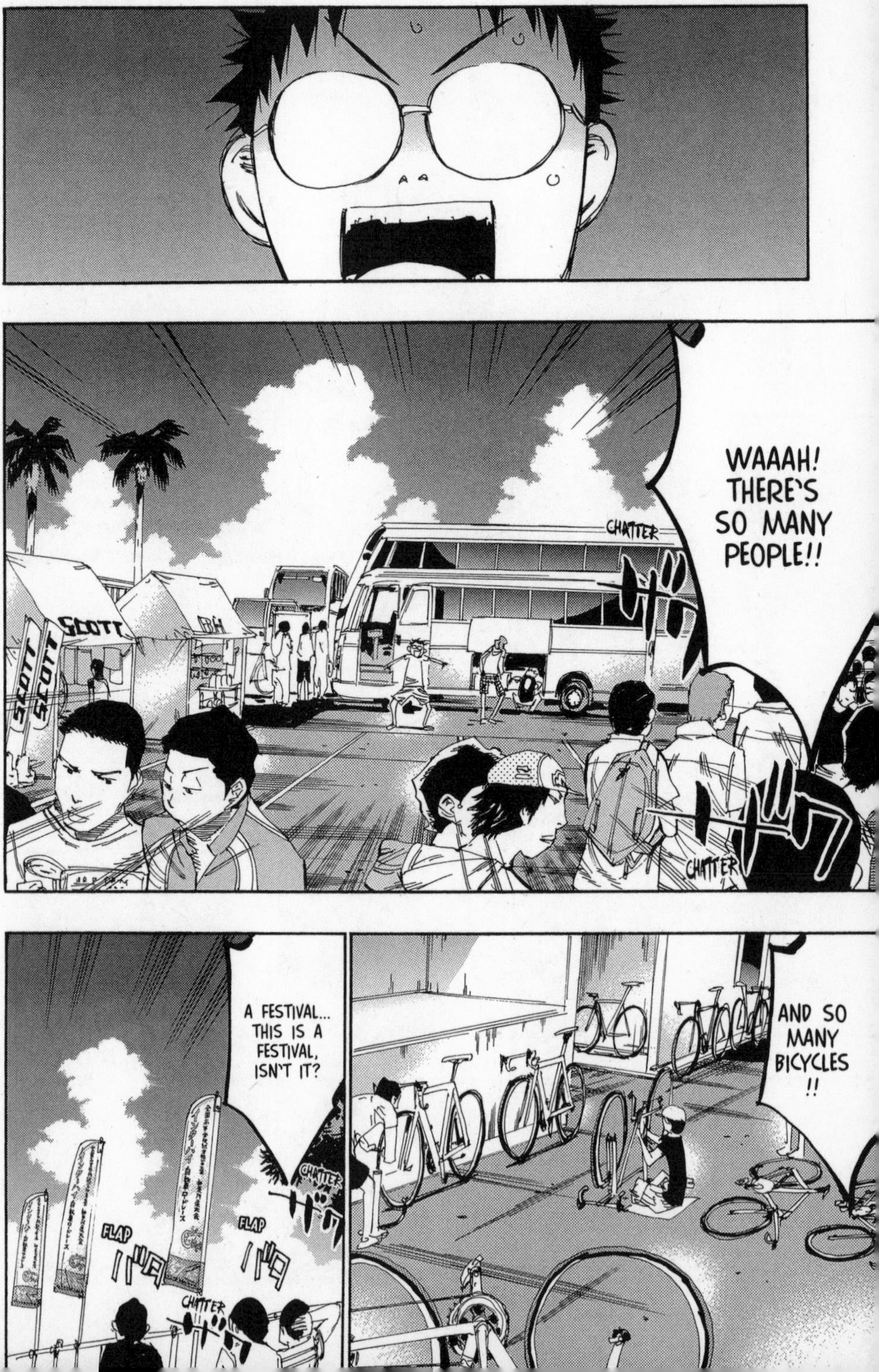
WAAAH! THERE'S SO MANY PEOPLE!!
CHATTER
CHATTER
AND SO MANY BICYCLES !!
A FESTIVAL... THIS IS A FESTIVAL, ISN'T IT?
CHATTER
FLAP
FLAP
CHATTER

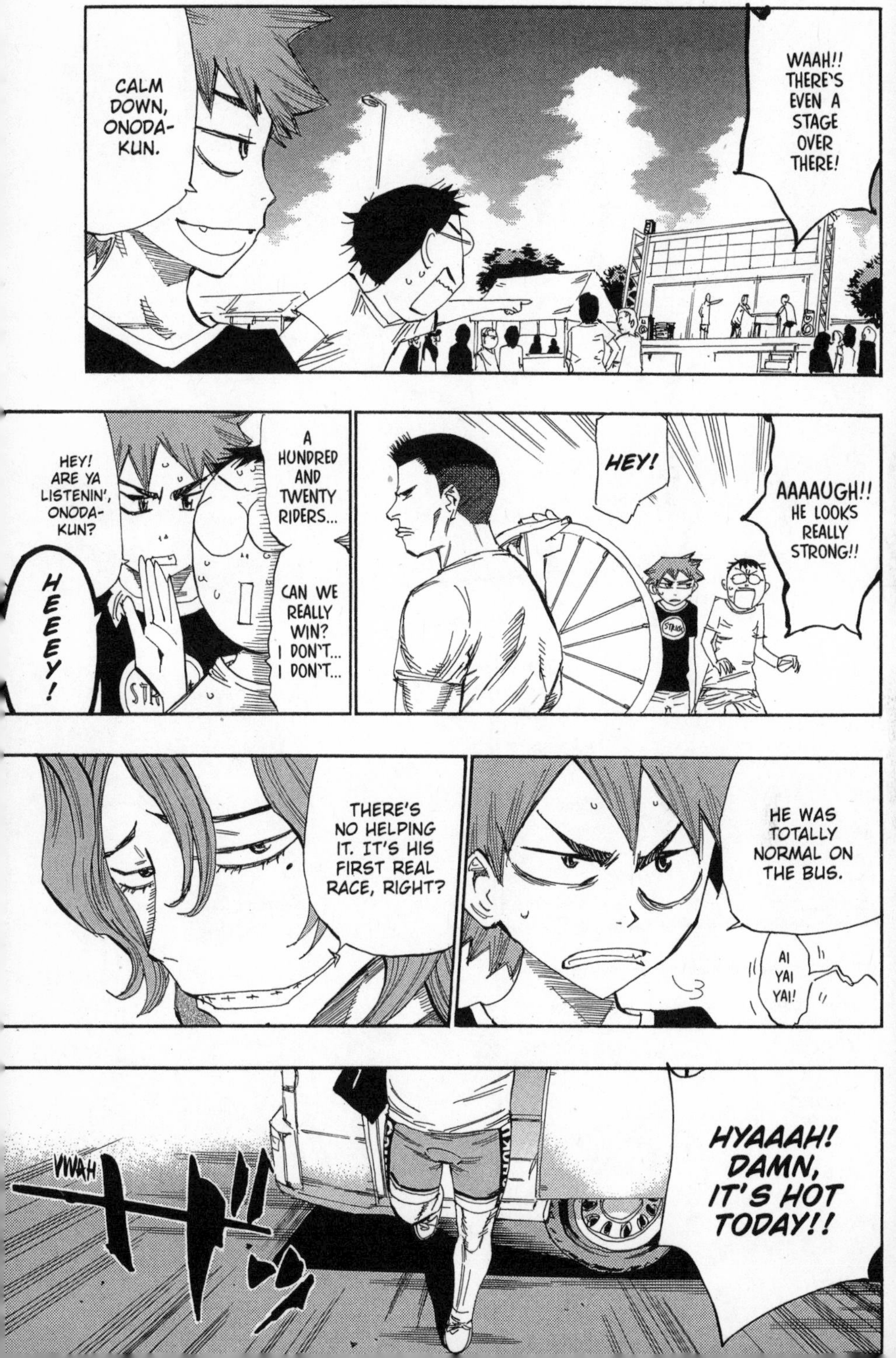
WAAH!! THERE'S EVEN A STAGE OVER THERE!
CALM DOWN, ONODA-KUN.
AAAAUGH!! HE LOOKS REALLY STRONG!!
HEY!
A HUNDRED AND TWENTY RIDERS...
CAN WE REALLY WIN? I DON'T... I DON'T...
HEY! ARE YA LISTENIN', ONODA-KUN?
HEEEEY!
HE WAS TOTALLY NORMAL ON THE BUS.
AI YAI YAI!
THERE'S NO HELPING IT. IT'S HIS FIRST REAL RACE, RIGHT?
HYAAAH! DAMN, IT'S HOT TODAY!!
VWAH

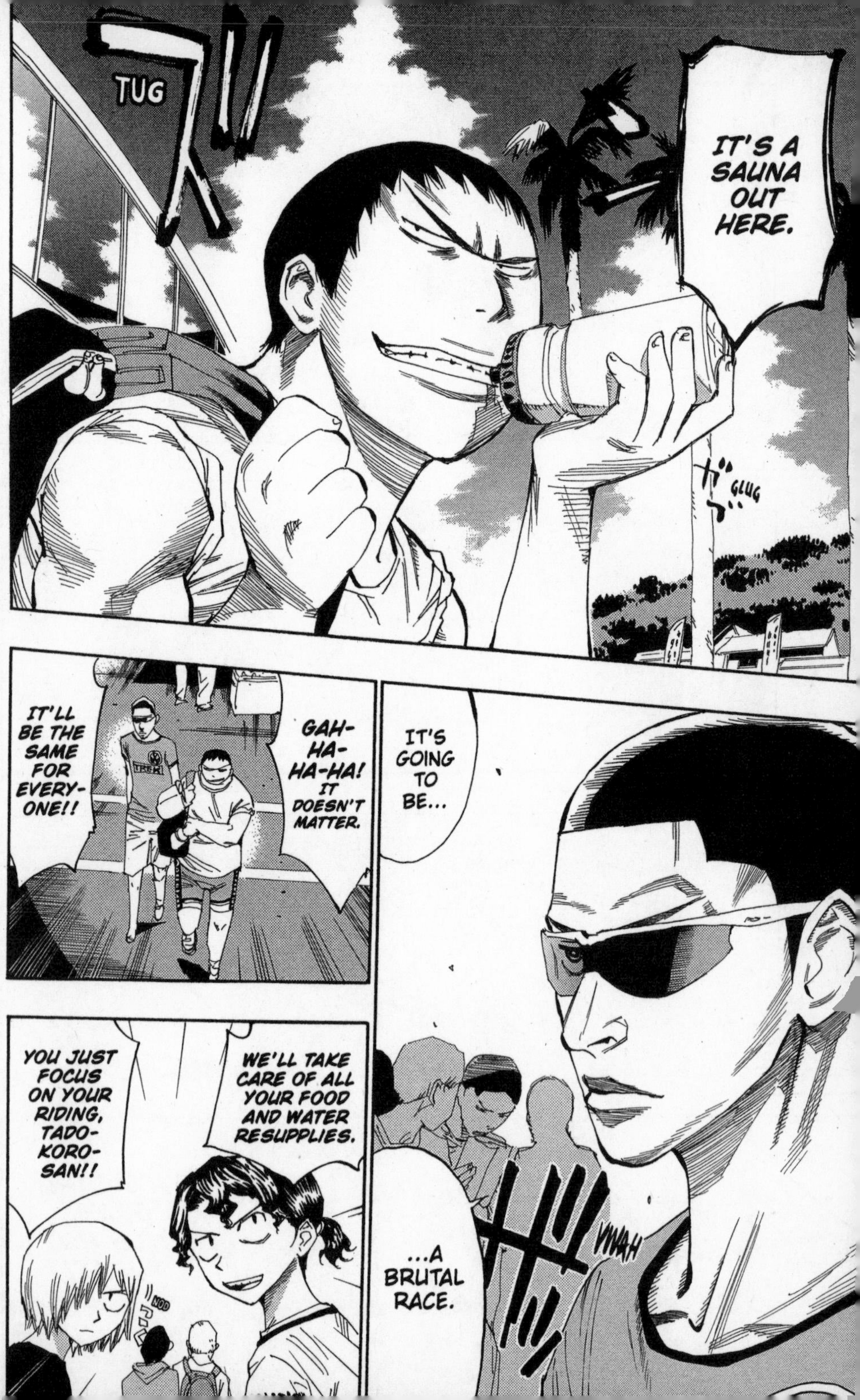
IT'S A SAUNA OUT HERE.
TUG
GLUG
IT'S GOING TO BE...
...A BRUTAL RACE.
VWAH
GAH-HA-HA-HA! IT DOESN'T MATTER.
IT'LL BE THE SAME FOR EVERYONE!!
WE'LL TAKE CARE OF ALL YOUR FOOD AND WATER RESUPPLIES.
YOU JUST FOCUS ON YOUR RIDING, TADOKORO-SAN!!
NOD

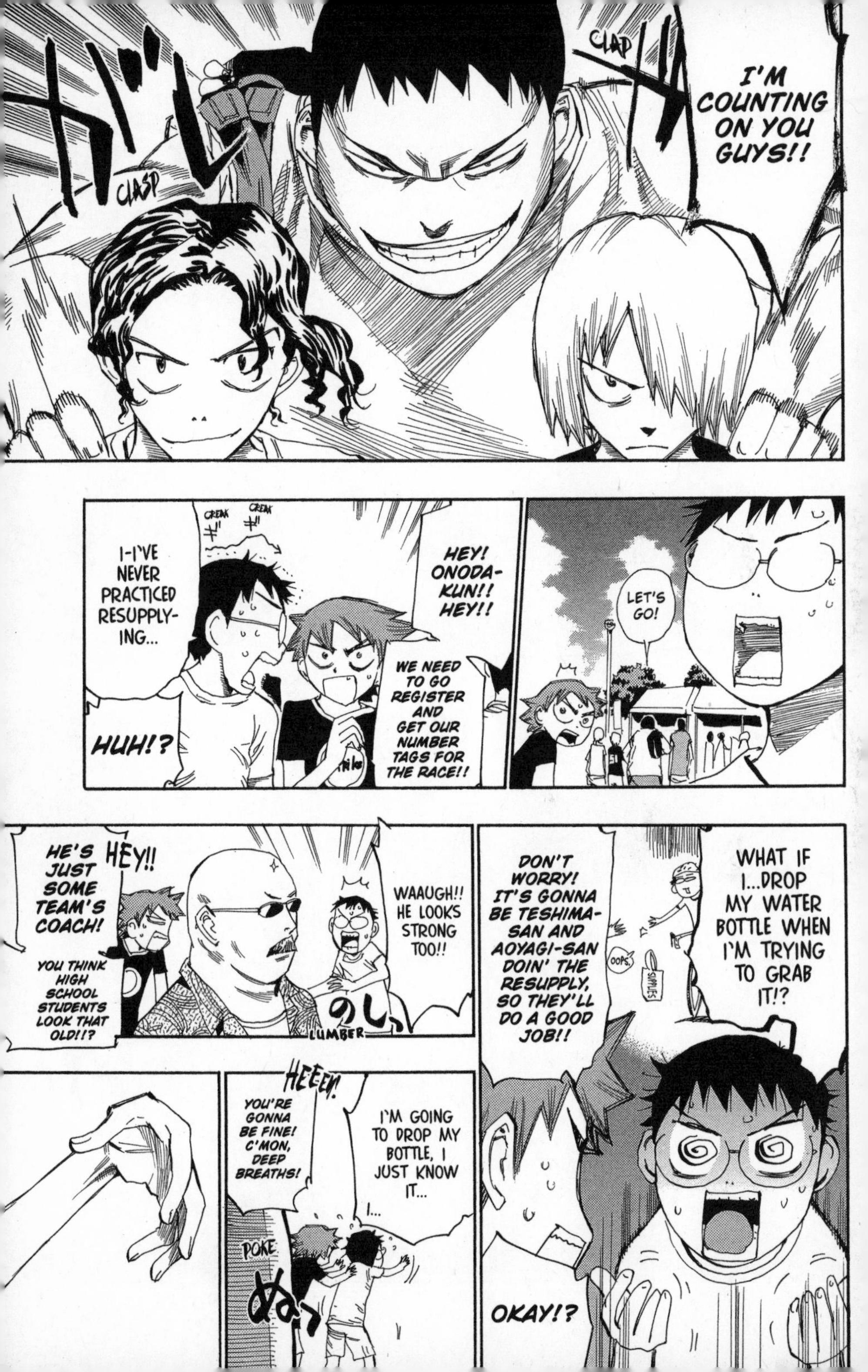
CLAP
I'M COUNTING ON YOU GUYS!!
CLASP
LET'S GO!
HEY! ONODA-KUN!! HEY!!
WE NEED TO GO REGISTER AND GET OUR NUMBER TAGS FOR THE RACE!!
CREAK
CREAK
I-I'VE NEVER PRACTICED RESUPPLYING...
HUH!?
WHAT IF I...DROP MY WATER BOTTLE WHEN I'M TRYING TO GRAB IT!?
OOPS.
SUPPLIES
DON'T WORRY! IT'S GONNA BE TESHIMA-SAN AND AOYAGI-SAN DOIN' THE RESUPPLY, SO THEY'LL DO A GOOD JOB!!
OKAY!?
WAAUGH!! HE LOOKS STRONG TOO!!
LUMBER
HEY!!
HE'S JUST SOME TEAM'S COACH!
YOU THINK HIGH SCHOOL STUDENTS LOOK THAT OLD!!?
HEEEY!
I'M GOING TO DROP MY BOTTLE, I JUST KNOW IT...
YOU'RE GONNA BE FINE! C'MON, DEEP BREATHS!
I...
POKE

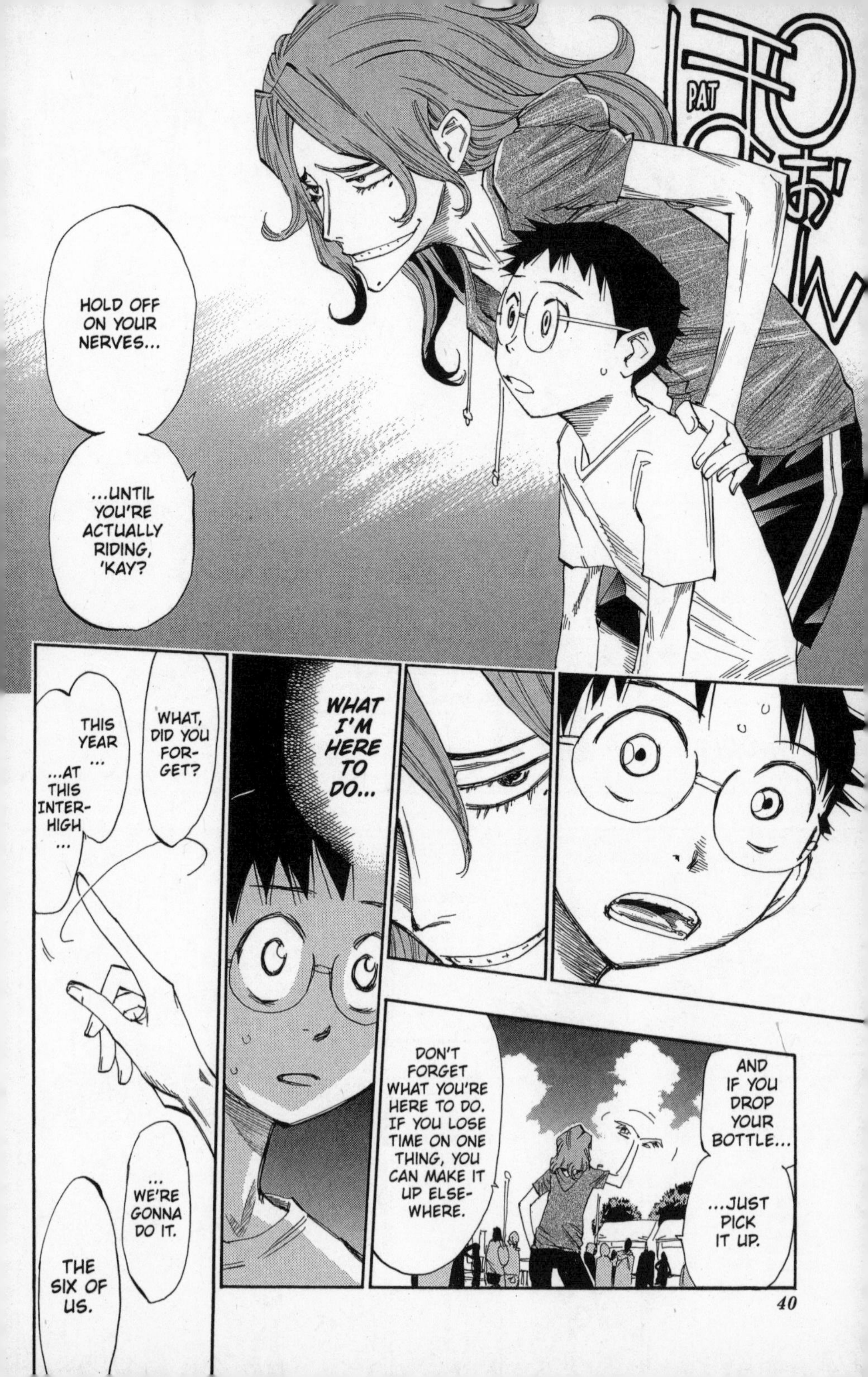
PAT
HOLD OFF ON YOUR NERVES...
...UNTIL YOU'RE ACTUALLY RIDING, 'KAY?
AND IF YOU DROP YOUR BOTTLE...
...JUST PICK IT UP.
DON'T FORGET WHAT YOU'RE HERE TO DO. IF YOU LOSE TIME ON ONE THING, YOU CAN MAKE IT UP ELSE-WHERE.
WHAT I'M HERE TO DO...
WHAT, DID YOU FOR-GET?
THIS YEAR...
...AT THIS INTER-HIGH...
...WE'RE GONNA DO IT.
THE SIX OF US.

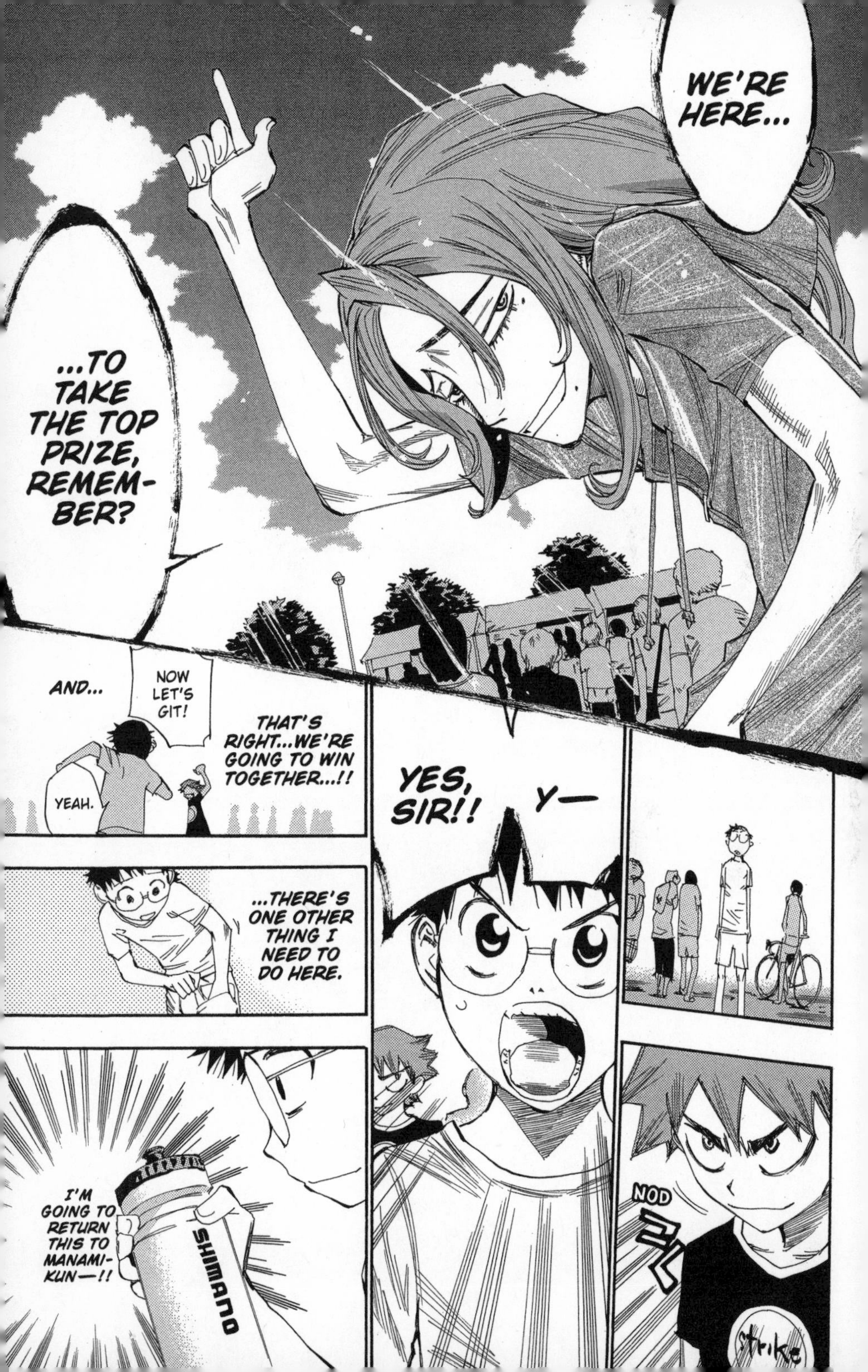
WE'RE HERE...
...TO TAKE THE TOP PRIZE, REMEMBER?
NOD
Strike
Y—
YES, SIR!!
NOW LET'S GIT!
YEAH.
THAT'S RIGHT...WE'RE GOING TO WIN TOGETHER...!!
AND...
...THERE'S ONE OTHER THING I NEED TO DO HERE.
I'M GOING TO RETURN THIS TO MANAMI-KUN—!!
SHIMANO

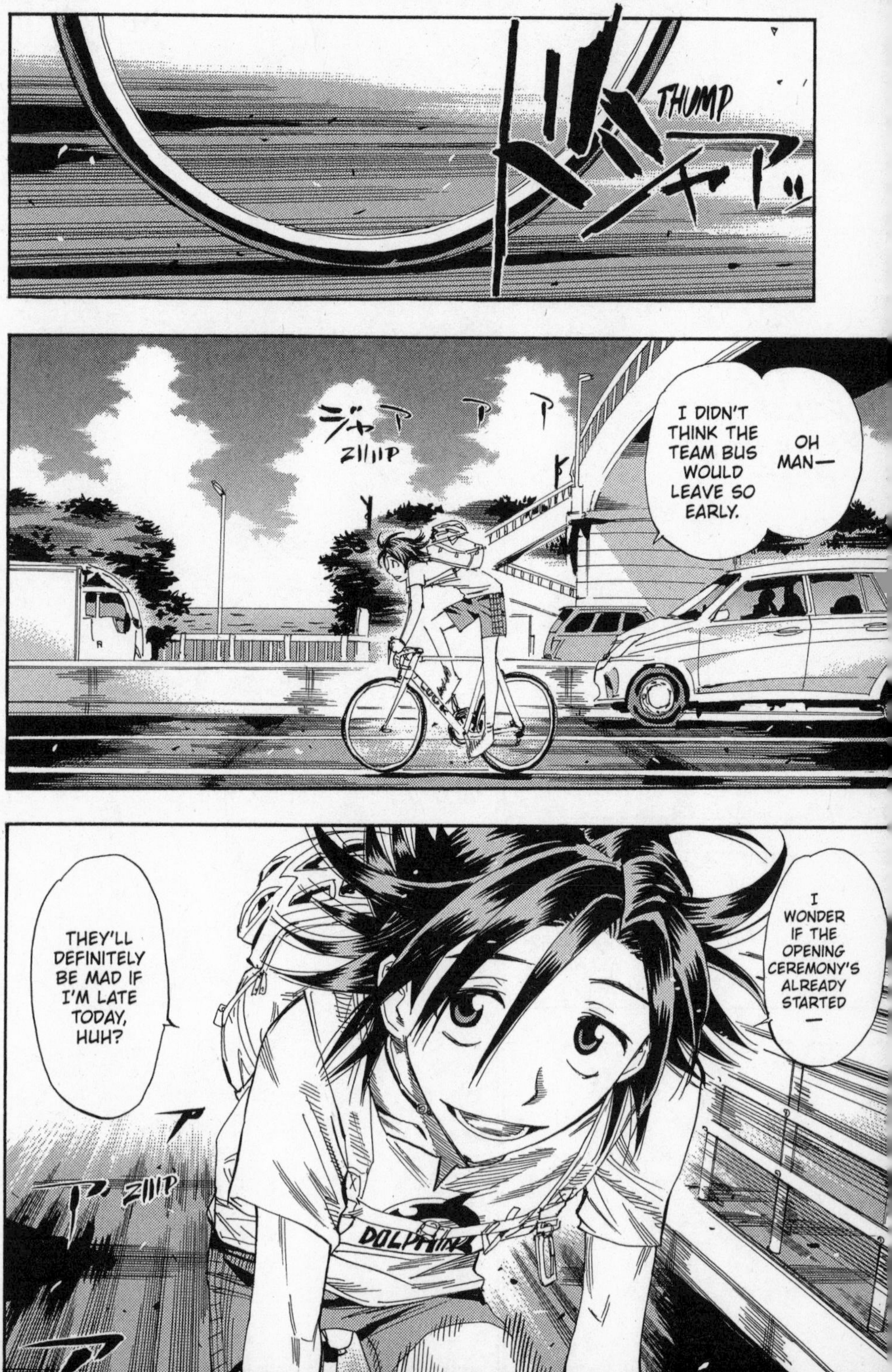
THUMP
OH MAN—
I DIDN'T THINK THE TEAM BUS WOULD LEAVE SO EARLY.
ZIIIIP
I WONDER IF THE OPENING CEREMONY'S ALREADY STARTED—
THEY'LL DEFINITELY BE MAD IF I'M LATE TODAY, HUH?
ZIIIP
DOLPHIN

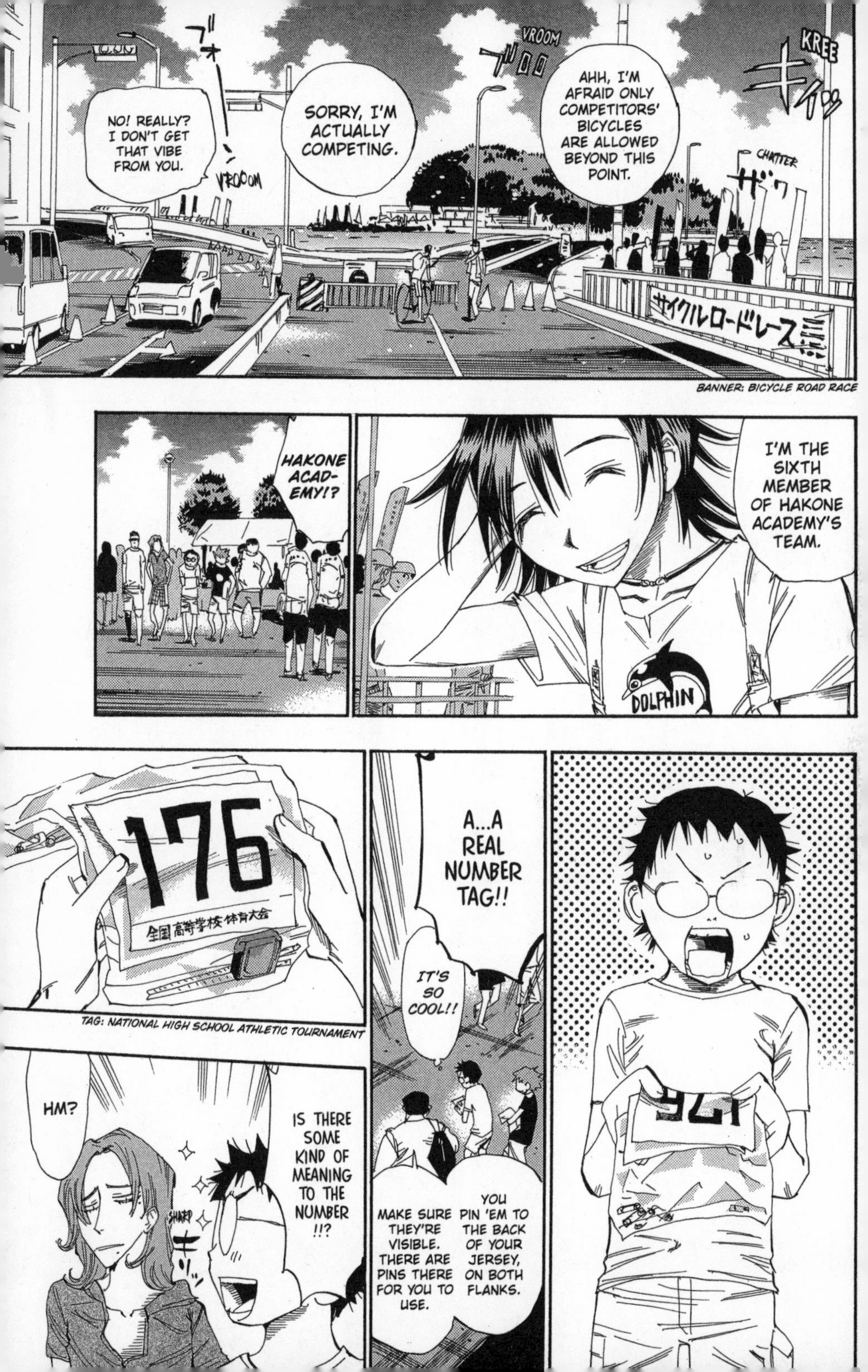
KREE
キイ
AHH, I'M AFRAID ONLY COMPETITORS' BICYCLES ARE ALLOWED BEYOND THIS POINT.
CHATTER
ザワ
VROOM
ブロロ
SORRY, I'M ACTUALLY COMPETING.
VROOOM
ブォー
NO! REALLY? I DON'T GET THAT VIBE FROM YOU.
サイクルロードレース
BANNER: BICYCLE ROAD RACE
I'M THE SIXTH MEMBER OF HAKONE ACADEMY'S TEAM.
DOLPHIN
HAKONE ACADEMY!?
A...A REAL NUMBER TAG!!
IT'S SO COOL!!
YOU PIN 'EM TO THE BACK OF YOUR JERSEY, ON BOTH FLANKS.
MAKE SURE THEY'RE VISIBLE. THERE ARE PINS THERE FOR YOU TO USE.
176
全国高等学校体育大会
TAG: NATIONAL HIGH SCHOOL ATHLETIC TOURNAMENT
IS THERE SOME KIND OF MEANING TO THE NUMBER!!?
SHARP
キッ
HM?

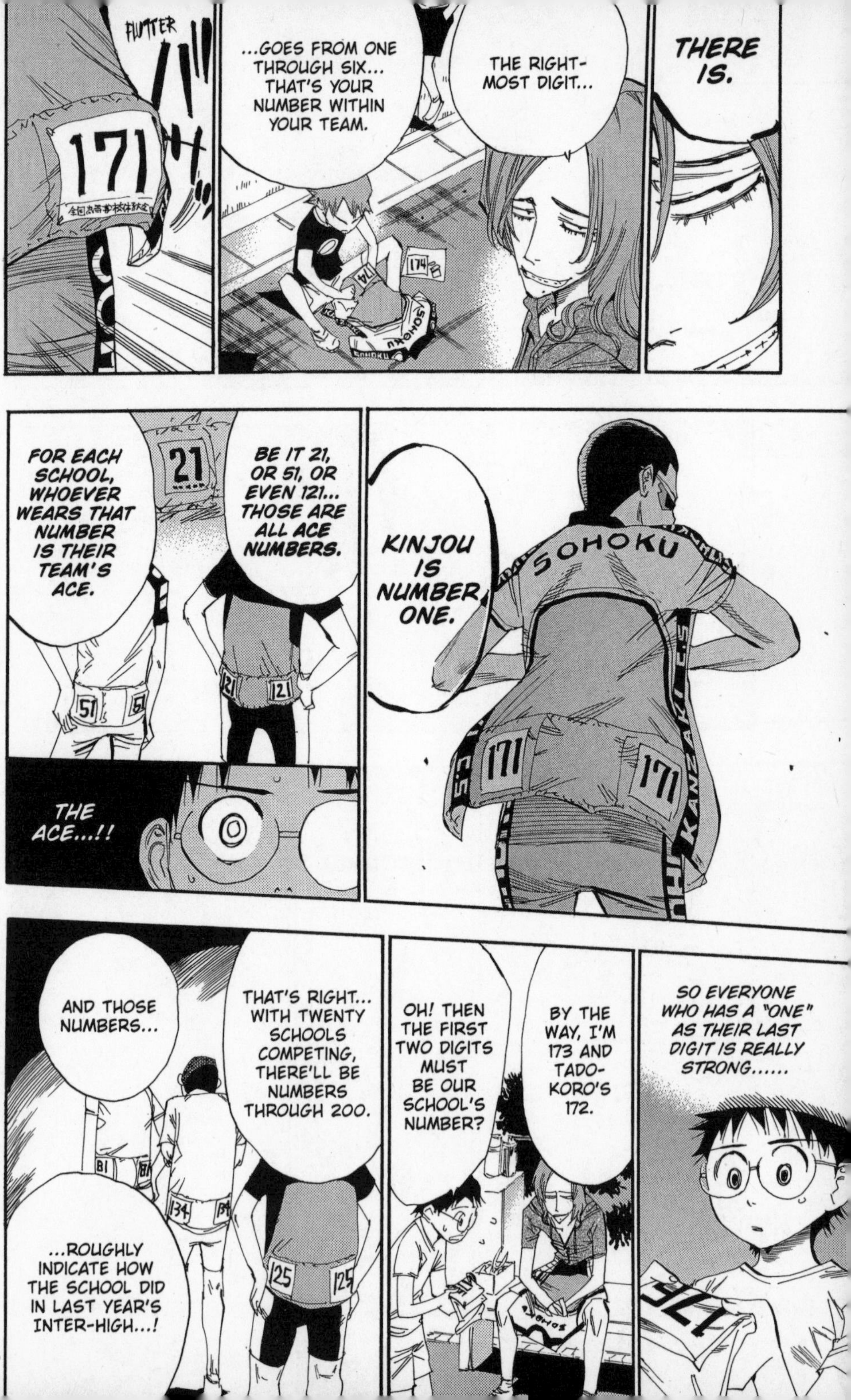
THERE IS.
THE RIGHT-MOST DIGIT...
...GOES FROM ONE THROUGH SIX... THAT'S YOUR NUMBER WITHIN YOUR TEAM.
FLUTTER
KINJOU IS NUMBER ONE.
BE IT 21, OR 51, OR EVEN 121... THOSE ARE ALL ACE NUMBERS.
FOR EACH SCHOOL, WHOEVER WEARS THAT NUMBER IS THEIR TEAM'S ACE.
THE ACE...!!
SO EVERYONE WHO HAS A "ONE" AS THEIR LAST DIGIT IS REALLY STRONG......
BY THE WAY, I'M 173 AND TADOKORO'S 172.
OH! THEN THE FIRST TWO DIGITS MUST BE OUR SCHOOL'S NUMBER?
THAT'S RIGHT... WITH TWENTY SCHOOLS COMPETING, THERE'LL BE NUMBERS THROUGH 200.
AND THOSE NUMBERS...
...ROUGHLY INDICATE HOW THE SCHOOL DID IN LAST YEAR'S INTER-HIGH...!

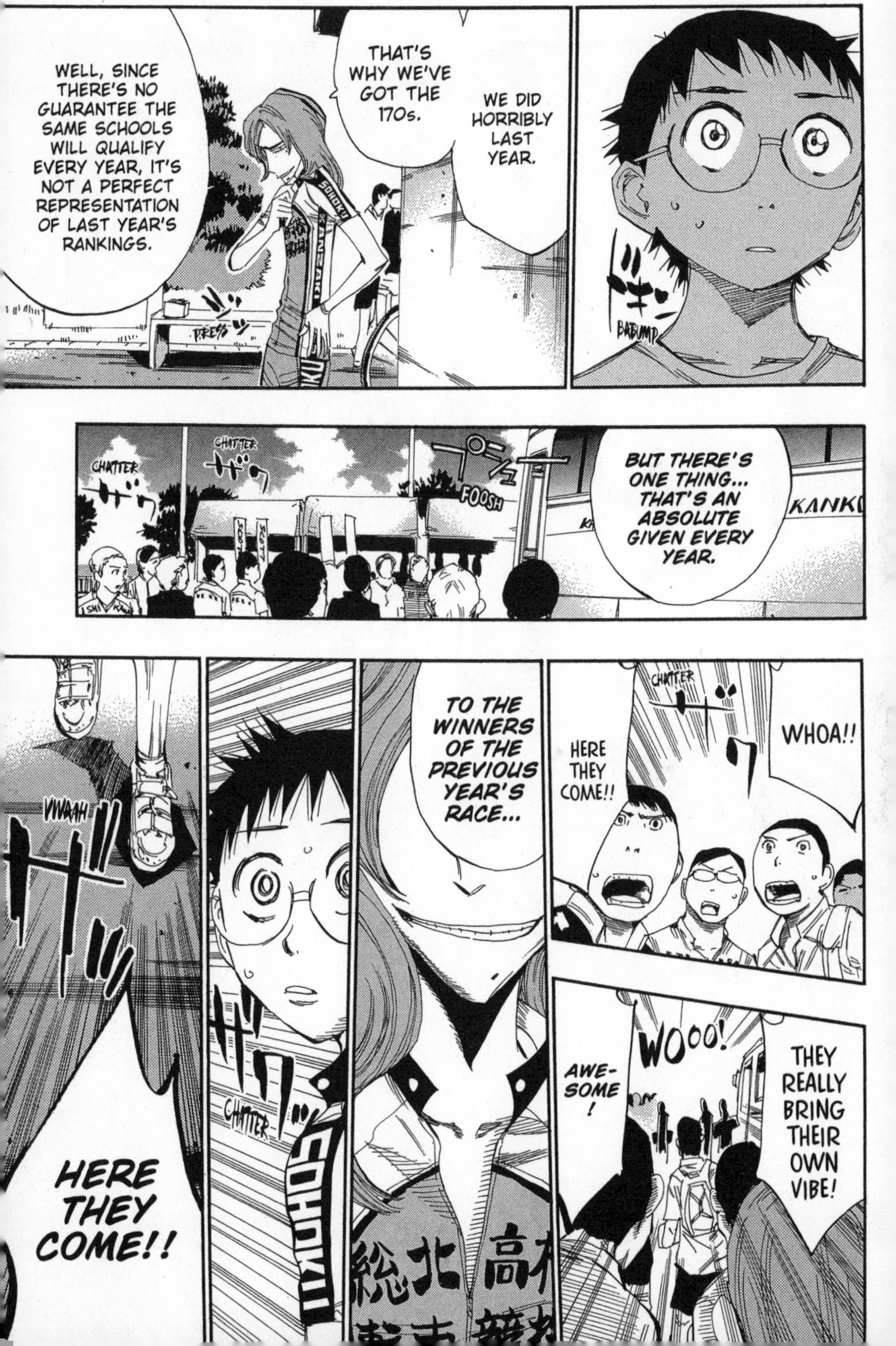
BABUMP
WE DID HORRIBLY LAST YEAR.
THAT'S WHY WE'VE GOT THE 170s.
WELL, SINCE THERE'S NO GUARANTEE THE SAME SCHOOLS WILL QUALIFY EVERY YEAR, IT'S NOT A PERFECT REPRESENTATION OF LAST YEAR'S RANKINGS.
PRESS
KANKO
BUT THERE'S ONE THING... THAT'S AN ABSOLUTE GIVEN EVERY YEAR.
FOOSH
CHATTER
CHATTER
WHOA!!
CHATTER
HERE THEY COME!!
THEY REALLY BRING THEIR OWN VIBE!
WOOO!
AWE-SOME!
TO THE WINNERS OF THE PREVIOUS YEAR'S RACE...
SOHOKU
総北高
CHATTER
VWAAH
HERE THEY COME!!

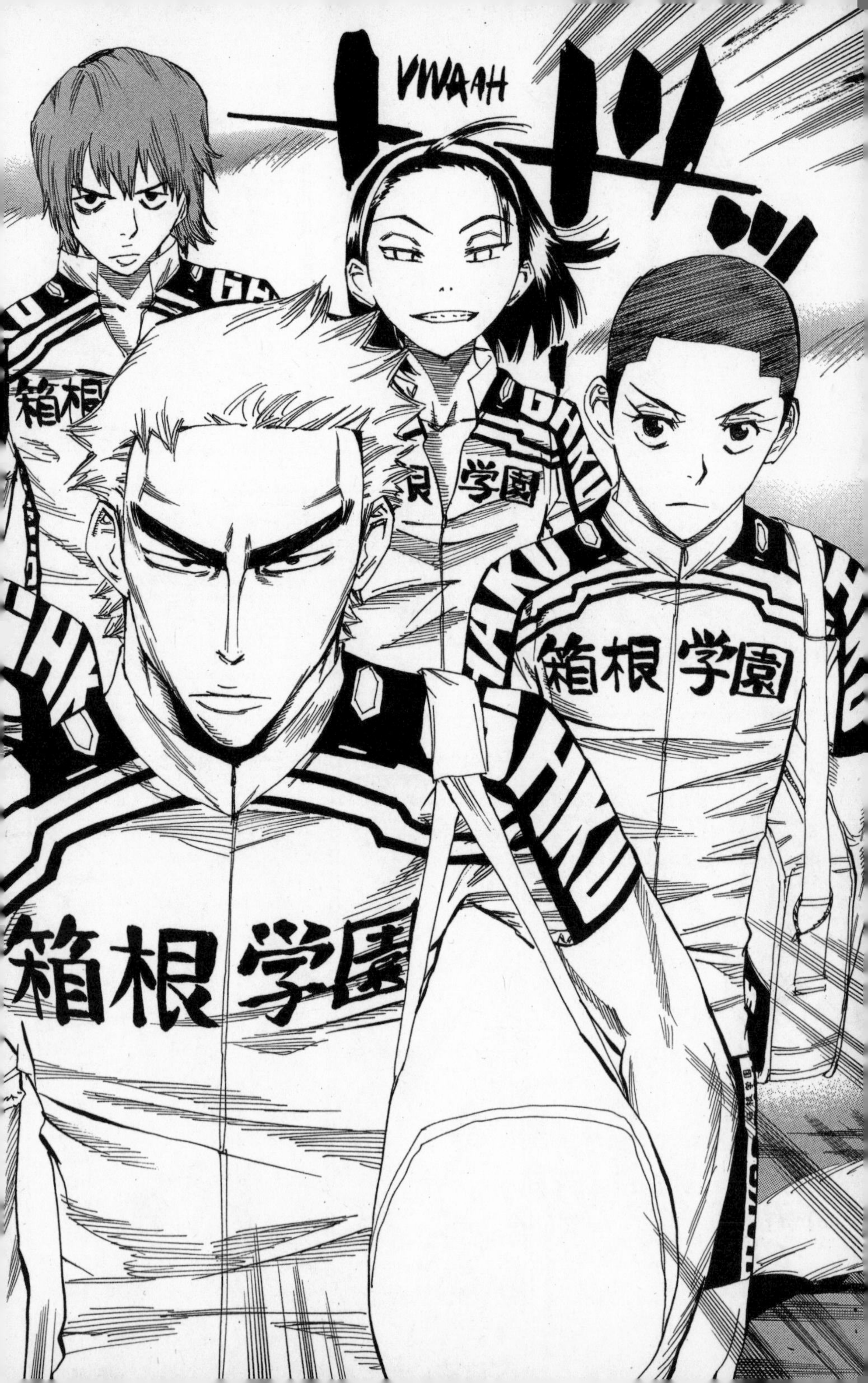
VWAAH
箱根学園

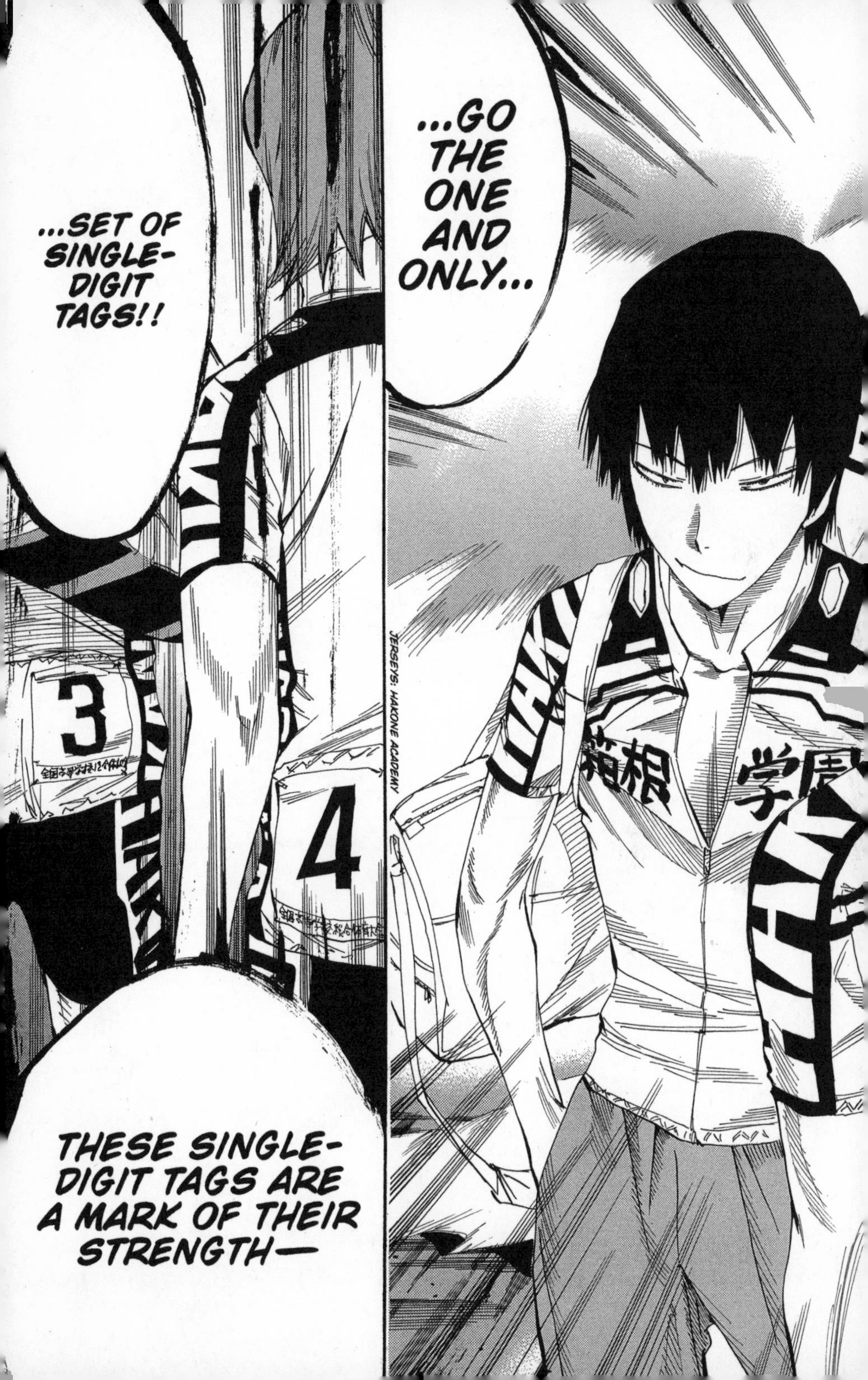
...GO THE ONE AND ONLY...
JERSEYS: HAKONE ACADEMY
...SET OF SINGLE-DIGIT TAGS!!
THESE SINGLE-DIGIT TAGS ARE A MARK OF THEIR STRENGTH—

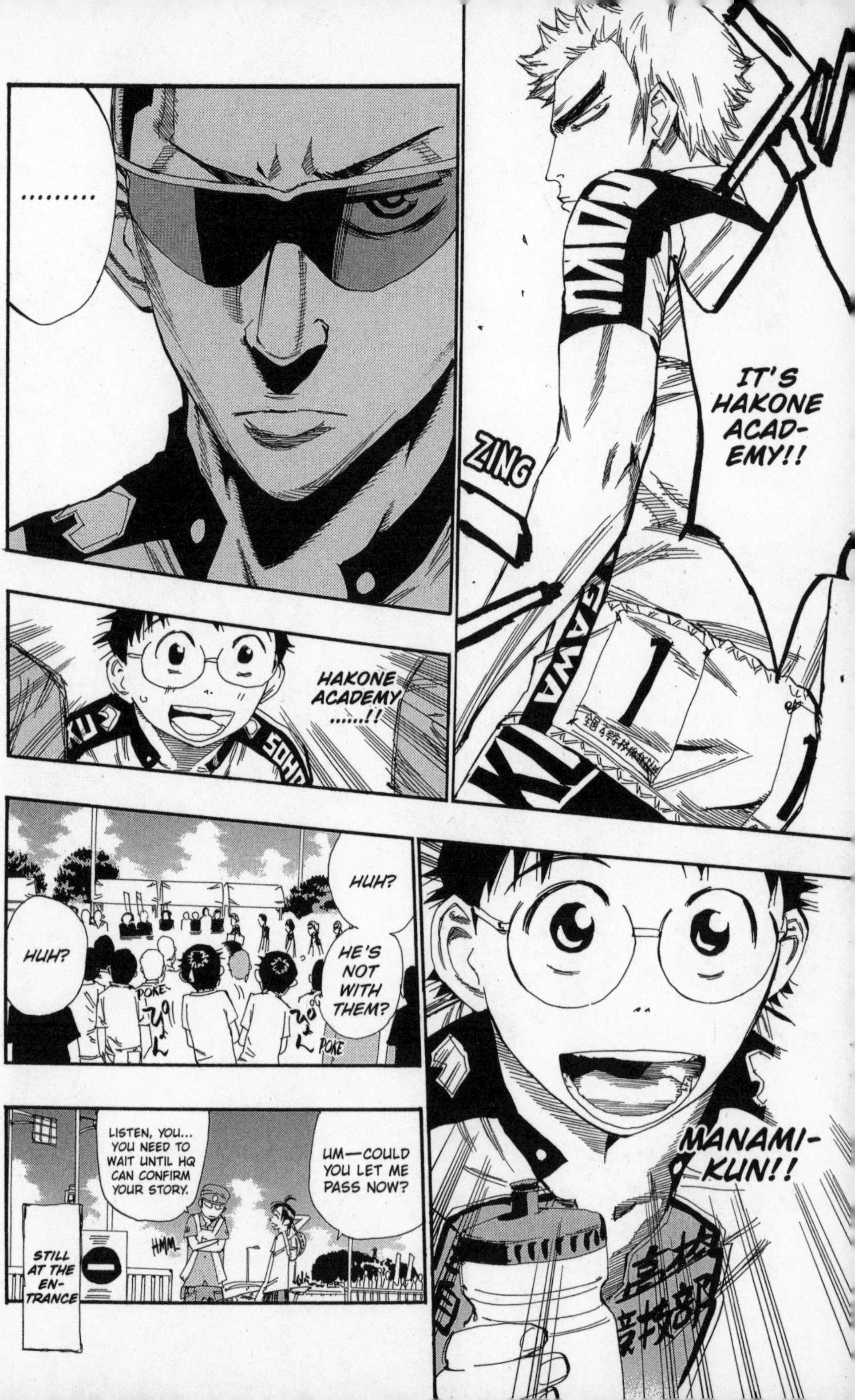
IT'S HAKONE ACAD-EMY!!
ZING
....
HAKONE ACADEMY ......!!
MANAMI-KUN!!
HUH?
HE'S NOT WITH THEM?
HUH?
POKE
POKE
UM—COULD YOU LET ME PASS NOW?
LISTEN, YOU... YOU NEED TO WAIT UNTIL HQ CAN CONFIRM YOUR STORY.
HMM
STILL AT THE EN-TRANCE

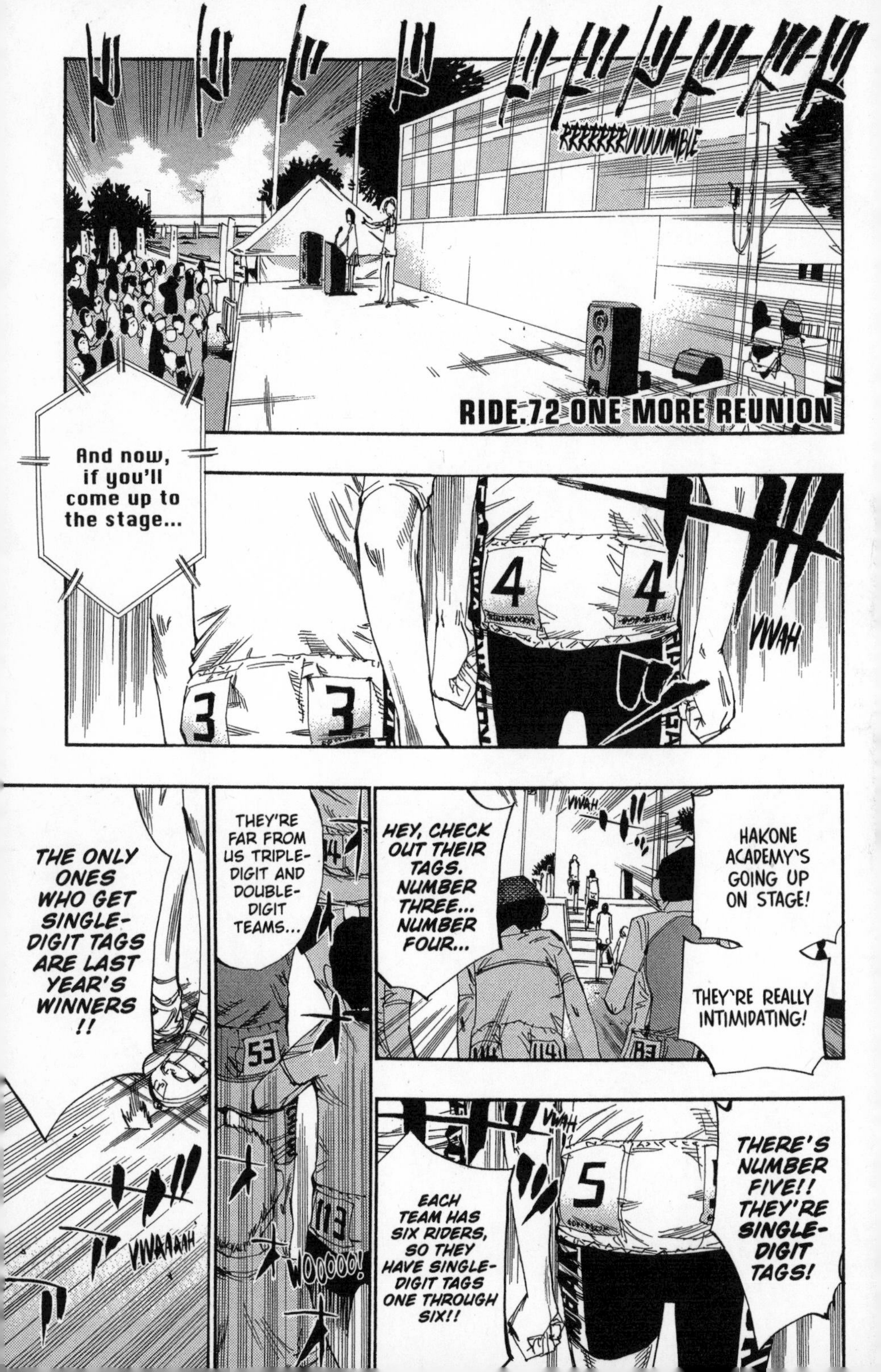
RRRRRRRUUUUUMBLE
RIDE.72 ONE MORE REUNION
And now, if you'll come up to the stage...
VWAH
HAKONE ACADEMY'S GOING UP ON STAGE!
THEY'RE REALLY INTIMIDATING!
HEY, CHECK OUT THEIR TAGS. NUMBER THREE... NUMBER FOUR...
VWAH
THERE'S NUMBER FIVE!! THEY'RE SINGLE-DIGIT TAGS!
EACH TEAM HAS SIX RIDERS, SO THEY HAVE SINGLE-DIGIT TAGS ONE THROUGH SIX!!
VWAH
THEY'RE FAR FROM US TRIPLE-DIGIT AND DOUBLE-DIGIT TEAMS...
WOOOOO!
THE ONLY ONES WHO GET SINGLE-DIGIT TAGS ARE LAST YEAR'S WINNERS!!
VWAAAAH

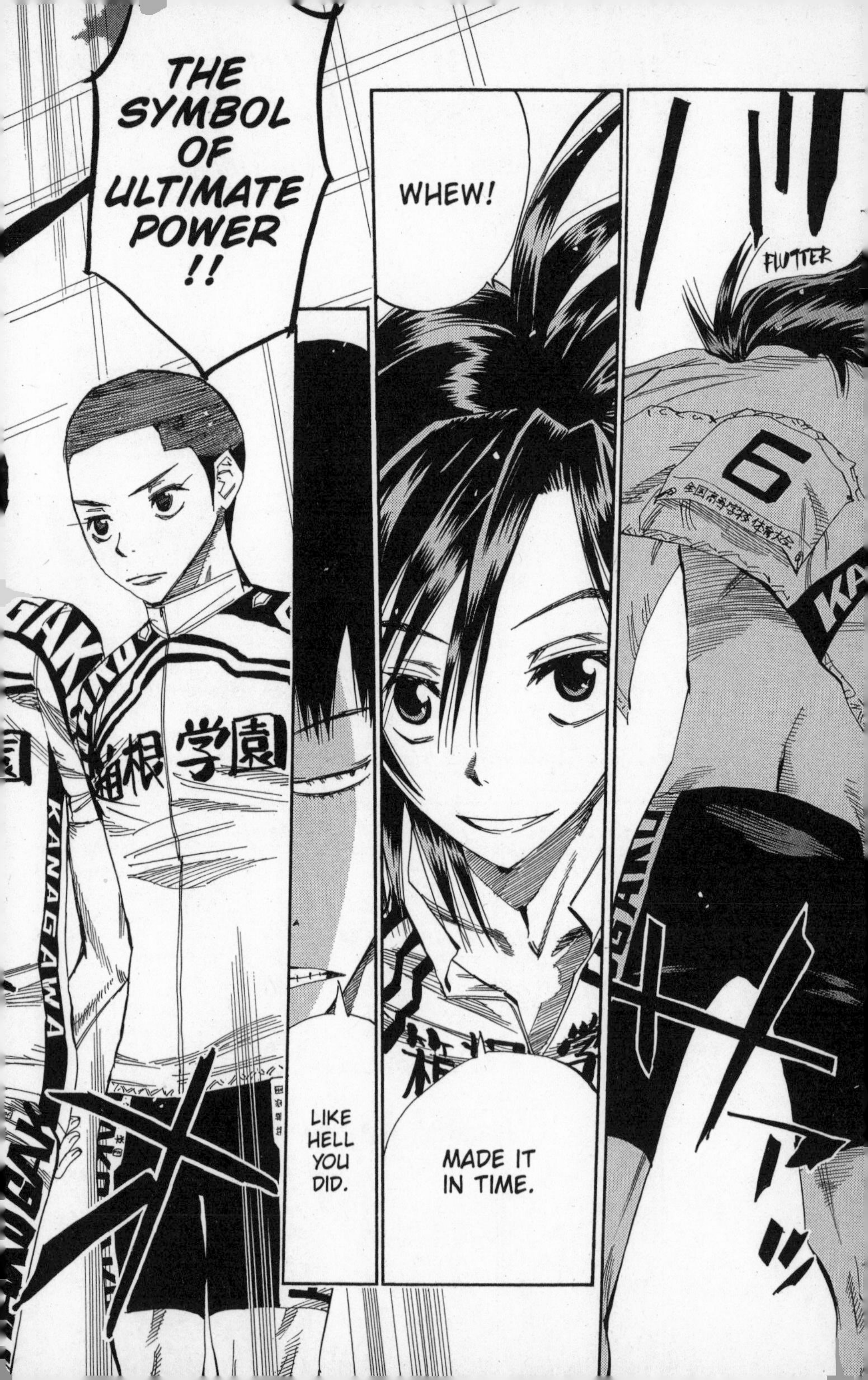
THE SYMBOL OF ULTIMATE POWER!!
FLUTTER
WHEW!
MADE IT IN TIME.
LIKE HELL YOU DID.

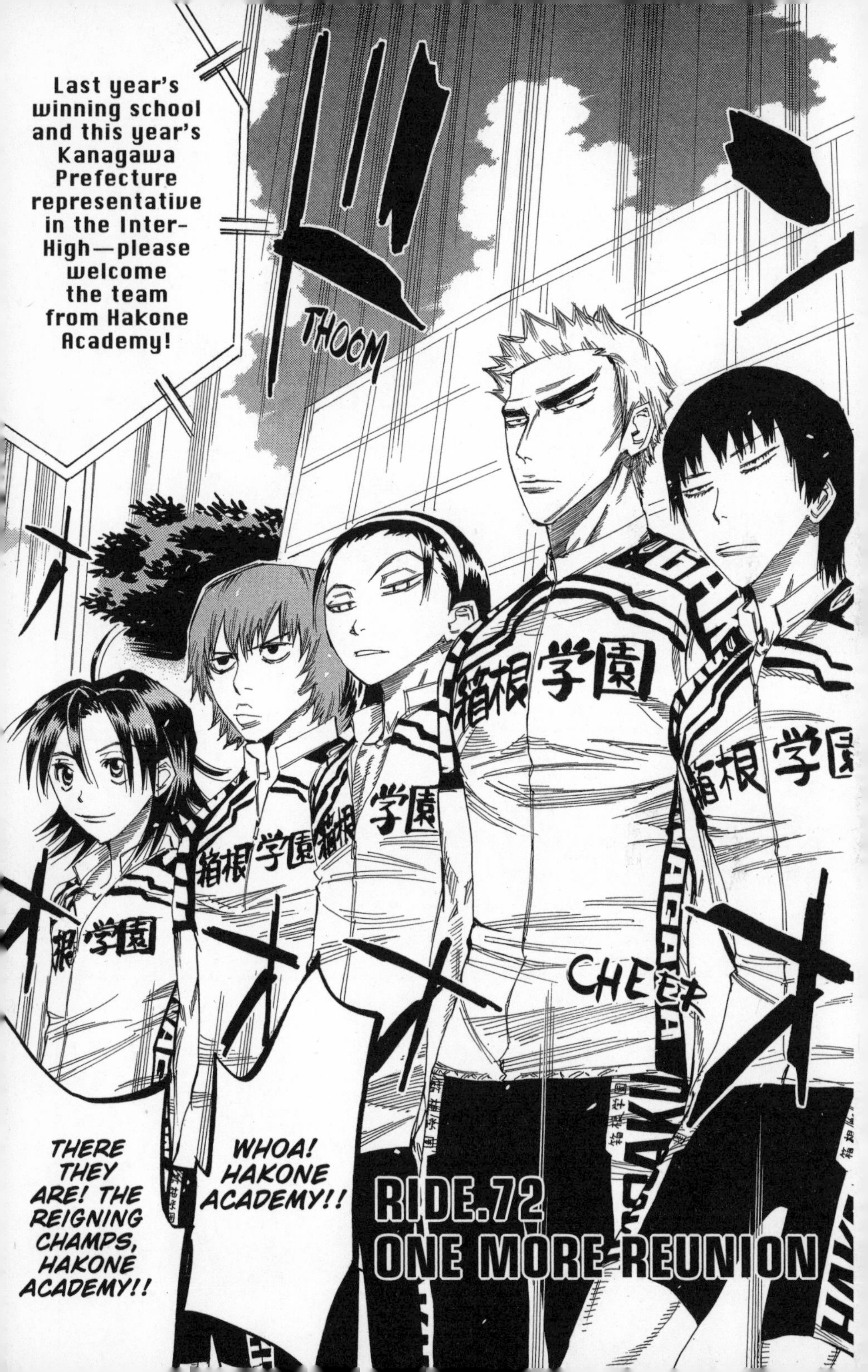
Last year's winning school and this year's Kanagawa Prefecture representative in the Inter-High—please welcome the team from Hakone Academy!
THOOM
CHEER
RIDE.72
ONE MORE REUNION
WHOA! HAKONE ACADEMY!!
THERE THEY ARE! THE REIGNING CHAMPS, HAKONE ACADEMY!!

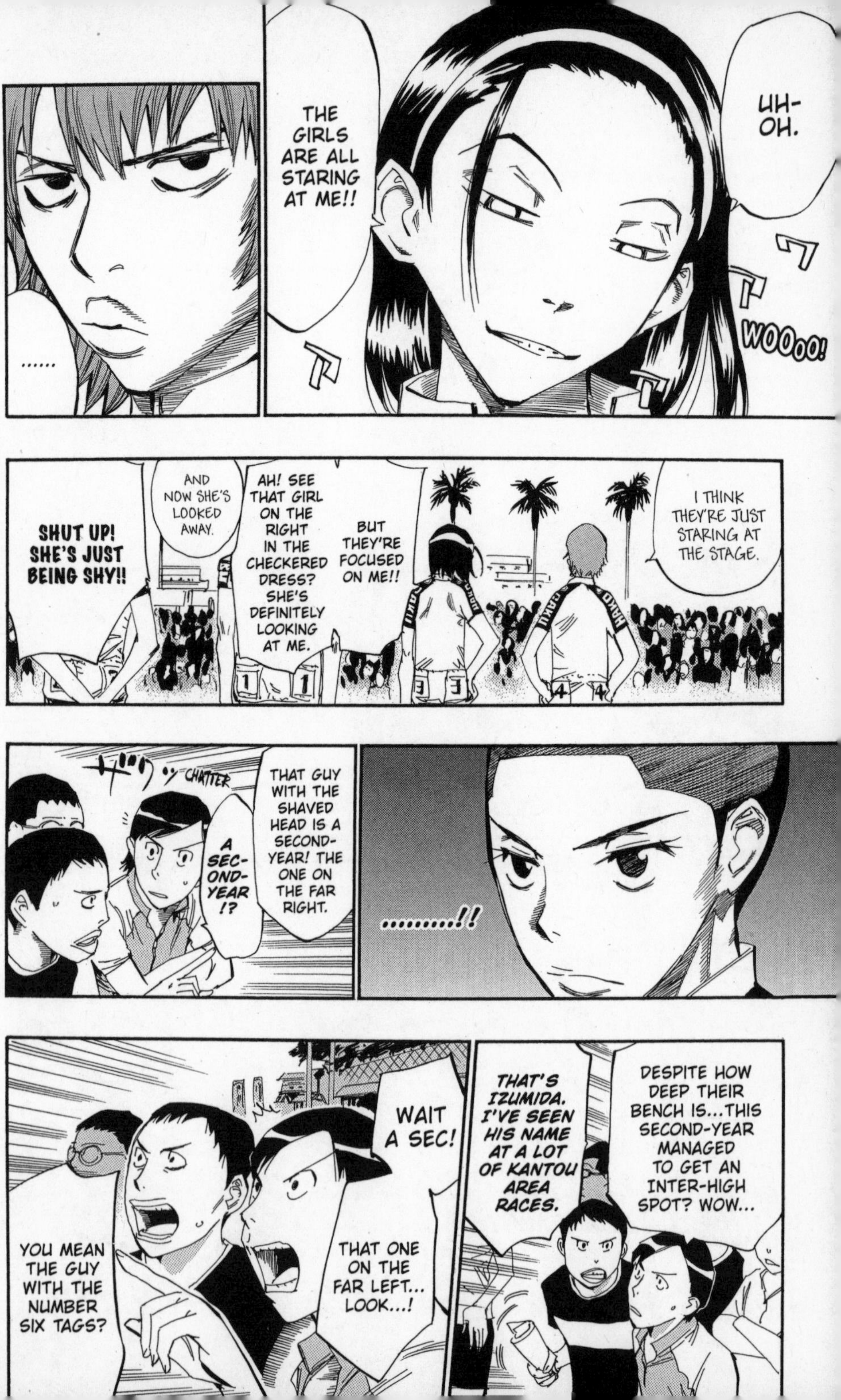
UH-OH.
THE GIRLS ARE ALL STARING AT ME!!
WOOOoo!
......
I THINK THEY'RE JUST STARING AT THE STAGE.
BUT THEY'RE FOCUSED ON ME!!
AH! SEE THAT GIRL ON THE RIGHT IN THE CHECKERED DRESS? SHE'S DEFINITELY LOOKING AT ME.
AND NOW SHE'S LOOKED AWAY.
SHUT UP! SHE'S JUST BEING SHY!!
..........!!
THAT GUY WITH THE SHAVED HEAD IS A SECOND-YEAR! THE ONE ON THE FAR RIGHT.
CHATTER
A SECOND-YEAR!?
DESPITE HOW DEEP THEIR BENCH IS...THIS SECOND-YEAR MANAGED TO GET AN INTER-HIGH SPOT? WOW...
THAT'S IZUMIDA. I'VE SEEN HIS NAME AT A LOT OF KANTOU AREA RACES.
WAIT A SEC!
THAT ONE ON THE FAR LEFT... LOOK...!
YOU MEAN THE GUY WITH THE NUMBER SIX TAGS?

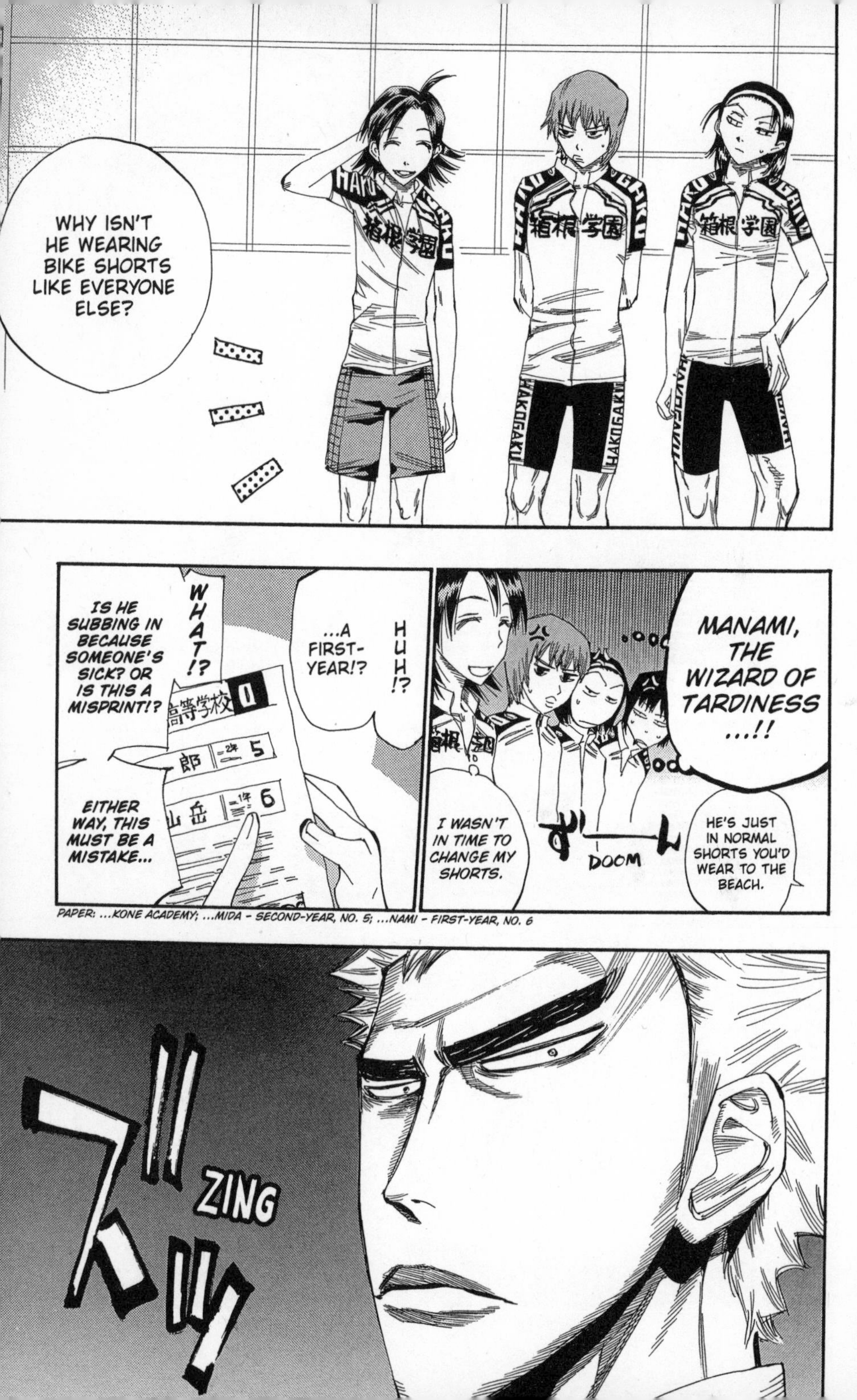
WHY ISN'T HE WEARING BIKE SHORTS LIKE EVERYONE ELSE?
MANAMI, THE WIZARD OF TARDINESS ...!!
HE'S JUST IN NORMAL SHORTS YOU'D WEAR TO THE BEACH.
DOOM
I WASN'T IN TIME TO CHANGE MY SHORTS.
HUH!?
...A FIRST-YEAR!?
WHAT!?
IS HE SUBBING IN BECAUSE SOMEONE'S SICK? OR IS THIS A MISPRINT!?
EITHER WAY, THIS MUST BE A MISTAKE...
PAPER: ...KONE ACADEMY; ...MIDA - SECOND-YEAR, NO. 5; ...NAMI - FIRST-YEAR, NO. 6
ZING

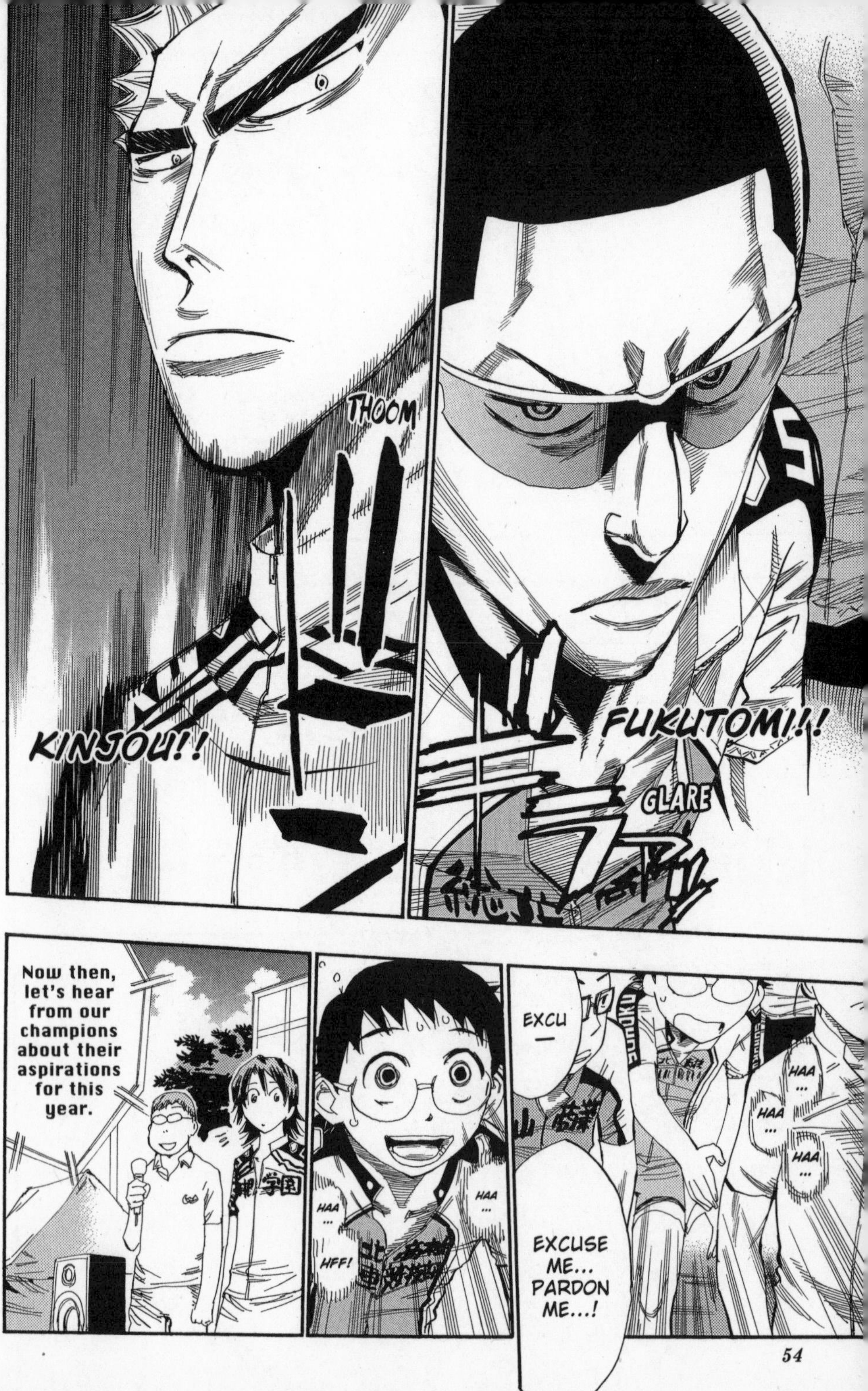
FUKUTOMI!!
GLARE
THOOM
KINJOU!!
EXCU—
HAA...
HAA...
HAA...
EXCUSE ME... PARDON ME...!
HAA...
HAA...
HFF!
Now then, let's hear from our champions about their aspirations for this year.

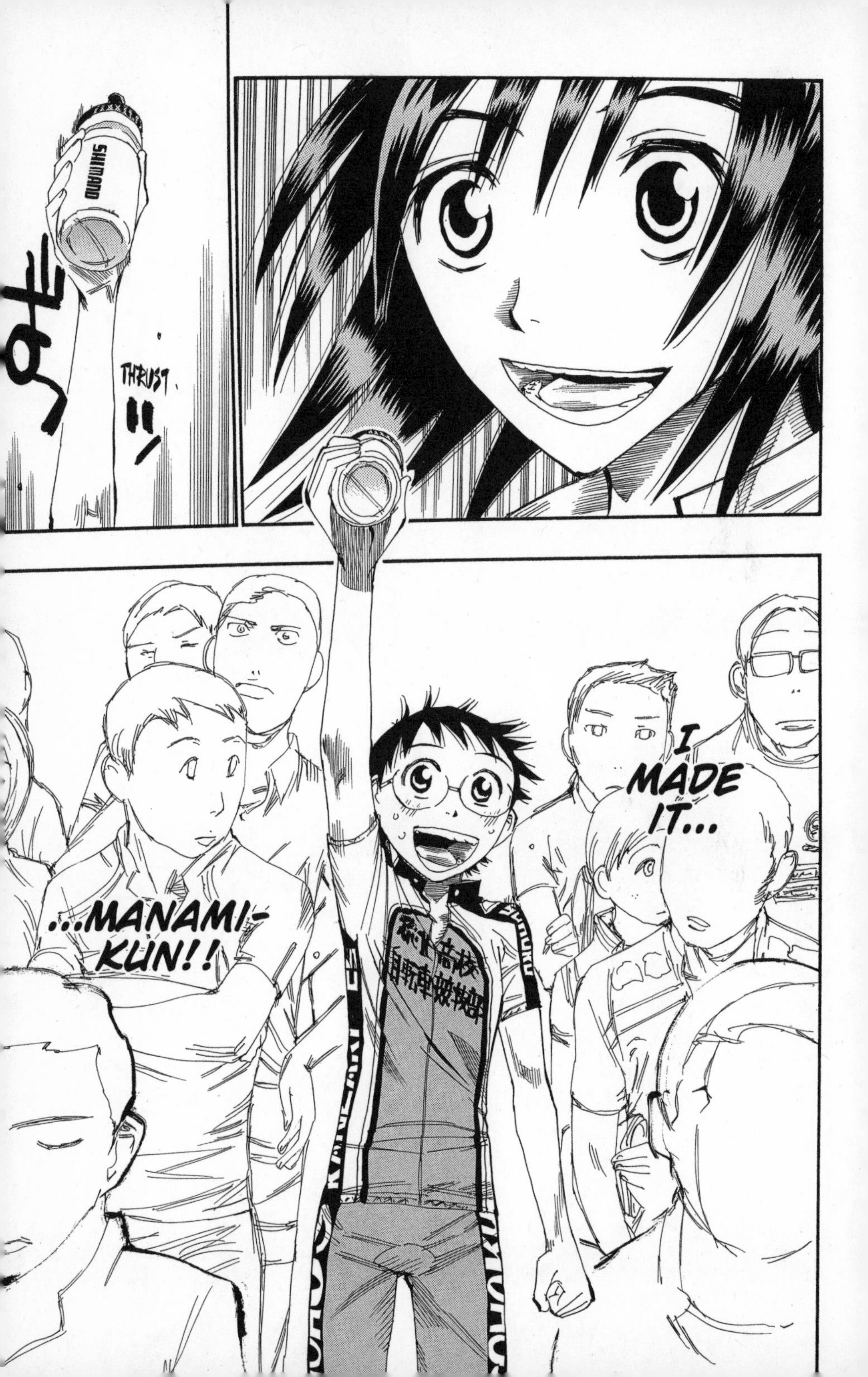
SHIMANO
THRUST
I MADE IT...
...MANAMI-KUN!!

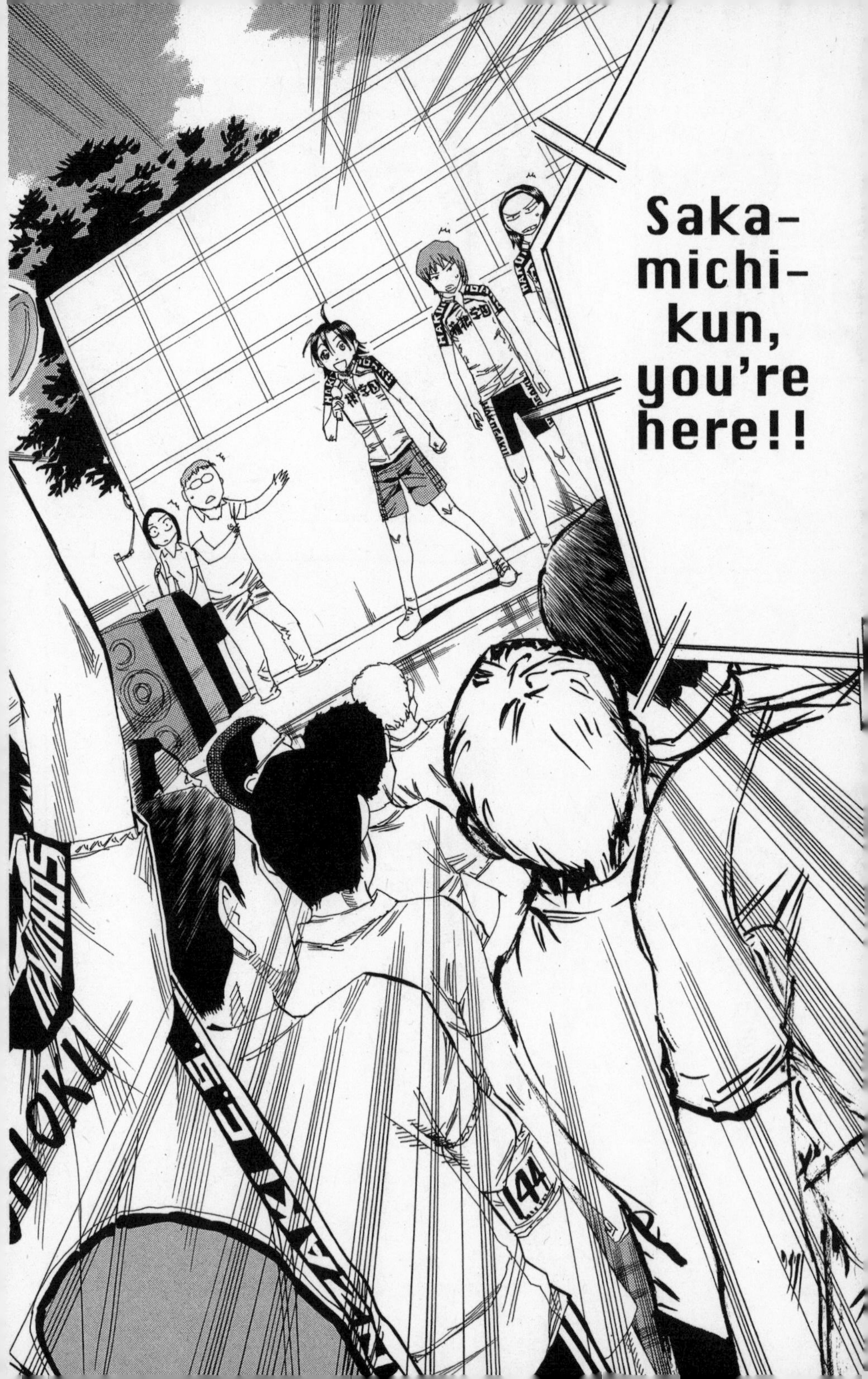
Saka-
michi-
kun,
you're
here!!

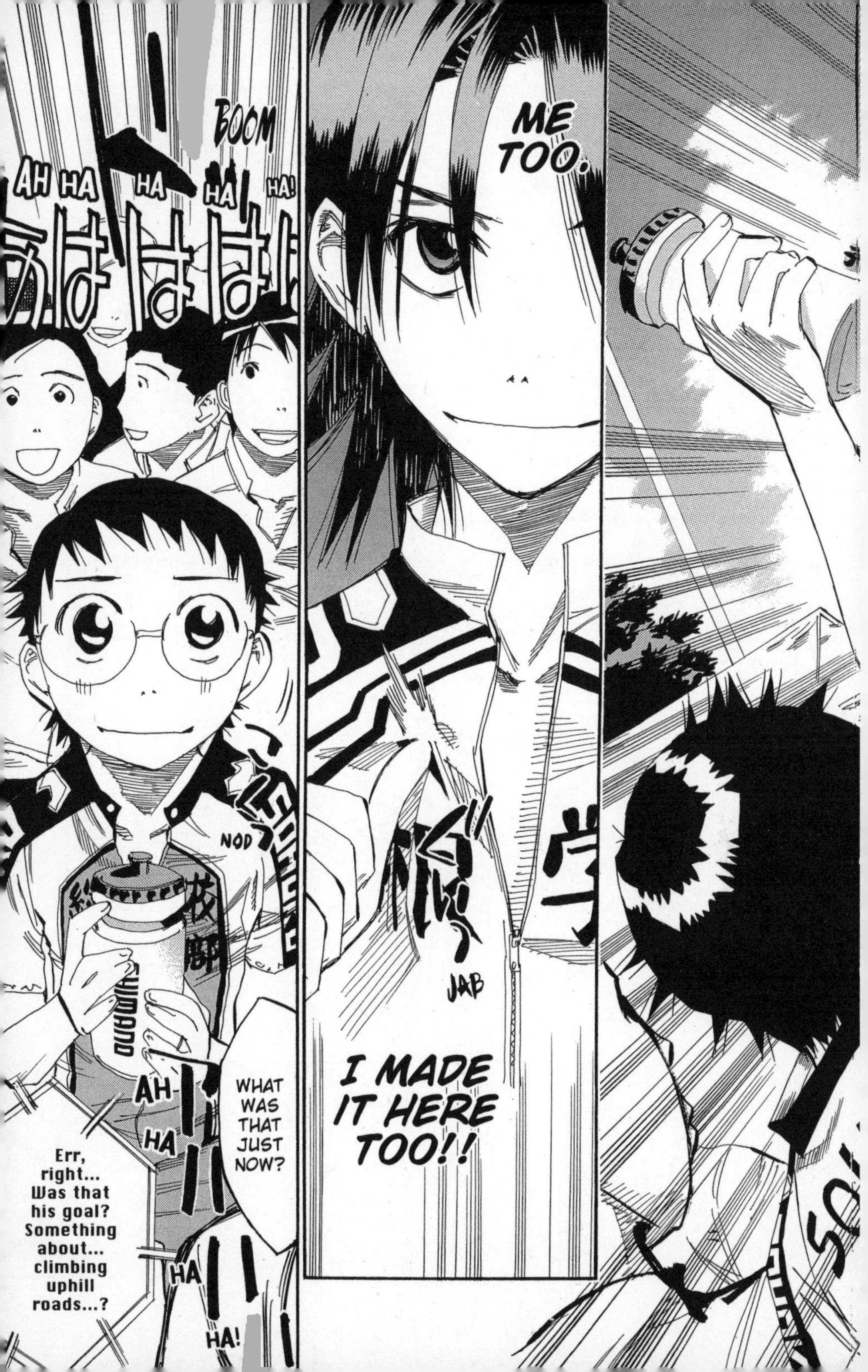
ME TOO.
JAB
I MADE IT HERE TOO!!
BOOM
AH HA HA HA HA!
NOD
WHAT WAS THAT JUST NOW?
Err, right... Was that his goal? Something about... climbing uphill roads...?
AH HA HA HA!

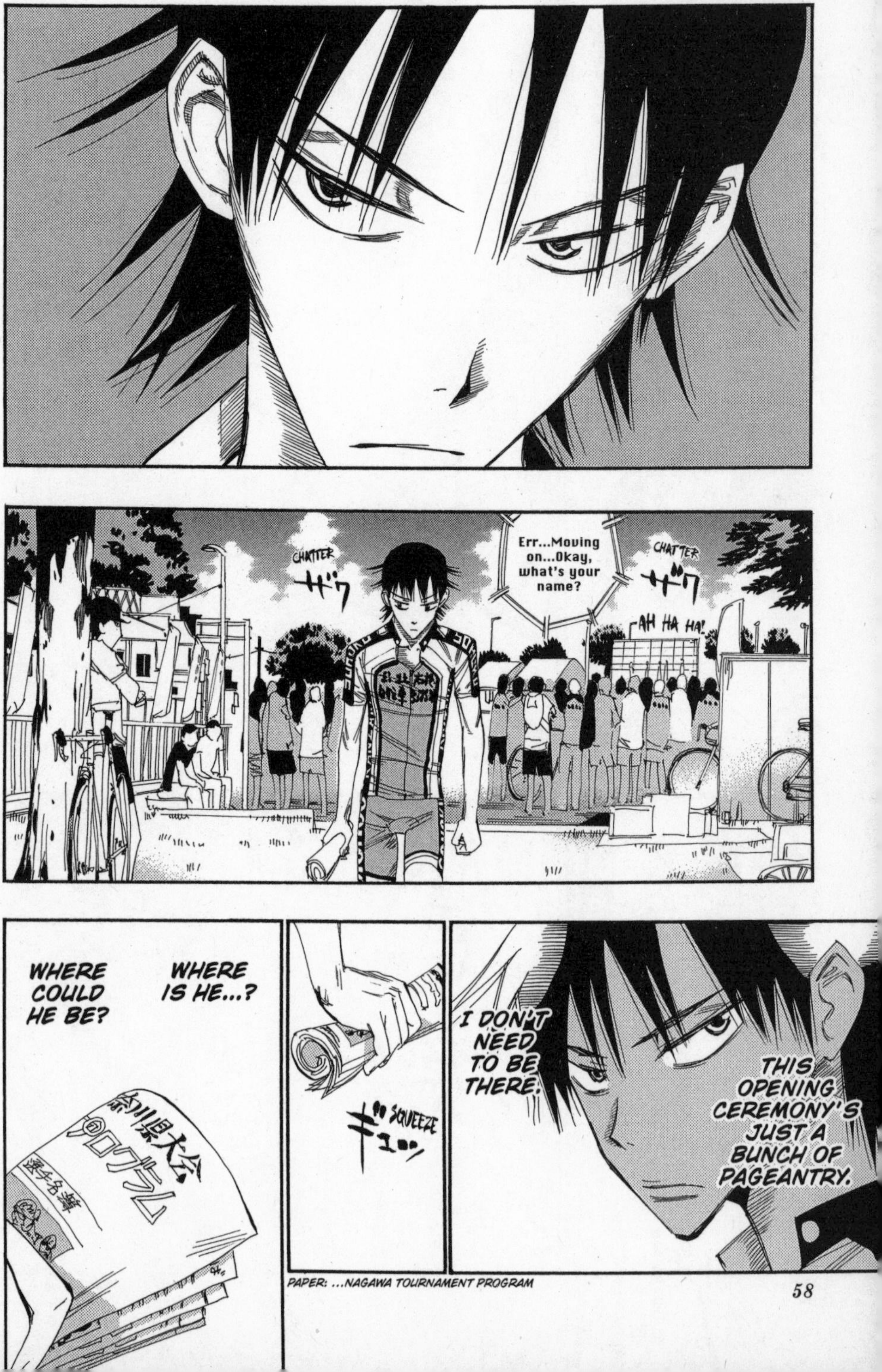
Err...Moving on...Okay, what's your name?
CHATTER
ザワ
AH HA HA!
CHATTER
ザワ
THIS OPENING CEREMONY'S JUST A BUNCH OF PAGEANTRY.
I DON'T NEED TO BE THERE.
SQUEEZE
ギュッ
WHERE IS HE...?
WHERE COULD HE BE?
川県大会
プログラム
選手名簿
PAPER: ...NAGAWA TOURNAMENT PROGRAM

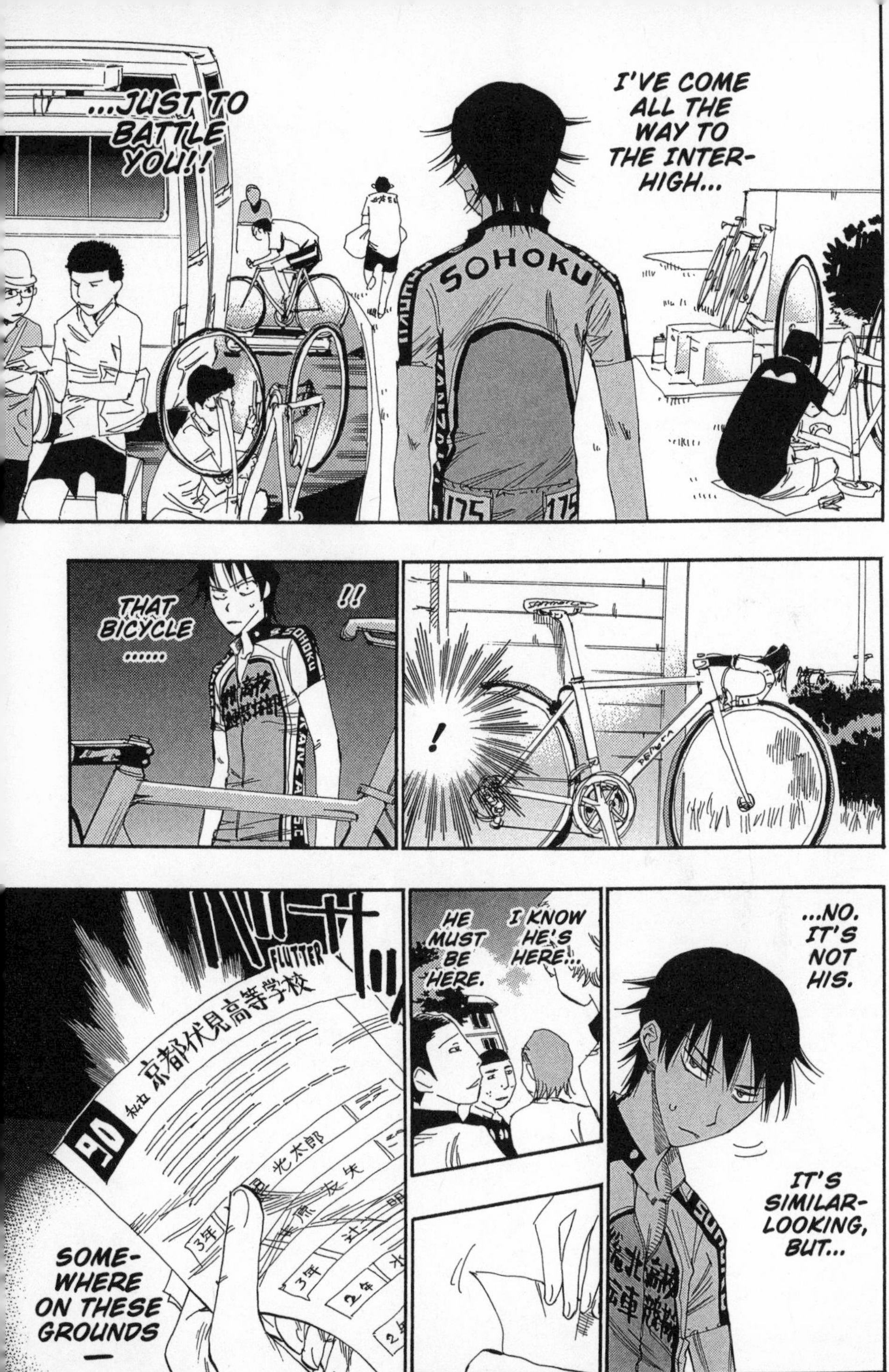
I'VE COME ALL THE WAY TO THE INTER-HIGH...
...JUST TO BATTLE YOU!!
SOHOKU
!
!!
THAT BICYCLE ......
...NO. IT'S NOT HIS.
IT'S SIMILAR-LOOKING, BUT...
I KNOW HE'S HERE...
HE MUST BE HERE.
FLUTTER
私立 京都伏見高等学校
SOME-WHERE ON THESE GROUNDS —

PAPER: PRIVATE KYOTO-FUSHIMI HIGH SCHOOL; THIRD-YEAR KOUTAROU ISHIGAKI; TOMOYA IHARA; THIRD-YEAR AKIHISA TSUJI; SECOND-YEAR NOBU...

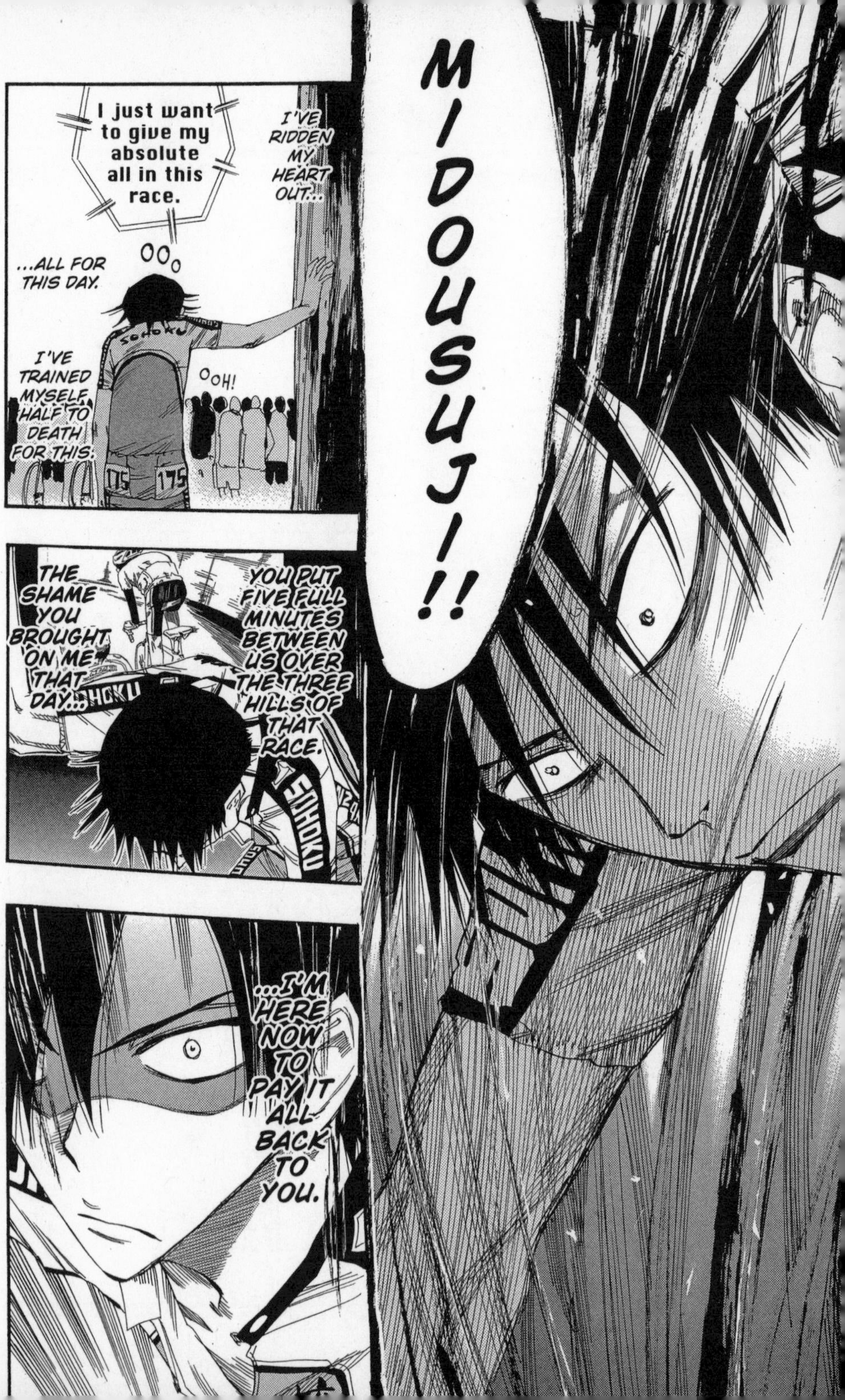
MIDOUSUJI!!
I'VE RIDDEN MY HEART OUT...
I just want to give my absolute all in this race.
OOo
...ALL FOR THIS DAY.
OOH!
I'VE TRAINED MYSELF HALF TO DEATH FOR THIS.
YOU PUT FIVE FULL MINUTES BETWEEN US OVER THE THREE HILLS OF THAT RACE.
THE SHAME YOU BROUGHT ON ME THAT DAY...
...I'M HERE NOW TO PAY IT ALL BACK TO YOU.

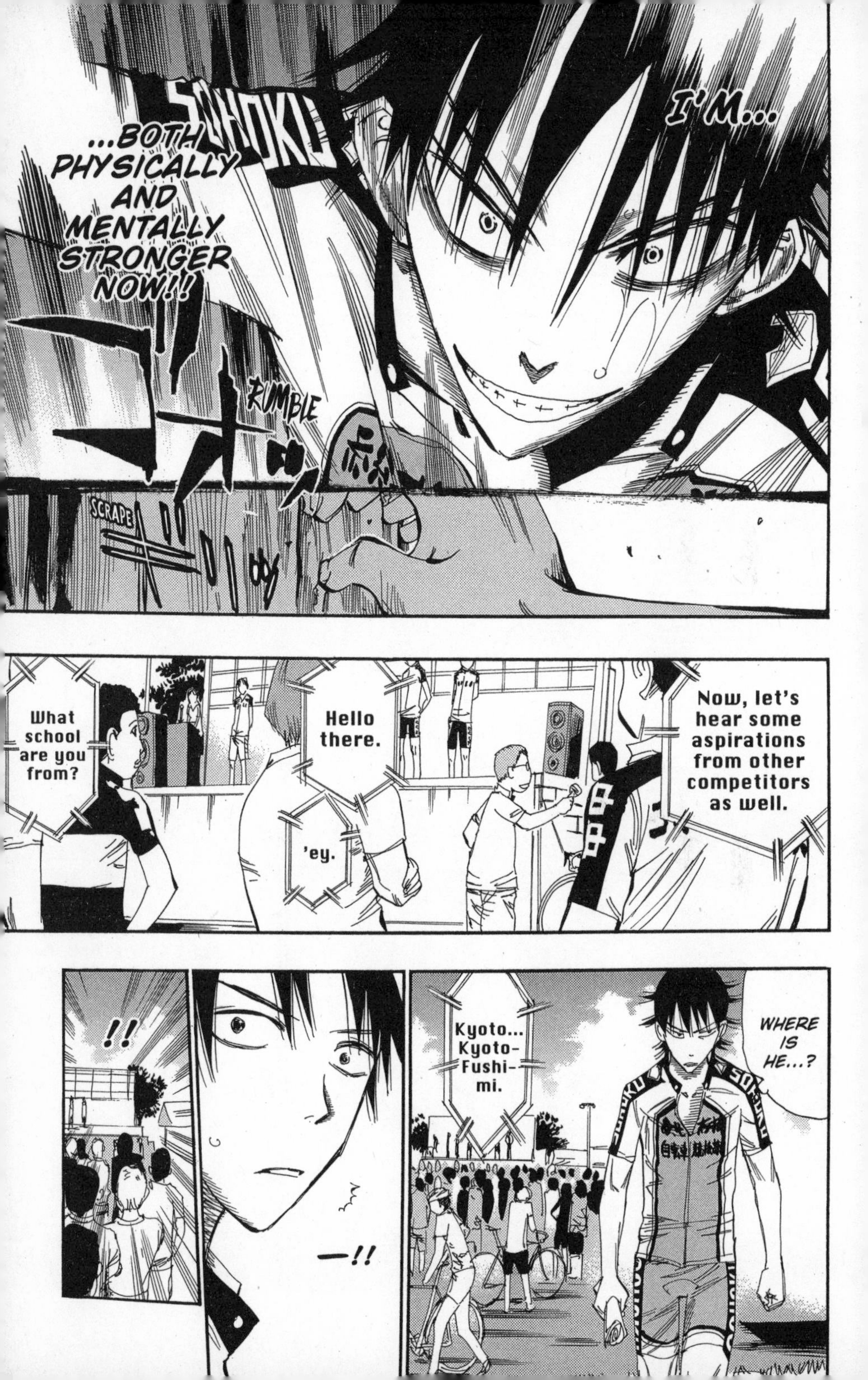
I'M...
...BOTH PHYSICALLY AND MENTALLY STRONGER NOW!!
SOHOKU
RUMBLE
SCRAPE
Now, let's hear some aspirations from other competitors as well.
Hello there.
'ey.
What school are you from?
WHERE IS HE...?
Kyoto... Kyoto-Fushimi.
—!!
!!

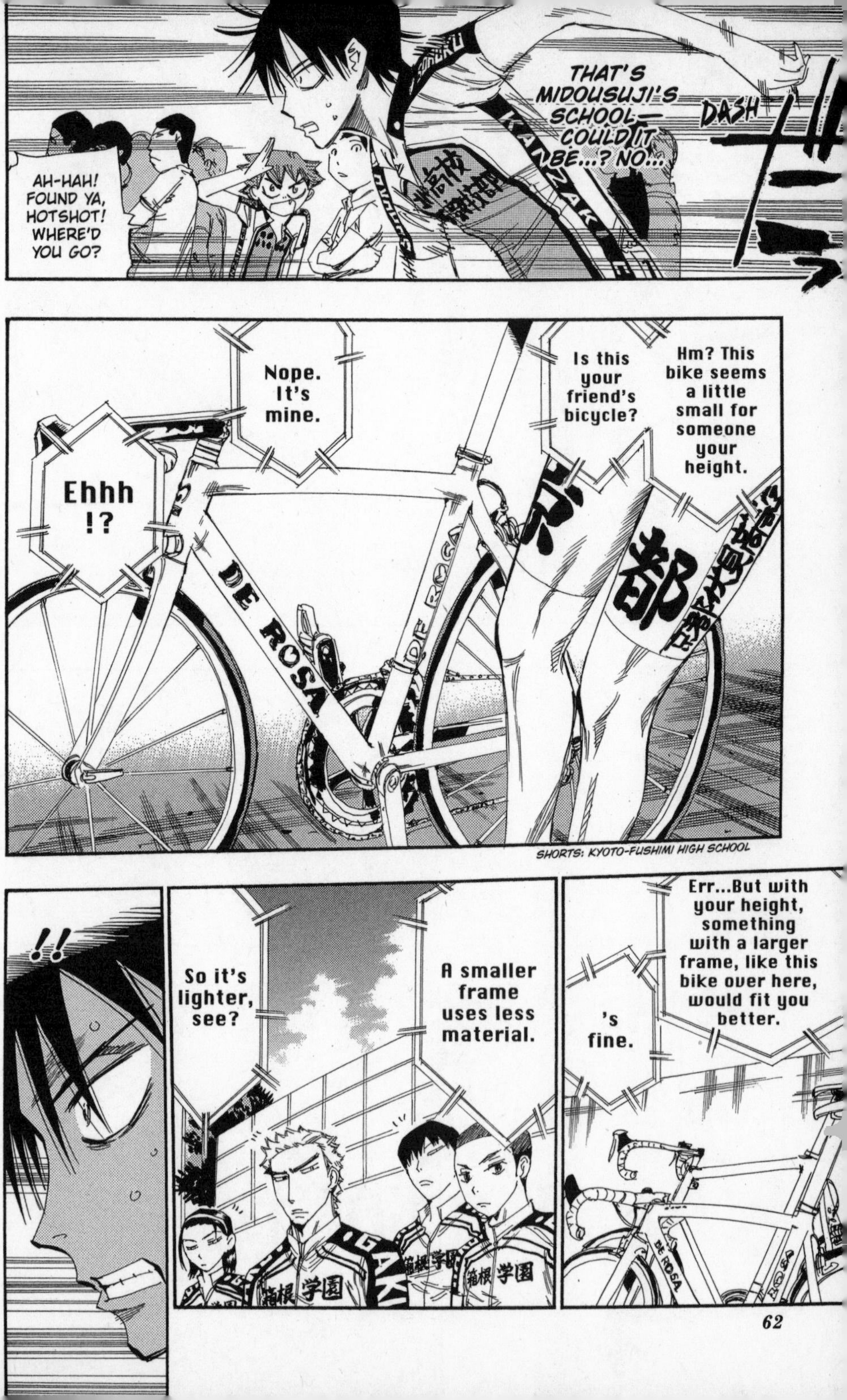
DASH
THAT'S MIDOUSUJI'S SCHOOL—COULD IT BE...? NO...
AH-HAH! FOUND YA, HOTSHOT! WHERE'D YOU GO?
Hm? This bike seems a little small for someone your height.
Is this your friend's bicycle?
Nope. It's mine.
Ehhh !?
SHORTS: KYOTO-FUSHIMI HIGH SCHOOL
Err...But with your height, something with a larger frame, like this bike over here, would fit you better.
's fine.
A smaller frame uses less material.
So it's lighter, see?
!!

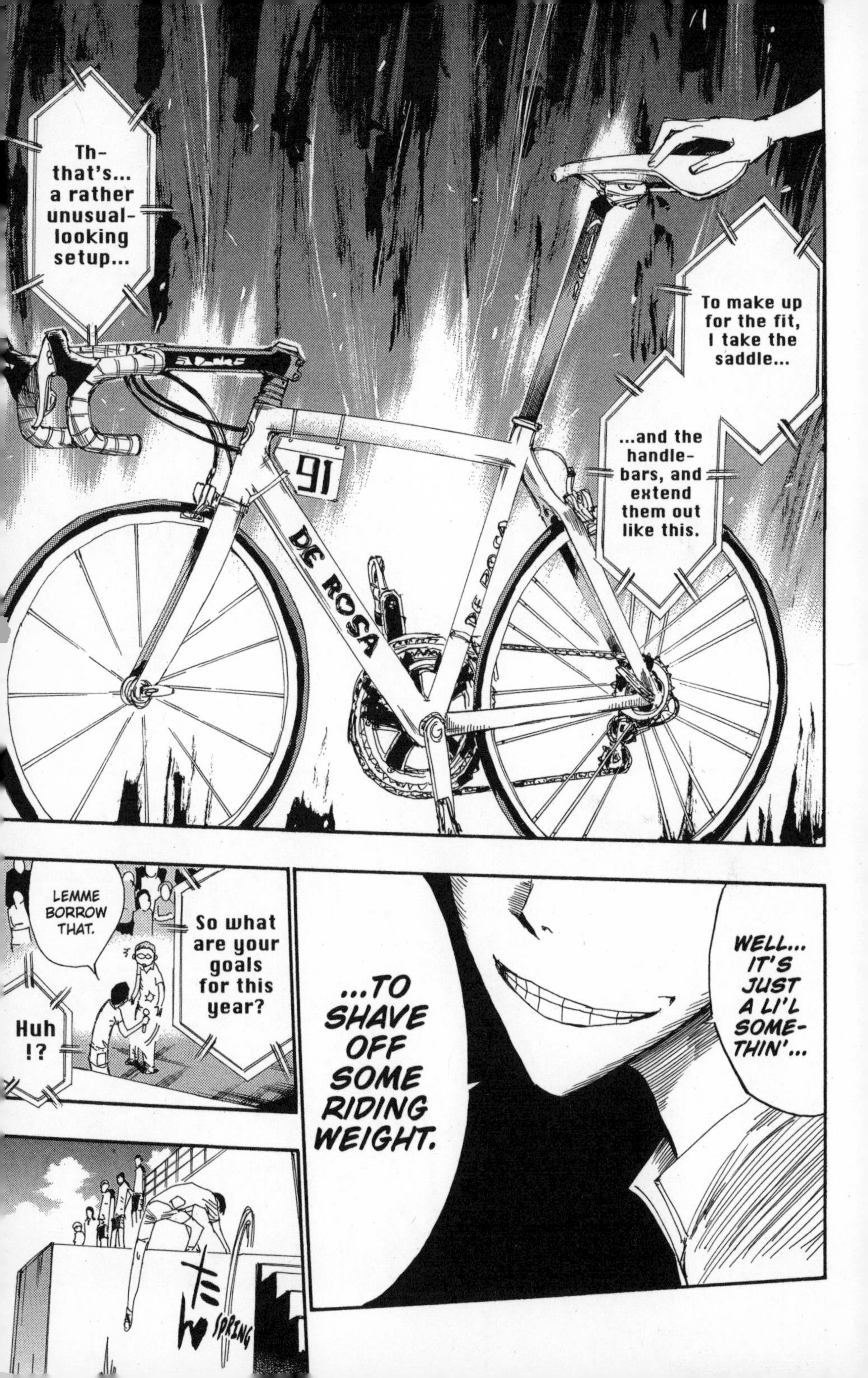
Th-that's... a rather unusual-looking setup...
To make up for the fit, I take the saddle...
...and the handlebars, and extend them out like this.
91
DE ROSA
DE ROSA
WELL... IT'S JUST A LI'L SOMETHIN'...
...TO SHAVE OFF SOME RIDING WEIGHT.
So what are your goals for this year?
LEMME BORROW THAT.
Huh!?
SPRING

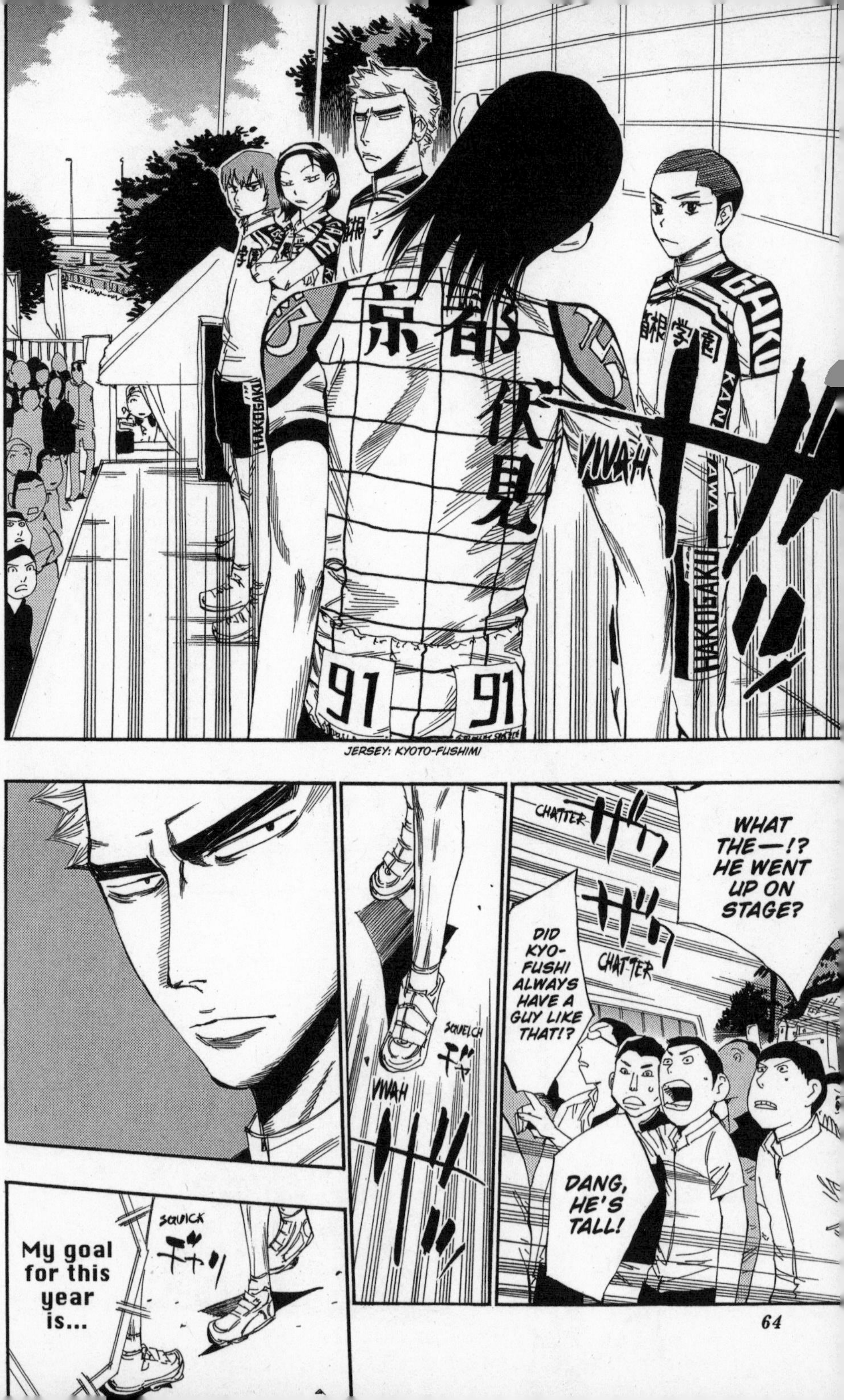
VWAH
京都伏見
箱根学園
HAKOGAKU
JERSEY: KYOTO-FUSHIMI
CHATTER
WHAT THE—!? HE WENT UP ON STAGE?
CHATTER
DID KYO-FUSHI ALWAYS HAVE A GUY LIKE THAT!?
DANG, HE'S TALL!
SQUELCH
VWAH
SQUICK
My goal for this year is...

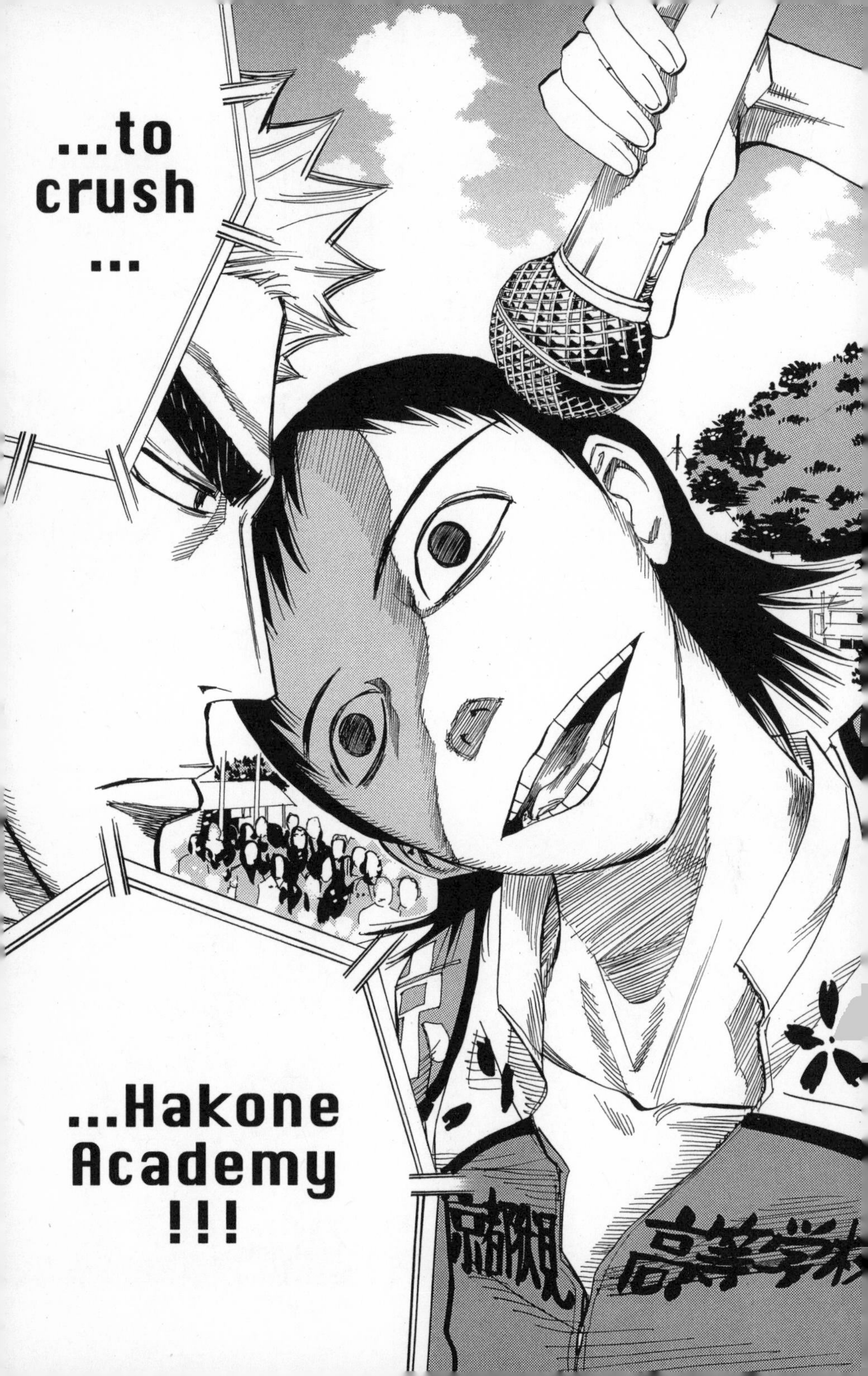
...to crush ...
...Hakone Academy !!!

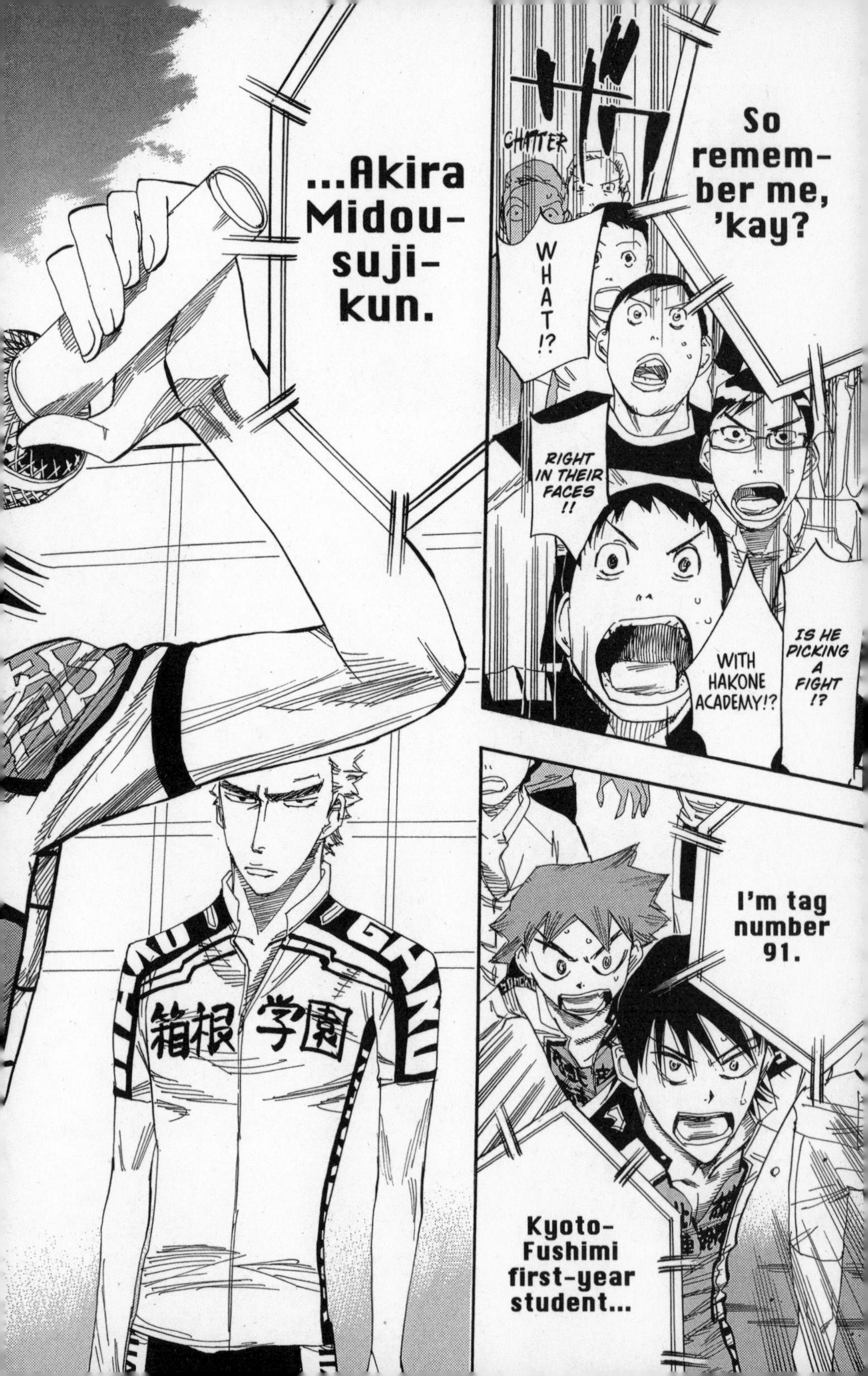
ザワ
CHATTER
So remem-ber me, 'kay?
WHAT!?
RIGHT IN THEIR FACES!!
IS HE PICKING A FIGHT!?
WITH HAKONE ACADEMY!?
I'm tag number 91.
Kyoto-Fushimi first-year student...
...Akira Midou-suji-kun.
箱根学園

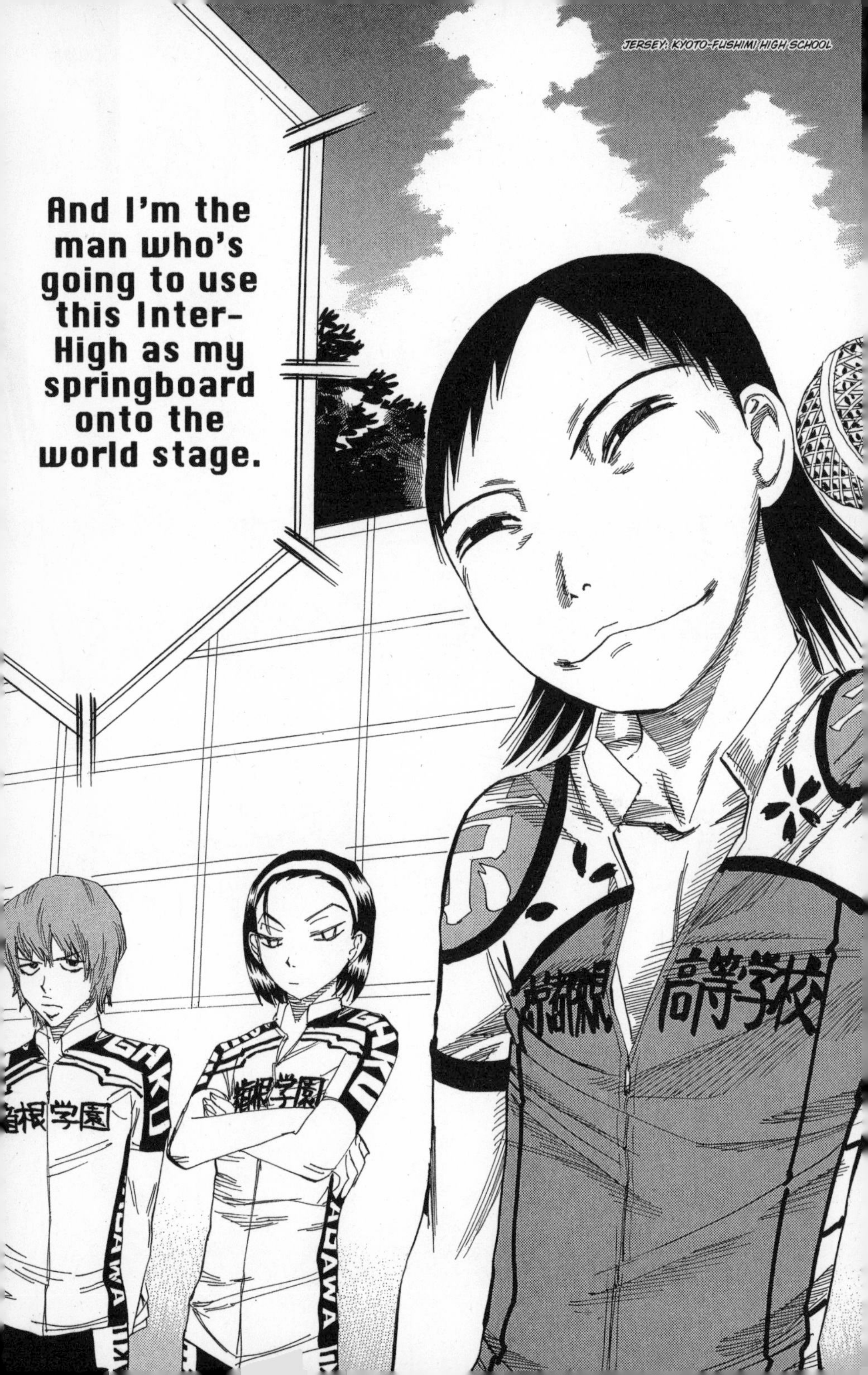
JERSEY: KYOTO-FUSHIMI HIGH SCHOOL
And I'm the man who's going to use this Inter-High as my springboard onto the world stage.
箱根学園
箱根学園
高等学校

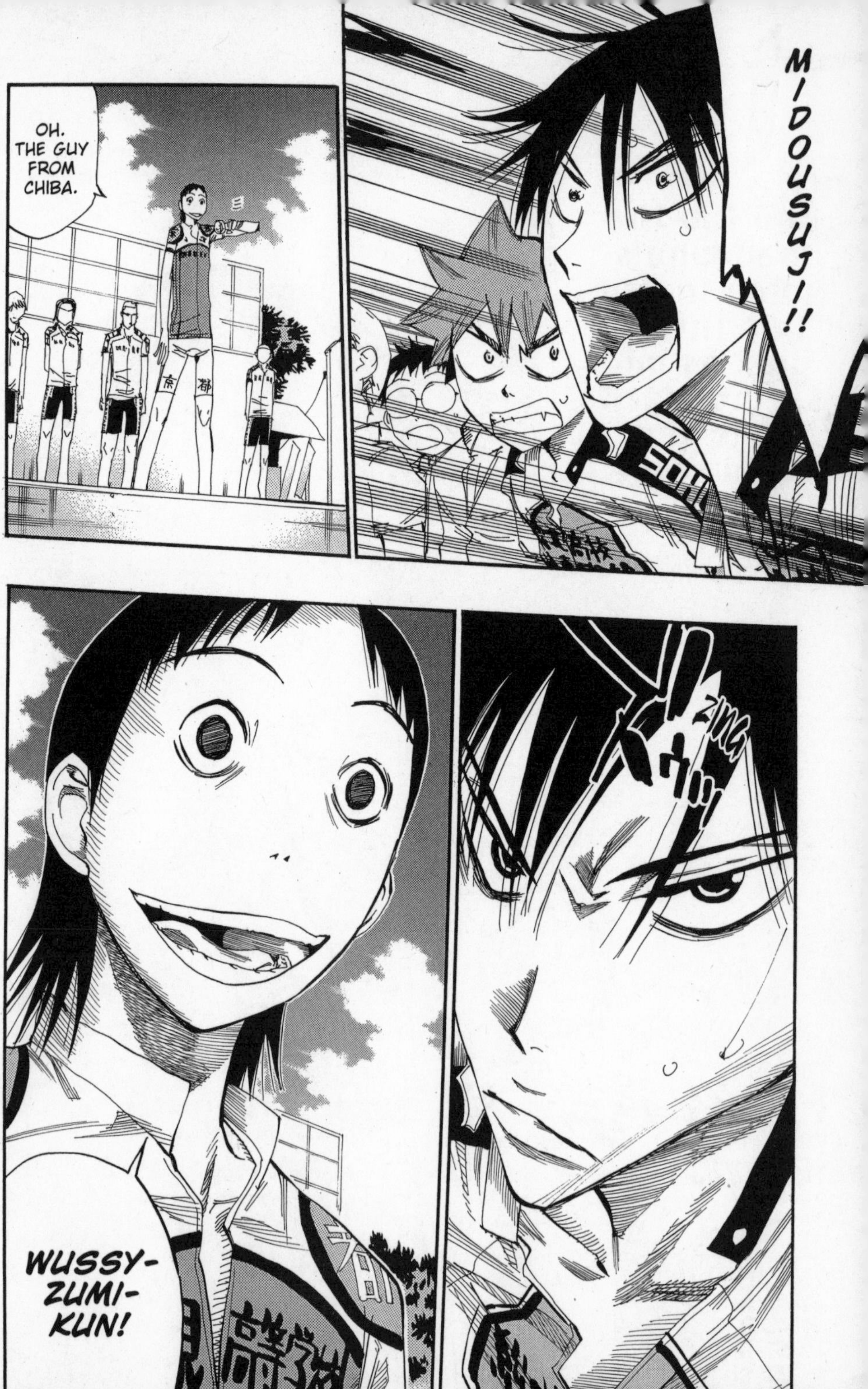
MIDOUSUJI!!
OH. THE GUY FROM CHIBA.
ZING
WUSSY-ZUMI-KUN!

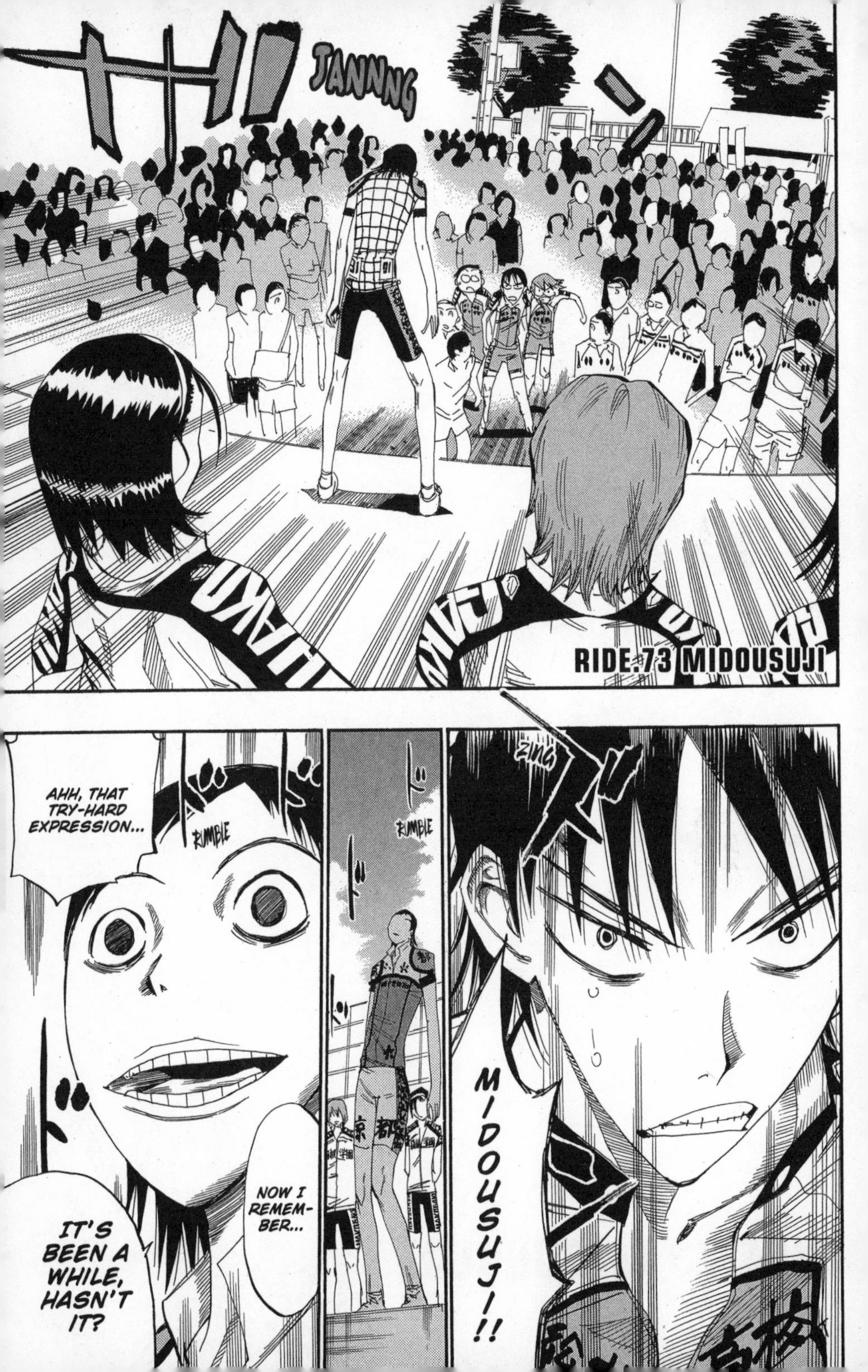
JANNNG
RIDE.73 MIDOUSUJI
ZING
MIDOUSUJI!!
RUMBLE
NOW I REMEMBER...
AHH, THAT TRY-HARD EXPRESSION...
RUMBLE
IT'S BEEN A WHILE, HASN'T IT?

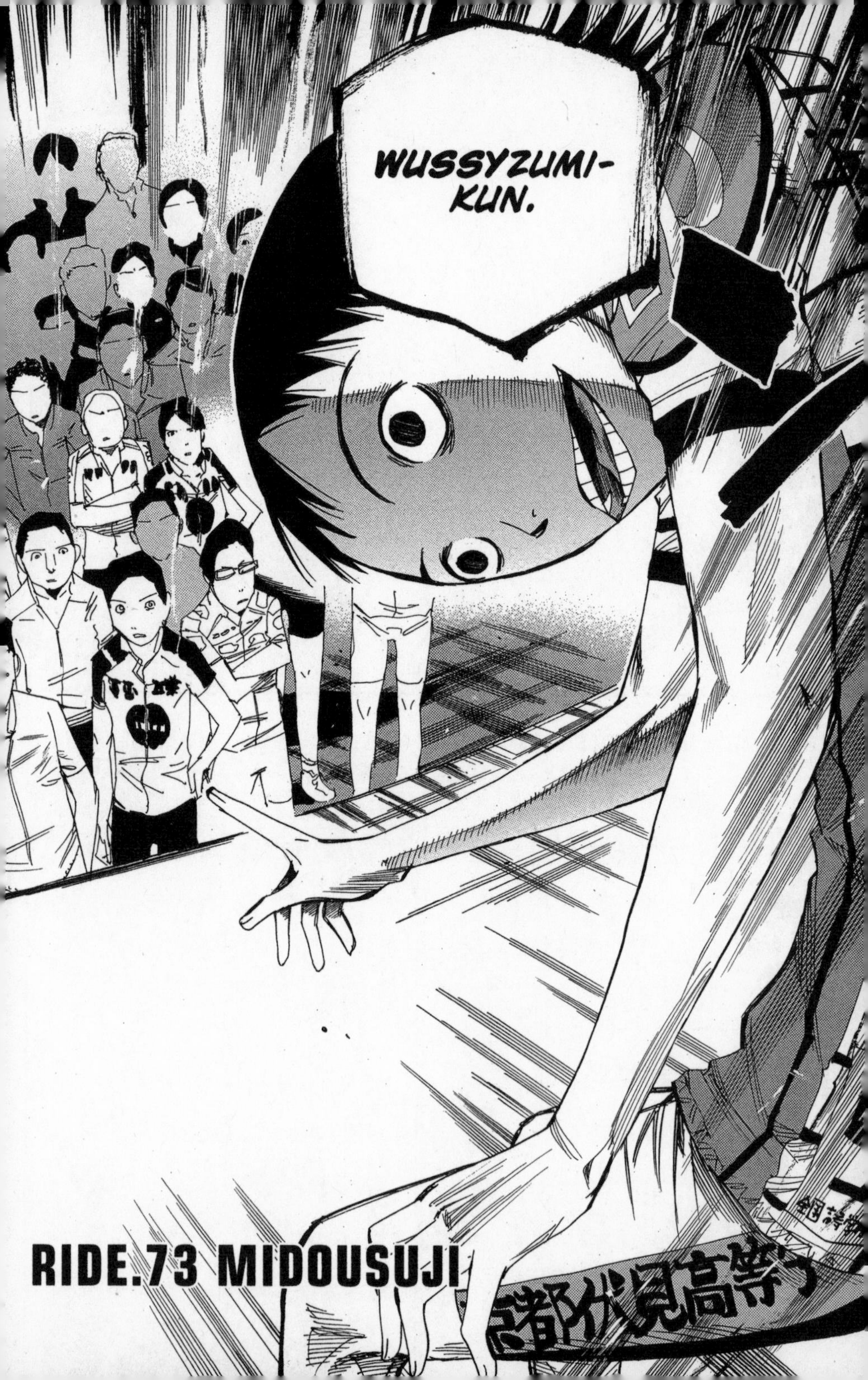
WUSSYZUMI-KUN.
RIDE.73 MIDOUSUJI
京都伏見高等学

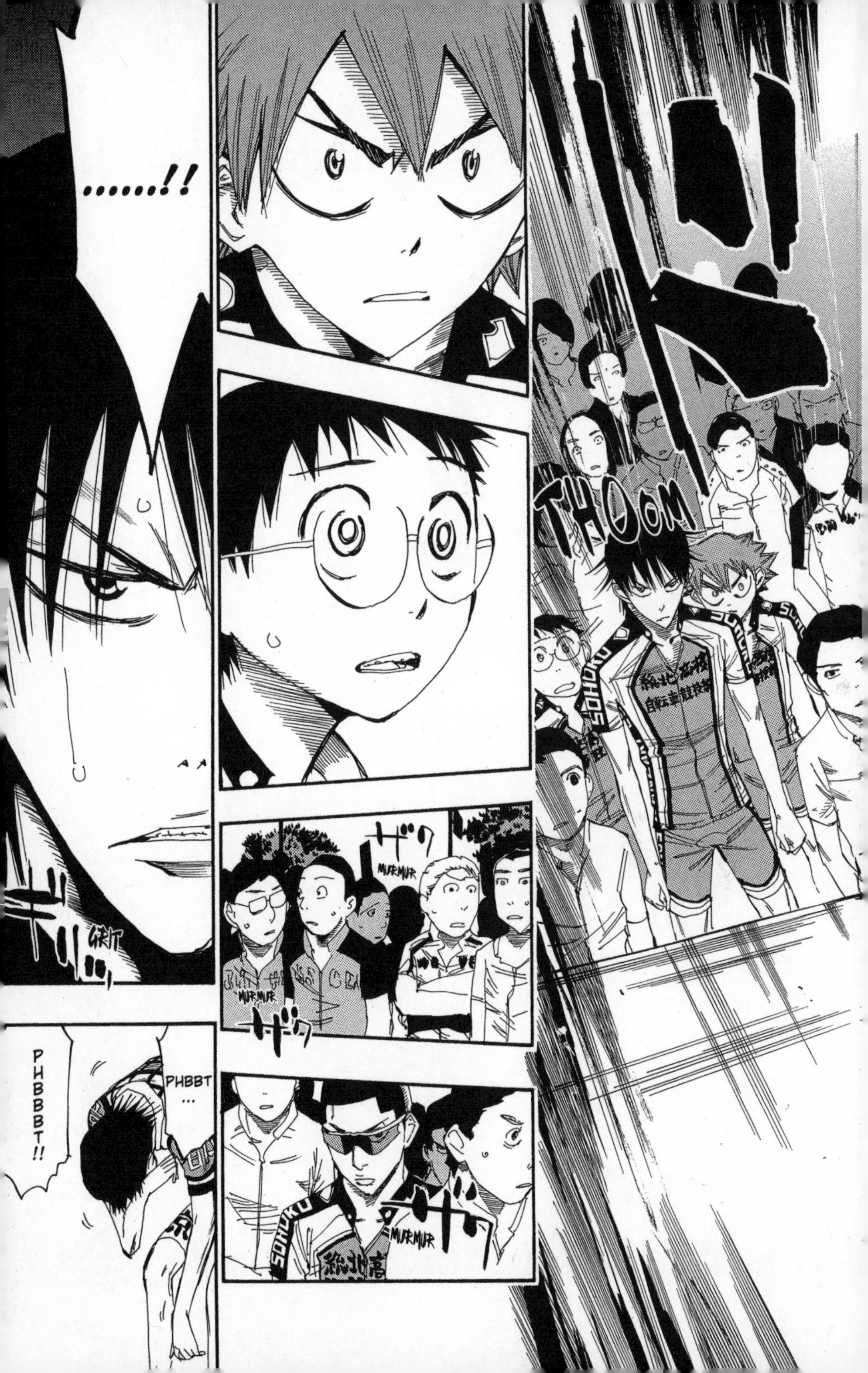
THOOM
MURMUR
MURMUR
MURMUR
......!!
GRIT
PHBBT
...
PHBBBT!!

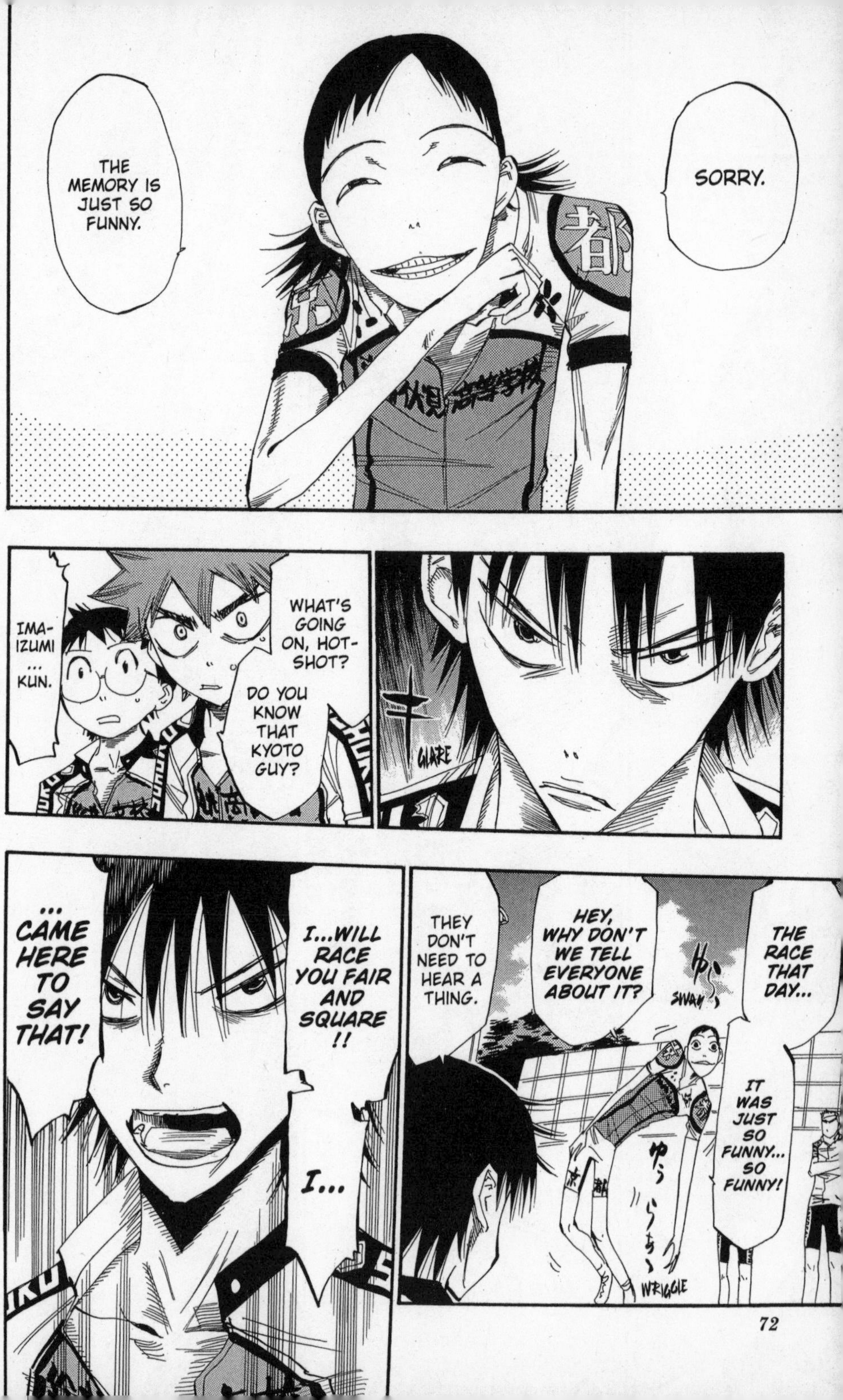
SORRY.
THE MEMORY IS JUST SO FUNNY.
GLARE
WHAT'S GOING ON, HOT-SHOT?
DO YOU KNOW THAT KYOTO GUY?
IMA-IZUMI ... KUN.
THE RACE THAT DAY...
HEY, WHY DON'T WE TELL EVERYONE ABOUT IT?
THEY DON'T NEED TO HEAR A THING.
SWAY
IT WAS JUST SO FUNNY... SO FUNNY!
WRIGGLE
I...WILL RACE YOU FAIR AND SQUARE!!
...CAME HERE TO SAY THAT!
I...

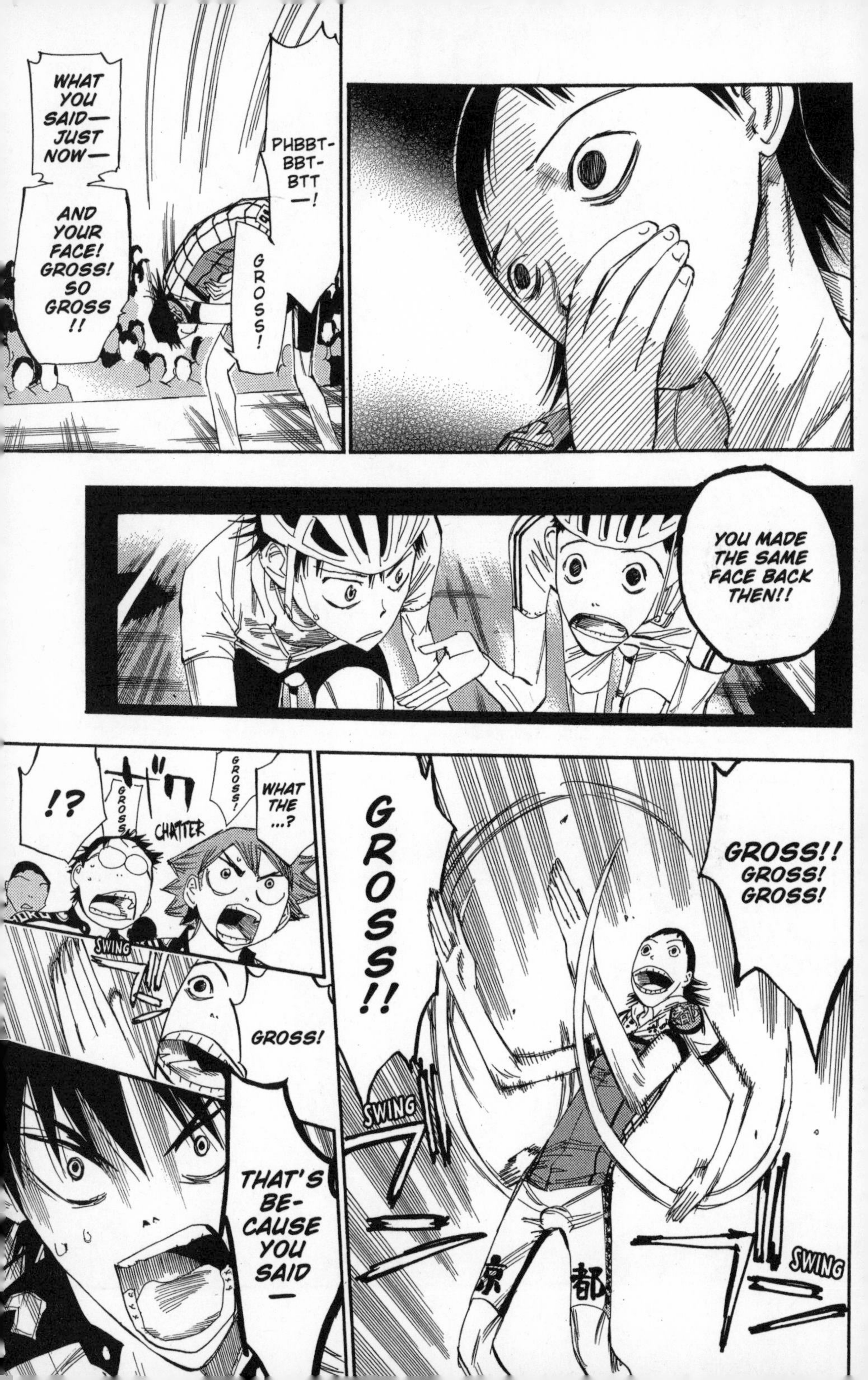
PHBBT-BBT-BTT—!
WHAT YOU SAID—JUST NOW—
GROSS!
AND YOUR FACE! GROSS! SO GROSS!!
YOU MADE THE SAME FACE BACK THEN!!
GROSS!! GROSS! GROSS!
GROSS!!
SWING
SWING
京都
WHAT THE ...?
GROSS!
GROSS
CHATTER
!?
SWING
GROSS!
THAT'S BE-CAUSE YOU SAID—

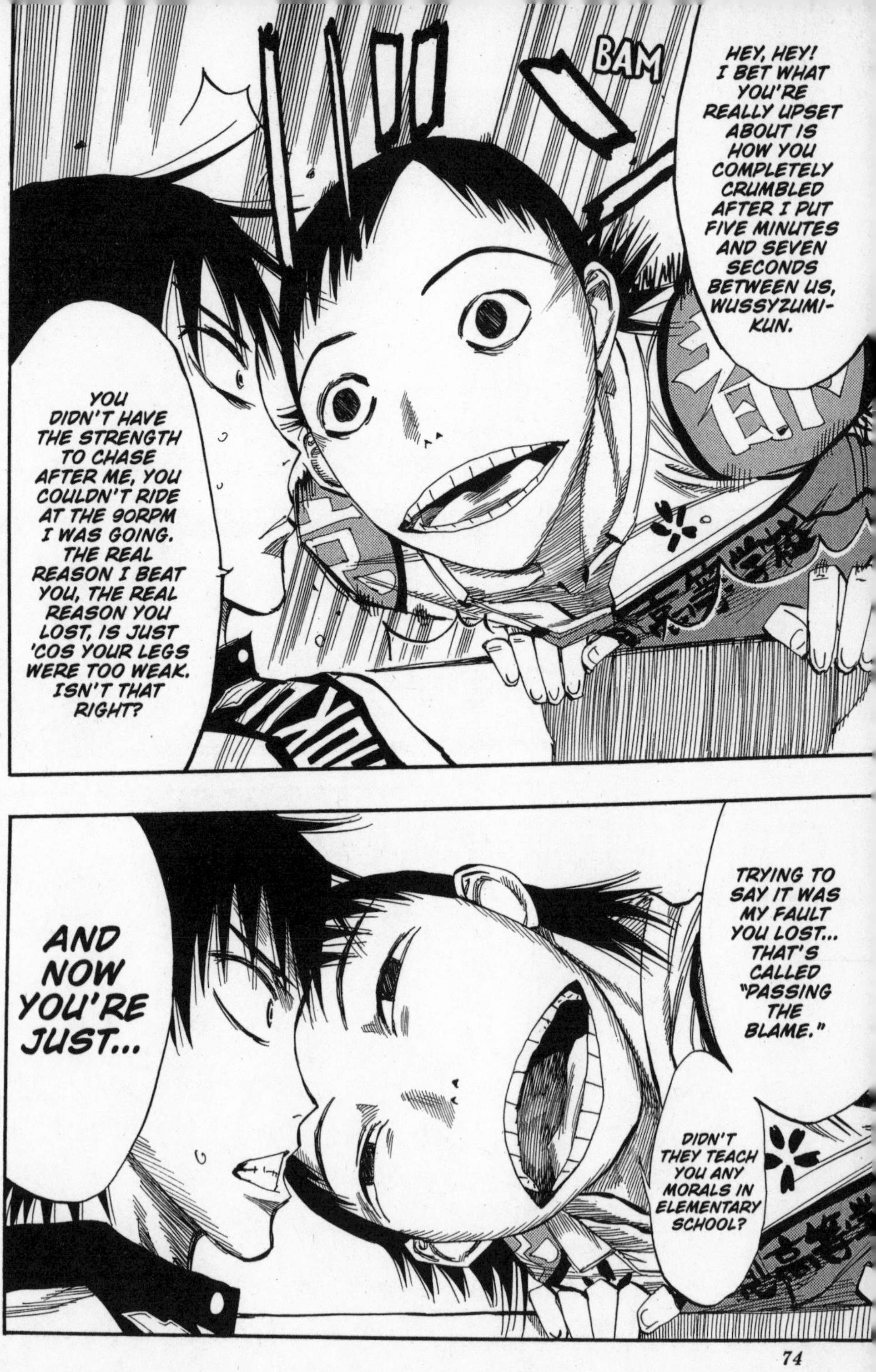
BAM
HEY, HEY! I BET WHAT YOU'RE REALLY UPSET ABOUT IS HOW YOU COMPLETELY CRUMBLED AFTER I PUT FIVE MINUTES AND SEVEN SECONDS BETWEEN US, WUSSYZUMI-KUN.
YOU DIDN'T HAVE THE STRENGTH TO CHASE AFTER ME, YOU COULDN'T RIDE AT THE 90RPM I WAS GOING. THE REAL REASON I BEAT YOU, THE REAL REASON YOU LOST, IS JUST 'COS YOUR LEGS WERE TOO WEAK. ISN'T THAT RIGHT?
TRYING TO SAY IT WAS MY FAULT YOU LOST... THAT'S CALLED "PASSING THE BLAME."
DIDN'T THEY TEACH YOU ANY MORALS IN ELEMENTARY SCHOOL?
AND NOW YOU'RE JUST...

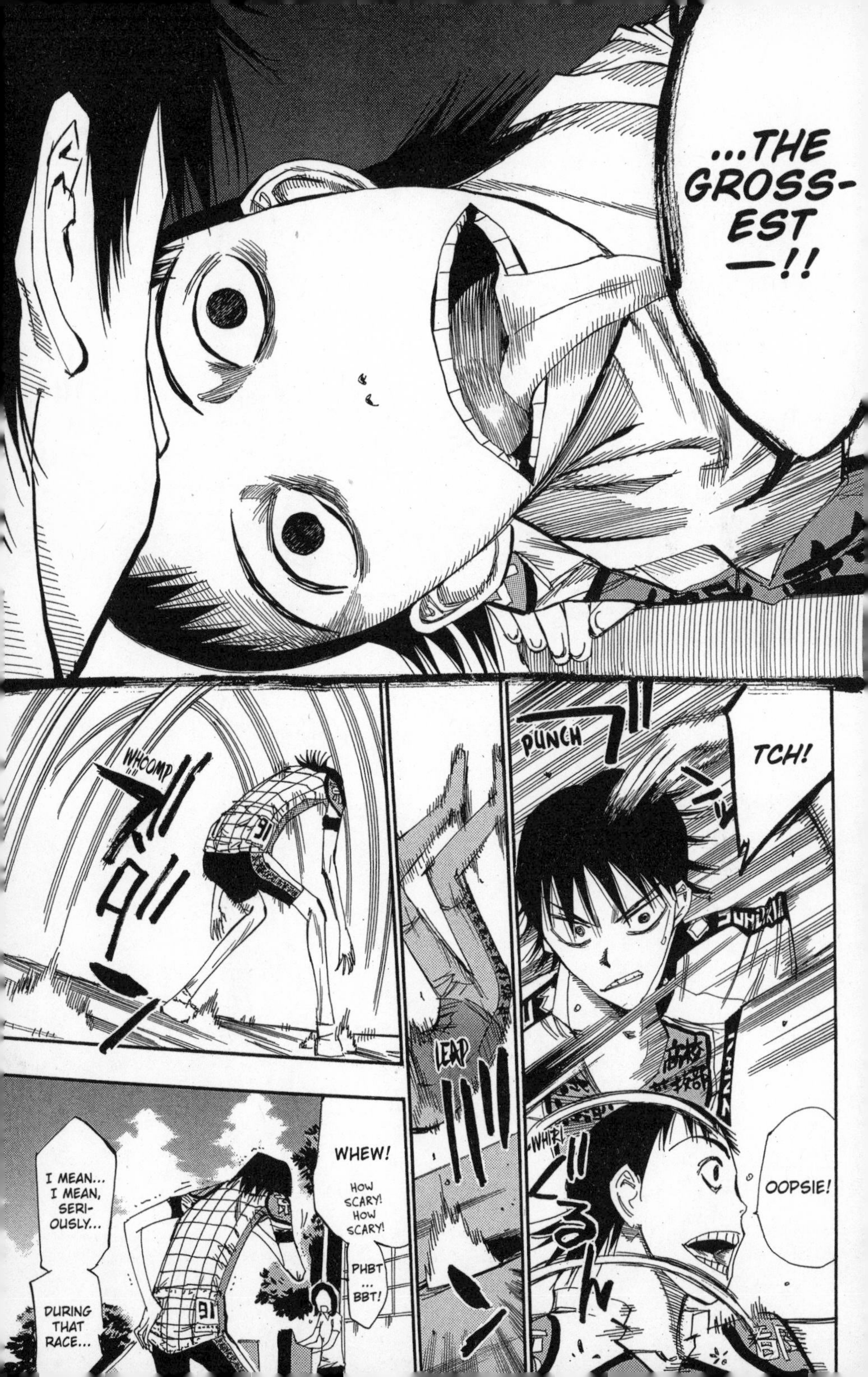
...THE GROSS-EST —!!
PUNCH
TCH!
LEAP
WHOOMP
WHIRL
OOPSIE!
WHEW!
HOW SCARY! HOW SCARY!
PHBT ... BBT!
I MEAN... I MEAN, SERI-OUSLY...
DURING THAT RACE...

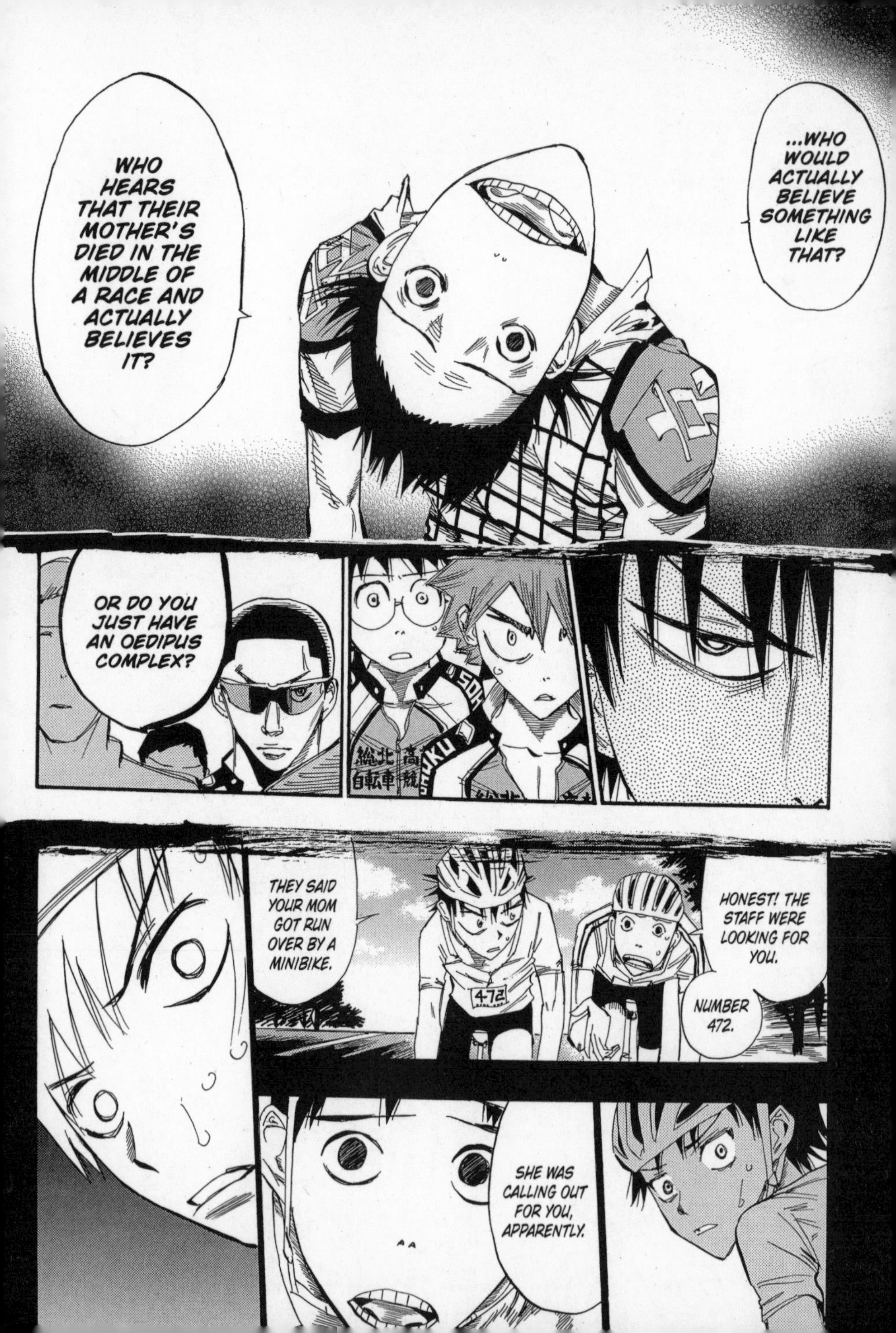
...WHO WOULD ACTUALLY BELIEVE SOMETHING LIKE THAT?
WHO HEARS THAT THEIR MOTHER'S DIED IN THE MIDDLE OF A RACE AND ACTUALLY BELIEVES IT?
OR DO YOU JUST HAVE AN OEDIPUS COMPLEX?
HONEST! THE STAFF WERE LOOKING FOR YOU.
NUMBER 472.
THEY SAID YOUR MOM GOT RUN OVER BY A MINIBIKE.
SHE WAS CALLING OUT FOR YOU, APPARENTLY.

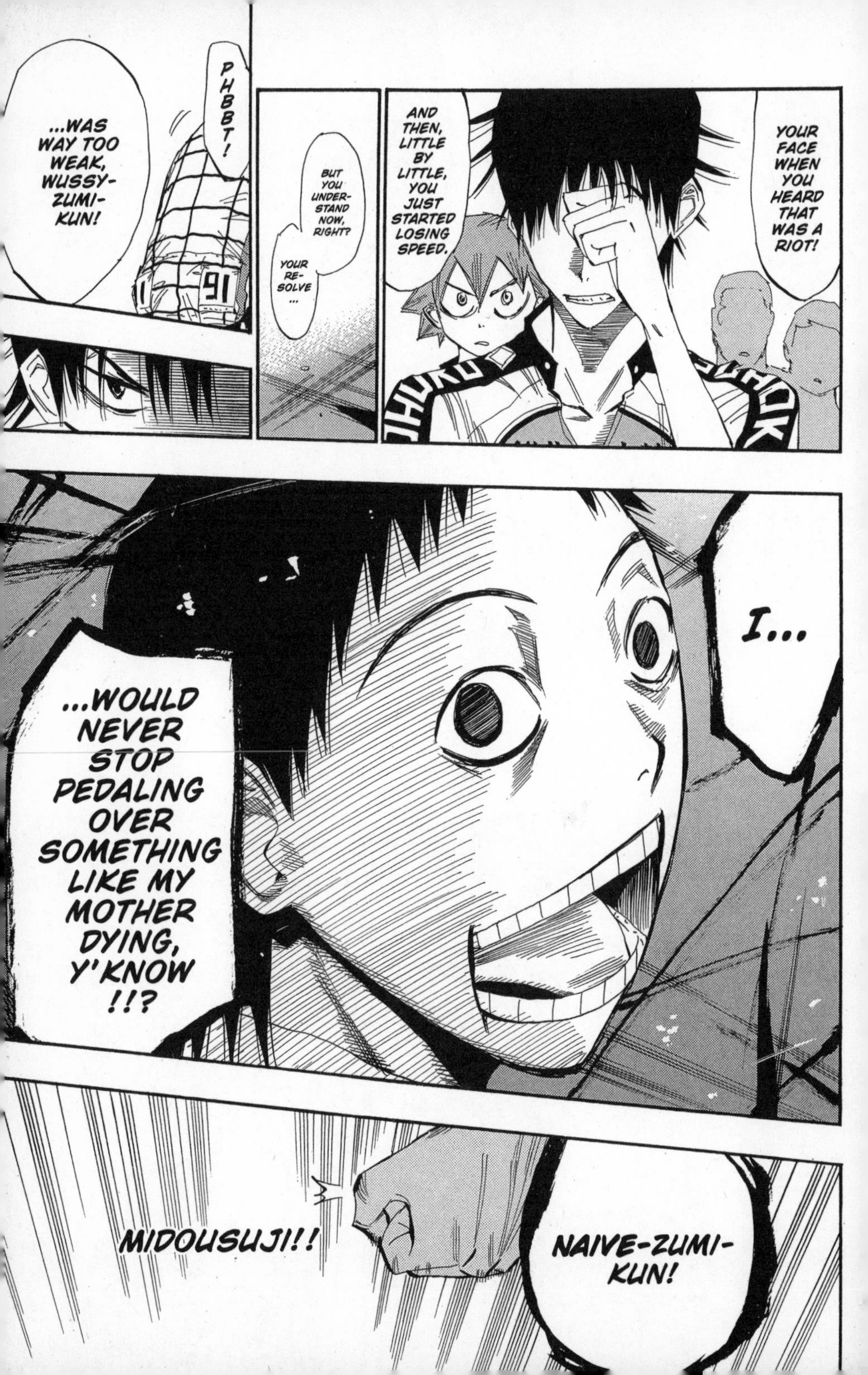
YOUR FACE WHEN YOU HEARD THAT WAS A RIOT!
AND THEN, LITTLE BY LITTLE, YOU JUST STARTED LOSING SPEED.
BUT YOU UNDERSTAND NOW, RIGHT?
YOUR RESOLVE...
PHBBT!
...WAS WAY TOO WEAK, WUSSY-ZUMI-KUN!
I...
...WOULD NEVER STOP PEDALING OVER SOMETHING LIKE MY MOTHER DYING, Y'KNOW!!?
NAIVE-ZUMI-KUN!
MIDOUSUJI!!

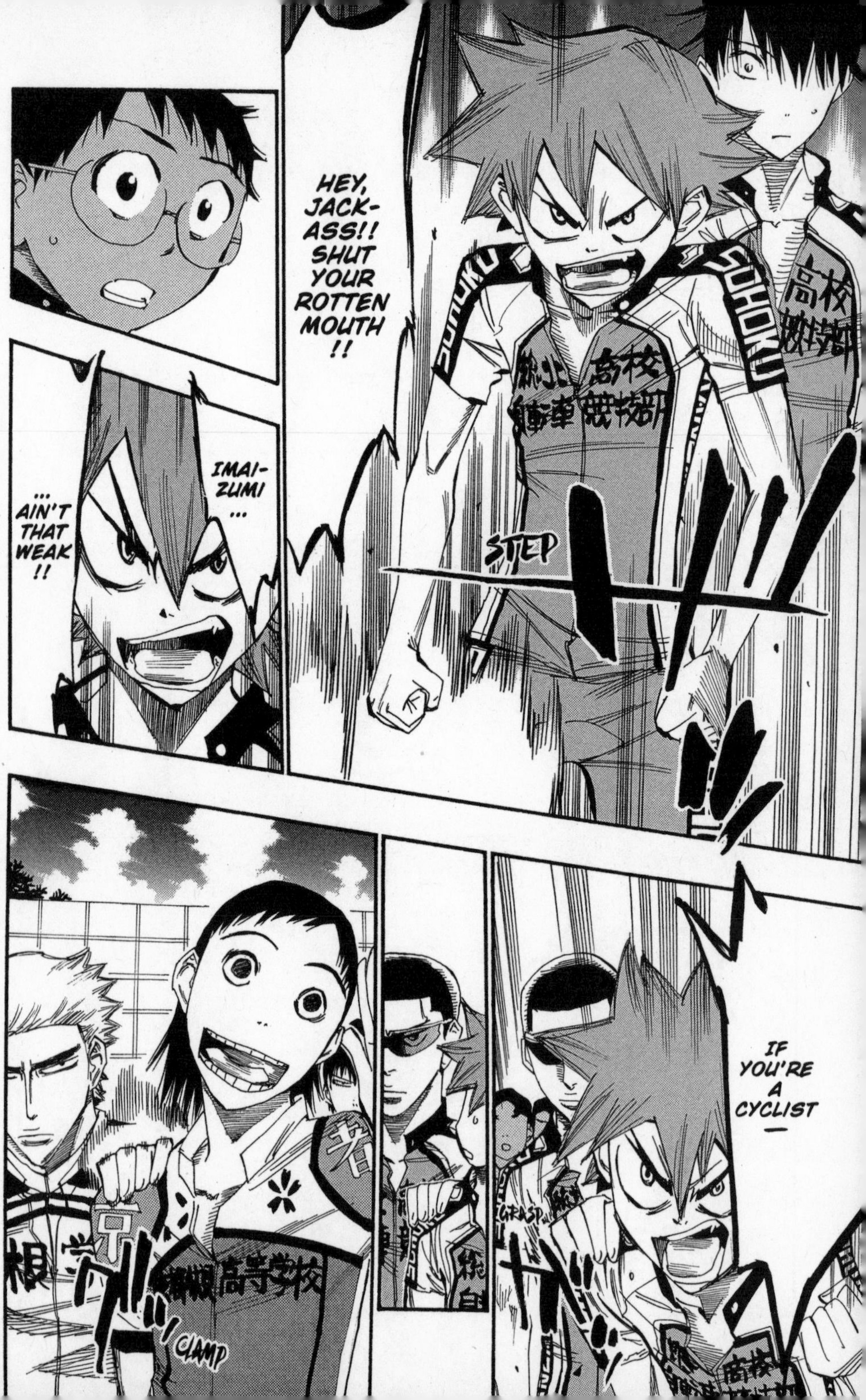
HEY, JACK-ASS!! SHUT YOUR ROTTEN MOUTH!!
STEP
IMAI-ZUMI...
...AIN'T THAT WEAK!!
IF YOU'RE A CYCLIST—
GRASP
CLAMP

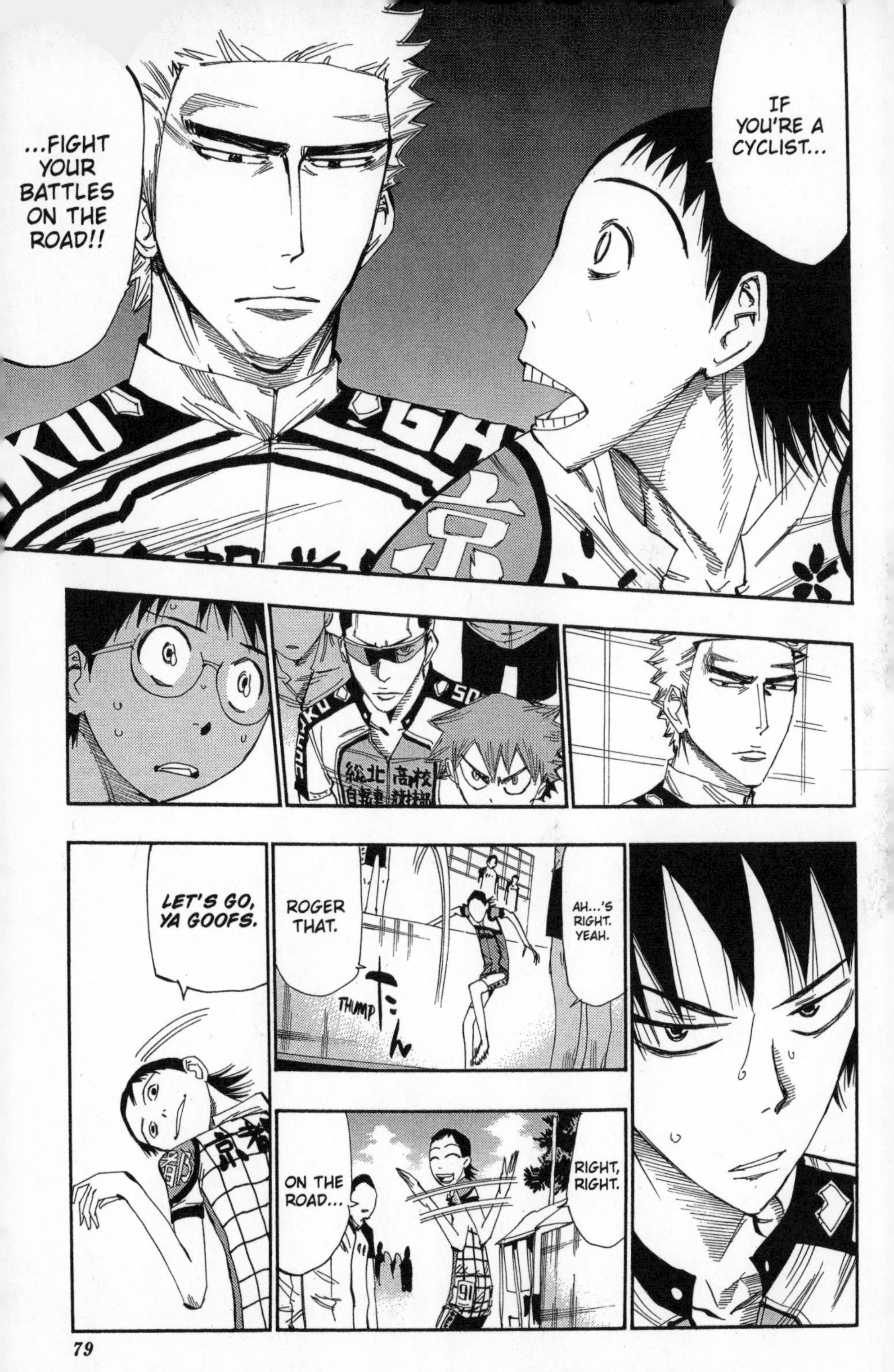
IF YOU'RE A CYCLIST...
...FIGHT YOUR BATTLES ON THE ROAD!!
AH...'S RIGHT. YEAH.
ROGER THAT.
THUMP
RIGHT, RIGHT.
ON THE ROAD...
LET'S GO, YA GOOFS.

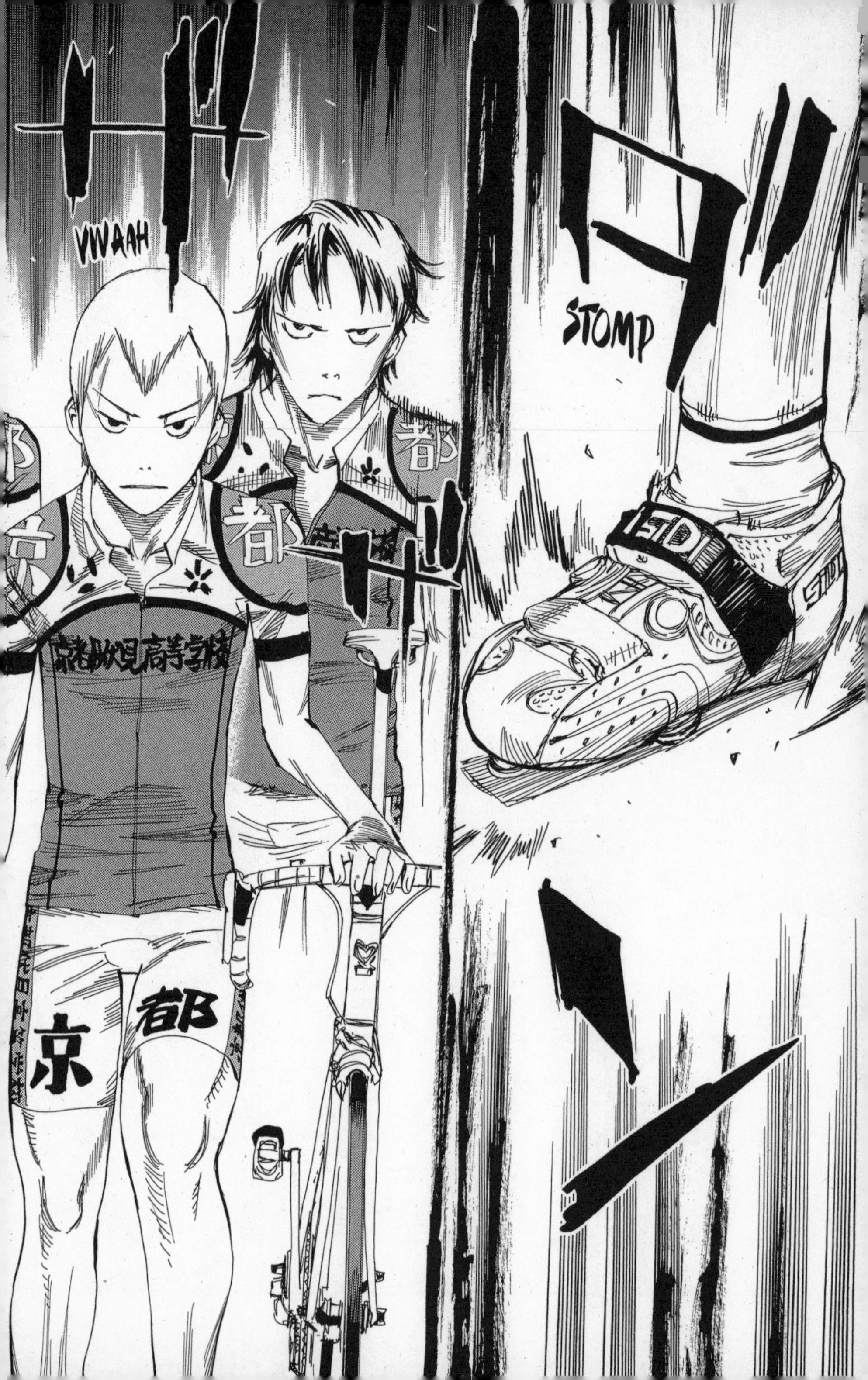
STOMP
VWAAH

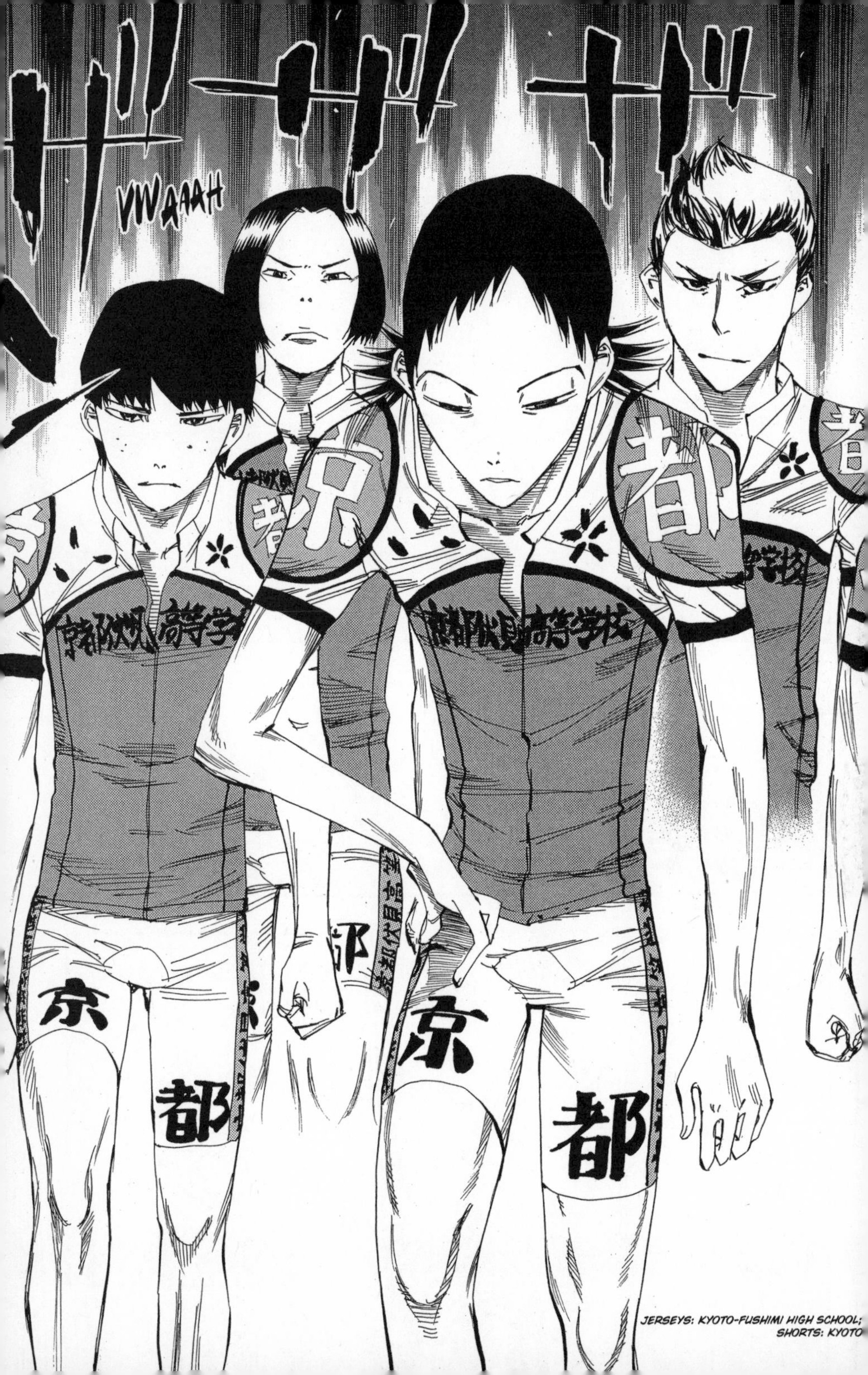
VWAAAH
JERSEYS: KYOTO-FUSHIMI HIGH SCHOOL;
SHORTS: KYOTO

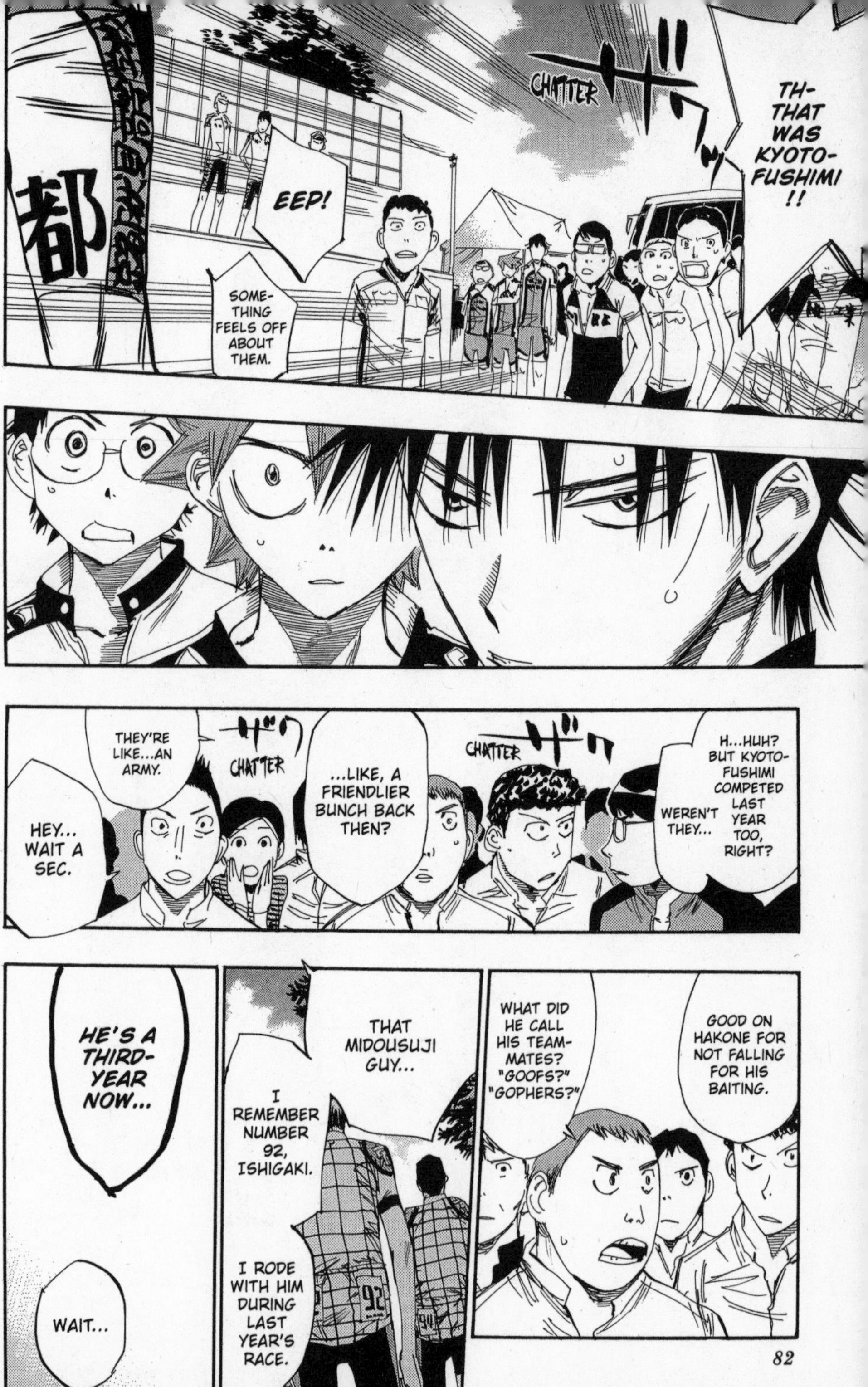
CHATTER
TH-THAT WAS KYOTO-FUSHIMI!!
EEP!
SOMETHING FEELS OFF ABOUT THEM.
H...HUH? BUT KYOTO-FUSHIMI COMPETED LAST YEAR TOO, RIGHT?
WEREN'T THEY...
CHATTER
...LIKE, A FRIENDLIER BUNCH BACK THEN?
CHATTER
THEY'RE LIKE...AN ARMY.
HEY... WAIT A SEC.
GOOD ON HAKONE FOR NOT FALLING FOR HIS BAITING.
WHAT DID HE CALL HIS TEAM-MATES? "GOOFS?" "GOPHERS?"
THAT MIDOUSUJI GUY...
I REMEMBER NUMBER 92, ISHIGAKI.
I RODE WITH HIM DURING LAST YEAR'S RACE.
HE'S A THIRD-YEAR NOW...
WAIT...

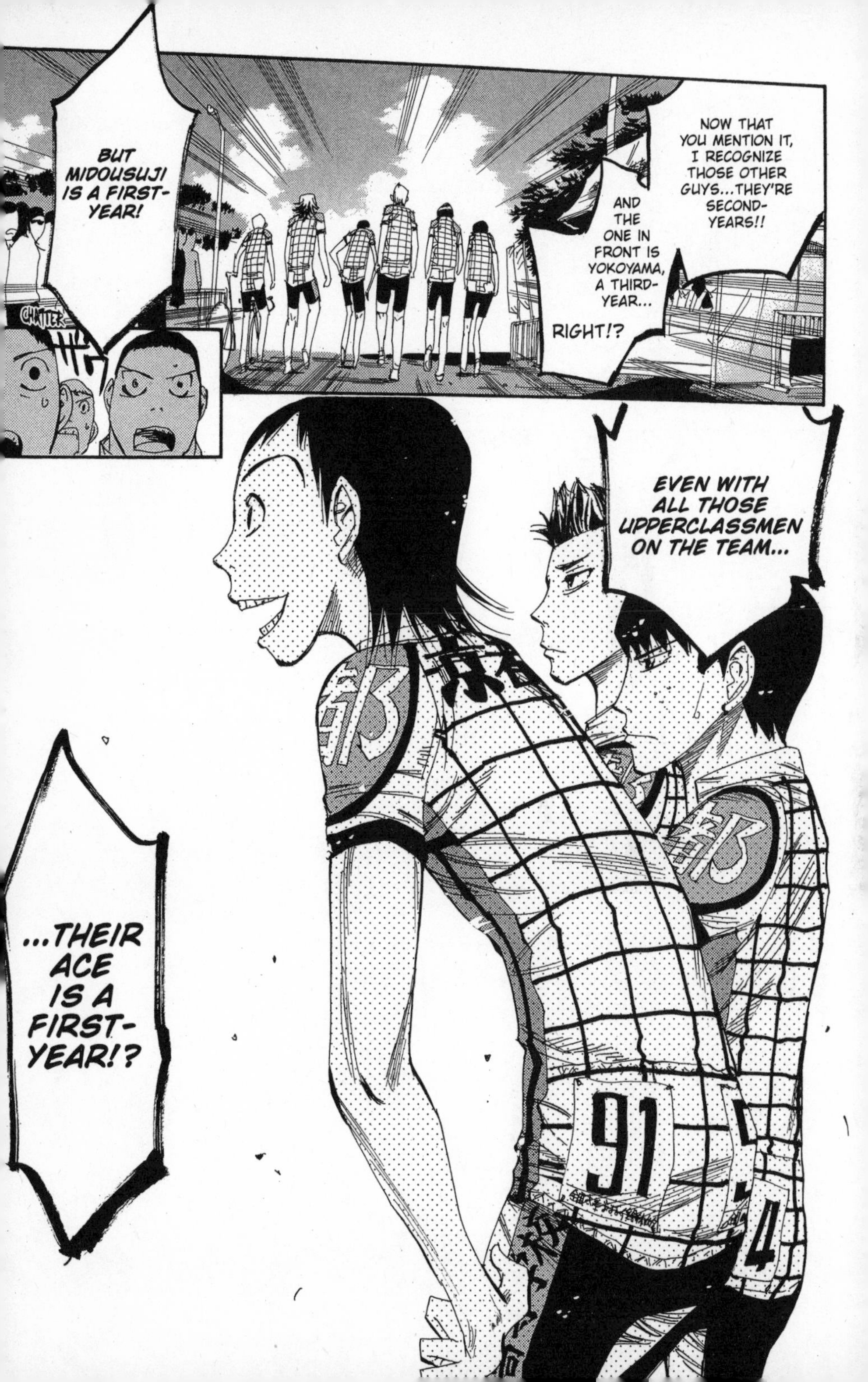
NOW THAT YOU MENTION IT, I RECOGNIZE THOSE OTHER GUYS...THEY'RE SECOND-YEARS!!
AND THE ONE IN FRONT IS YOKOYAMA, A THIRD-YEAR...
RIGHT!?
BUT MIDOUSUJI IS A FIRST-YEAR!
EVEN WITH ALL THOSE UPPERCLASSMEN ON THE TEAM...
...THEIR ACE IS A FIRST-YEAR!?

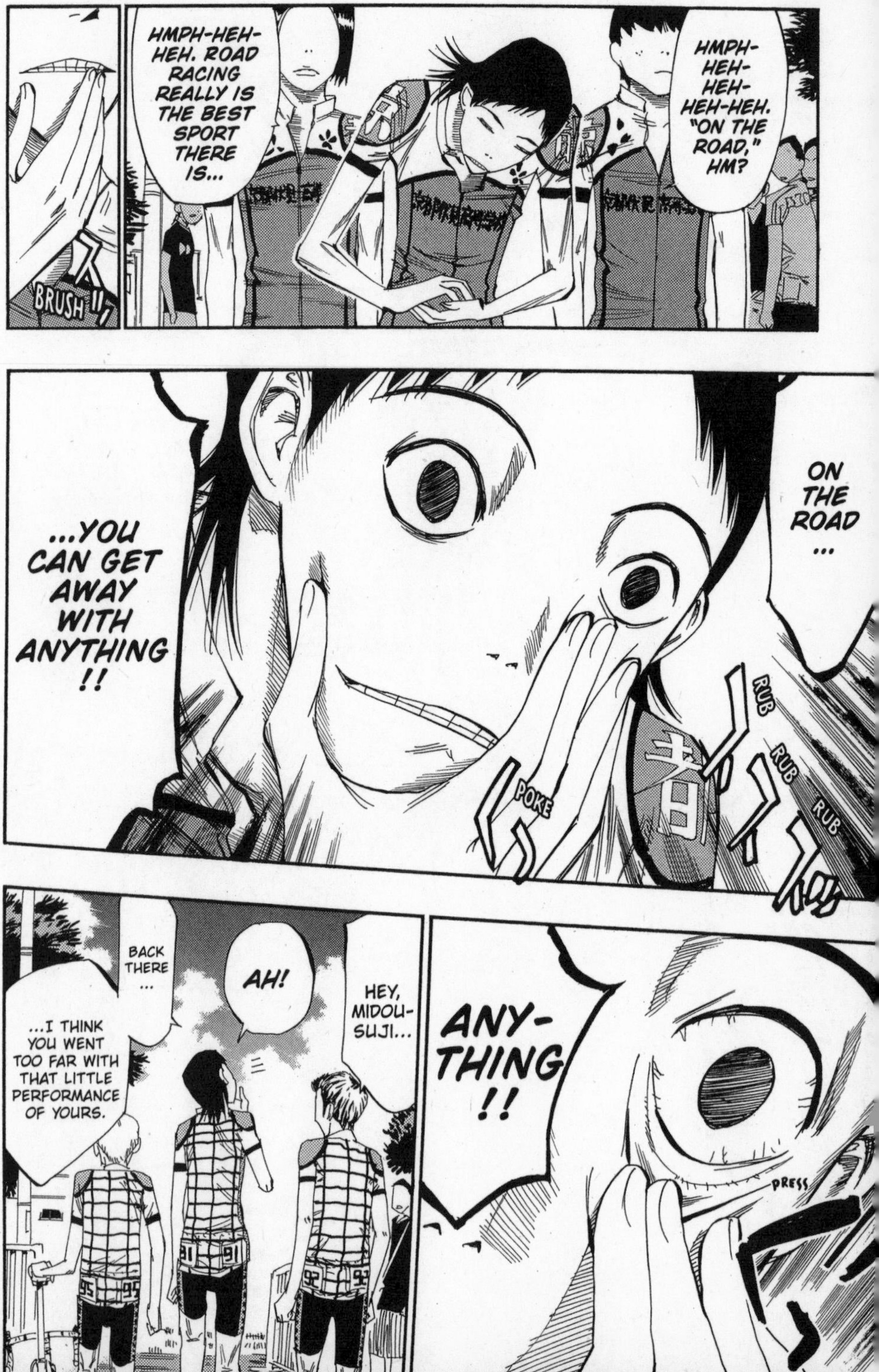
HMPH-HEH-HEH-HEH-HEH. "ON THE ROAD," HM?
HMPH-HEH-HEH. ROAD RACING REALLY IS THE BEST SPORT THERE IS...
BRUSH
ON THE ROAD ...
RUB
RUB
RUB
POKE
...YOU CAN GET AWAY WITH ANYTHING !!
ANY-THING !!
PRESS
HEY, MIDOU-SUJI...
AH!
BACK THERE ...
...I THINK YOU WENT TOO FAR WITH THAT LITTLE PERFORMANCE OF YOURS.

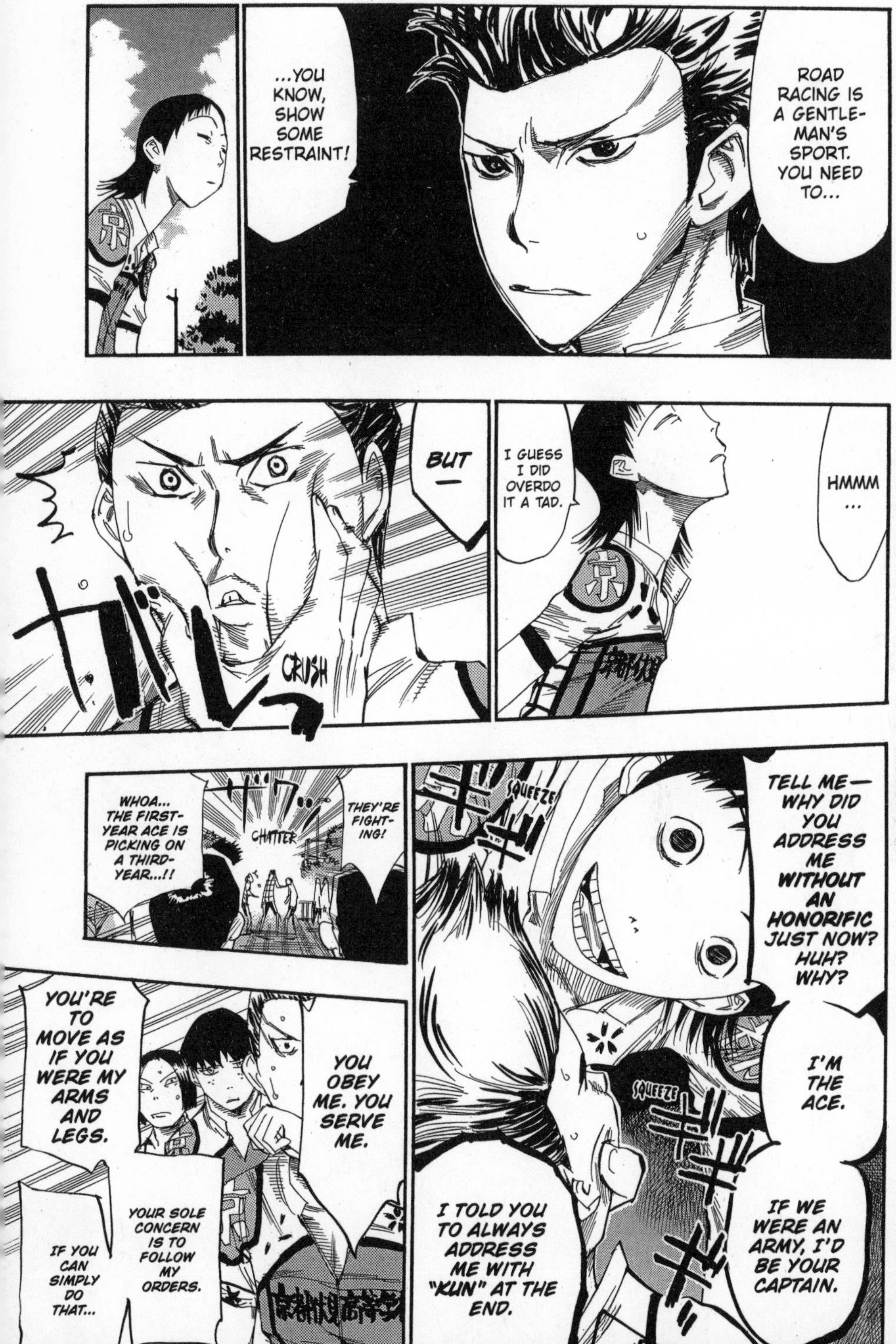
ROAD RACING IS A GENTLEMAN'S SPORT. YOU NEED TO...
...YOU KNOW, SHOW SOME RESTRAINT!
HMMM...
I GUESS I DID OVERDO IT A TAD.
BUT—
CRUSH
SQUEEZE
TELL ME—WHY DID YOU ADDRESS ME WITHOUT AN HONORIFIC JUST NOW? HUH? WHY?
I'M THE ACE.
SQUEEZE
IF WE WERE AN ARMY, I'D BE YOUR CAPTAIN.
I TOLD YOU TO ALWAYS ADDRESS ME WITH "KUN" AT THE END.
THEY'RE FIGHTING!
CHATTER
WHOA... THE FIRST-YEAR ACE IS PICKING ON A THIRD-YEAR...!!
YOU OBEY ME. YOU SERVE ME.
YOU'RE TO MOVE AS IF YOU WERE MY ARMS AND LEGS.
YOUR SOLE CONCERN IS TO FOLLOW MY ORDERS.
IF YOU CAN SIMPLY DO THAT...

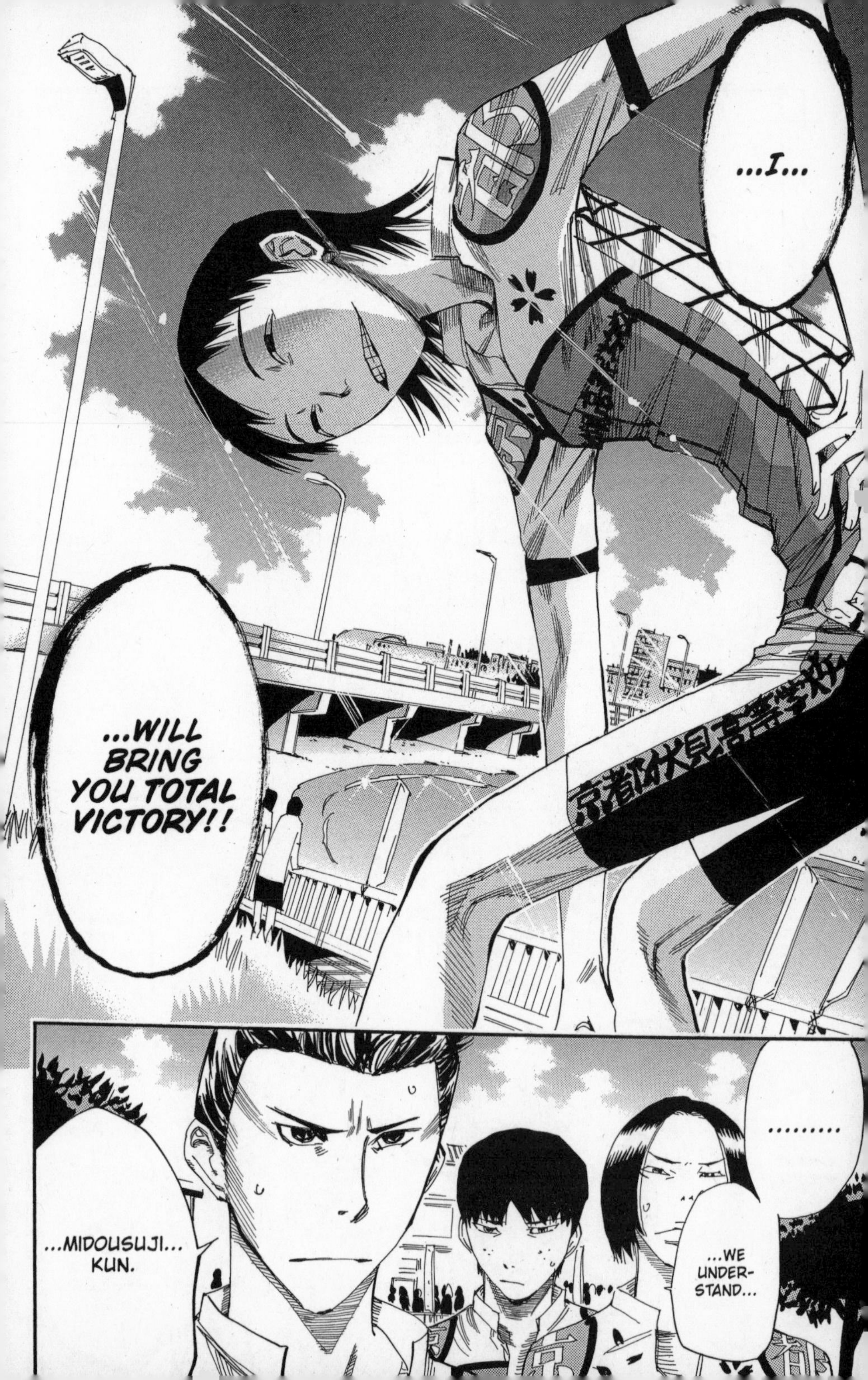
...I...
...WILL BRING YOU TOTAL VICTORY!!
....
...WE UNDER-STAND...
...MIDOUSUJI... KUN.

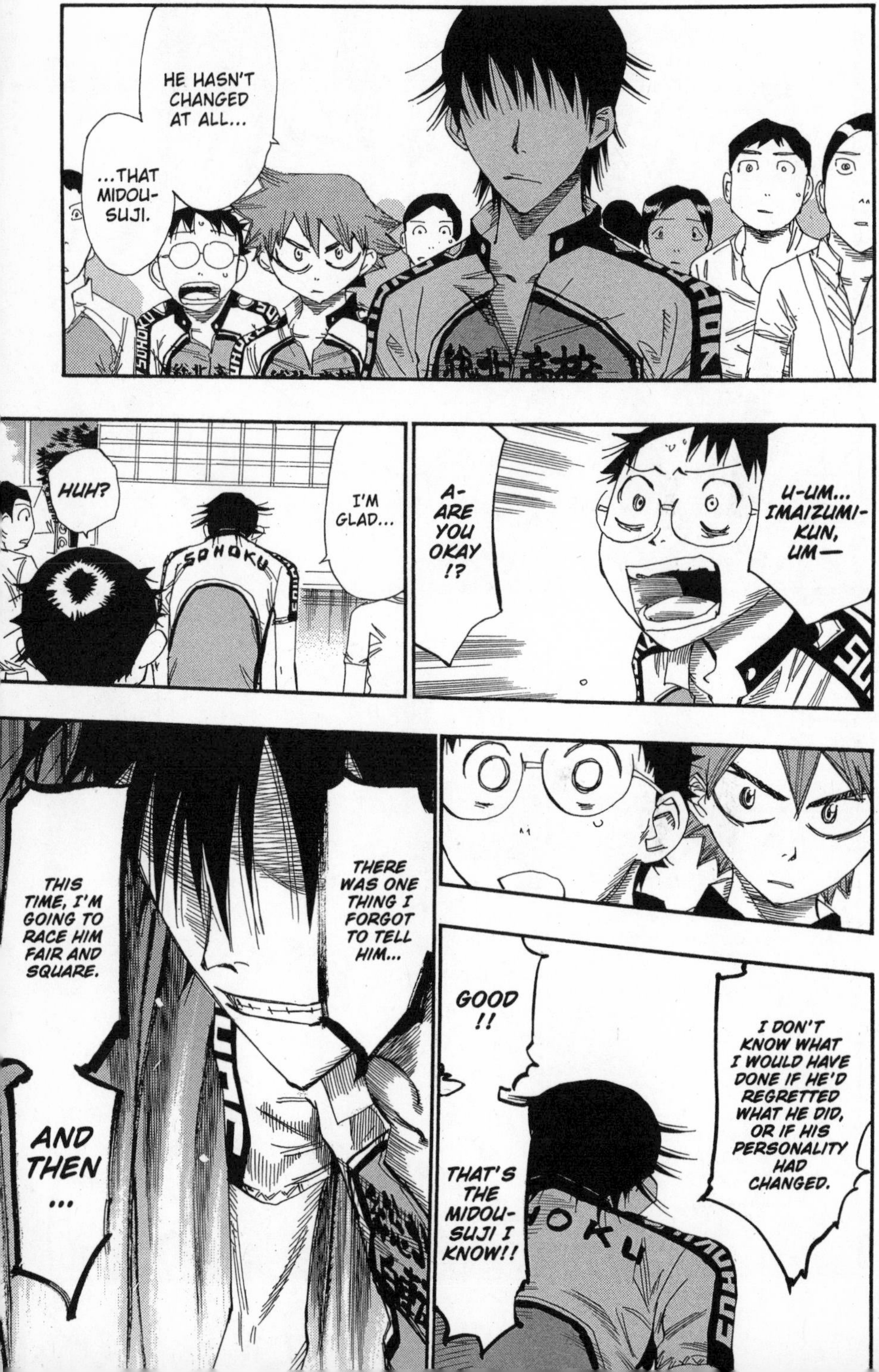
HE HASN'T CHANGED AT ALL...
...THAT MIDOU-SUJI.
U-UM... IMAIZUMI-KUN, UM—
A-ARE YOU OKAY!?
I'M GLAD...
HUH?
I DON'T KNOW WHAT I WOULD HAVE DONE IF HE'D REGRETTED WHAT HE DID, OR IF HIS PERSONALITY HAD CHANGED.
GOOD!!
THAT'S THE MIDOU-SUJI I KNOW!!
THERE WAS ONE THING I FORGOT TO TELL HIM...
THIS TIME, I'M GOING TO RACE HIM FAIR AND SQUARE.
AND THEN...

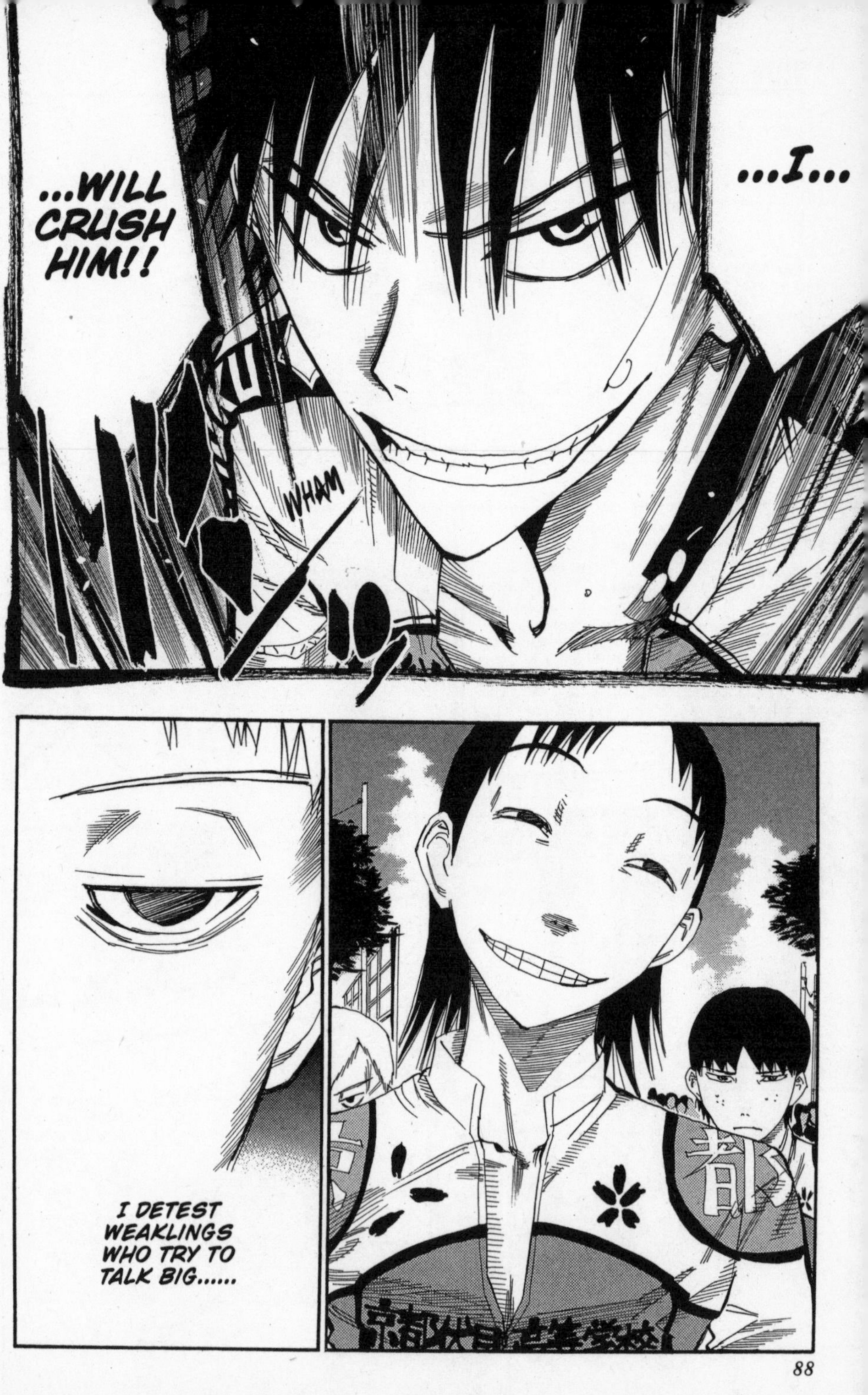
...I...
...WILL CRUSH HIM!!
WHAM
I DETEST WEAKLINGS WHO TRY TO TALK BIG......

RIDE.74 STARTING RHYTHM

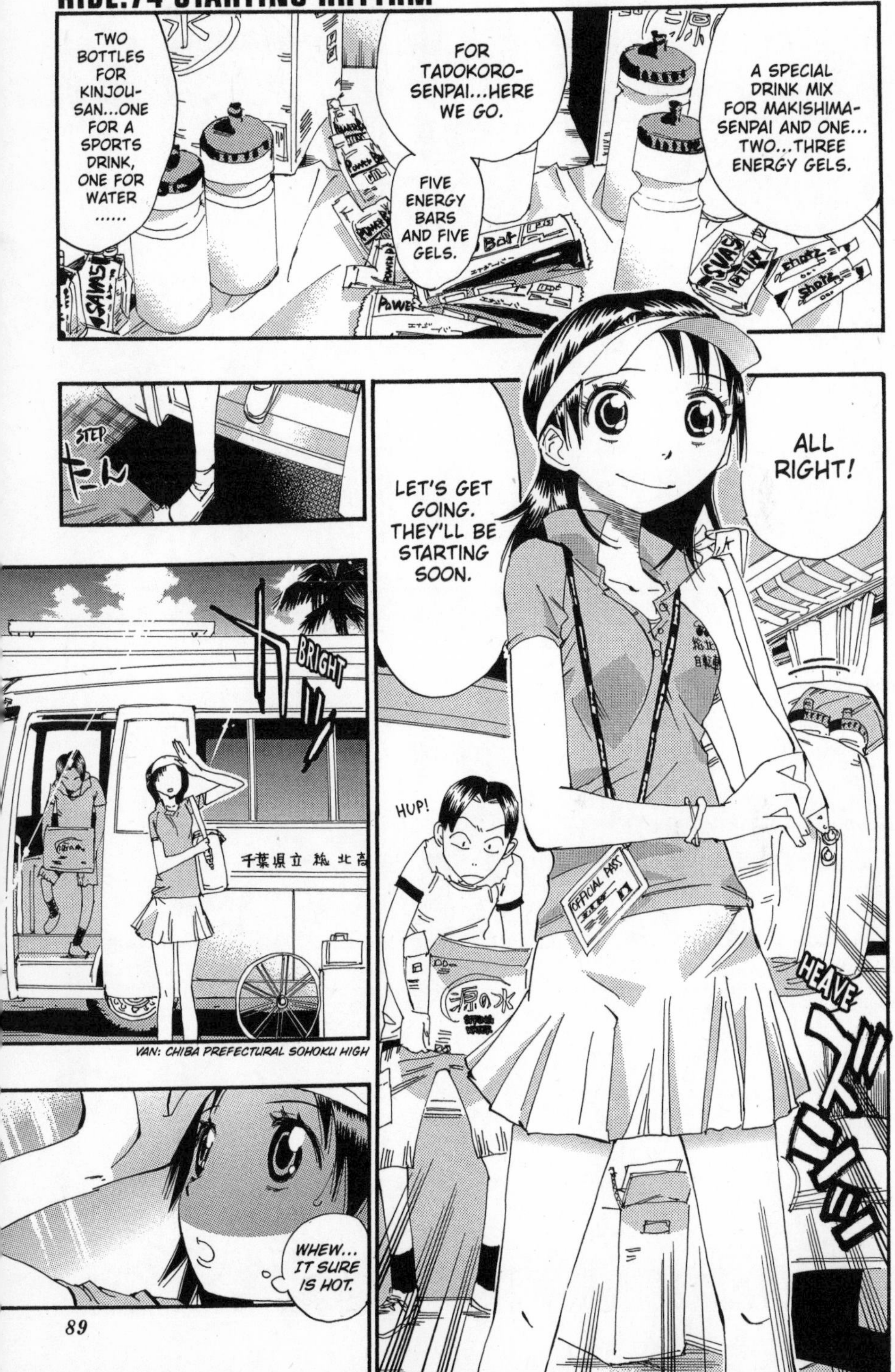
A SPECIAL DRINK MIX FOR MAKISHIMA-SENPAI AND ONE... TWO...THREE ENERGY GELS.
FOR TADOKORO-SENPAI...HERE WE GO.
FIVE ENERGY BARS AND FIVE GELS.
TWO BOTTLES FOR KINJOU-SAN...ONE FOR A SPORTS DRINK, ONE FOR WATER ......
ALL RIGHT!
LET'S GET GOING. THEY'LL BE STARTING SOON.
HUP!
OFFICIAL PASS
HEAVE
STEP
BRIGHT
VAN: CHIBA PREFECTURAL SOHOKU HIGH
WHEW... IT SURE IS HOT.

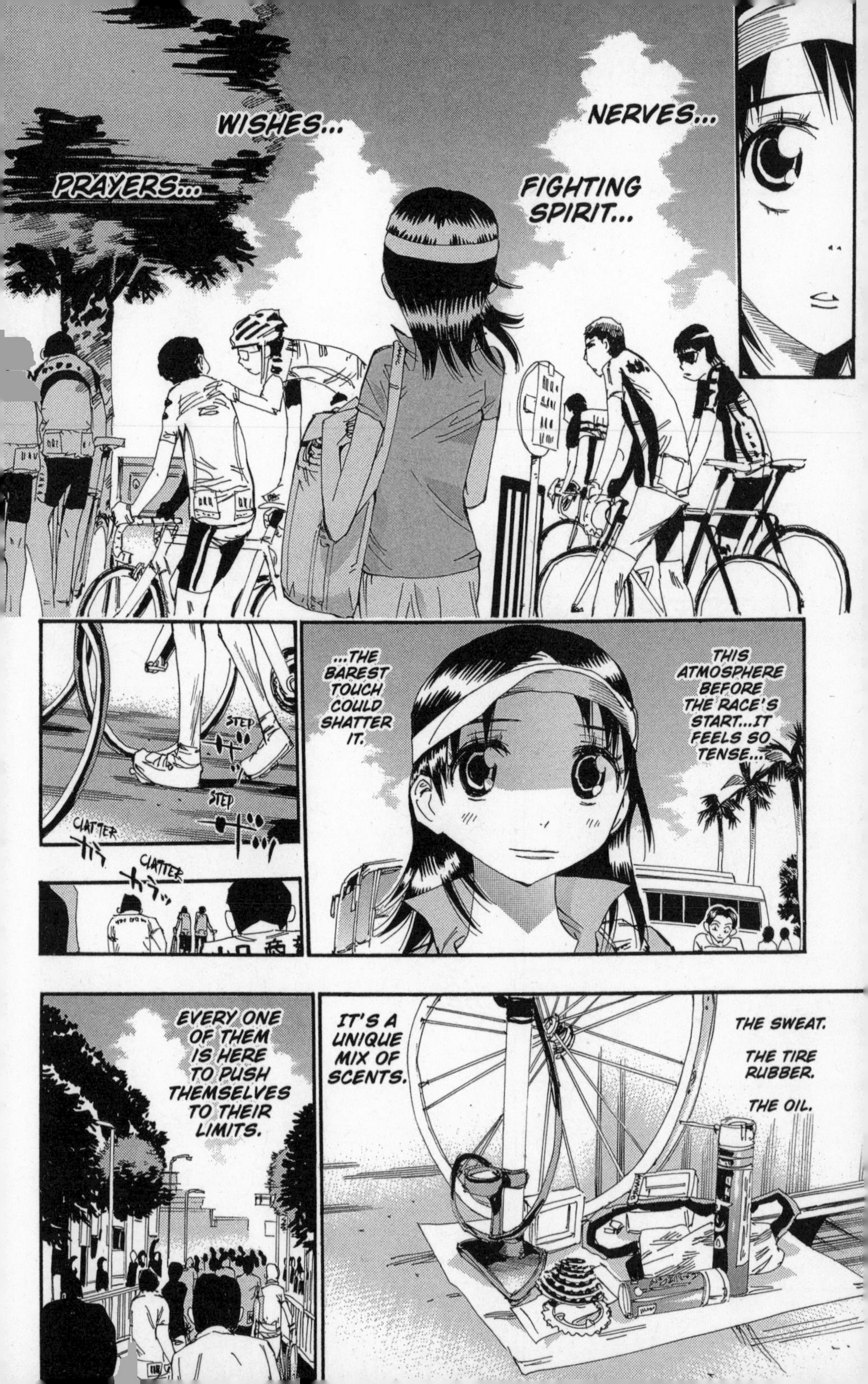
NERVES...
FIGHTING SPIRIT...
WISHES...
PRAYERS...
THIS ATMOSPHERE BEFORE THE RACE'S START...IT FEELS SO TENSE...
...THE BAREST TOUCH COULD SHATTER IT.
STEP
STEP
CLATTER
CLATTER
THE SWEAT.
THE TIRE RUBBER.
THE OIL.
IT'S A UNIQUE MIX OF SCENTS.
EVERY ONE OF THEM IS HERE TO PUSH THEMSELVES TO THEIR LIMITS.

THE RHYTHM'S STARTING TO BUILD—

ONE'S FEELINGS TOWARD ONESELF

BUZZ BUZZ BUZZ

ONE'S FEELINGS TOWARD THE FINISH LINE...

ONE'S FEELINGS TOWARD OTHERS...

ONE'S SENSE OF STILL-NESS...

ONE'S SENSE OF INTENSITY...

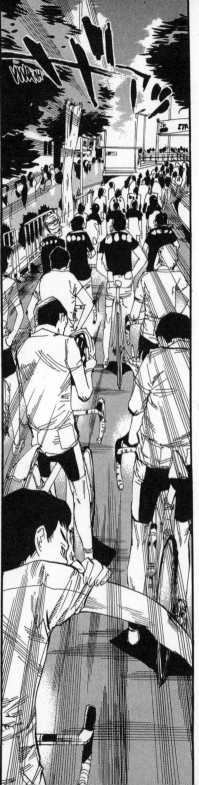

HOLDING ALL THESE DIFFERENT EMOTIONS INSIDE...

...EACH OF THEM WILL FACE THE START LINE...

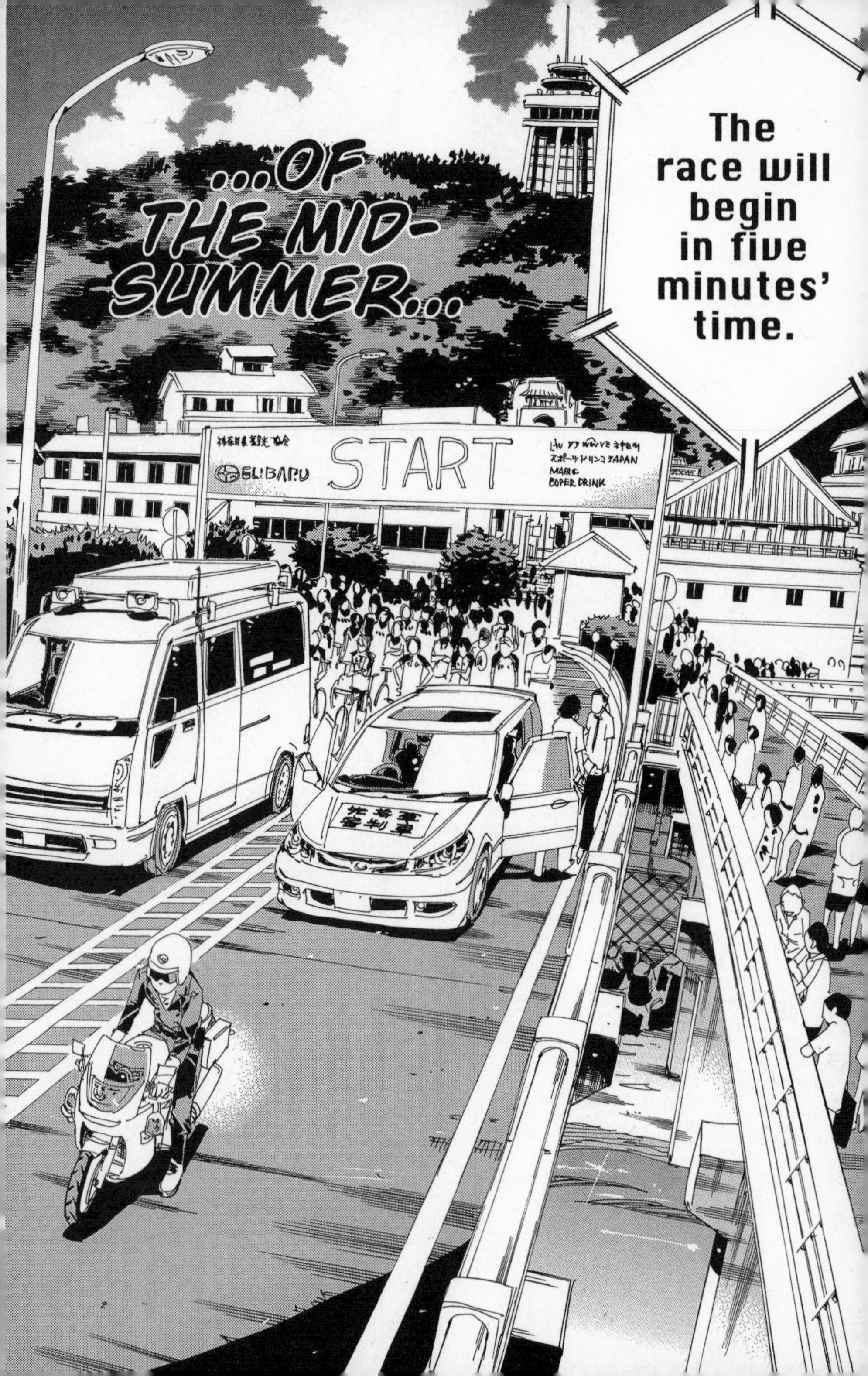
The race will begin in five minutes' time.
...OF THE MID-SUMMER...
START

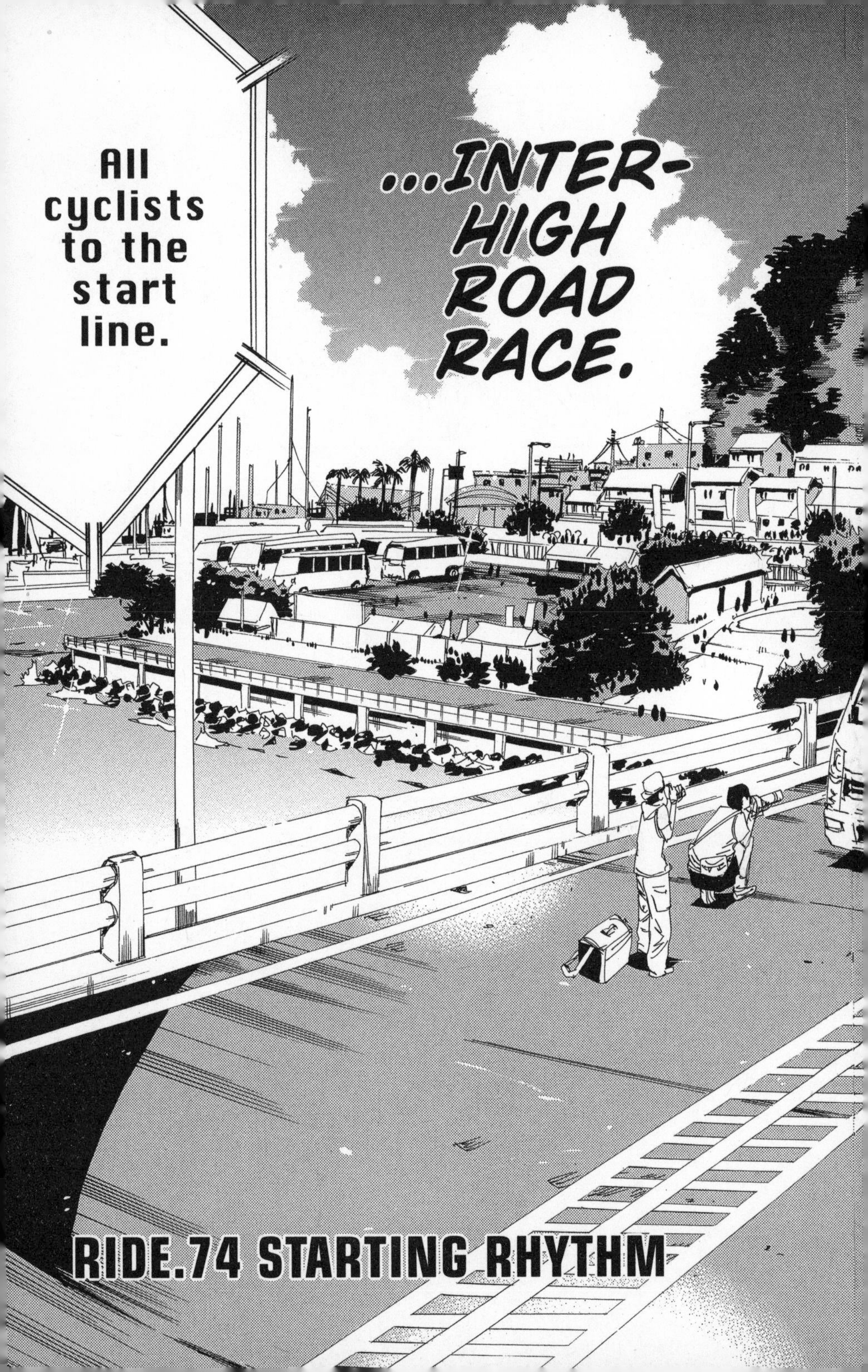
...INTER-HIGH ROAD RACE.
All cyclists to the start line.
RIDE.74 STARTING RHYTHM

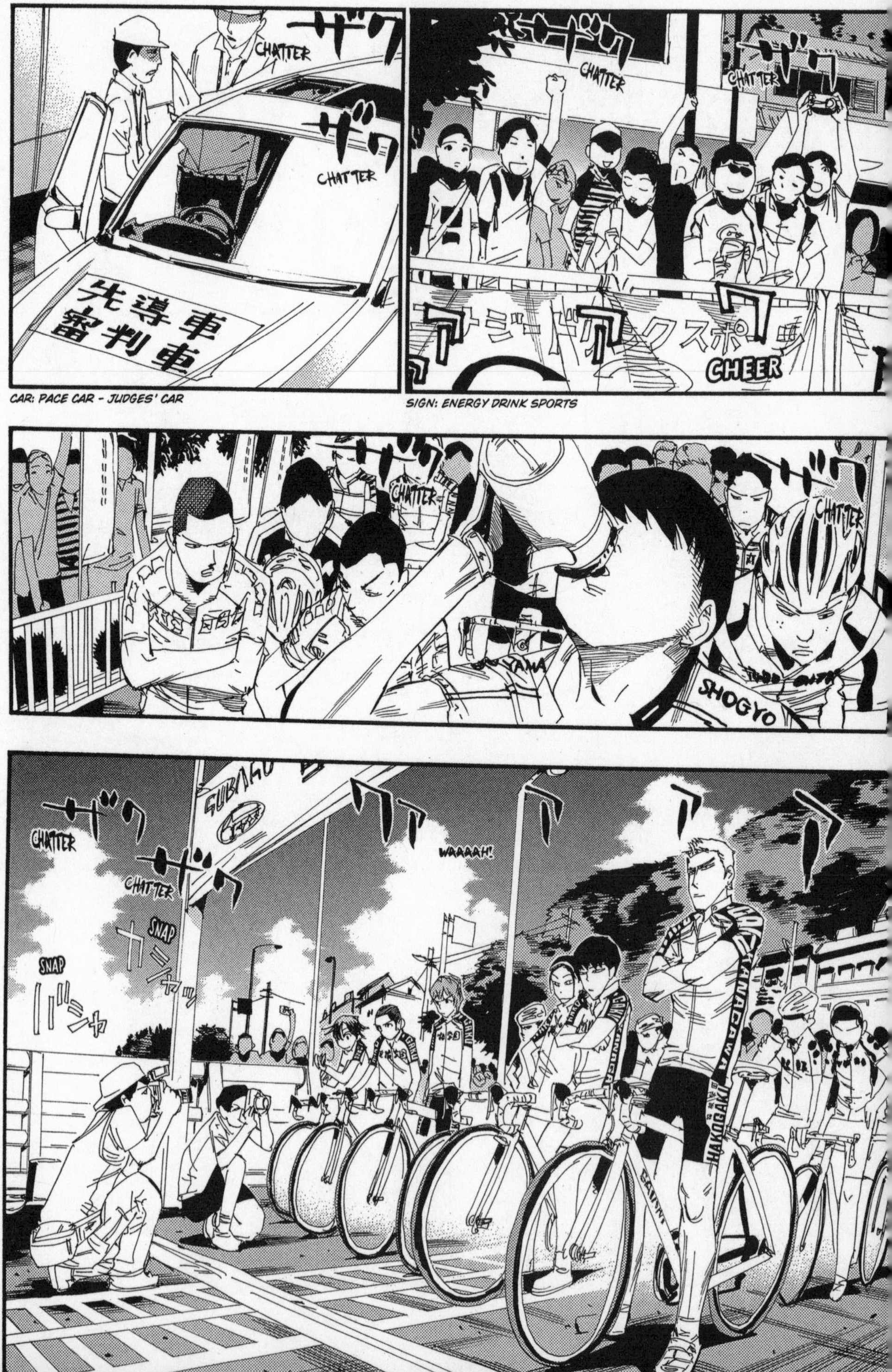

ザワ
CHATTER
ザワ
CHATTER
ザワ
CHATTER
CHEER
SIGN: ENERGY DRINK SPORTS
ザワ
CHATTER
ザワ
CHATTER
先導車
審判車
CAR: PACE CAR - JUDGES' CAR
ザワ
CHATTER
CHATTER
SHOGYO
WAAAAH!
ザワ
CHATTER
ザワ
CHATTER
カシャッ
SNAP
バシャ
SNAP
HAKOGAKU

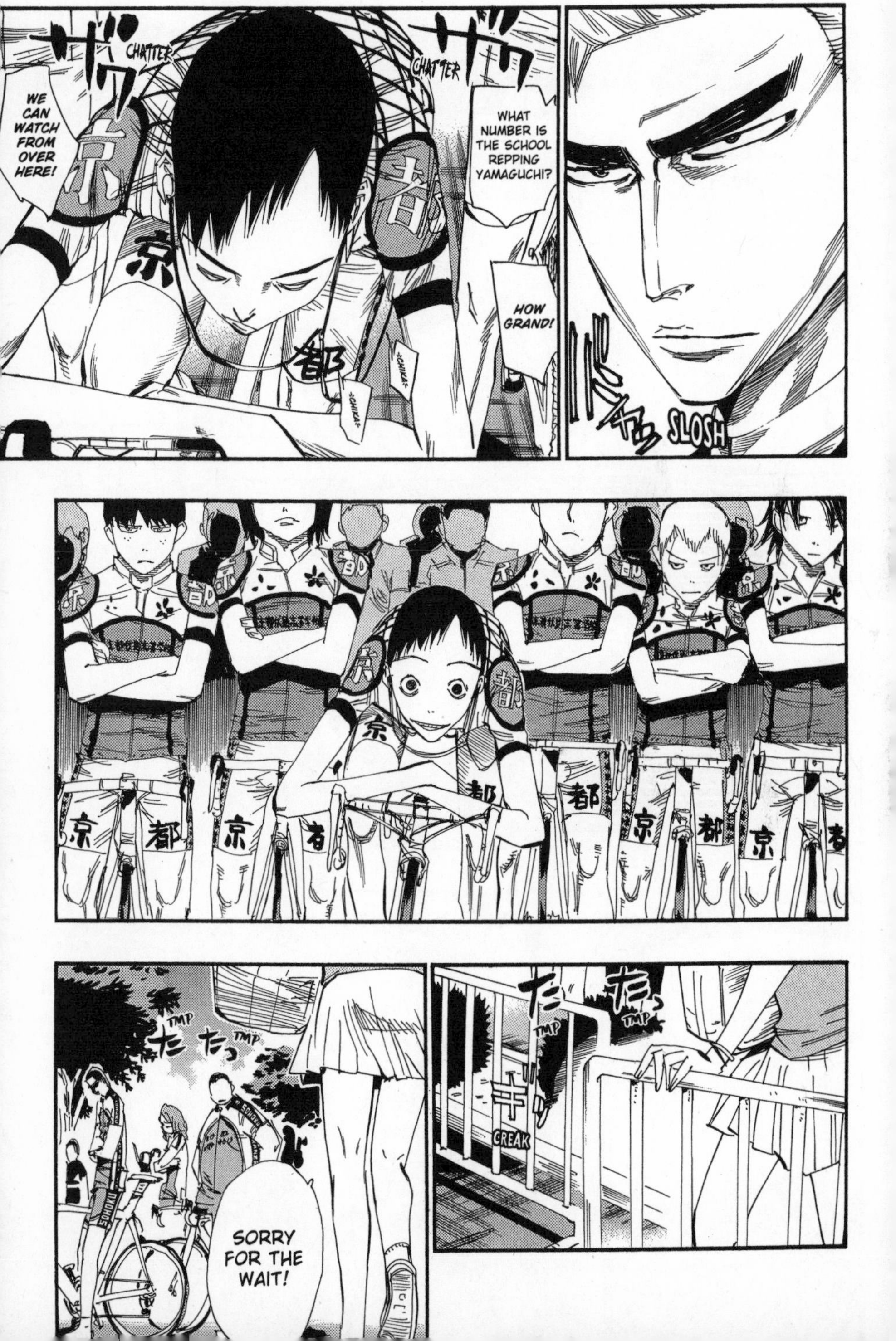
SLOSH
CHATTER
WHAT NUMBER IS THE SCHOOL REPPING YAMAGUCHI?
CHATTER
WE CAN WATCH FROM OVER HERE!
HOW GRAND!
TMP
TMP
CREAK
TMP
TMP
SORRY FOR THE WAIT!

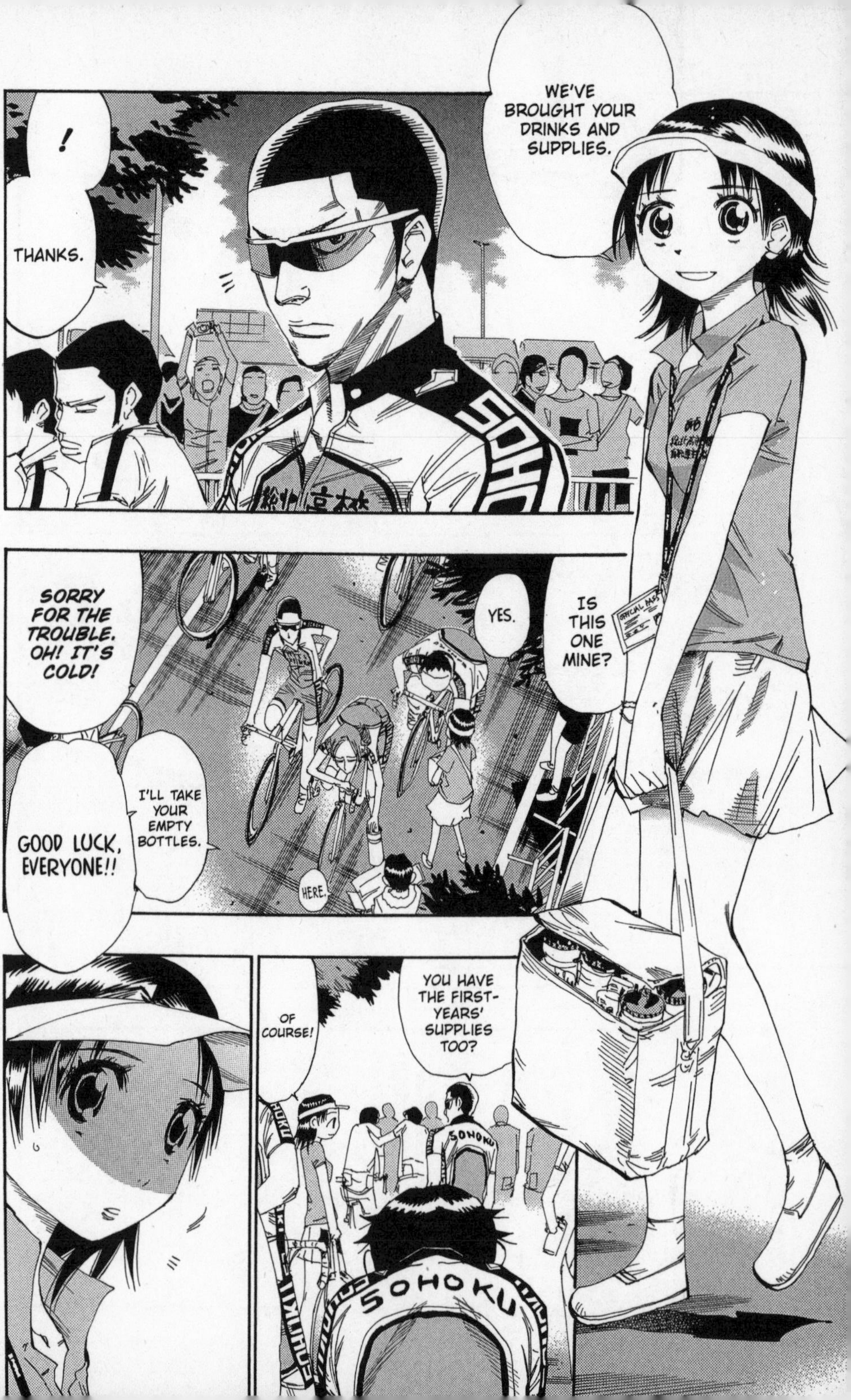
WE'VE BROUGHT YOUR DRINKS AND SUPPLIES.
!
THANKS.
IS THIS ONE MINE?
YES.
SORRY FOR THE TROUBLE. OH! IT'S COLD!
I'LL TAKE YOUR EMPTY BOTTLES.
HERE.
GOOD LUCK, EVERYONE!!
YOU HAVE THE FIRST-YEARS' SUPPLIES TOO?
OF COURSE!

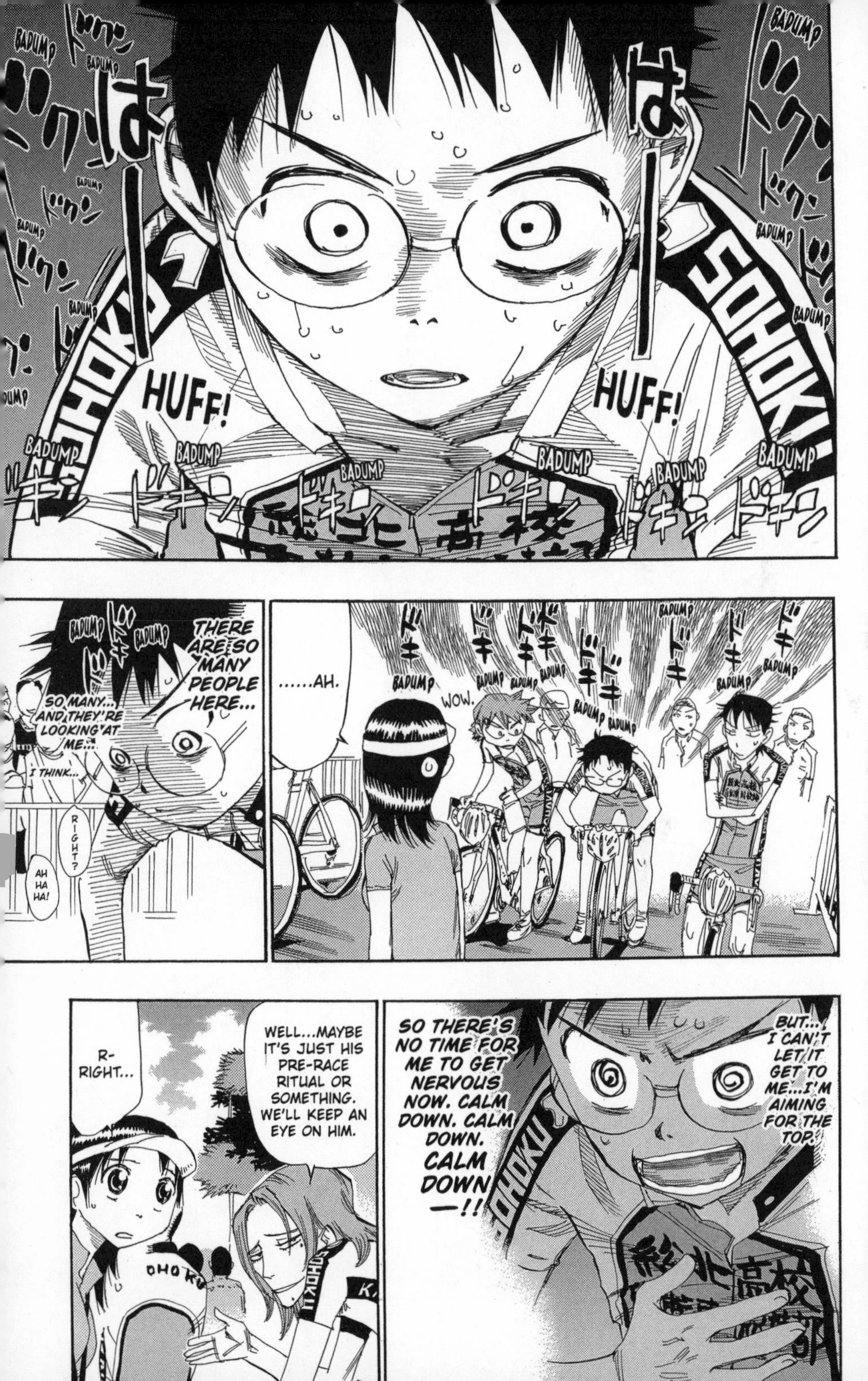
BADUMP
HUFF!
HUFF!
BADUMP
BADUMP
......AH.
BADUMP
WOW.
THERE ARE SO MANY PEOPLE HERE...
SO MANY... AND THEY'RE LOOKING AT ME...
I THINK...
RIGHT?
AH HA HA!
BUT...! I CAN'T LET IT GET TO ME...I'M AIMING FOR THE TOP.
SO THERE'S NO TIME FOR ME TO GET NERVOUS NOW. CALM DOWN. CALM DOWN. CALM DOWN—!!
WELL...MAYBE IT'S JUST HIS PRE-RACE RITUAL OR SOMETHING. WE'LL KEEP AN EYE ON HIM.
R-RIGHT...

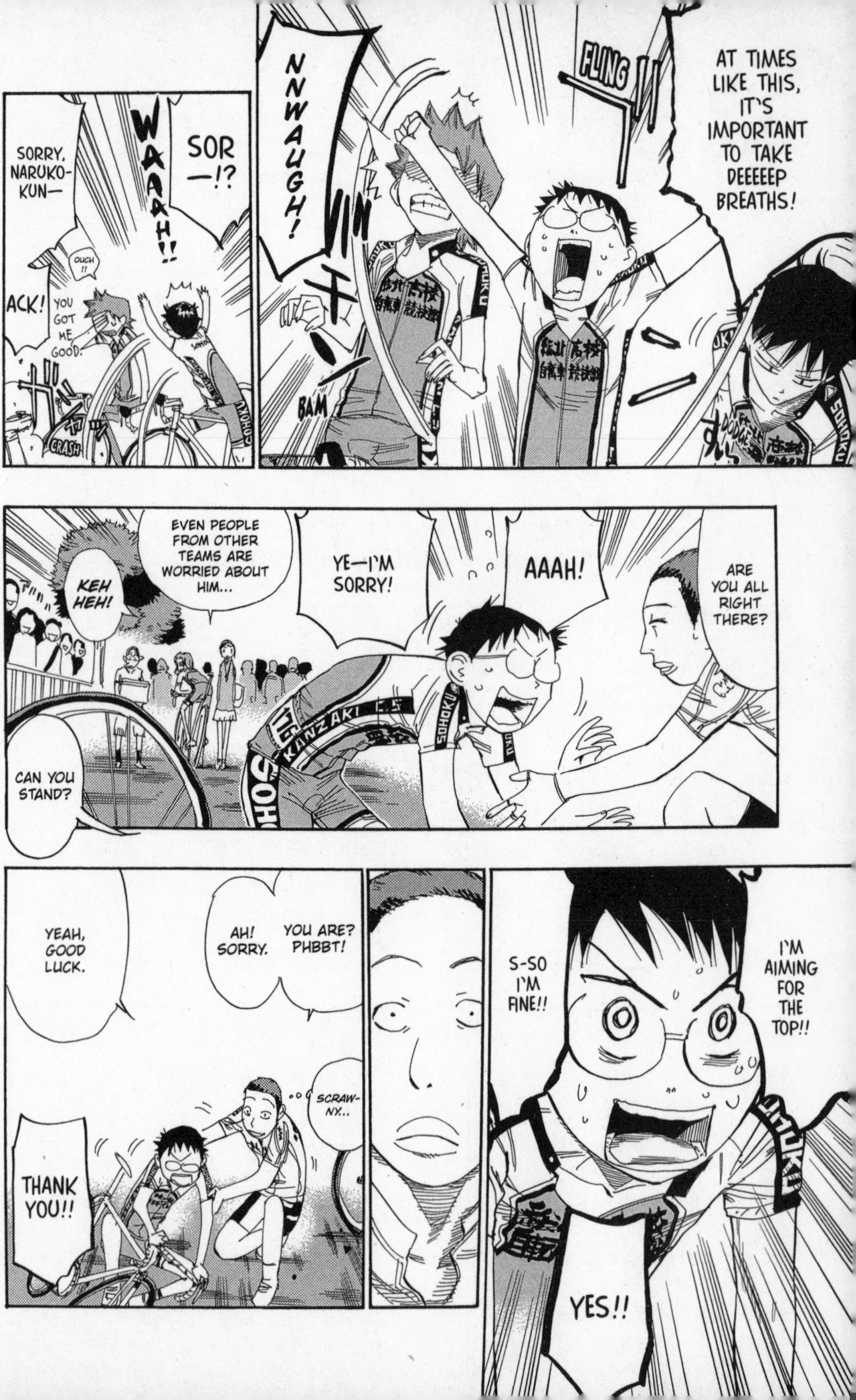
AT TIMES LIKE THIS, IT'S IMPORTANT TO TAKE DEEEEEP BREATHS!
FLING
NNWAUGH!
VIN
BAM
DODGE
SOR—!?
WAAAH!!
SORRY, NARUKO-KUN—
OUCH!!
ACK!
YOU GOT ME GOOD!
CRASH
ARE YOU ALL RIGHT THERE?
AAAH!
YE—I'M SORRY!
EVEN PEOPLE FROM OTHER TEAMS ARE WORRIED ABOUT HIM...
KEH HEH!
CAN YOU STAND?
I'M AIMING FOR THE TOP!!
S-SO I'M FINE!!
YES!!
YOU ARE? PHBBT!
AH! SORRY.
YEAH, GOOD LUCK.
SCRAWNY...
THANK YOU!!

HAAAHH...

HAAH!...

HAAH!...

HAAH!...

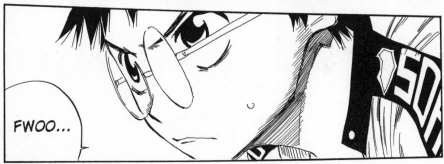

FWOO...

FALLING DOWN MIGHT'VE HELPED HIM CALM HIS NERVES.

HUH?

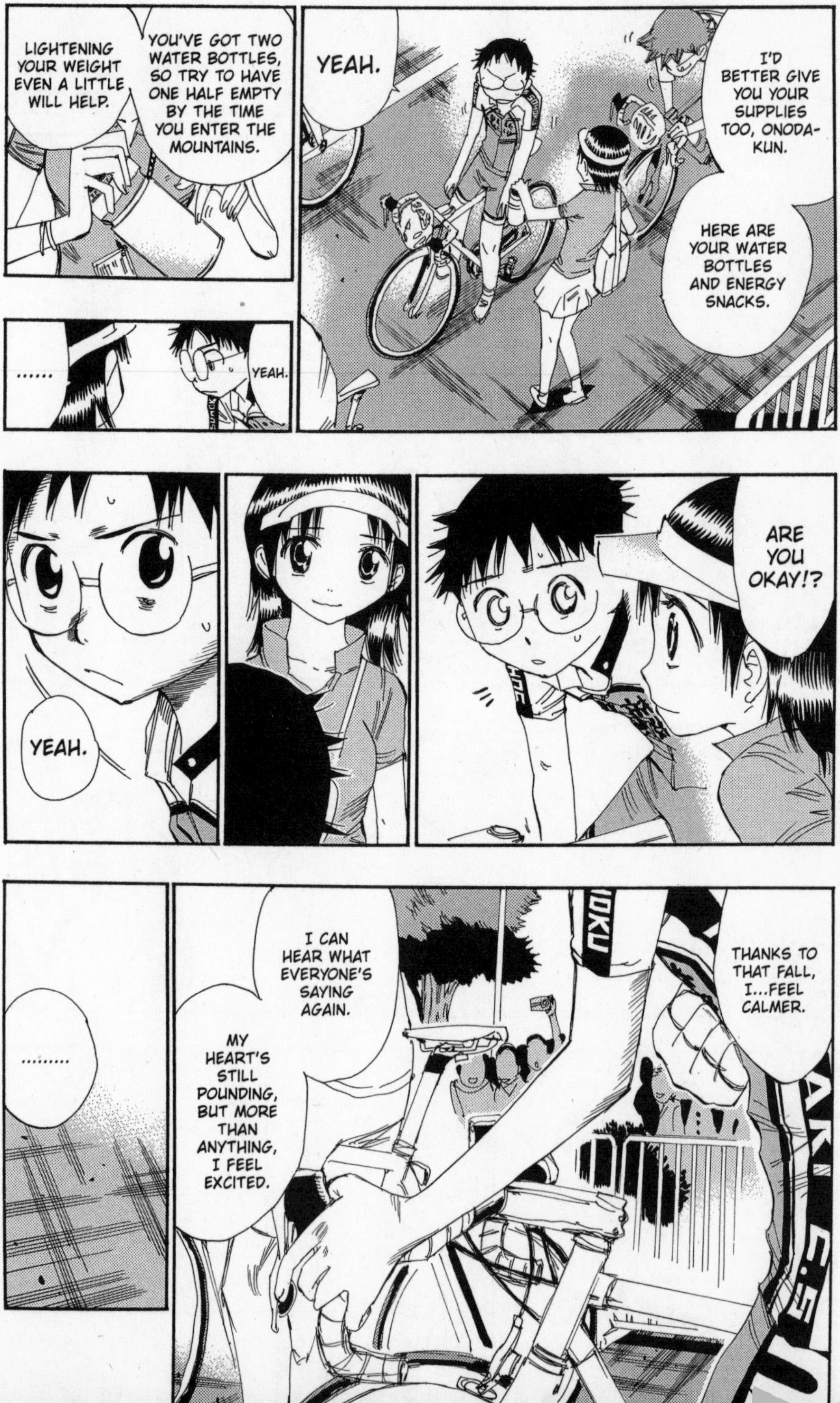
I'D BETTER GIVE YOU YOUR SUPPLIES TOO, ONODA-KUN.
HERE ARE YOUR WATER BOTTLES AND ENERGY SNACKS.
YEAH.
YOU'VE GOT TWO WATER BOTTLES, SO TRY TO HAVE ONE HALF EMPTY BY THE TIME YOU ENTER THE MOUNTAINS.
LIGHTENING YOUR WEIGHT EVEN A LITTLE WILL HELP.
YEAH.
......
ARE YOU OKAY!?
YEAH.
THANKS TO THAT FALL, I...FEEL CALMER.
I CAN HEAR WHAT EVERYONE'S SAYING AGAIN.
MY HEART'S STILL POUNDING, BUT MORE THAN ANYTHING, I FEEL EXCITED.
....

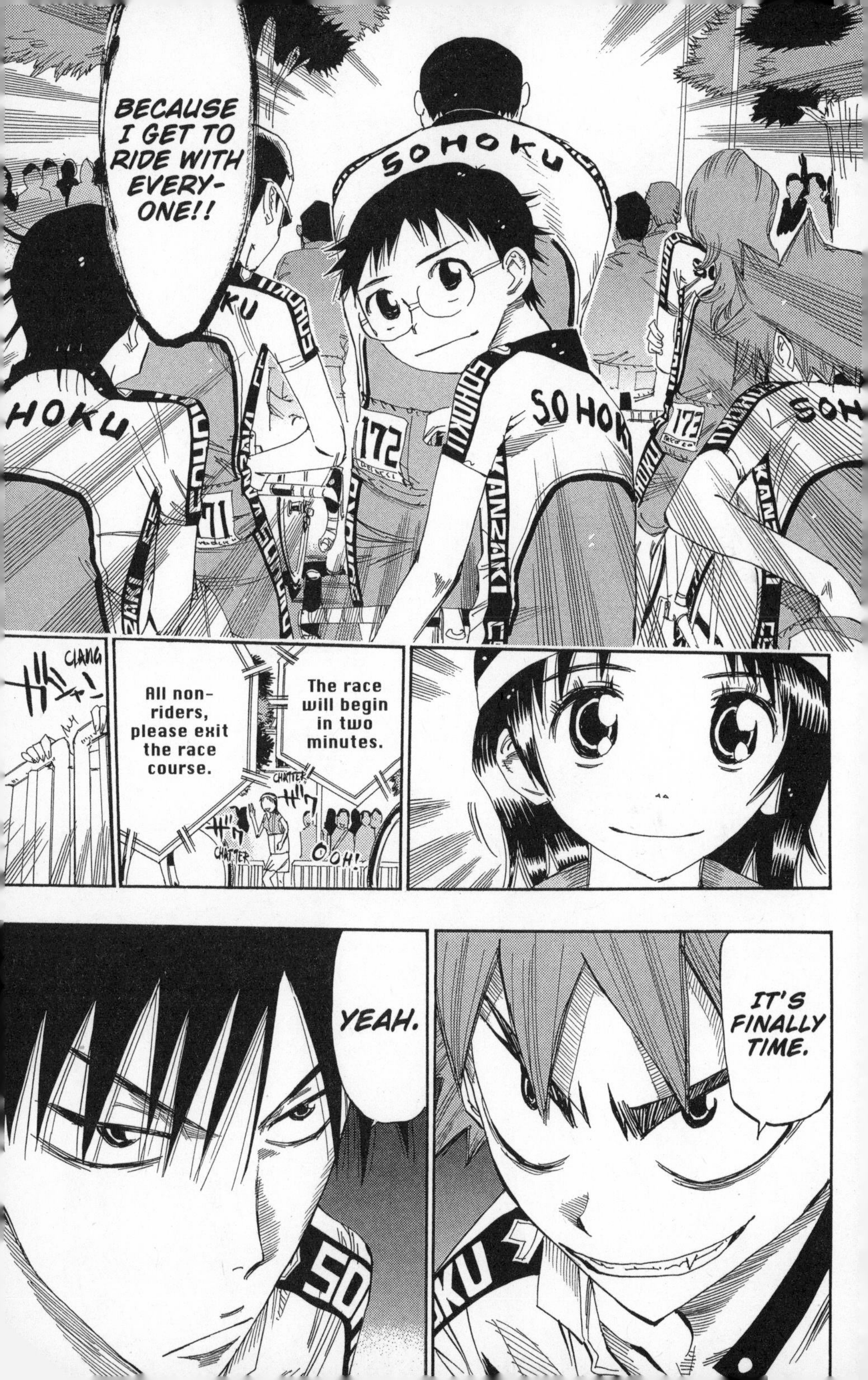
BECAUSE I GET TO RIDE WITH EVERY-ONE!!
The race will begin in two minutes.
All non-riders, please exit the race course.
CHATTER
OOH!
CHATTER
CLANG
IT'S FINALLY TIME.
YEAH.

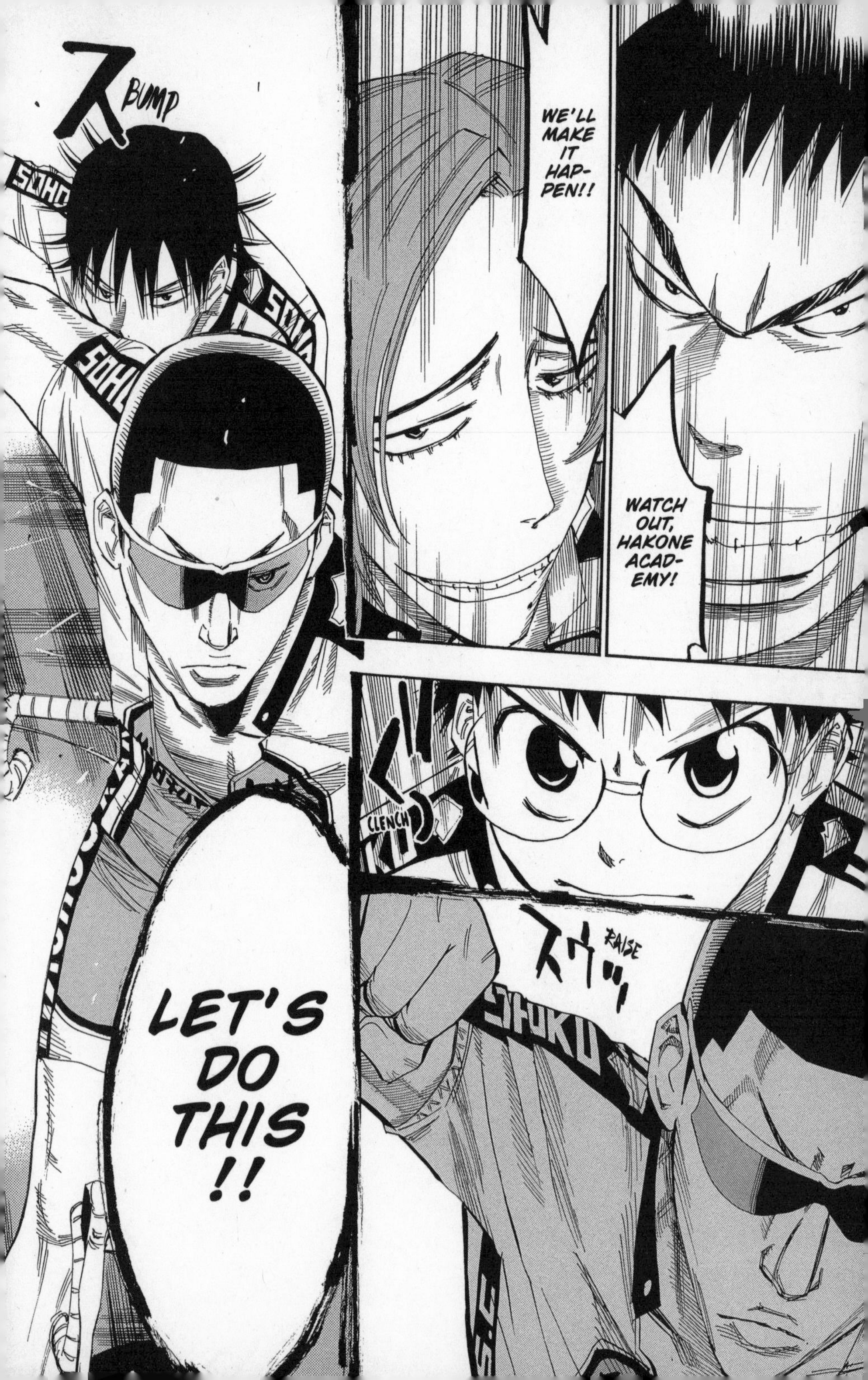
WATCH OUT, HAKONE ACADEMY!
WE'LL MAKE IT HAPPEN!!
CLENCH
RAISE
BUMP
LET'S DO THIS!!

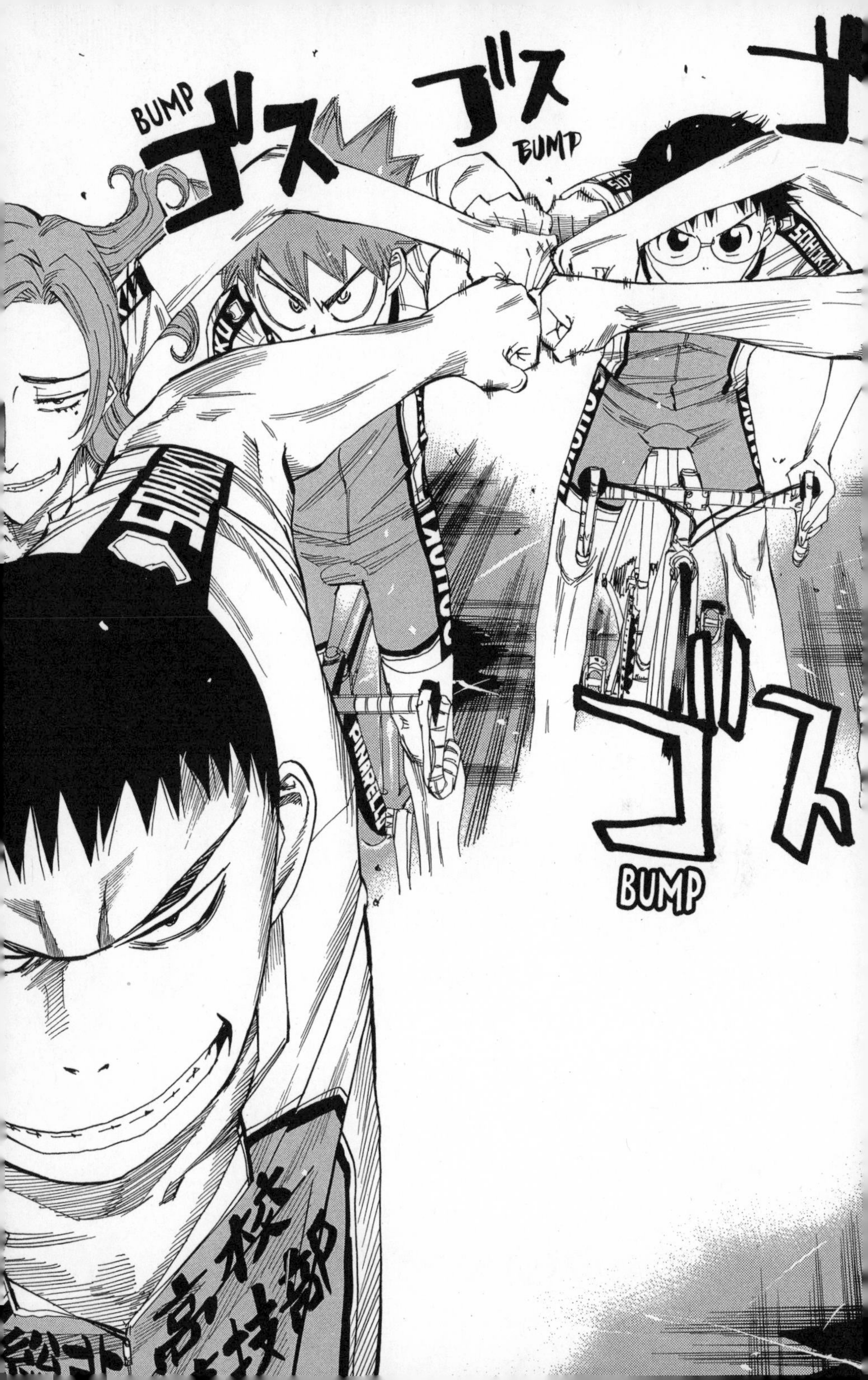
ゴ
ゴス
BUMP
ゴス
BUMP
ゴス
BUMP

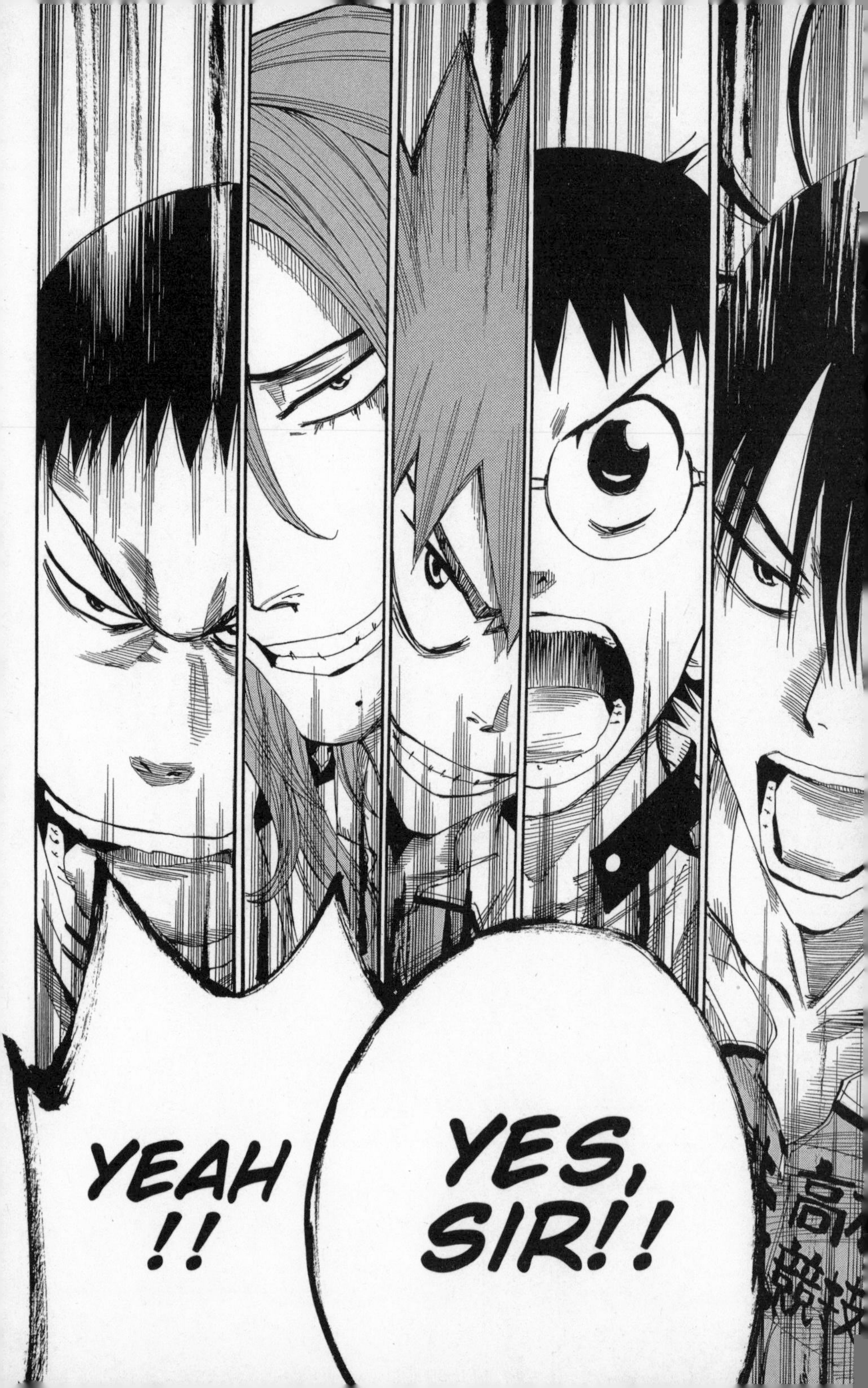
YES, SIR!!
YEAH!!

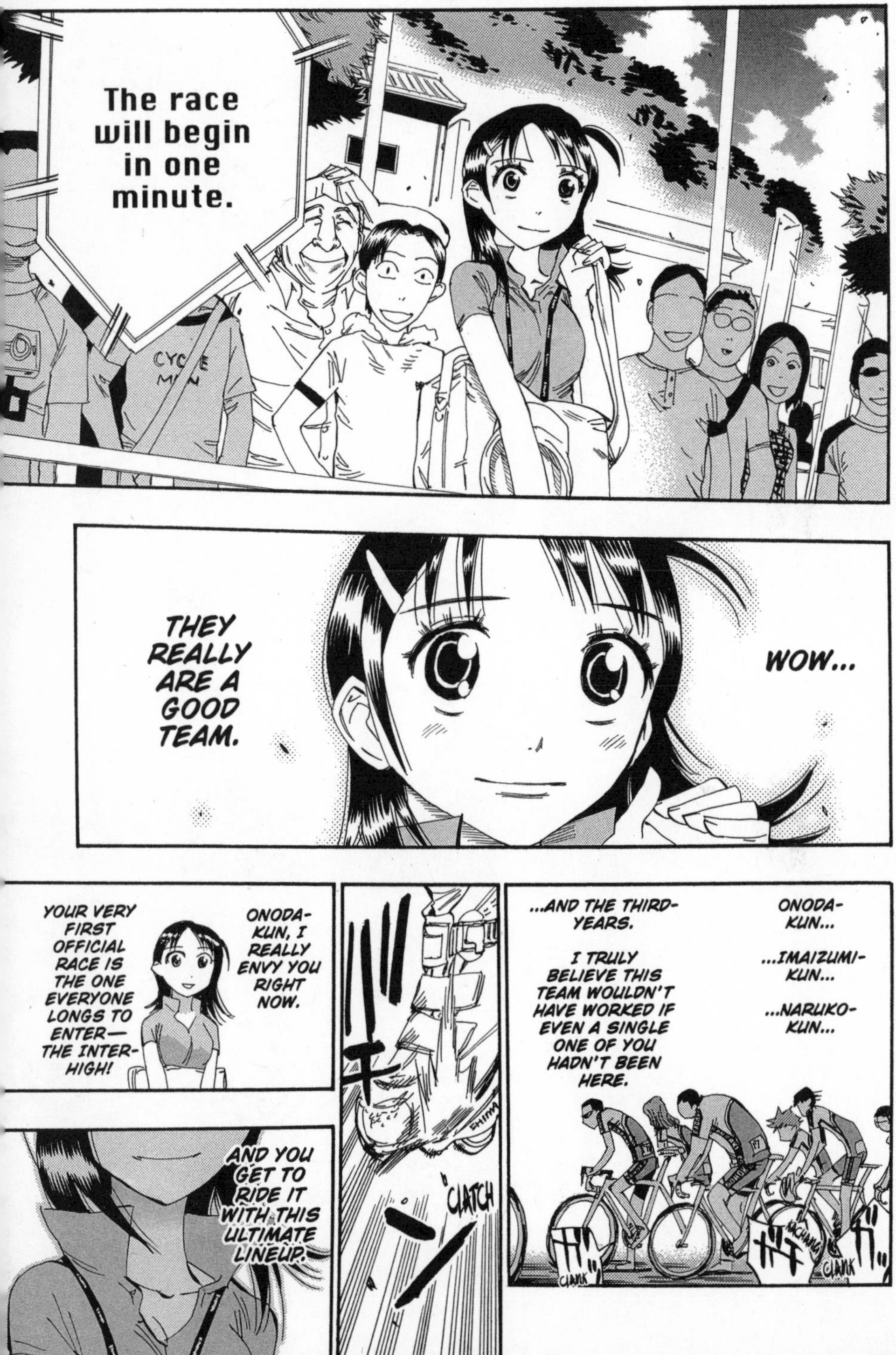
The race will begin in one minute.
WOW...
THEY REALLY ARE A GOOD TEAM.
ONODA-KUN...
...IMAIZUMI-KUN...
...NARUKO-KUN...
...AND THE THIRD-YEARS.
I TRULY BELIEVE THIS TEAM WOULDN'T HAVE WORKED IF EVEN A SINGLE ONE OF YOU HADN'T BEEN HERE.
KACHANG
CLANK
CLANK
CLATCH
ONODA-KUN, I REALLY ENVY YOU RIGHT NOW.
YOUR VERY FIRST OFFICIAL RACE IS THE ONE EVERYONE LONGS TO ENTER—THE INTER-HIGH!
AND YOU GET TO RIDE IT WITH THIS ULTIMATE LINEUP.

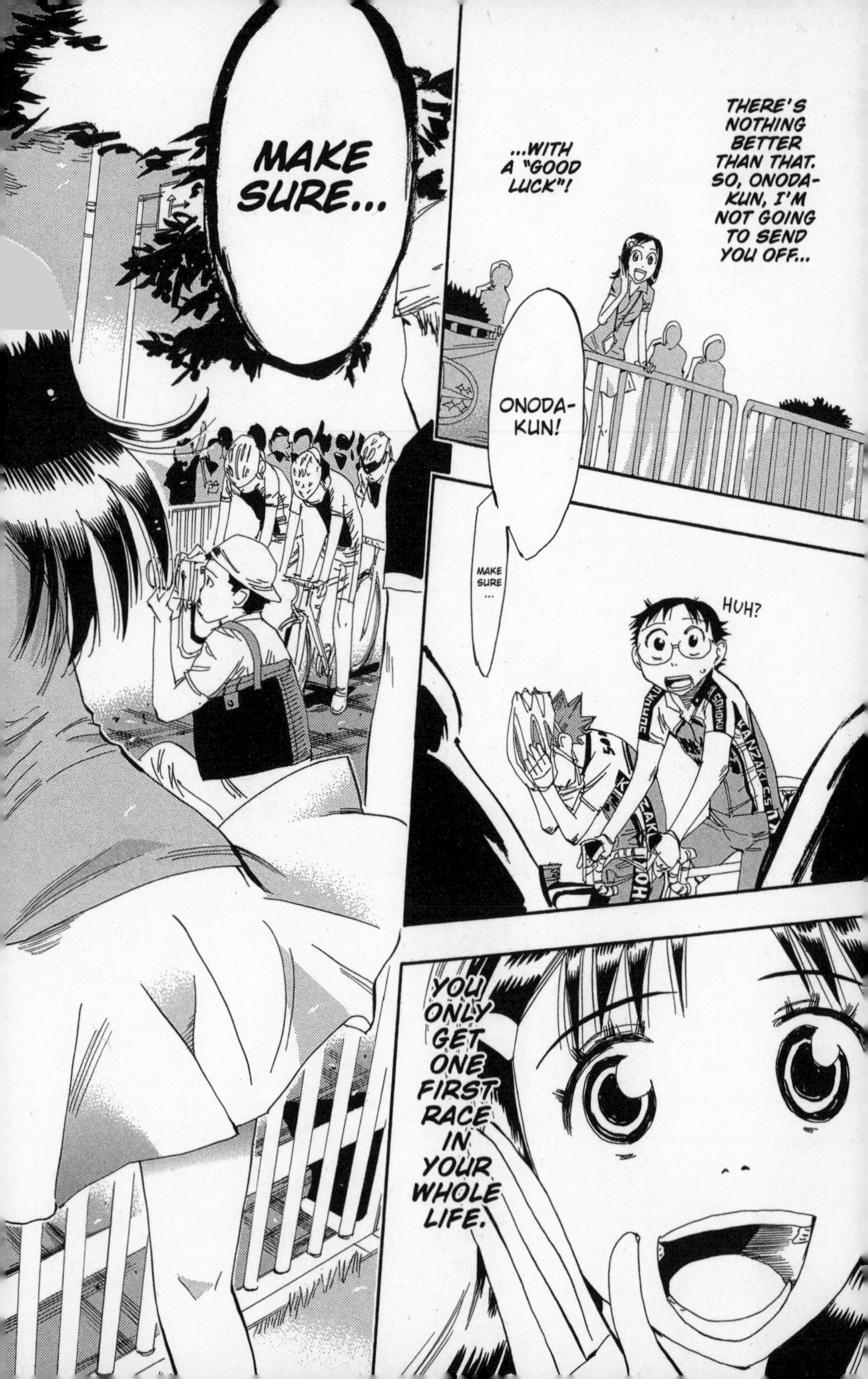
THERE'S NOTHING BETTER THAN THAT. SO, ONODA-KUN, I'M NOT GOING TO SEND YOU OFF...
...WITH A "GOOD LUCK"!
ONODA-KUN!
MAKE SURE ...
HUH?
YOU ONLY GET ONE FIRST RACE IN YOUR WHOLE LIFE.
MAKE SURE...

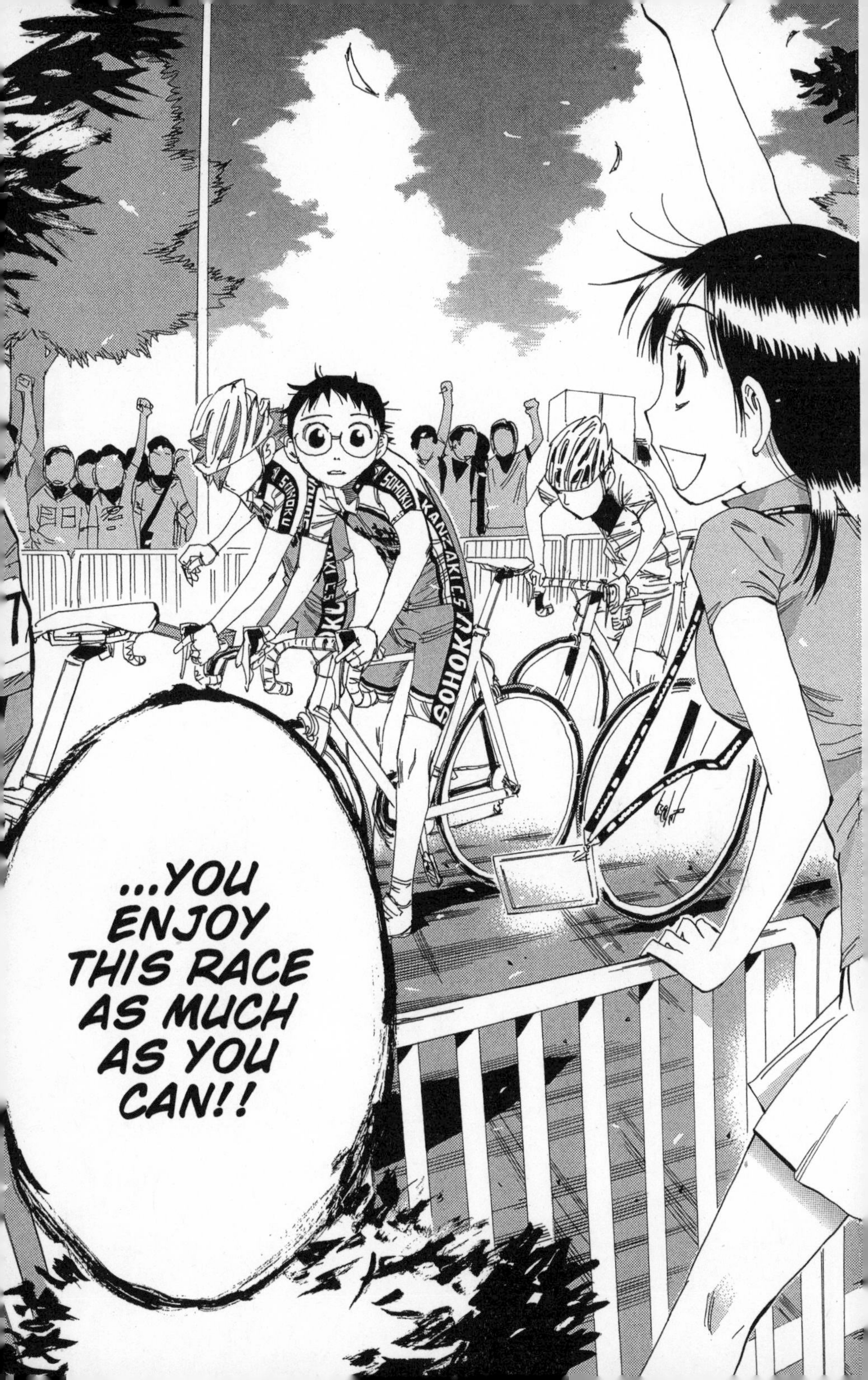
...YOU ENJOY THIS RACE AS MUCH AS YOU CAN!!

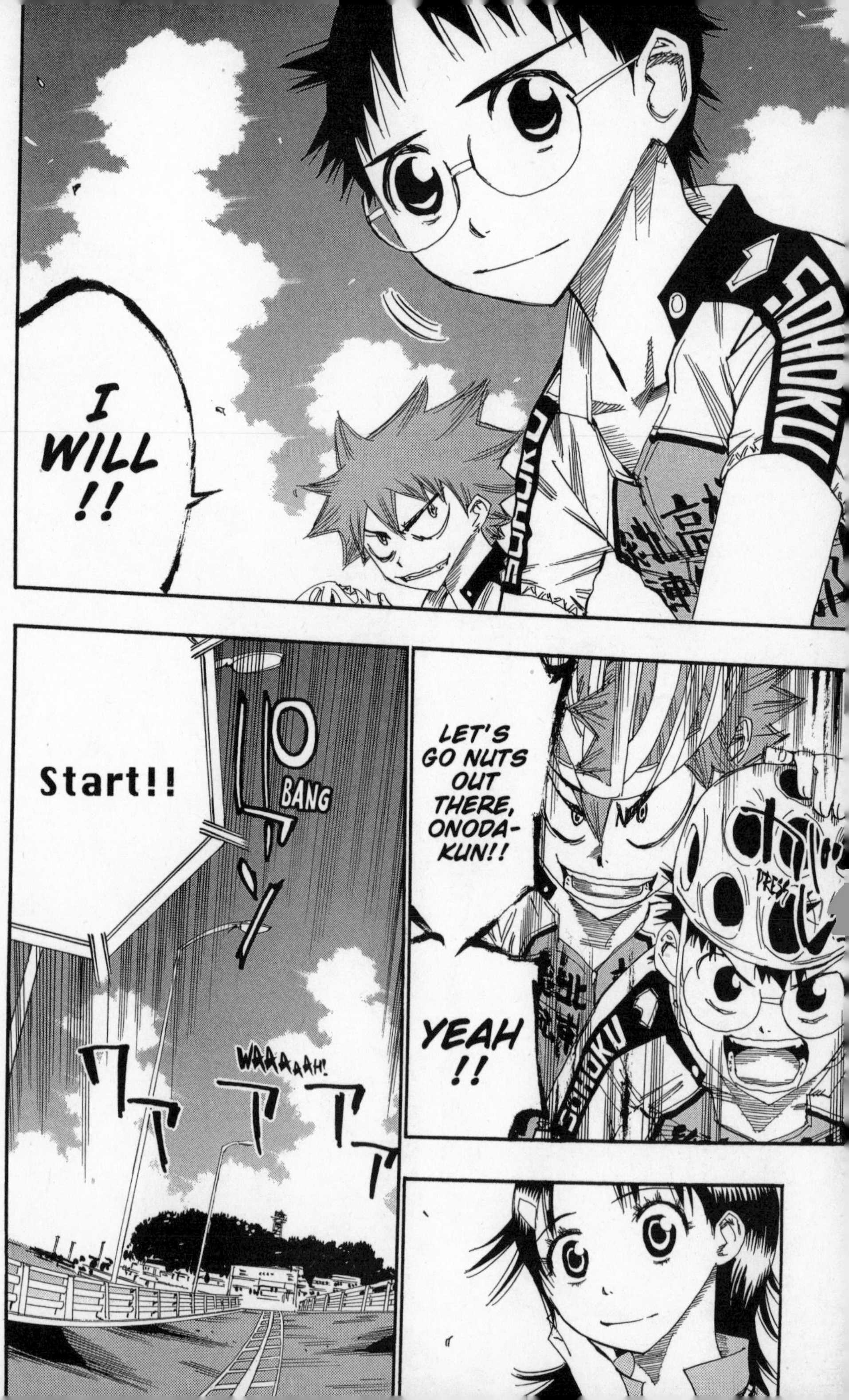
I WILL!!
LET'S GO NUTS OUT THERE, ONODA-KUN!!
YEAH!!
Start!!
BANG
WAAAAAH!

RIDE.75 THE START LINE

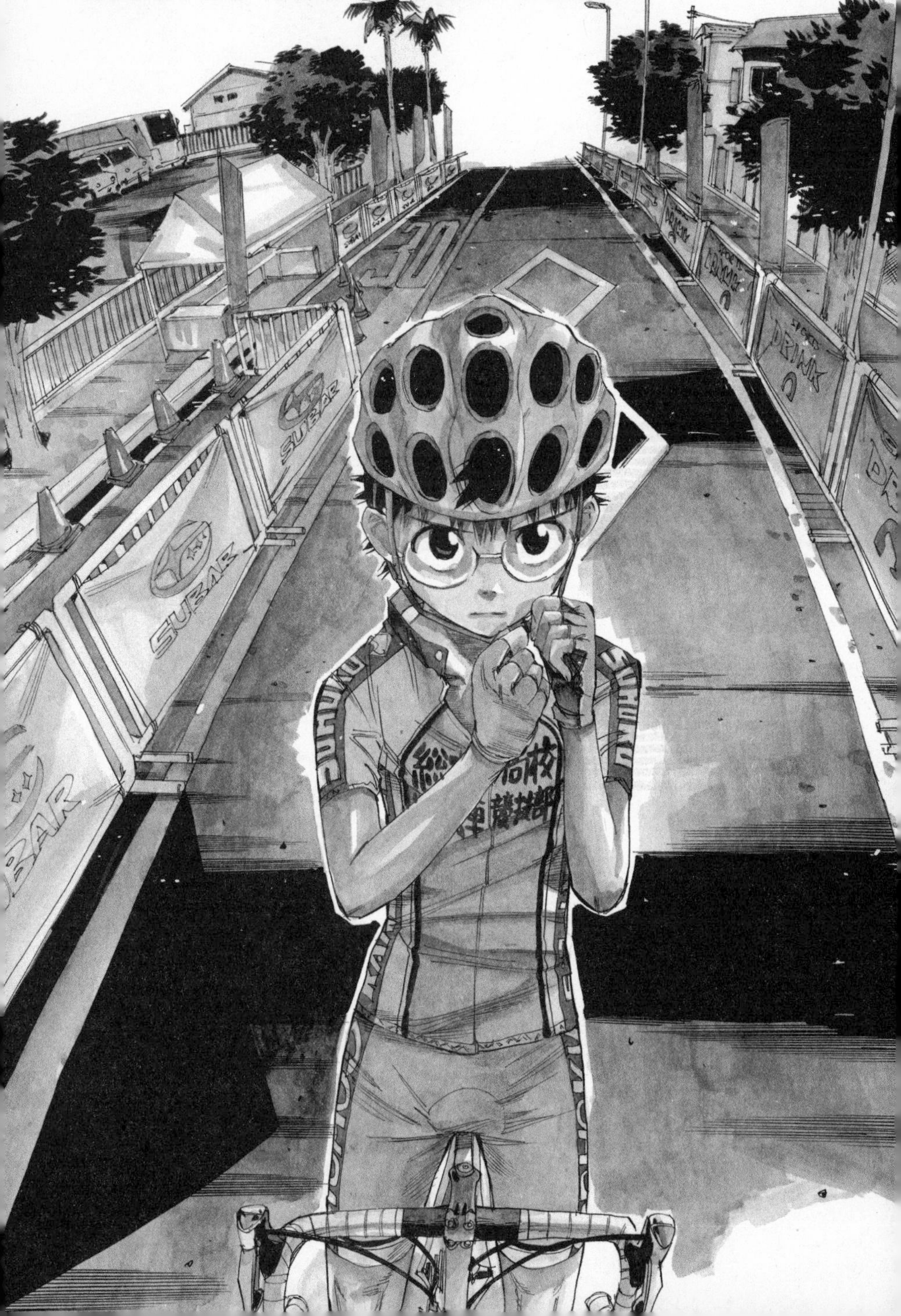
SUBAR
DRINK

YOWAMUSHI PEDAL

SOHOKU MEMBERS

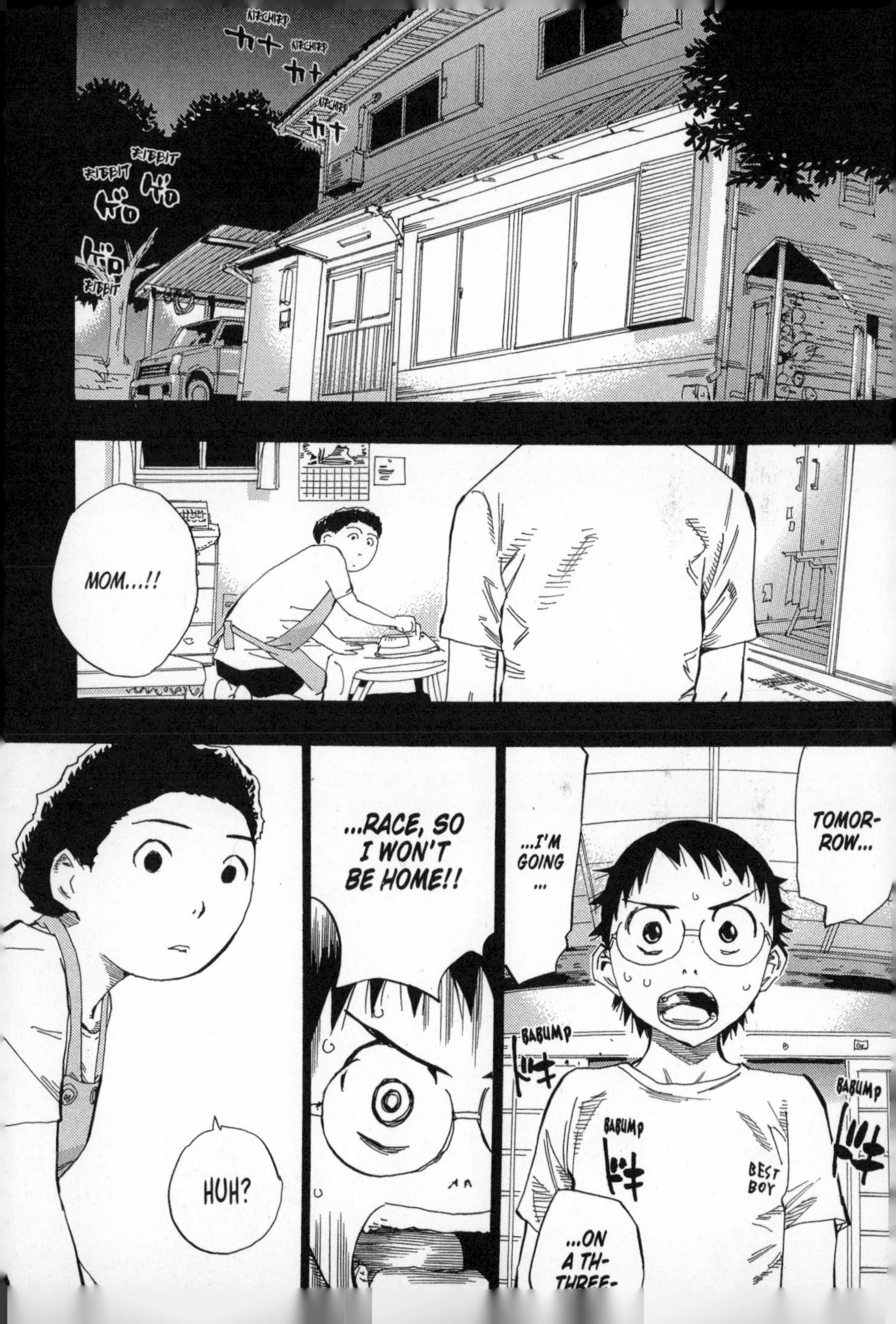
KIRCHIRP
カナ
KIRCHIRP
カナ
KIRCHIRP
カナ
RIBBIT
ゲロ
RIBBIT
ゲロ
ゲロ
RIBBIT
MOM...!!
TOMOR-ROW...
...I'M GOING ...
...ON A TH- THREE-
BABUMP
ドキ
BABUMP
ドキ
BABUMP
ドキ
BEST BOY
...RACE, SO I WON'T BE HOME!!
HUH?

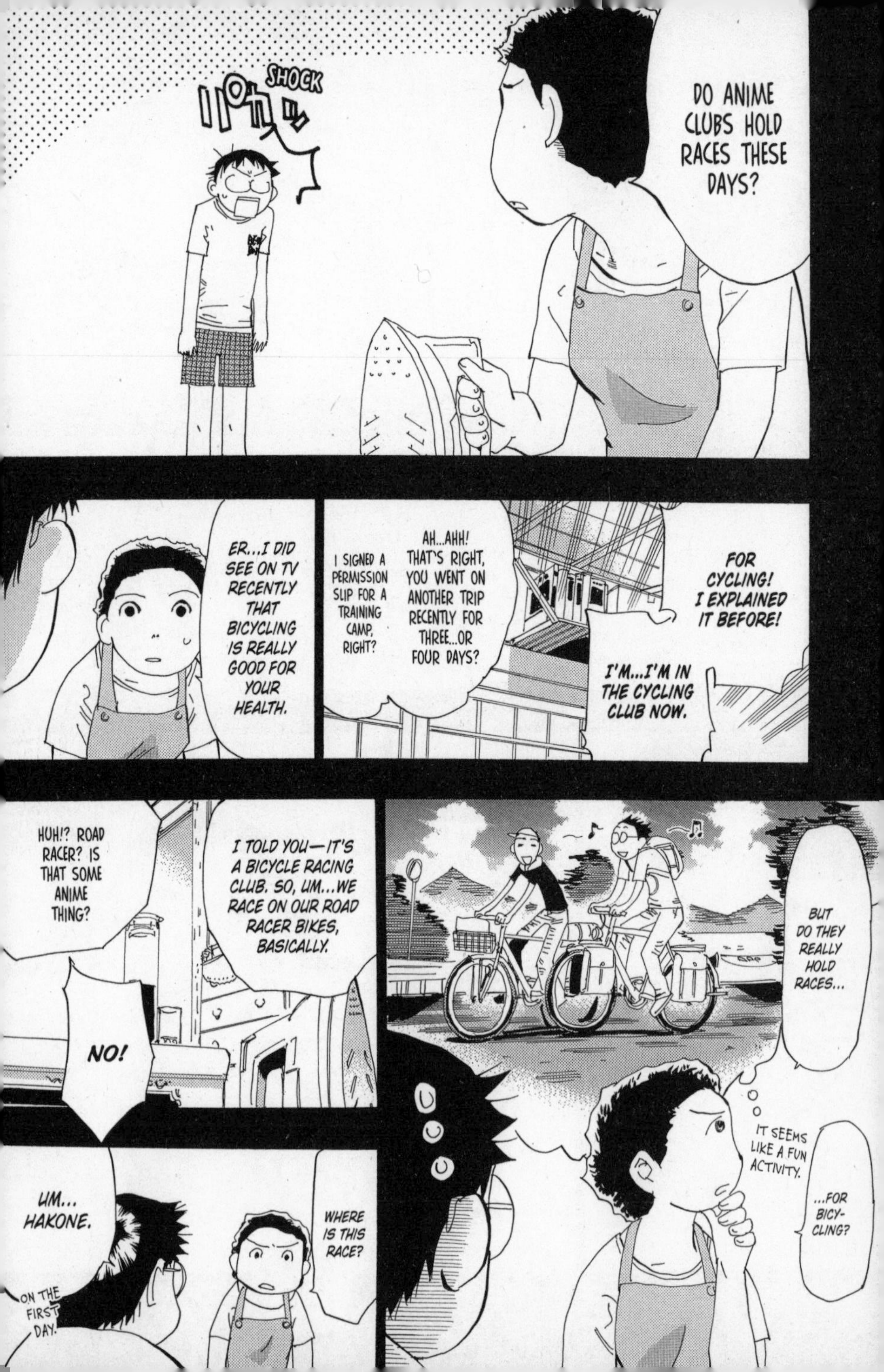
DO ANIME CLUBS HOLD RACES THESE DAYS?
SHOCK
FOR CYCLING! I EXPLAINED IT BEFORE!
I'M...I'M IN THE CYCLING CLUB NOW.
AH...AHH! THAT'S RIGHT, YOU WENT ON ANOTHER TRIP RECENTLY FOR THREE...OR FOUR DAYS?
I SIGNED A PERMISSION SLIP FOR A TRAINING CAMP, RIGHT?
ER...I DID SEE ON TV RECENTLY THAT BICYCLING IS REALLY GOOD FOR YOUR HEALTH.
BUT DO THEY REALLY HOLD RACES...
IT SEEMS LIKE A FUN ACTIVITY.
...FOR BICY-CLING?
I TOLD YOU—IT'S A BICYCLE RACING CLUB. SO, UM...WE RACE ON OUR ROAD RACER BIKES, BASICALLY.
HUH!? ROAD RACER? IS THAT SOME ANIME THING?
NO!
WHERE IS THIS RACE?
UM... HAKONE.
ON THE FIRST DAY.

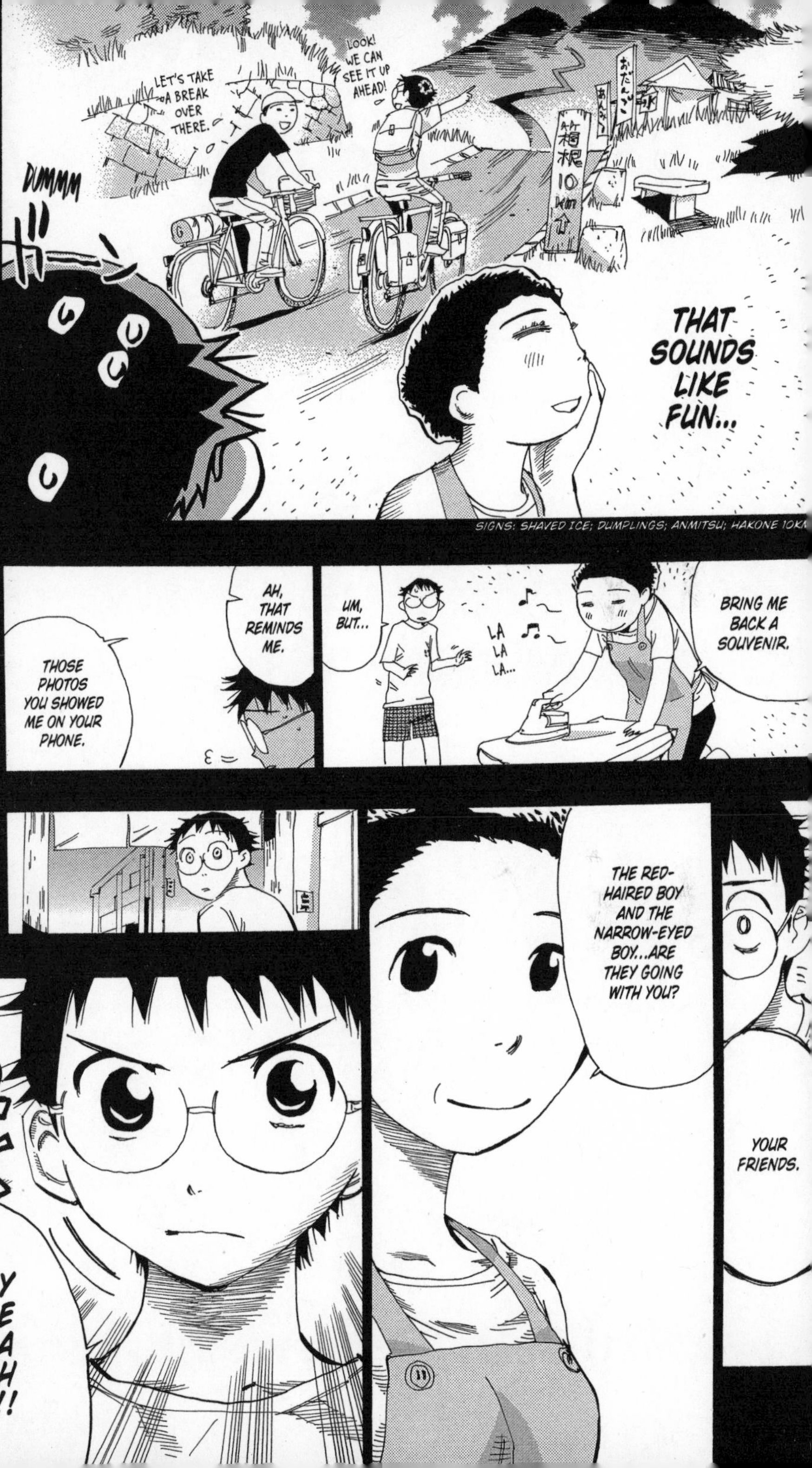
THAT SOUNDS LIKE FUN...
LOOK! WE CAN SEE IT UP AHEAD!
LET'S TAKE A BREAK OVER THERE.
DUMMMM
SIGNS: SHAVED ICE; DUMPLINGS; ANMITSU; HAKONE 10KM
BRING ME BACK A SOUVENIR.
LA LA LA...
UM, BUT...
AH, THAT REMINDS ME.
THOSE PHOTOS YOU SHOWED ME ON YOUR PHONE.
YOUR FRIENDS.
THE RED-HAIRED BOY AND THE NARROW-EYED BOY...ARE THEY GOING WITH YOU?
NOD
YEAH!!

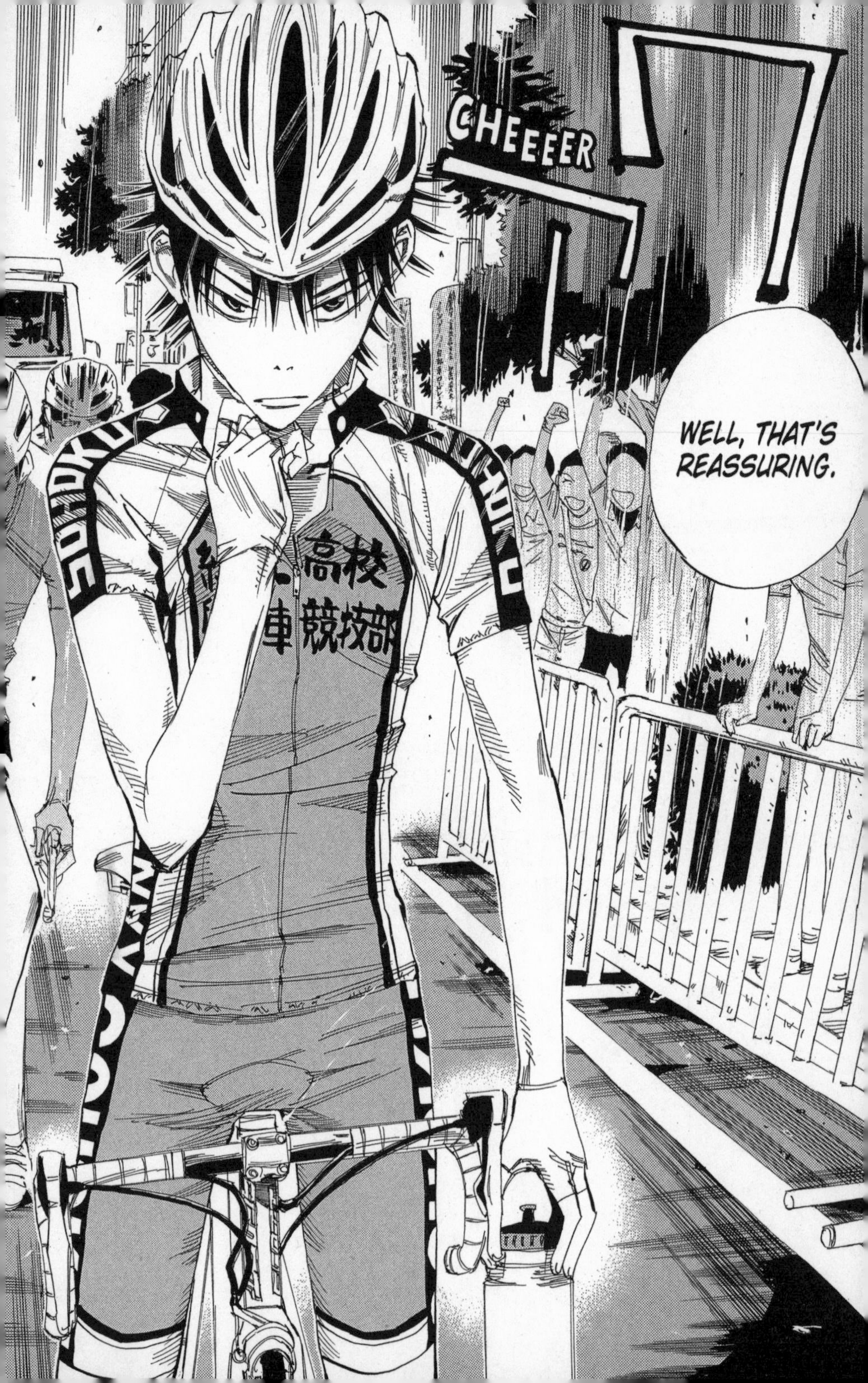
CHEEEER
WELL, THAT'S REASSURING.
SOHOKU
高校
車競技部

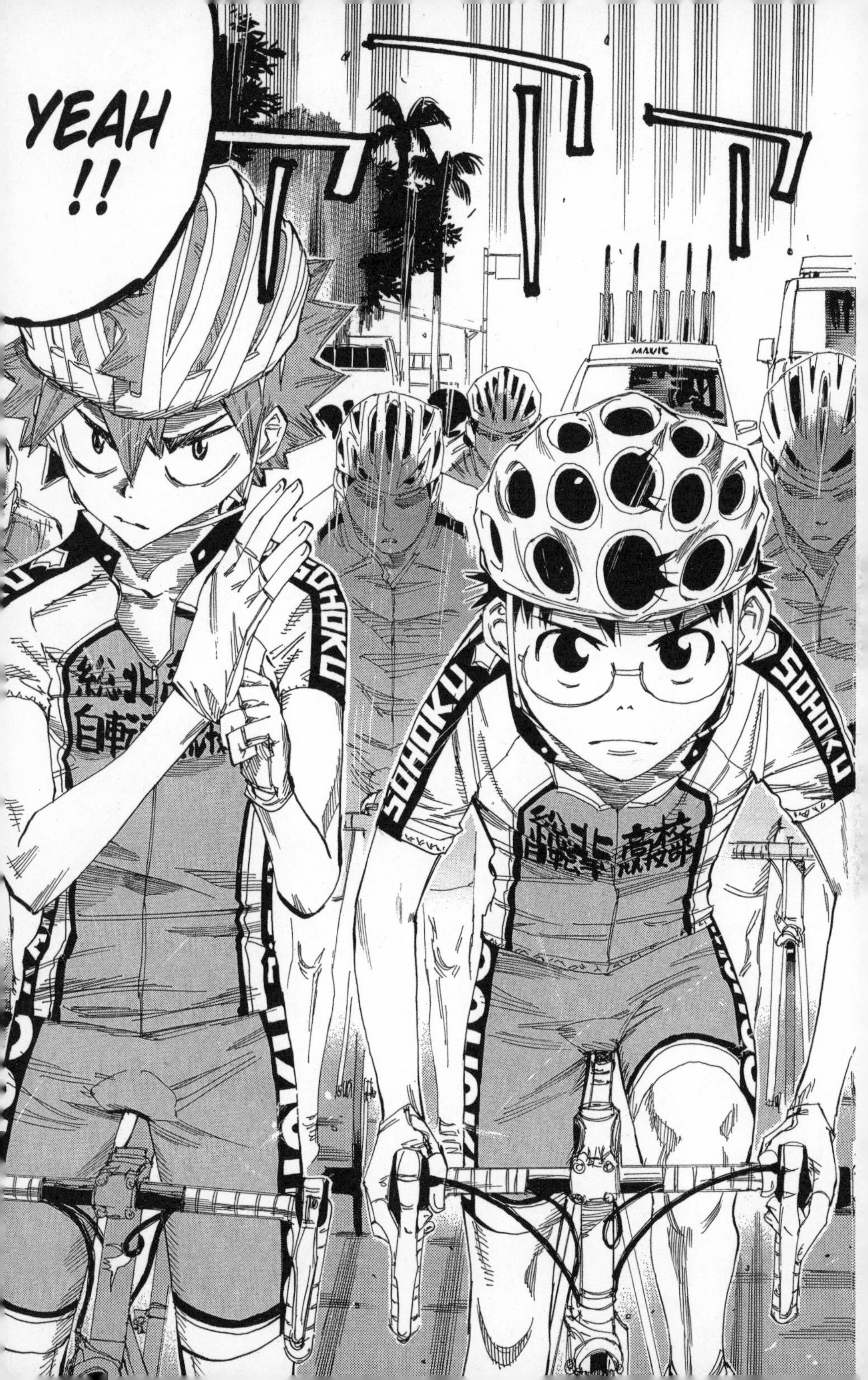
YEAH !!
MAVIC
SOHOKU

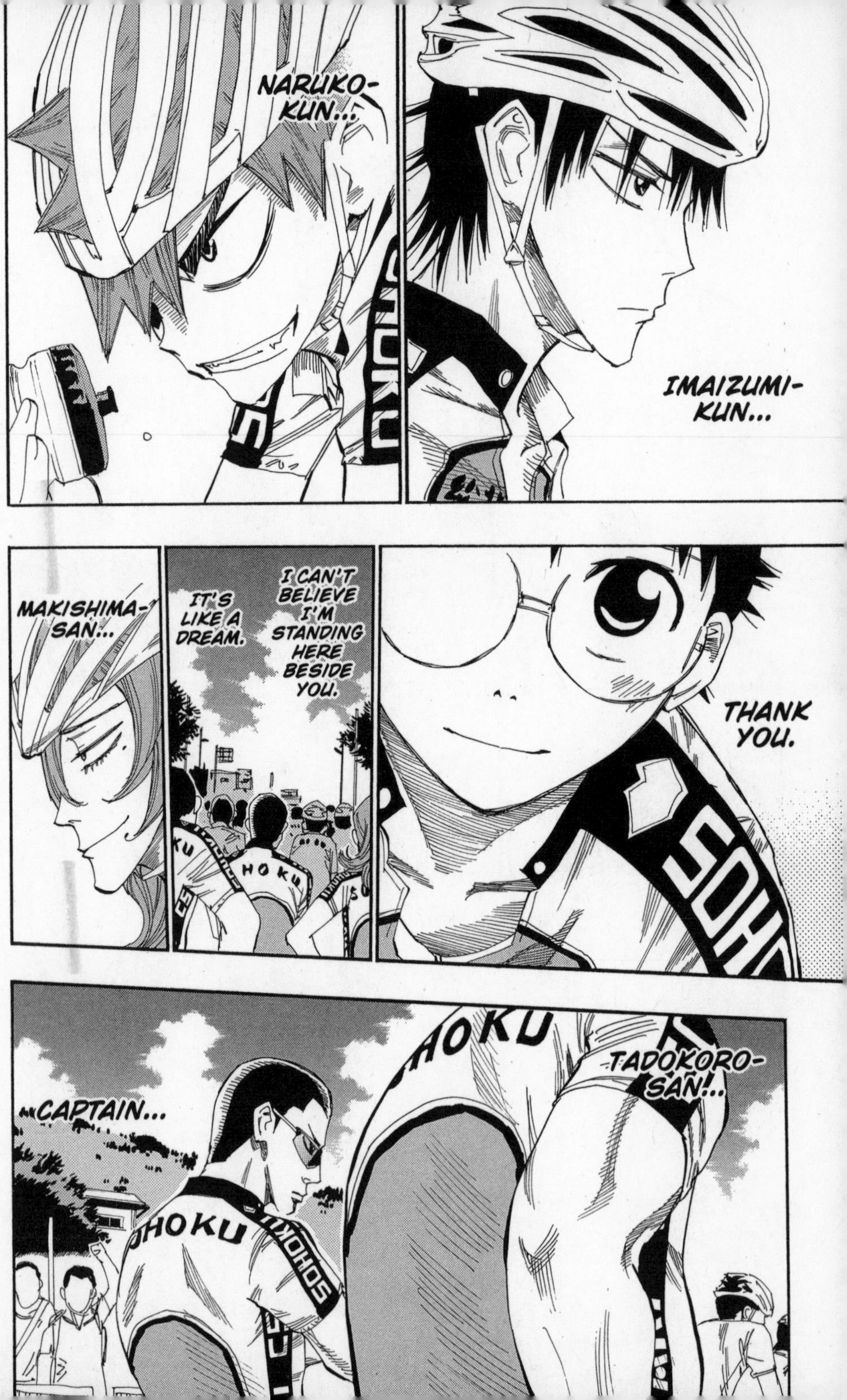
IMAIZUMI-KUN...
NARUKO-KUN...
THANK YOU.
I CAN'T BELIEVE I'M STANDING HERE BESIDE YOU.
IT'S LIKE A DREAM.
MAKISHIMA-SAN...
TADOKORO-SAN...
...CAPTAIN...

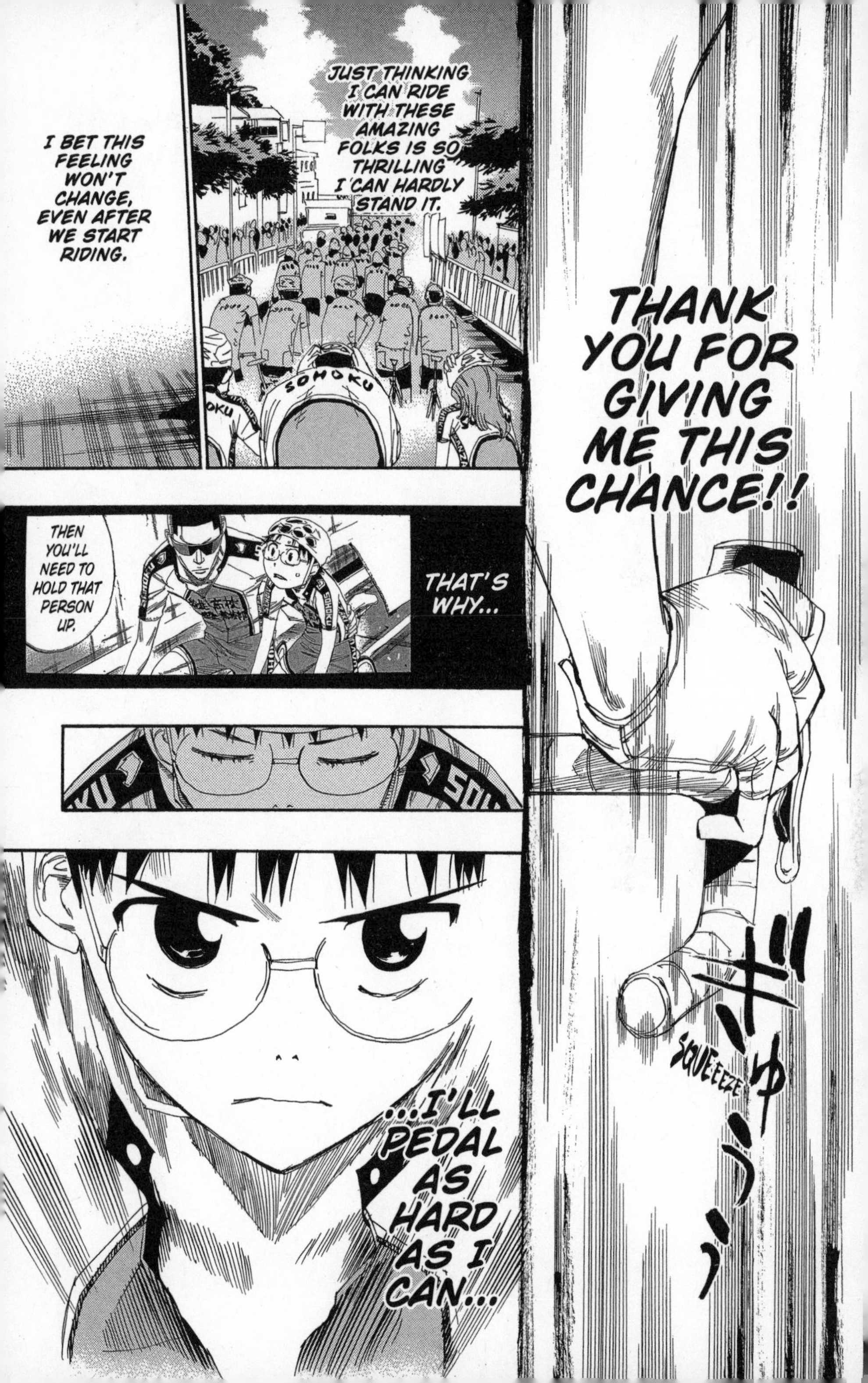
THANK YOU FOR GIVING ME THIS CHANCE!!
ぎゅうう
SQUEEZE
JUST THINKING I CAN RIDE WITH THESE AMAZING FOLKS IS SO THRILLING I CAN HARDLY STAND IT.
I BET THIS FEELING WON'T CHANGE, EVEN AFTER WE START RIDING.
SOHOKU
THAT'S WHY...
THEN YOU'LL NEED TO HOLD THAT PERSON UP.
...I'LL PEDAL AS HARD AS I CAN...

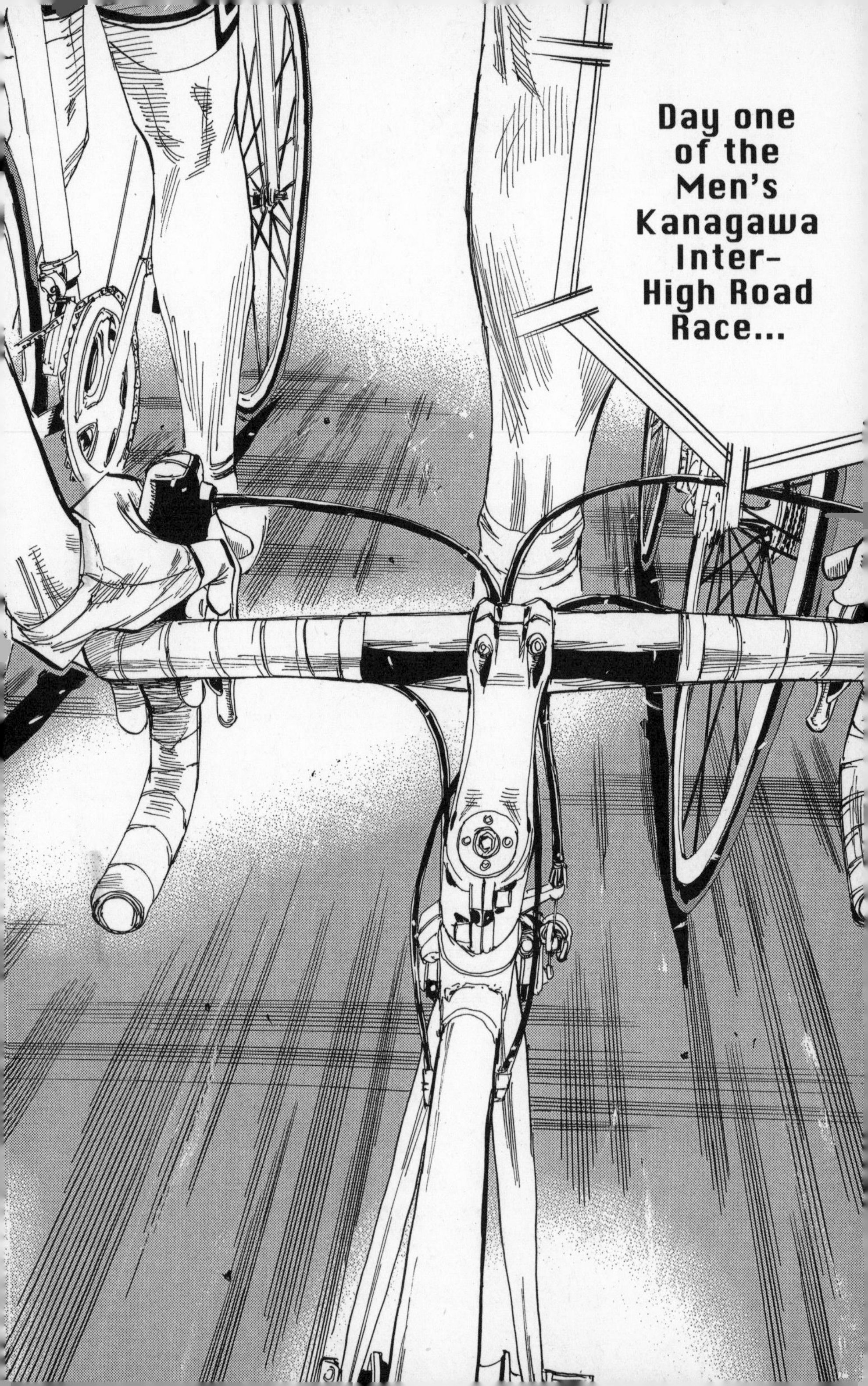
Day one of the Men's Kanagawa Inter-High Road Race...

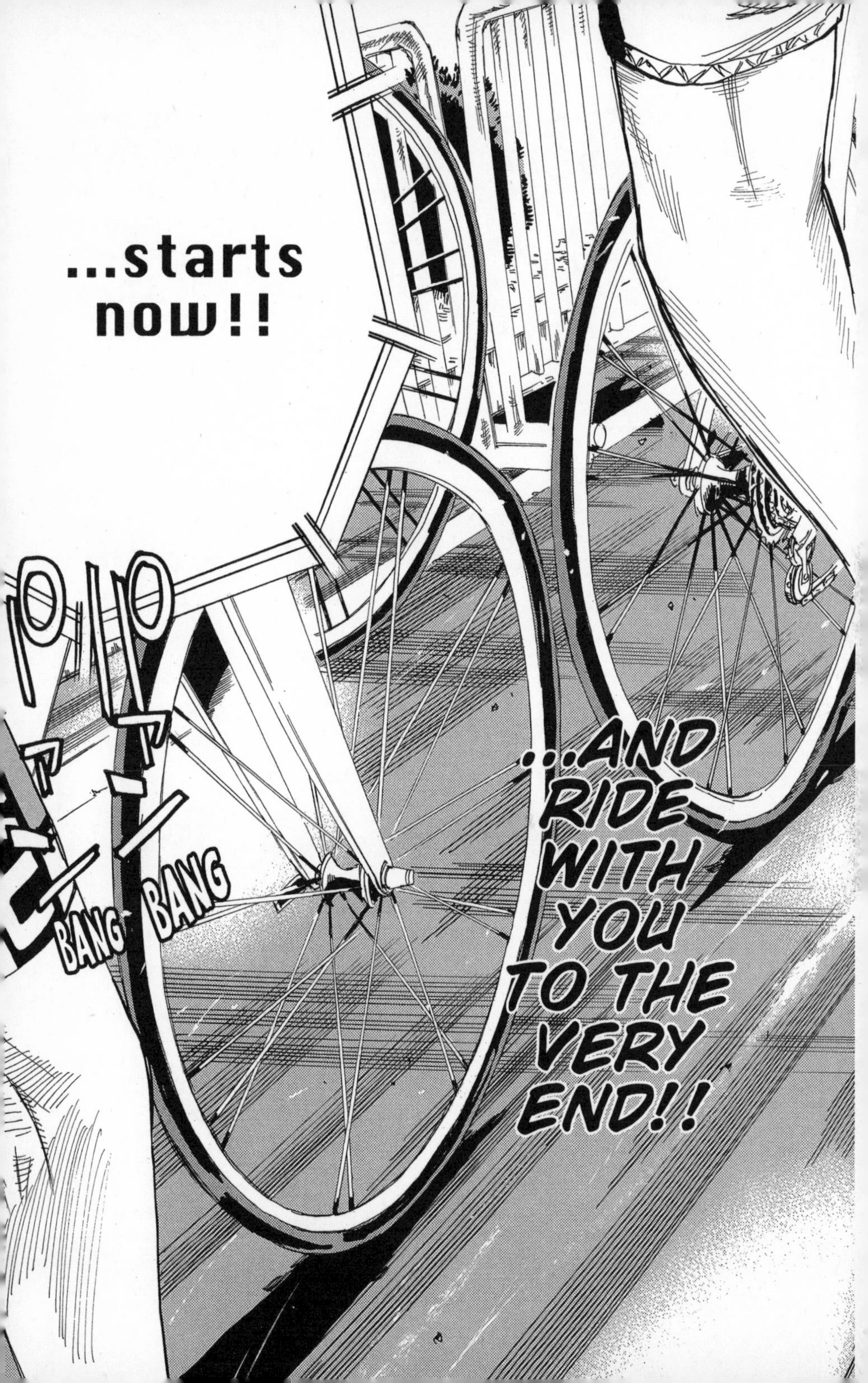
...starts now!!
...AND RIDE WITH YOU TO THE VERY END!!
BANG BANG

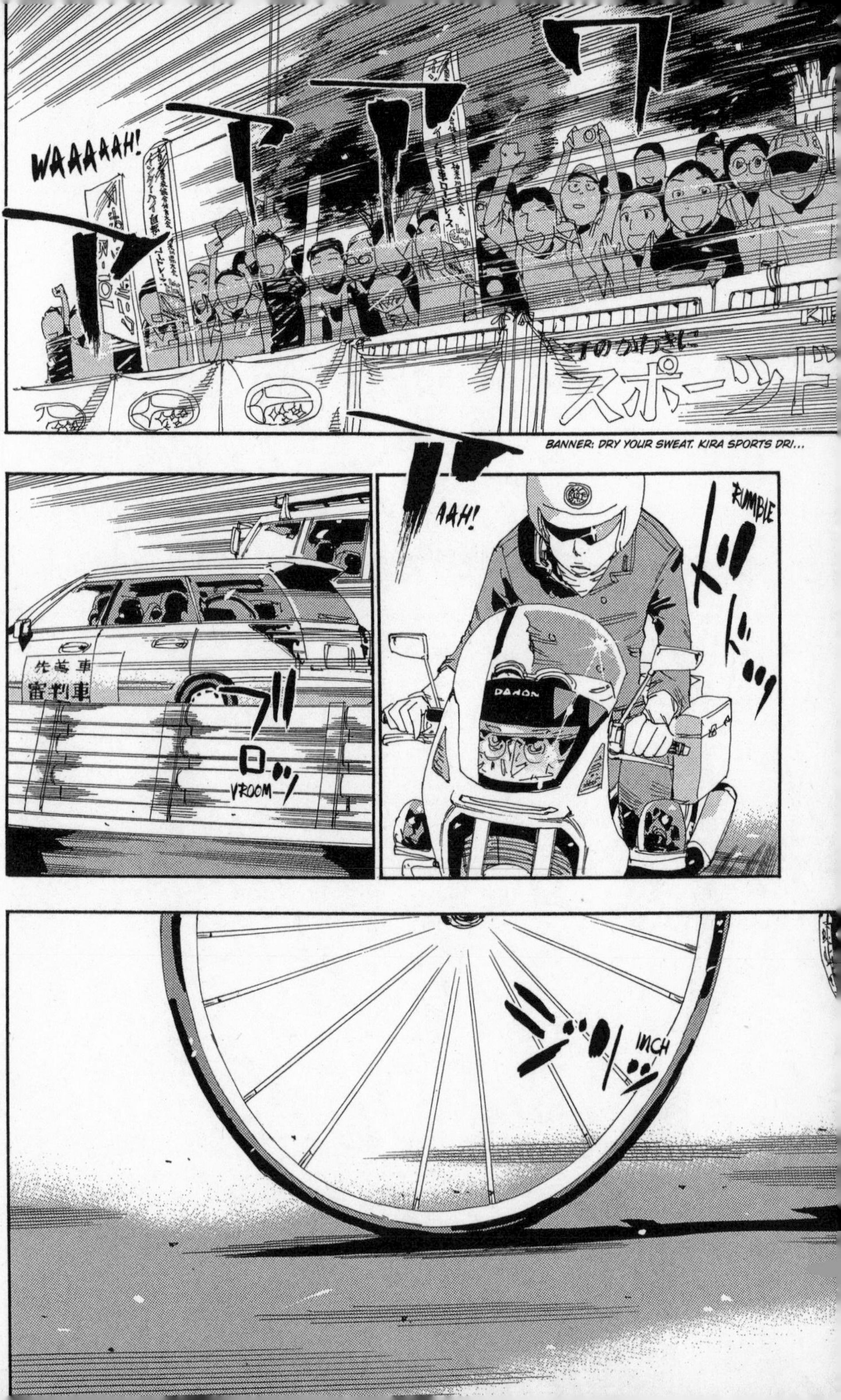
WAAAAAH!
BANNER: DRY YOUR SWEAT. KIRA SPORTS DRI...
AAH!
RUMBLE
先導車
審判車
VROOM
INCH

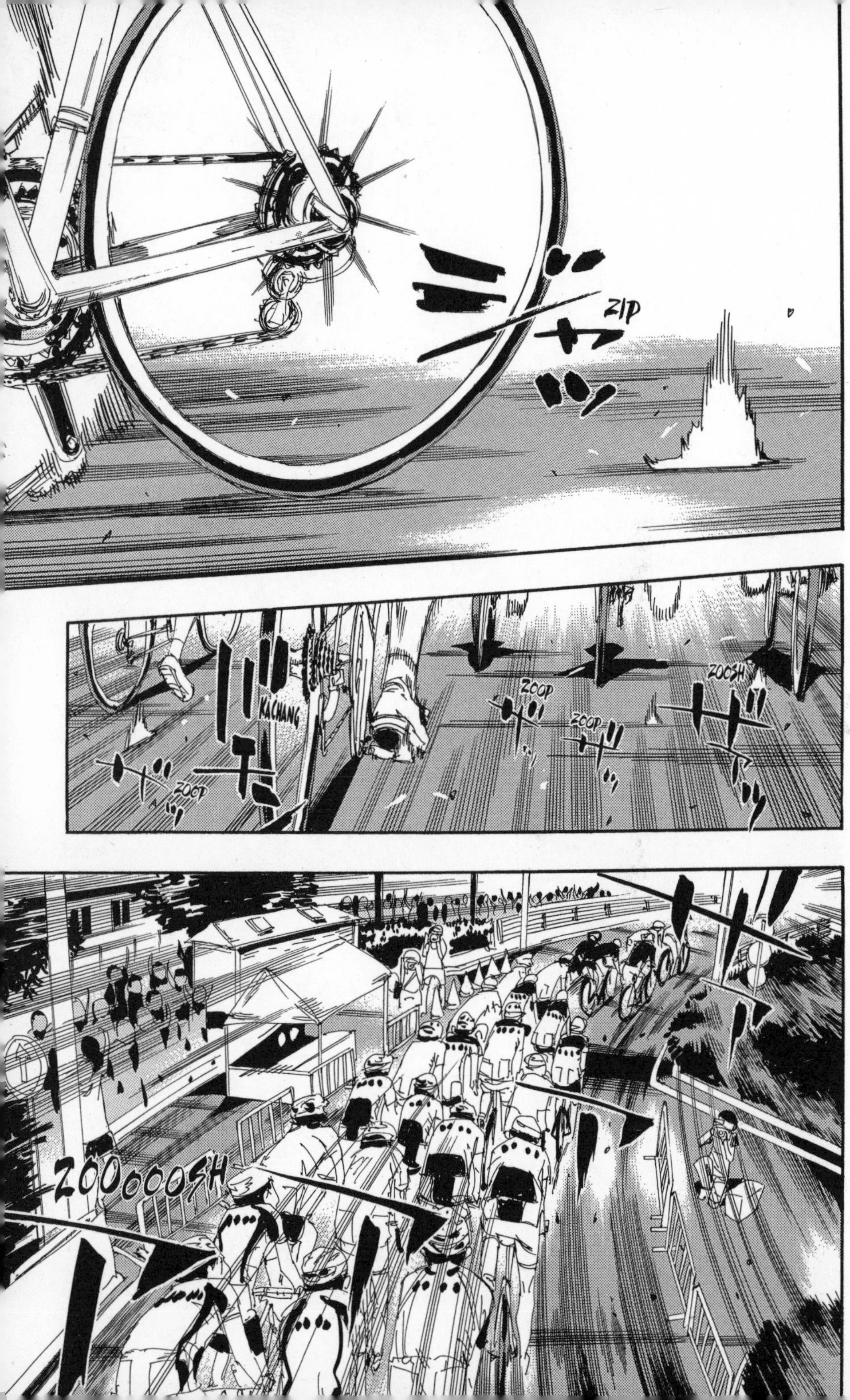
ZIP
ZOOSH
ZOOP
ZOOP
KACHANG
ZOOP
ZOOOOOOSH

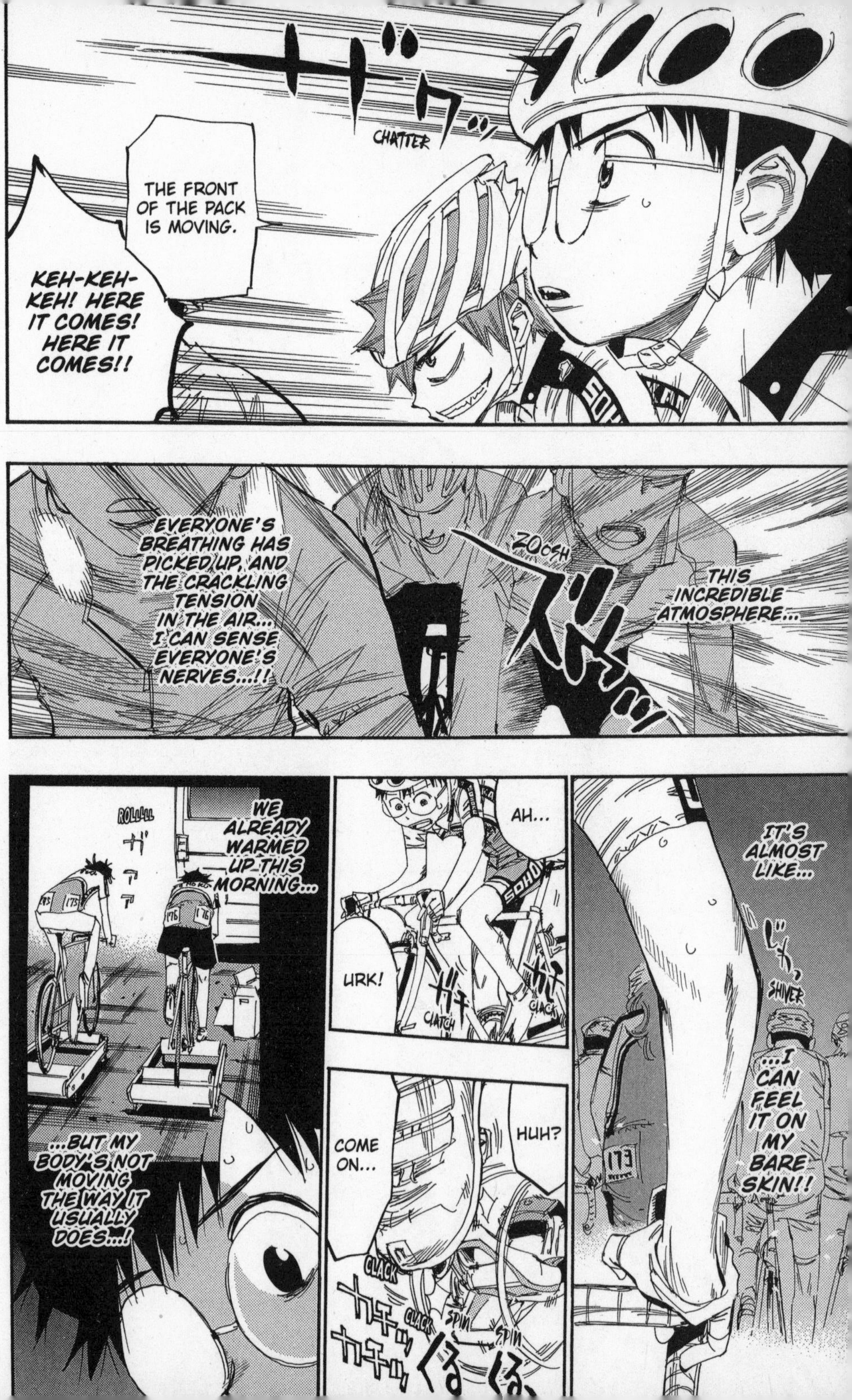
CHATTER
THE FRONT OF THE PACK IS MOVING.
KEH-KEH-KEH! HERE IT COMES! HERE IT COMES!!
ZOOSH
THIS INCREDIBLE ATMOSPHERE...
EVERYONE'S BREATHING HAS PICKED UP, AND THE CRACKLING TENSION IN THE AIR... I CAN SENSE EVERYONE'S NERVES...!!
IT'S ALMOST LIKE...
SHIVER
...I CAN FEEL IT ON MY BARE SKIN!!
AH...
URK!
CLACK
CLATCH
HUH?
COME ON...
CLACK
CLACK
SPIN
SPIN
WE ALREADY WARMED UP THIS MORNING...
ROLLLL
...BUT MY BODY'S NOT MOVING THE WAY IT USUALLY DOES...!

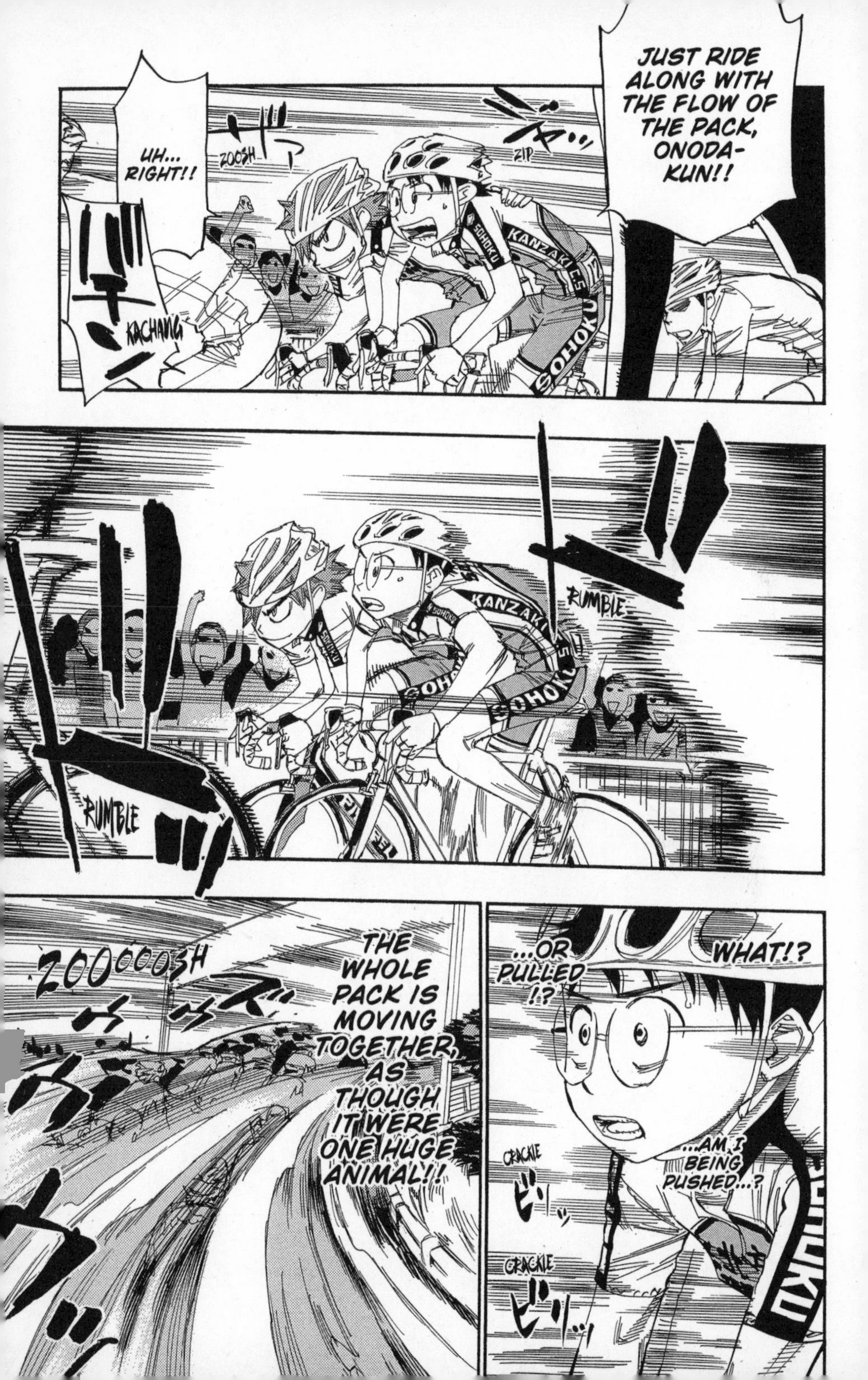
JUST RIDE ALONG WITH THE FLOW OF THE PACK, ONODA-KUN!!
ZIP
ZOOSH
UH... RIGHT!!
KACHANG
RUMBLE
RUMBLE
WHAT!?
...AM I BEING PUSHED...?
...OR PULLED !?
CRACKLE
CRACKLE
THE WHOLE PACK IS MOVING TOGETHER, AS THOUGH IT WERE ONE HUGE ANIMAL!!
ZOOOOOOSH

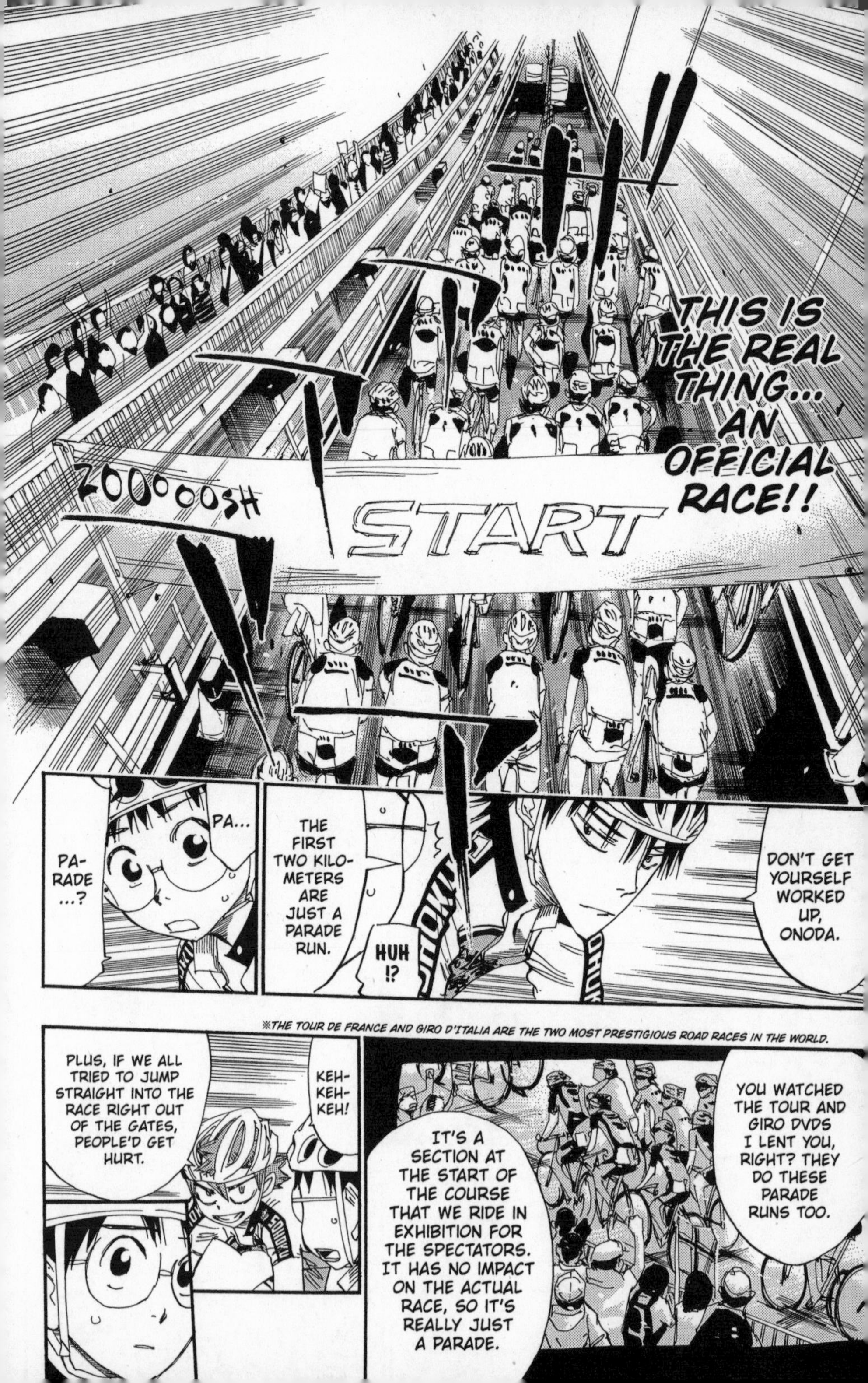
THIS IS THE REAL THING... AN OFFICIAL RACE!!
START
ZOOOOOOSH
DON'T GET YOURSELF WORKED UP, ONODA.
THE FIRST TWO KILOMETERS ARE JUST A PARADE RUN.
HUH!?
PA...
PARADE ...?
※THE TOUR DE FRANCE AND GIRO D'ITALIA ARE THE TWO MOST PRESTIGIOUS ROAD RACES IN THE WORLD.
YOU WATCHED THE TOUR AND GIRO DVDS I LENT YOU, RIGHT? THEY DO THESE PARADE RUNS TOO.
IT'S A SECTION AT THE START OF THE COURSE THAT WE RIDE IN EXHIBITION FOR THE SPECTATORS. IT HAS NO IMPACT ON THE ACTUAL RACE, SO IT'S REALLY JUST A PARADE.
KEH-KEH-KEH!
PLUS, IF WE ALL TRIED TO JUMP STRAIGHT INTO THE RACE RIGHT OUT OF THE GATES, PEOPLE'D GET HURT.

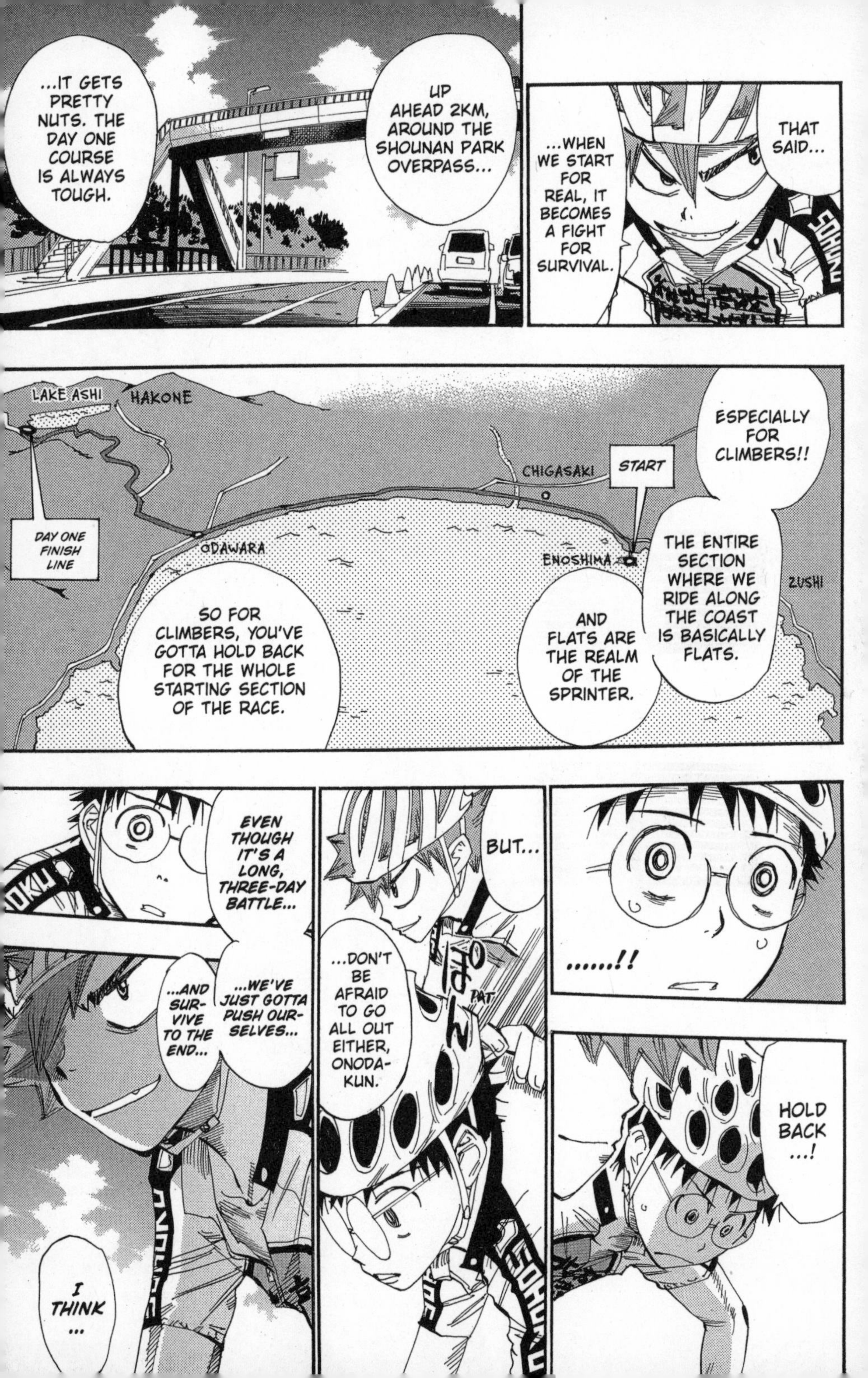
THAT SAID...
...WHEN WE START FOR REAL, IT BECOMES A FIGHT FOR SURVIVAL.
UP AHEAD 2KM, AROUND THE SHOUNAN PARK OVERPASS...
...IT GETS PRETTY NUTS. THE DAY ONE COURSE IS ALWAYS TOUGH.
ESPECIALLY FOR CLIMBERS!!
ZUSHI
START
THE ENTIRE SECTION WHERE WE RIDE ALONG THE COAST IS BASICALLY FLATS.
ENOSHIMA
CHIGASAKI
AND FLATS ARE THE REALM OF THE SPRINTER.
HAKONE
LAKE ASHI
ODAWARA
DAY ONE FINISH LINE
SO FOR CLIMBERS, YOU'VE GOTTA HOLD BACK FOR THE WHOLE STARTING SECTION OF THE RACE.
......!!
HOLD BACK ...!
BUT...
PAT
...DON'T BE AFRAID TO GO ALL OUT EITHER, ONODA-KUN.
EVEN THOUGH IT'S A LONG, THREE-DAY BATTLE...
...WE'VE JUST GOTTA PUSH OURSELVES...
...AND SURVIVE TO THE END...
I THINK ...

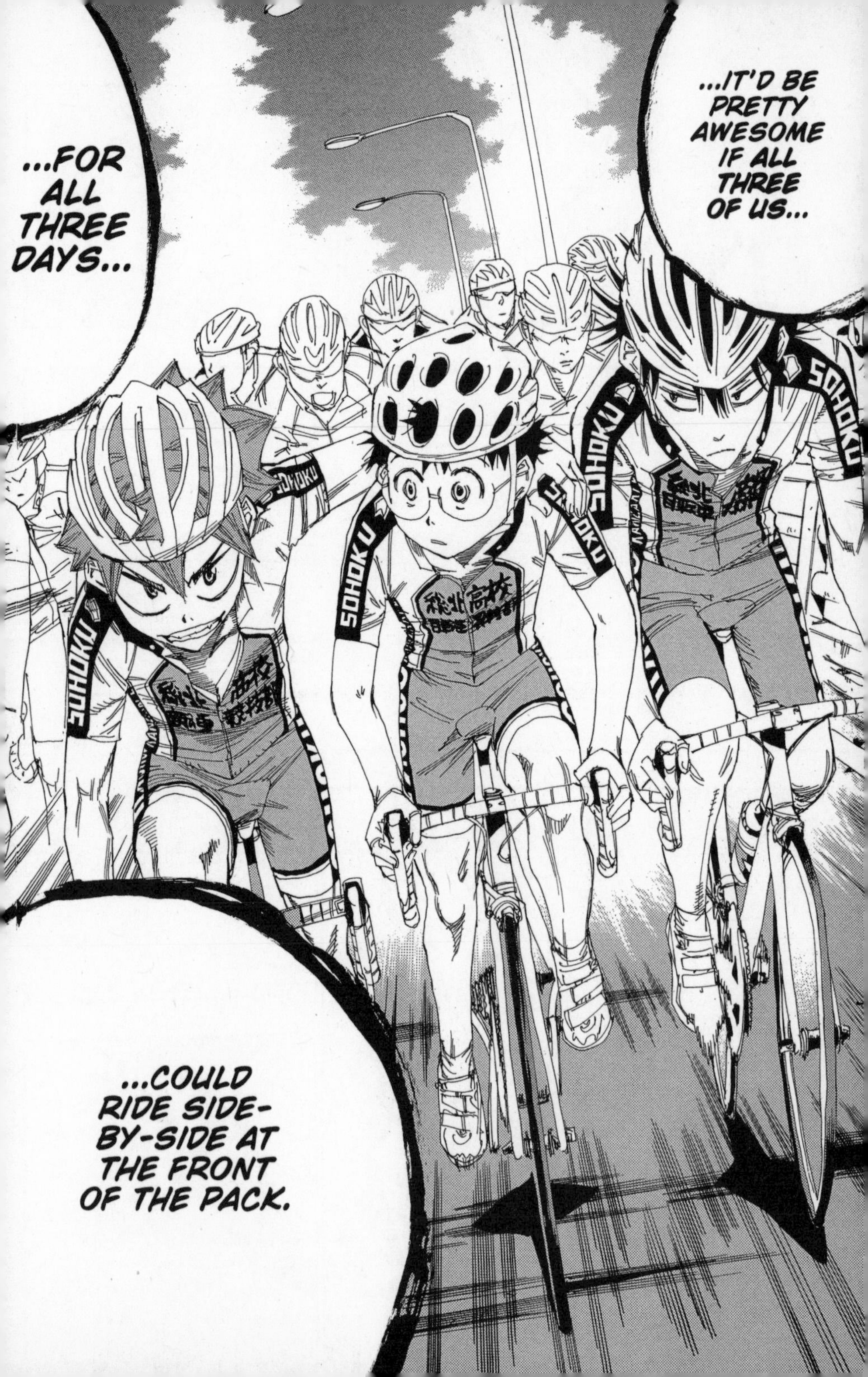
...IT'D BE PRETTY AWESOME IF ALL THREE OF US...
...FOR ALL THREE DAYS...
...COULD RIDE SIDE-BY-SIDE AT THE FRONT OF THE PACK.

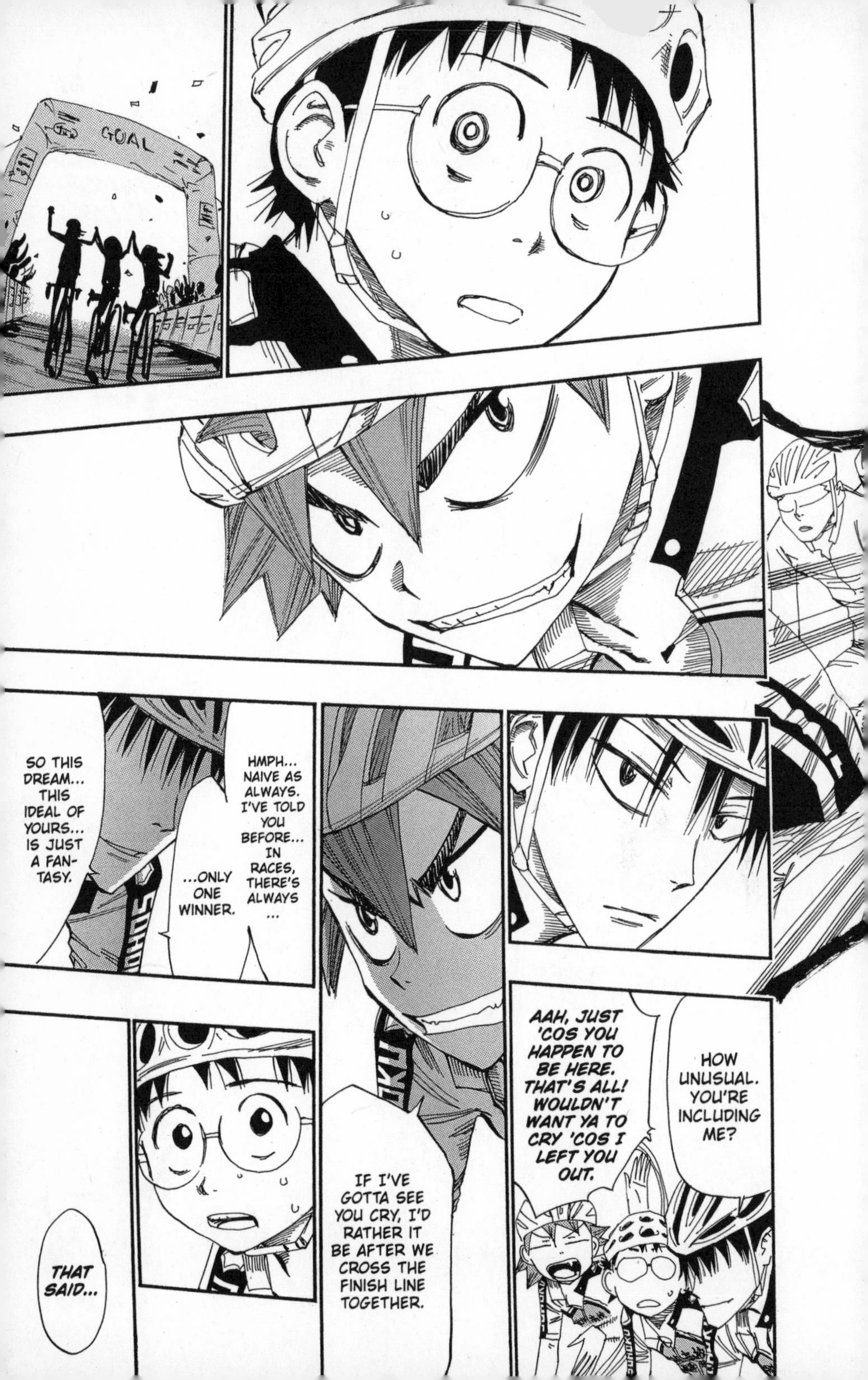
GOAL
HMPH... NAIVE AS ALWAYS. I'VE TOLD YOU BEFORE... IN RACES, THERE'S ALWAYS...
...ONLY ONE WINNER.
SO THIS DREAM... THIS IDEAL OF YOURS... IS JUST A FAN-TASY.
THAT SAID...
IF I'VE GOTTA SEE YOU CRY, I'D RATHER IT BE AFTER WE CROSS THE FINISH LINE TOGETHER.
HOW UNUSUAL. YOU'RE INCLUDING ME?
AAH, JUST 'COS YOU HAPPEN TO BE HERE. THAT'S ALL! WOULDN'T WANT YA TO CRY 'COS I LEFT YOU OUT.

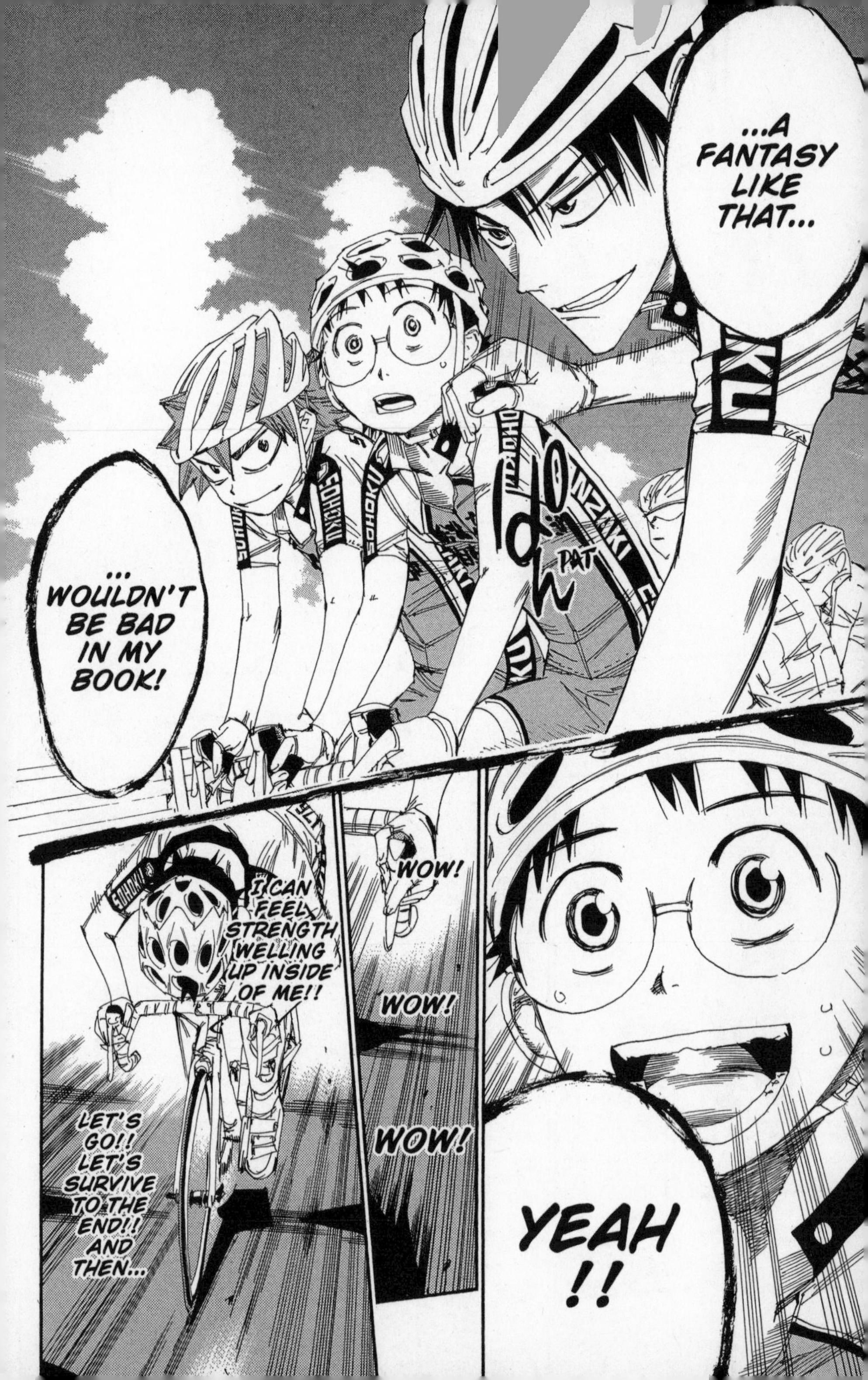
...A FANTASY LIKE THAT...
PAT
...WOULDN'T BE BAD IN MY BOOK!
YEAH!!
WOW!
WOW!
WOW!
I CAN FEEL STRENGTH WELLING UP INSIDE OF ME!!
LET'S GO!! LET'S SURVIVE TO THE END!! AND THEN...

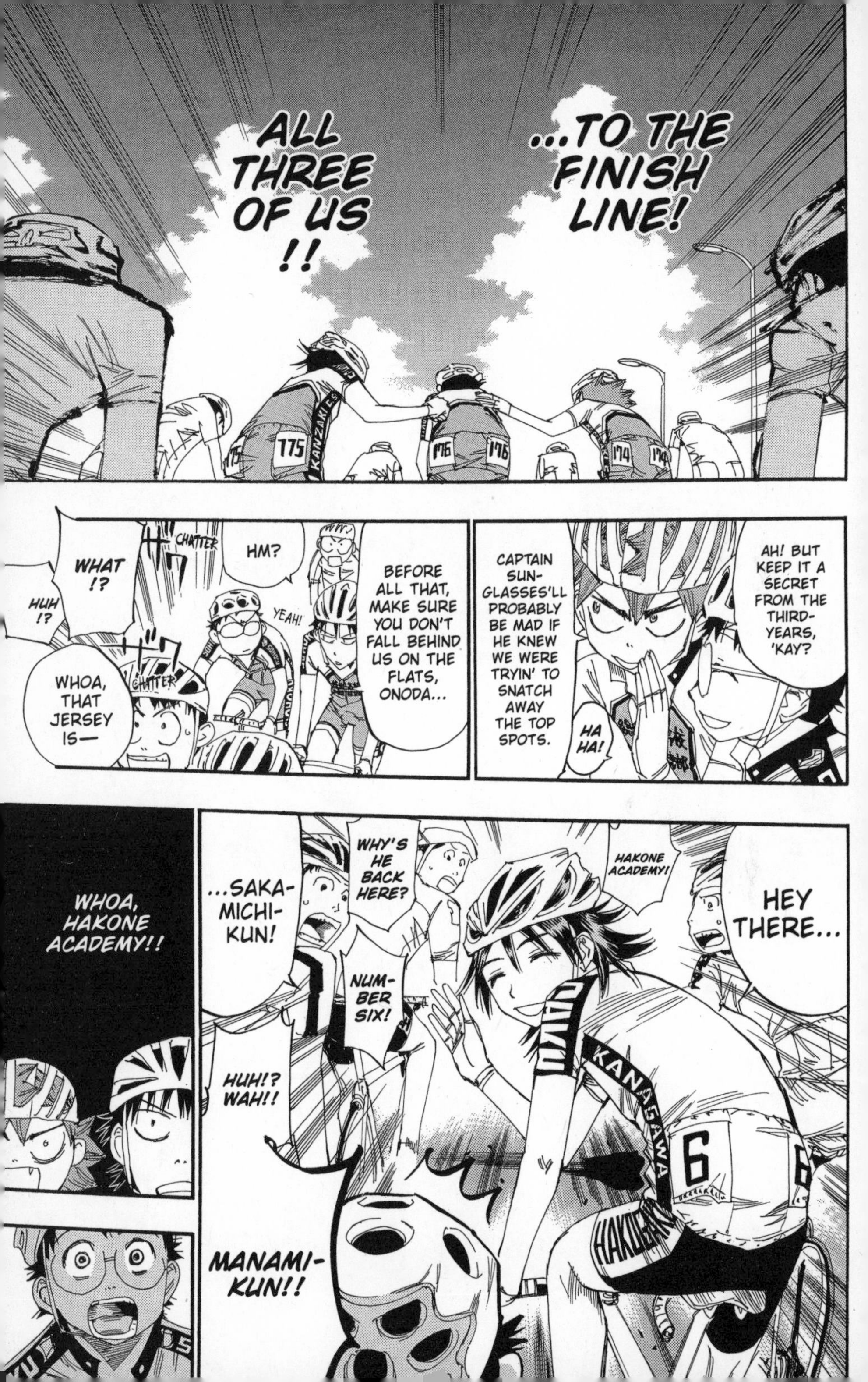
ALL THREE OF US !!
...TO THE FINISH LINE!
AH! BUT KEEP IT A SECRET FROM THE THIRD-YEARS, 'KAY?
CAPTAIN SUN-GLASSES'LL PROBABLY BE MAD IF HE KNEW WE WERE TRYIN' TO SNATCH AWAY THE TOP SPOTS.
HA HA!
BEFORE ALL THAT, MAKE SURE YOU DON'T FALL BEHIND US ON THE FLATS, ONODA...
HM?
YEAH!
CHATTER
WHAT !?
HUH !?
CHATTER
WHOA, THAT JERSEY IS—
HEY THERE...
HAKONE ACADEMY!
WHY'S HE BACK HERE?
...SAKA-MICHI-KUN!
NUMBER SIX!
HUH!? WAH!!
MANAMI-KUN!!
WHOA, HAKONE ACADEMY!!

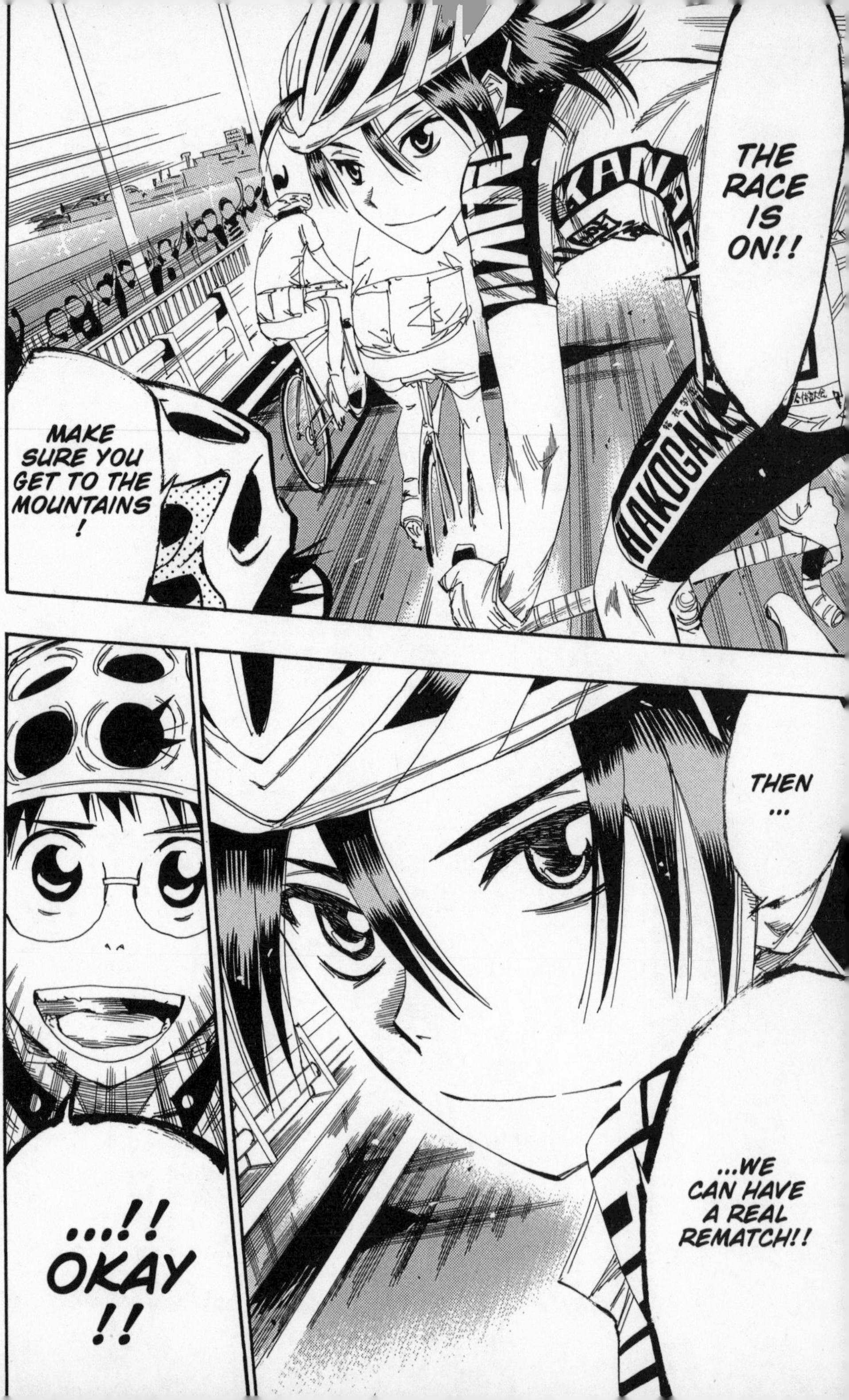
THE RACE IS ON!!
MAKE SURE YOU GET TO THE MOUNTAINS!
THEN...
...WE CAN HAVE A REAL REMATCH!!
...!! OKAY!!

RIDE.76 TOP SPRINTER!!

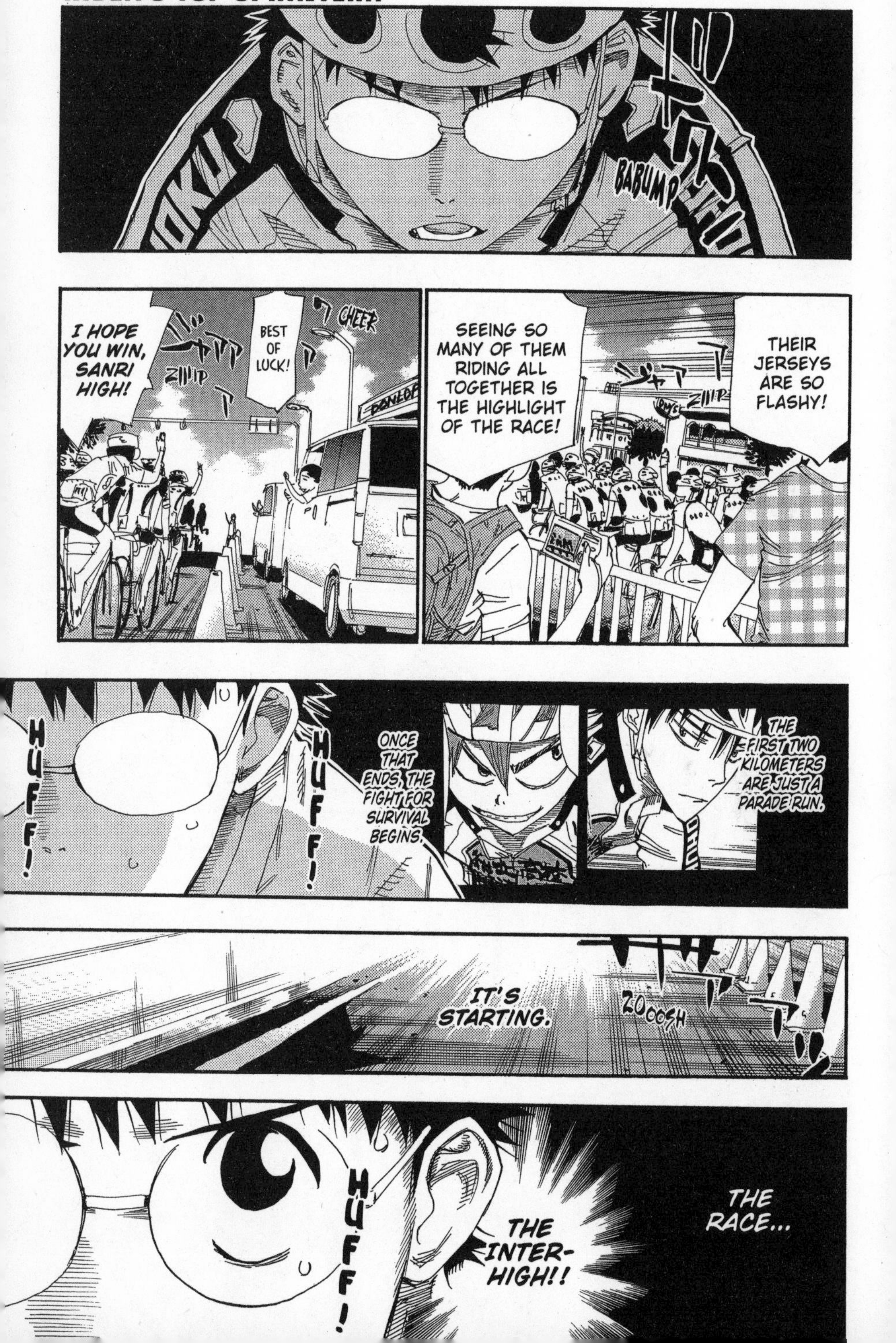
BABUMP
THEIR JERSEYS ARE SO FLASHY!
ZIIIP
SEEING SO MANY OF THEM RIDING ALL TOGETHER IS THE HIGHLIGHT OF THE RACE!
CHEER
BEST OF LUCK!
ZIIIP
I HOPE YOU WIN, SANRI HIGH!
THE FIRST TWO KILOMETERS ARE JUST A PARADE RUN.
ONCE THAT ENDS, THE FIGHT FOR SURVIVAL BEGINS.
HUFF!
HUFF!
ZOOOSH
IT'S STARTING.
THE RACE...
THE INTER-HIGH!!
HUFF!

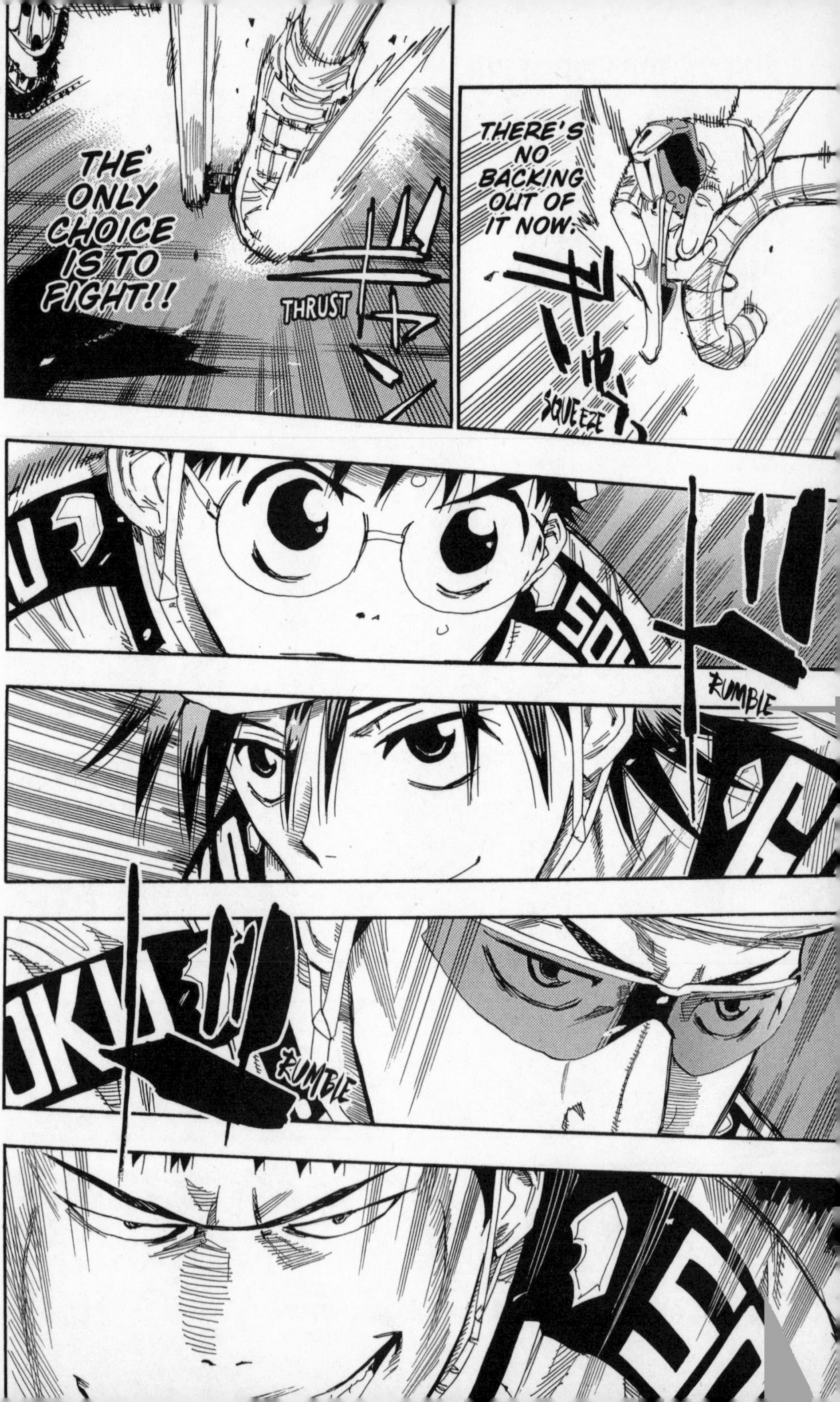
THERE'S NO BACKING OUT OF IT NOW.
SQUEEZE
THE ONLY CHOICE IS TO FIGHT!!
THRUST
RUMBLE
RUMBLE

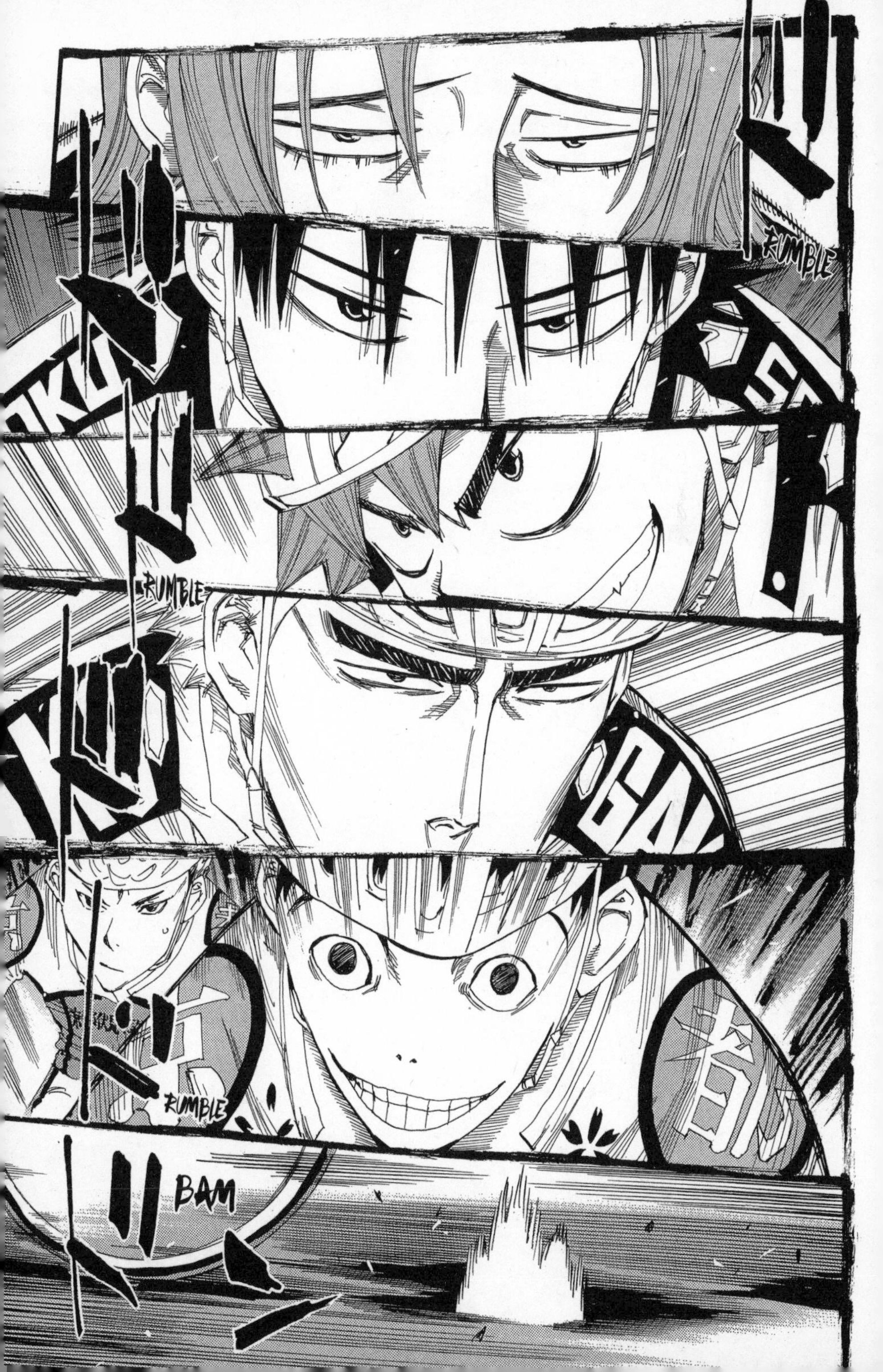
RUMBLE
RUMBLE
RUMBLE
BAM

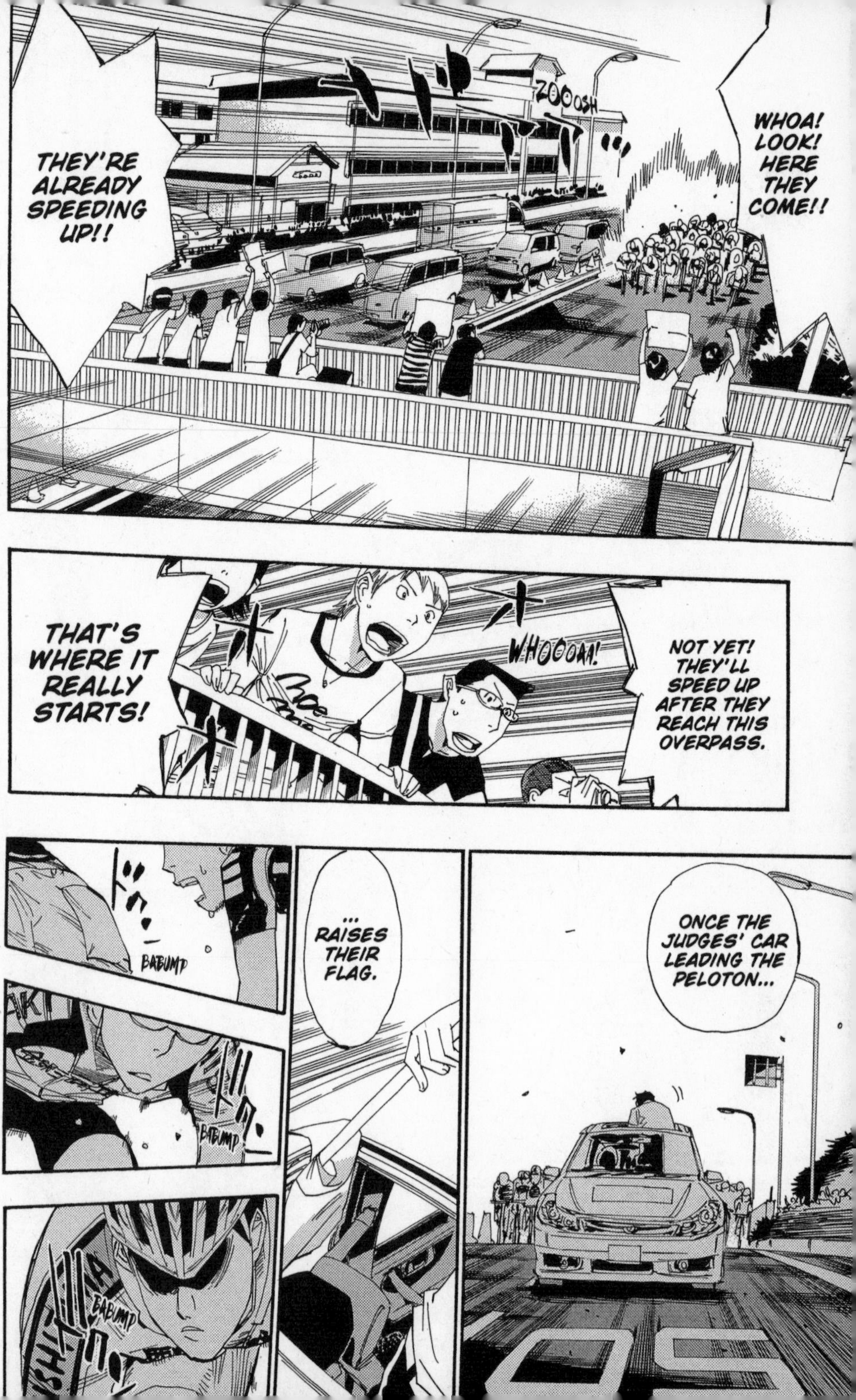
WHOA! LOOK! HERE THEY COME!!
ZOOOSH
THEY'RE ALREADY SPEEDING UP!!
NOT YET! THEY'LL SPEED UP AFTER THEY REACH THIS OVERPASS.
WHOOOAA!
THAT'S WHERE IT REALLY STARTS!
ONCE THE JUDGES' CAR LEADING THE PELOTON...
...RAISES THEIR FLAG.
BABUMP
BABUMP
BABUMP

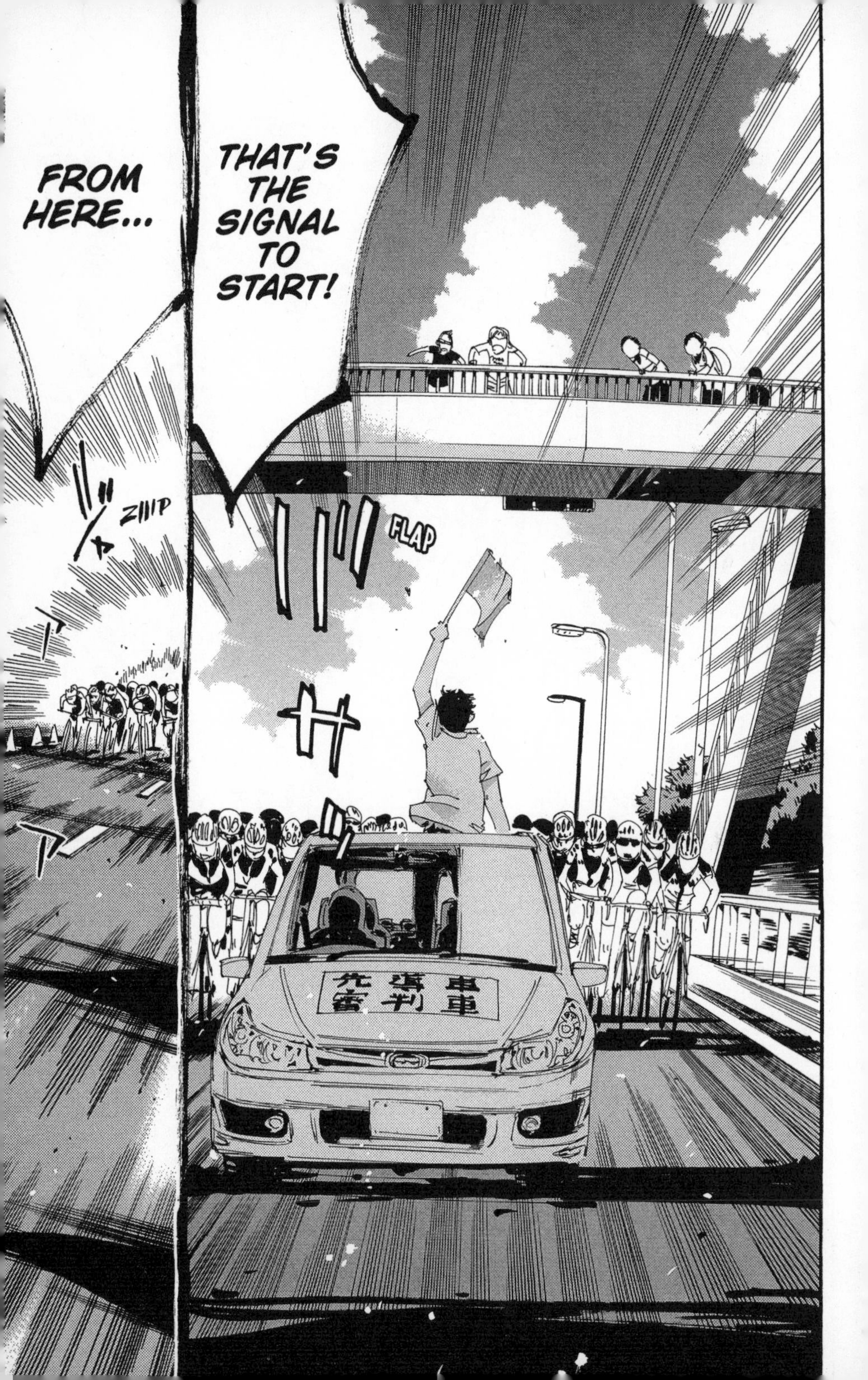
THAT'S THE SIGNAL TO START!
FLAP
先導車
審判車
FROM HERE...
ZIIIP

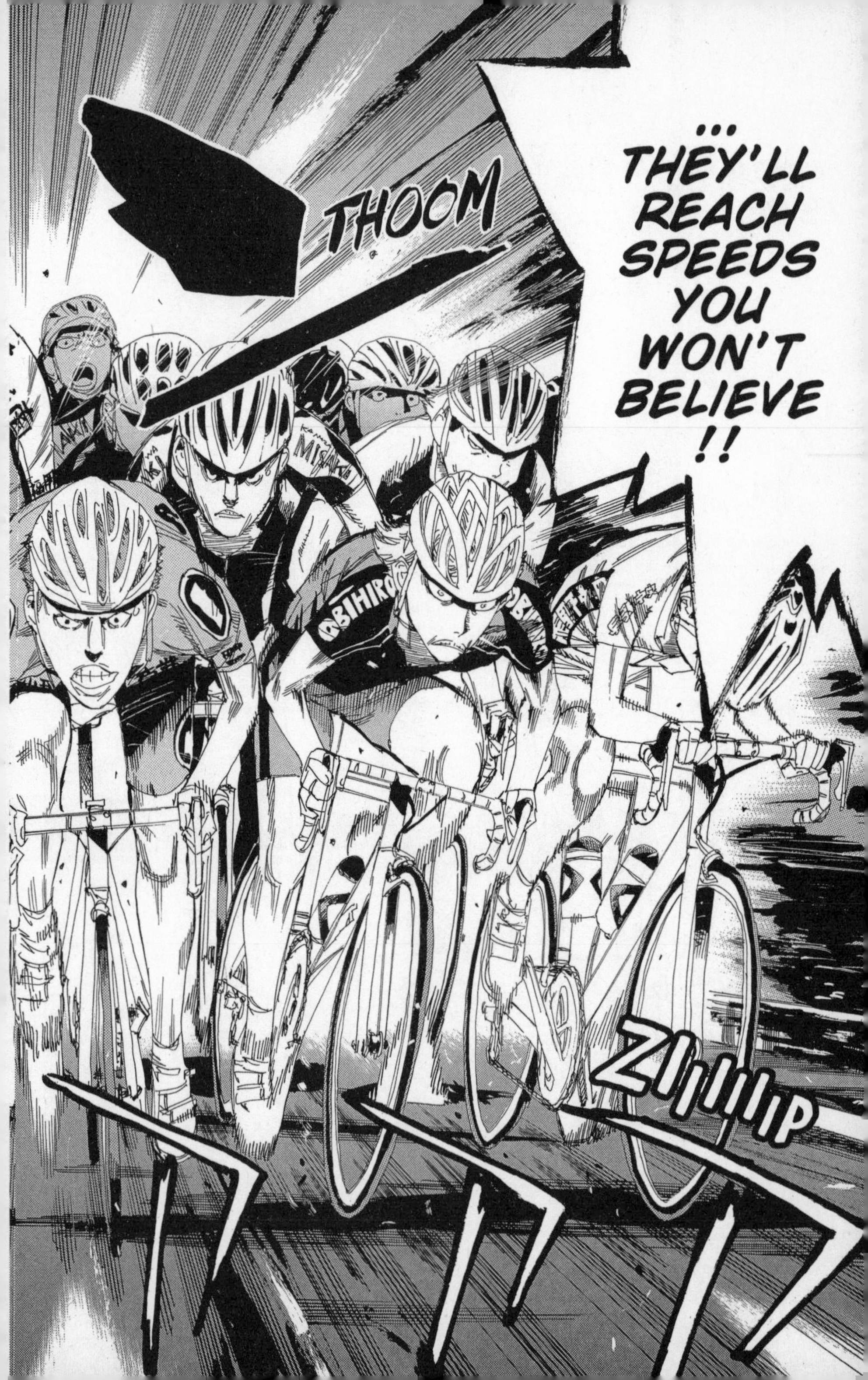
...THEY'LL REACH SPEEDS YOU WON'T BELIEVE!!
THOOM
ZIIIIIIP

RIDE.76 TOP SPRINTER!!

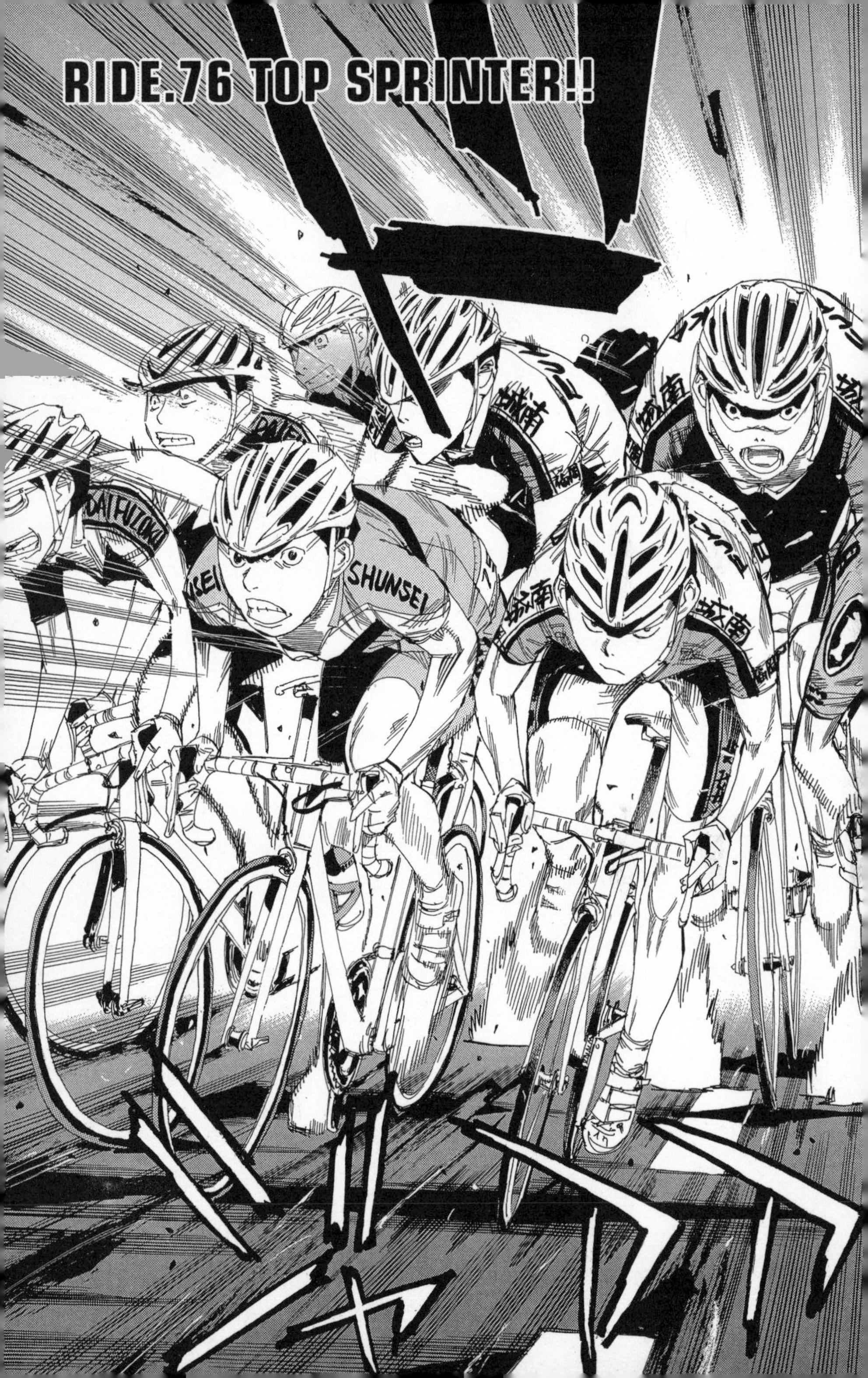
SHUNSEI

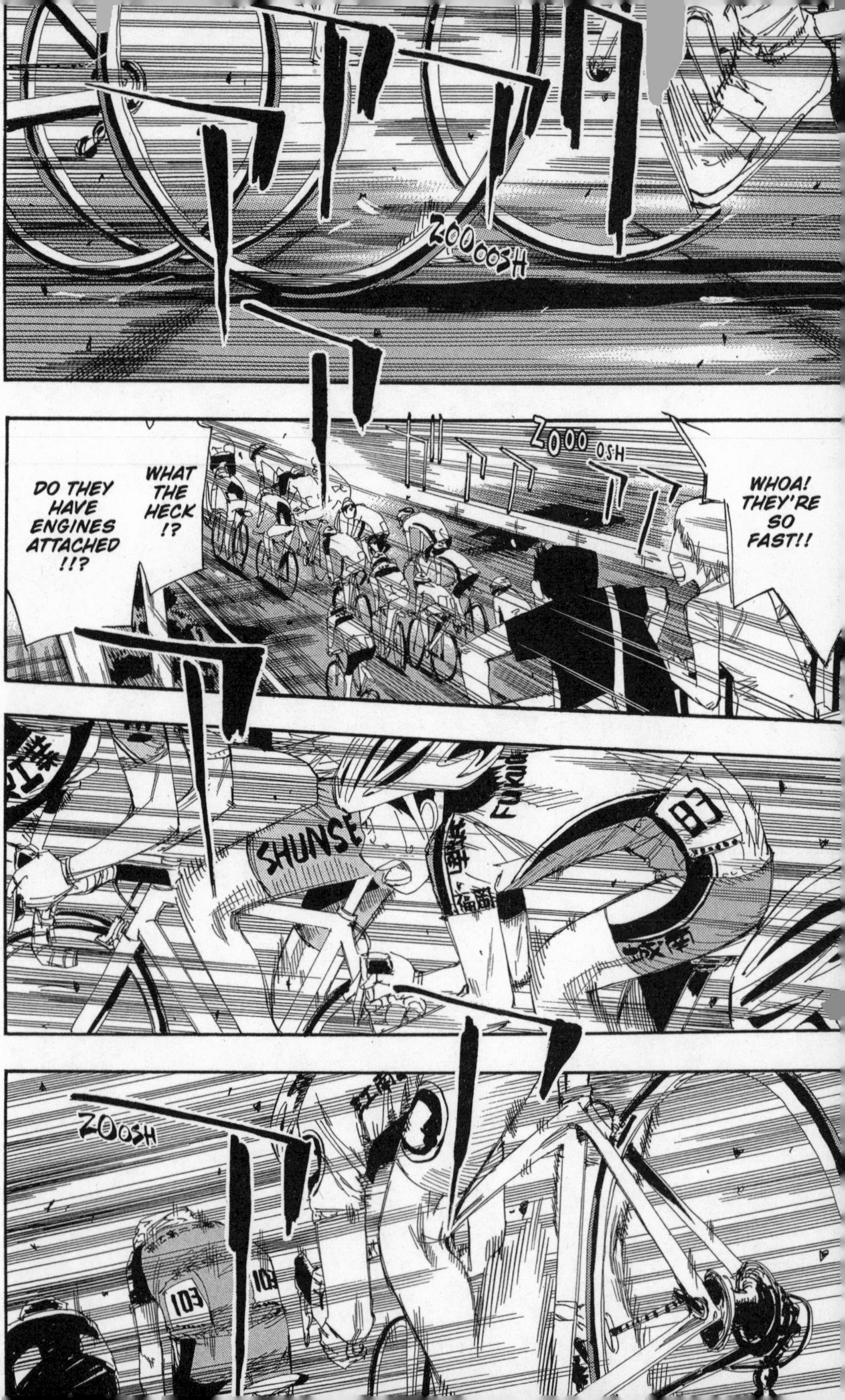
ZOOOOSH
WHOA! THEY'RE SO FAST!!
ZOOO OSH
WHAT THE HECK !?
DO THEY HAVE ENGINES ATTACHED !!?
ZOOSH

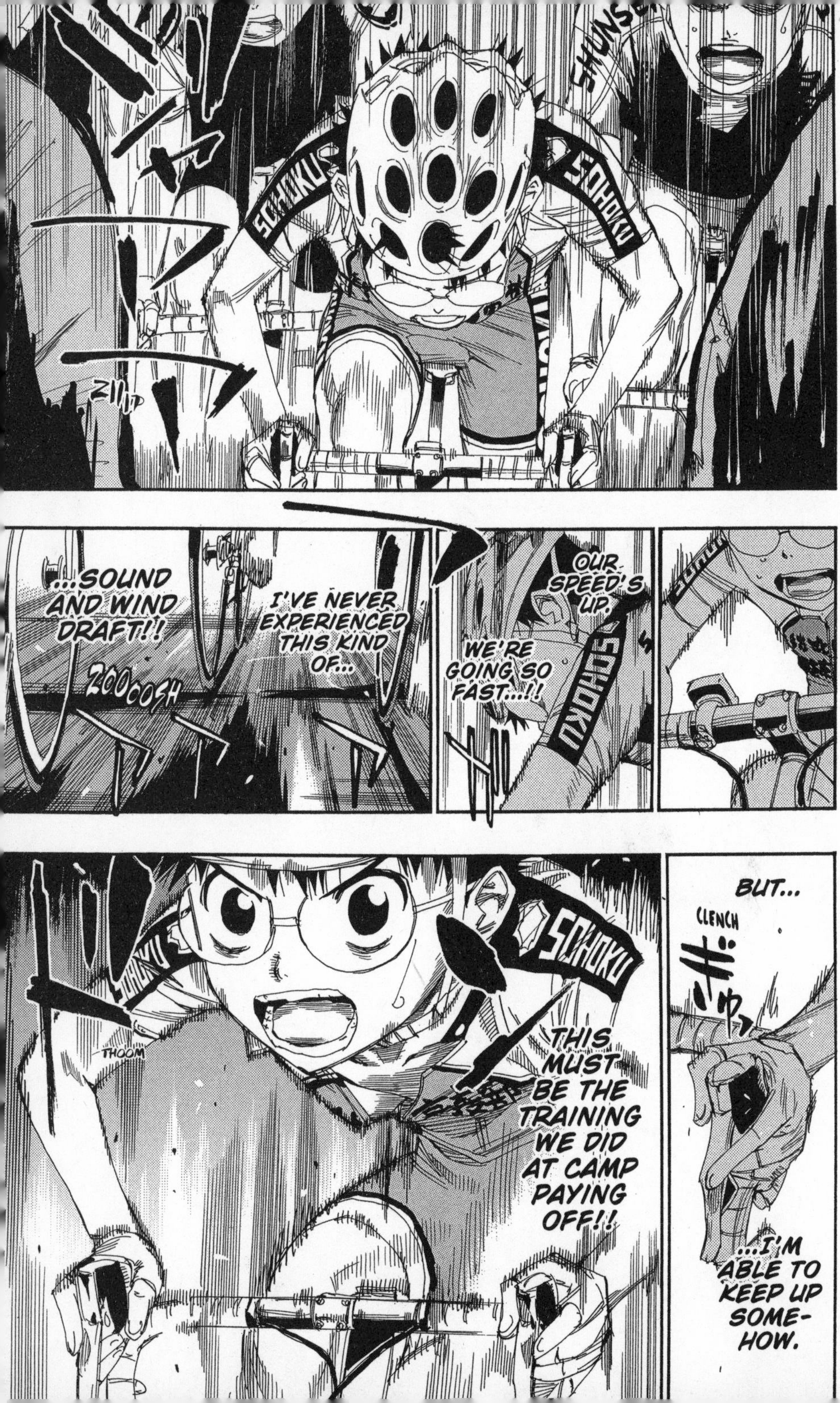
OUR SPEED'S UP.
WE'RE GOING SO FAST...!!
I'VE NEVER EXPERIENCED THIS KIND OF...
...SOUND AND WIND DRAFT!!
ZOOOOSH
BUT...
CLENCH
...I'M ABLE TO KEEP UP SOME-HOW.
THIS MUST BE THE TRAINING WE DID AT CAMP PAYING OFF!!
THOOM

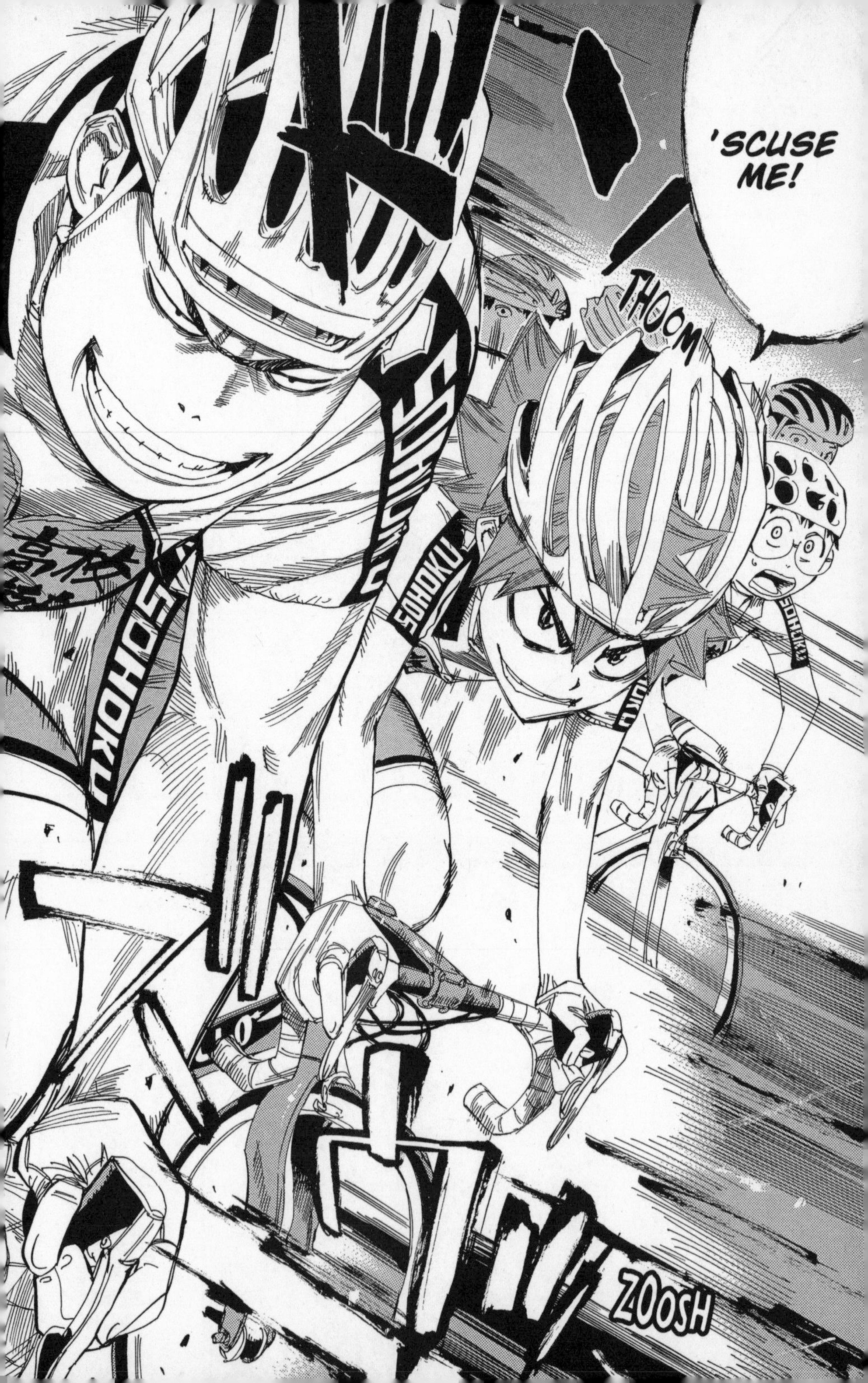
'SCUSE ME!
THOOM
ZOOSH

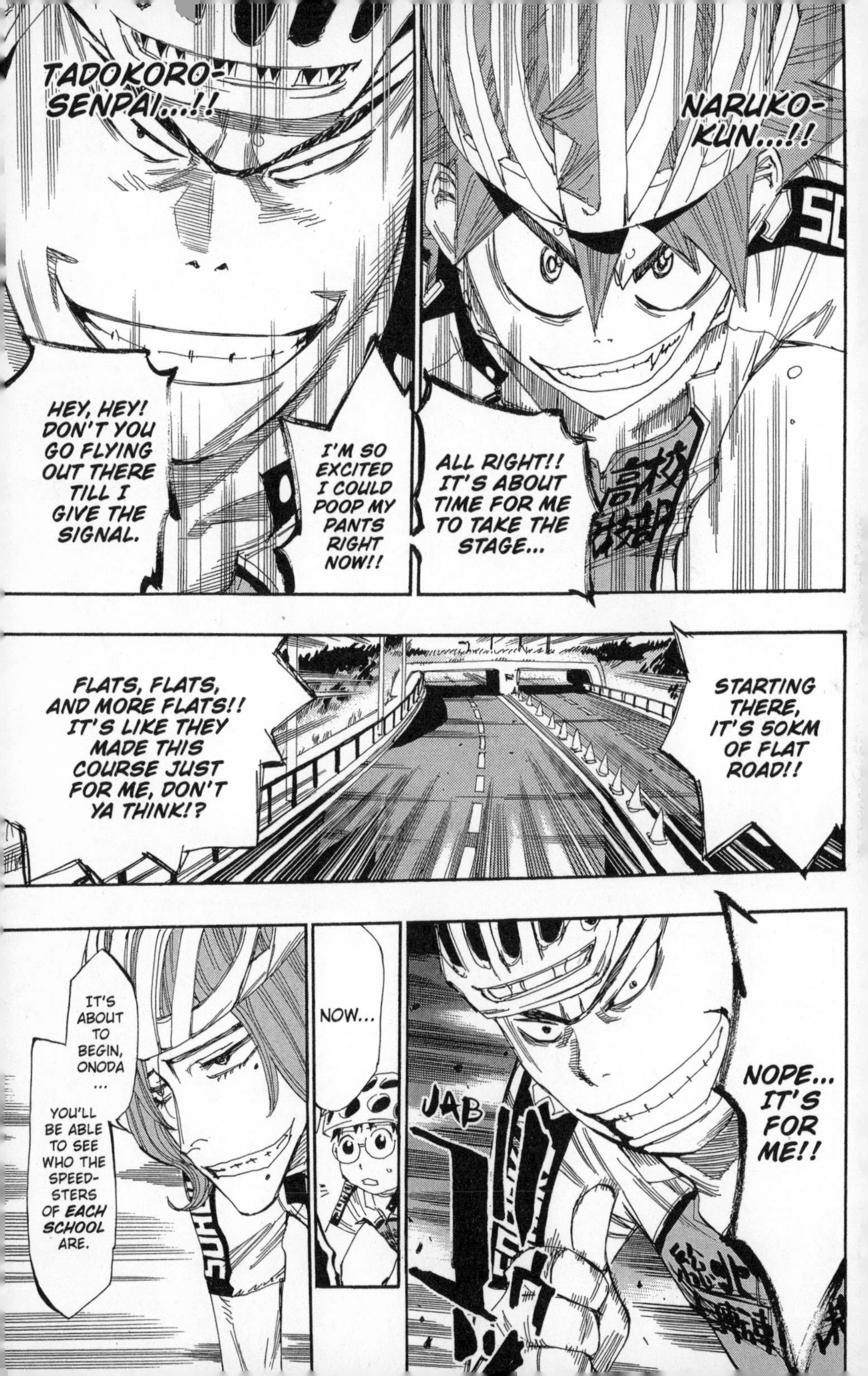
NARUKO-KUN...!!
ALL RIGHT!! IT'S ABOUT TIME FOR ME TO TAKE THE STAGE...
TADOKORO-SENPAI...!!
I'M SO EXCITED I COULD POOP MY PANTS RIGHT NOW!!
HEY, HEY! DON'T YOU GO FLYING OUT THERE TILL I GIVE THE SIGNAL.
STARTING THERE, IT'S 50KM OF FLAT ROAD!!
FLATS, FLATS, AND MORE FLATS!! IT'S LIKE THEY MADE THIS COURSE JUST FOR ME, DON'T YA THINK!?
NOPE... IT'S FOR ME!!
JAB
NOW...
IT'S ABOUT TO BEGIN, ONODA...
YOU'LL BE ABLE TO SEE WHO THE SPEED-STERS OF EACH SCHOOL ARE.

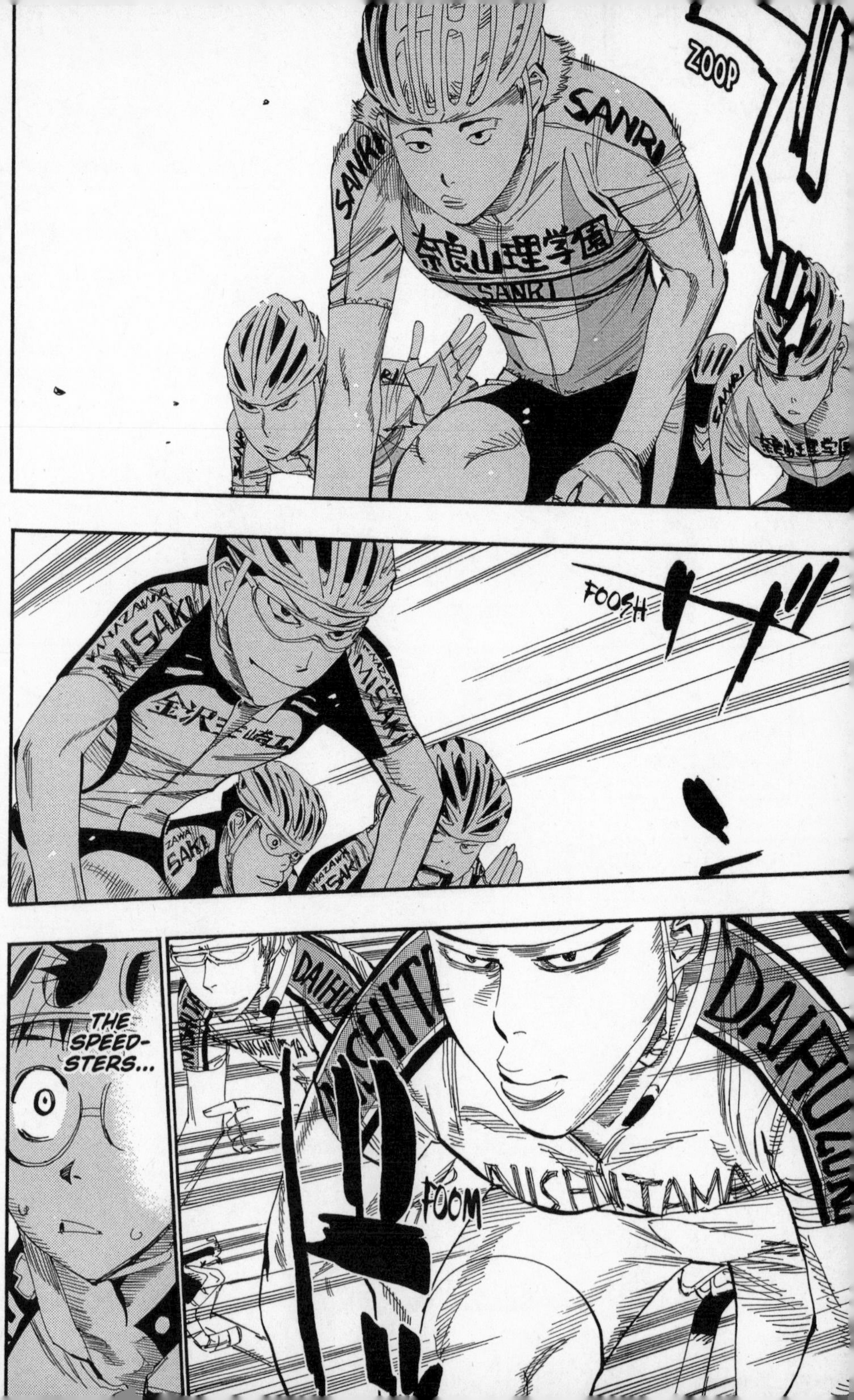
ZOOP
FOOSH
FOOM
THE SPEED-STERS...

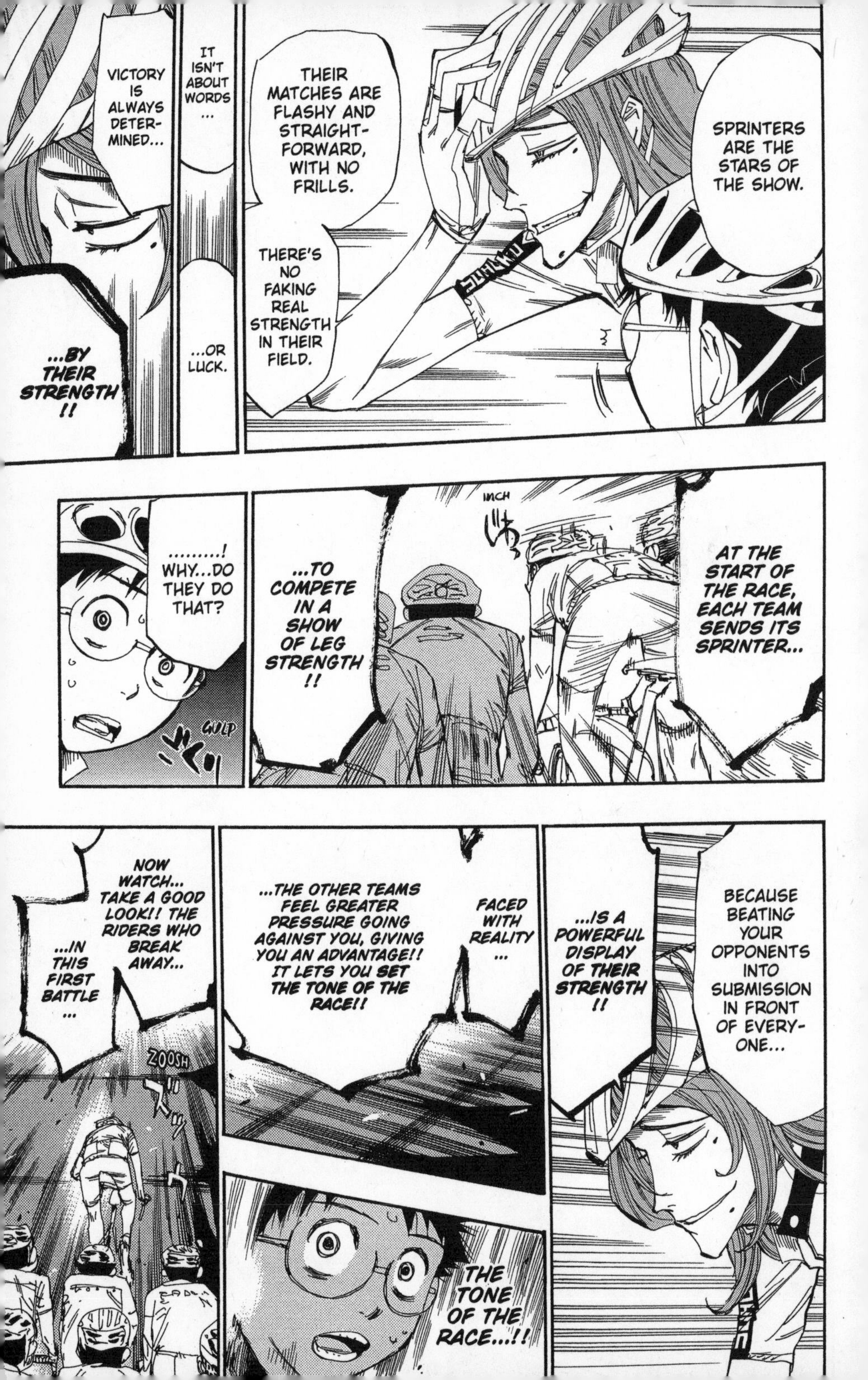
SPRINTERS ARE THE STARS OF THE SHOW.
THEIR MATCHES ARE FLASHY AND STRAIGHT-FORWARD, WITH NO FRILLS.
THERE'S NO FAKING REAL STRENGTH IN THEIR FIELD.
IT ISN'T ABOUT WORDS...
...OR LUCK.
VICTORY IS ALWAYS DETER-MINED...
...BY THEIR STRENGTH!!
AT THE START OF THE RACE, EACH TEAM SENDS ITS SPRINTER...
INCH
...TO COMPETE IN A SHOW OF LEG STRENGTH!!
.........! WHY...DO THEY DO THAT?
GULP
BECAUSE BEATING YOUR OPPONENTS INTO SUBMISSION IN FRONT OF EVERY-ONE...
...IS A POWERFUL DISPLAY OF THEIR STRENGTH!!
FACED WITH REALITY...
...THE OTHER TEAMS FEEL GREATER PRESSURE GOING AGAINST YOU, GIVING YOU AN ADVANTAGE!! IT LETS YOU SET THE TONE OF THE RACE!!
THE TONE OF THE RACE...!!
NOW WATCH... TAKE A GOOD LOOK!! THE RIDERS WHO BREAK AWAY...
...IN THIS FIRST BATTLE...
ZOOSH

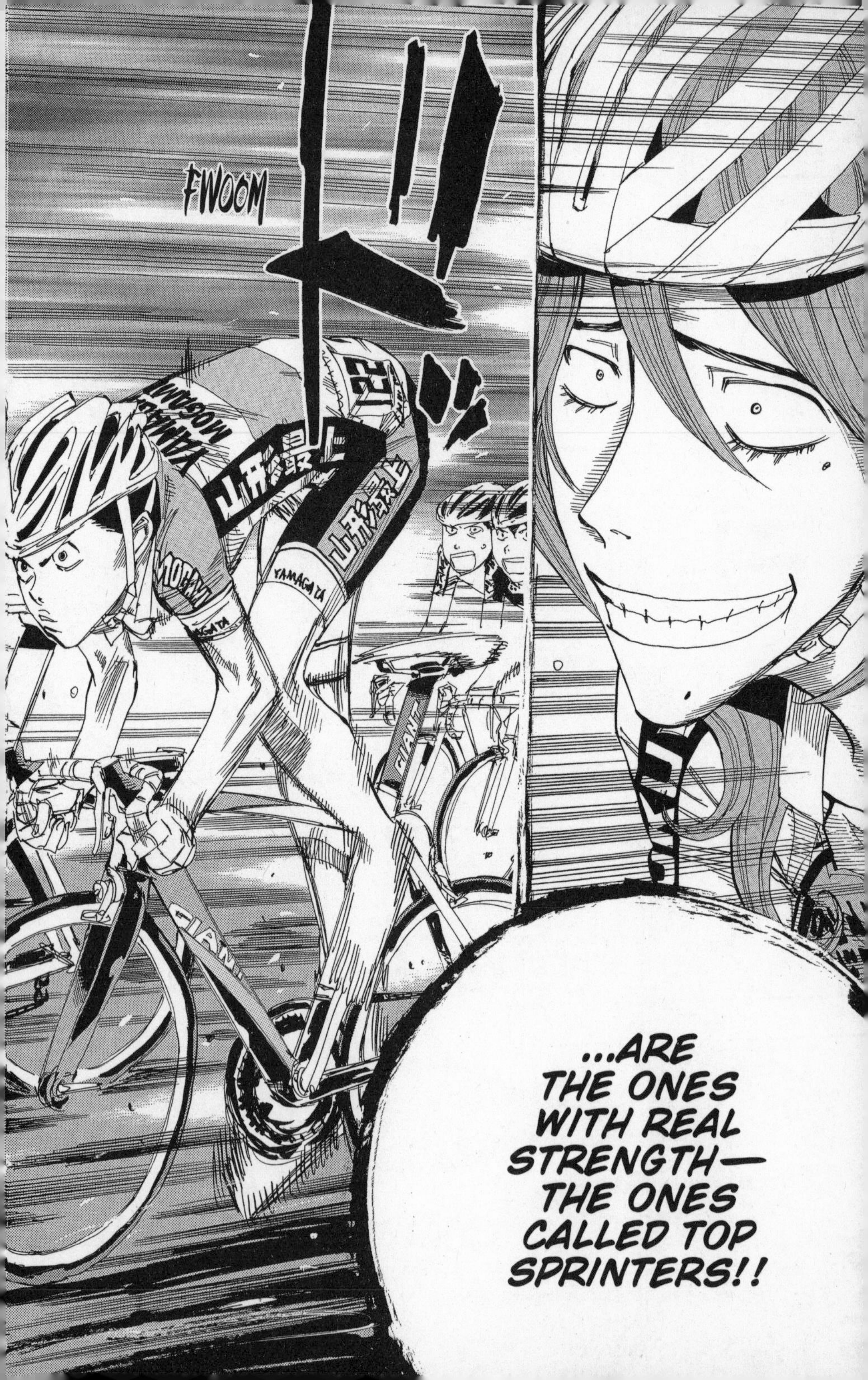

...ARE THE ONES WITH REAL STRENGTH— THE ONES CALLED TOP SPRINTERS!!
FWOOM

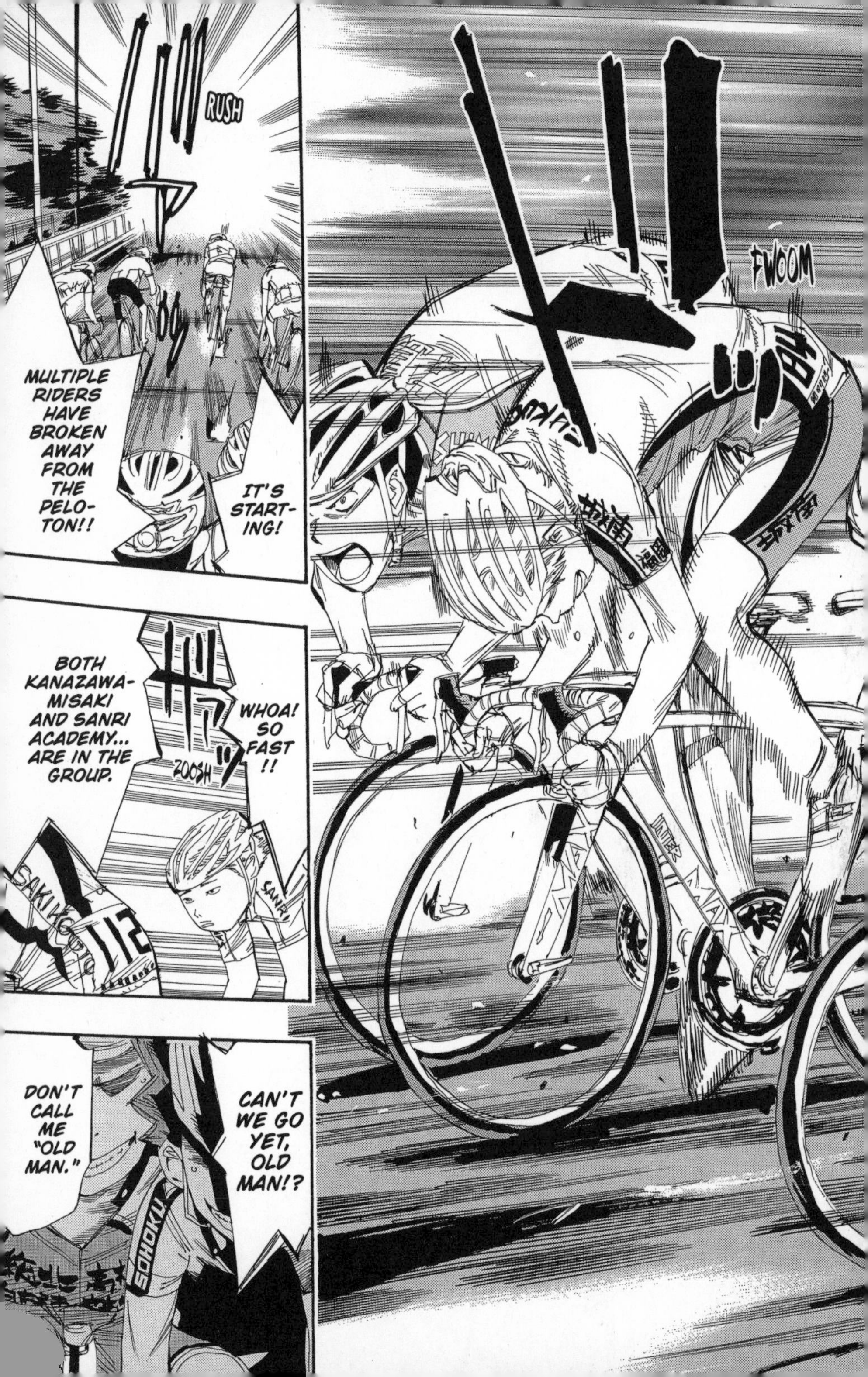
FWOOM
RUSH
IT'S STARTING!
MULTIPLE RIDERS HAVE BROKEN AWAY FROM THE PELOTON!!
WHOA! SO FAST!!
ZOOSH
BOTH KANAZAWA-MISAKI AND SANRI ACADEMY... ARE IN THE GROUP.
CAN'T WE GO YET, OLD MAN!?
DON'T CALL ME "OLD MAN."

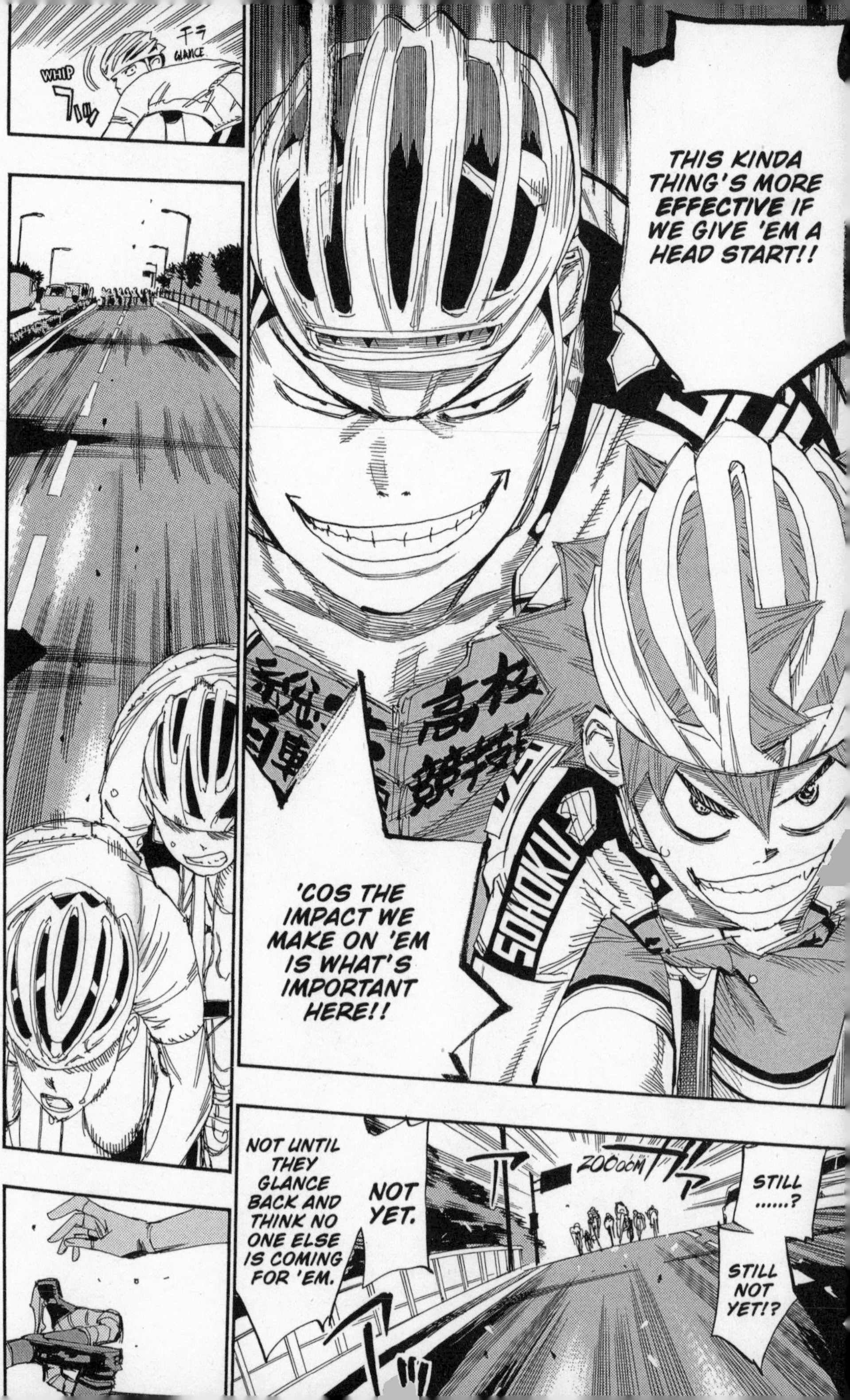

THIS KINDA THING'S MORE EFFECTIVE IF WE GIVE 'EM A HEAD START!!
'COS THE IMPACT WE MAKE ON 'EM IS WHAT'S IMPORTANT HERE!!
SOHOKU
チラ
GLANCE
WHIP
フッ
STILL ......?
STILL NOT YET!?
ZOOOOM
NOT YET.
NOT UNTIL THEY GLANCE BACK AND THINK NO ONE ELSE IS COMING FOR 'EM.

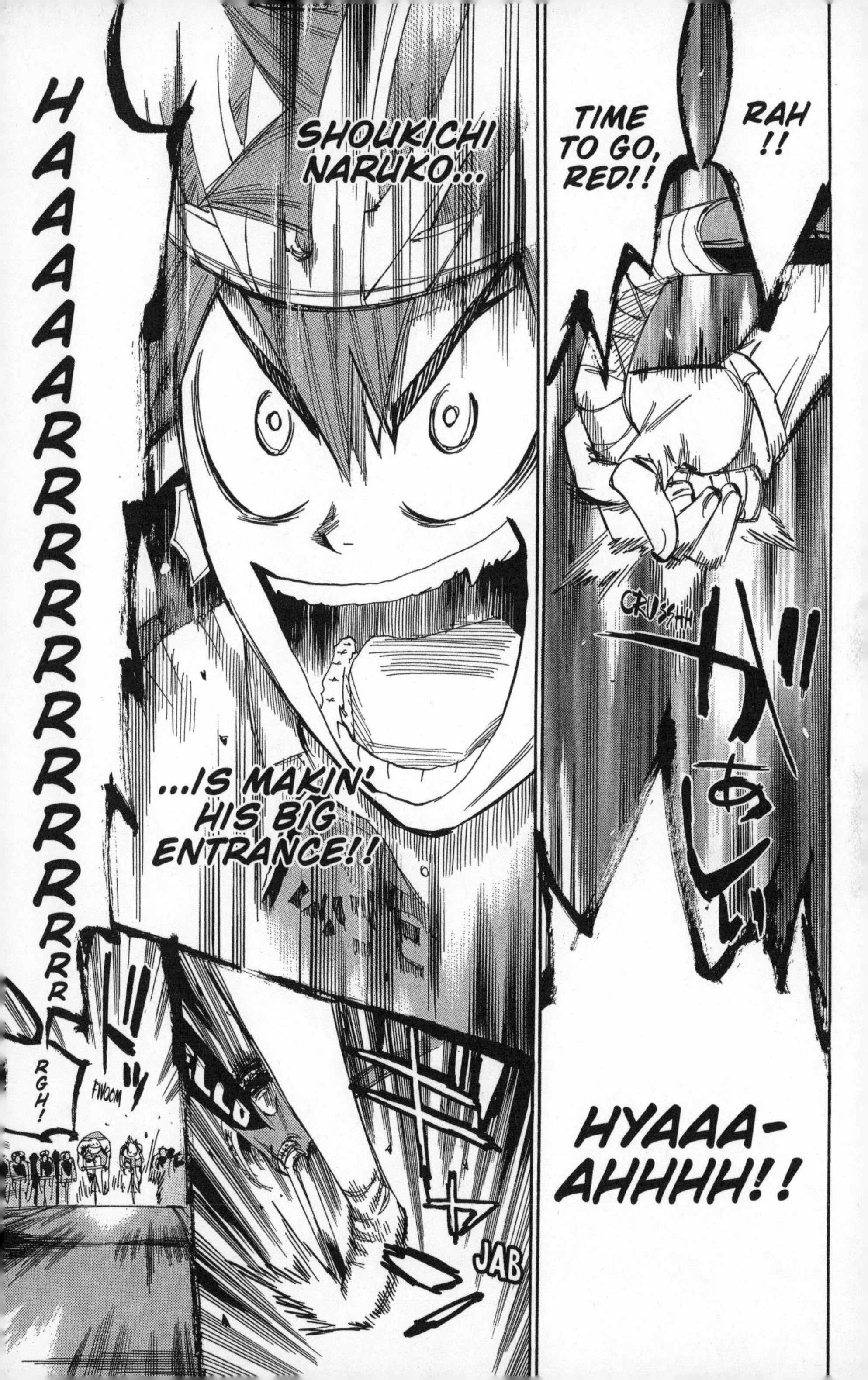
RAH!!
TIME TO GO, RED!!
CRUSHH
HYAAA-AHHHH!!
HAAAAAARRRRRRRRRRRRrr
SHOUKICHI NARUKO...
...IS MAKIN' HIS BIG ENTRANCE!!
RGH!
FWOOM
JAB

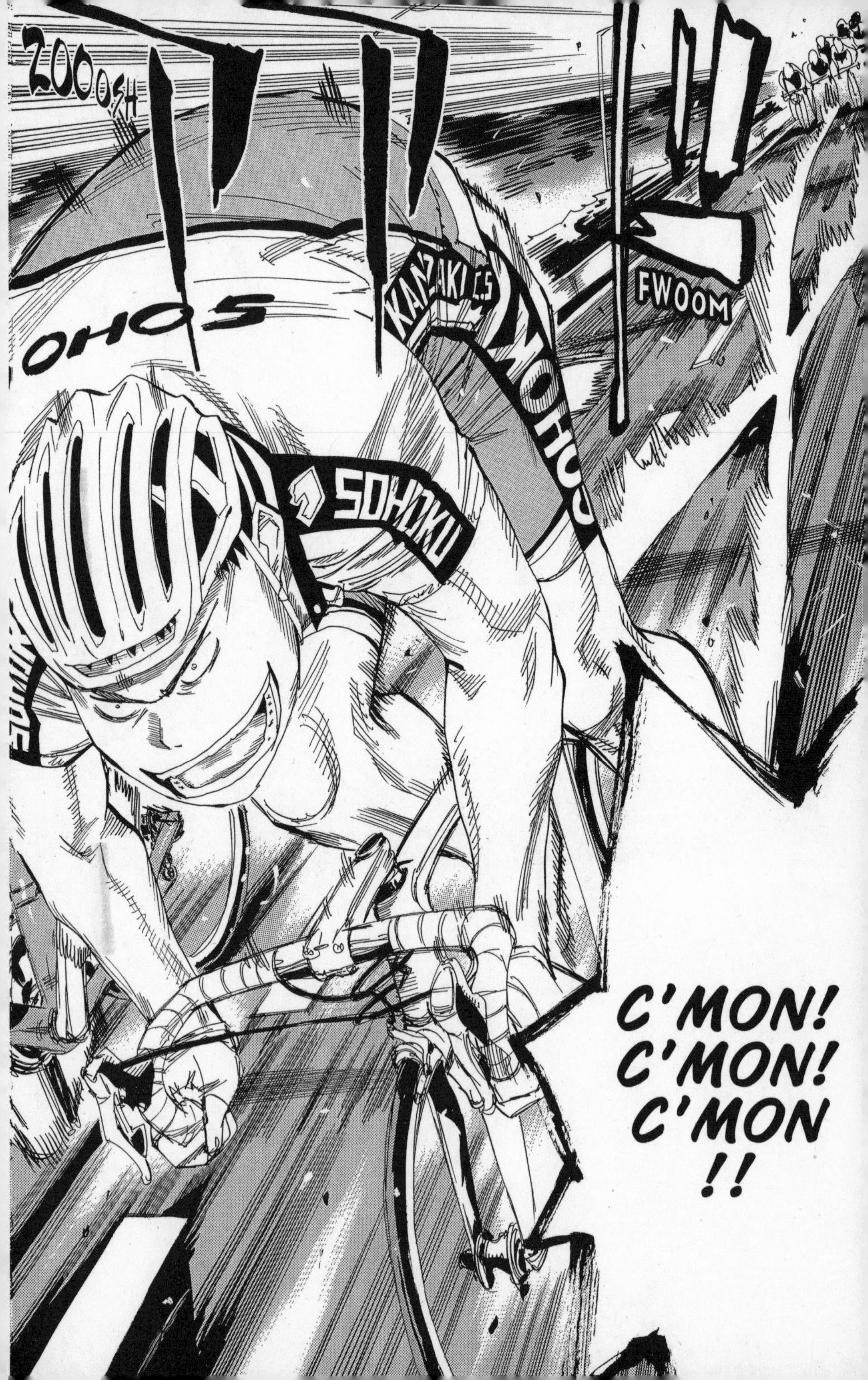
ZOOOSH
FWOOM
SOHOKU
C'MON! C'MON! C'MON !!

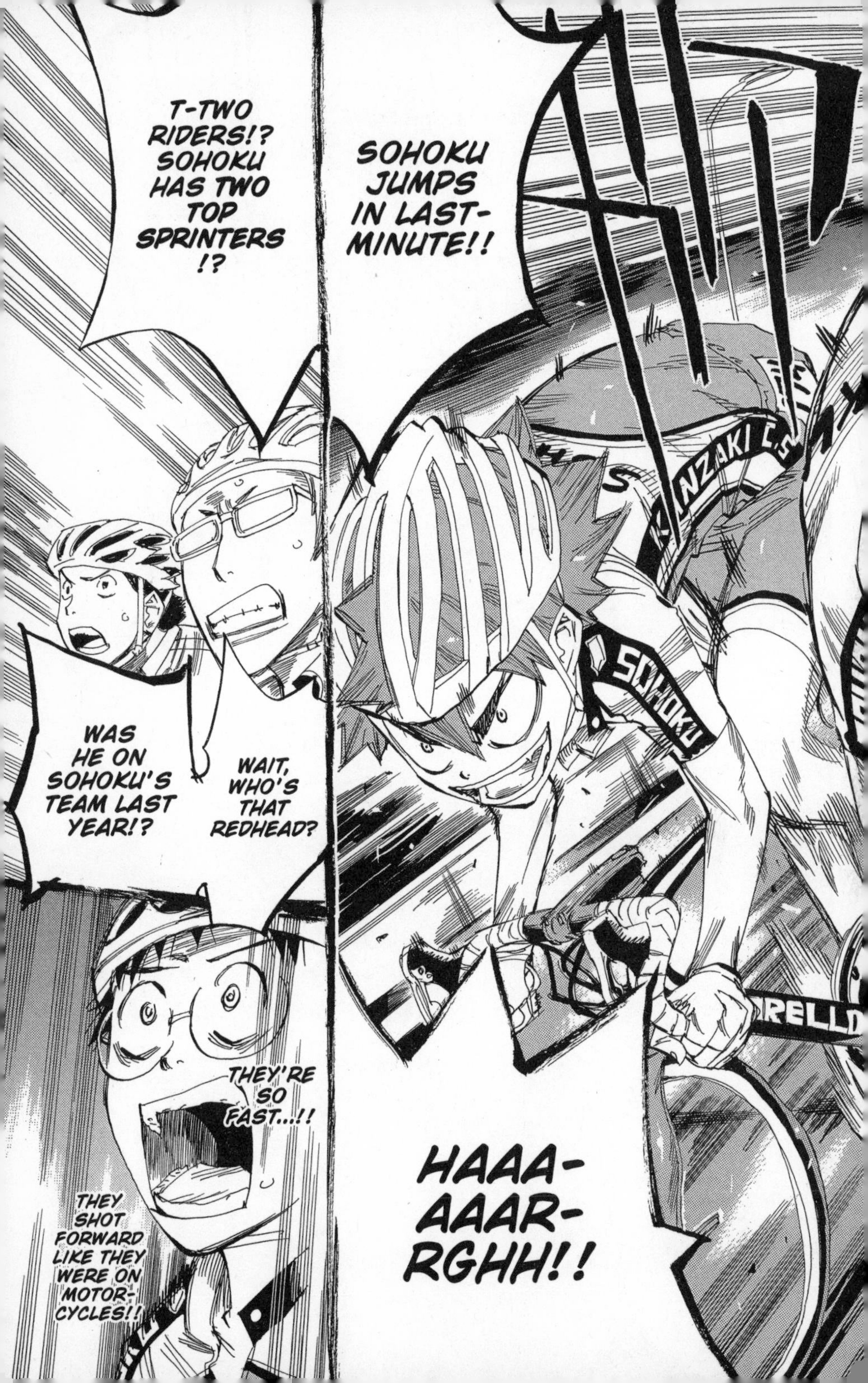
SOHOKU JUMPS IN LAST-MINUTE!!
HAAA-AAAR-RGHH!!
KANZAKI C.S
SOHOKU
T-TWO RIDERS!? SOHOKU HAS TWO TOP SPRINTERS!?
WAIT, WHO'S THAT REDHEAD?
WAS HE ON SOHOKU'S TEAM LAST YEAR!?
THEY'RE SO FAST...!!
THEY SHOT FORWARD LIKE THEY WERE ON MOTOR-CYCLES!!

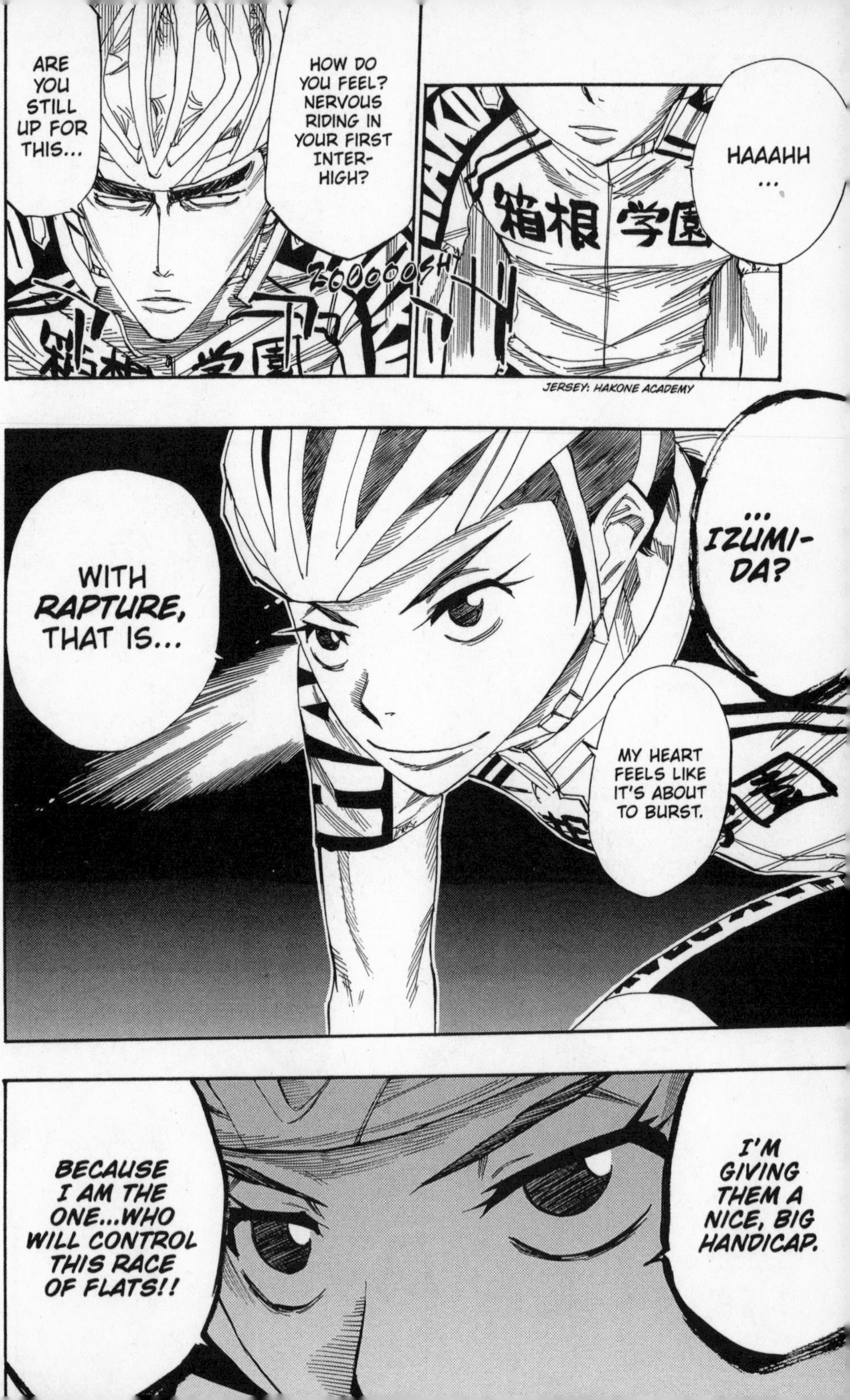
HAAAHH...
箱根学園
HOW DO YOU FEEL? NERVOUS RIDING IN YOUR FIRST INTER-HIGH?
ARE YOU STILL UP FOR THIS...
ZOOOOOOSH
JERSEY: HAKONE ACADEMY
...IZUMIDA?
MY HEART FEELS LIKE IT'S ABOUT TO BURST.
WITH *RAPTURE*, THAT IS...
I'M GIVING THEM A NICE, BIG HANDICAP.
BECAUSE I AM THE ONE...WHO WILL CONTROL THIS RACE OF FLATS!!

RIDE.77 RACE!!

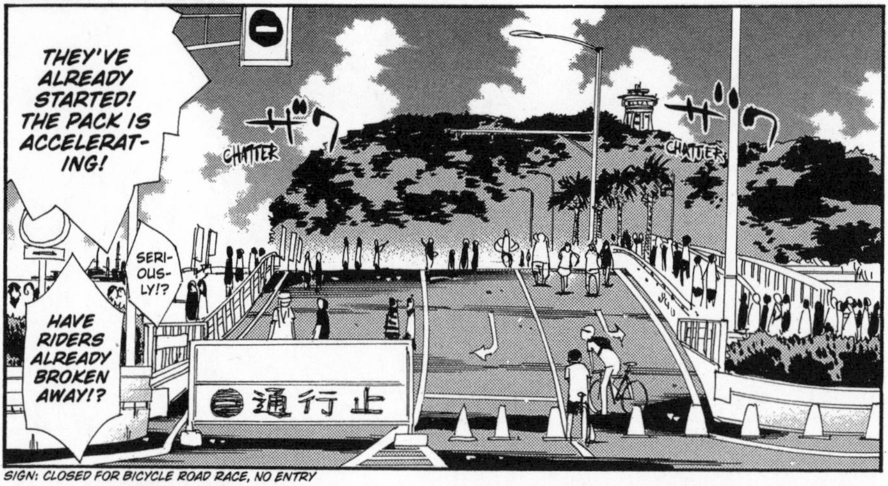
CHATTER
CHATTER
THEY'VE ALREADY STARTED! THE PACK IS ACCELERATING!
SERIOUSLY!?
HAVE RIDERS ALREADY BROKEN AWAY!?
通行止

SIGN: CLOSED FOR BICYCLE ROAD RACE, NO ENTRY

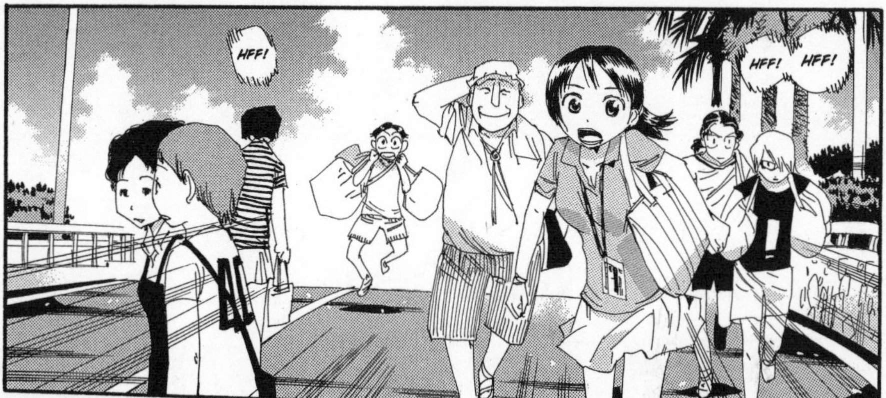
HFF! HFF!
HFF!

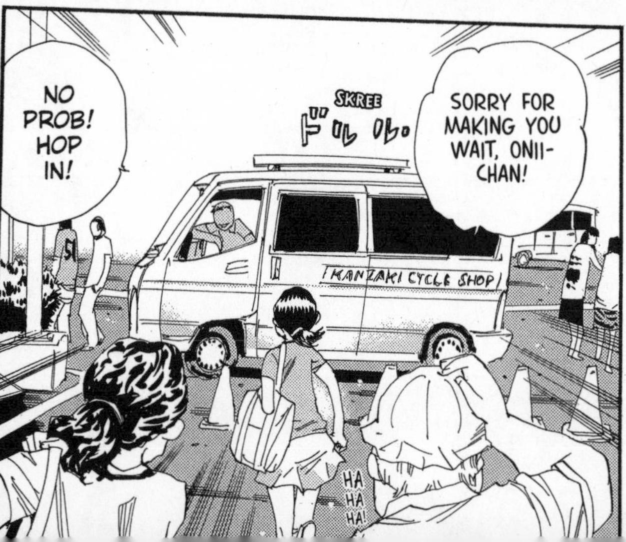
SORRY FOR MAKING YOU WAIT, ONII-CHAN!
SKREE
NO PROB! HOP IN!
KANZAKI CYCLE SHOP
HA HA HA HA!

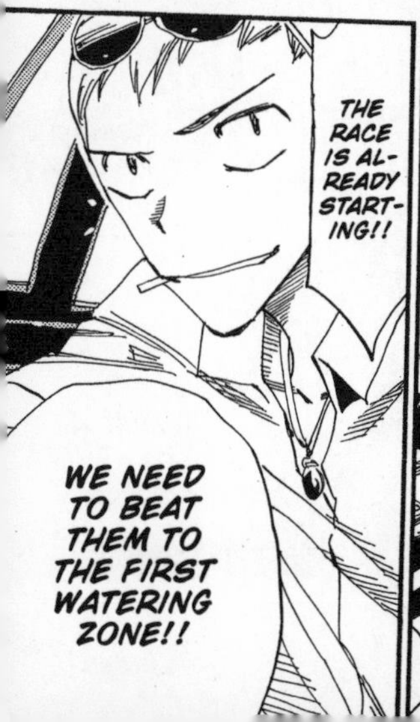
THE RACE IS ALREADY STARTING!!
WE NEED TO BEAT THEM TO THE FIRST WATERING ZONE!!

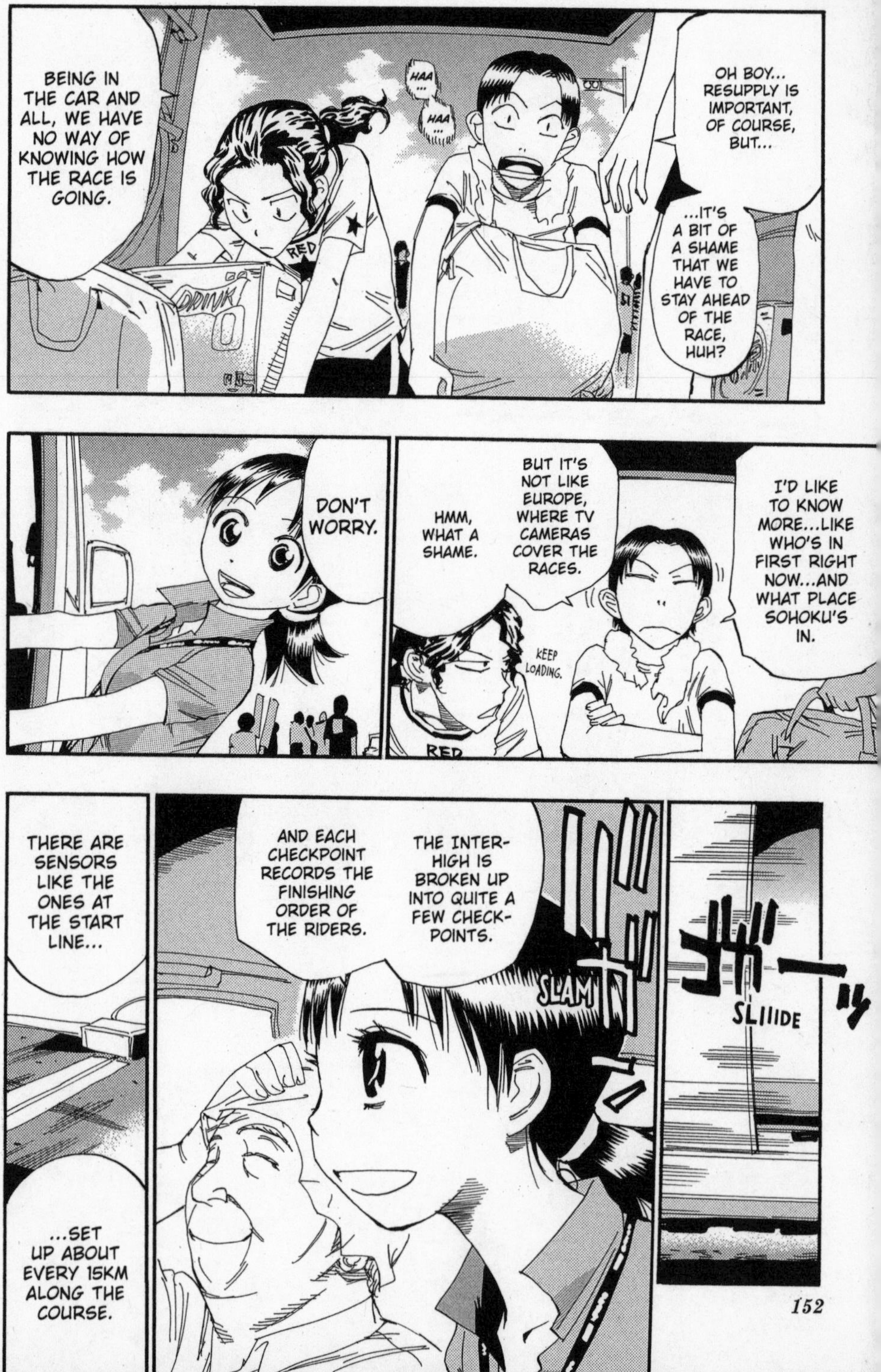
OH BOY... RESUPPLY IS IMPORTANT, OF COURSE, BUT...
HAA... HAA...
...IT'S A BIT OF A SHAME THAT WE HAVE TO STAY AHEAD OF THE RACE, HUH?
BEING IN THE CAR AND ALL, WE HAVE NO WAY OF KNOWING HOW THE RACE IS GOING.
I'D LIKE TO KNOW MORE...LIKE WHO'S IN FIRST RIGHT NOW...AND WHAT PLACE SOHOKU'S IN.
BUT IT'S NOT LIKE EUROPE, WHERE TV CAMERAS COVER THE RACES.
HMM, WHAT A SHAME.
KEEP LOADING.
DON'T WORRY.
SLIIIDE
THE INTER-HIGH IS BROKEN UP INTO QUITE A FEW CHECK-POINTS.
AND EACH CHECKPOINT RECORDS THE FINISHING ORDER OF THE RIDERS.
SLAM
THERE ARE SENSORS LIKE THE ONES AT THE START LINE...
...SET UP ABOUT EVERY 15KM ALONG THE COURSE.

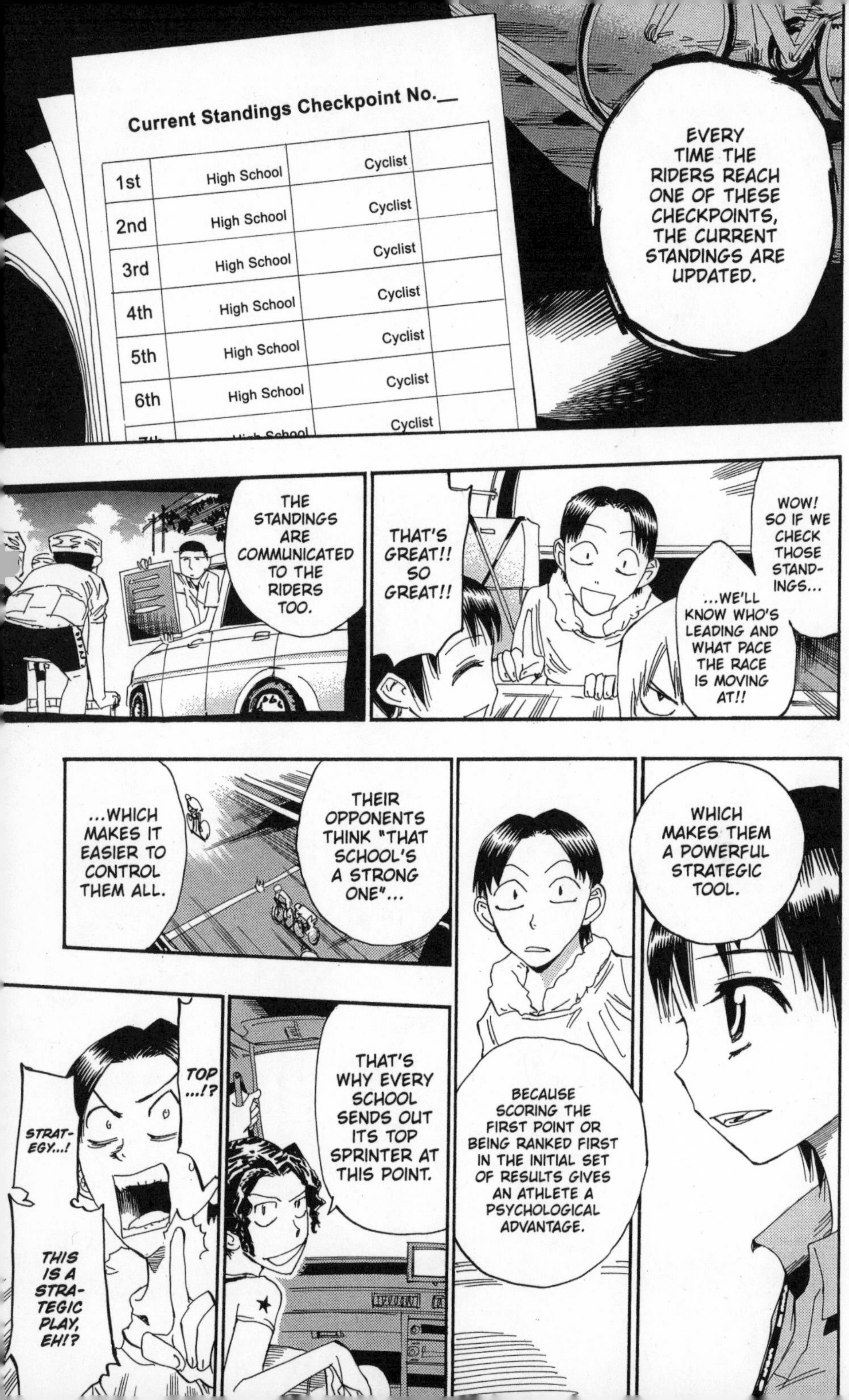
EVERY TIME THE RIDERS REACH ONE OF THESE CHECKPOINTS, THE CURRENT STANDINGS ARE UPDATED.
Current Standings Checkpoint No.__
1st High School Cyclist
2nd High School Cyclist
3rd High School Cyclist
4th High School Cyclist
5th High School Cyclist
6th High School Cyclist
Cyclist
WOW! SO IF WE CHECK THOSE STAND-INGS...
...WE'LL KNOW WHO'S LEADING AND WHAT PACE THE RACE IS MOVING AT!!
THAT'S GREAT!! SO GREAT!!
THE STANDINGS ARE COMMUNICATED TO THE RIDERS TOO.
WHICH MAKES THEM A POWERFUL STRATEGIC TOOL.
BECAUSE SCORING THE FIRST POINT OR BEING RANKED FIRST IN THE INITIAL SET OF RESULTS GIVES AN ATHLETE A PSYCHOLOGICAL ADVANTAGE.
THEIR OPPONENTS THINK "THAT SCHOOL'S A STRONG ONE"...
...WHICH MAKES IT EASIER TO CONTROL THEM ALL.
THAT'S WHY EVERY SCHOOL SENDS OUT ITS TOP SPRINTER AT THIS POINT.
TOP ...!?
STRAT-EGY...!
THIS IS A STRA-TEGIC PLAY, EH!?

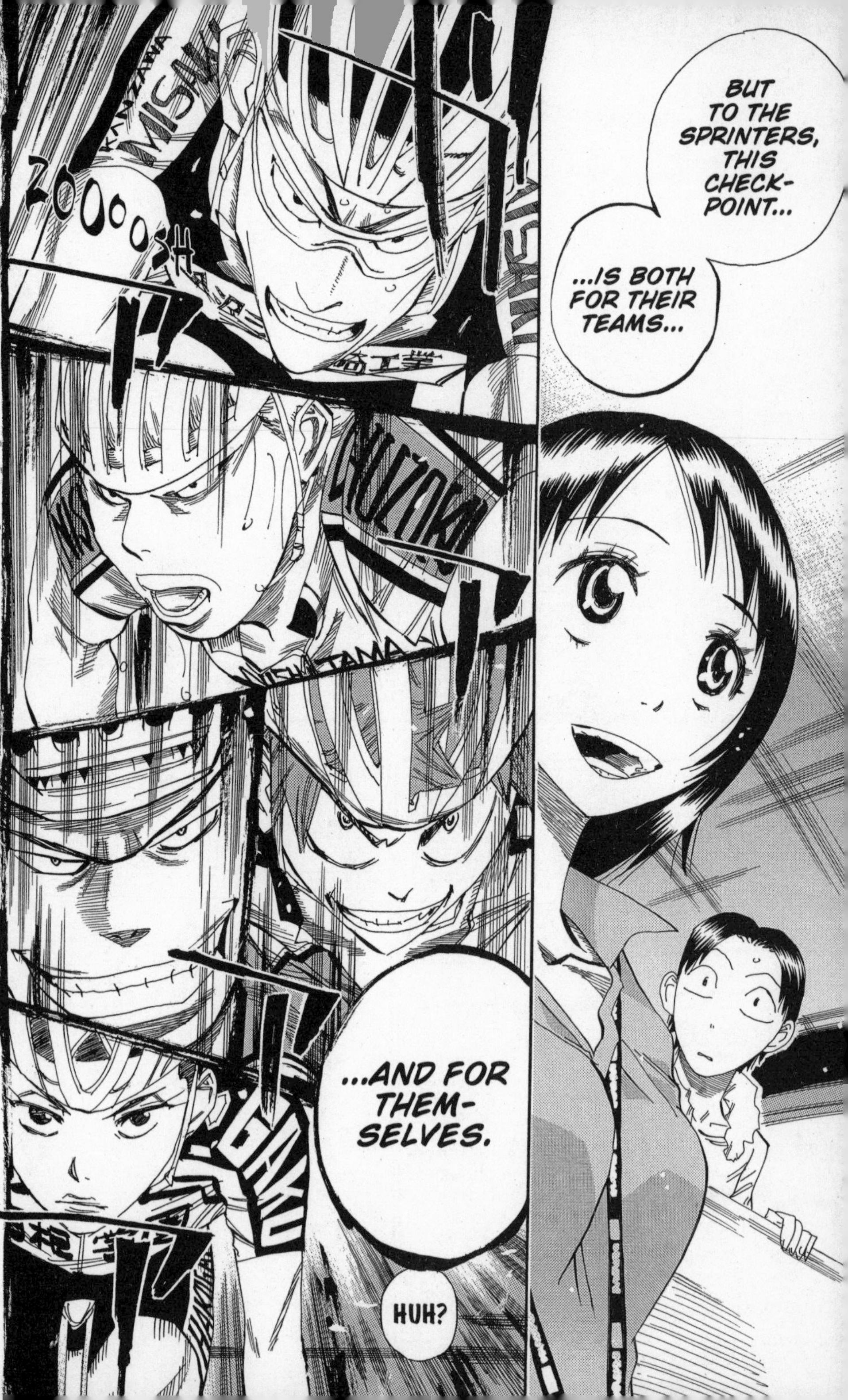
BUT TO THE SPRINTERS, THIS CHECKPOINT...
...IS BOTH FOR THEIR TEAMS...
ZOOOOSH
...AND FOR THEMSELVES.
HUH?

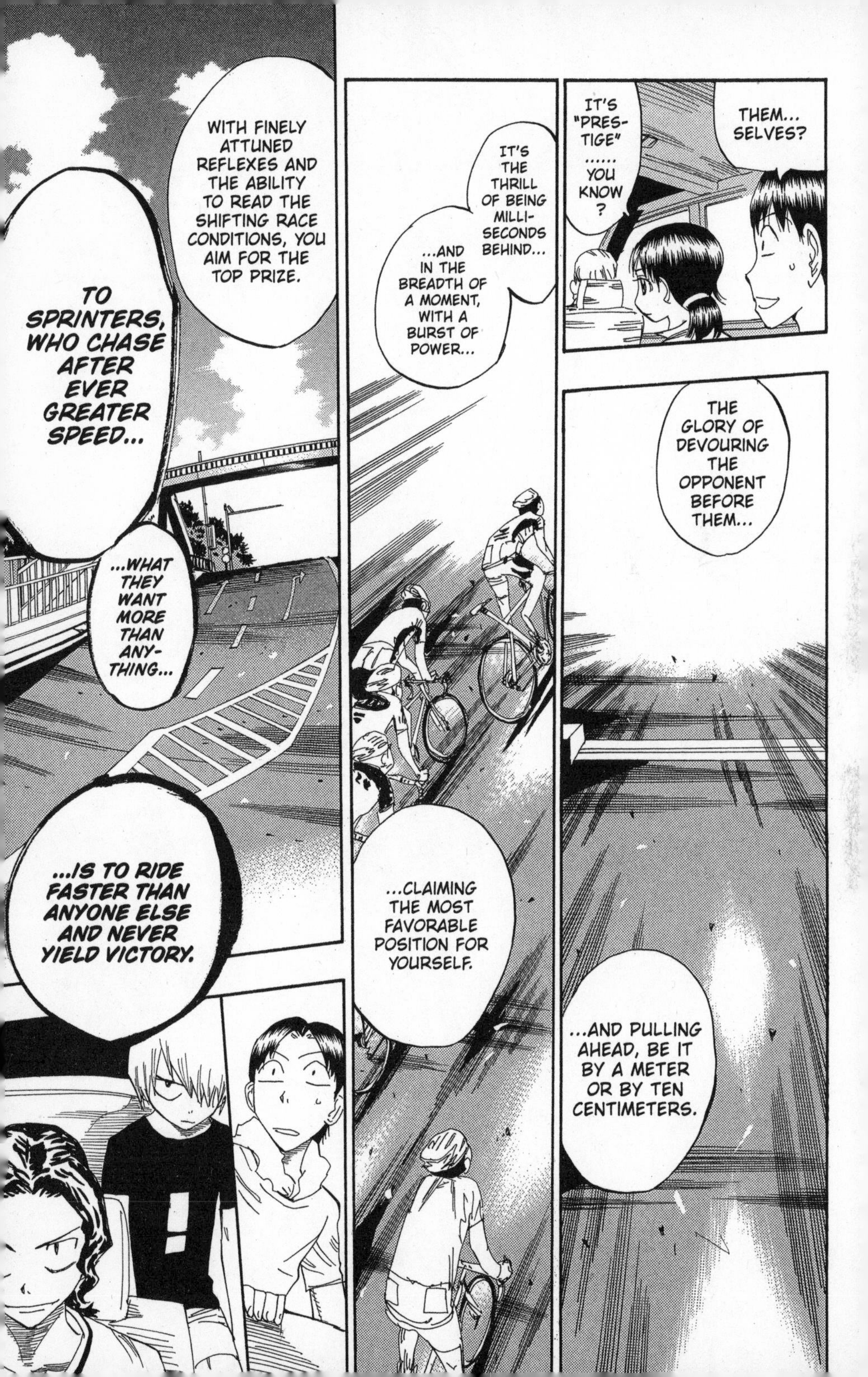
THEM... SELVES?
IT'S "PRES-TIGE" ...... YOU KNOW?
THE GLORY OF DEVOURING THE OPPONENT BEFORE THEM...
...AND PULLING AHEAD, BE IT BY A METER OR BY TEN CENTIMETERS.
IT'S THE THRILL OF BEING MILLI-SECONDS BEHIND...
...AND IN THE BREADTH OF A MOMENT, WITH A BURST OF POWER...
...CLAIMING THE MOST FAVORABLE POSITION FOR YOURSELF.
WITH FINELY ATTUNED REFLEXES AND THE ABILITY TO READ THE SHIFTING RACE CONDITIONS, YOU AIM FOR THE TOP PRIZE.
TO SPRINTERS, WHO CHASE AFTER EVER GREATER SPEED...
...WHAT THEY WANT MORE THAN ANY-THING...
...IS TO RIDE FASTER THAN ANYONE ELSE AND NEVER YIELD VICTORY.

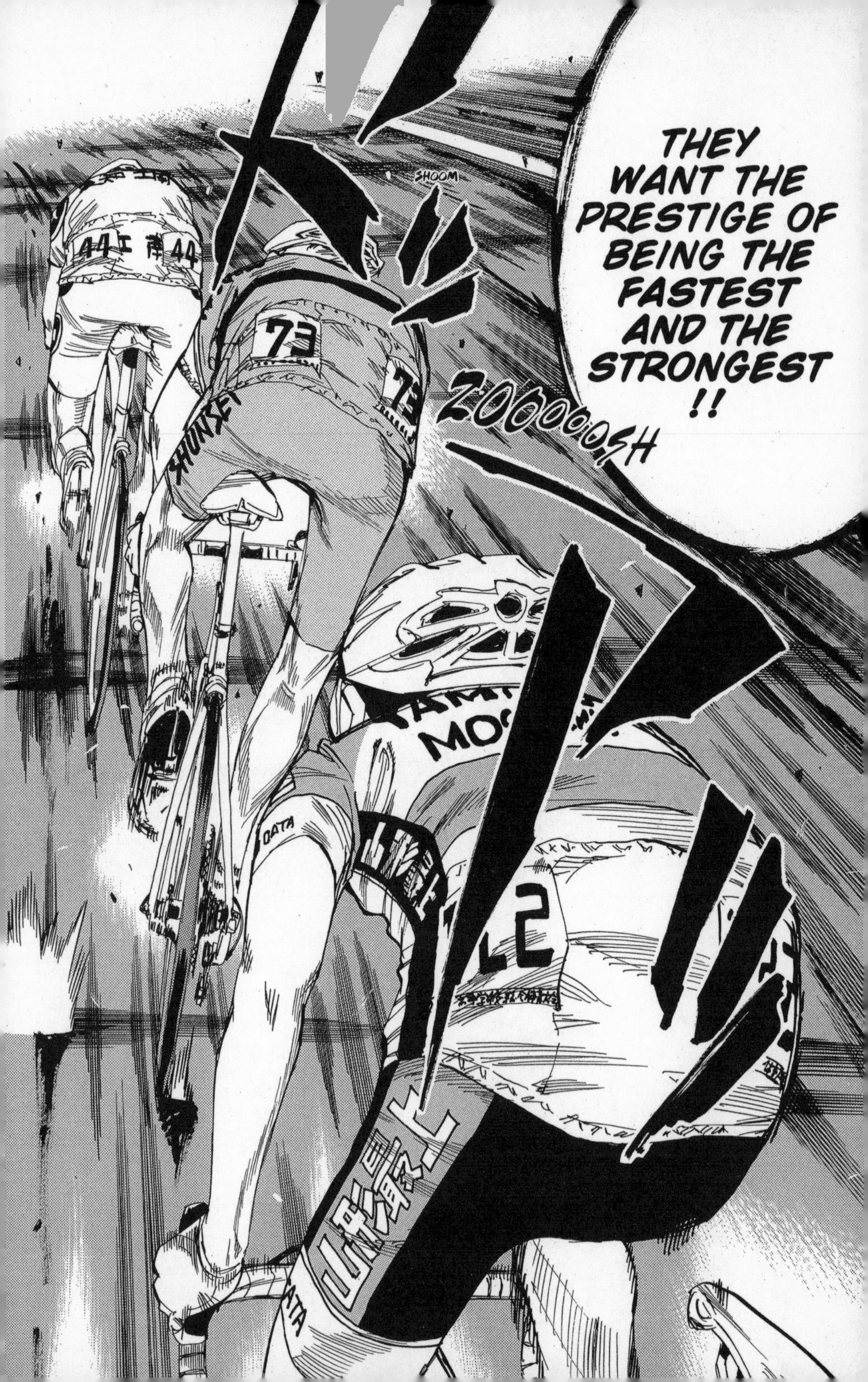
THEY WANT THE PRESTIGE OF BEING THE FASTEST AND THE STRONGEST!!
SHOOM
ZOOOOOOSH

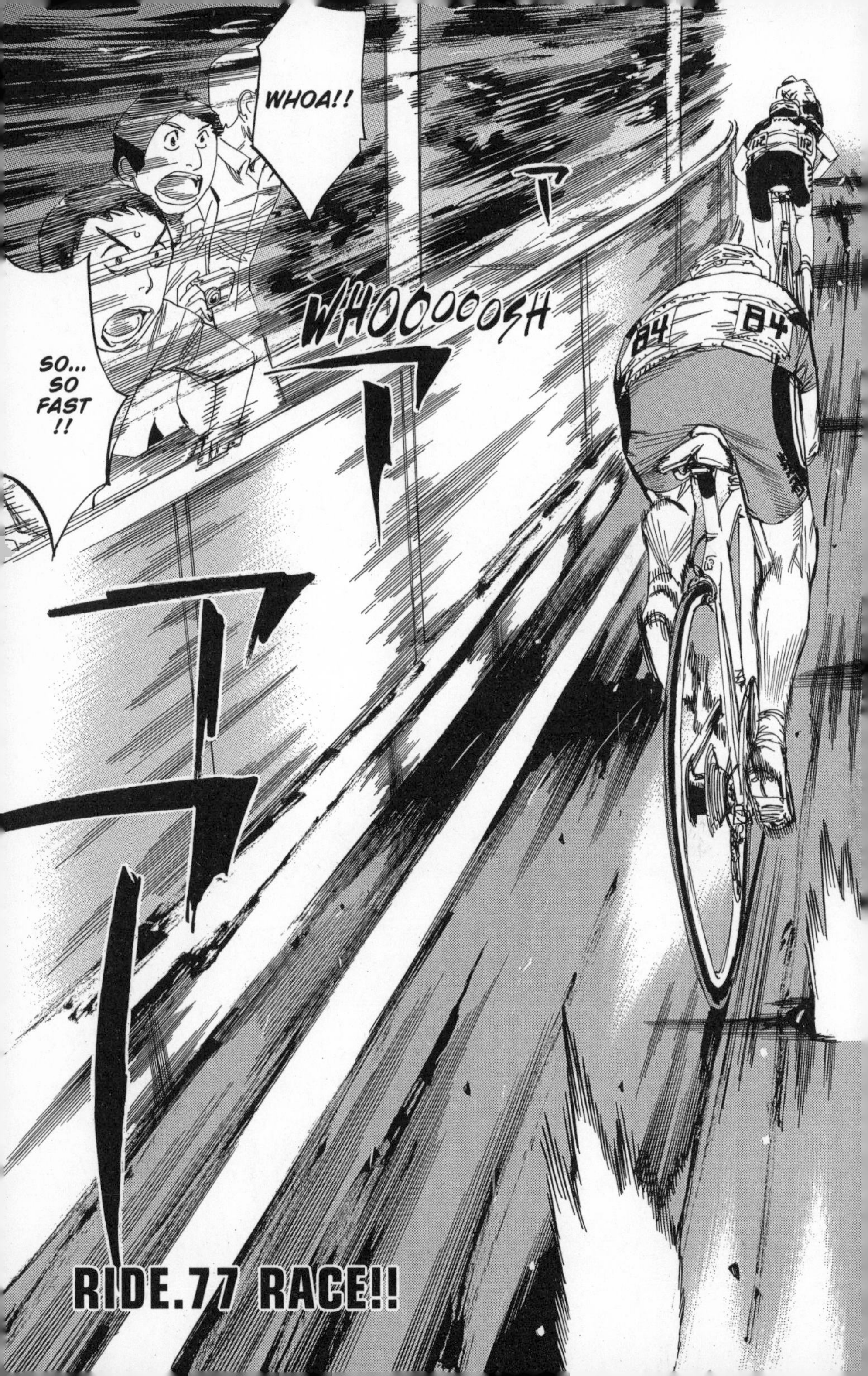
WHOA!!
SO... SO FAST !!
WHOOOOOSH
RIDE.77 RACE!!

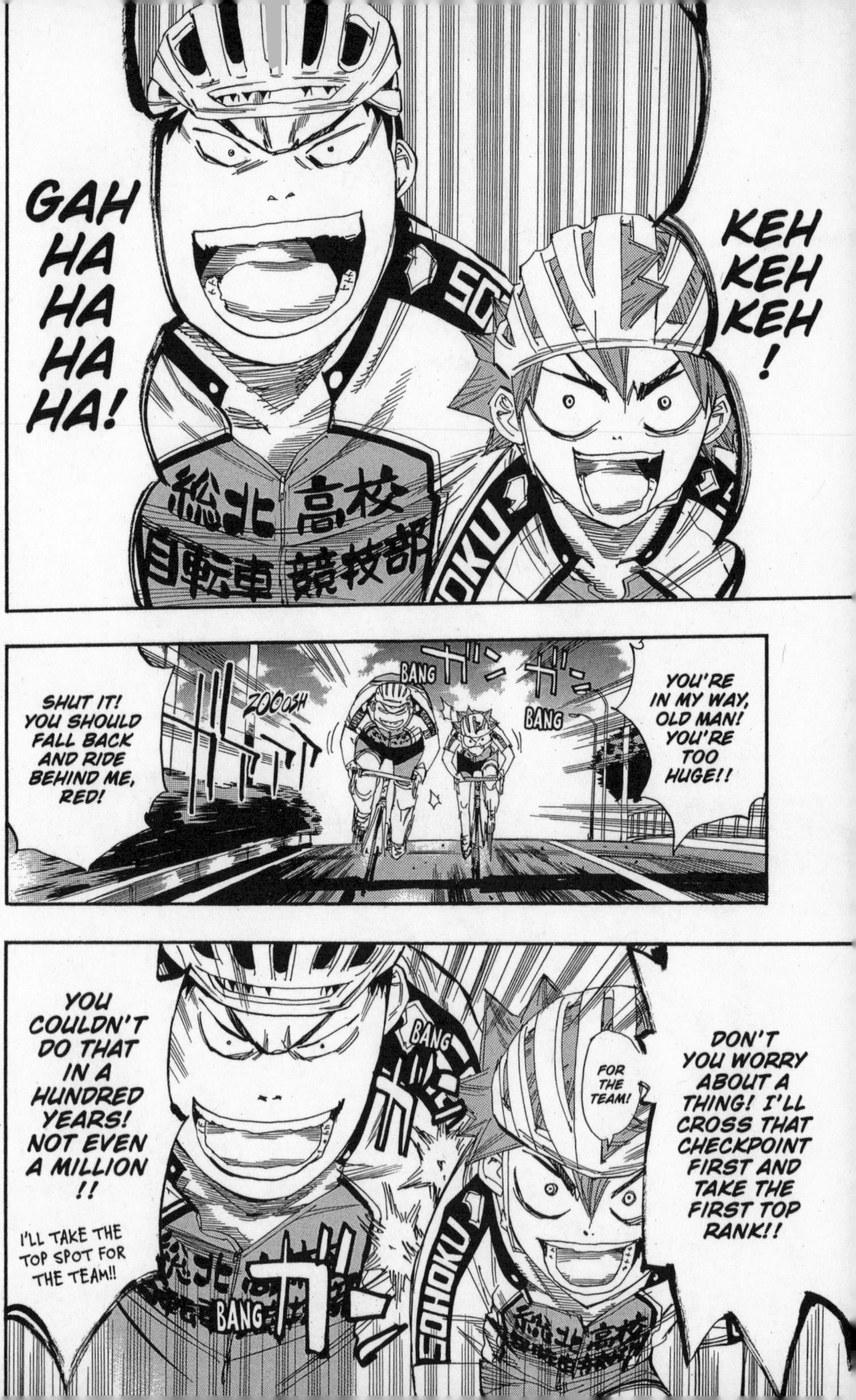
KEH KEH KEH!
GAH HA HA HA HA HA!
総北高校 自転車競技部
BANG
BANG
YOU'RE IN MY WAY, OLD MAN! YOU'RE TOO HUGE!!
ZOOOOSH
SHUT IT! YOU SHOULD FALL BACK AND RIDE BEHIND ME, RED!
DON'T YOU WORRY ABOUT A THING! I'LL CROSS THAT CHECKPOINT FIRST AND TAKE THE FIRST TOP RANK!!
FOR THE TEAM!
BANG
YOU COULDN'T DO THAT IN A HUNDRED YEARS! NOT EVEN A MILLION!!
I'LL TAKE THE TOP SPOT FOR THE TEAM!!
BANG

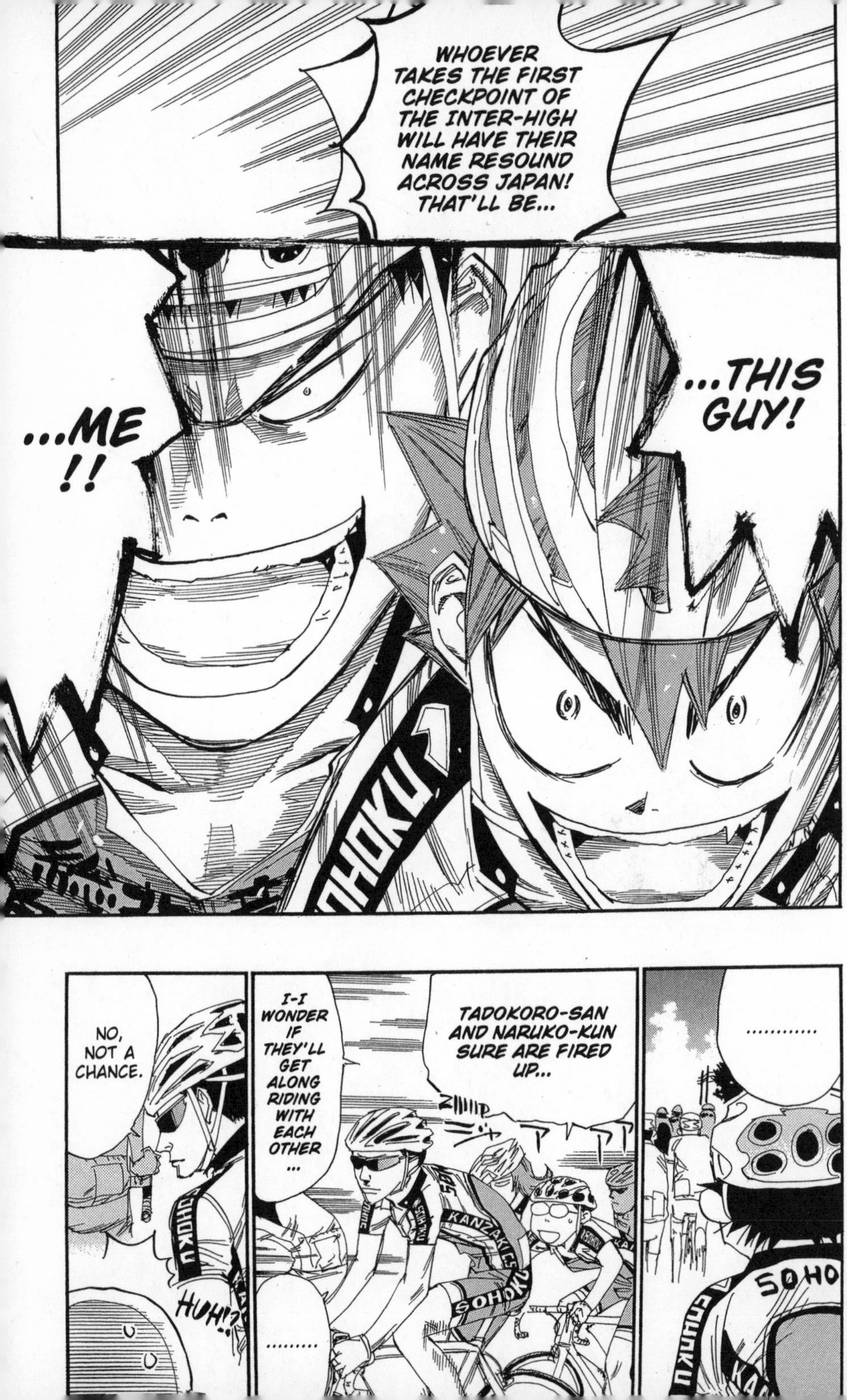
WHOEVER TAKES THE FIRST CHECKPOINT OF THE INTER-HIGH WILL HAVE THEIR NAME RESOUND ACROSS JAPAN! THAT'LL BE...
...THIS GUY!
...ME !!
....
TADOKORO-SAN AND NARUKO-KUN SURE ARE FIRED UP...
I-I WONDER IF THEY'LL GET ALONG RIDING WITH EACH OTHER ...
....
NO, NOT A CHANCE.
HUH!?

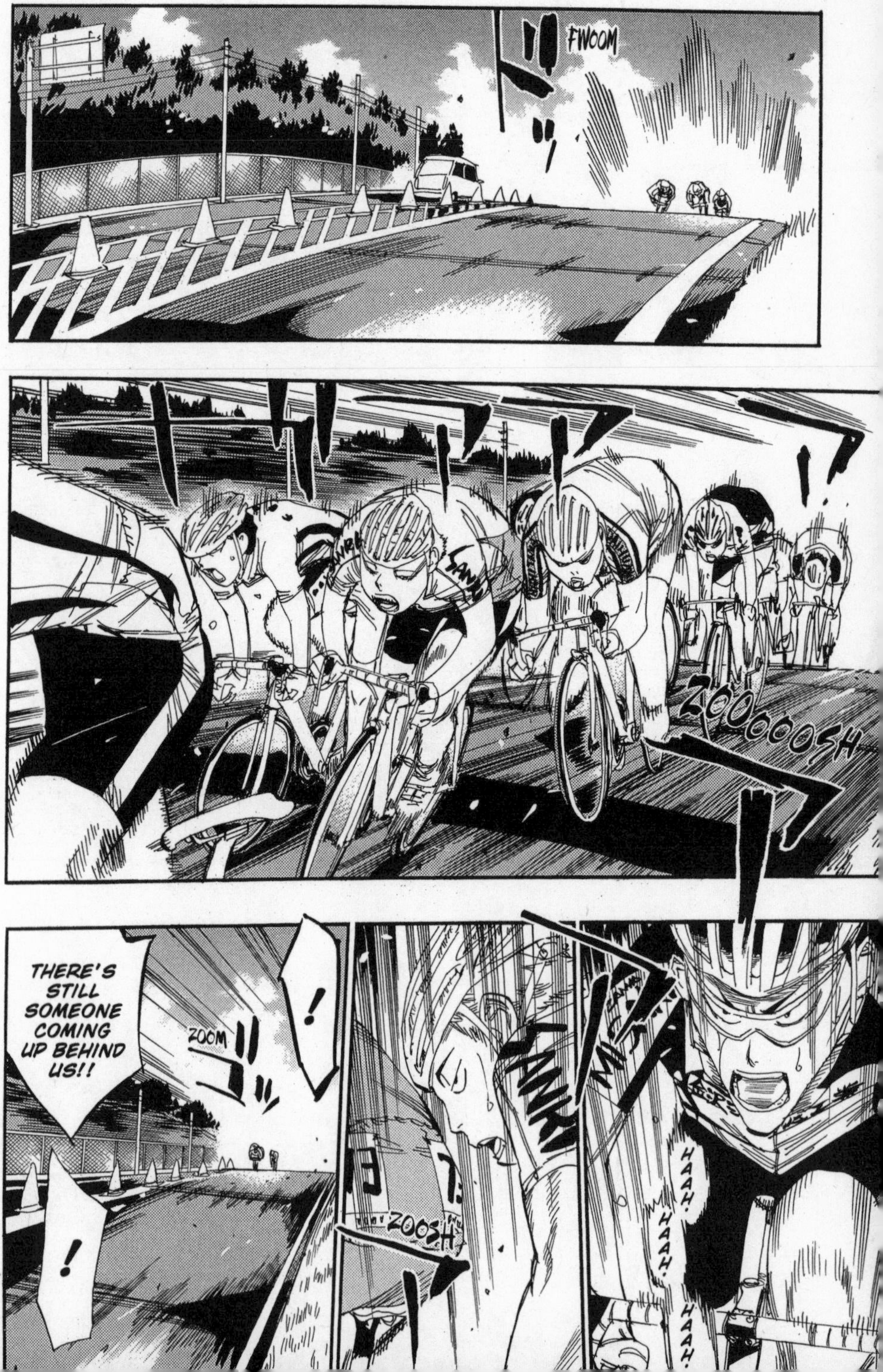
FWOOM
ZOOOOOOSH
HAAAH! HAAAH! HAAAH! HAAAH!
ZOOSH
THERE'S STILL SOMEONE COMING UP BEHIND US!!
ZOOM
!
!

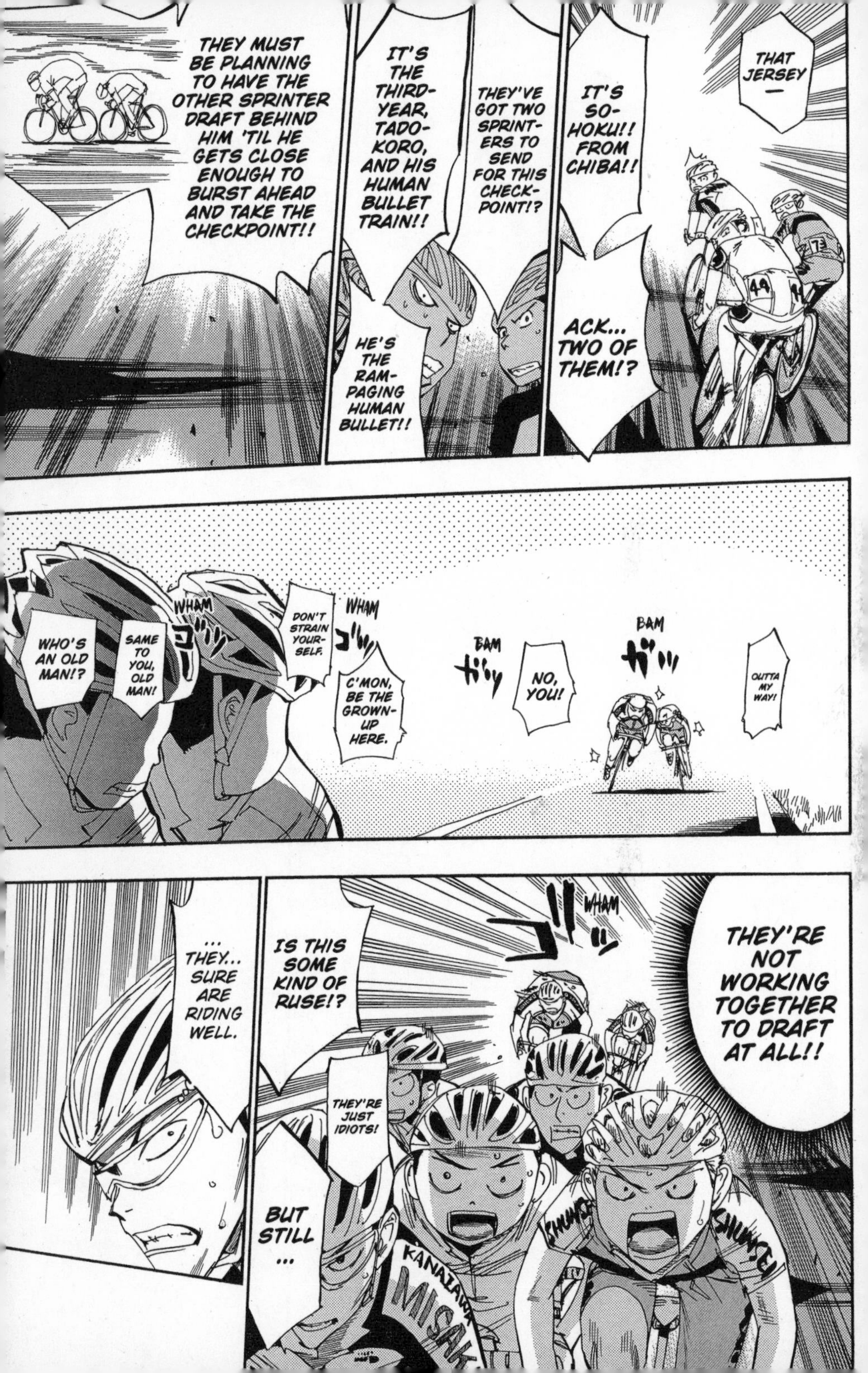
THAT JERSEY —
IT'S SO-HOKU!! FROM CHIBA!!
ACK... TWO OF THEM!?
THEY'VE GOT TWO SPRINT-ERS TO SEND FOR THIS CHECK-POINT!?
IT'S THE THIRD-YEAR, TADO-KORO, AND HIS HUMAN BULLET TRAIN!!
HE'S THE RAM-PAGING HUMAN BULLET!!
THEY MUST BE PLANNING TO HAVE THE OTHER SPRINTER DRAFT BEHIND HIM 'TIL HE GETS CLOSE ENOUGH TO BURST AHEAD AND TAKE THE CHECKPOINT!!
OUTTA MY WAY!
BAM
NO, YOU!
BAM
C'MON, BE THE GROWN-UP HERE.
DON'T STRAIN YOUR-SELF.
WHAM
SAME TO YOU, OLD MAN!
WHAM
WHO'S AN OLD MAN!?
THEY'RE NOT WORKING TOGETHER TO DRAFT AT ALL!!
WHAM
IS THIS SOME KIND OF RUSE!?
THEY'RE JUST IDIOTS!
BUT STILL ...
... THEY... SURE ARE RIDING WELL.

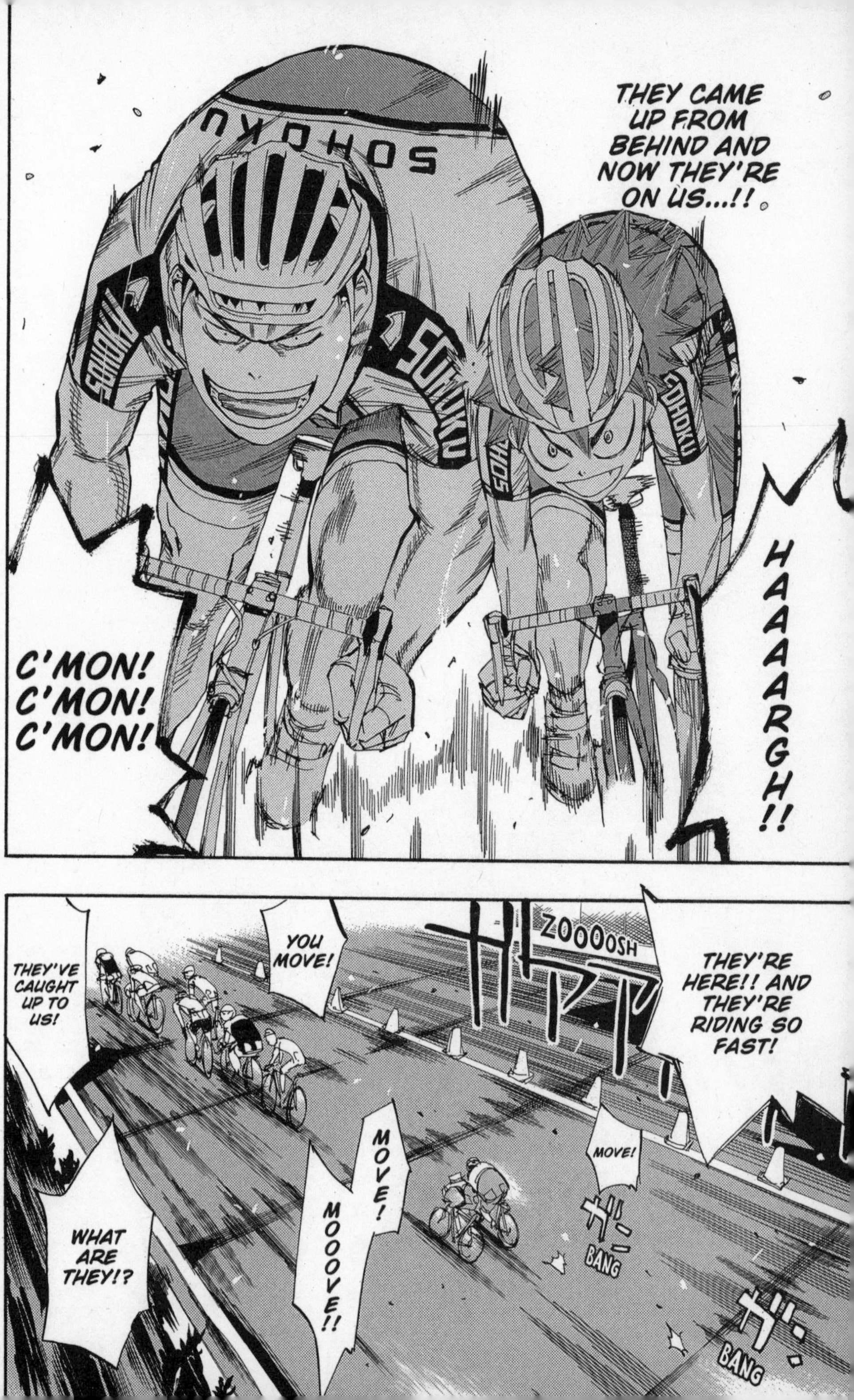
THEY CAME UP FROM BEHIND AND NOW THEY'RE ON US...!!
HAAAARGH!!
C'MON! C'MON! C'MON!
THEY'RE HERE!! AND THEY'RE RIDING SO FAST!
ZOOOOOSH
YOU MOVE!
THEY'VE CAUGHT UP TO US!
MOVE!
MOVE! MOOOOVE!!
BANG
WHAT ARE THEY!?
BANG

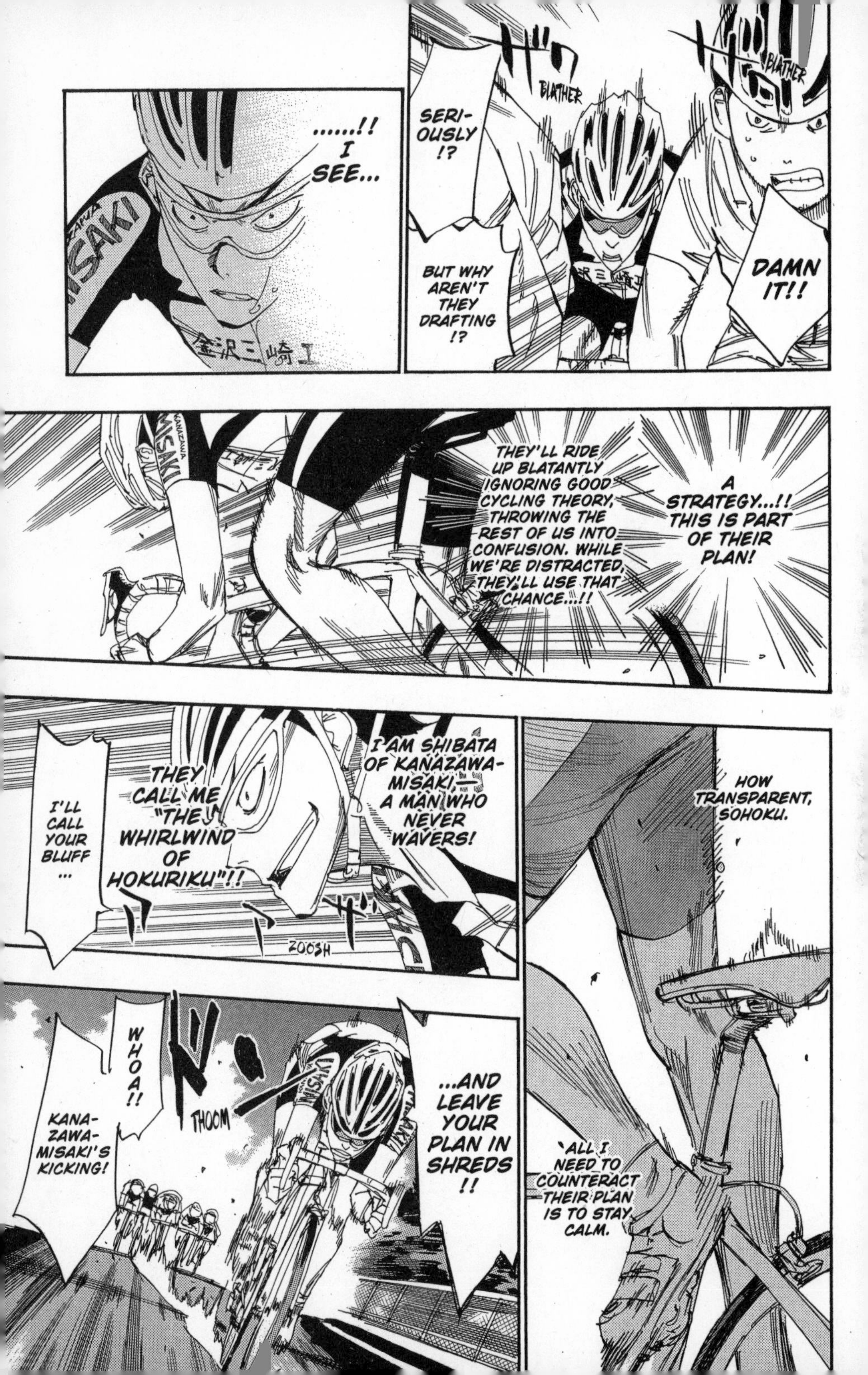
BLATHER
BLATHER
DAMN IT!!
SERI-OUSLY!?
BUT WHY AREN'T THEY DRAFTING!?
......!! I SEE...
A STRATEGY...!! THIS IS PART OF THEIR PLAN!
THEY'LL RIDE UP BLATANTLY IGNORING GOOD CYCLING THEORY, THROWING THE REST OF US INTO CONFUSION. WHILE WE'RE DISTRACTED, THEY'LL USE THAT CHANCE...!!
HOW TRANSPARENT, SOHOKU.
ALL I NEED TO COUNTERACT THEIR PLAN IS TO STAY CALM.
I AM SHIBATA OF KANAZAWA-MISAKI, A MAN WHO NEVER WAVERS!
THEY CALL ME "THE WHIRLWIND OF HOKURIKU"!!
I'LL CALL YOUR BLUFF...
ZOOSH
...AND LEAVE YOUR PLAN IN SHREDS!!
THOOM
WHOA!!
KANA-ZAWA-MISAKI'S KICKING!

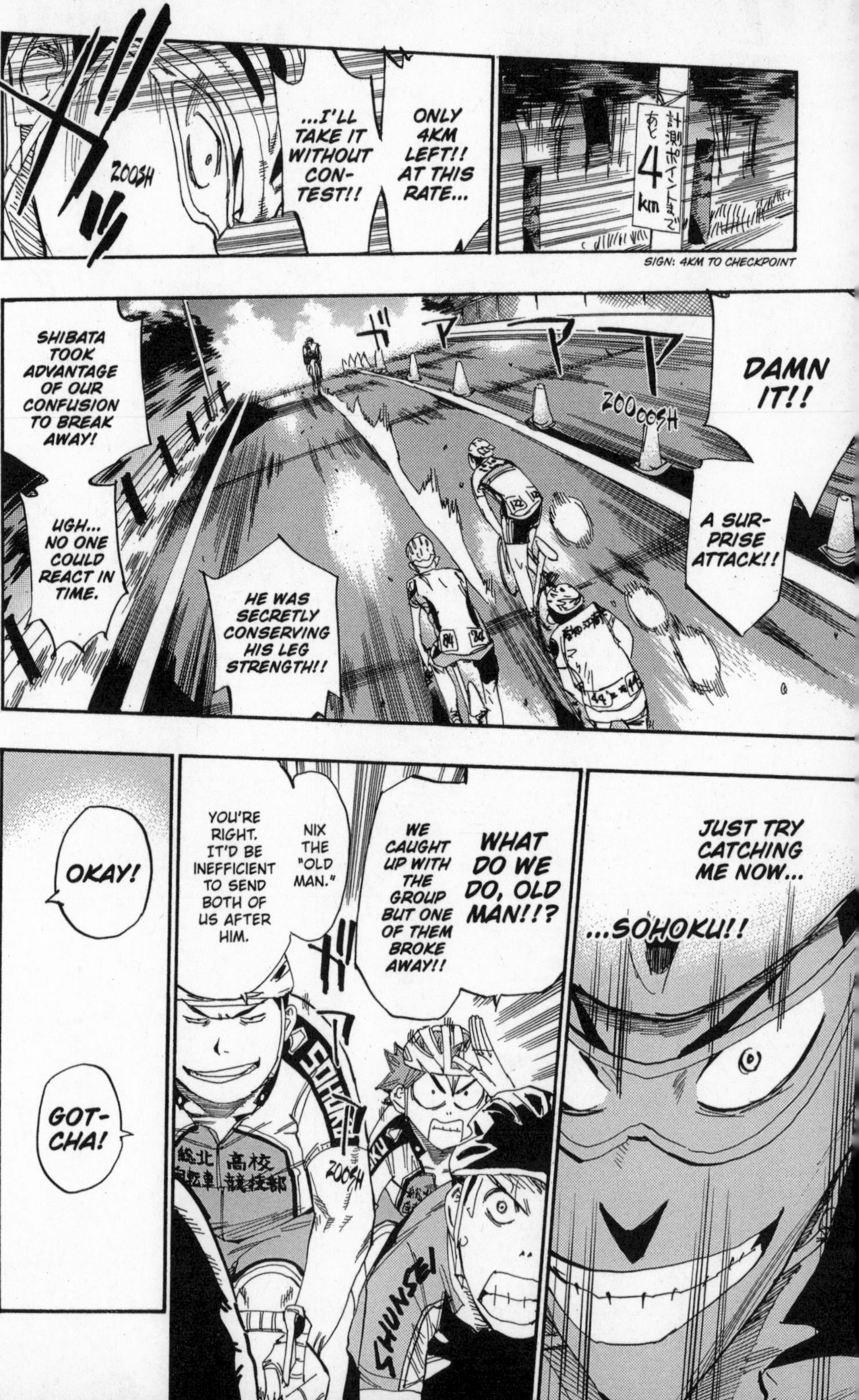
計測ポイントまで あと 4 km
SIGN: 4KM TO CHECKPOINT
ONLY 4KM LEFT!! AT THIS RATE...
...I'LL TAKE IT WITHOUT CON-TEST!!
ZOOSH
DAMN IT!!
ギャアーア
ZOOOOSH
A SUR-PRISE ATTACK!!
SHIBATA TOOK ADVANTAGE OF OUR CONFUSION TO BREAK AWAY!
HE WAS SECRETLY CONSERVING HIS LEG STRENGTH!!
UGH... NO ONE COULD REACT IN TIME.
JUST TRY CATCHING ME NOW...
...SOHOKU!!
SHUNSEI
WHAT DO WE DO, OLD MAN!!?
WE CAUGHT UP WITH THE GROUP BUT ONE OF THEM BROKE AWAY!!
NIX THE "OLD MAN."
YOU'RE RIGHT. IT'D BE INEFFICIENT TO SEND BOTH OF US AFTER HIM.
ZOOSH
総北高校自転車競技部
SOHOKU
OKAY!
GOT-CHA!

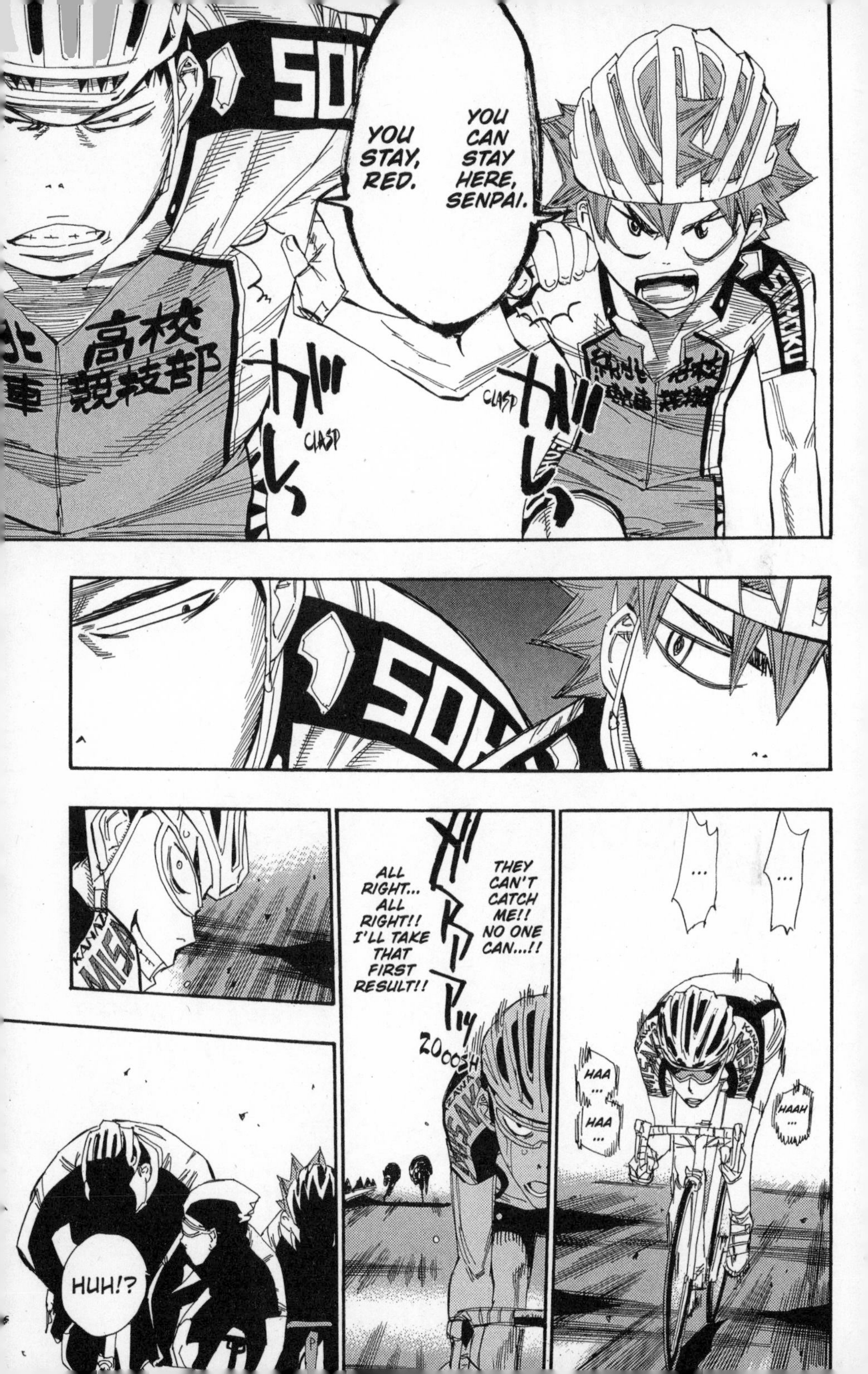
YOU CAN STAY HERE, SENPAI.
YOU STAY, RED.
CLASP
CLASP
...
...
HAAH...
HAA... HAA...
THEY CAN'T CATCH ME!! NO ONE CAN...!!
ALL RIGHT... ALL RIGHT!! I'LL TAKE THAT FIRST RESULT!!
ZOOOSH
HUH!?

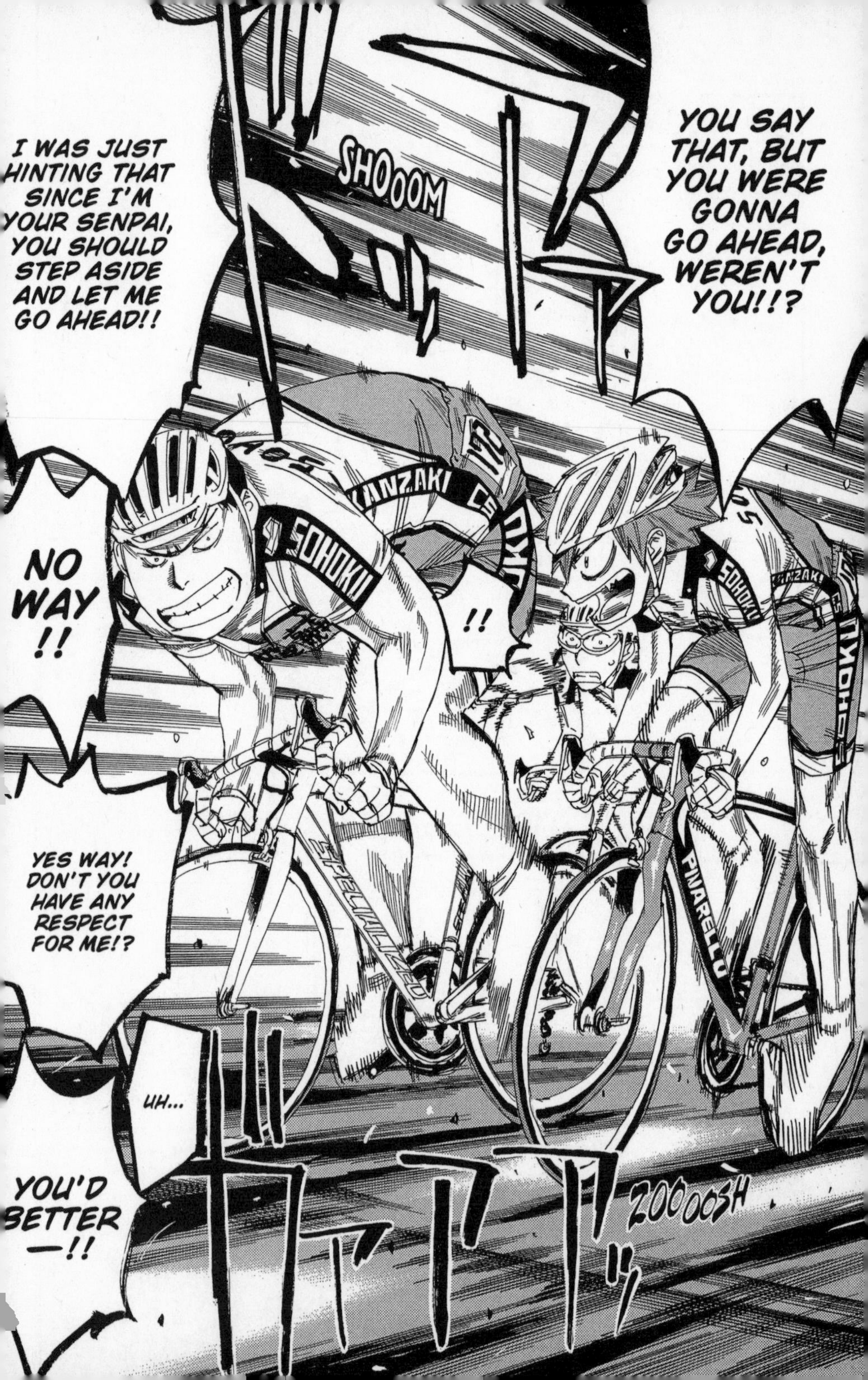
YOU SAY THAT, BUT YOU WERE GONNA GO AHEAD, WEREN'T YOU!!?
SHOOOM
I WAS JUST HINTING THAT SINCE I'M YOUR SENPAI, YOU SHOULD STEP ASIDE AND LET ME GO AHEAD!!
!!
NO WAY!!
YES WAY! DON'T YOU HAVE ANY RESPECT FOR ME!?
ZOOOOSH
UH...
YOU'D BETTER—!!

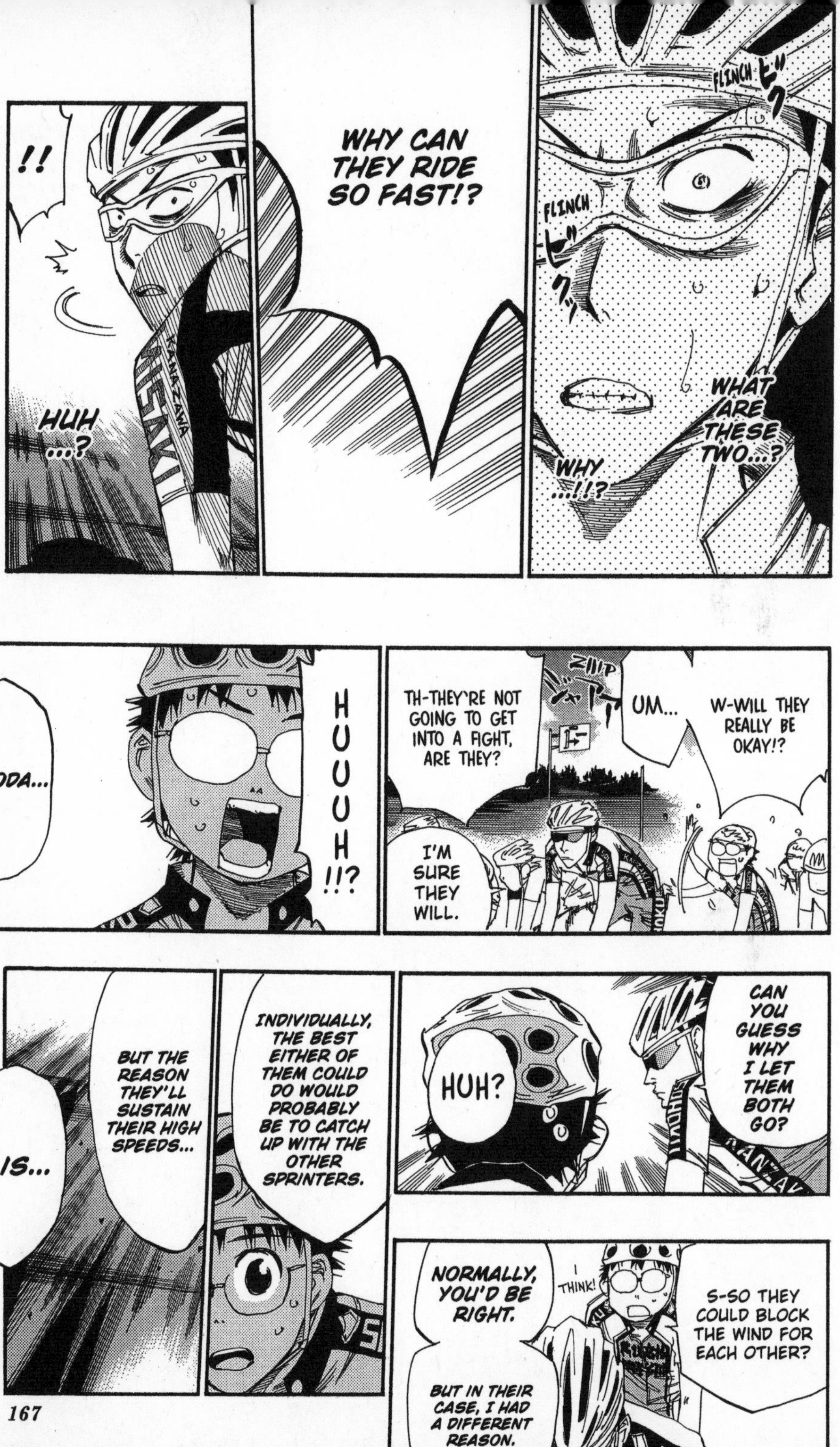
FLINCH
FLINCH
WHAT ARE THESE TWO...?
WHY ...!!?
WHY CAN THEY RIDE SO FAST!?
!!
HUH ...?
W-WILL THEY REALLY BE OKAY!?
UM...
TH-THEY'RE NOT GOING TO GET INTO A FIGHT, ARE THEY?
ZIIIP
I'M SURE THEY WILL.
HUUUH!!?
ONODA...
CAN YOU GUESS WHY I LET THEM BOTH GO?
HUH?
S-SO THEY COULD BLOCK THE WIND FOR EACH OTHER?
I THINK!
NORMALLY, YOU'D BE RIGHT.
BUT IN THEIR CASE, I HAD A DIFFERENT REASON.
INDIVIDUALLY, THE BEST EITHER OF THEM COULD DO WOULD PROBABLY BE TO CATCH UP WITH THE OTHER SPRINTERS.
BUT THE REASON THEY'LL SUSTAIN THEIR HIGH SPEEDS...
...IS...

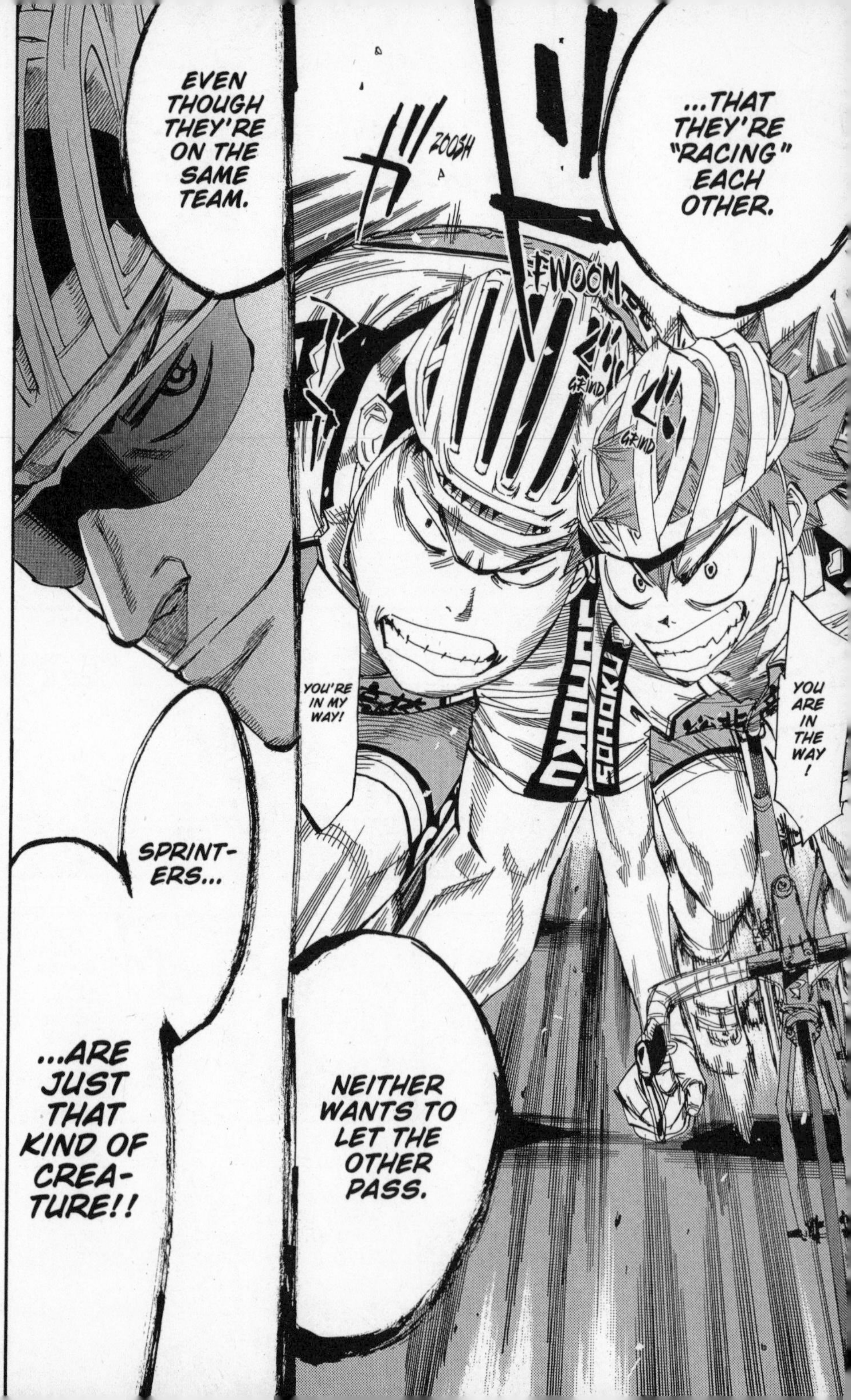
...THAT THEY'RE "RACING" EACH OTHER.
ZOOSH
FWOOM
GRIND
GRIND
YOU ARE IN THE WAY!
YOU'RE IN MY WAY!
SOHOKU
SOHOKU
NEITHER WANTS TO LET THE OTHER PASS.
EVEN THOUGH THEY'RE ON THE SAME TEAM.
SPRINT-ERS...
...ARE JUST THAT KIND OF CREA-TURE!!

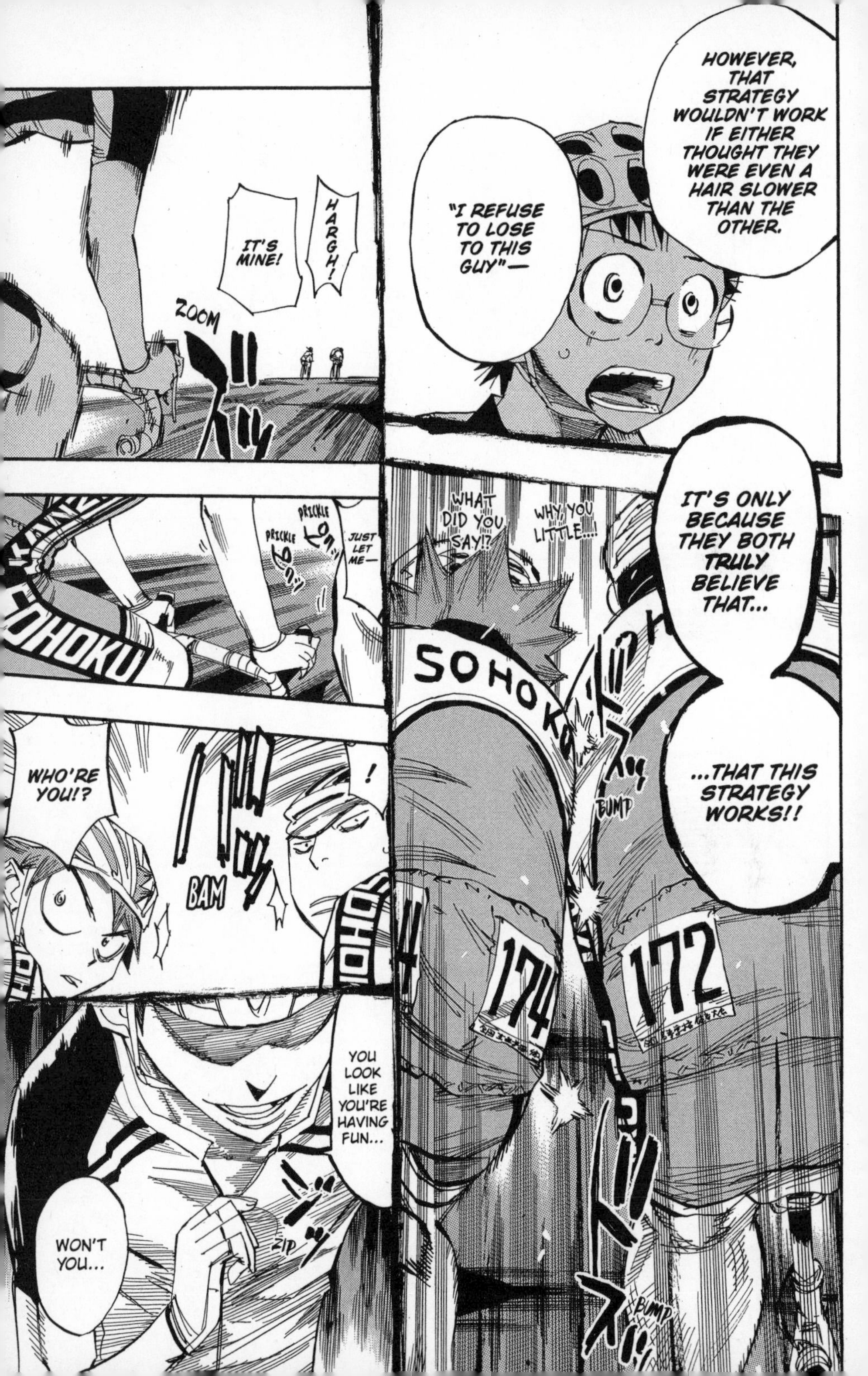
HOWEVER, THAT STRATEGY WOULDN'T WORK IF EITHER THOUGHT THEY WERE EVEN A HAIR SLOWER THAN THE OTHER.
"I REFUSE TO LOSE TO THIS GUY"—
HARGH!
IT'S MINE!
ZOOM
IT'S ONLY BECAUSE THEY BOTH TRULY BELIEVE THAT...
WHY, YOU LITTLE...!
WHAT DID YOU SAY!?
SOHOKU
BUMP
...THAT THIS STRATEGY WORKS!!
174
172
BUMP
JUST LET ME—
PRICKLE
PRICKLE
SOHOKU
!
BAM
WHO'RE YOU!?
YOU LOOK LIKE YOU'RE HAVING FUN...
ZIP
WON'T YOU...

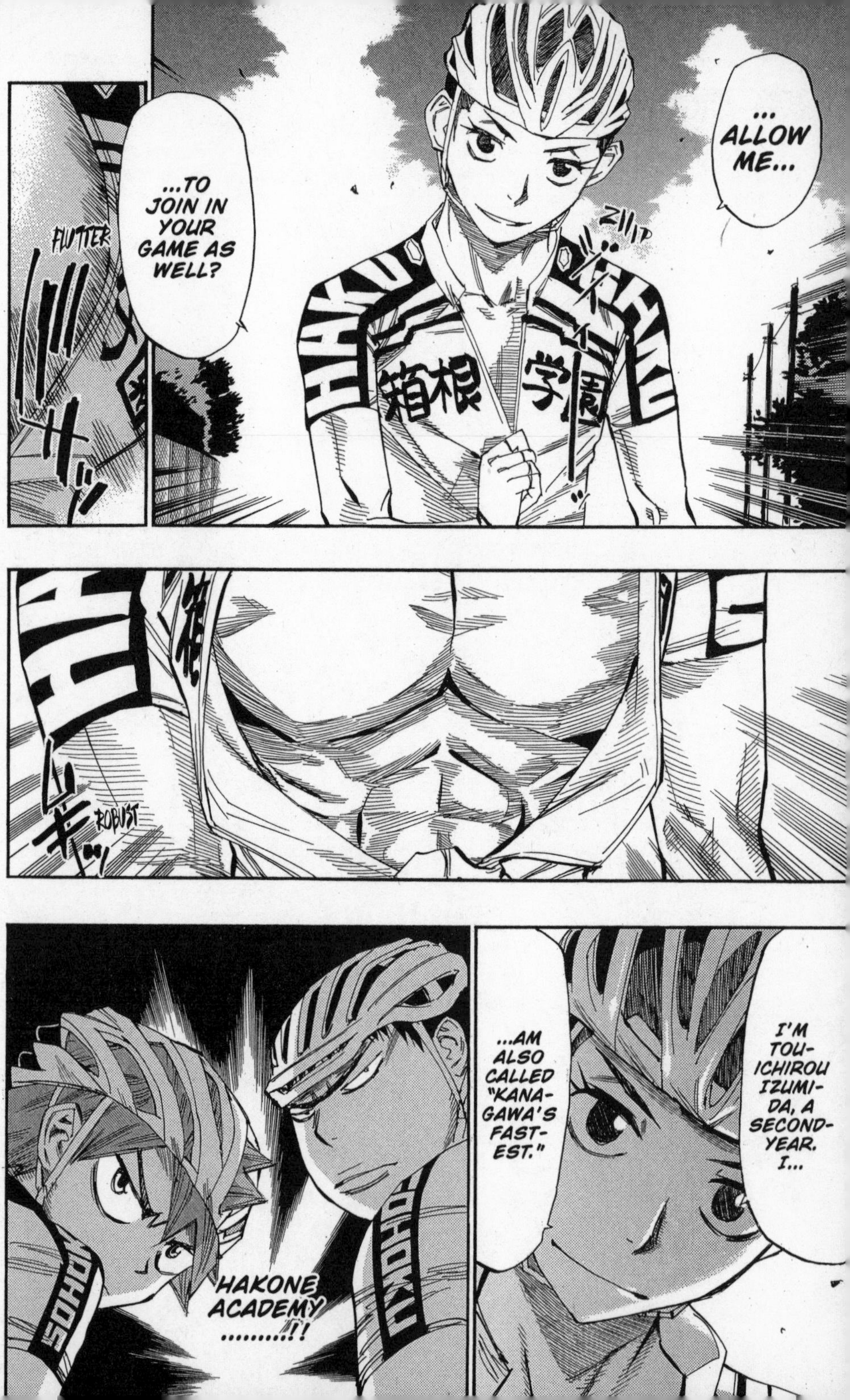
... ALLOW ME...
ZIIIP
...TO JOIN IN YOUR GAME AS WELL?
FLUTTER
ROBUST
I'M TOUICHIROU IZUMIDA, A SECOND-YEAR. I...
...AM ALSO CALLED "KANAGAWA'S FASTEST."
HAKONE ACADEMY ....!!

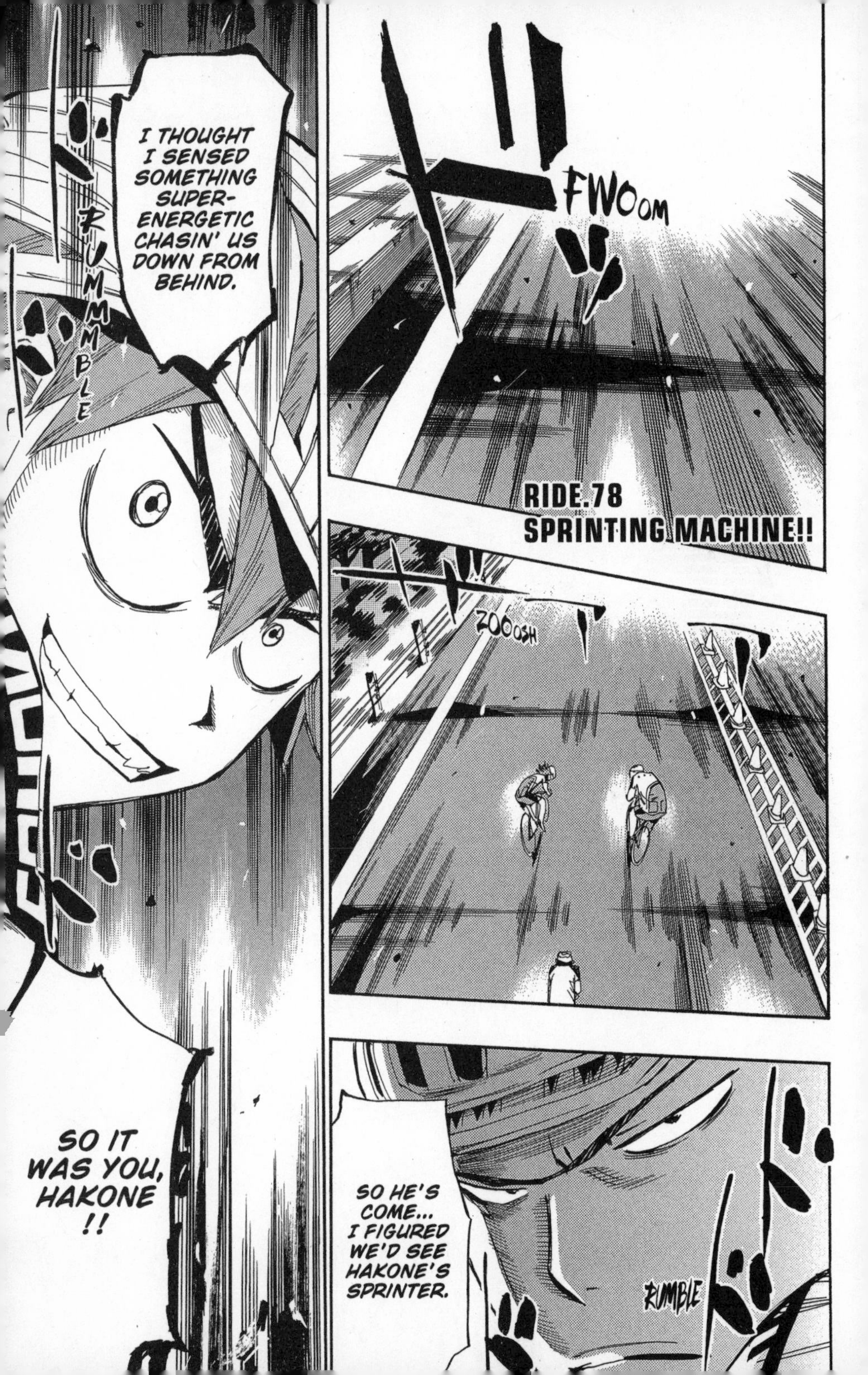
FWOOM
RIDE.78
SPRINTING MACHINE!!
ZOOOSH
SO HE'S COME... I FIGURED WE'D SEE HAKONE'S SPRINTER.
RUMBLE
I THOUGHT I SENSED SOMETHING SUPER-ENERGETIC CHASIN' US DOWN FROM BEHIND.
RUMMMMBLE
SO IT WAS YOU, HAKONE !!

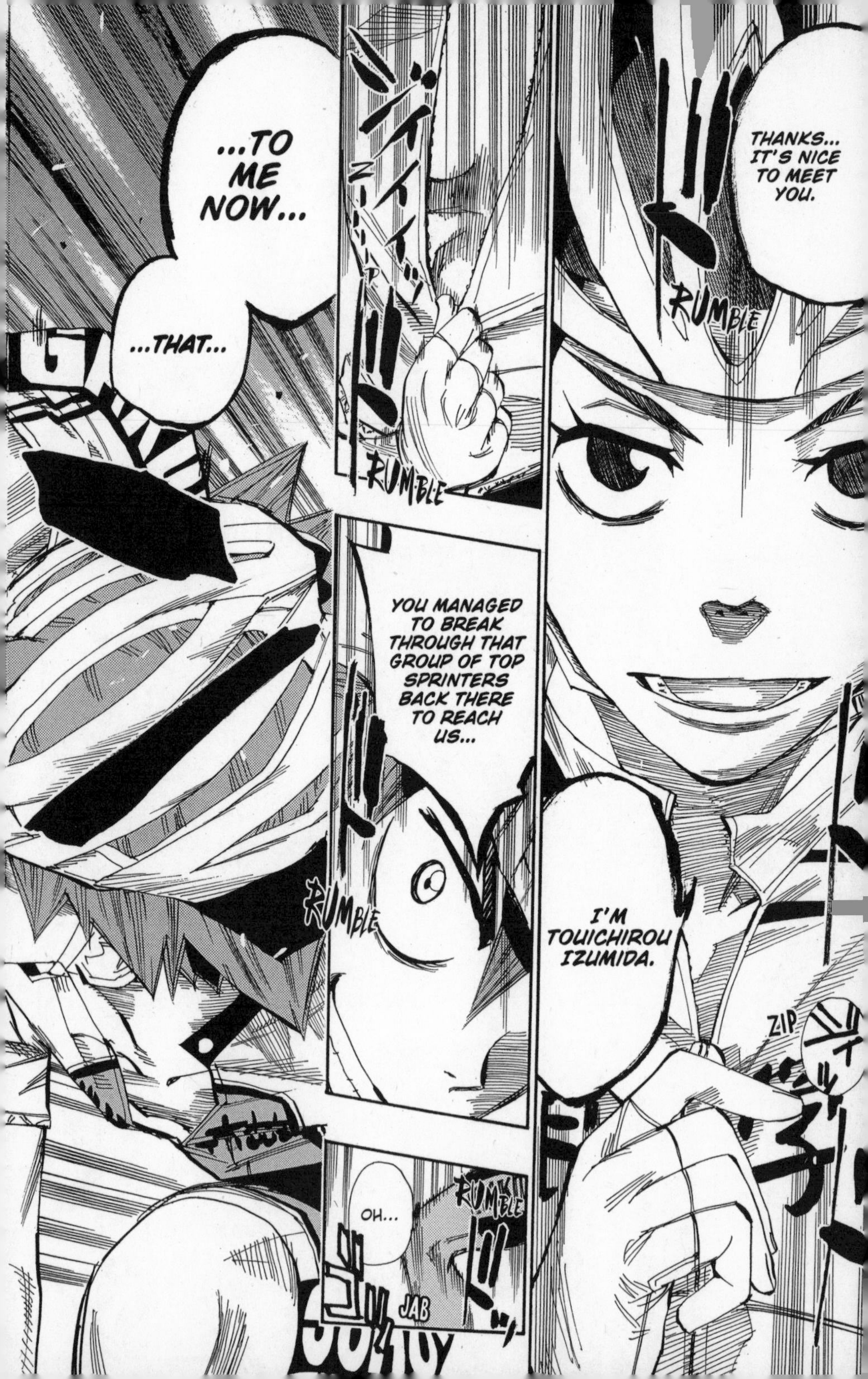
THANKS... IT'S NICE TO MEET YOU.
RUMBLE
I'M TOUICHIROU IZUMIDA.
ZIP
RUMBLE
YOU MANAGED TO BREAK THROUGH THAT GROUP OF TOP SPRINTERS BACK THERE TO REACH US...
RUMBLE
RUMBLE
OH...
JAB
...TO ME NOW...
...THAT...

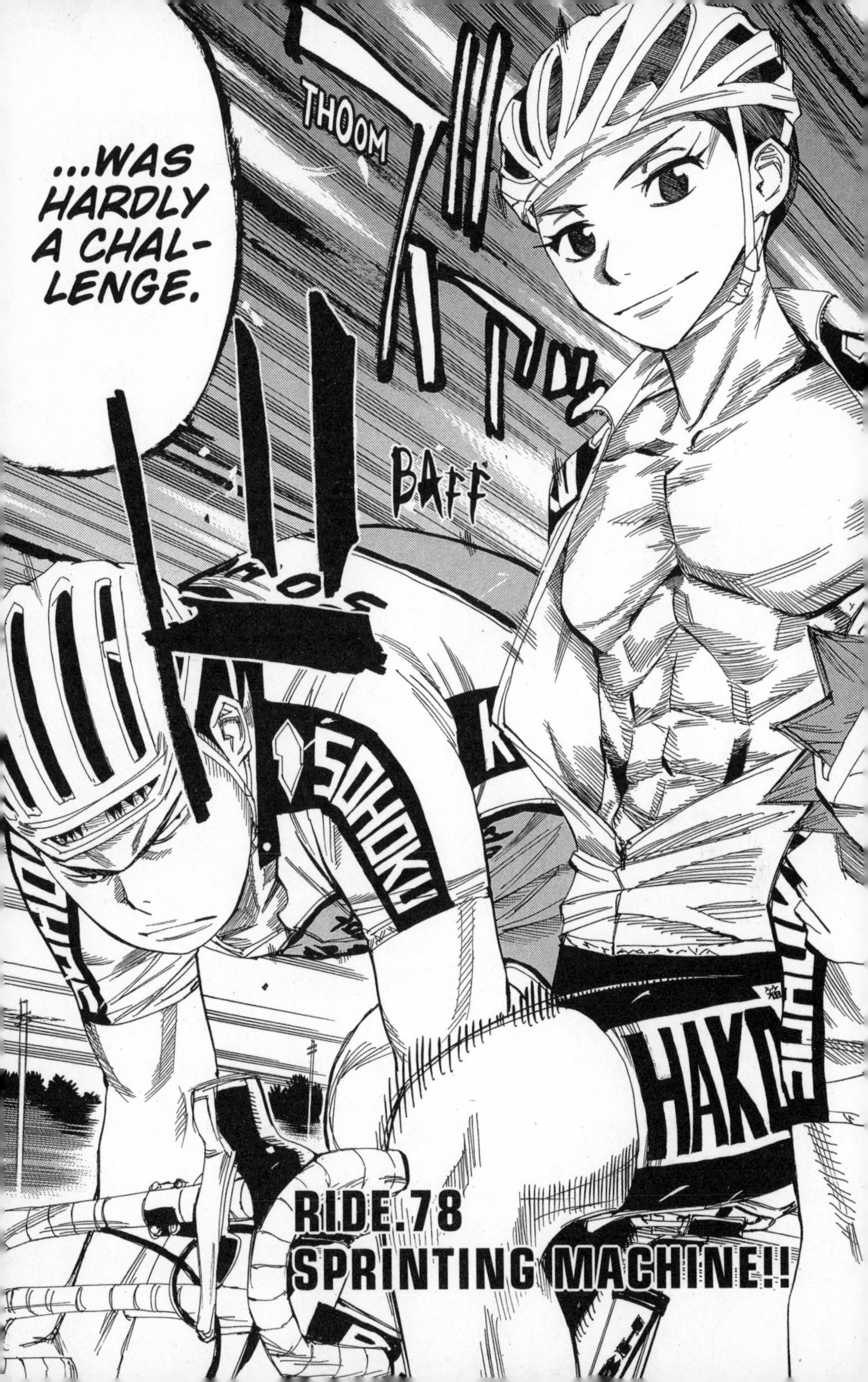
...WAS HARDLY A CHAL-LENGE.
THOOM
BAFF
SOHOKU
HAKO
RIDE.78
SPRINTING MACHINE!!

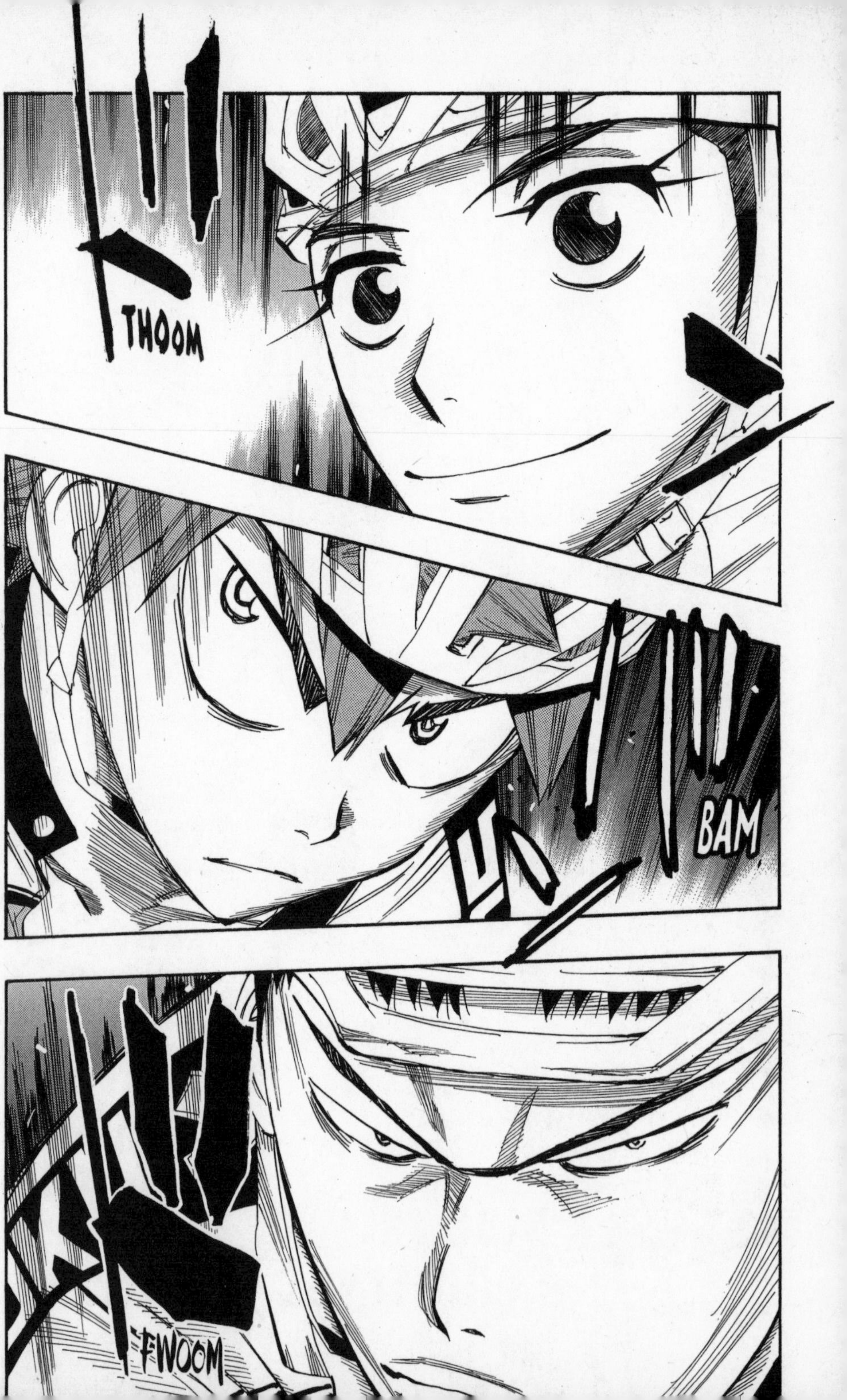
THOOM
BAM
FWOOM

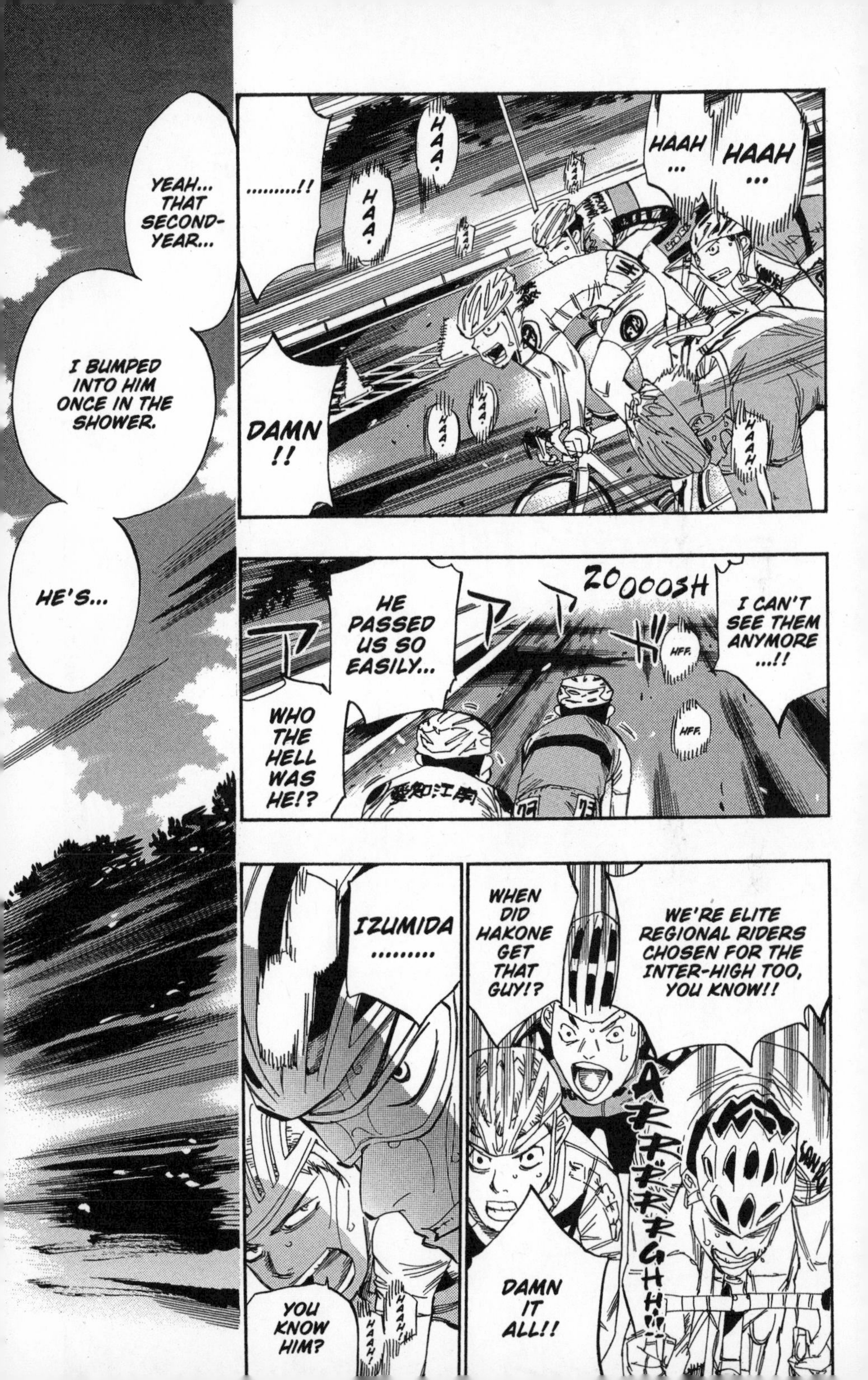
HAAH...
HAAH...
HAA. HAA.
.........!!
DAMN!!
HAA.
HAAH.
ZOOOOSH
I CAN'T SEE THEM ANYMORE...!!
HFF.
HFF.
HE PASSED US SO EASILY...
WHO THE HELL WAS HE!?
WE'RE ELITE REGIONAL RIDERS CHOSEN FOR THE INTER-HIGH TOO, YOU KNOW!!
WHEN DID HAKONE GET THAT GUY!?
ARRRRRGH
DAMN IT ALL!!
IZUMIDA.........
HAAH
HAAH
YOU KNOW HIM?
YEAH... THAT SECOND-YEAR...
I BUMPED INTO HIM ONCE IN THE SHOWER.
HE'S...

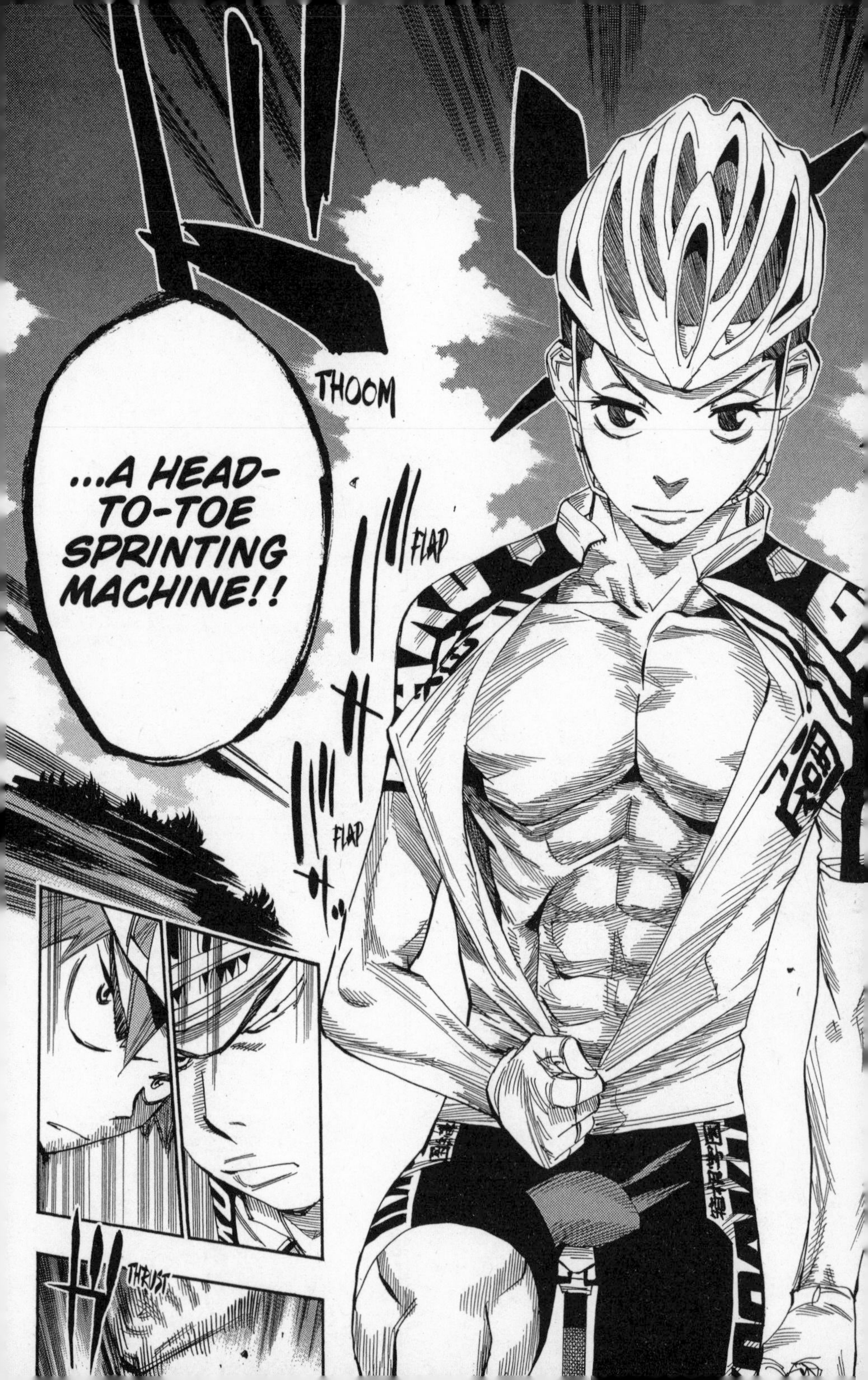
THOOM
...A HEAD-TO-TOE SPRINTING MACHINE!!
FLAP
FLAP
THRUST

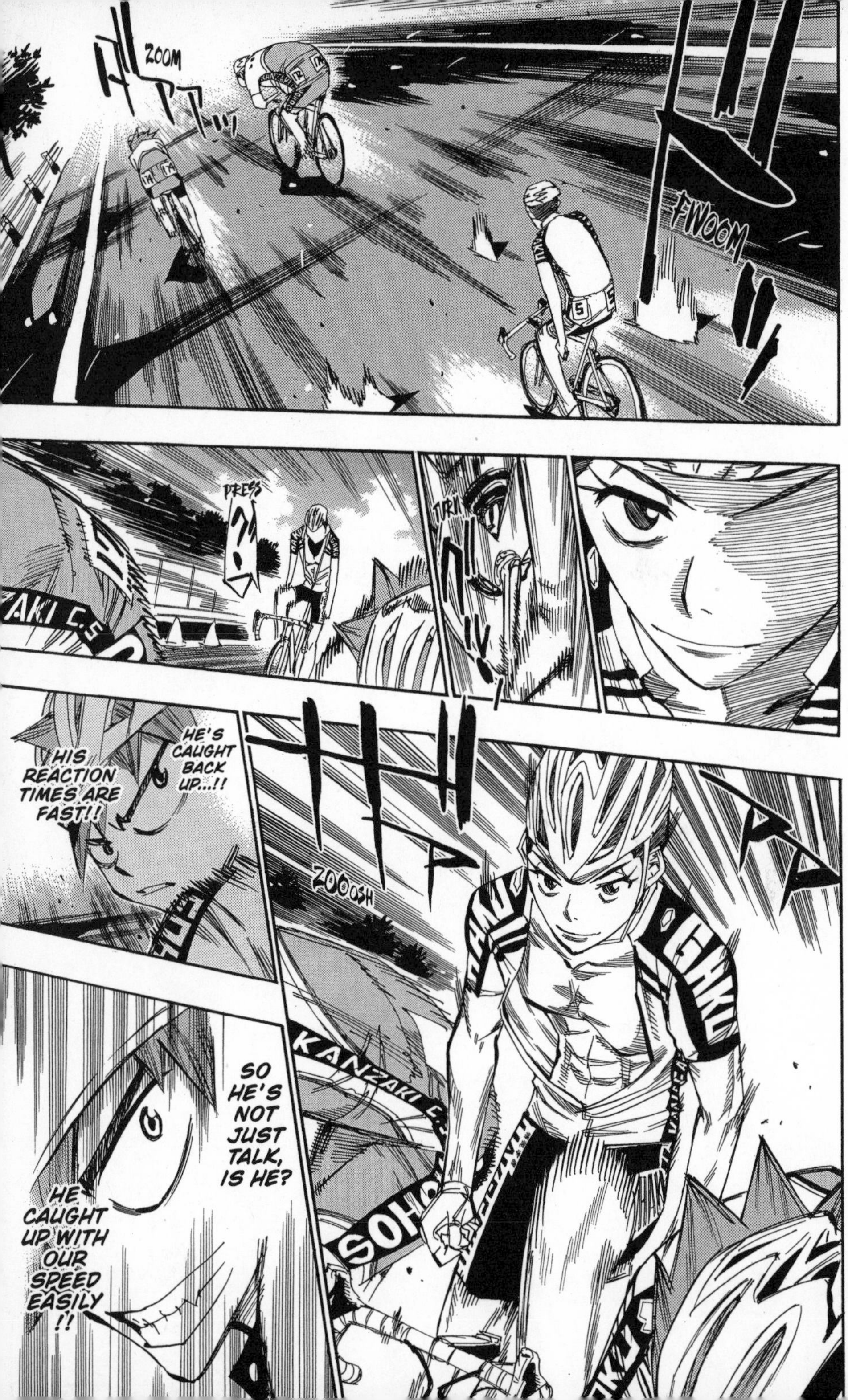
FWOOM
ZOOM
TURN
PRESS
ZOOOSH
HE'S CAUGHT BACK UP...!!
HIS REACTION TIMES ARE FAST!!
SO HE'S NOT JUST TALK, IS HE?
HE CAUGHT UP WITH OUR SPEED EASILY!!

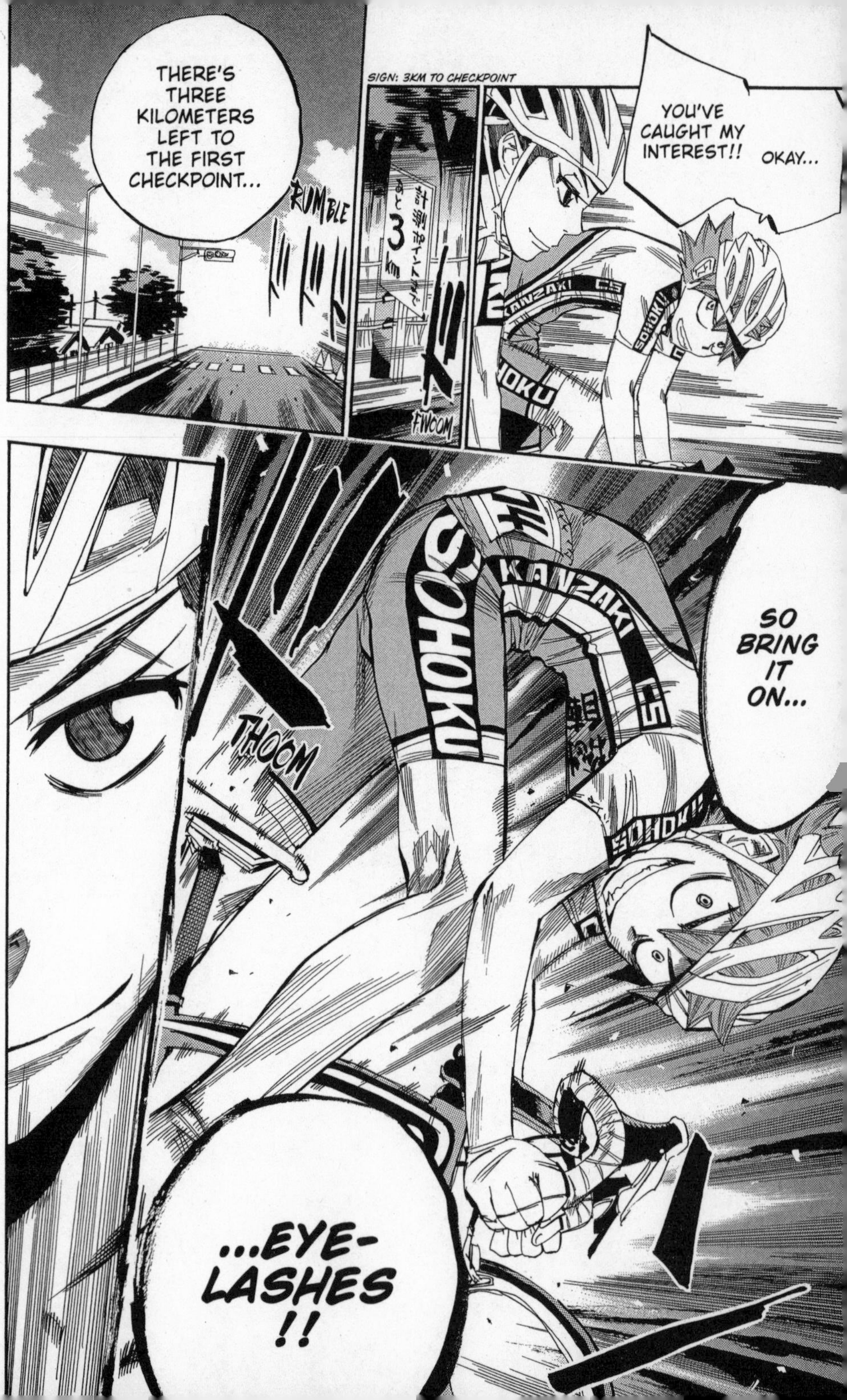
OKAY...
YOU'VE CAUGHT MY INTEREST!!
SIGN: 3KM TO CHECKPOINT
計測ポイントまで
あと3km
FWOOM
THERE'S THREE KILOMETERS LEFT TO THE FIRST CHECKPOINT...
RUMBLE
SO BRING IT ON...
THOOM
...EYE-LASHES!!

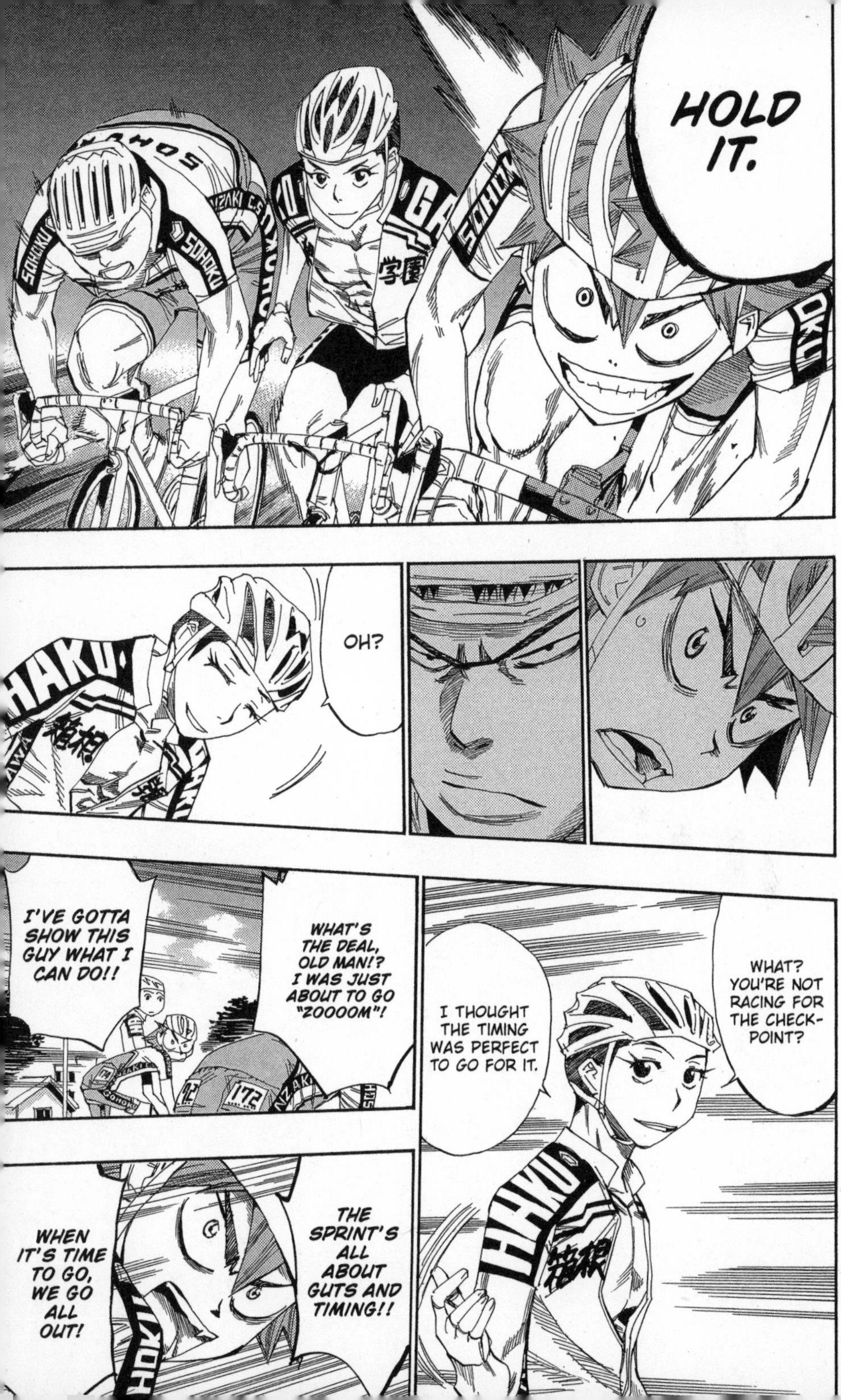
HOLD IT.
OH?
WHAT? YOU'RE NOT RACING FOR THE CHECK-POINT?
I THOUGHT THE TIMING WAS PERFECT TO GO FOR IT.
WHAT'S THE DEAL, OLD MAN!? I WAS JUST ABOUT TO GO "ZOOOOM"!
I'VE GOTTA SHOW THIS GUY WHAT I CAN DO!!
THE SPRINT'S ALL ABOUT GUTS AND TIMING!!
WHEN IT'S TIME TO GO, WE GO ALL OUT!

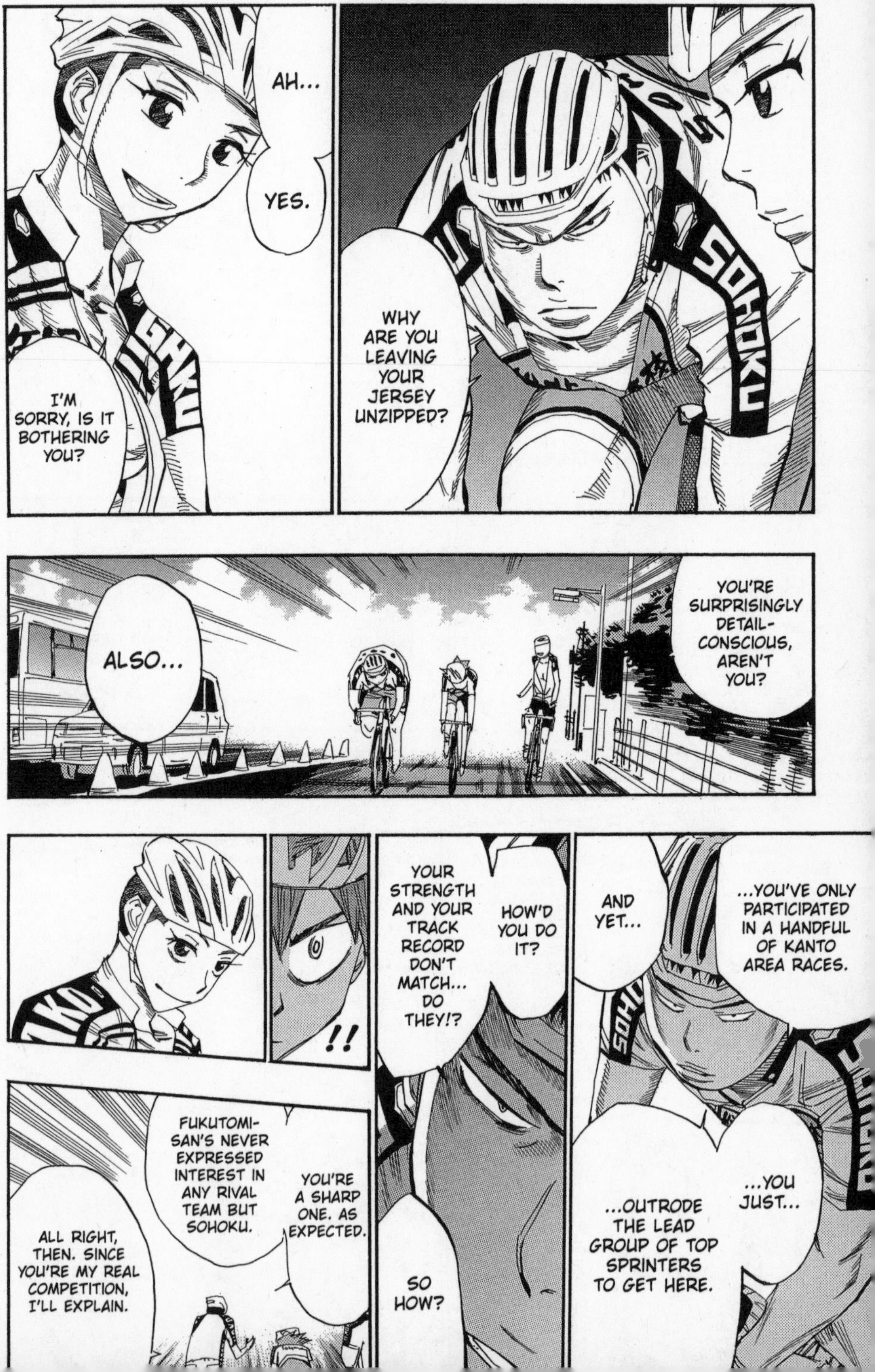
WHY ARE YOU LEAVING YOUR JERSEY UNZIPPED?
AH...
YES.
I'M SORRY, IS IT BOTHERING YOU?
YOU'RE SURPRISINGLY DETAIL-CONSCIOUS, AREN'T YOU?
ALSO...
...YOU'VE ONLY PARTICIPATED IN A HANDFUL OF KANTO AREA RACES.
AND YET...
...YOU JUST...
...OUTRODE THE LEAD GROUP OF TOP SPRINTERS TO GET HERE.
HOW'D YOU DO IT?
YOUR STRENGTH AND YOUR TRACK RECORD DON'T MATCH... DO THEY!?
SO HOW?
!!
YOU'RE A SHARP ONE. AS EXPECTED.
FUKUTOMI-SAN'S NEVER EXPRESSED INTEREST IN ANY RIVAL TEAM BUT SOHOKU.
ALL RIGHT, THEN. SINCE YOU'RE MY REAL COMPETITION, I'LL EXPLAIN.

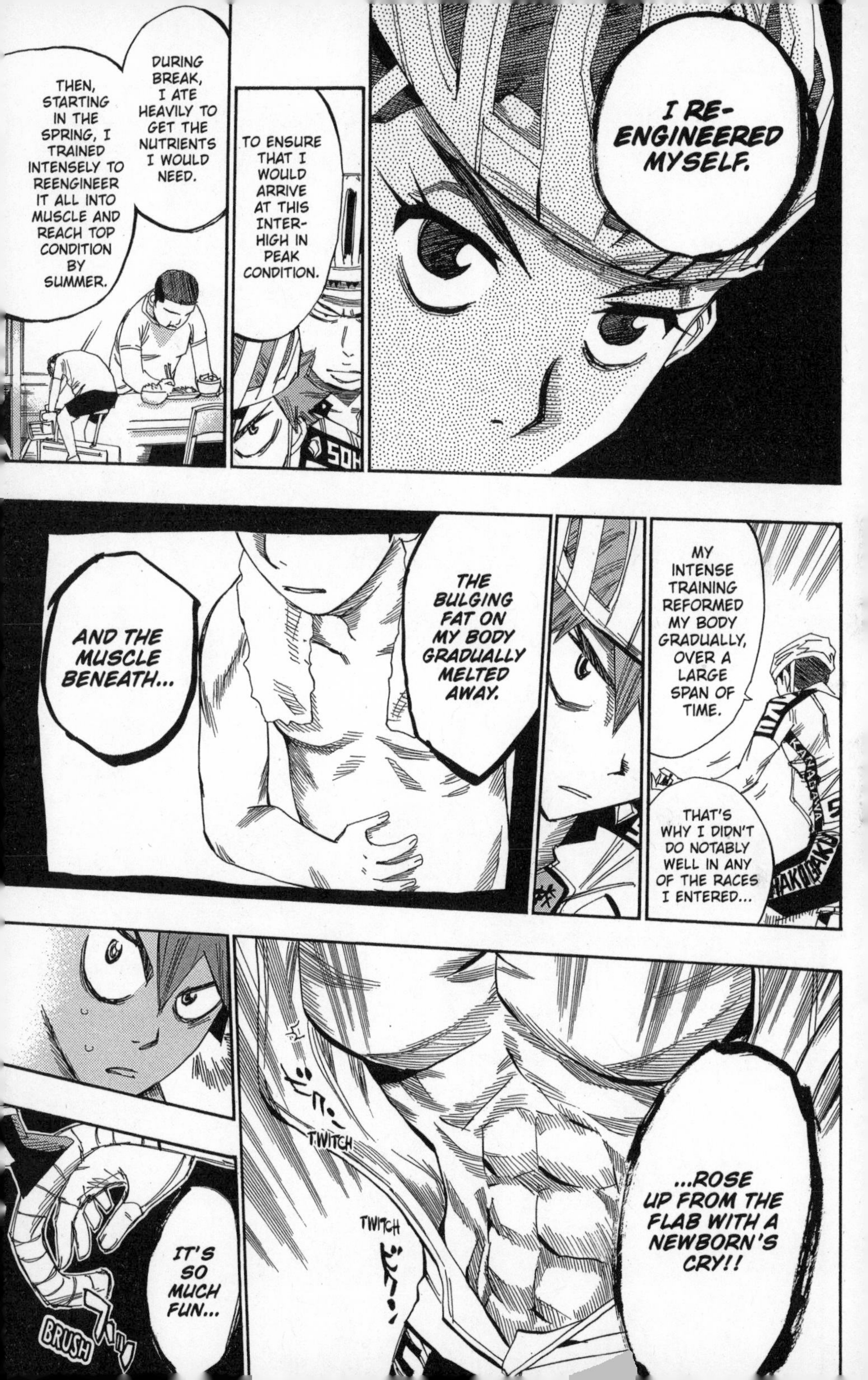
I RE-ENGINEERED MYSELF.
TO ENSURE THAT I WOULD ARRIVE AT THIS INTER-HIGH IN PEAK CONDITION.
DURING BREAK, I ATE HEAVILY TO GET THE NUTRIENTS I WOULD NEED.
THEN, STARTING IN THE SPRING, I TRAINED INTENSELY TO REENGINEER IT ALL INTO MUSCLE AND REACH TOP CONDITION BY SUMMER.
MY INTENSE TRAINING REFORMED MY BODY GRADUALLY, OVER A LARGE SPAN OF TIME.
THAT'S WHY I DIDN'T DO NOTABLY WELL IN ANY OF THE RACES I ENTERED...
THE BULGING FAT ON MY BODY GRADUALLY MELTED AWAY.
AND THE MUSCLE BENEATH...
TWITCH
...ROSE UP FROM THE FLAB WITH A NEWBORN'S CRY!!
TWITCH
IT'S SO MUCH FUN...
BRUSH

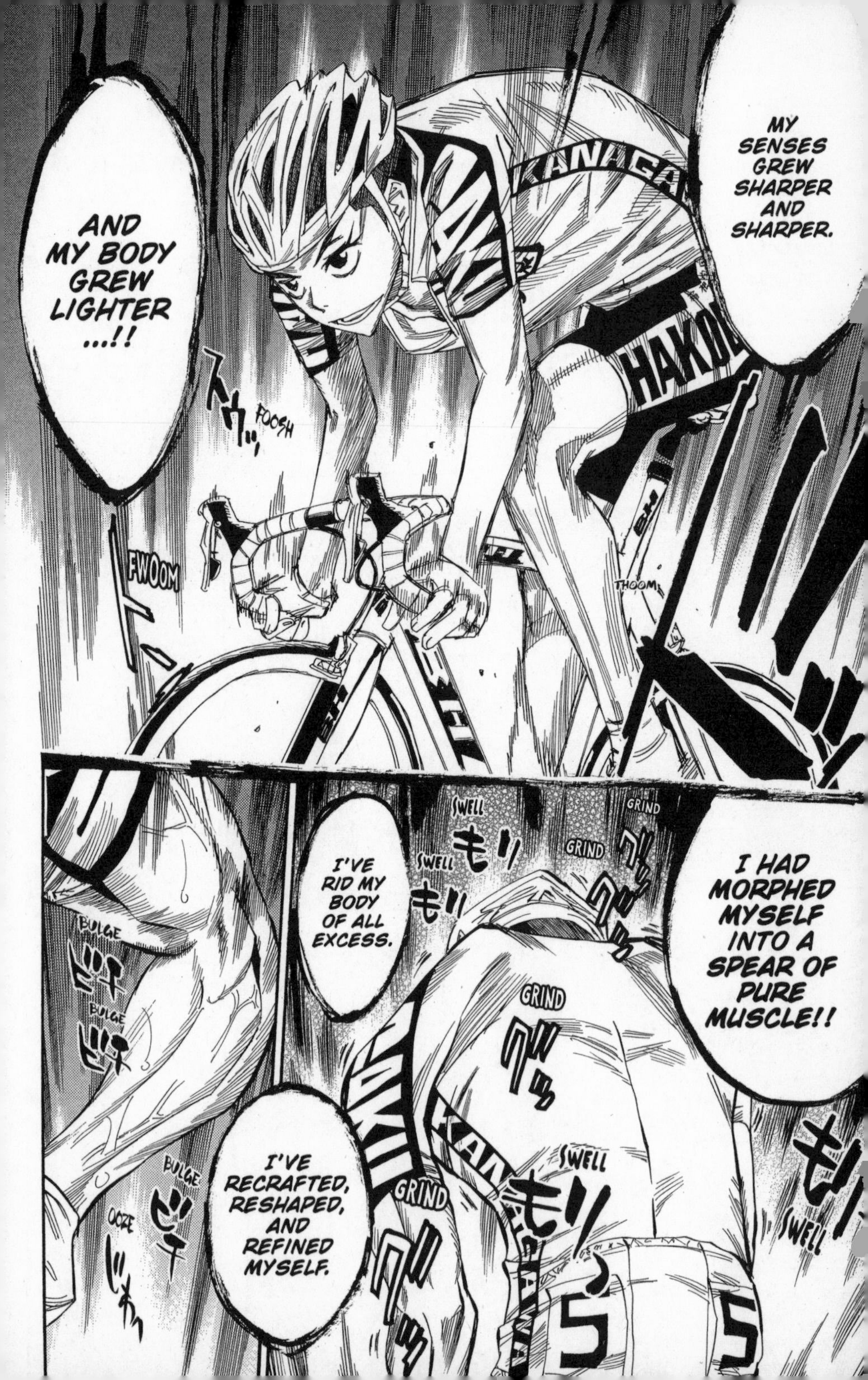
MY SENSES GREW SHARPER AND SHARPER.
AND MY BODY GREW LIGHTER...!!
THOOM
FOOSH
FWOOM
I HAD MORPHED MYSELF INTO A SPEAR OF PURE MUSCLE!!
GRIND
GRIND
SWELL
SWELL
I'VE RID MY BODY OF ALL EXCESS.
SWELL
GRIND
SWELL
GRIND
I'VE RECRAFTED, RESHAPED, AND REFINED MYSELF.
BULGE
BULGE
BULGE
OOZE

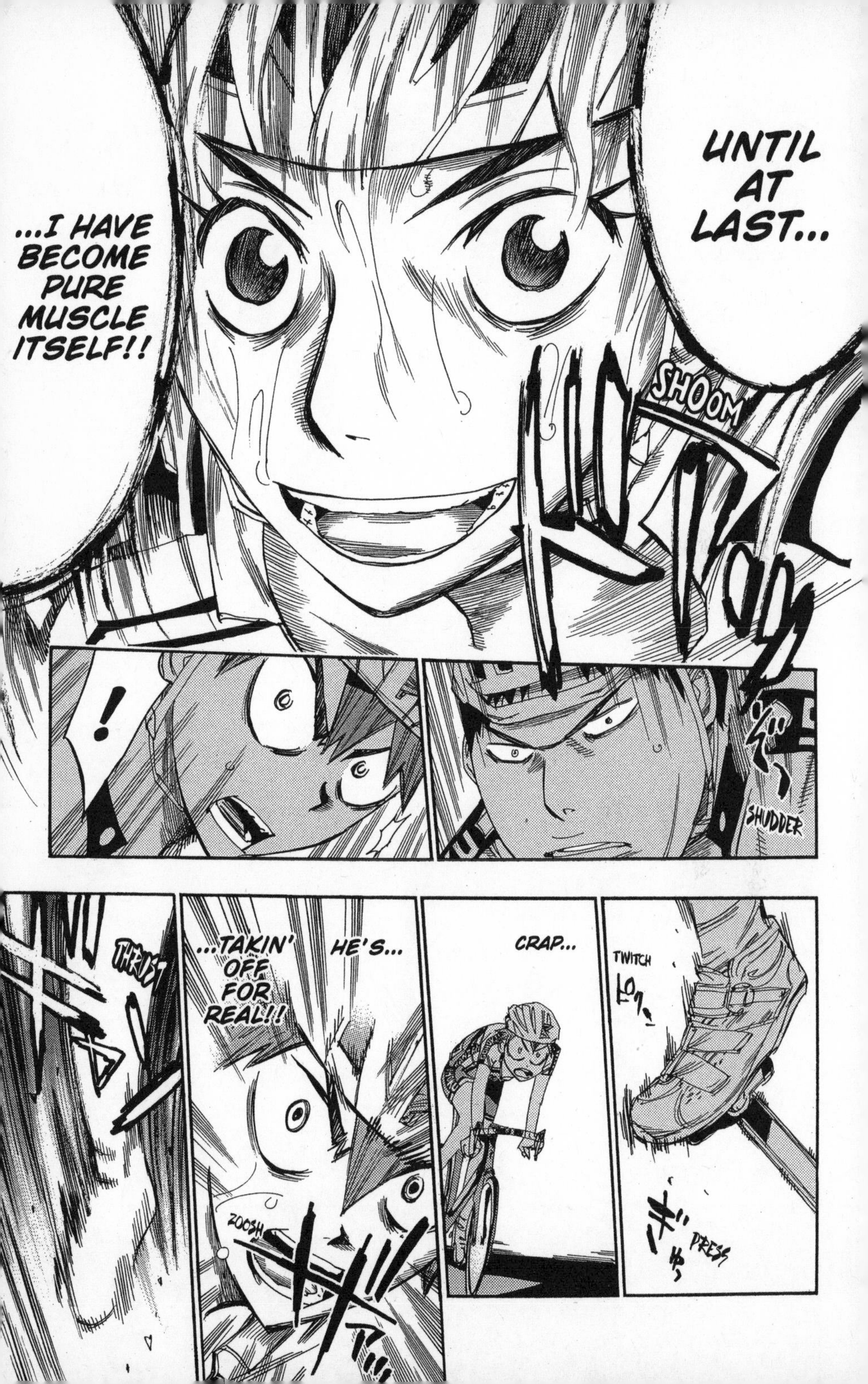
UNTIL AT LAST...
...I HAVE BECOME PURE MUSCLE ITSELF!!
SHOOM
SHUDDER
!
TWITCH
PRESS
CRAP...
HE'S...
...TAKIN' OFF FOR REAL!!
ZOOSH
THRUST

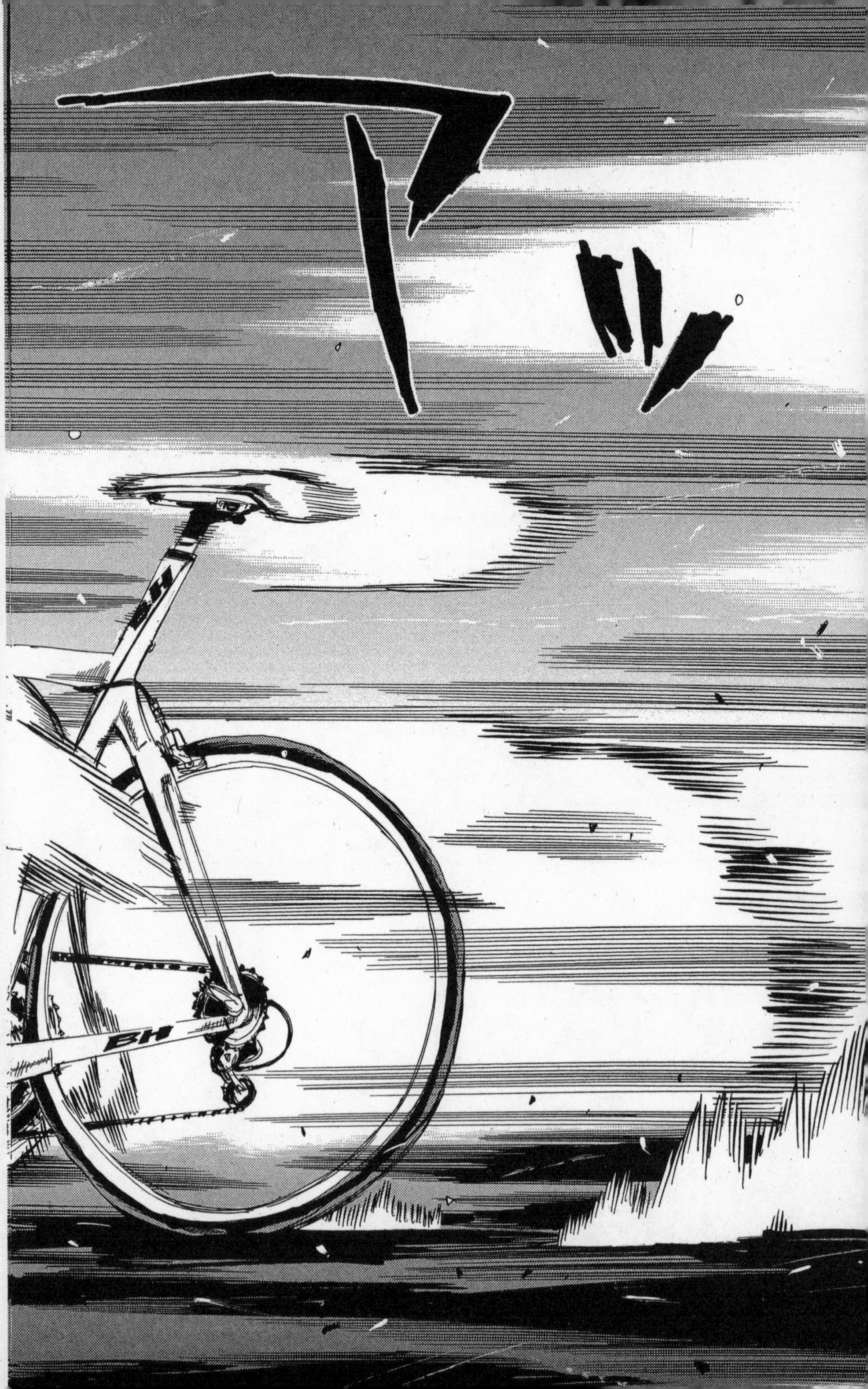
アッ

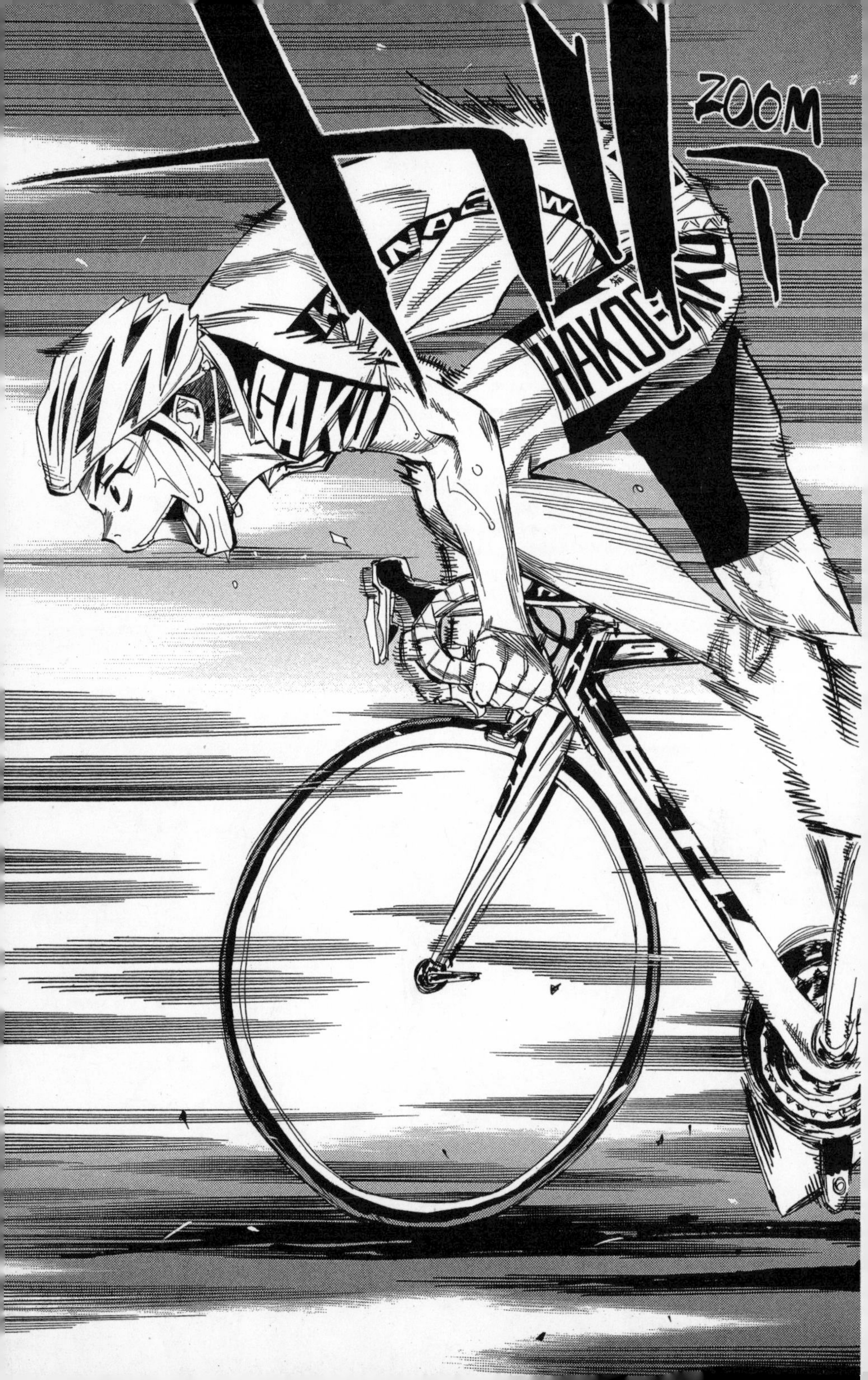
ZOOM

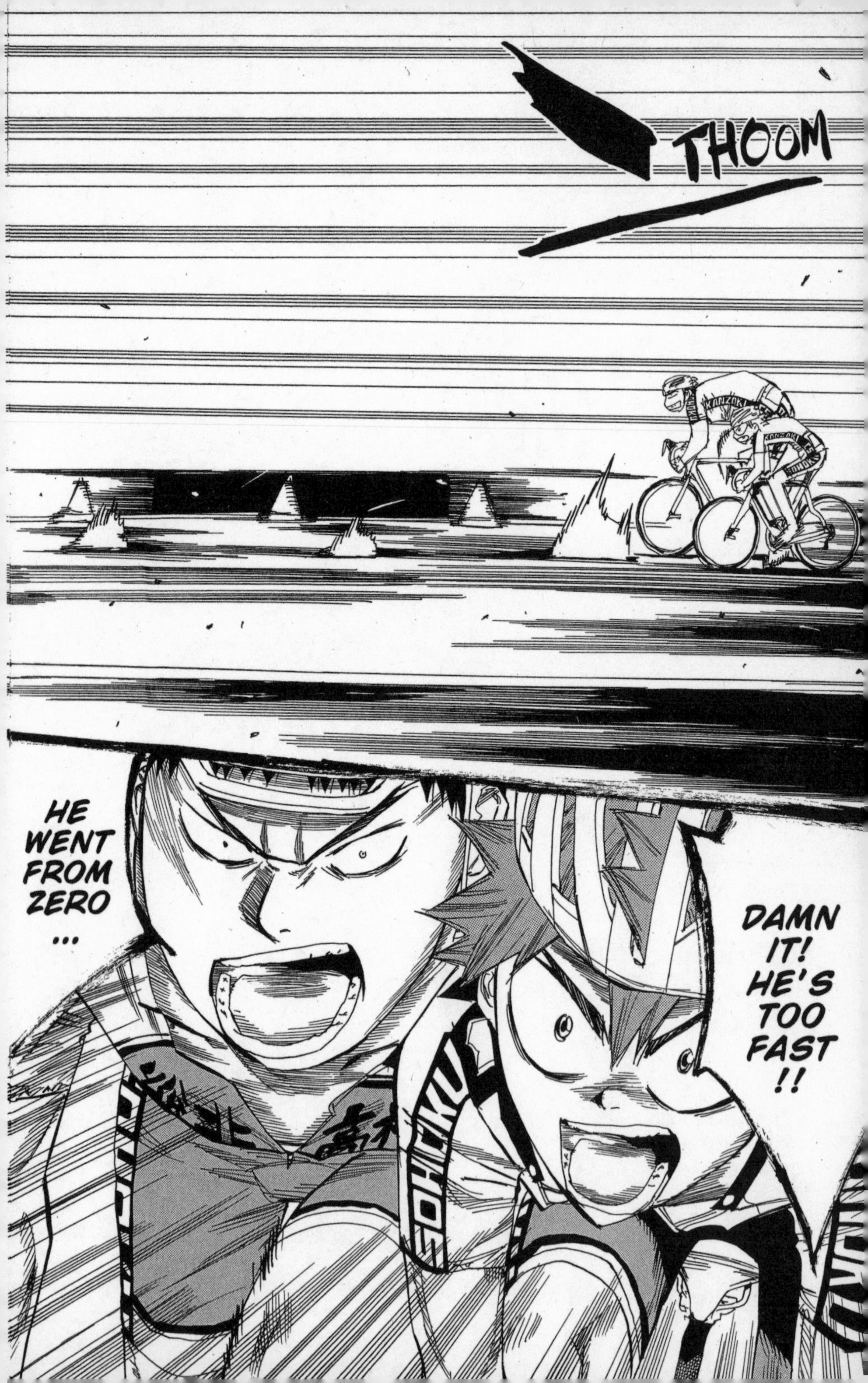
THOOM
DAMN IT! HE'S TOO FAST!!
HE WENT FROM ZERO...

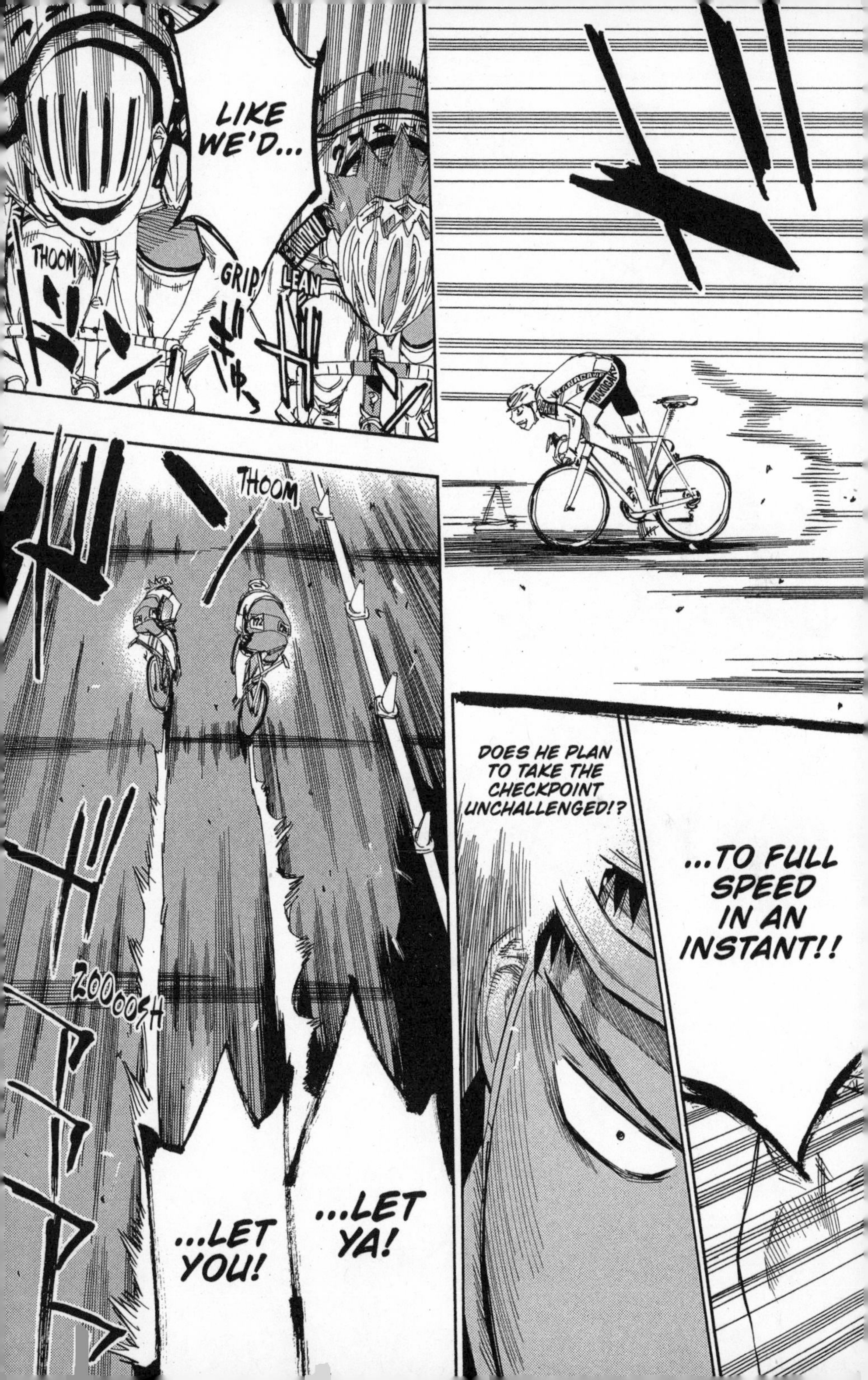
LIKE WE'D...
THOOM
LEAN
GRIP
THOOM
ZOOOOSH
...LET YA!
...LET YOU!
DOES HE PLAN TO TAKE THE CHECKPOINT UNCHALLENGED!?
...TO FULL SPEED IN AN INSTANT!!

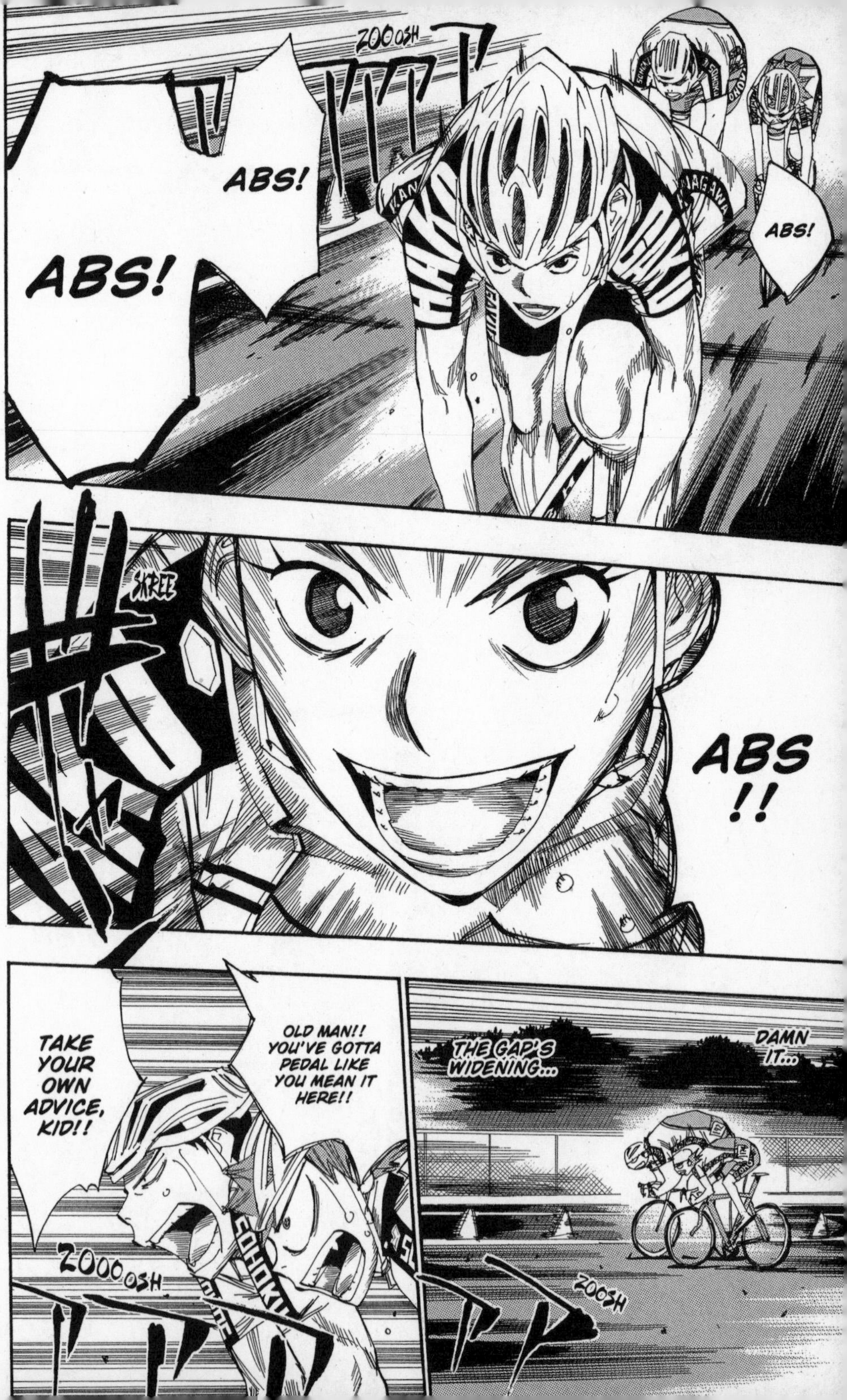
ZOOOSH
ABS!
ABS!
ABS!
ABS !!
SKREE
DAMN IT...
THE GAP'S WIDENING...
ZOOSH
OLD MAN!! YOU'VE GOTTA PEDAL LIKE YOU MEAN IT HERE!!
TAKE YOUR OWN ADVICE, KID!!
ZOOOOSH

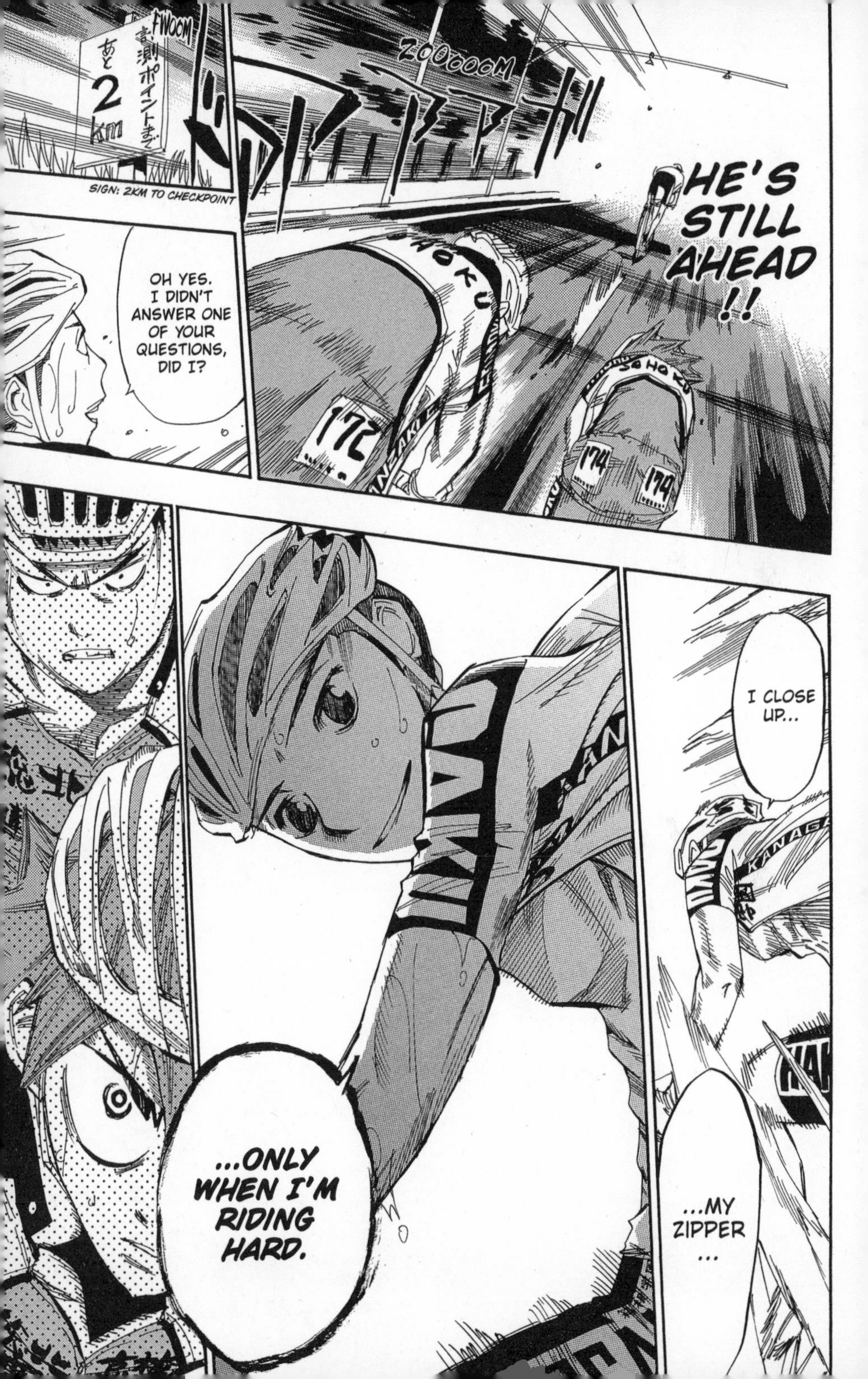
ZOOOOOM
HE'S STILL AHEAD!!
FWOOM
計測ポイントまで
あと 2 km
SIGN: 2KM TO CHECKPOINT
OH YES. I DIDN'T ANSWER ONE OF YOUR QUESTIONS, DID I?
I CLOSE UP...
...MY ZIPPER ...
...ONLY WHEN I'M RIDING HARD.

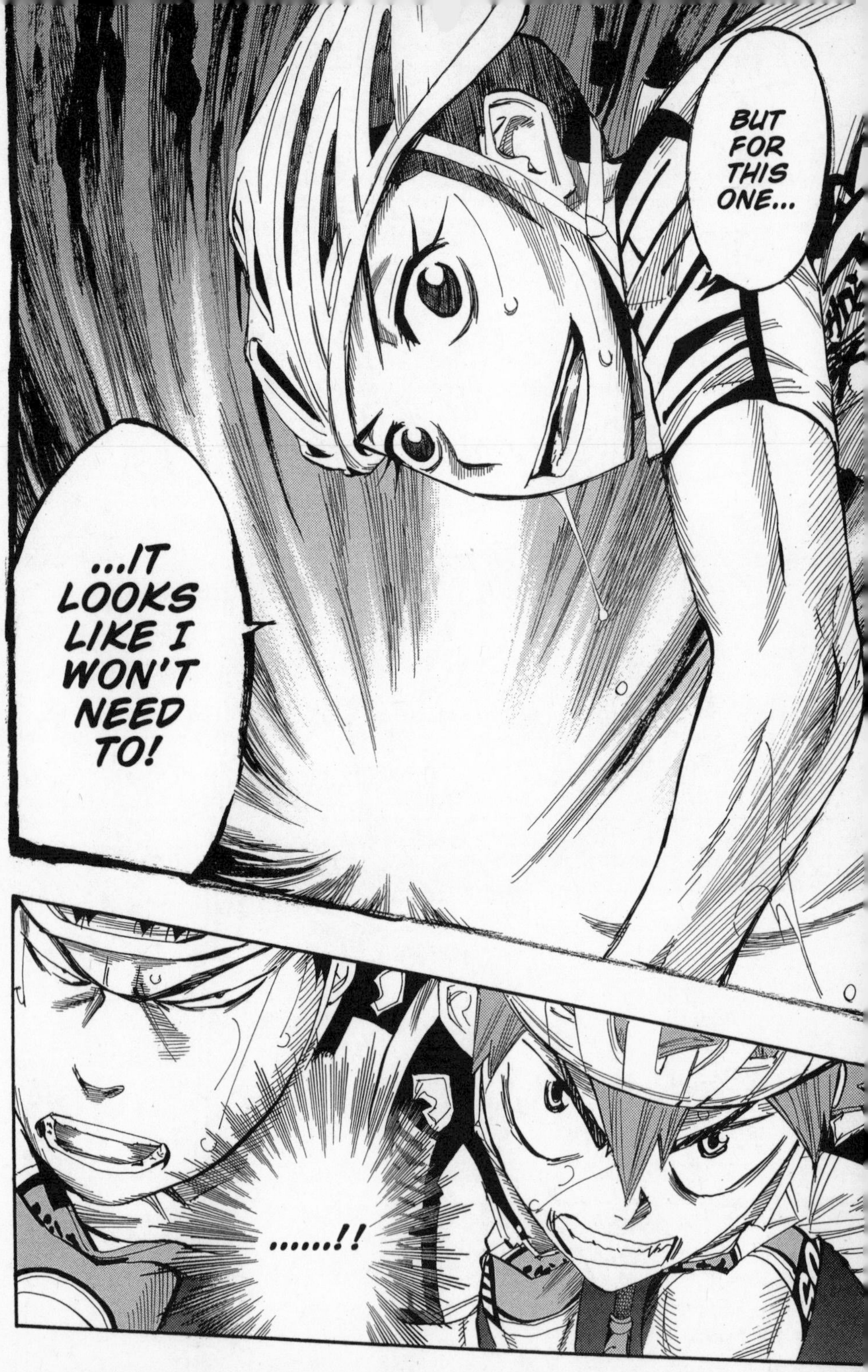
BUT FOR THIS ONE...
...IT LOOKS LIKE I WON'T NEED TO!
......!!

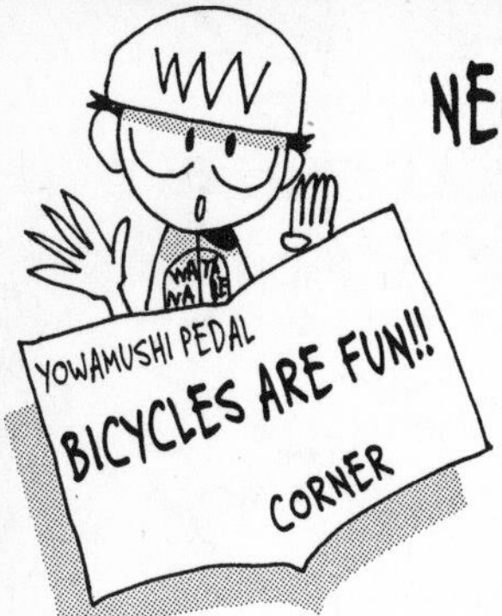
YOWAMUSHI PEDAL
BICYCLES ARE FUN!!
CORNER

NECESSITIES FOR RIDING A ROAD BIKE:

A CHAT ABOUT NECESSARY MUSCLES

JUST AS SOMEONE WHO DOESN'T EXERCISE REGULARLY CAN'T JUMP UP AND RUN A FULL MARATHON, TO RIDE A ROAD BIKE—WHICH IS, AFTER ALL, A TOOL ONE USES TO COMPETE IN THE SPORT OF ROAD RACING—ONE DOES NEED TO DO A LITTLE TRAINING.

YOU'VE DECIDED YOU'RE GOING TO BUY A ROAD BIKE AND ASK YOUR FRIEND TO LET YOU TRY THEIRS OUT, BUT...

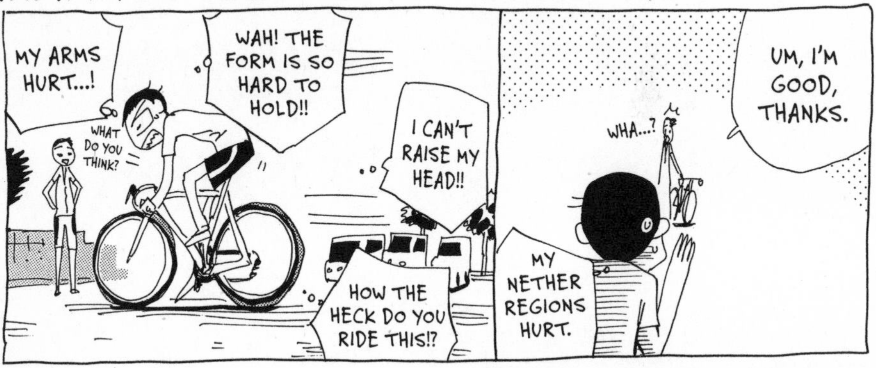
UM, I'M GOOD, THANKS.
WHA...?
MY NETHER REGIONS HURT.
I CAN'T RAISE MY HEAD!!
WAH! THE FORM IS SO HARD TO HOLD!!
MY ARMS HURT...!
WHAT DO YOU THINK?
HOW THE HECK DO YOU RIDE THIS!?

HAS THIS HAPPENED TO ANYONE...?

OR MAYBE, YOU'VE GONE AND BOUGHT IT ALREADY, BUT...

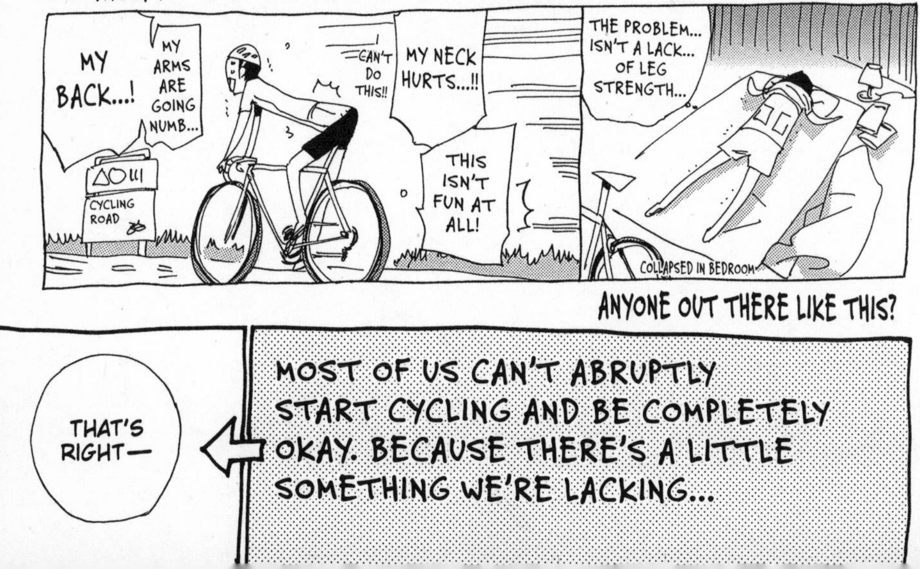
THE PROBLEM... ISN'T A LACK... OF LEG STRENGTH...
COLLAPSED IN BEDROOM
MY NECK HURTS...!!
THIS ISN'T FUN AT ALL!
CAN'T DO THIS!!
MY ARMS ARE GOING NUMB...
MY BACK...!
CYCLING ROAD

ANYONE OUT THERE LIKE THIS?

MOST OF US CAN'T ABRUPTLY START CYCLING AND BE COMPLETELY OKAY. BECAUSE THERE'S A LITTLE SOMETHING WE'RE LACKING...

THAT'S RIGHT—

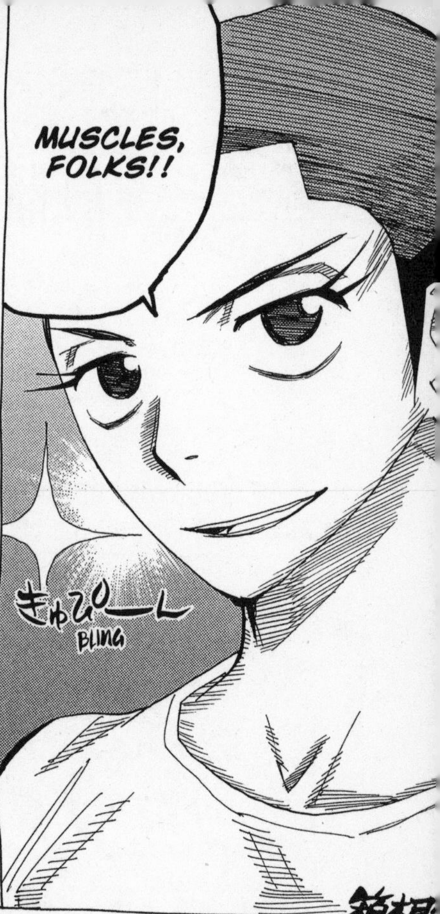
MUSCLES, FOLKS!!
きゅぴーーん
BLING
SHIRT: HAKONE ACADEMY

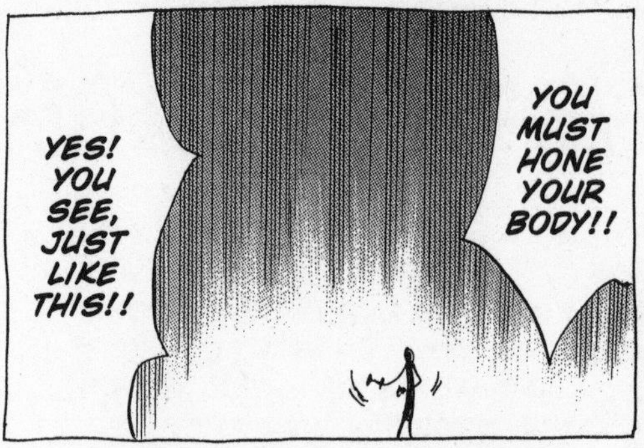
YOU MUST HONE YOUR BODY!!
YES! YOU SEE, JUST LIKE THIS!!

HIS CASE IS A BIT EXCESSIVE...

TO RIDE A ROAD BIKE, YOU WILL NEED TO USE MUSCLES YOU LIKELY DON'T USE MUCH NORMALLY.

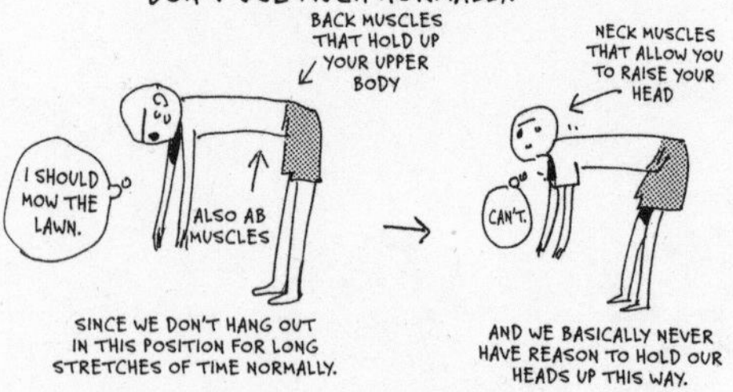
BACK MUSCLES THAT HOLD UP YOUR UPPER BODY
I SHOULD MOW THE LAWN.
ALSO AB MUSCLES
SINCE WE DON'T HANG OUT IN THIS POSITION FOR LONG STRETCHES OF TIME NORMALLY.
NECK MUSCLES THAT ALLOW YOU TO RAISE YOUR HEAD
CAN'T.
AND WE BASICALLY NEVER HAVE REASON TO HOLD OUR HEADS UP THIS WAY.

BUT THERE'S NO SPECIAL EXERCISE YOU NEED TO DO IN ORDER TO RIDE A ROAD BIKE.

JUST RIDE YOUR BIKE LITTLE BY LITTLE EVERY DAY AND YOU WILL NATURALLY BUILD UP THESE MUSCLES.

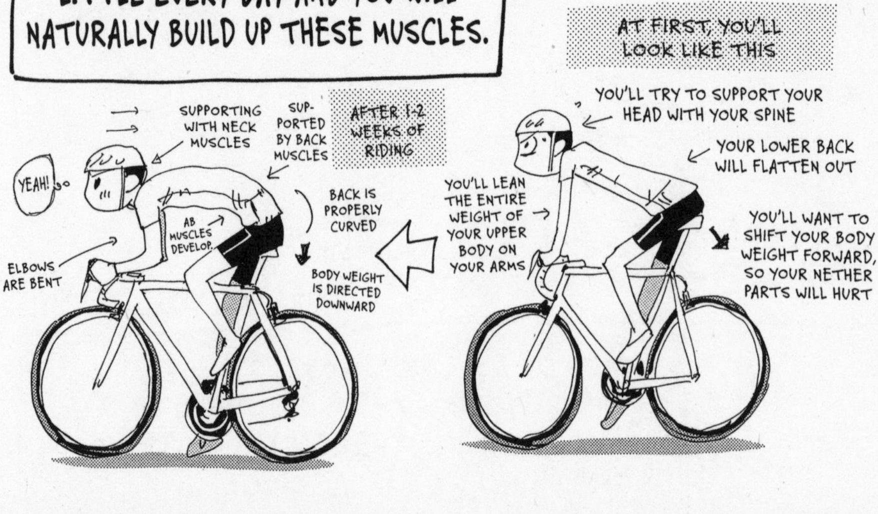
AT FIRST, YOU'LL LOOK LIKE THIS
YOU'LL TRY TO SUPPORT YOUR HEAD WITH YOUR SPINE
YOUR LOWER BACK WILL FLATTEN OUT
YOU'LL LEAN THE ENTIRE WEIGHT OF YOUR UPPER BODY ON YOUR ARMS
YOU'LL WANT TO SHIFT YOUR BODY WEIGHT FORWARD, SO YOUR NETHER PARTS WILL HURT
AFTER 1-2 WEEKS OF RIDING
SUPPORTING WITH NECK MUSCLES
SUP-PORTED BY BACK MUSCLES
YEAH!
AB MUSCLES DEVELOP.
ELBOWS ARE BENT
BACK IS PROPERLY CURVED
BODY WEIGHT IS DIRECTED DOWNWARD

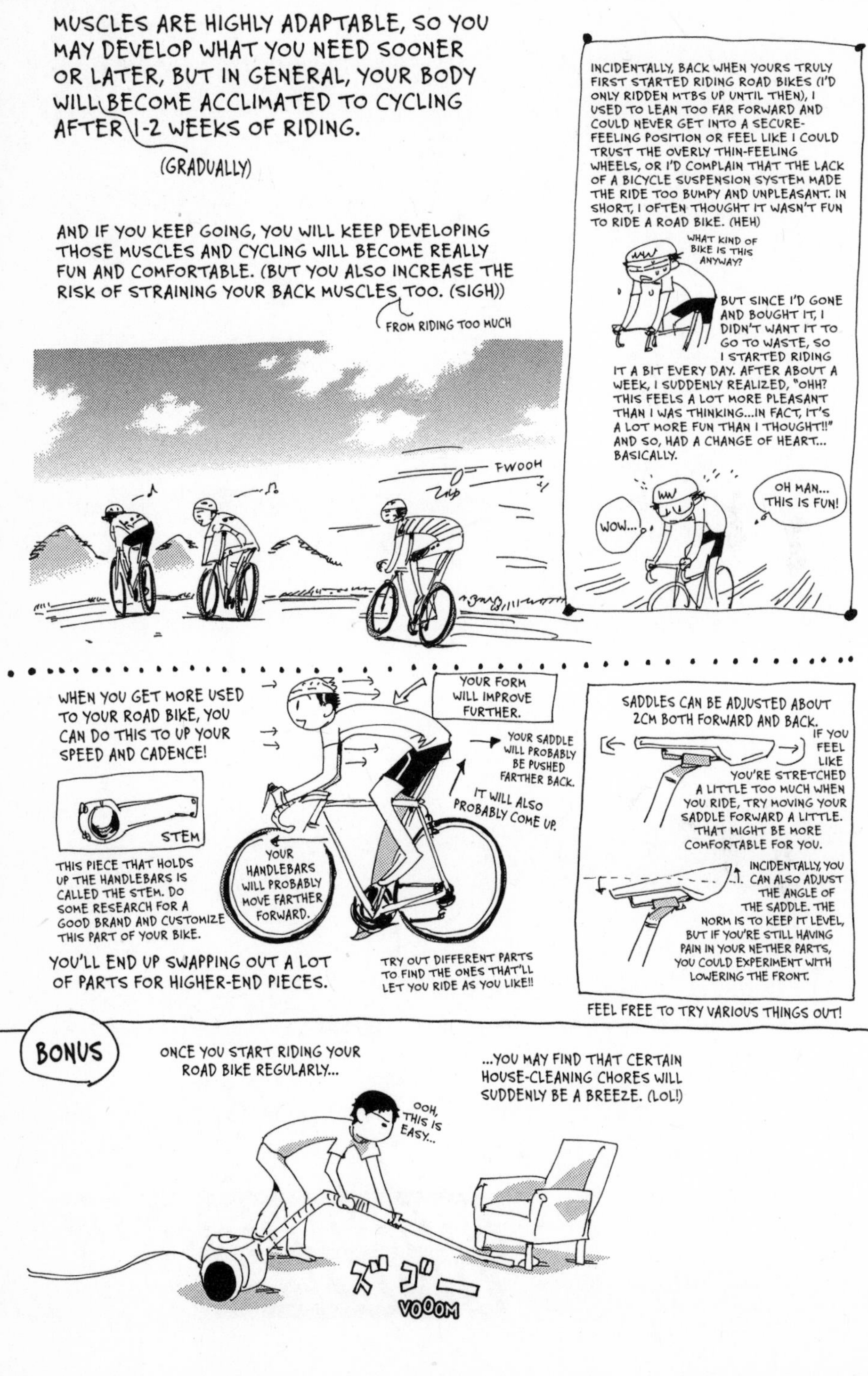
INCIDENTALLY, BACK WHEN YOURS TRULY FIRST STARTED RIDING ROAD BIKES (I'D ONLY RIDDEN MTBS UP UNTIL THEN), I USED TO LEAN TOO FAR FORWARD AND COULD NEVER GET INTO A SECURE-FEELING POSITION OR FEEL LIKE I COULD TRUST THE OVERLY THIN-FEELING WHEELS, OR I'D COMPLAIN THAT THE LACK OF A BICYCLE SUSPENSION SYSTEM MADE THE RIDE TOO BUMPY AND UNPLEASANT. IN SHORT, I OFTEN THOUGHT IT WASN'T FUN TO RIDE A ROAD BIKE. (HEH)
WHAT KIND OF BIKE IS THIS ANYWAY?
BUT SINCE I'D GONE AND BOUGHT IT, I DIDN'T WANT IT TO GO TO WASTE, SO I STARTED RIDING IT A BIT EVERY DAY. AFTER ABOUT A WEEK, I SUDDENLY REALIZED, "OHH? THIS FEELS A LOT MORE PLEASANT THAN I WAS THINKING...IN FACT, IT'S A LOT MORE FUN THAN I THOUGHT!!" AND SO, HAD A CHANGE OF HEART... BASICALLY.
OH MAN... THIS IS FUN!
WOW...
MUSCLES ARE HIGHLY ADAPTABLE, SO YOU MAY DEVELOP WHAT YOU NEED SOONER OR LATER, BUT IN GENERAL, YOUR BODY WILL BECOME ACCLIMATED TO CYCLING AFTER 1-2 WEEKS OF RIDING.
(GRADUALLY)
AND IF YOU KEEP GOING, YOU WILL KEEP DEVELOPING THOSE MUSCLES AND CYCLING WILL BECOME REALLY FUN AND COMFORTABLE. (BUT YOU ALSO INCREASE THE RISK OF STRAINING YOUR BACK MUSCLES TOO. (SIGH))
FROM RIDING TOO MUCH
FWOOH
SADDLES CAN BE ADJUSTED ABOUT 2CM BOTH FORWARD AND BACK.
IF YOU FEEL LIKE YOU'RE STRETCHED A LITTLE TOO MUCH WHEN YOU RIDE, TRY MOVING YOUR SADDLE FORWARD A LITTLE. THAT MIGHT BE MORE COMFORTABLE FOR YOU.
INCIDENTALLY, YOU CAN ALSO ADJUST THE ANGLE OF THE SADDLE. THE NORM IS TO KEEP IT LEVEL, BUT IF YOU'RE STILL HAVING PAIN IN YOUR NETHER PARTS, YOU COULD EXPERIMENT WITH LOWERING THE FRONT.
FEEL FREE TO TRY VARIOUS THINGS OUT!
YOUR FORM WILL IMPROVE FURTHER.
YOUR SADDLE WILL PROBABLY BE PUSHED FARTHER BACK.
IT WILL ALSO PROBABLY COME UP.
WHEN YOU GET MORE USED TO YOUR ROAD BIKE, YOU CAN DO THIS TO UP YOUR SPEED AND CADENCE!
STEM
YOUR HANDLEBARS WILL PROBABLY MOVE FARTHER FORWARD.
THIS PIECE THAT HOLDS UP THE HANDLEBARS IS CALLED THE STEM. DO SOME RESEARCH FOR A GOOD BRAND AND CUSTOMIZE THIS PART OF YOUR BIKE.
TRY OUT DIFFERENT PARTS TO FIND THE ONES THAT'LL LET YOU RIDE AS YOU LIKE!!
YOU'LL END UP SWAPPING OUT A LOT OF PARTS FOR HIGHER-END PIECES.
BONUS
ONCE YOU START RIDING YOUR ROAD BIKE REGULARLY...
...YOU MAY FIND THAT CERTAIN HOUSE-CLEANING CHORES WILL SUDDENLY BE A BREEZE. (LOL!)
OOH, THIS IS EASY...
ズゴー
VOOOM

YOWAMUSHI PEDAL

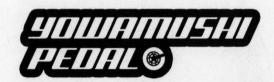

RIDE.79 ATONEMENT

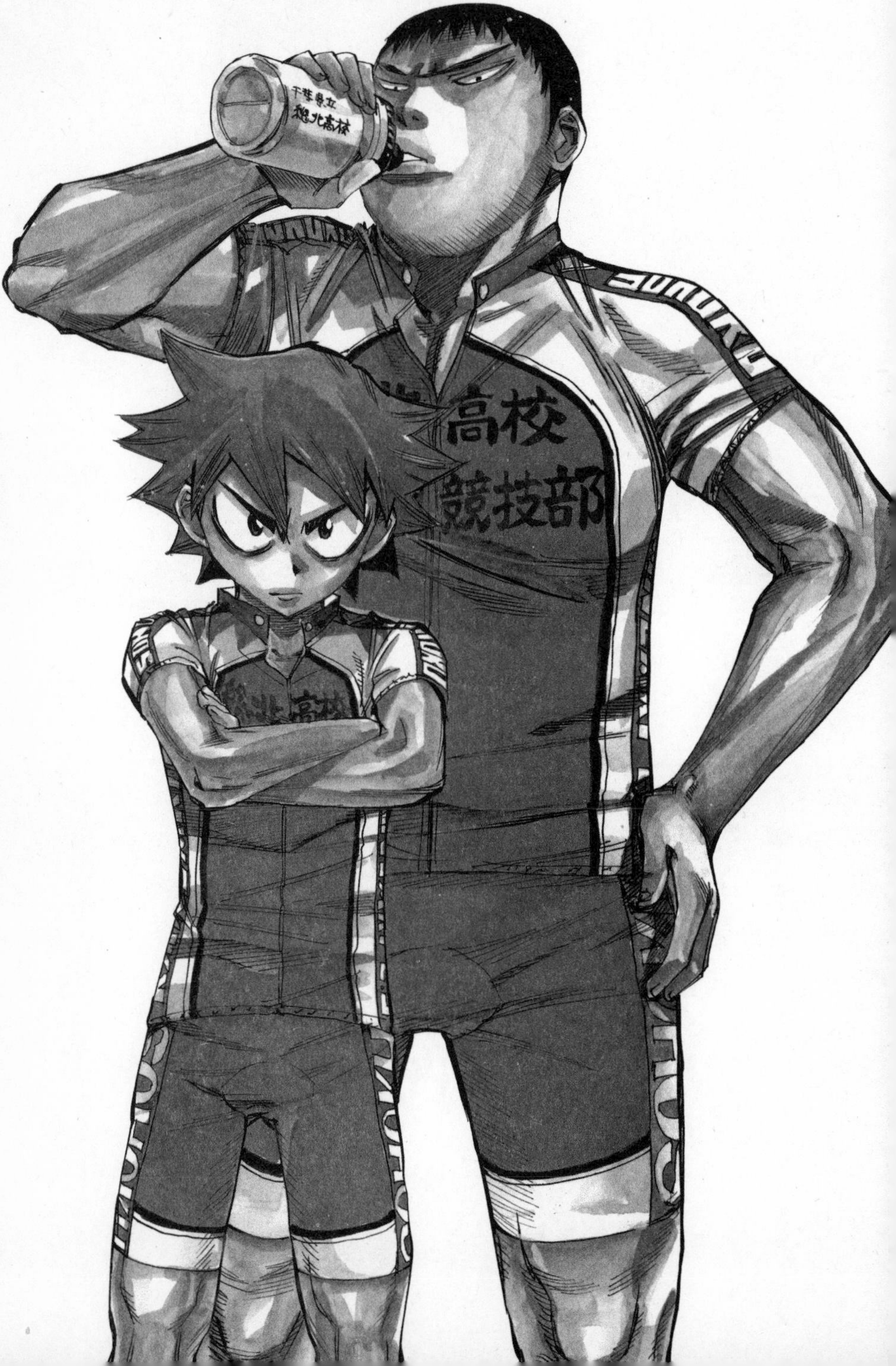
千葉県立
総北高校
高校
競技部

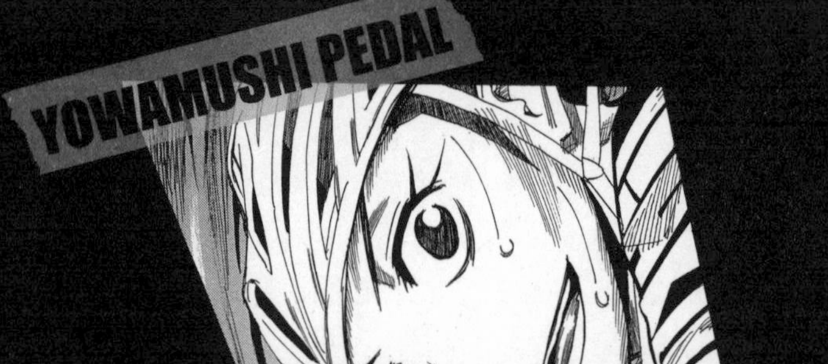
YOWAMUSHI PEDAL
IZUMIDA

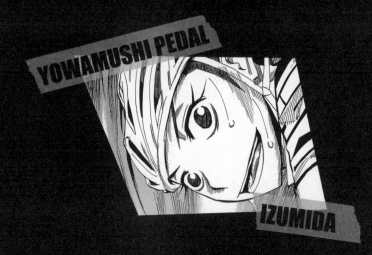

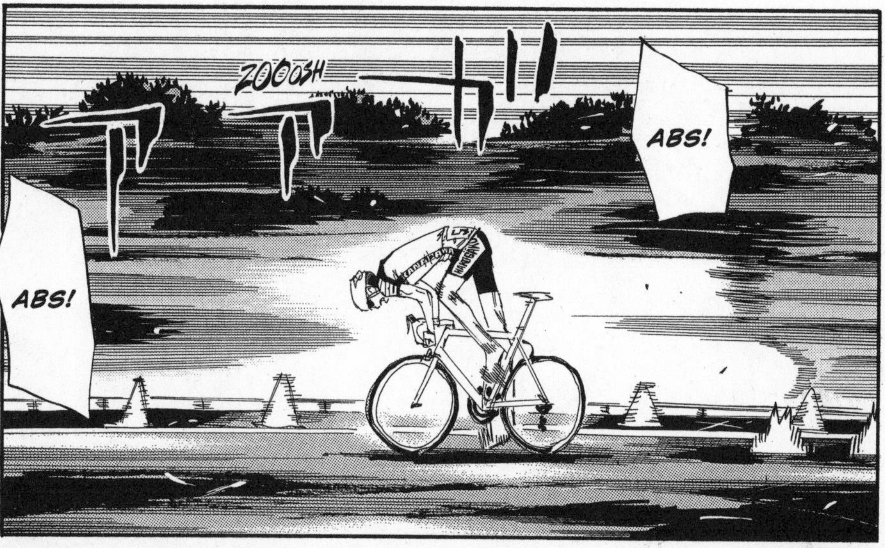
ABS!
ZOOOSH
ABS!

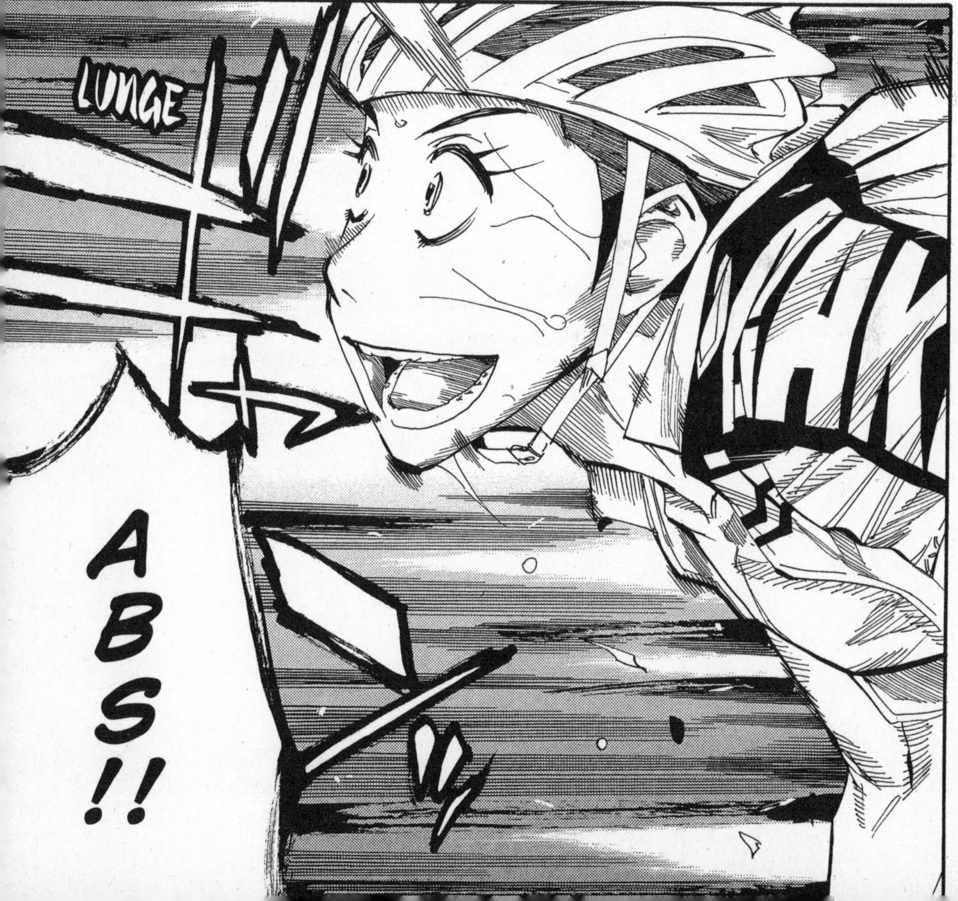
LUNGE
ABS!!

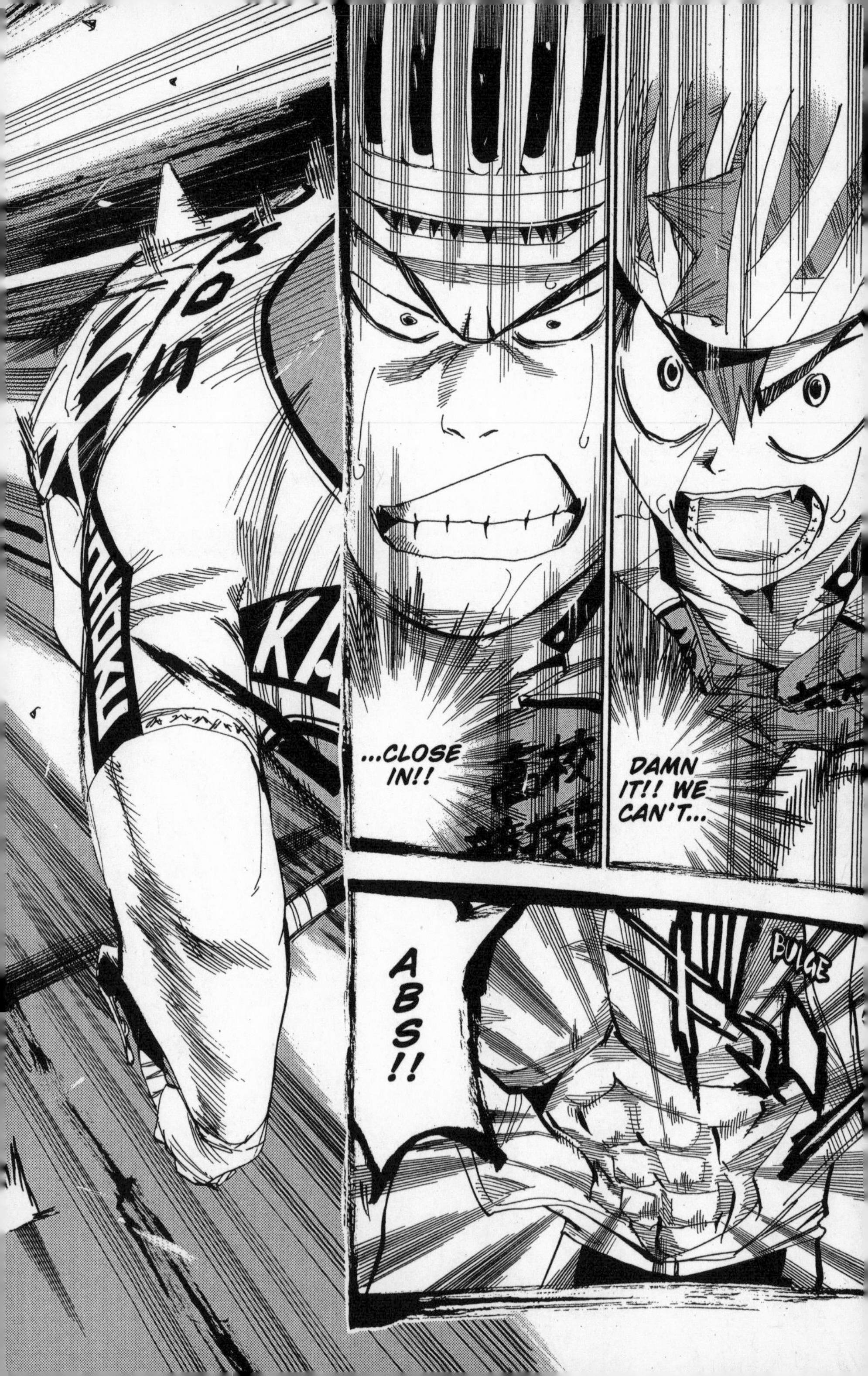
DAMN IT!! WE CAN'T...
...CLOSE IN!!
BULGE
ABS!!

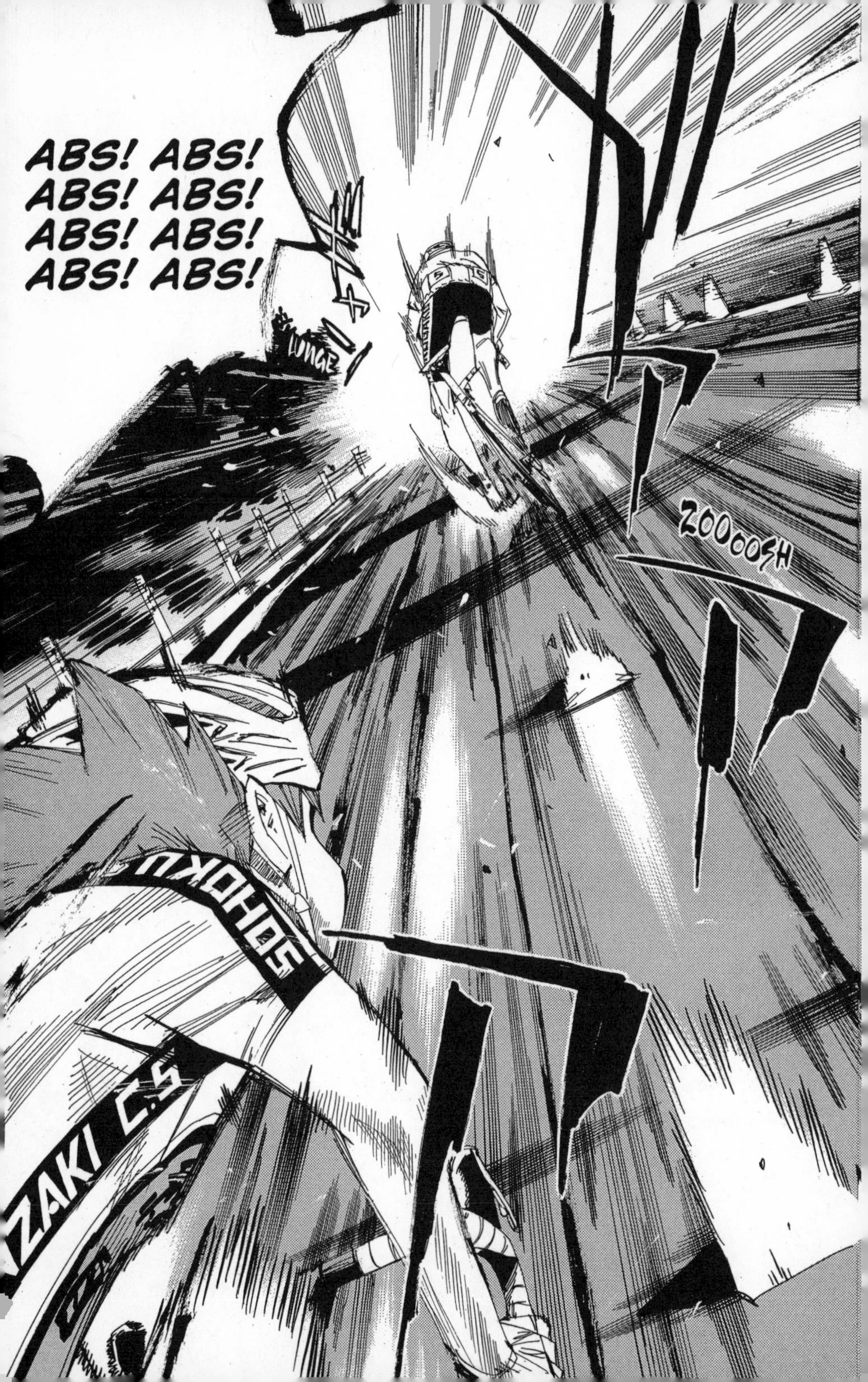
ABS! ABS!
ABS! ABS!
ABS! ABS!
ABS! ABS!
LUNGE
ZOOOOSH
SOHOKU
ZAKI C.S

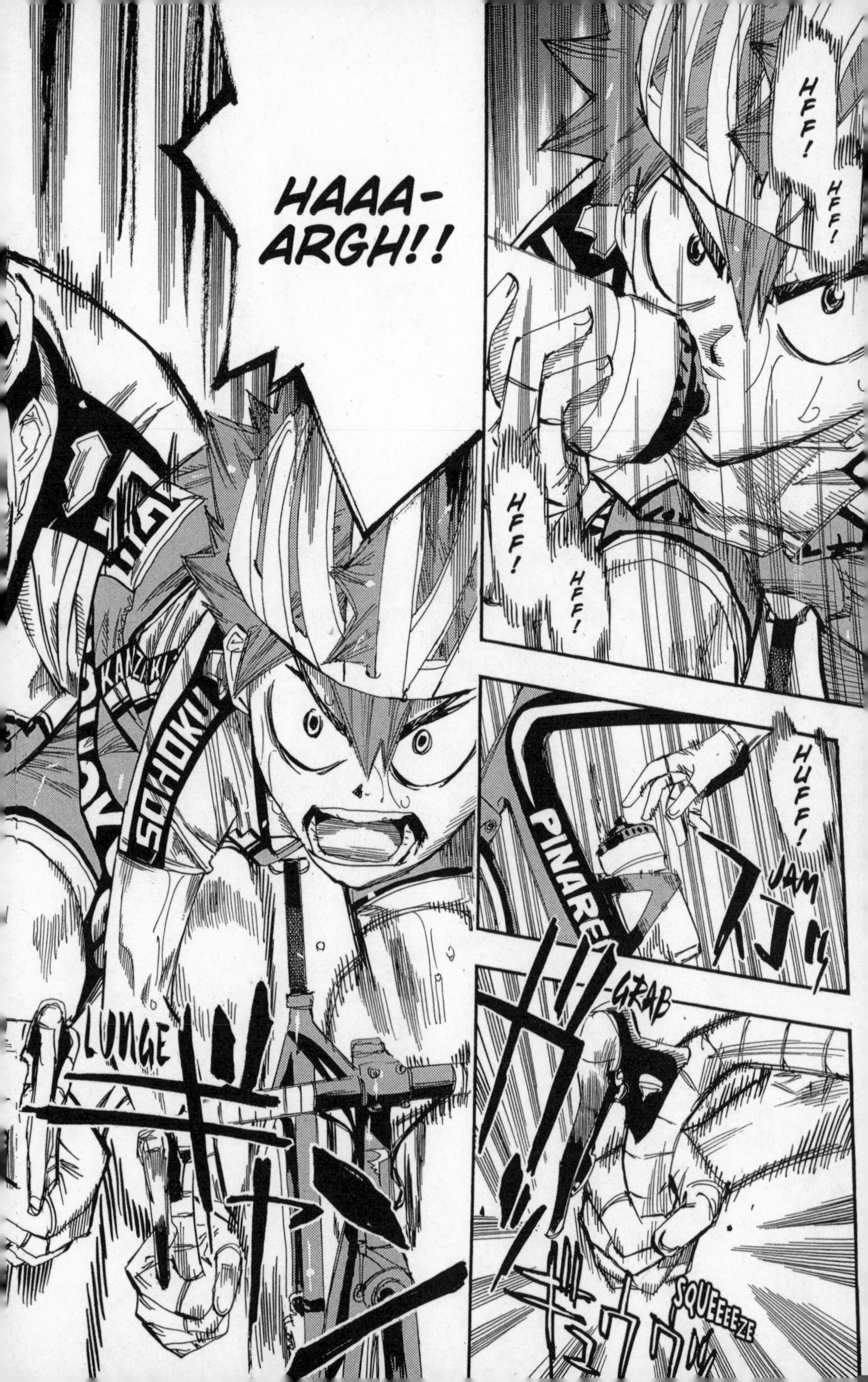
HFF!
HFF!
HFF!
HFF!
HUFF!
JAM
GRAB
SQUEEEEZE
HAAA-
ARGH!!
LUNGE

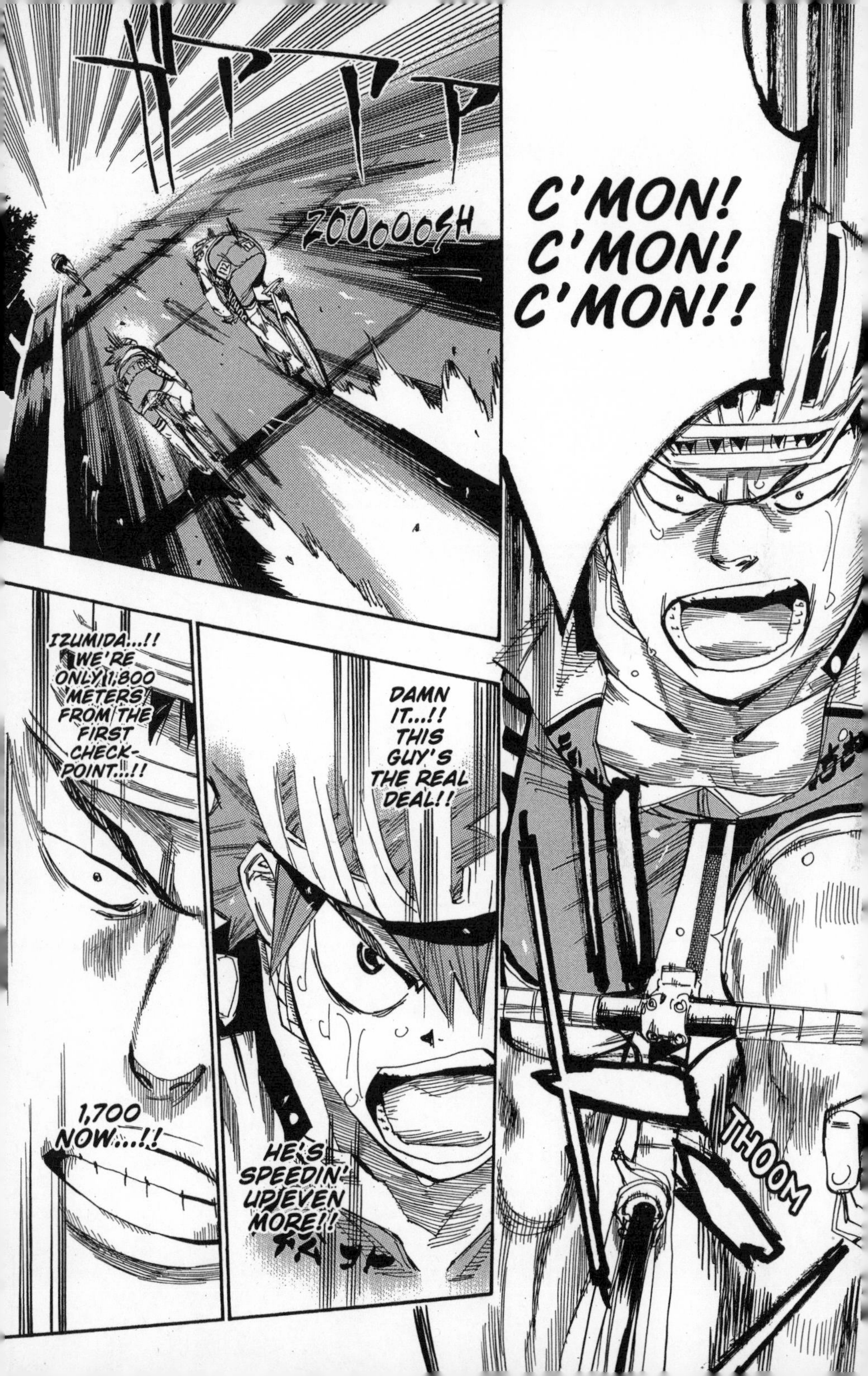
C'MON! C'MON! C'MON!!
THOOM
ZOOOOOSH
DAMN IT...!! THIS GUY'S THE REAL DEAL!!
HE'S SPEEDIN' UP EVEN MORE!!
IZUMIDA...!! WE'RE ONLY 1,800 METERS FROM THE FIRST CHECK-POINT...!!
1,700 NOW...!!

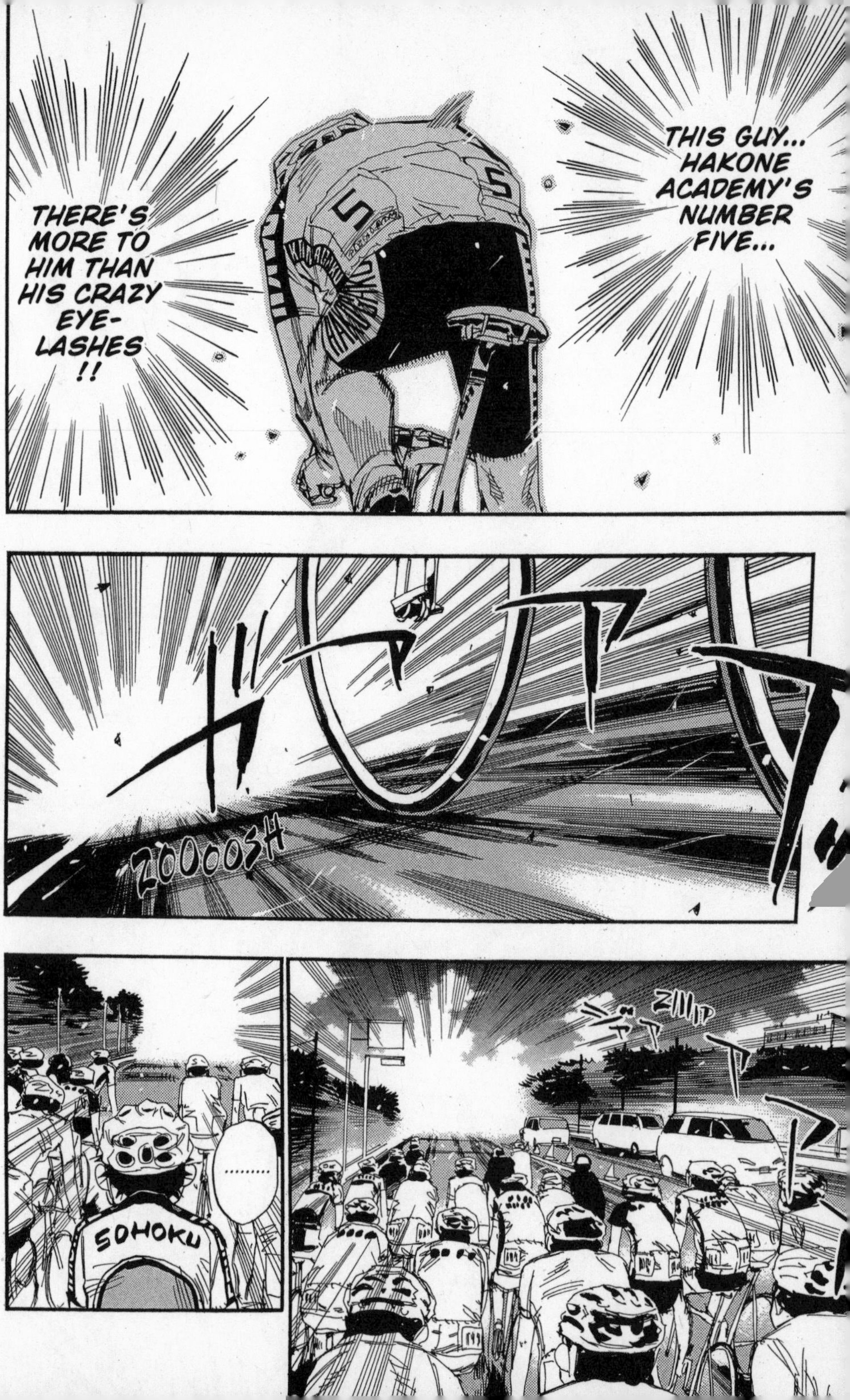
THIS GUY... HAKONE ACADEMY'S NUMBER FIVE...
THERE'S MORE TO HIM THAN HIS CRAZY EYE-LASHES !!
ZOOOOSH
ZIIIIP
....

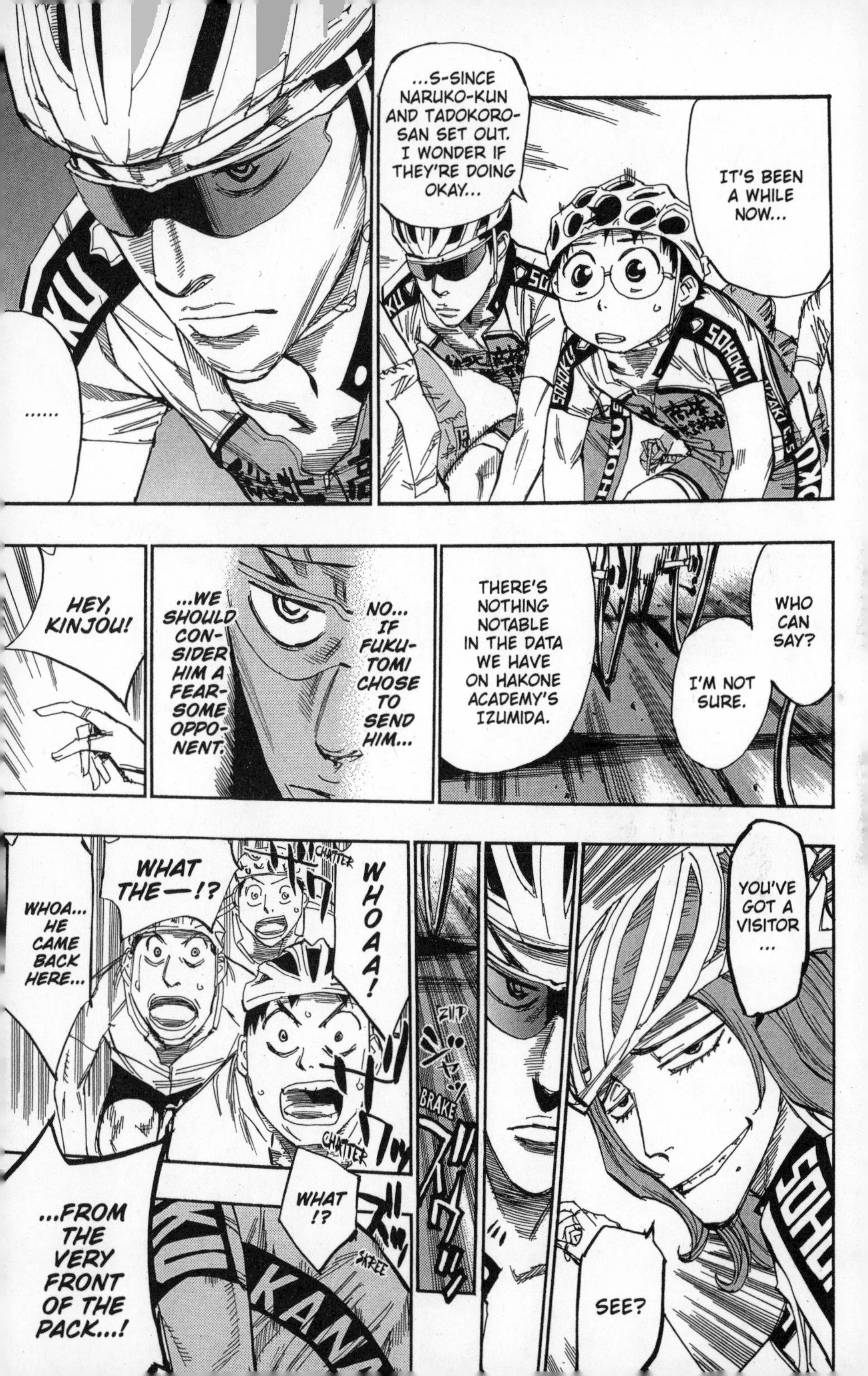
IT'S BEEN A WHILE NOW...
...S-SINCE NARUKO-KUN AND TADOKORO-SAN SET OUT. I WONDER IF THEY'RE DOING OKAY...
......
WHO CAN SAY?
I'M NOT SURE.
THERE'S NOTHING NOTABLE IN THE DATA WE HAVE ON HAKONE ACADEMY'S IZUMIDA.
NO... IF FUKUTOMI CHOSE TO SEND HIM...
...WE SHOULD CONSIDER HIM A FEARSOME OPPONENT.
HEY, KINJOU!
YOU'VE GOT A VISITOR...
ZIIP
BRAKE
SEE?
WHOAA!
CHATTER
WHAT THE—!?
WHOA... HE CAME BACK HERE...
CHATTER
WHAT!?
SKREE
...FROM THE VERY FRONT OF THE PACK...!

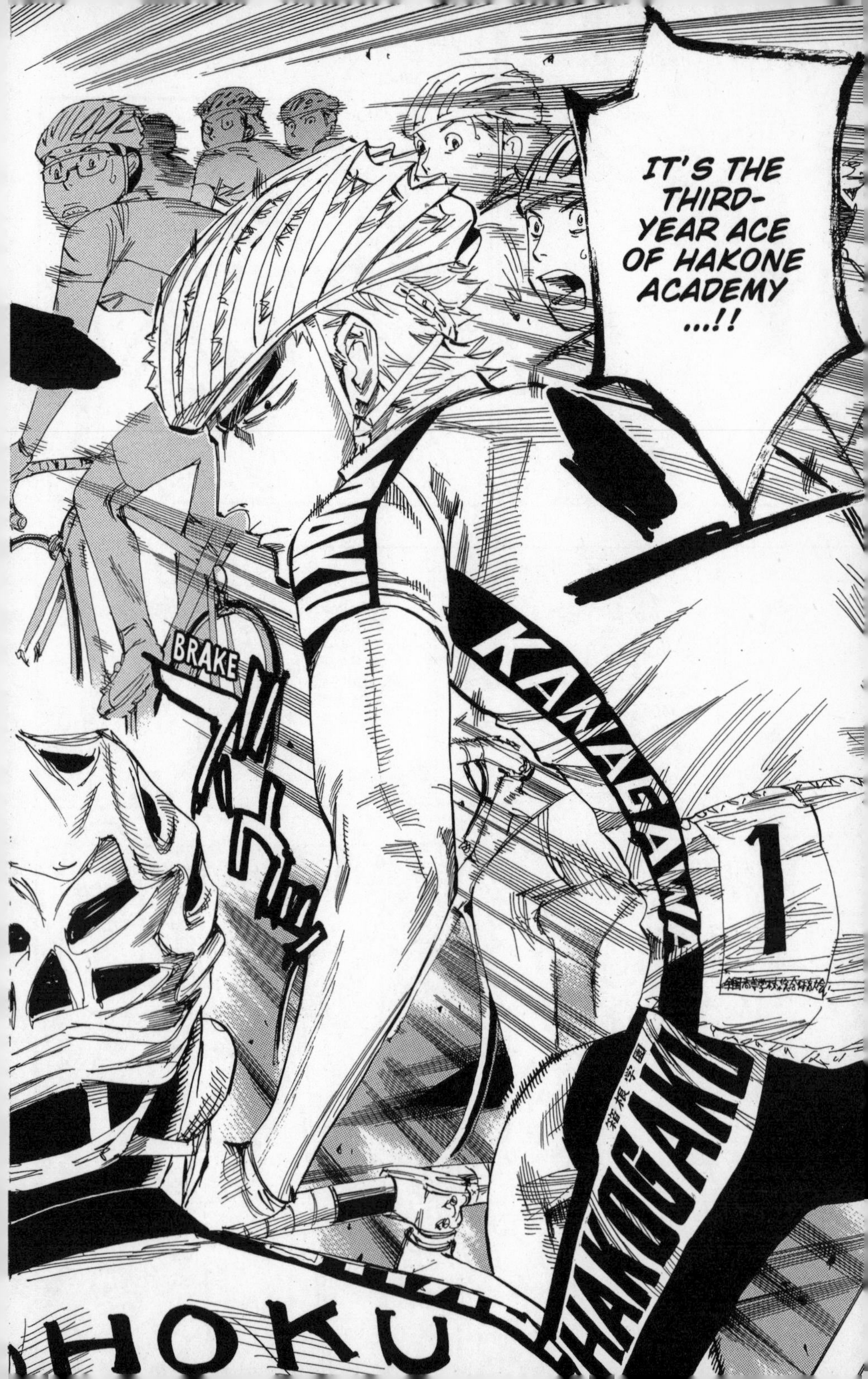
IT'S THE THIRD-YEAR ACE OF HAKONE ACADEMY ...!!
BRAKE
KANAGAWA
1
HAKOGAKU
箱根学園
HOKU

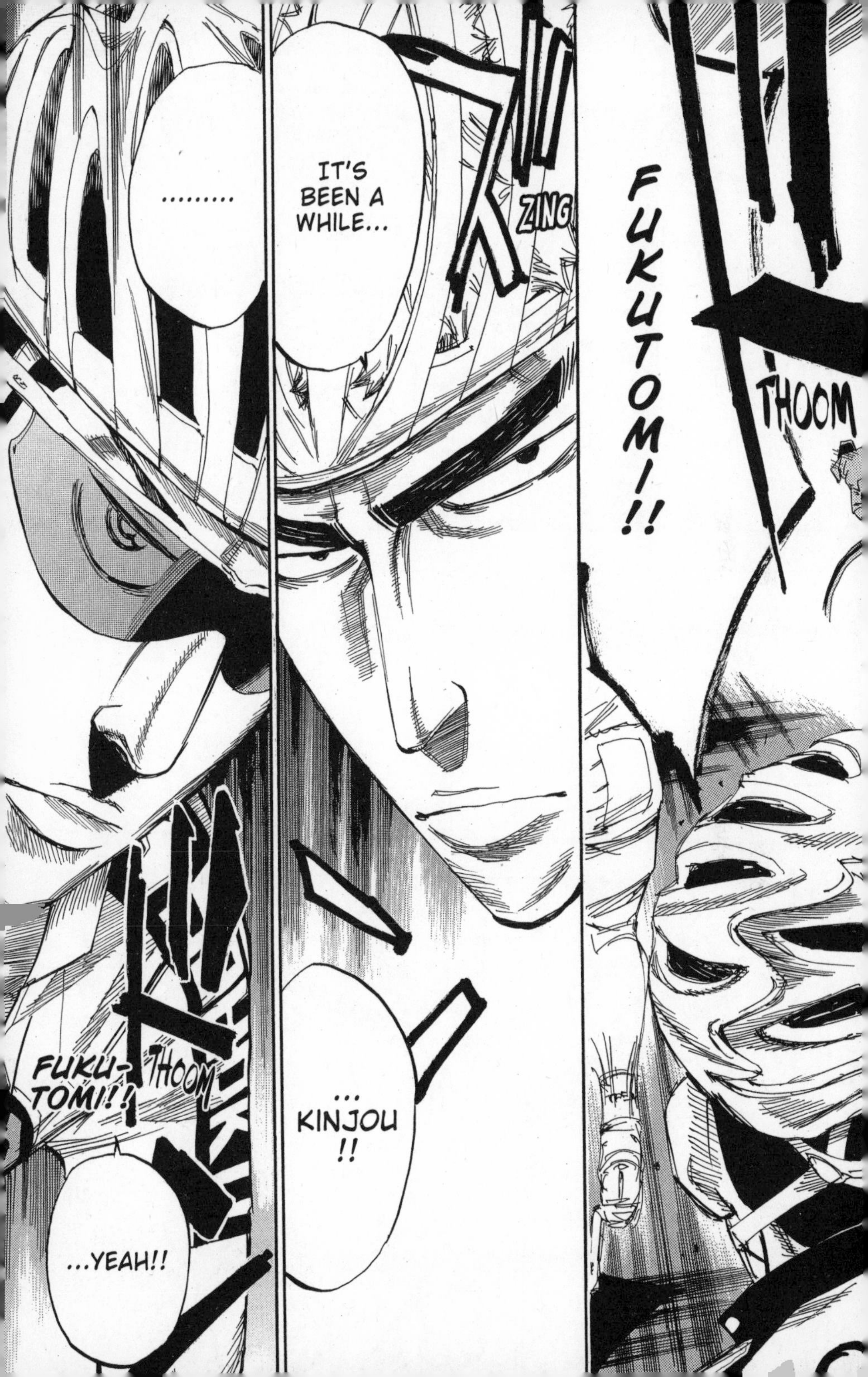
FUKUTOMI!!
THOOM
ZING
IT'S BEEN A WHILE...
...KINJOU!!
....
THOOM
FUKU-TOMI!!
...YEAH!!

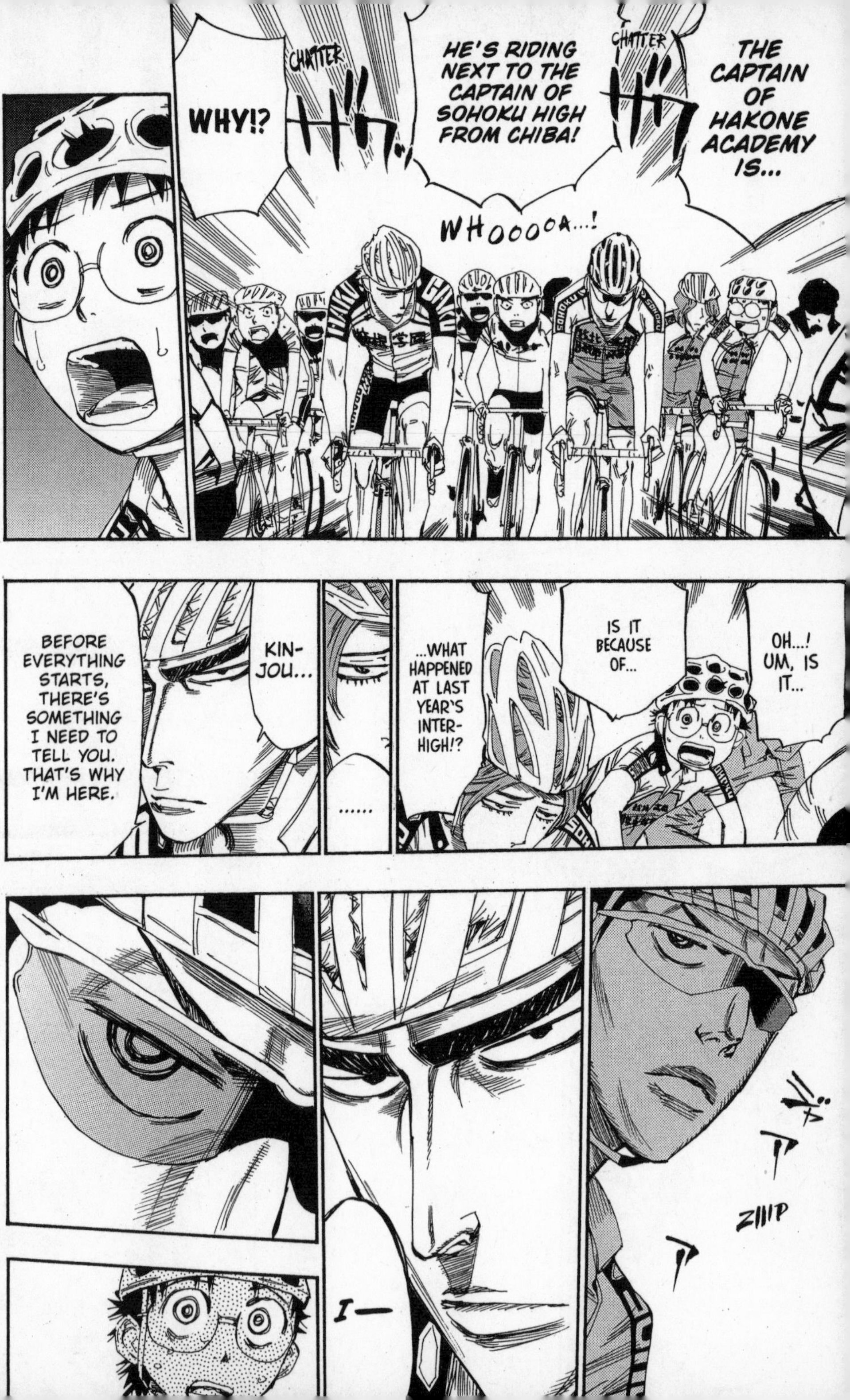
THE CAPTAIN OF HAKONE ACADEMY IS...
CHATTER
HE'S RIDING NEXT TO THE CAPTAIN OF SOHOKU HIGH FROM CHIBA!
CHATTER
WHY!?
WHOOOOA...!
OH...! UM, IS IT...
IS IT BECAUSE OF...
...WHAT HAPPENED AT LAST YEAR'S INTER-HIGH!?
KIN-JOU...
......
BEFORE EVERYTHING STARTS, THERE'S SOMETHING I NEED TO TELL YOU. THAT'S WHY I'M HERE.
ZIIIP
I—

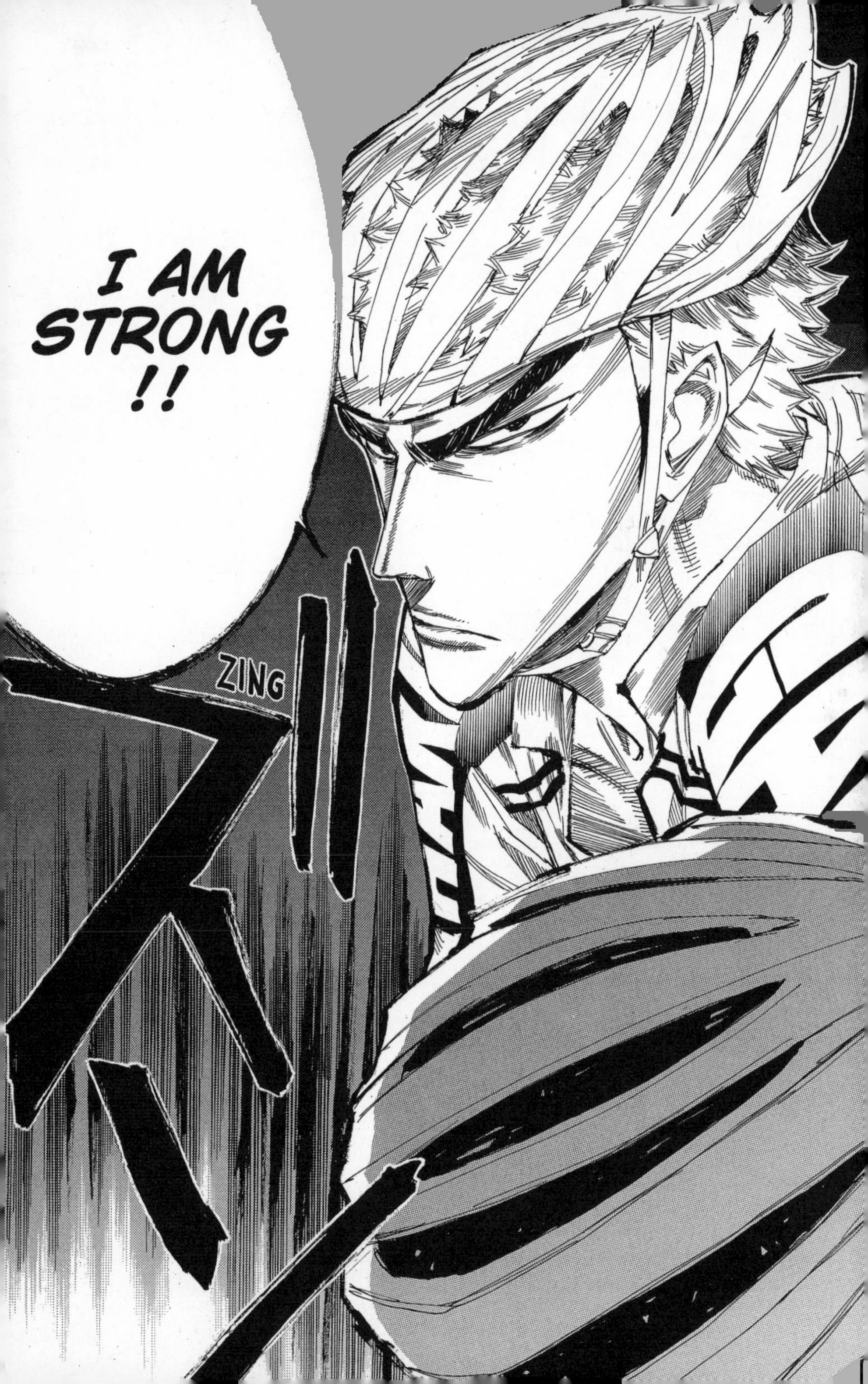
I AM STRONG !!
ZING

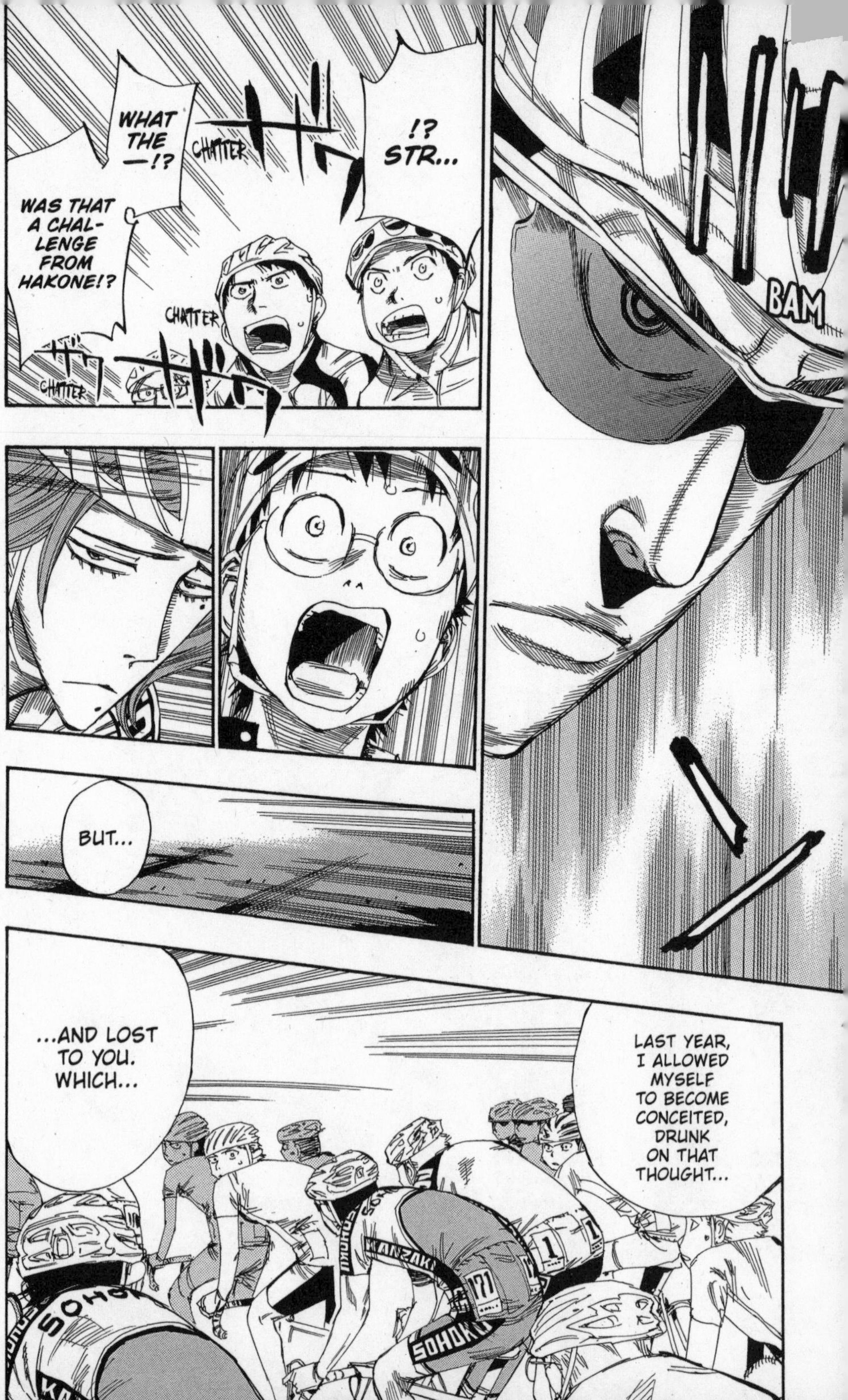
BAM
!? STR...
WHAT THE—!?
CHATTER
WAS THAT A CHALLENGE FROM HAKONE!?
CHATTER
CHATTER
BUT...
LAST YEAR, I ALLOWED MYSELF TO BECOME CONCEITED, DRUNK ON THAT THOUGHT...
...AND LOST TO YOU. WHICH...

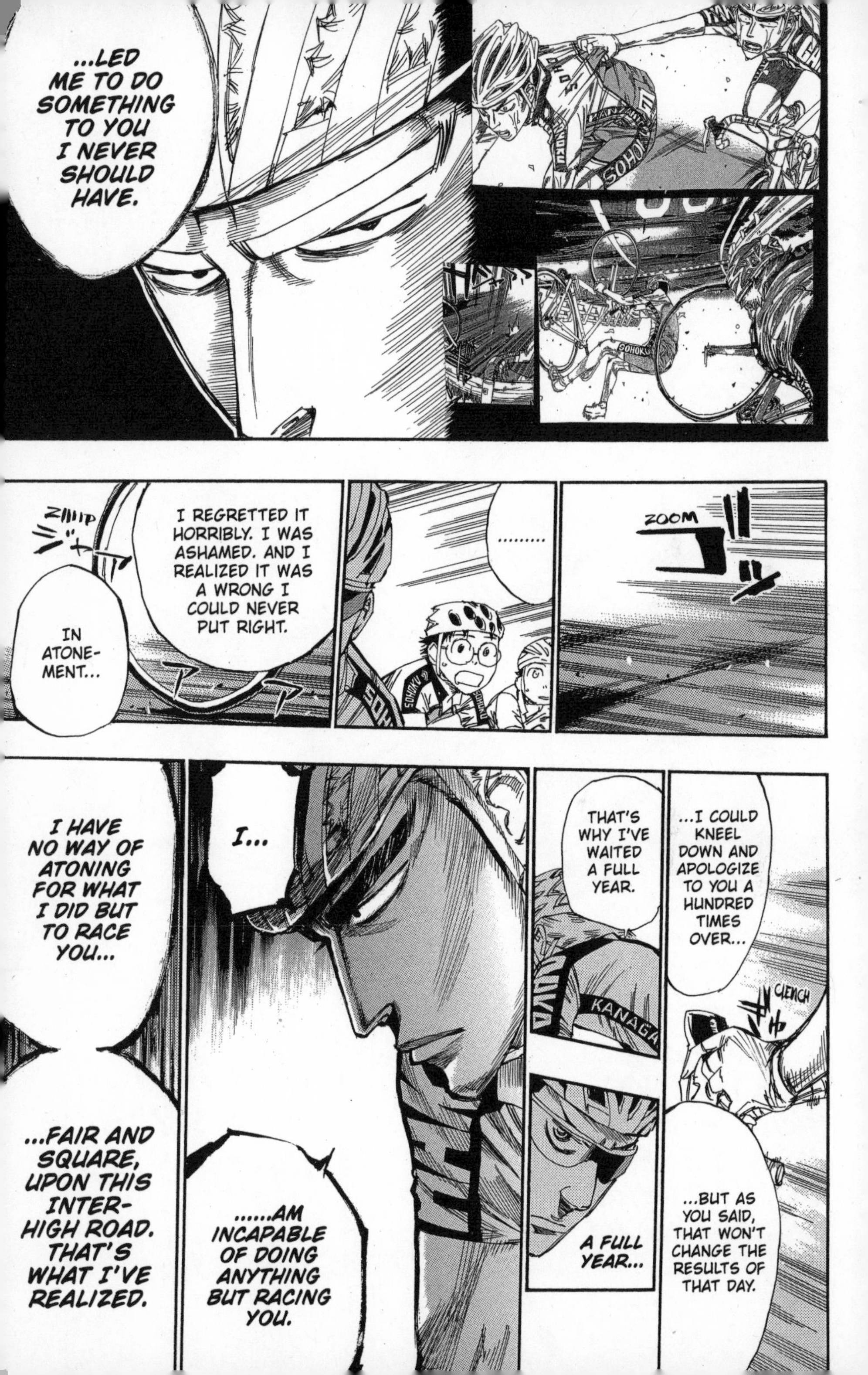
...LED ME TO DO SOMETHING TO YOU I NEVER SHOULD HAVE.
ZOOM
....
ZIIIIP
I REGRETTED IT HORRIBLY. I WAS ASHAMED. AND I REALIZED IT WAS A WRONG I COULD NEVER PUT RIGHT.
IN ATONE-MENT...
...I COULD KNEEL DOWN AND APOLOGIZE TO YOU A HUNDRED TIMES OVER...
CLENCH
...BUT AS YOU SAID, THAT WON'T CHANGE THE RESULTS OF THAT DAY.
THAT'S WHY I'VE WAITED A FULL YEAR.
A FULL YEAR...
I...
......AM INCAPABLE OF DOING ANYTHING BUT RACING YOU.
I HAVE NO WAY OF ATONING FOR WHAT I DID BUT TO RACE YOU...
...FAIR AND SQUARE, UPON THIS INTER-HIGH ROAD. THAT'S WHAT I'VE REALIZED.

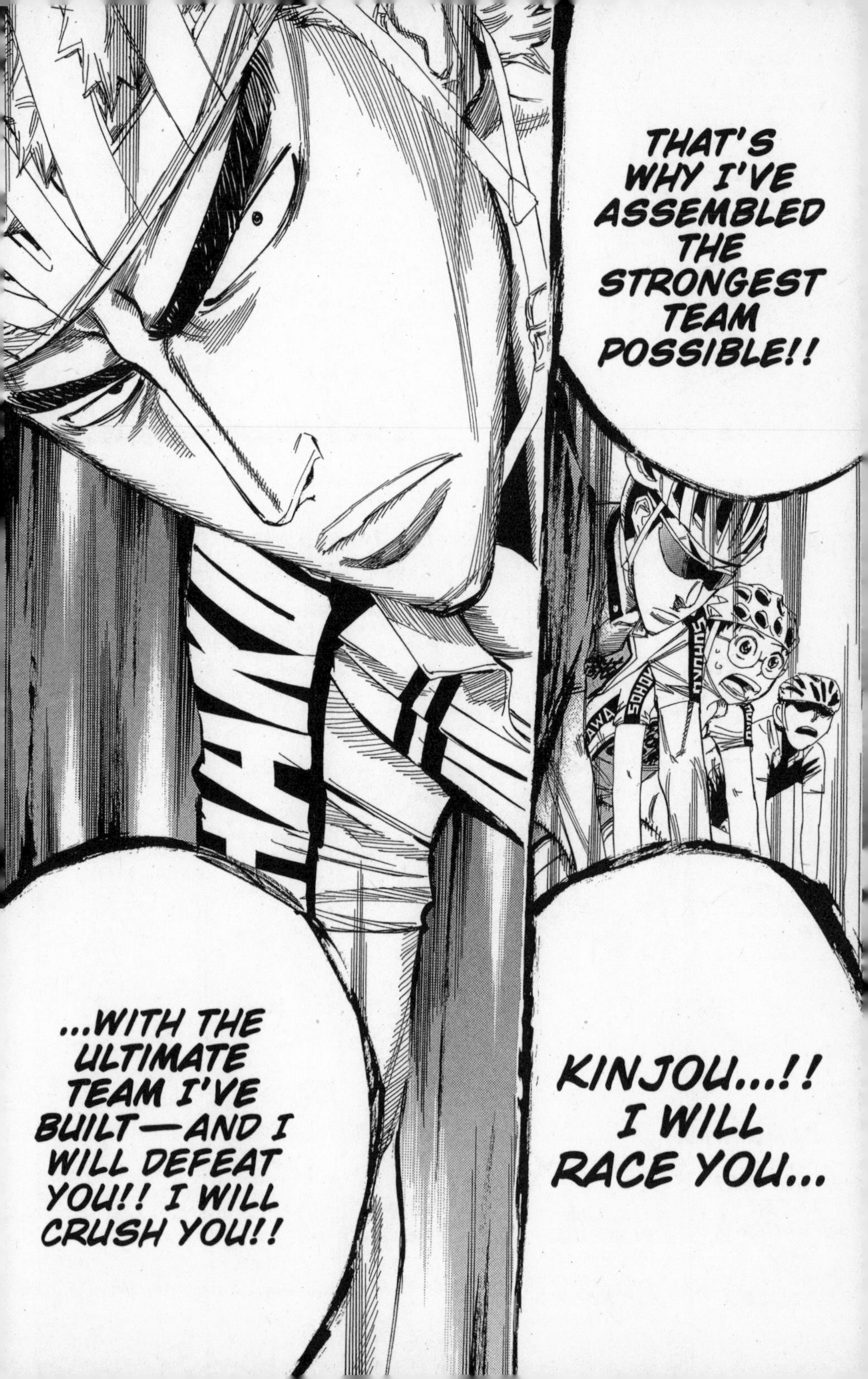
THAT'S WHY I'VE ASSEMBLED THE STRONGEST TEAM POSSIBLE!!
KINJOU...!! I WILL RACE YOU...
...WITH THE ULTIMATE TEAM I'VE BUILT—AND I WILL DEFEAT YOU!! I WILL CRUSH YOU!!

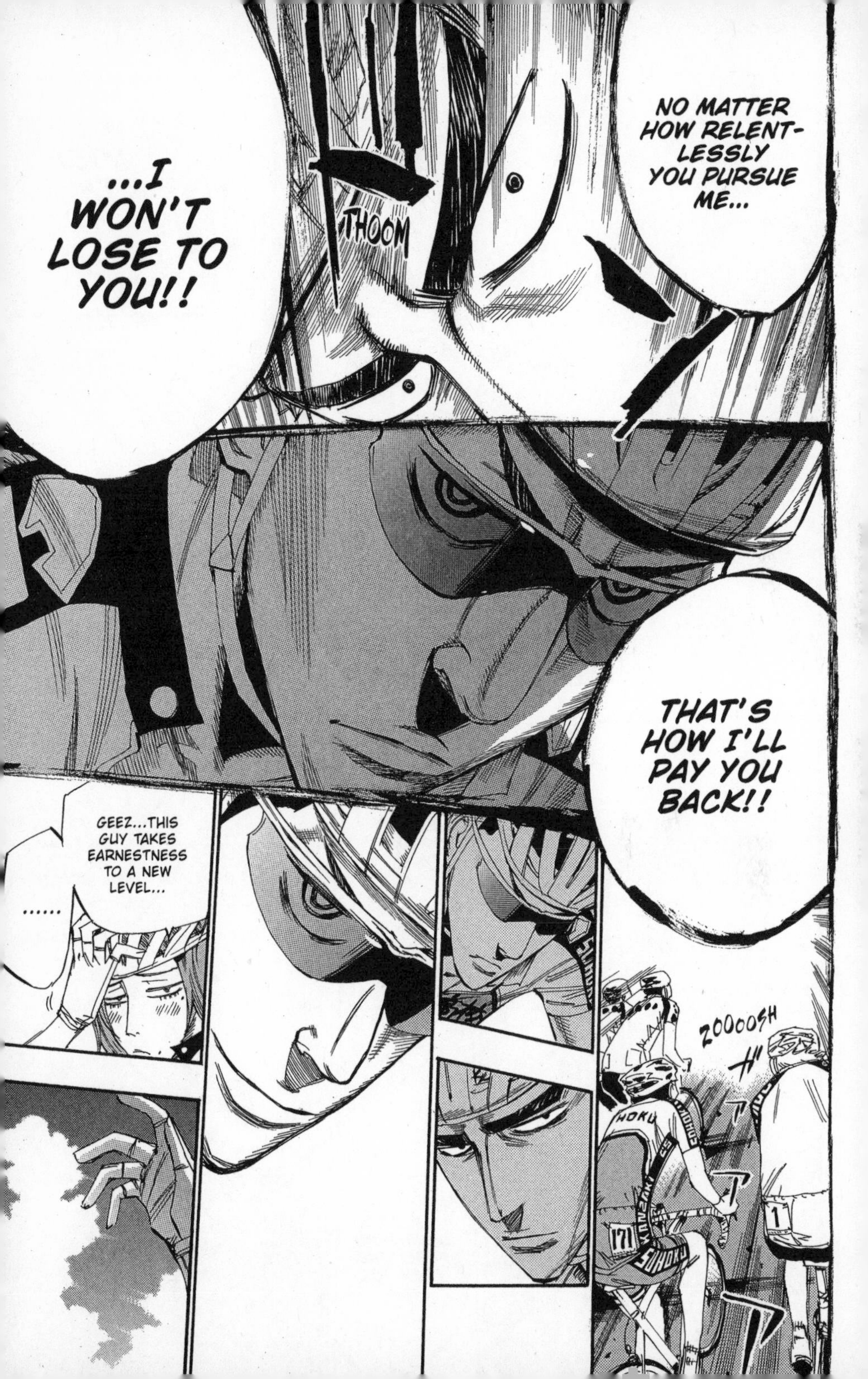
NO MATTER HOW RELENT-LESSLY YOU PURSUE ME...
THOOM
...I WON'T LOSE TO YOU!!
THAT'S HOW I'LL PAY YOU BACK!!
ZOOOOSH
GEEZ...THIS GUY TAKES EARNESTNESS TO A NEW LEVEL...
......

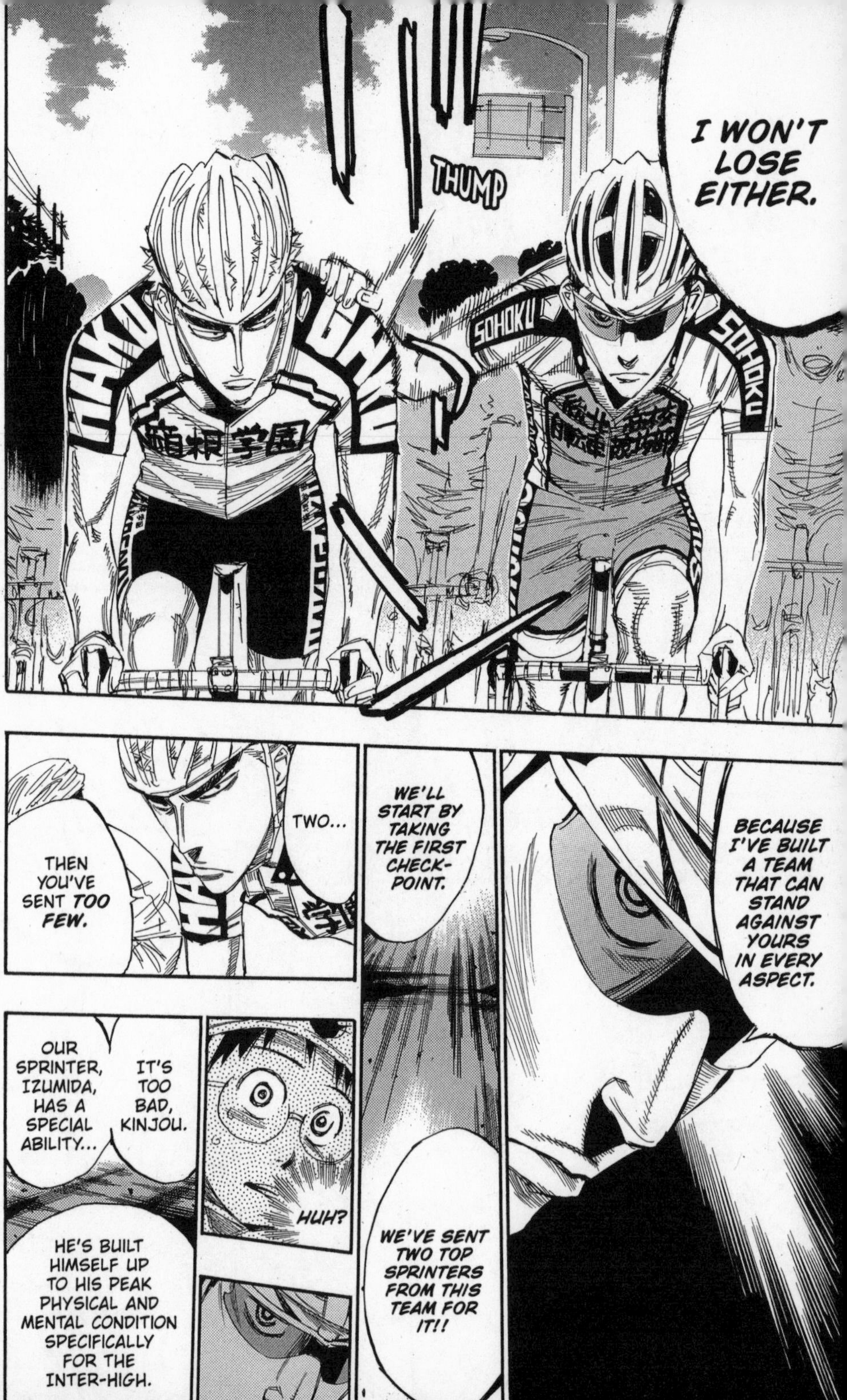
I WON'T LOSE EITHER.
THUMP
BECAUSE I'VE BUILT A TEAM THAT CAN STAND AGAINST YOURS IN EVERY ASPECT.
WE'LL START BY TAKING THE FIRST CHECK-POINT.
WE'VE SENT TWO TOP SPRINTERS FROM THIS TEAM FOR IT!!
TWO...
THEN YOU'VE SENT TOO FEW.
IT'S TOO BAD, KINJOU.
HUH?
OUR SPRINTER, IZUMIDA, HAS A SPECIAL ABILITY...
HE'S BUILT HIMSELF UP TO HIS PEAK PHYSICAL AND MENTAL CONDITION SPECIFICALLY FOR THE INTER-HIGH.

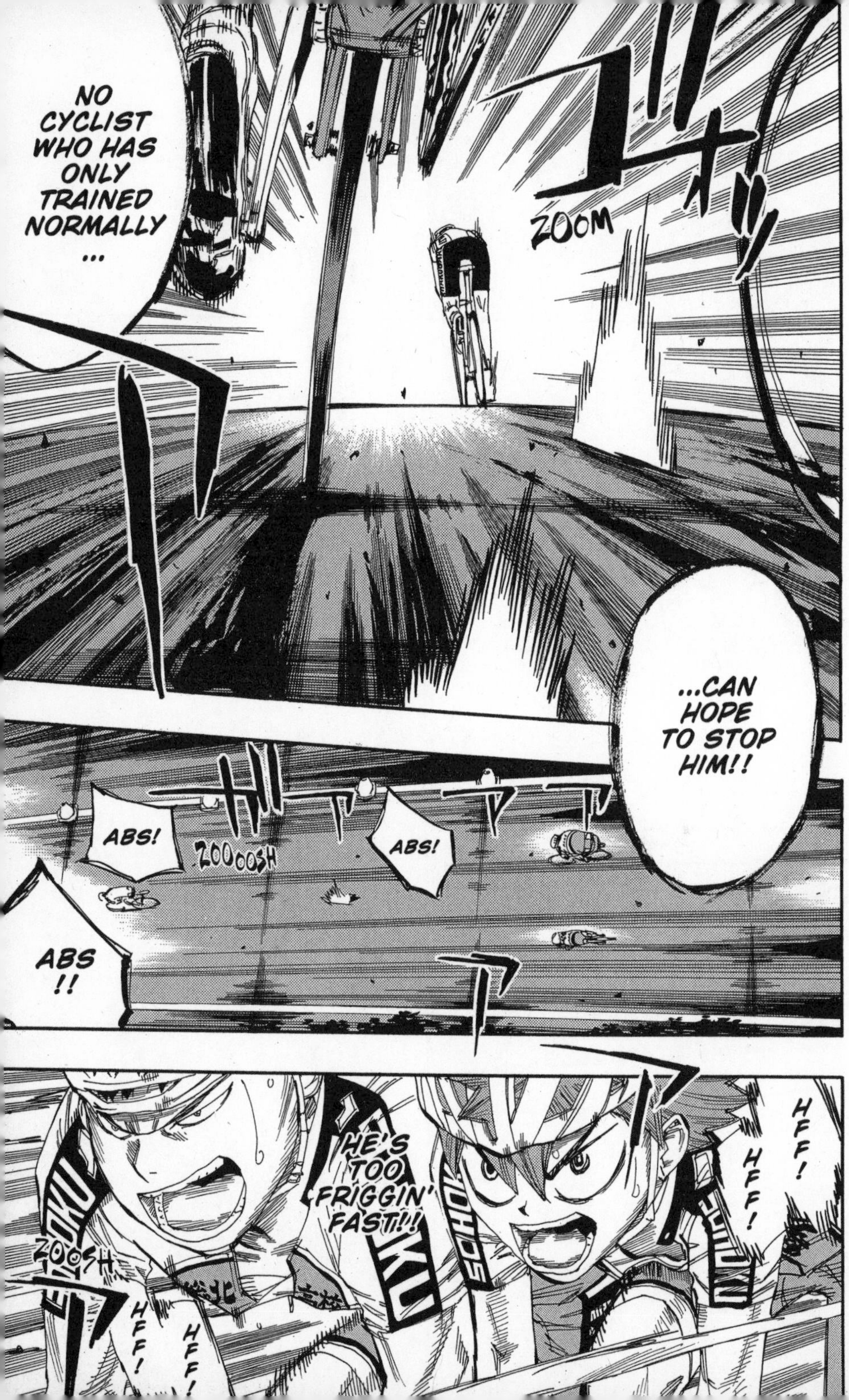
ZOOM
NO CYCLIST WHO HAS ONLY TRAINED NORMALLY ...
...CAN HOPE TO STOP HIM!!
ABS!
ZOOOOSH
ABS!
ABS !!
HFF! HFF!
HE'S TOO FRIGGIN' FAST!!
ZOOSH
HFF! HFF!

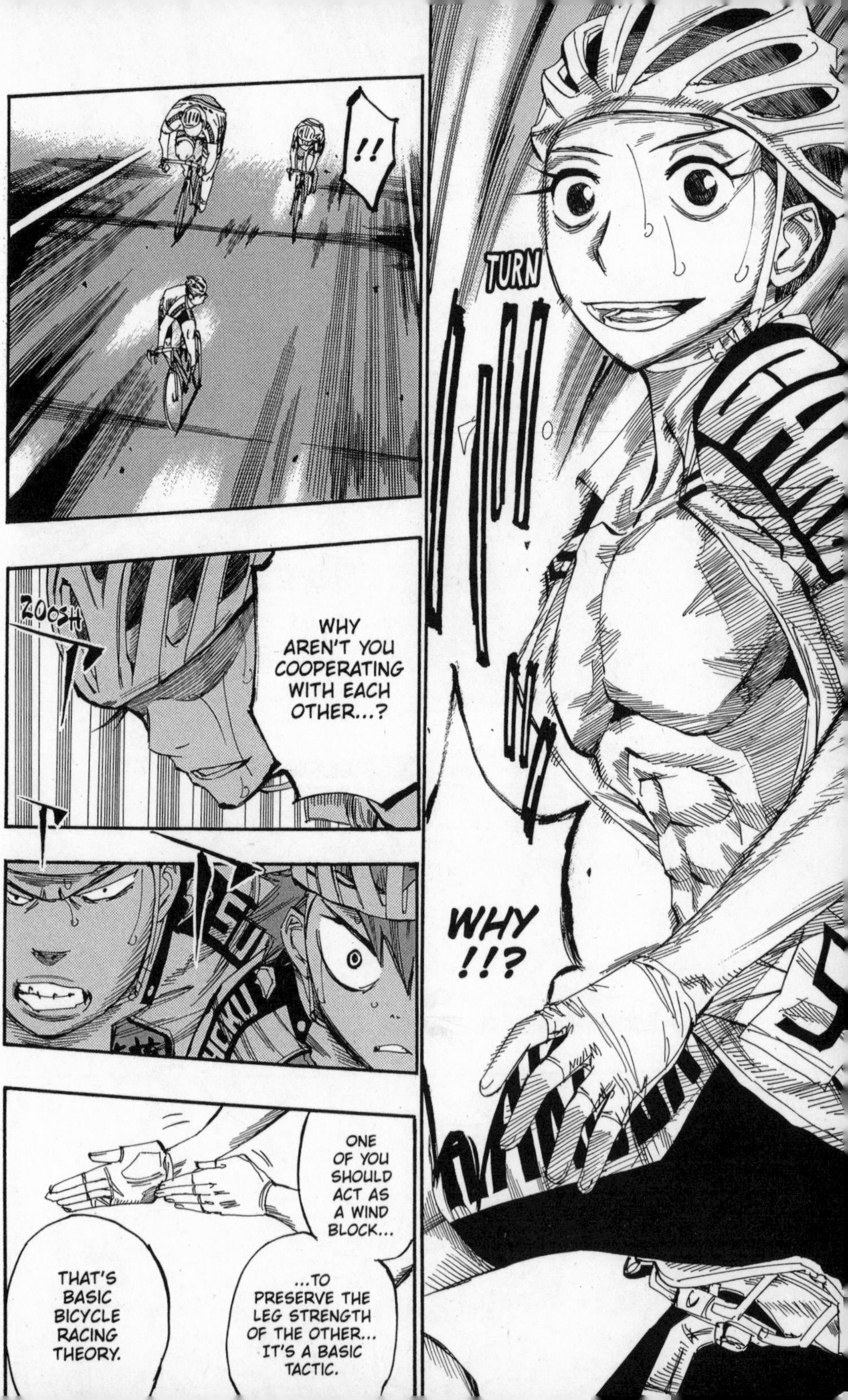

TURN
WHY !!?
!!
ZOOSH
WHY AREN'T YOU COOPERATING WITH EACH OTHER...?
ONE OF YOU SHOULD ACT AS A WIND BLOCK...
...TO PRESERVE THE LEG STRENGTH OF THE OTHER... IT'S A BASIC TACTIC.
THAT'S BASIC BICYCLE RACING THEORY.

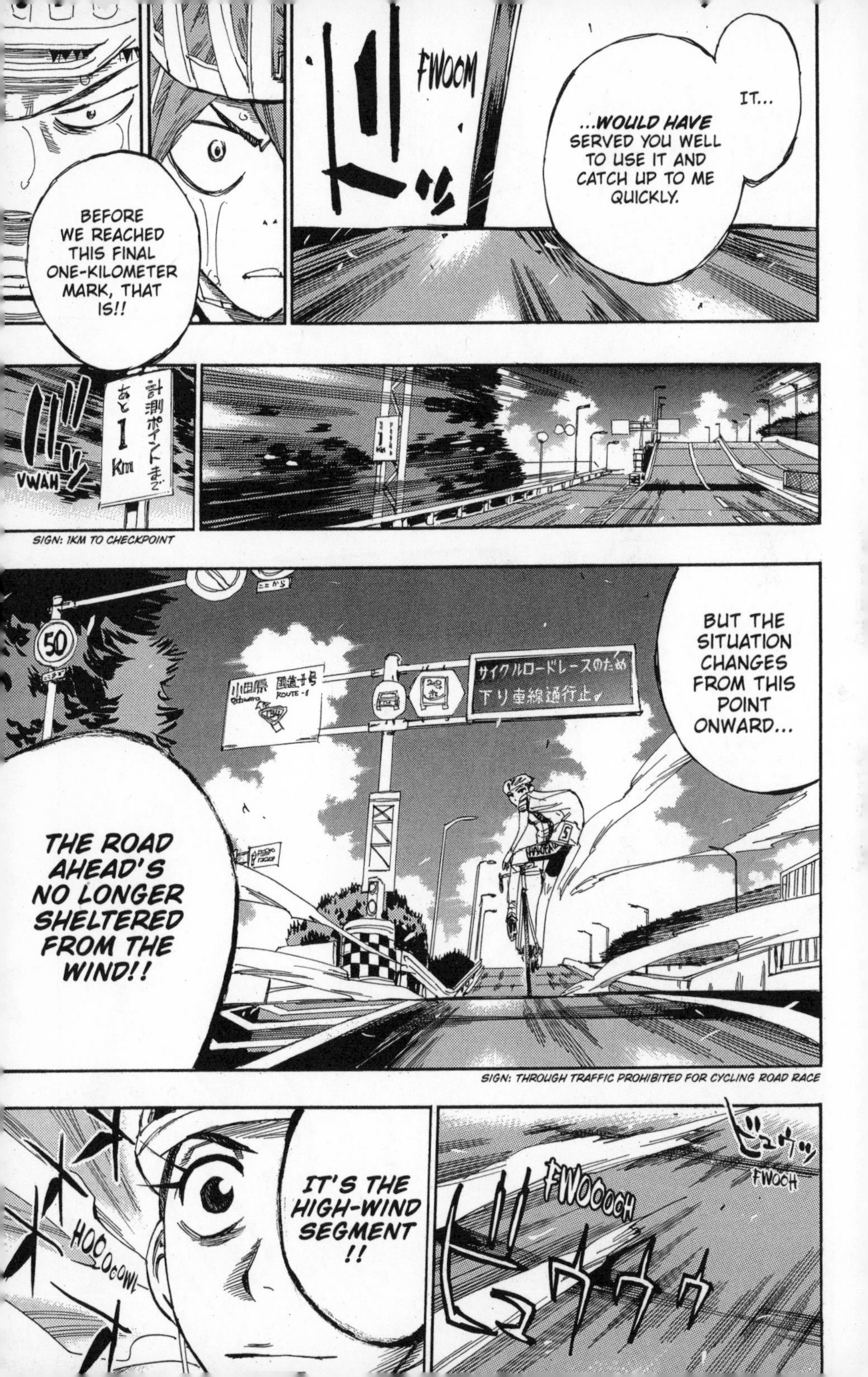
IT...
...WOULD HAVE SERVED YOU WELL TO USE IT AND CATCH UP TO ME QUICKLY.
FWOOM
BEFORE WE REACHED THIS FINAL ONE-KILOMETER MARK, THAT IS!!
計測ポイントまで あと1Km
VWAH
SIGN: 1KM TO CHECKPOINT
BUT THE SITUATION CHANGES FROM THIS POINT ONWARD...
サイクルロードレースのため 下り車線通行止
小田原 国道一号 ROUTE-1
50
THE ROAD AHEAD'S NO LONGER SHELTERED FROM THE WIND!!
SIGN: THROUGH TRAFFIC PROHIBITED FOR CYCLING ROAD RACE
FWOOOCH
FWOCH
IT'S THE HIGH-WIND SEGMENT!!
HOOOOOWL

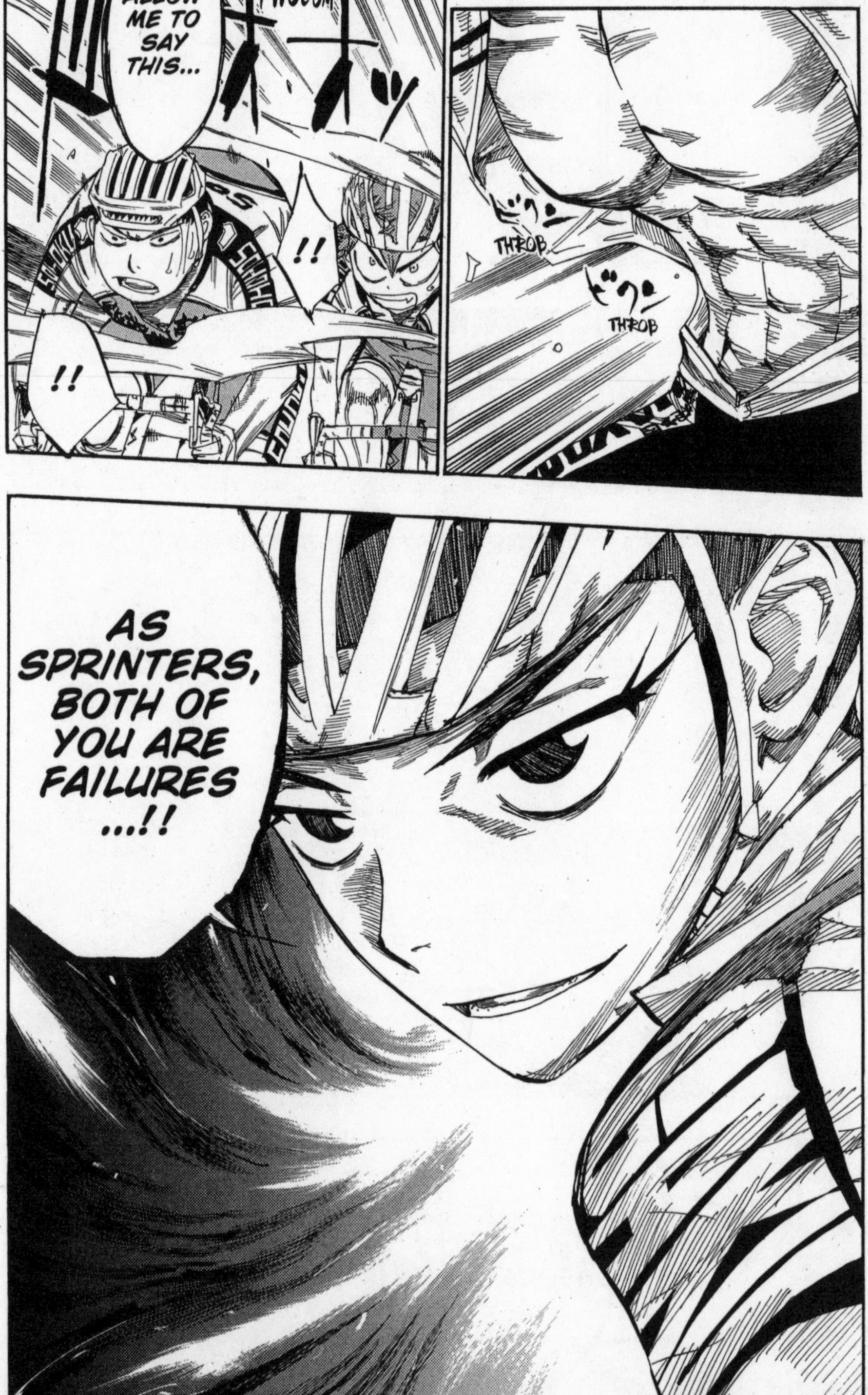
THROB
THROB
ALLOW ME TO SAY THIS...
FWOOOM
!!
!!
AS SPRINTERS, BOTH OF YOU ARE FAILURES ...!!

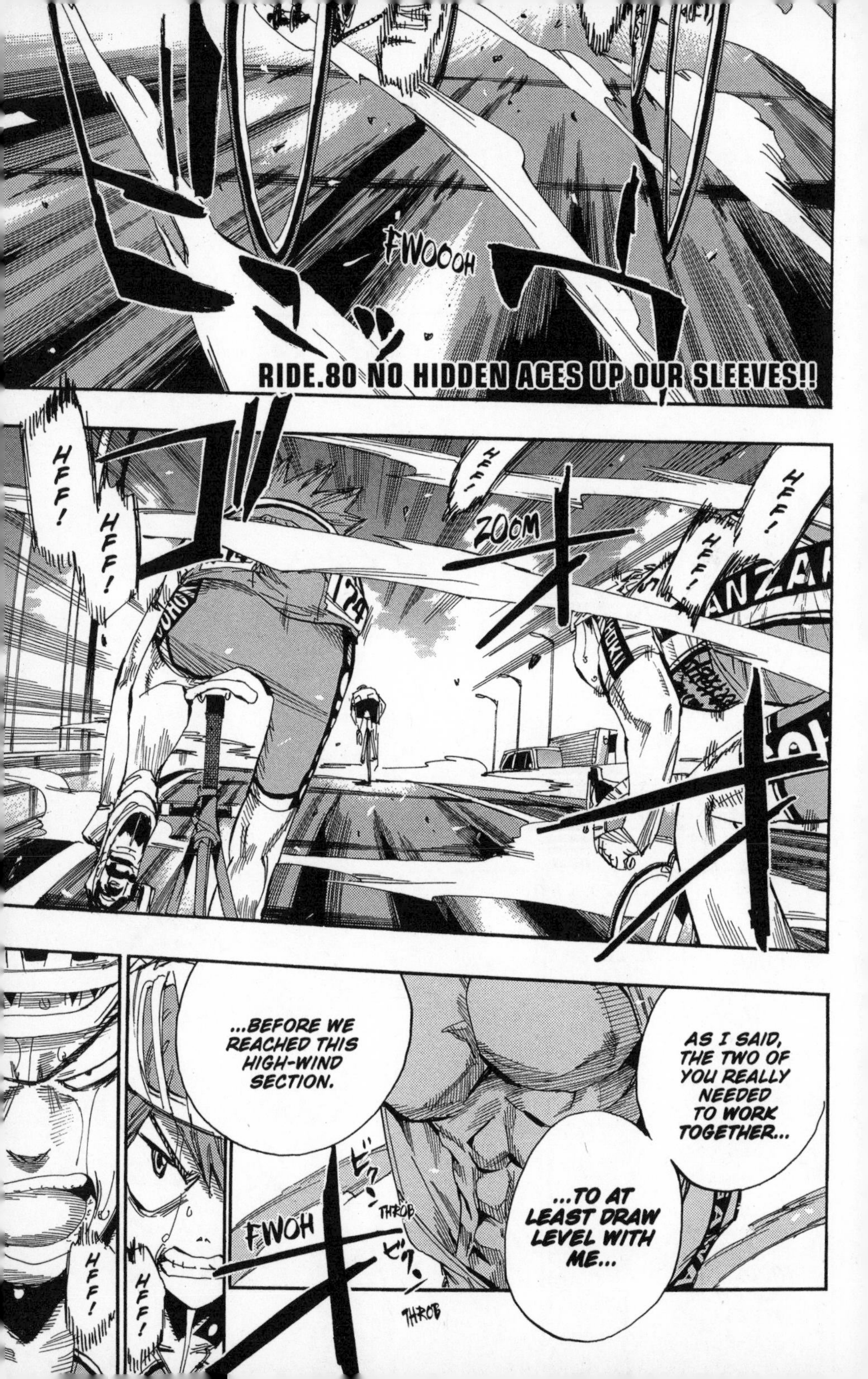
FWOOOH
RIDE.80 NO HIDDEN ACES UP OUR SLEEVES!!
HFF!
HFF!
ZOOM
HFF!
HFF!
HFF!
AS I SAID, THE TWO OF YOU REALLY NEEDED TO WORK TOGETHER...
...TO AT LEAST DRAW LEVEL WITH ME...
...BEFORE WE REACHED THIS HIGH-WIND SECTION.
THROB
THROB
FWOH
HFF!
HFF!

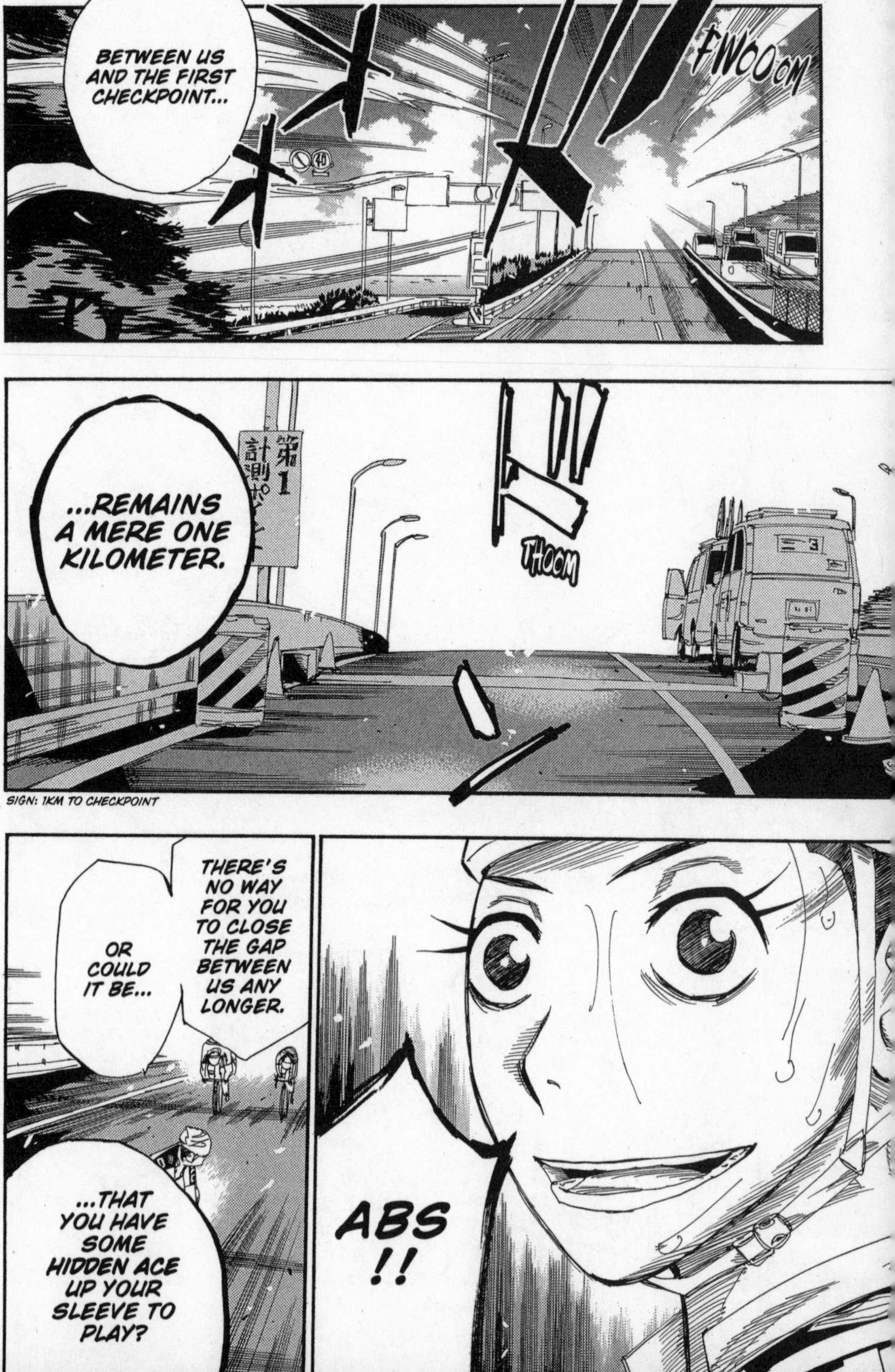
FWOOOM
BETWEEN US AND THE FIRST CHECKPOINT...
THOOM
...REMAINS A MERE ONE KILOMETER.
ABS !!
THERE'S NO WAY FOR YOU TO CLOSE THE GAP BETWEEN US ANY LONGER.
OR COULD IT BE...
...THAT YOU HAVE SOME HIDDEN ACE UP YOUR SLEEVE TO PLAY?
SIGN: 1KM TO CHECKPOINT

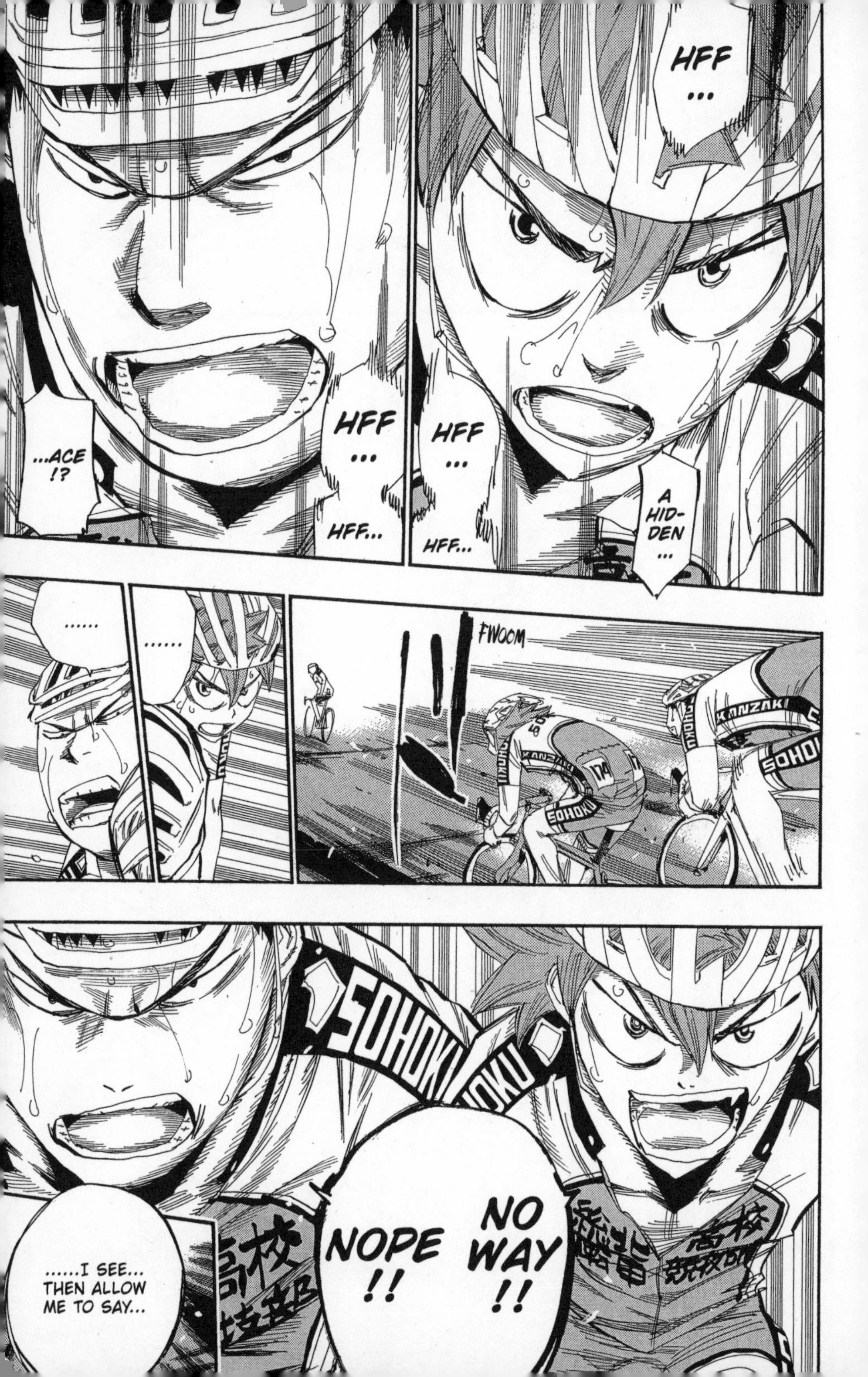
HFF ...
HFF ...
A HID-DEN ...
HFF...
HFF ...
...ACE !?
HFF...
FWOOM
......
......
NO WAY !!
NOPE !!
......I SEE... THEN ALLOW ME TO SAY...

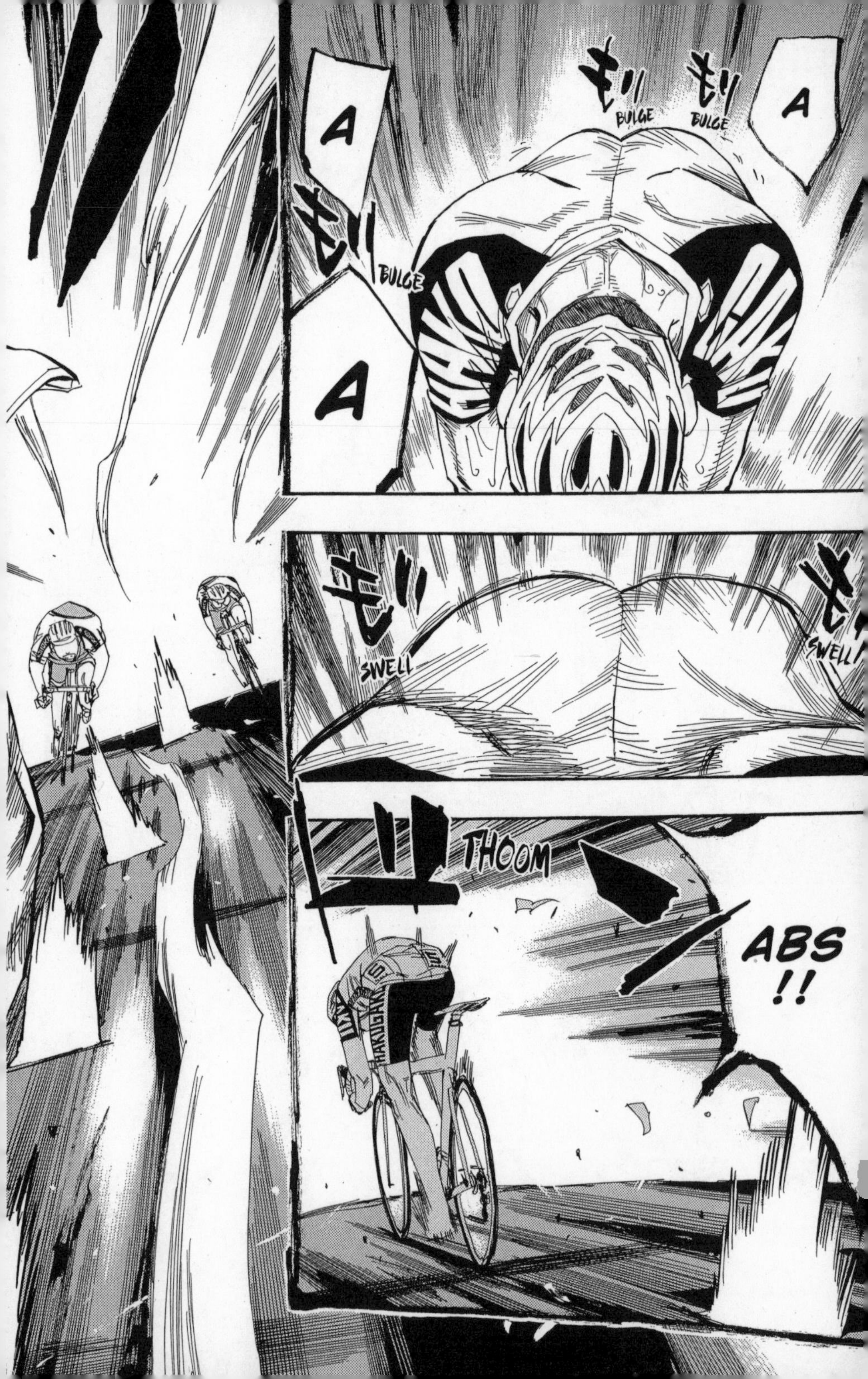

A
もり
BULGE
もり
BULGE
A
もり
BULGE
A
もり
SWELL
もり
SWELL
THOOM
ABS!!

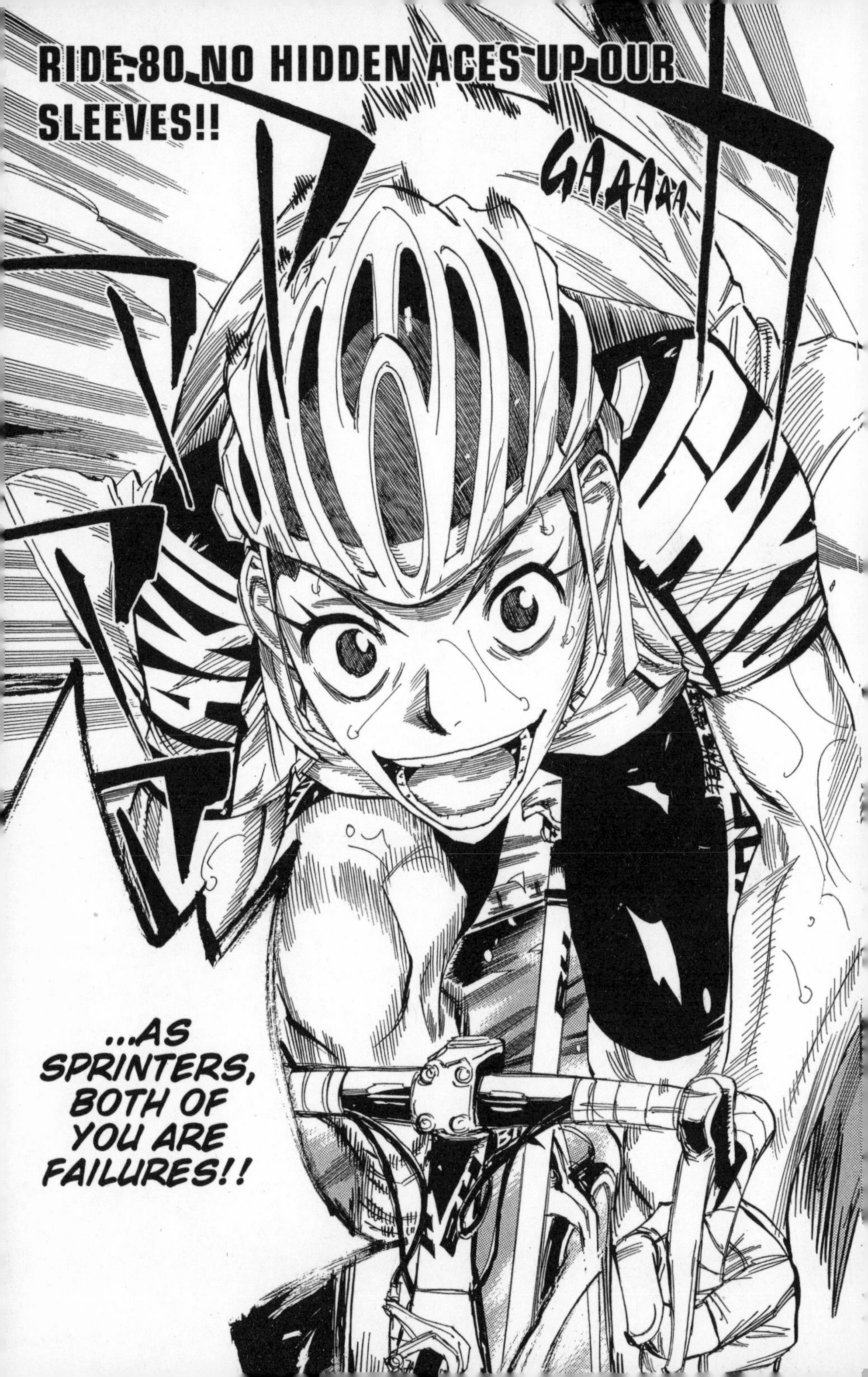
RIDE.80 NO HIDDEN ACES UP OUR SLEEVES!!
GAAAAA
...AS SPRINTERS, BOTH OF YOU ARE FAILURES!!

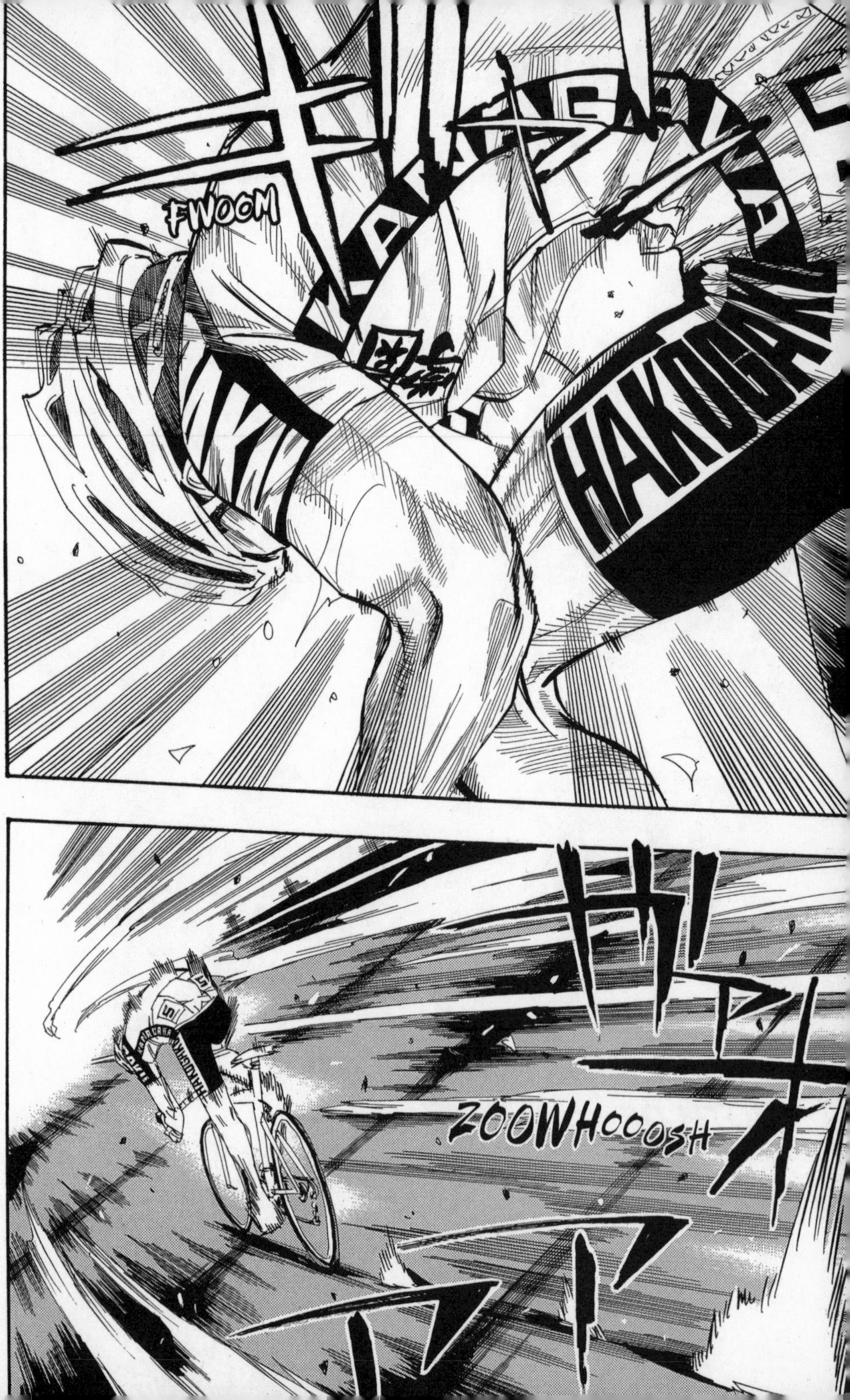
FWOOM
ZOOWHOOOSH

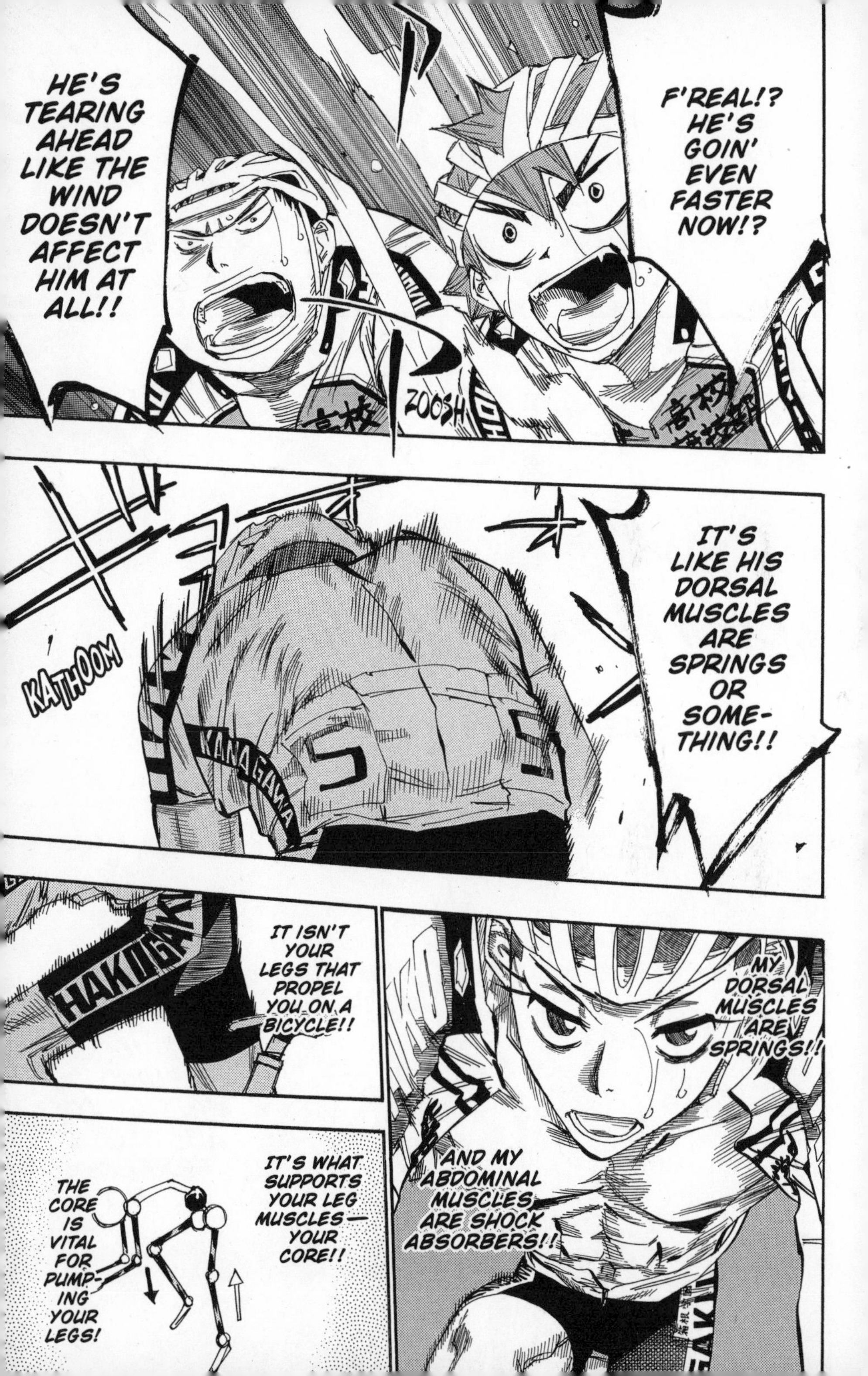
F'REAL!? HE'S GOIN' EVEN FASTER NOW!?
HE'S TEARING AHEAD LIKE THE WIND DOESN'T AFFECT HIM AT ALL!!
ZOOSH
IT'S LIKE HIS DORSAL MUSCLES ARE SPRINGS OR SOME-THING!!
KANAGAWA
KATHOOM
MY DORSAL MUSCLES ARE SPRINGS!!
AND MY ABDOMINAL MUSCLES ARE SHOCK ABSORBERS!!
IT ISN'T YOUR LEGS THAT PROPEL YOU ON A BICYCLE!!
IT'S WHAT SUPPORTS YOUR LEG MUSCLES—YOUR CORE!!
THE CORE IS VITAL FOR PUMP-ING YOUR LEGS!

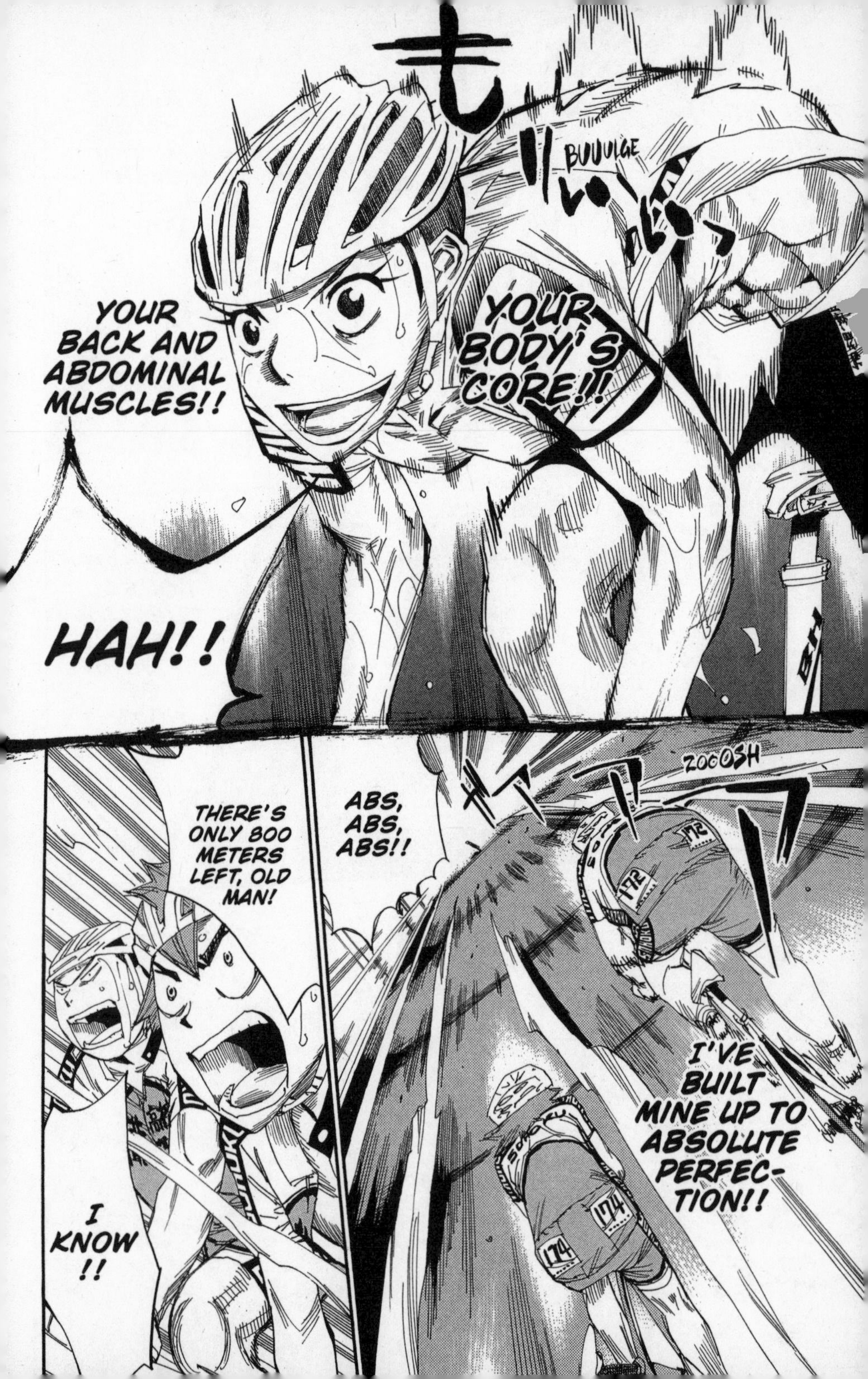
BUUUULGE
YOUR BODY'S CORE!!
YOUR BACK AND ABDOMINAL MUSCLES!!
HAH!!
ZOOOSH
ABS, ABS, ABS!!
I'VE BUILT MINE UP TO ABSOLUTE PERFEC-TION!!
THERE'S ONLY 800 METERS LEFT, OLD MAN!
I KNOW!!

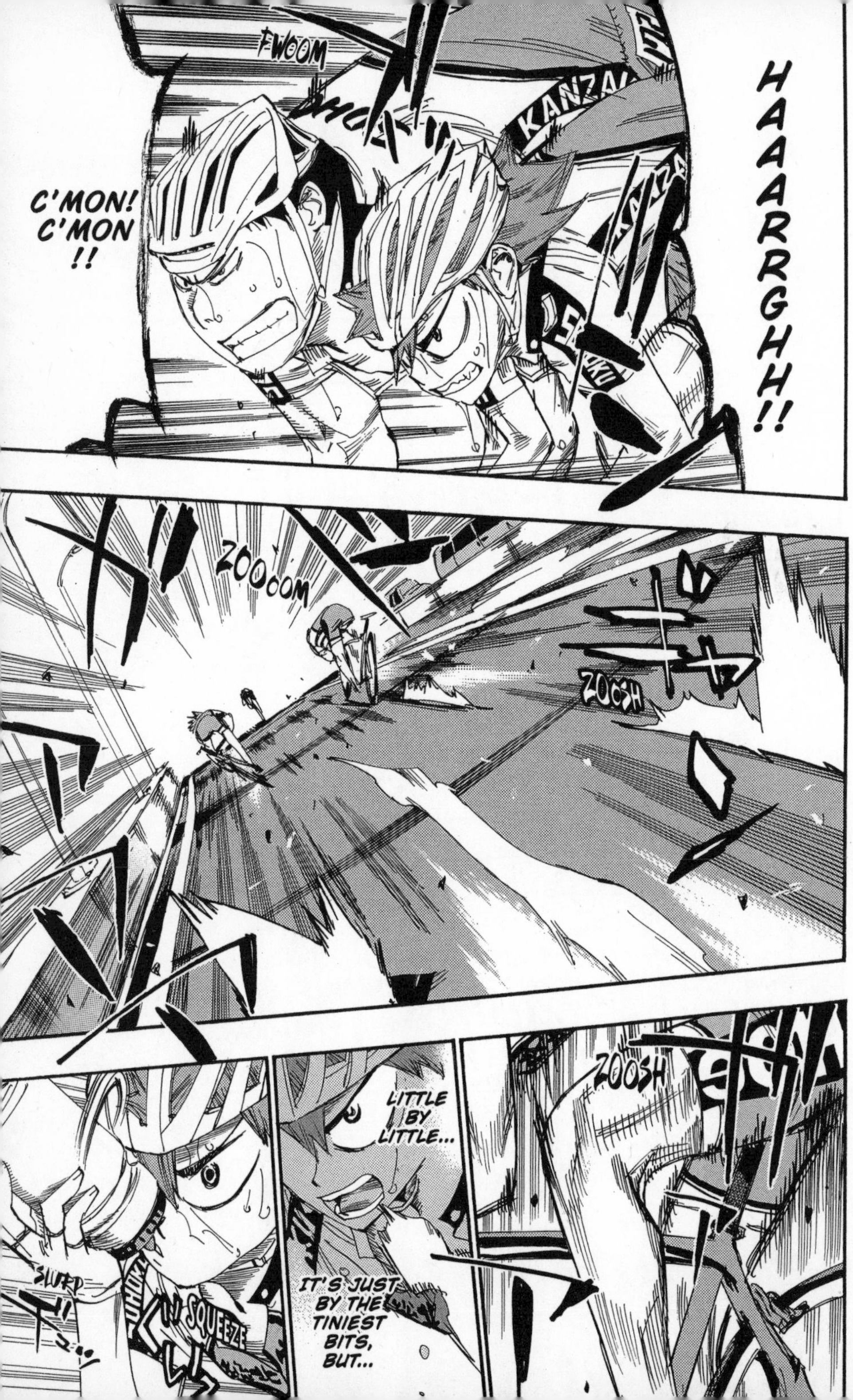
HAAAARRGHH!!
FWOOM
C'MON! C'MON!!
ZOOOOM
ZOOSH
ZOOSH
LITTLE BY LITTLE...
IT'S JUST BY THE TINIEST BITS, BUT...
SLURP
SQUEEZE

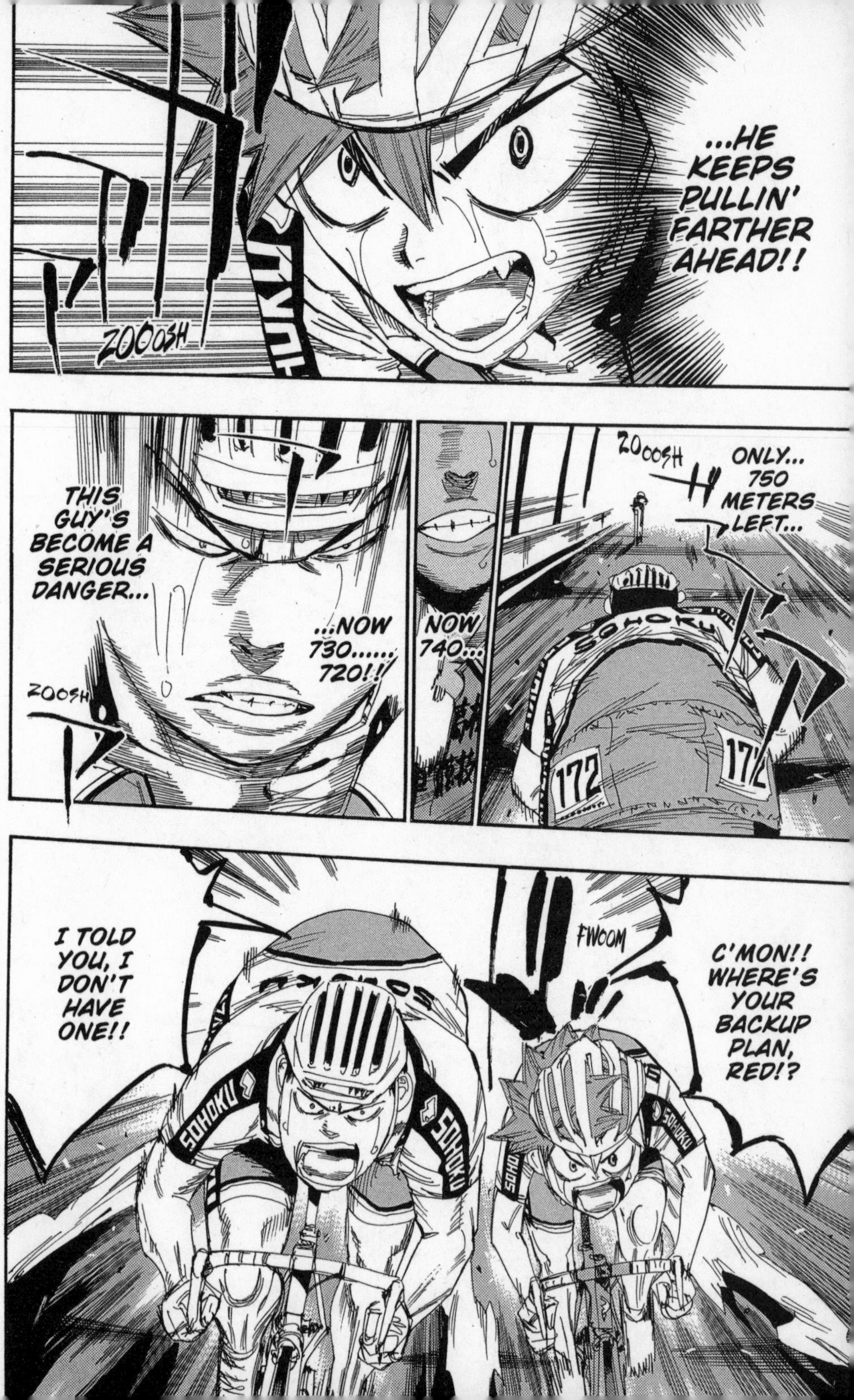
...HE KEEPS PULLIN' FARTHER AHEAD!!
ZOOOSH
ZOOOSH
ONLY... 750 METERS LEFT...
172
172
NOW 740...
THIS GUY'S BECOME A SERIOUS DANGER...
...NOW 730...... 720!!
ZOOSH
C'MON!! WHERE'S YOUR BACKUP PLAN, RED!?
FWOOM
I TOLD YOU, I DON'T HAVE ONE!!

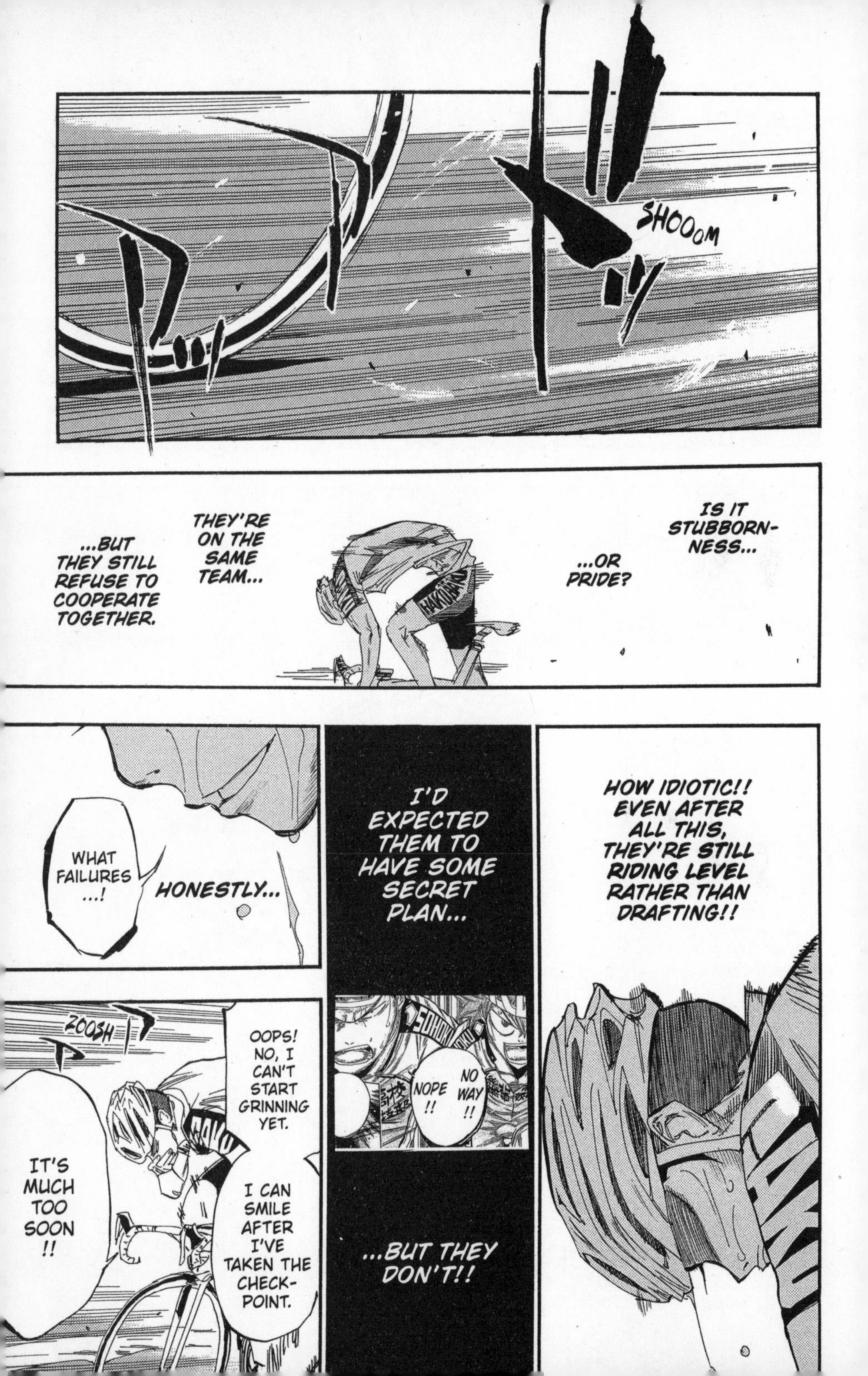
SHOOOM
IS IT STUBBORNNESS...
...OR PRIDE?
THEY'RE ON THE SAME TEAM...
...BUT THEY STILL REFUSE TO COOPERATE TOGETHER.
HOW IDIOTIC!! EVEN AFTER ALL THIS, THEY'RE STILL RIDING LEVEL RATHER THAN DRAFTING!!
I'D EXPECTED THEM TO HAVE SOME SECRET PLAN...
NO WAY!!
NOPE!!
...BUT THEY DON'T!!
HONESTLY...
WHAT FAILURES...!
ZOOSH
OOPS! NO, I CAN'T START GRINNING YET.
I CAN SMILE AFTER I'VE TAKEN THE CHECKPOINT.
IT'S MUCH TOO SOON!!

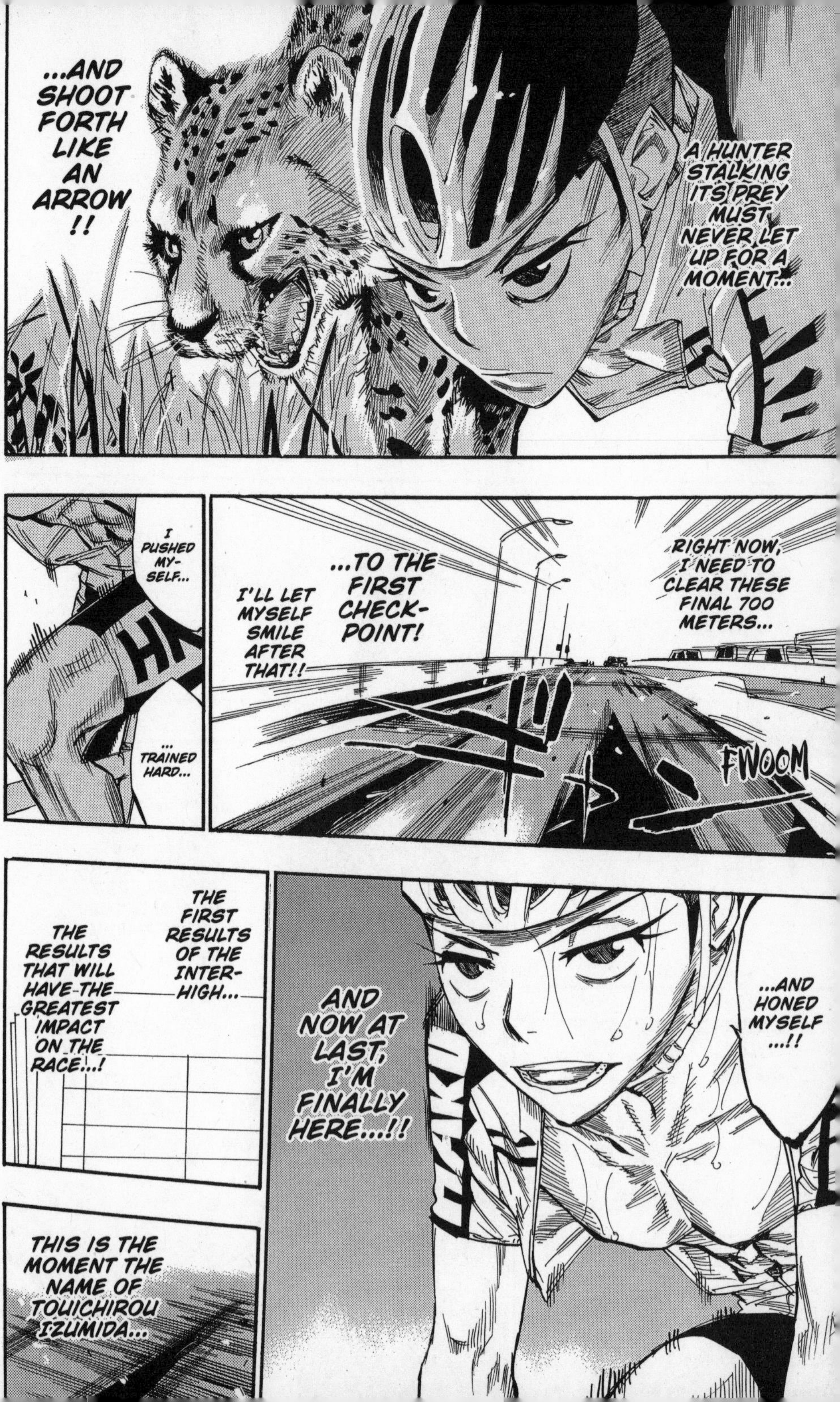
A HUNTER STALKING ITS PREY MUST NEVER LET UP FOR A MOMENT...
...AND SHOOT FORTH LIKE AN ARROW!!
RIGHT NOW, I NEED TO CLEAR THESE FINAL 700 METERS...
...TO THE FIRST CHECK-POINT!
I'LL LET MYSELF SMILE AFTER THAT!!
FWOOM
I PUSHED MY-SELF...
...TRAINED HARD...
...AND HONED MYSELF...!!
AND NOW AT LAST, I'M FINALLY HERE...!!
THE FIRST RESULTS OF THE INTER-HIGH...
THE RESULTS THAT WILL HAVE THE GREATEST IMPACT ON THE RACE...!
THIS IS THE MOMENT THE NAME OF TOUICHIROU IZUMIDA...

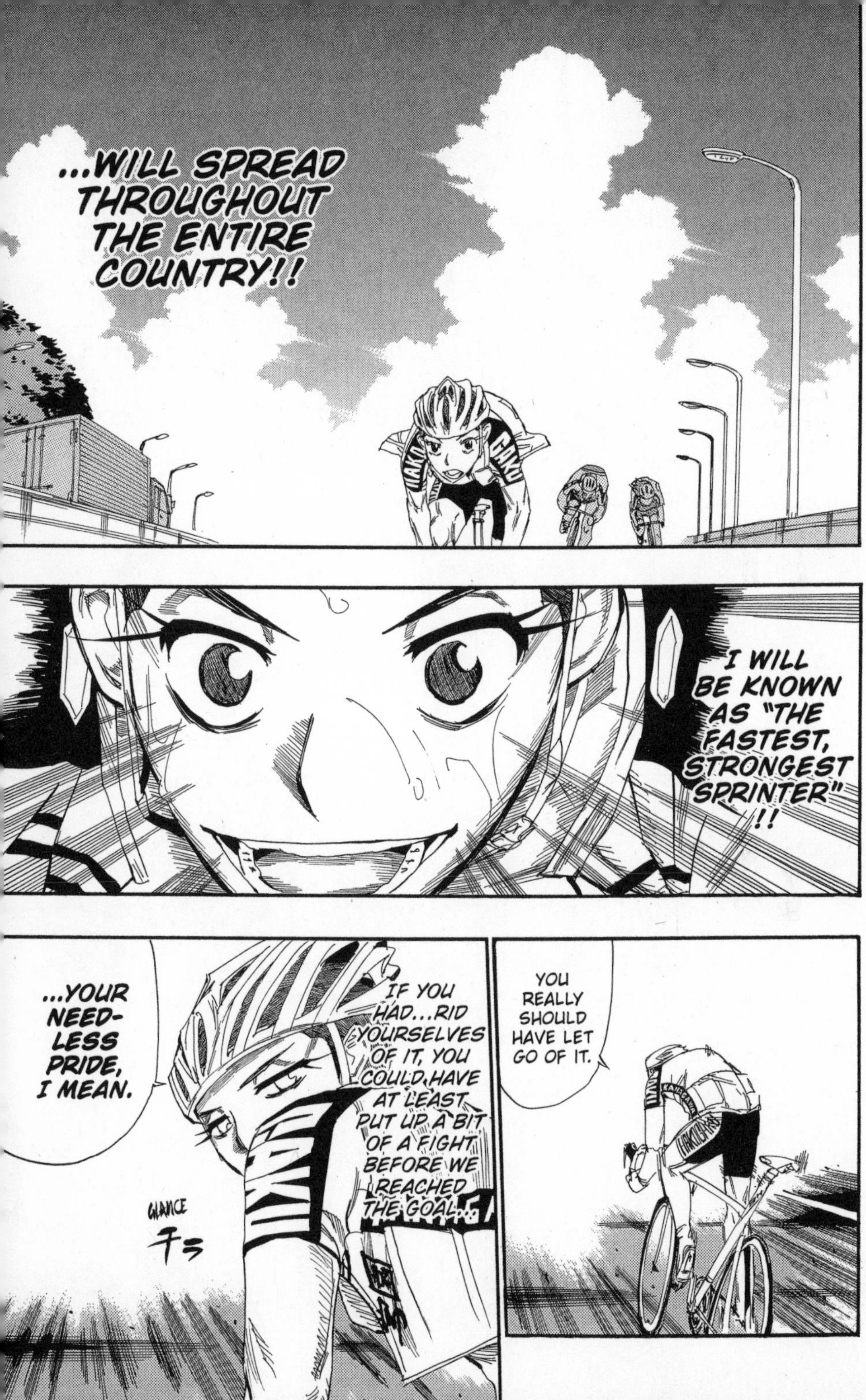
...WILL SPREAD THROUGHOUT THE ENTIRE COUNTRY!!
I WILL BE KNOWN AS "THE FASTEST, STRONGEST SPRINTER"!!
YOU REALLY SHOULD HAVE LET GO OF IT.
...YOUR NEED-LESS PRIDE, I MEAN.
IF YOU HAD...RID YOURSELVES OF IT, YOU COULD HAVE AT LEAST PUT UP A BIT OF A FIGHT BEFORE WE REACHED THE GOAL...
GLANCE

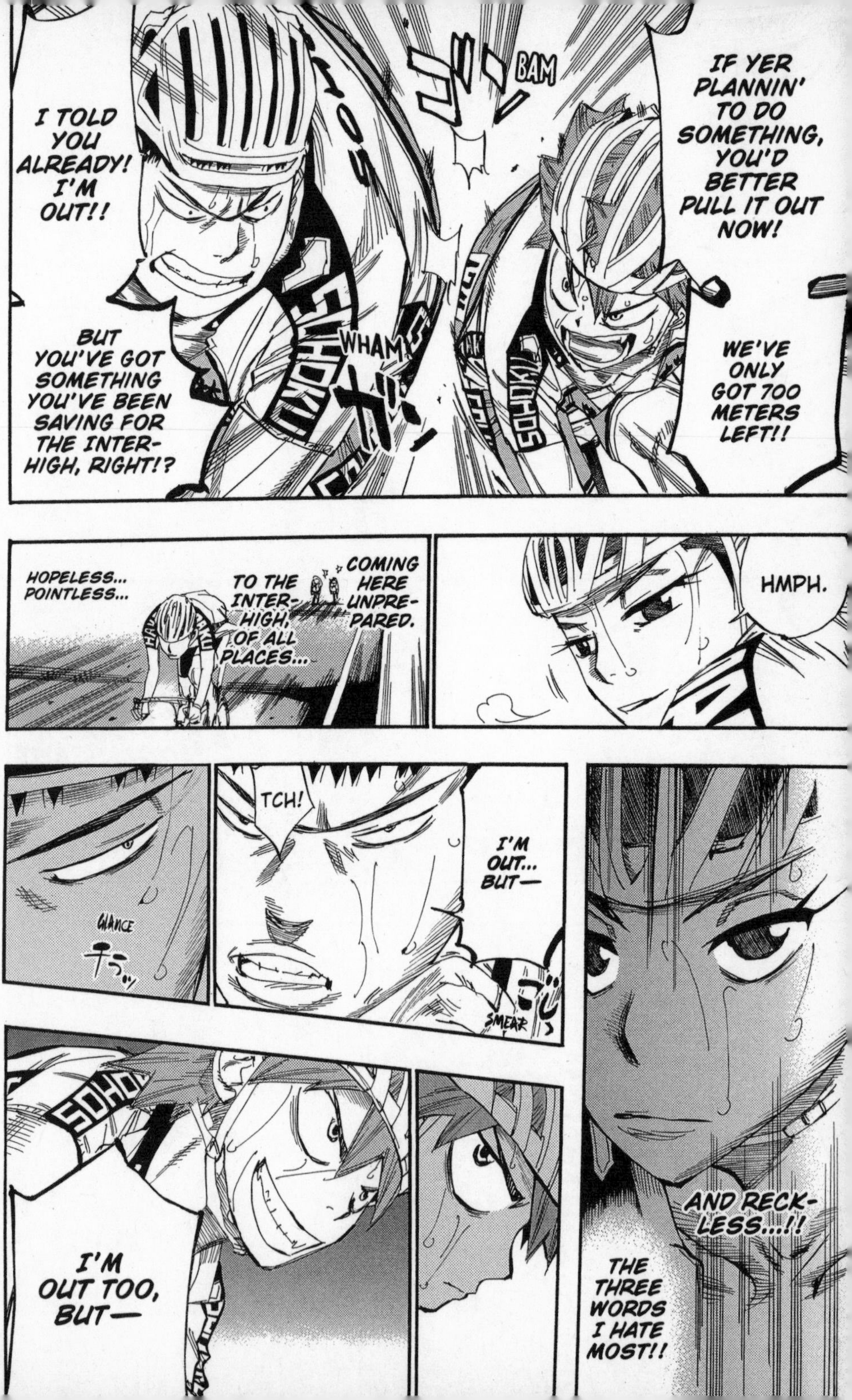
IF YER PLANNIN' TO DO SOMETHING, YOU'D BETTER PULL IT OUT NOW!
BAM
WE'VE ONLY GOT 700 METERS LEFT!!
I TOLD YOU ALREADY! I'M OUT!!
WHAM
BUT YOU'VE GOT SOMETHING YOU'VE BEEN SAVING FOR THE INTER-HIGH, RIGHT!?
HMPH.
COMING HERE UNPREPARED.
TO THE INTER-HIGH, OF ALL PLACES...
HOPELESS... POINTLESS...
AND RECK-LESS...!!
THE THREE WORDS I HATE MOST!!
TCH!
I'M OUT... BUT—
SMEAR
GLANCE
I'M OUT TOO, BUT—

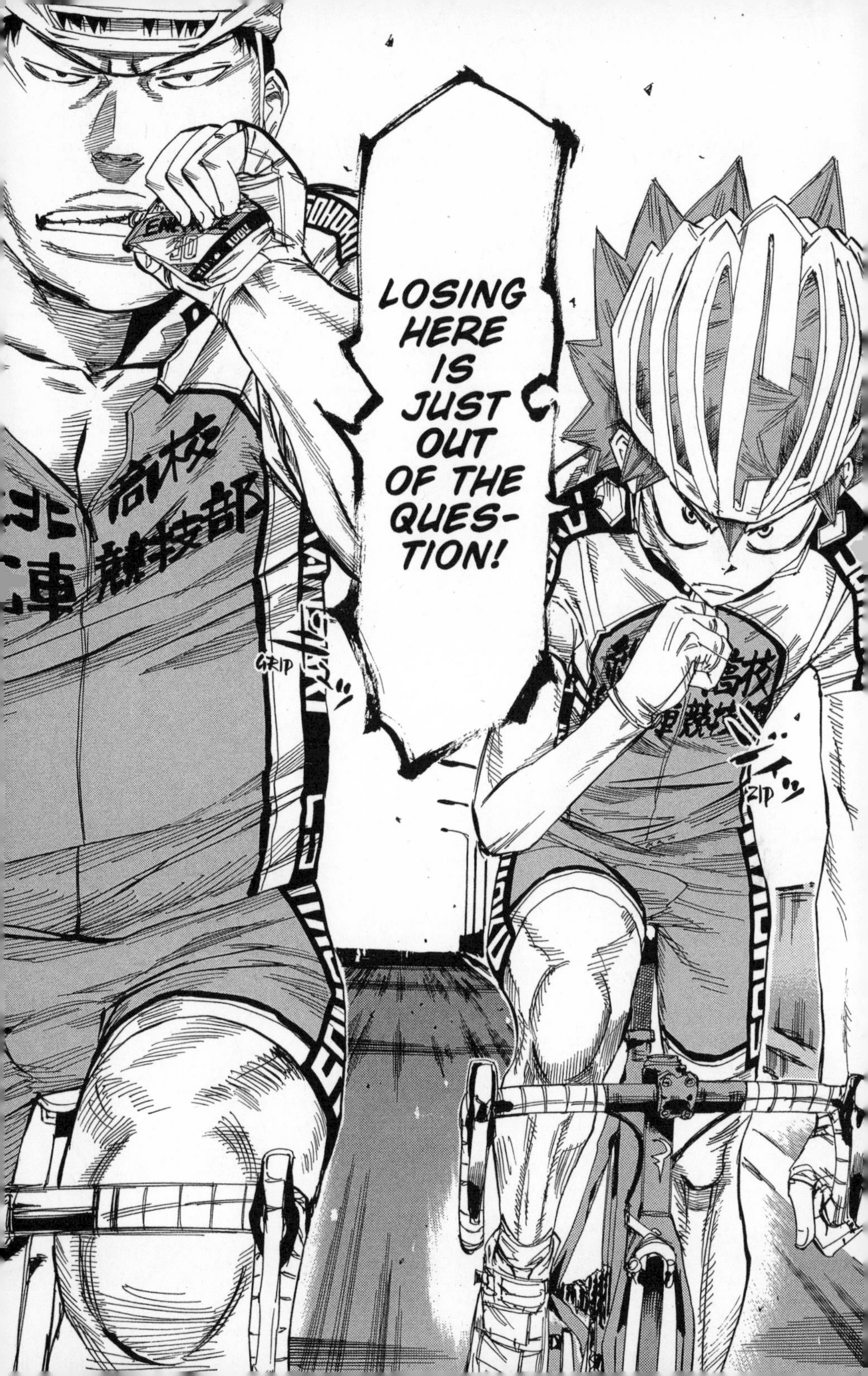
ZIP
LOSING HERE IS JUST OUT OF THE QUES-TION!
GRIP

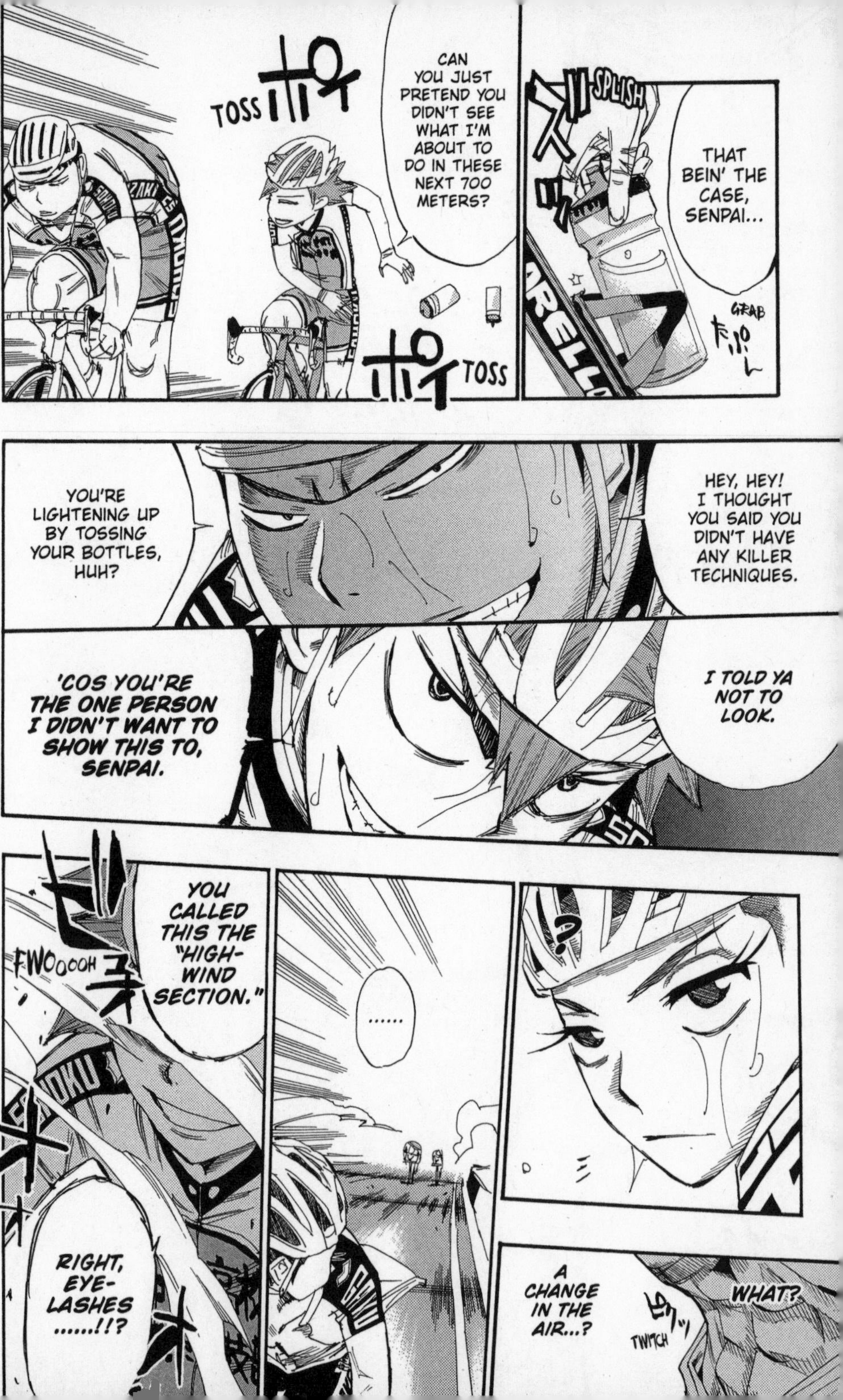
SPLISH
THAT BEIN' THE CASE, SENPAI...
GRAB
TOSS
CAN YOU JUST PRETEND YOU DIDN'T SEE WHAT I'M ABOUT TO DO IN THESE NEXT 700 METERS?
TOSS
HEY, HEY! I THOUGHT YOU SAID YOU DIDN'T HAVE ANY KILLER TECHNIQUES.
YOU'RE LIGHTENING UP BY TOSSING YOUR BOTTLES, HUH?
I TOLD YA NOT TO LOOK.
'COS YOU'RE THE ONE PERSON I DIDN'T WANT TO SHOW THIS TO, SENPAI.
?
WHAT?
TWITCH
A CHANGE IN THE AIR...?
......
FWOooOH
YOU CALLED THIS THE "HIGH-WIND SECTION."
RIGHT, EYE-LASHES ......!!?

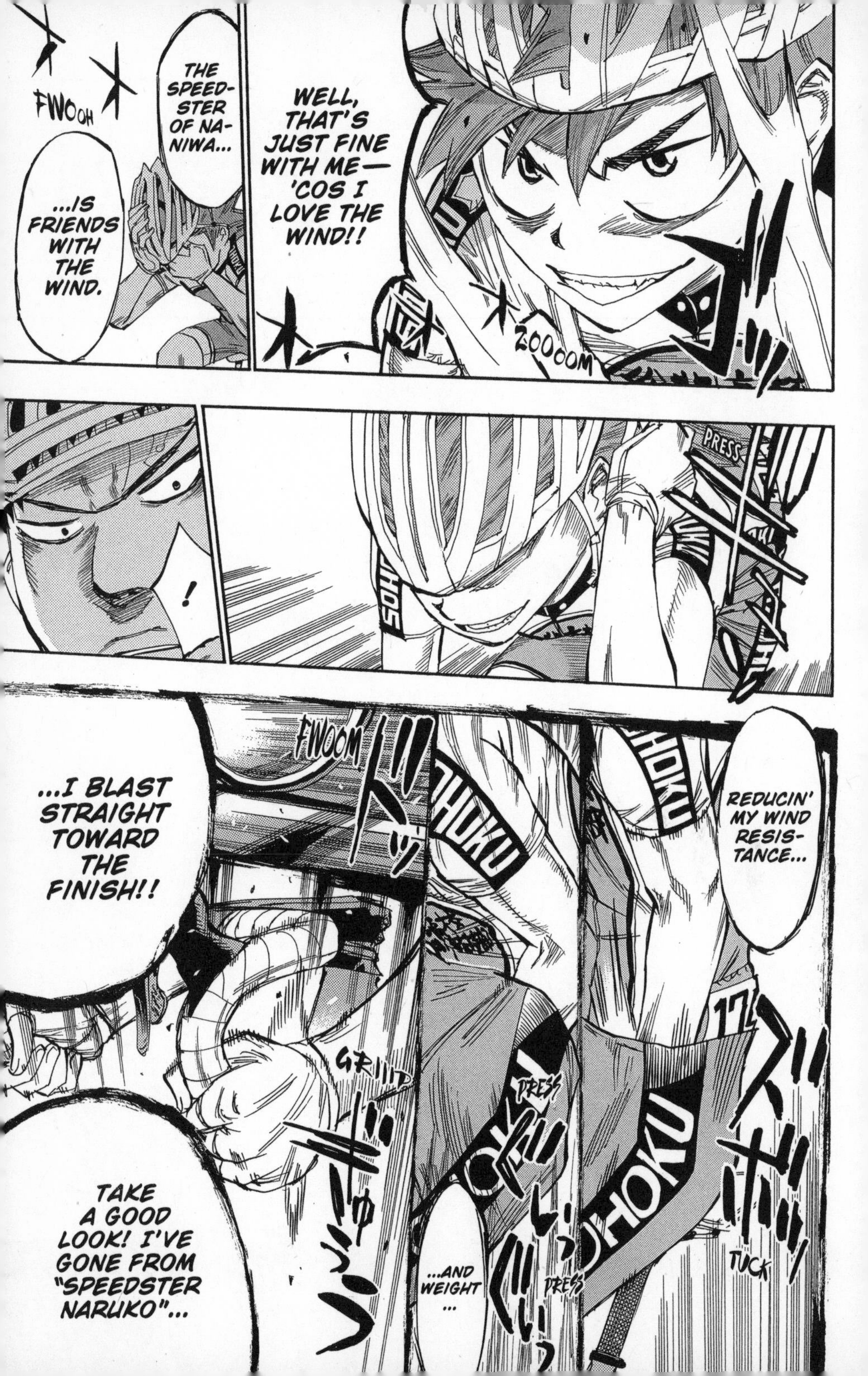
WELL, THAT'S JUST FINE WITH ME— 'COS I LOVE THE WIND!!
ZOOOOM
FWOOH
THE SPEEDSTER OF NANIWA...
...IS FRIENDS WITH THE WIND.
PRESS
!
REDUCIN' MY WIND RESISTANCE...
TUCK
PRESS
PRESS
...AND WEIGHT ...
GRIIID
FWOOM
...I BLAST STRAIGHT TOWARD THE FINISH!!
TAKE A GOOD LOOK! I'VE GONE FROM "SPEEDSTER NARUKO"...

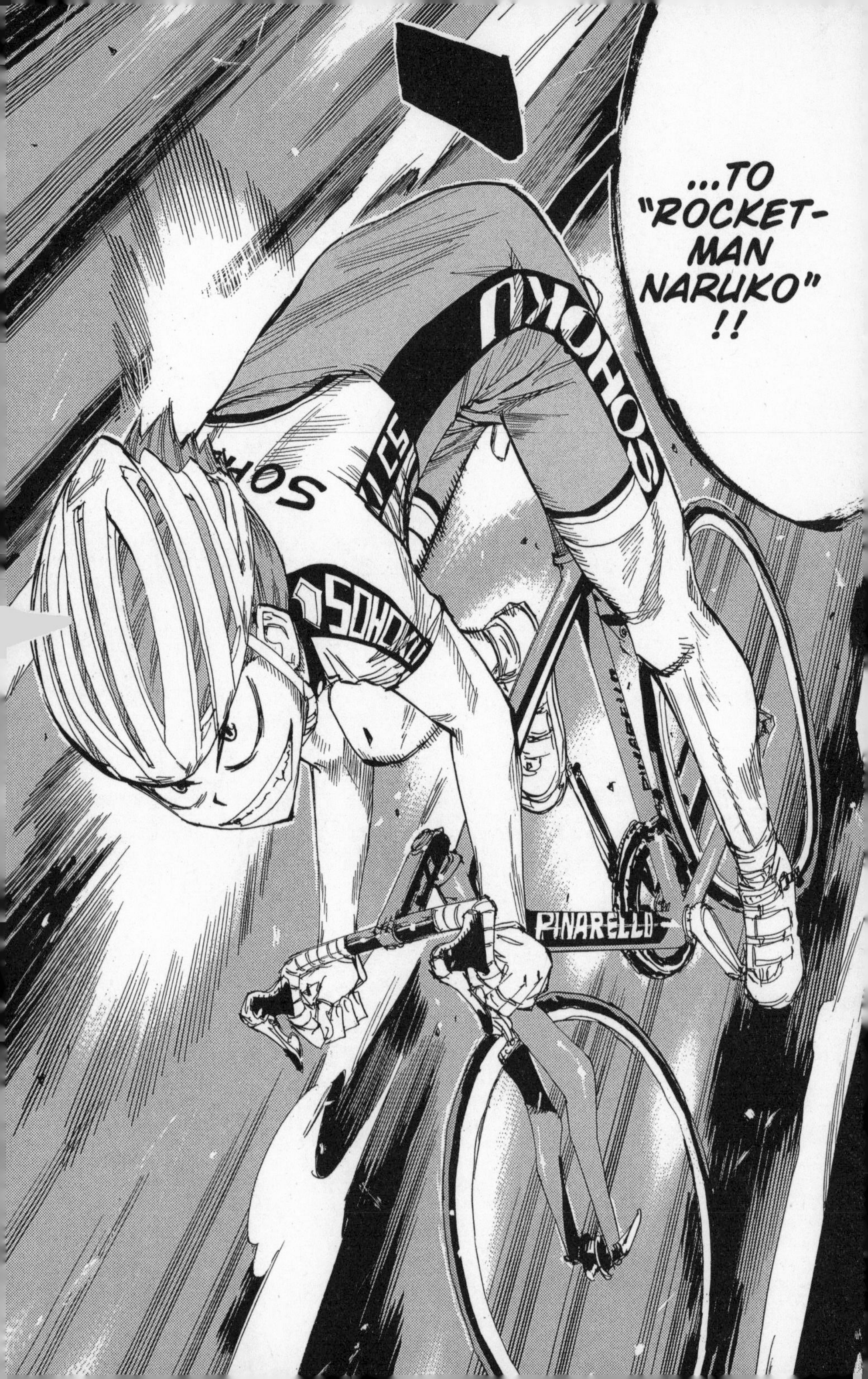
...TO "ROCKET-MAN NARUKO"!!
SOHOKU
SOHOKU
SOHOKU
PINARELLO

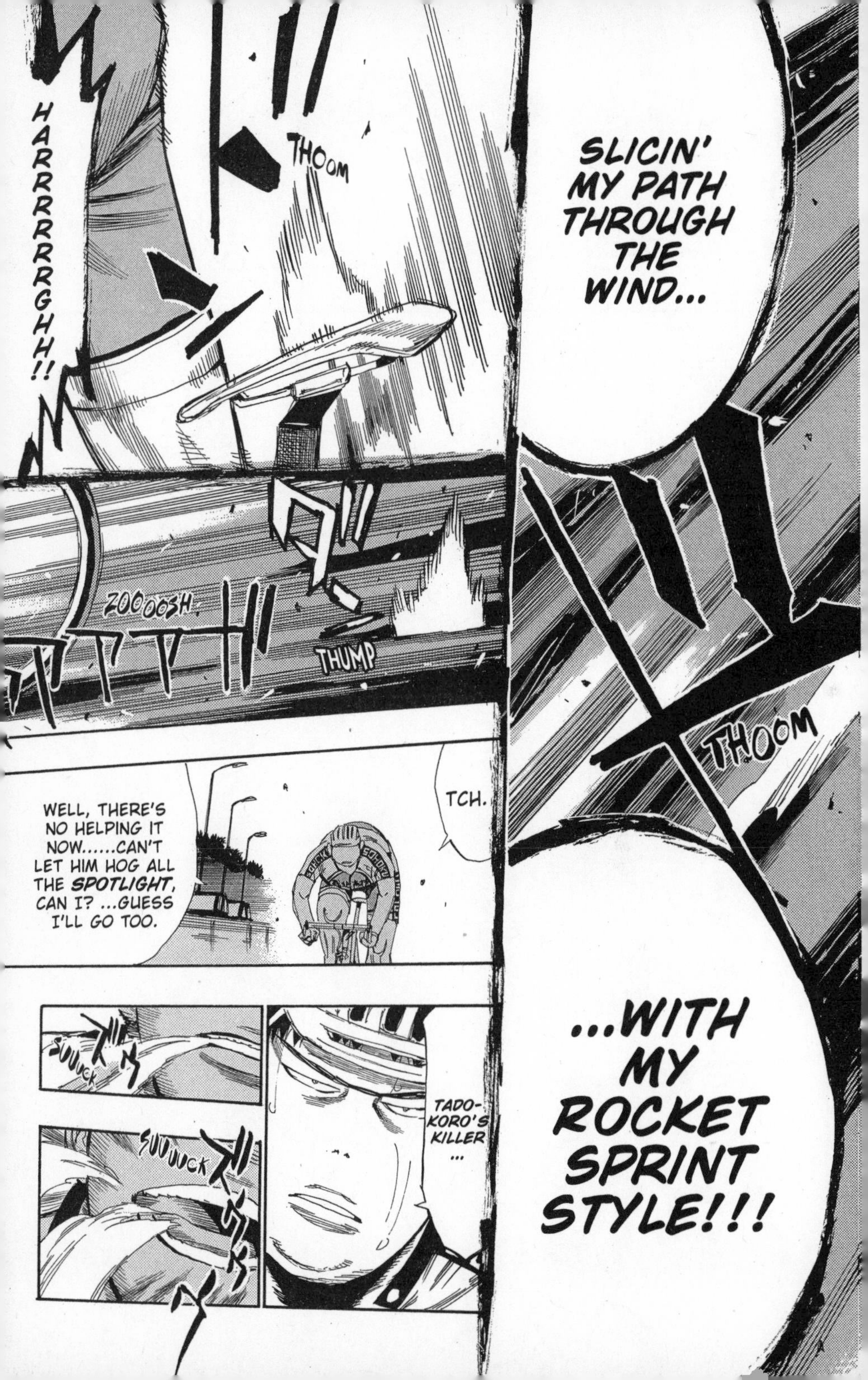
SLICIN' MY PATH THROUGH THE WIND...
THOOM
...WITH MY ROCKET SPRINT STYLE!!!
HARRRRRRGHH!!
THOOM
ZOOOOSH
THUMP
TCH.
WELL, THERE'S NO HELPING IT NOW......CAN'T LET HIM HOG ALL THE *SPOTLIGHT*, CAN I? ...GUESS I'LL GO TOO.
TADO-KORO'S KILLER ...
SUUUCK
SUUUUCK

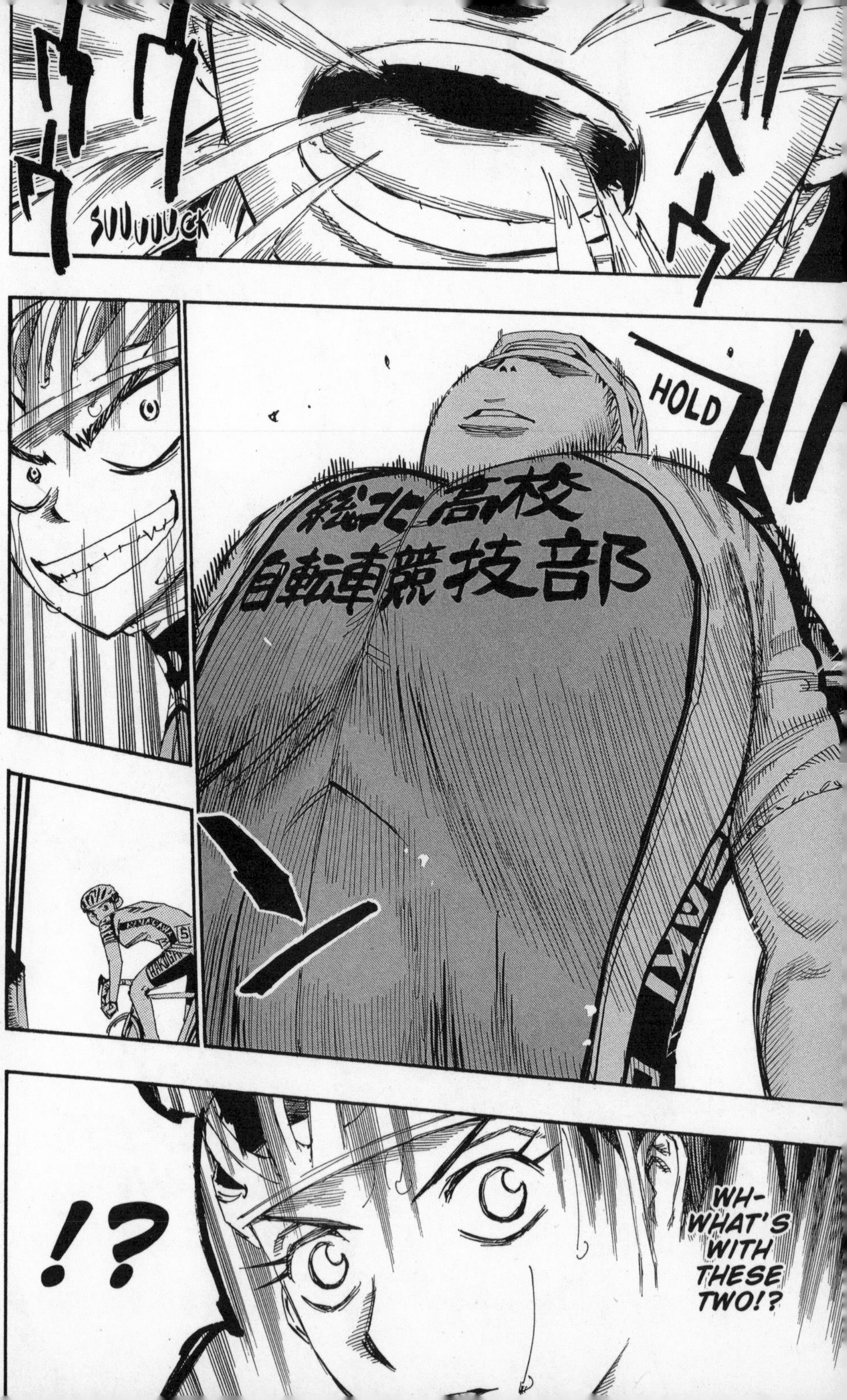
SUUUUUCK
HOLD
総北高校
自転車競技部
WH-WHAT'S WITH THESE TWO!?
!?

RIDE.81 TREMBLING IZUMIDA

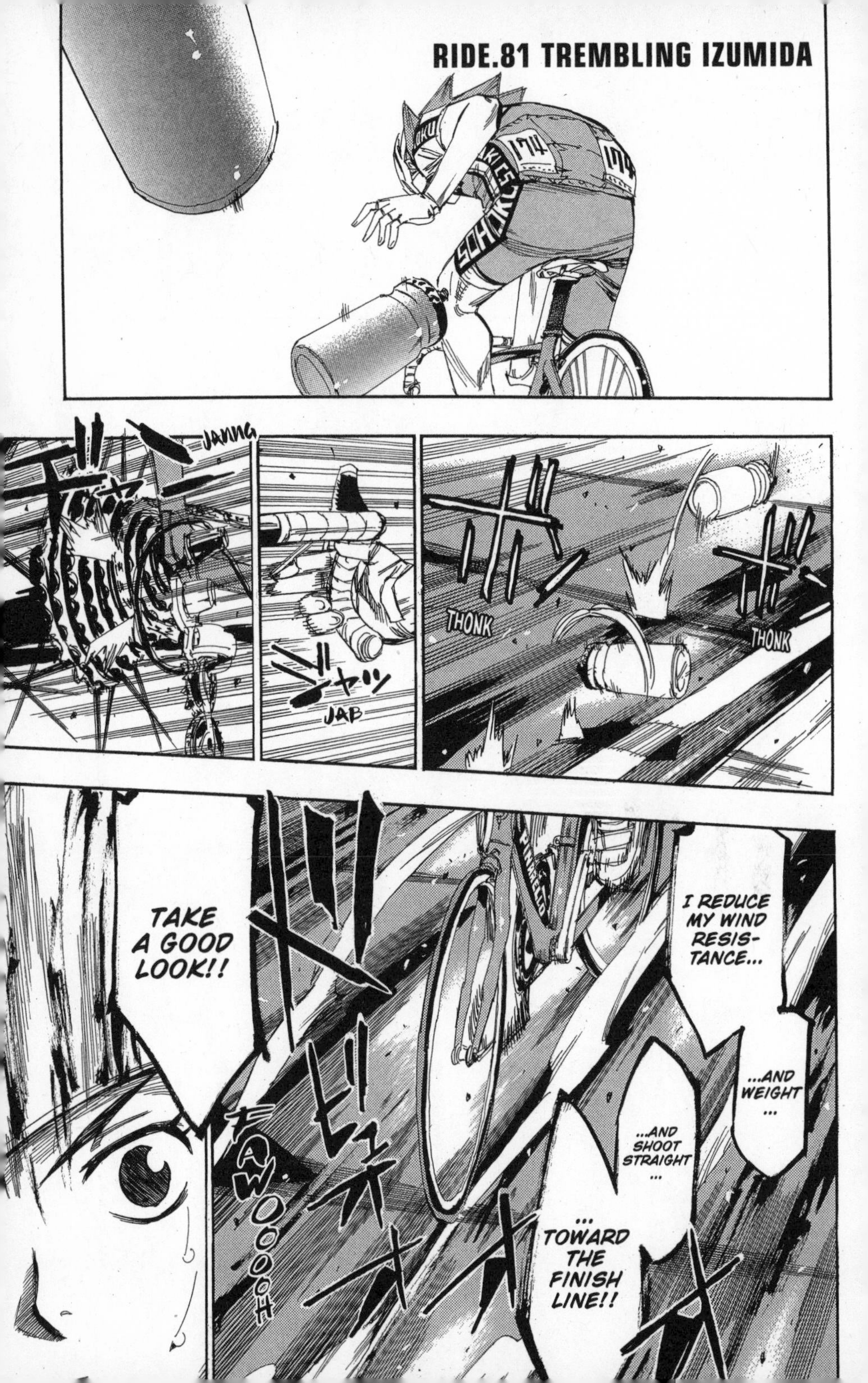
THONK
THONK
JAB
JANNG
I REDUCE MY WIND RESIS-TANCE...
...AND WEIGHT...
...AND SHOOT STRAIGHT...
...TOWARD THE FINISH LINE!!
TAKE A GOOD LOOK!!
FWOOOOOOH

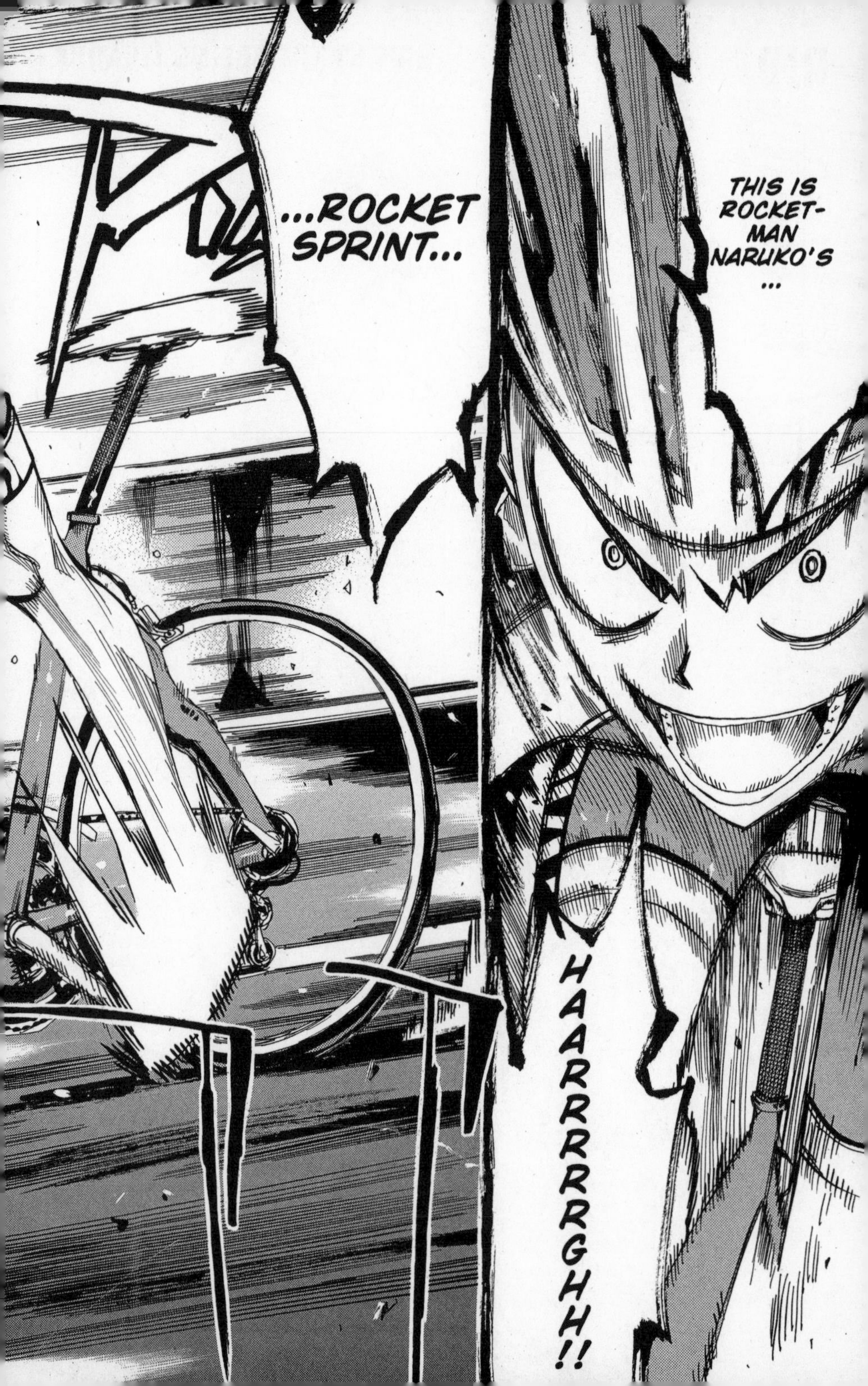
THIS IS ROCKET-MAN NARUKO'S ...
HAARRRRGHH!!
...ROCKET SPRINT...

RIDE.81 TREMBLING IZUMIDA

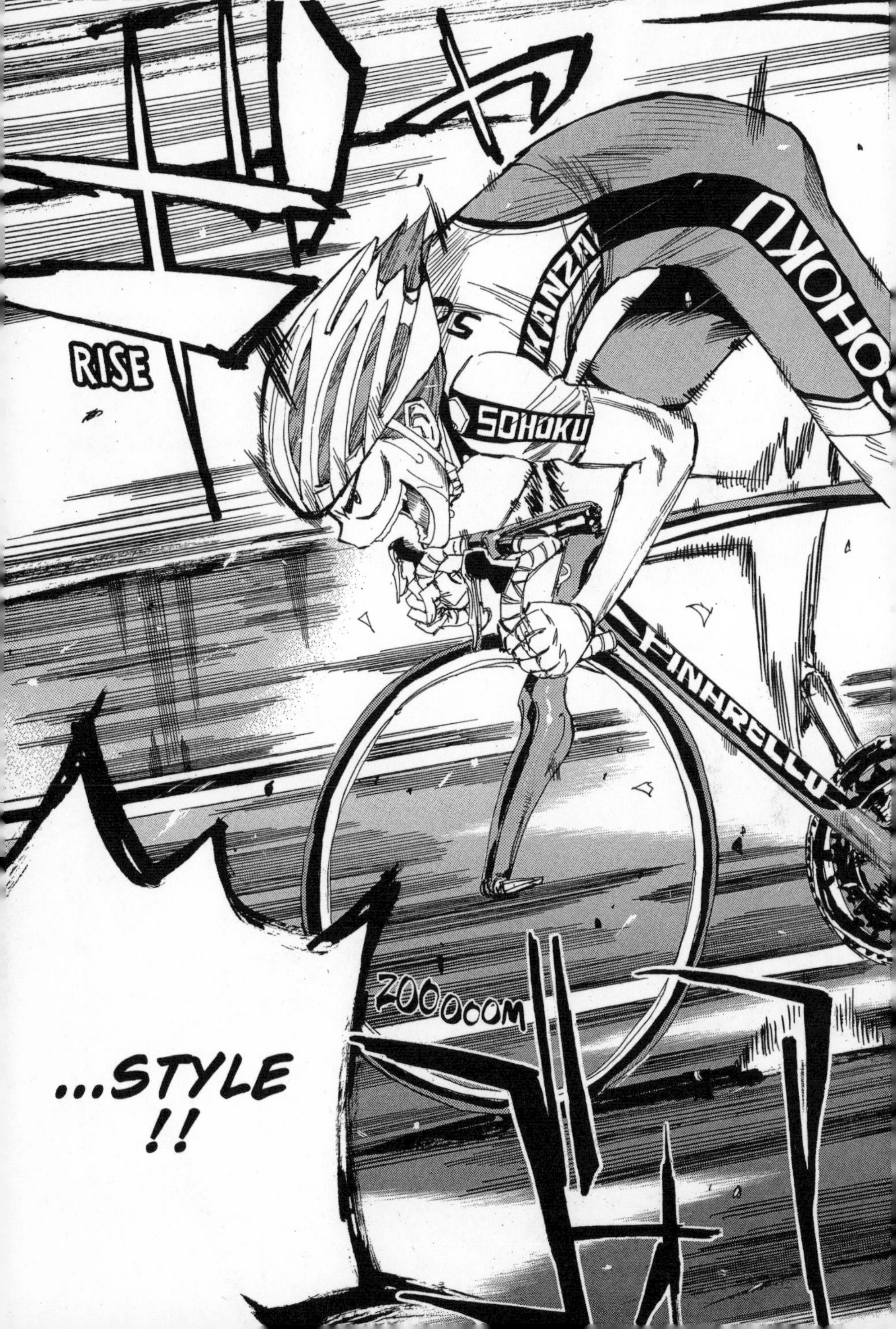
RISE
ZOOOOOM
...STYLE !!

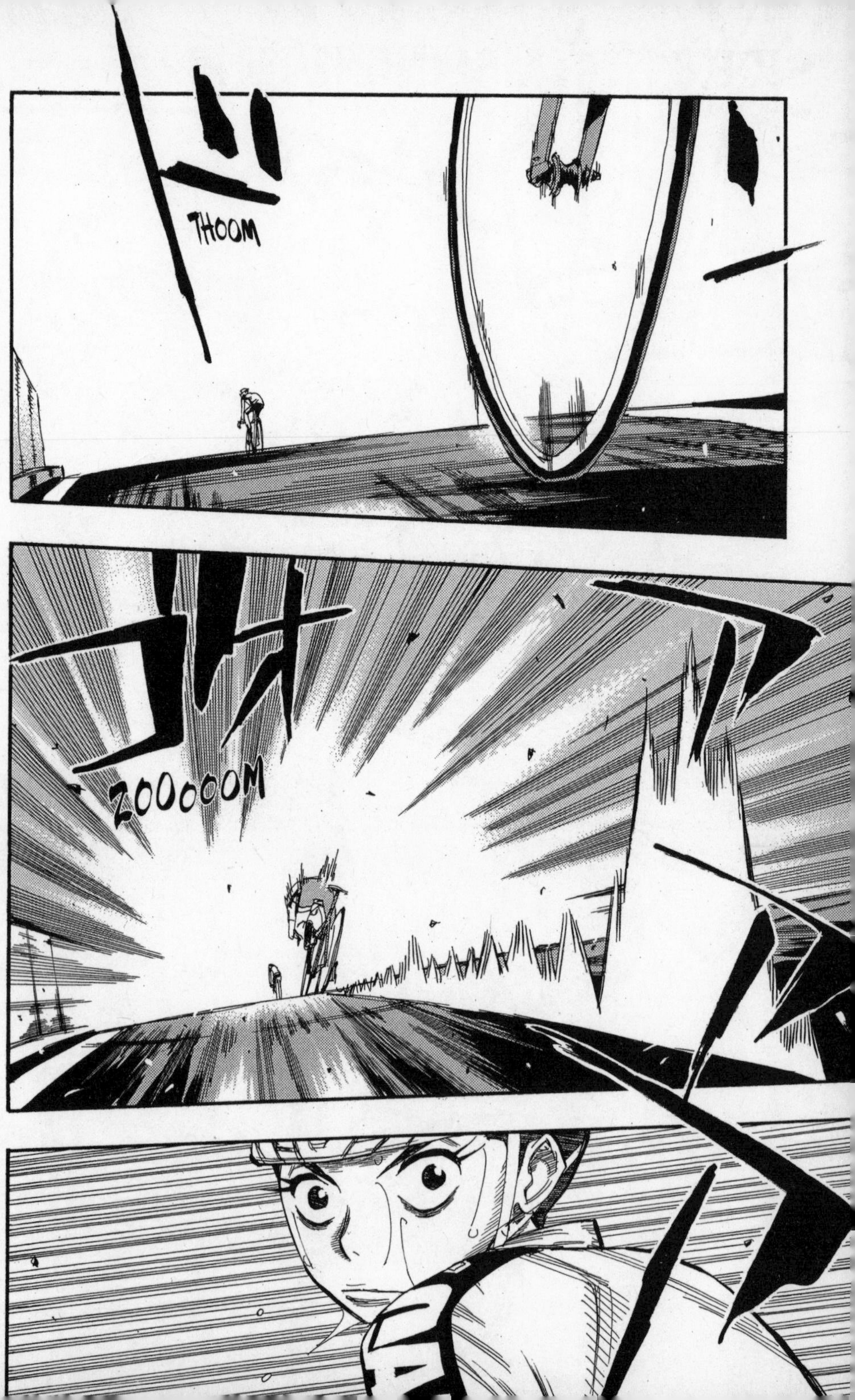
THOOM
ZOOOOOM

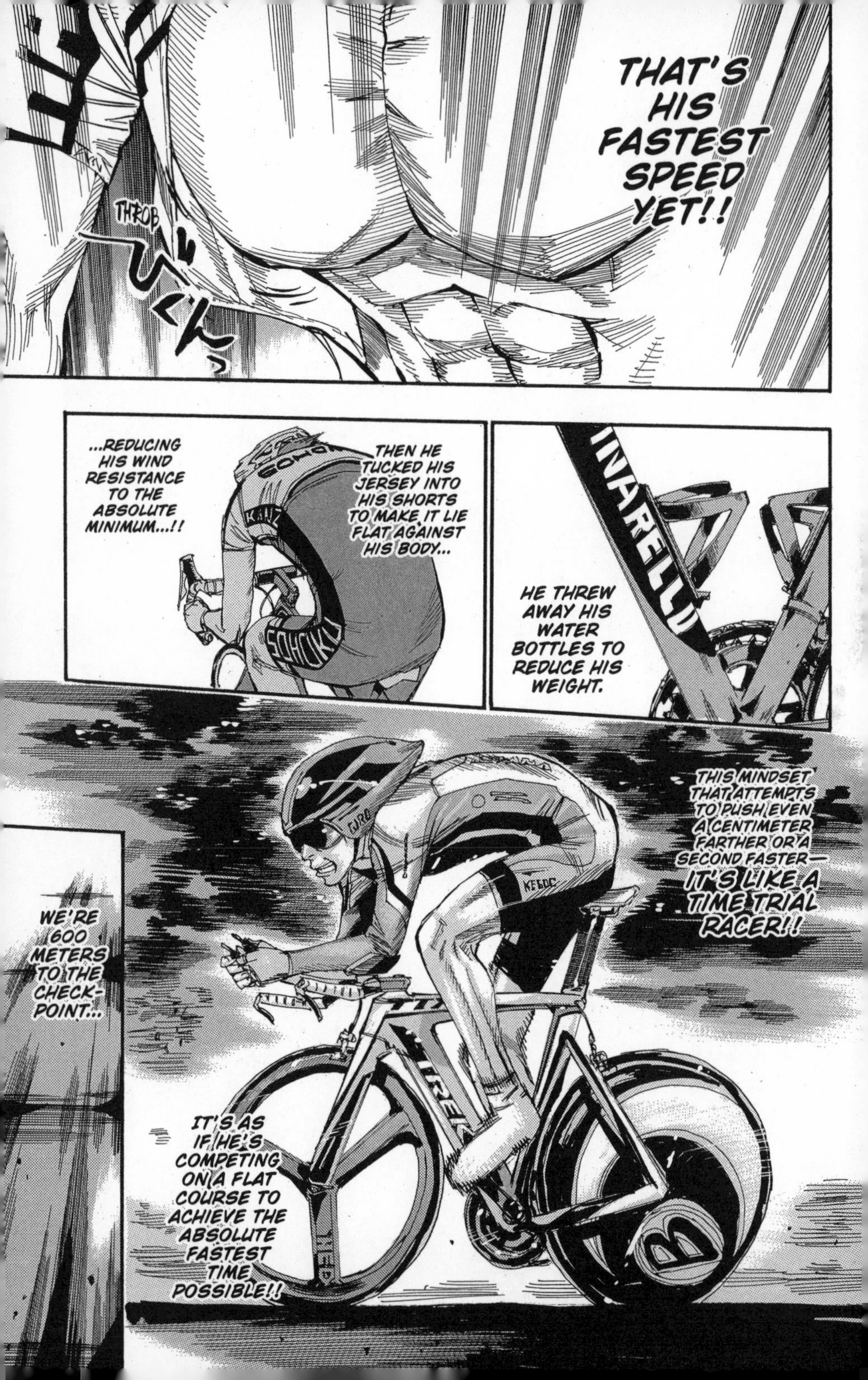
THAT'S HIS FASTEST SPEED YET!!
THROB
HE THREW AWAY HIS WATER BOTTLES TO REDUCE HIS WEIGHT.
THEN HE TUCKED HIS JERSEY INTO HIS SHORTS TO MAKE IT LIE FLAT AGAINST HIS BODY...
...REDUCING HIS WIND RESISTANCE TO THE ABSOLUTE MINIMUM...!!
THIS MINDSET THAT ATTEMPTS TO PUSH EVEN A CENTIMETER FARTHER OR A SECOND FASTER— IT'S LIKE A TIME TRIAL RACER!!
IT'S AS IF HE'S COMPETING ON A FLAT COURSE TO ACHIEVE THE ABSOLUTE FASTEST TIME POSSIBLE!!
WE'RE 600 METERS TO THE CHECK-POINT...

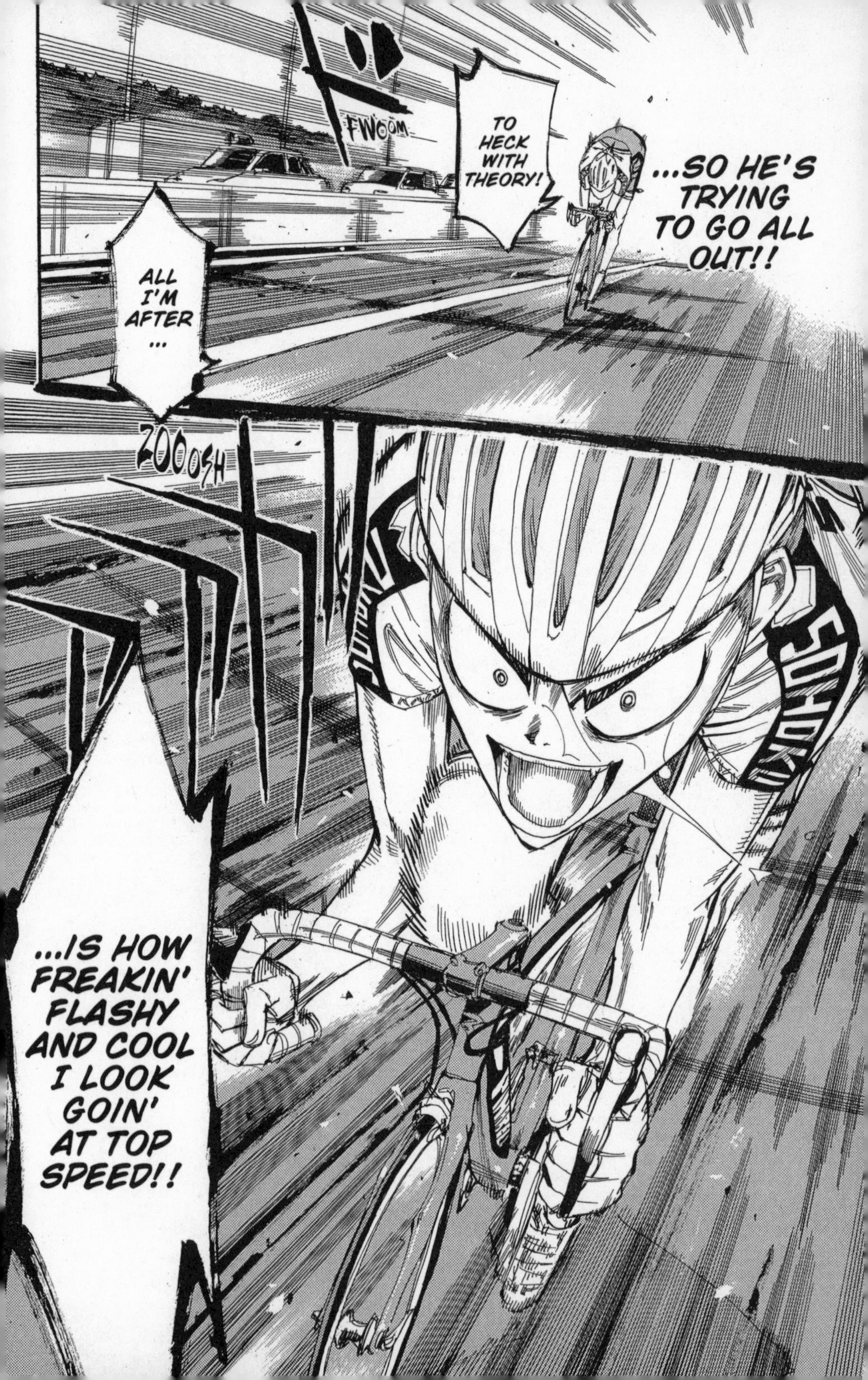
...SO HE'S TRYING TO GO ALL OUT!!
TO HECK WITH THEORY!
FWOOM
ALL I'M AFTER...
ZOOOSH
...IS HOW FREAKIN' FLASHY AND COOL I LOOK GOIN' AT TOP SPEED!!

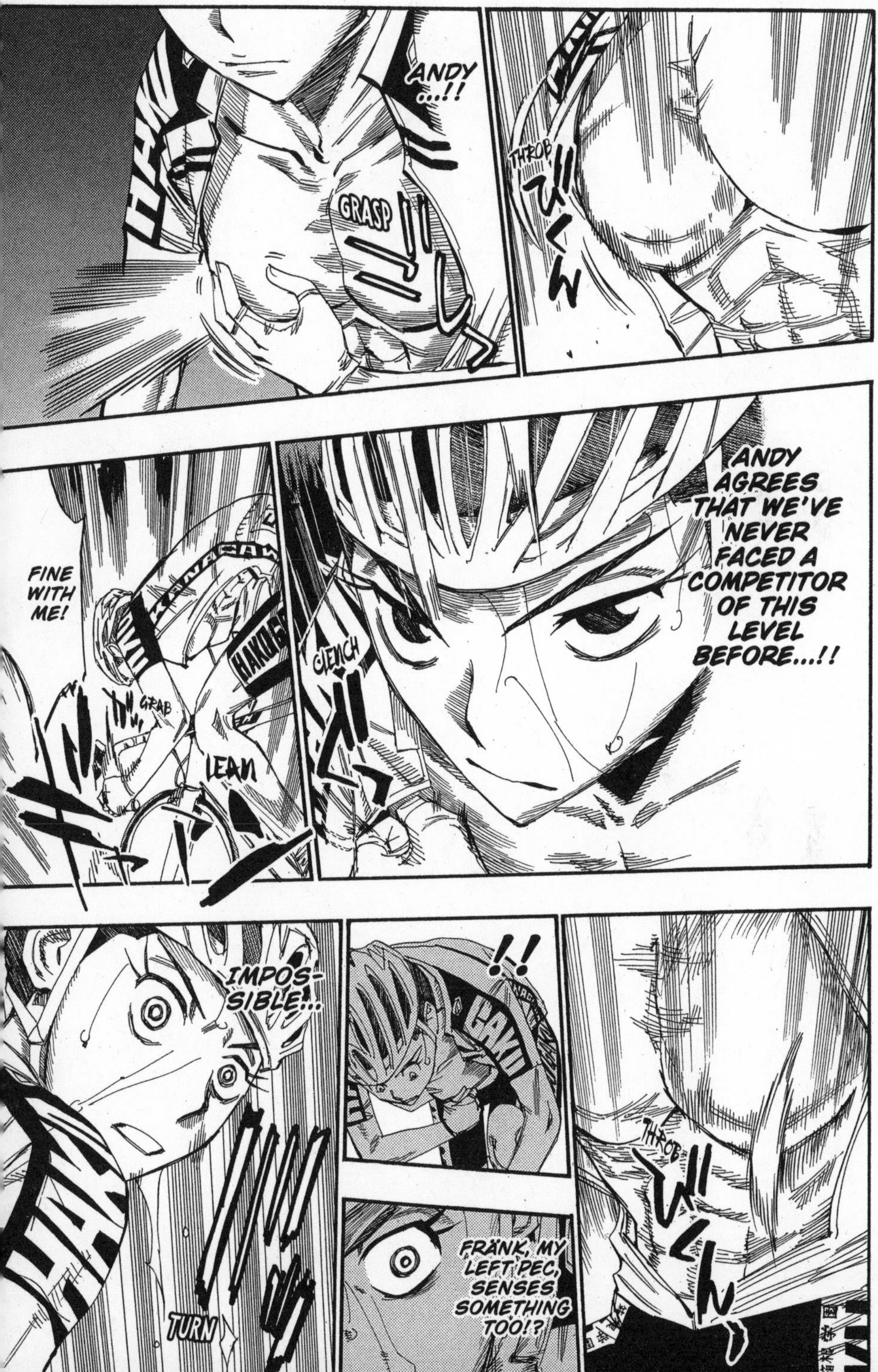
THROB
ANDY ...!!
GRASP
ANDY AGREES THAT WE'VE NEVER FACED A COMPETITOR OF THIS LEVEL BEFORE...!!
CLENCH
FINE WITH ME!
GRAB
LEAN
THROB
!!
FRÄNK, MY LEFT PEC, SENSES SOMETHING TOO!?
IMPOS-SIBLE...
TURN

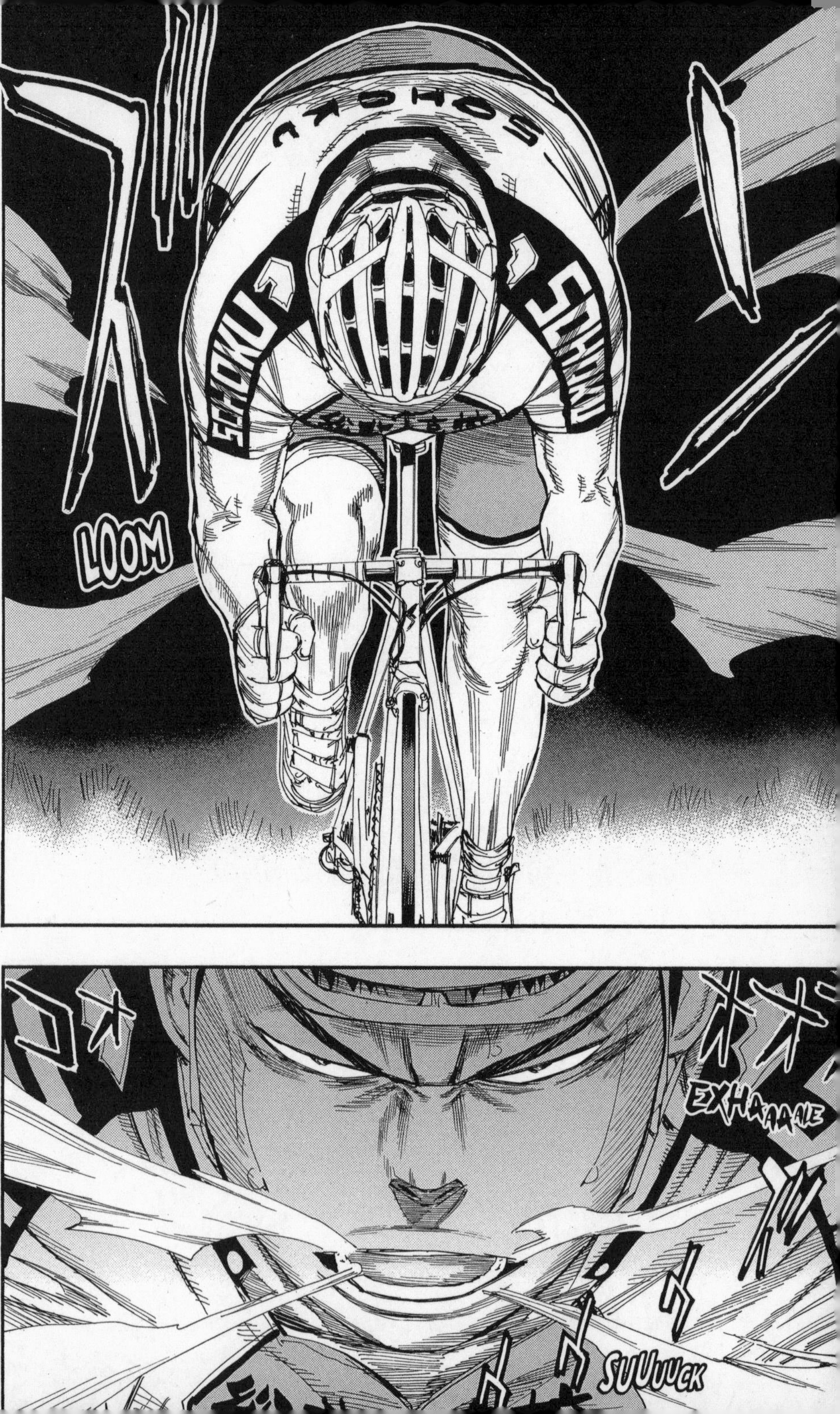
LOOM
EXHAAAALE
SUUUUCK

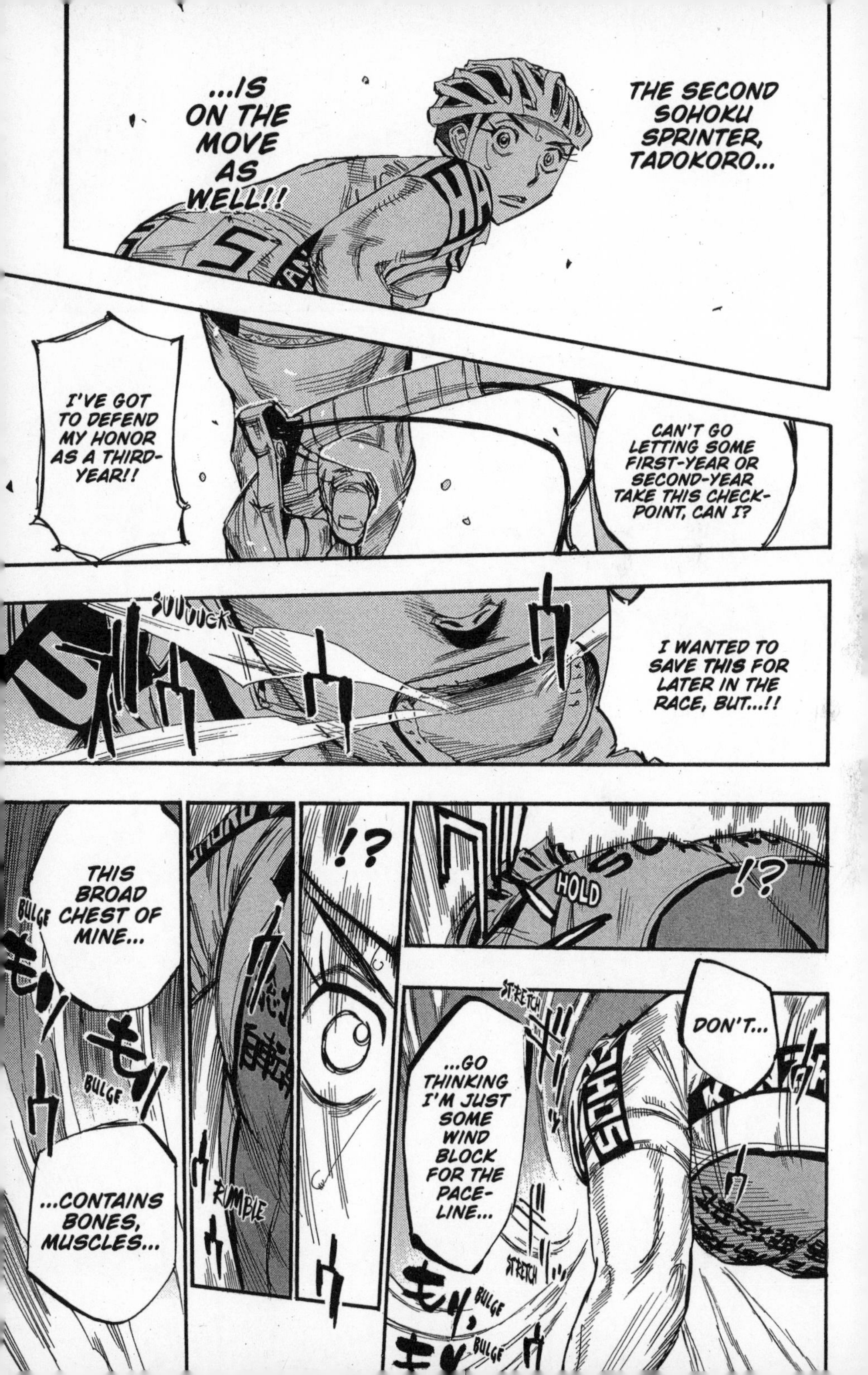
THE SECOND SOHOKU SPRINTER, TADOKORO...
...IS ON THE MOVE AS WELL!!
CAN'T GO LETTING SOME FIRST-YEAR OR SECOND-YEAR TAKE THIS CHECK-POINT, CAN I?
I'VE GOT TO DEFEND MY HONOR AS A THIRD-YEAR!!
I WANTED TO SAVE THIS FOR LATER IN THE RACE, BUT...!!
SUUUUCK
!?
HOLD
DON'T...
...GO THINKING I'M JUST SOME WIND BLOCK FOR THE PACE-LINE...
STRETCH
STRETCH
BULGE
BULGE
!?
RUMBLE
THIS BROAD CHEST OF MINE...
BULGE
BULGE
...CONTAINS BONES, MUSCLES...

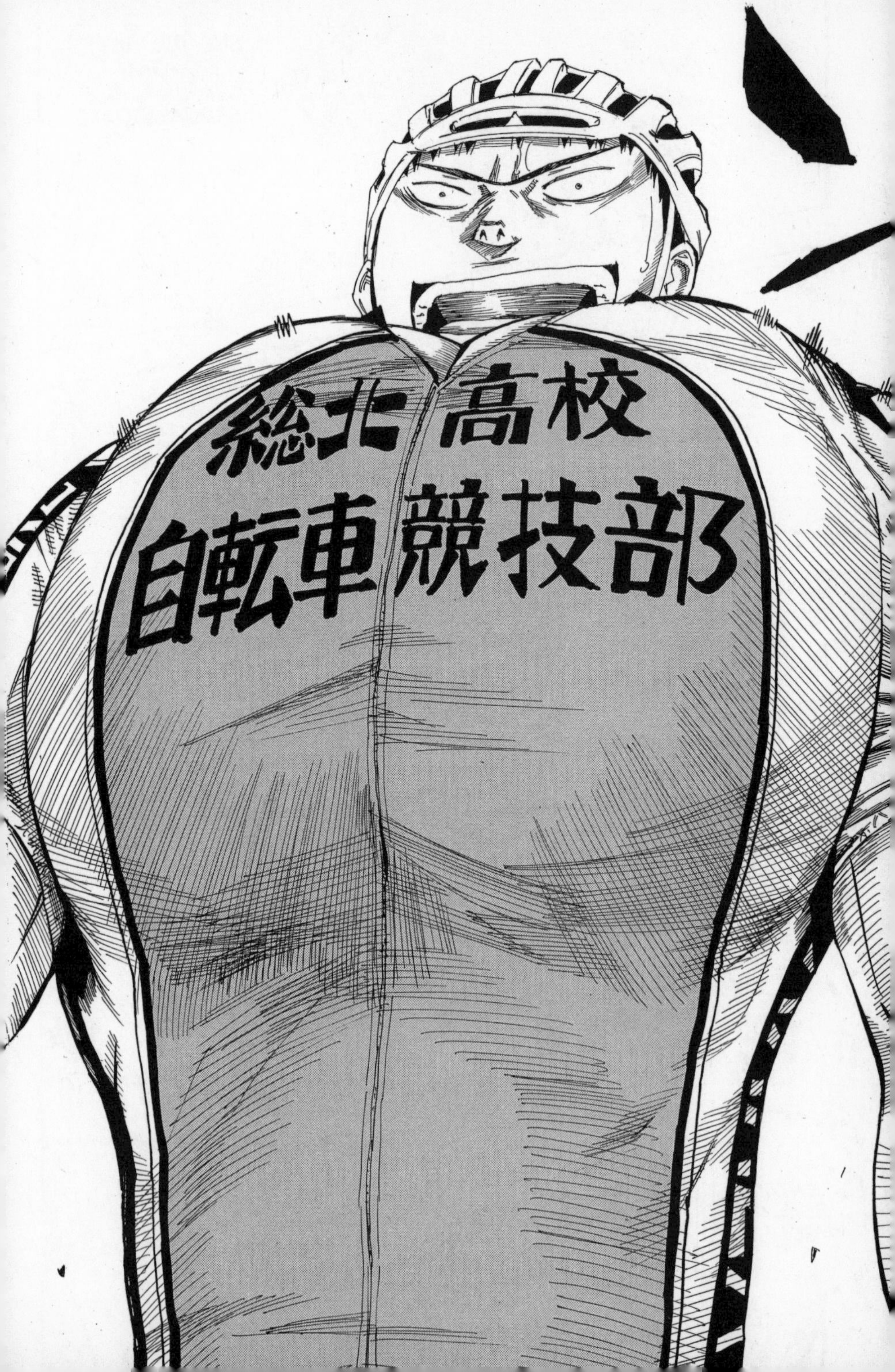
総北高校
自転車競技部

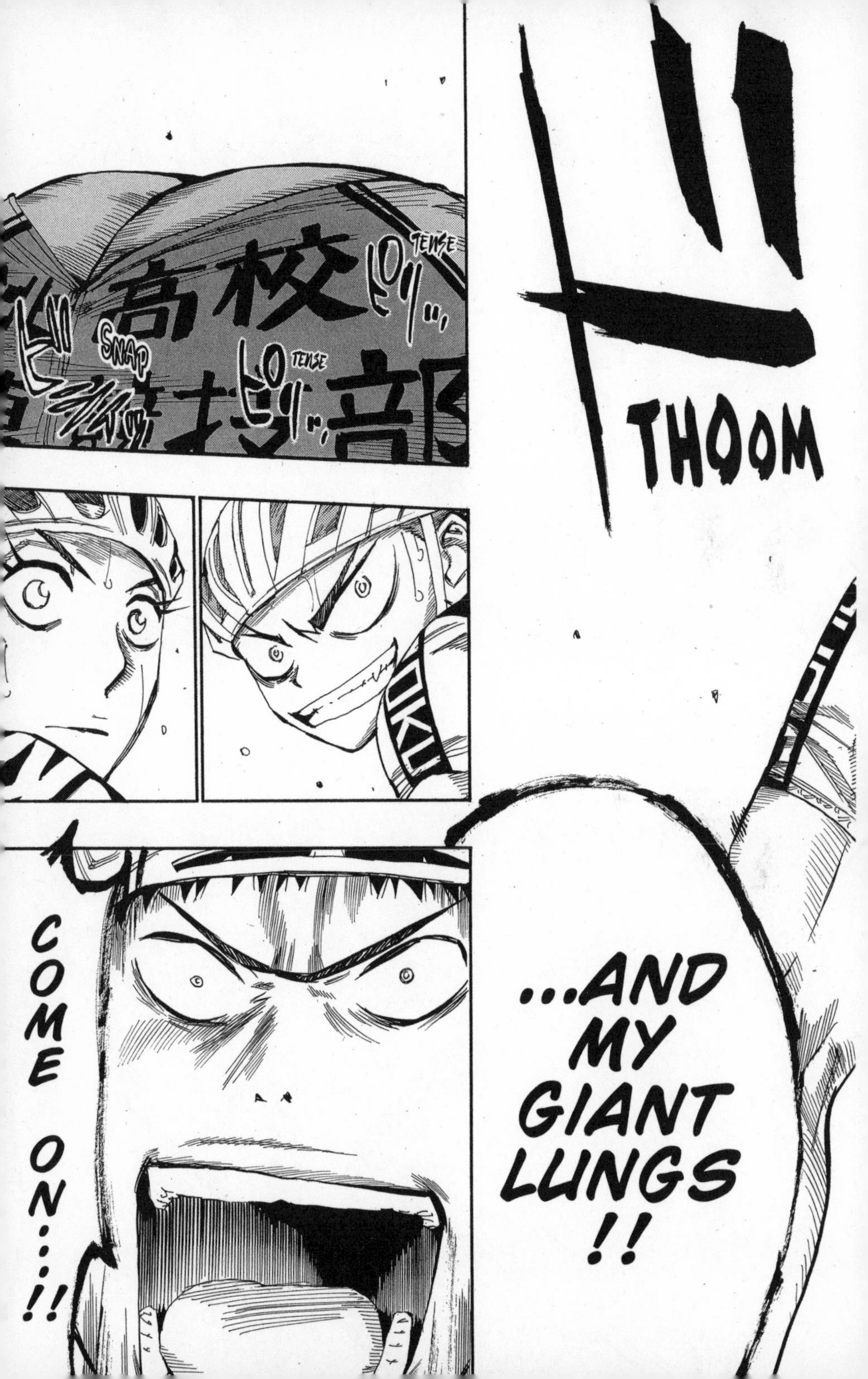
THOOM
...AND MY GIANT LUNGS!!
TENSE
TENSE
SNAP
COME ON...!!

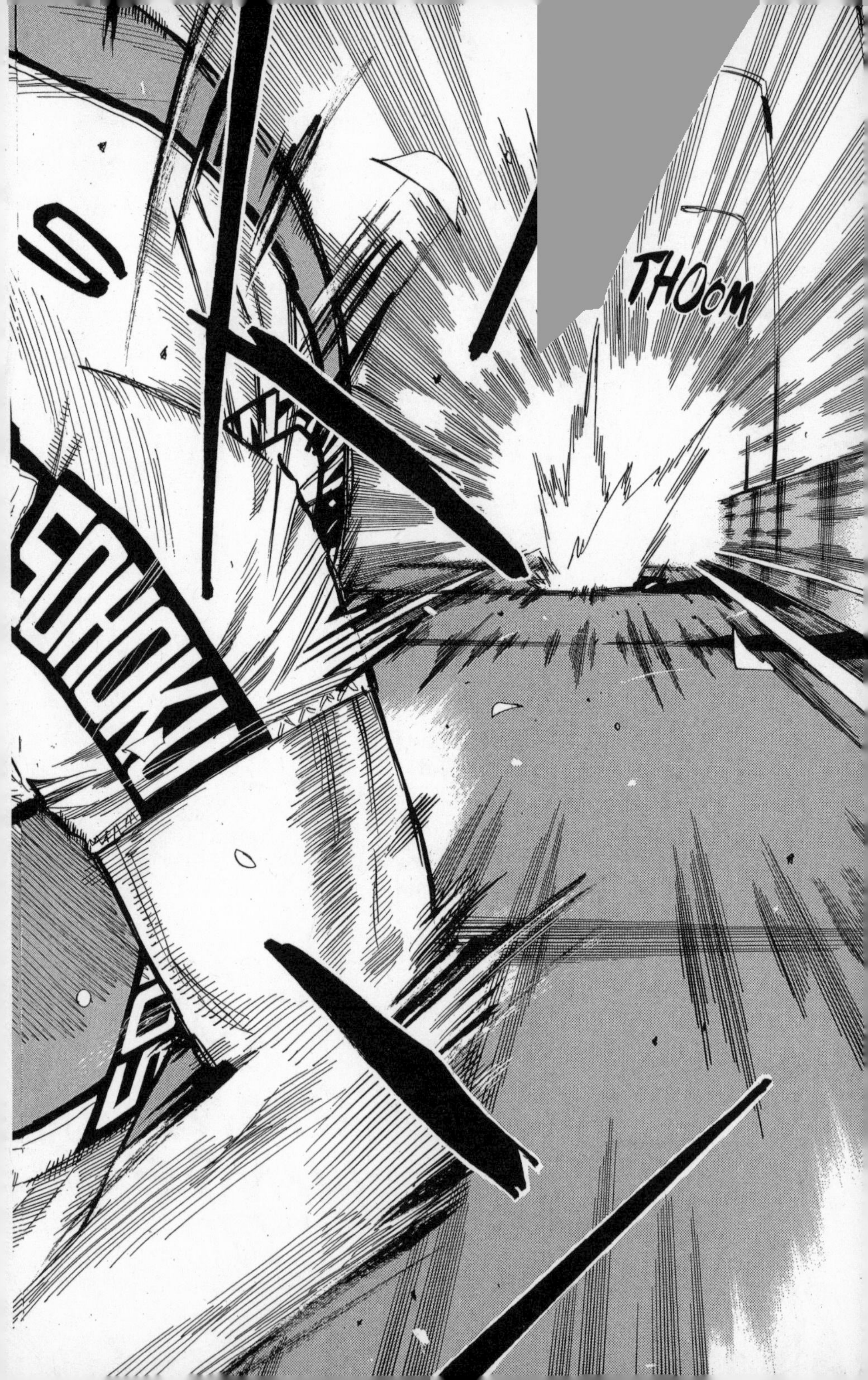
THOOM
SCHOK!

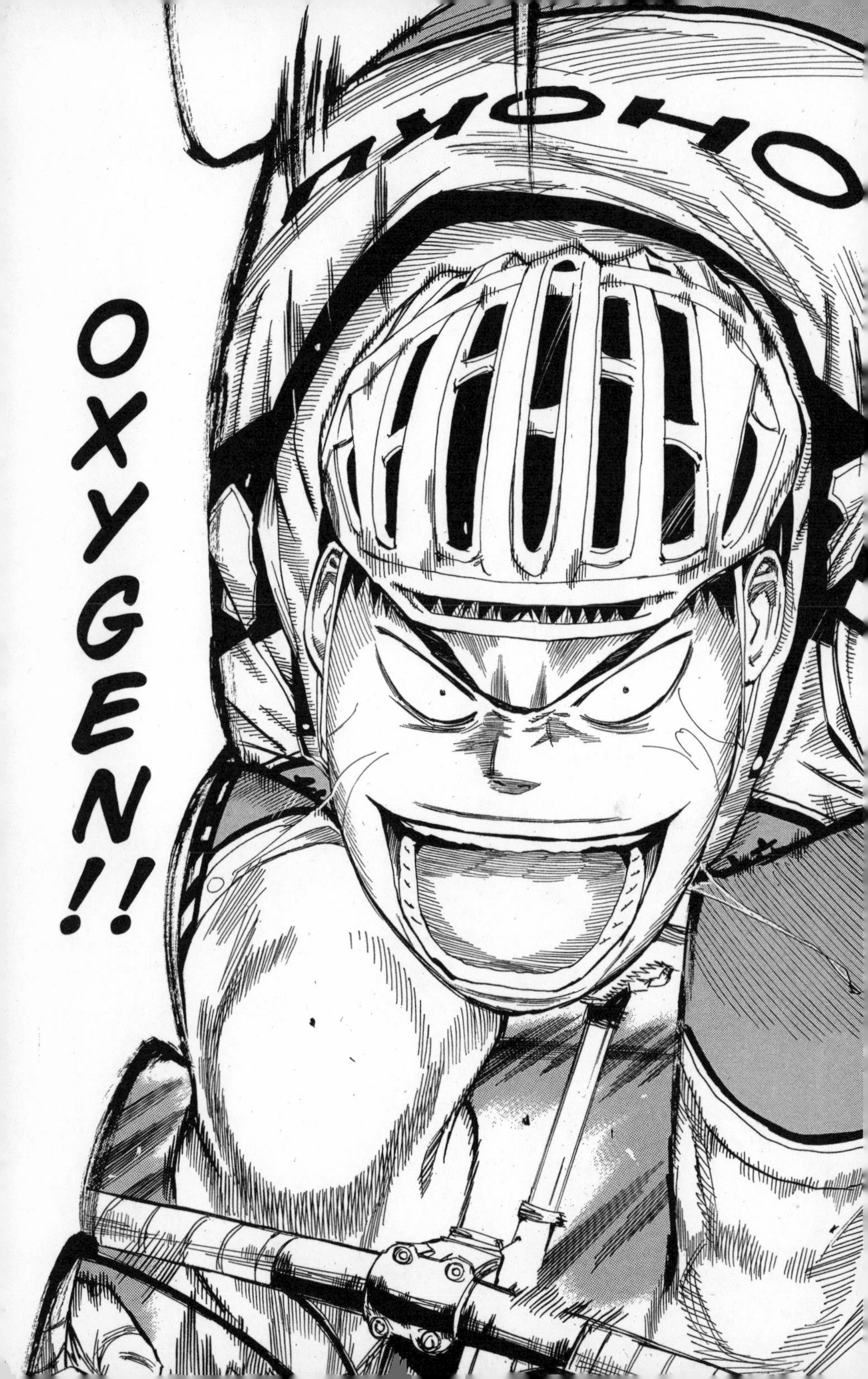
OXYGEN!!

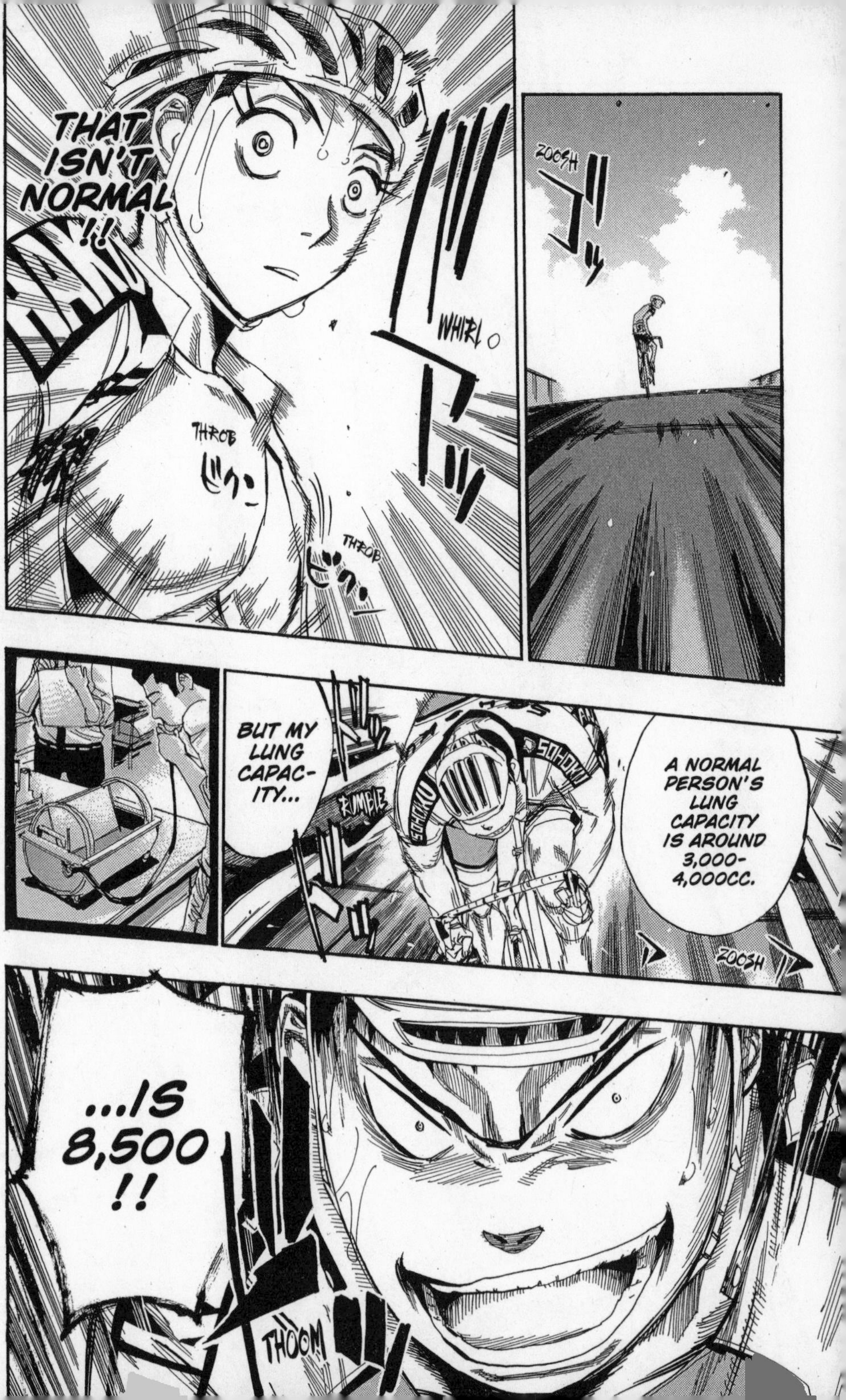

ZOOSH
ゴッ
THAT ISN'T NORMAL!!
WHIRL
THROB
ビクッ
THROB
ビクッ
A NORMAL PERSON'S LUNG CAPACITY IS AROUND 3,000-4,000CC.
ZOOSH
RUMBLE
BUT MY LUNG CAPACITY...
...IS 8,500!!
THOOM

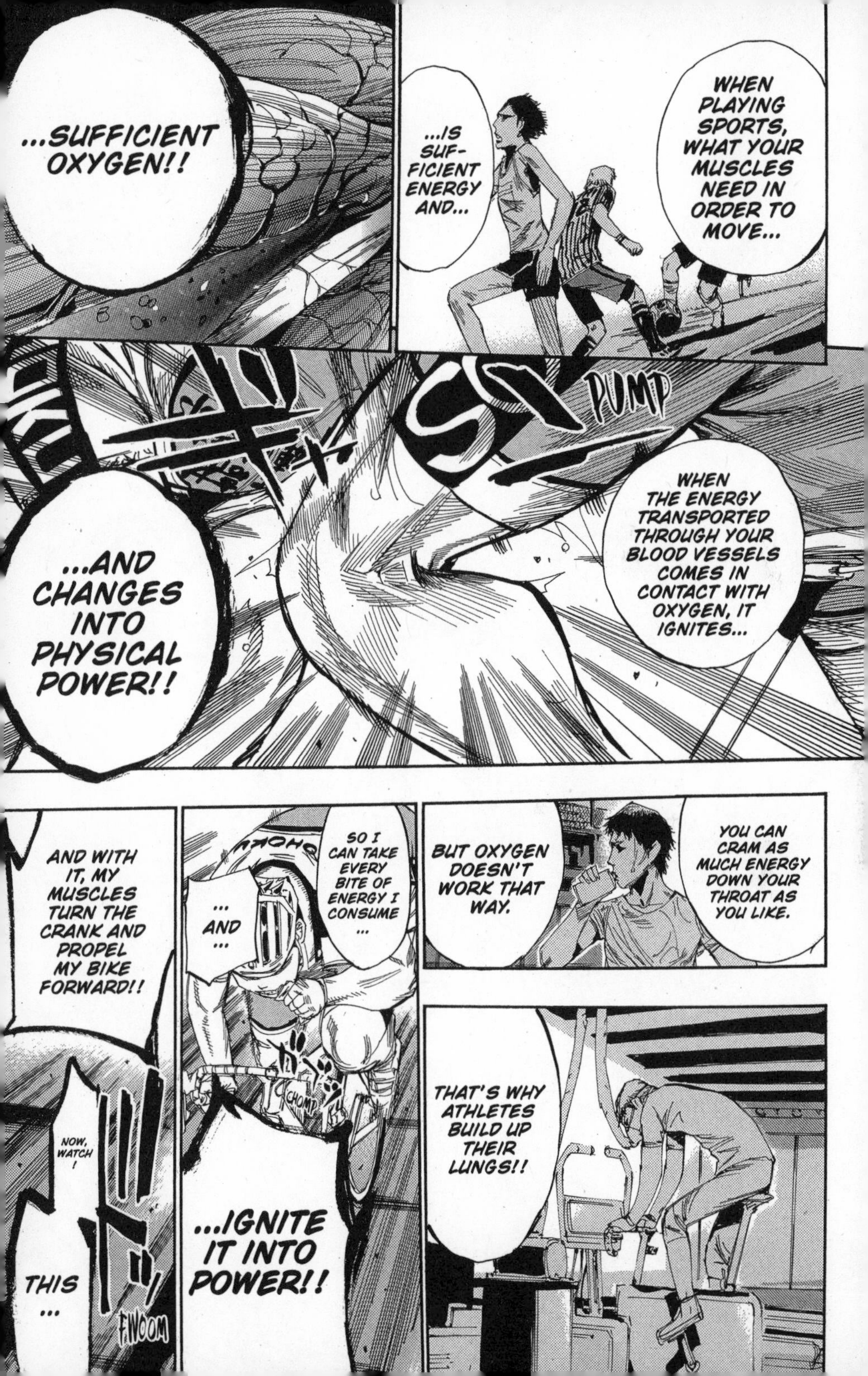
WHEN PLAYING SPORTS, WHAT YOUR MUSCLES NEED IN ORDER TO MOVE...
...IS SUF-FICIENT ENERGY AND...
...SUFFICIENT OXYGEN!!
PUMP
WHEN THE ENERGY TRANSPORTED THROUGH YOUR BLOOD VESSELS COMES IN CONTACT WITH OXYGEN, IT IGNITES...
...AND CHANGES INTO PHYSICAL POWER!!
YOU CAN CRAM AS MUCH ENERGY DOWN YOUR THROAT AS YOU LIKE.
BUT OXYGEN DOESN'T WORK THAT WAY.
THAT'S WHY ATHLETES BUILD UP THEIR LUNGS!!
SO I CAN TAKE EVERY BITE OF ENERGY I CONSUME...
...AND...
CHOMP
...IGNITE IT INTO POWER!!
AND WITH IT, MY MUSCLES TURN THE CRANK AND PROPEL MY BIKE FORWARD!!
NOW, WATCH!
THIS...
FWOOM

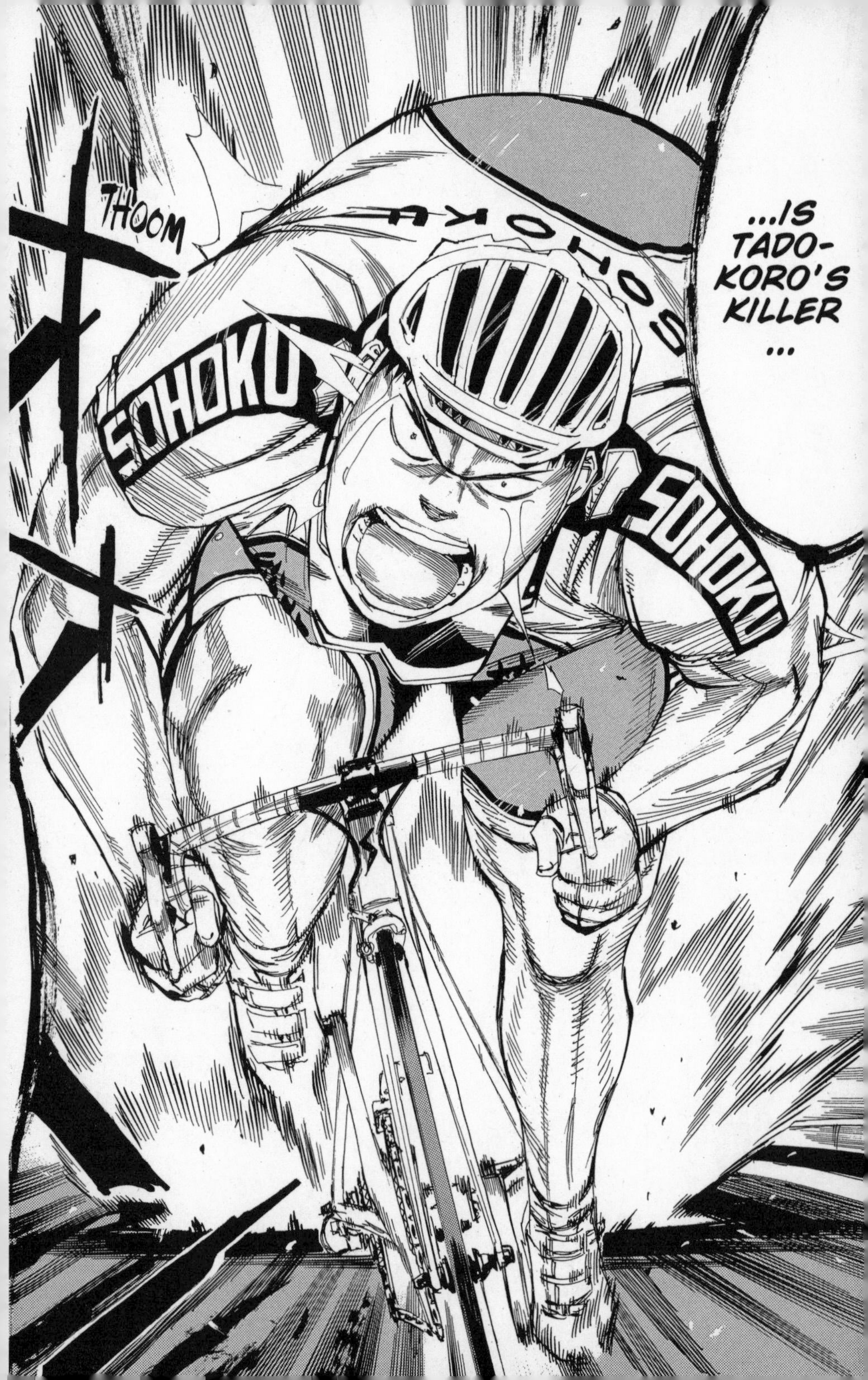
...IS TADO-KORO'S KILLER ...
THOOM
SOHOKU
SOHOKU
SOHOKU

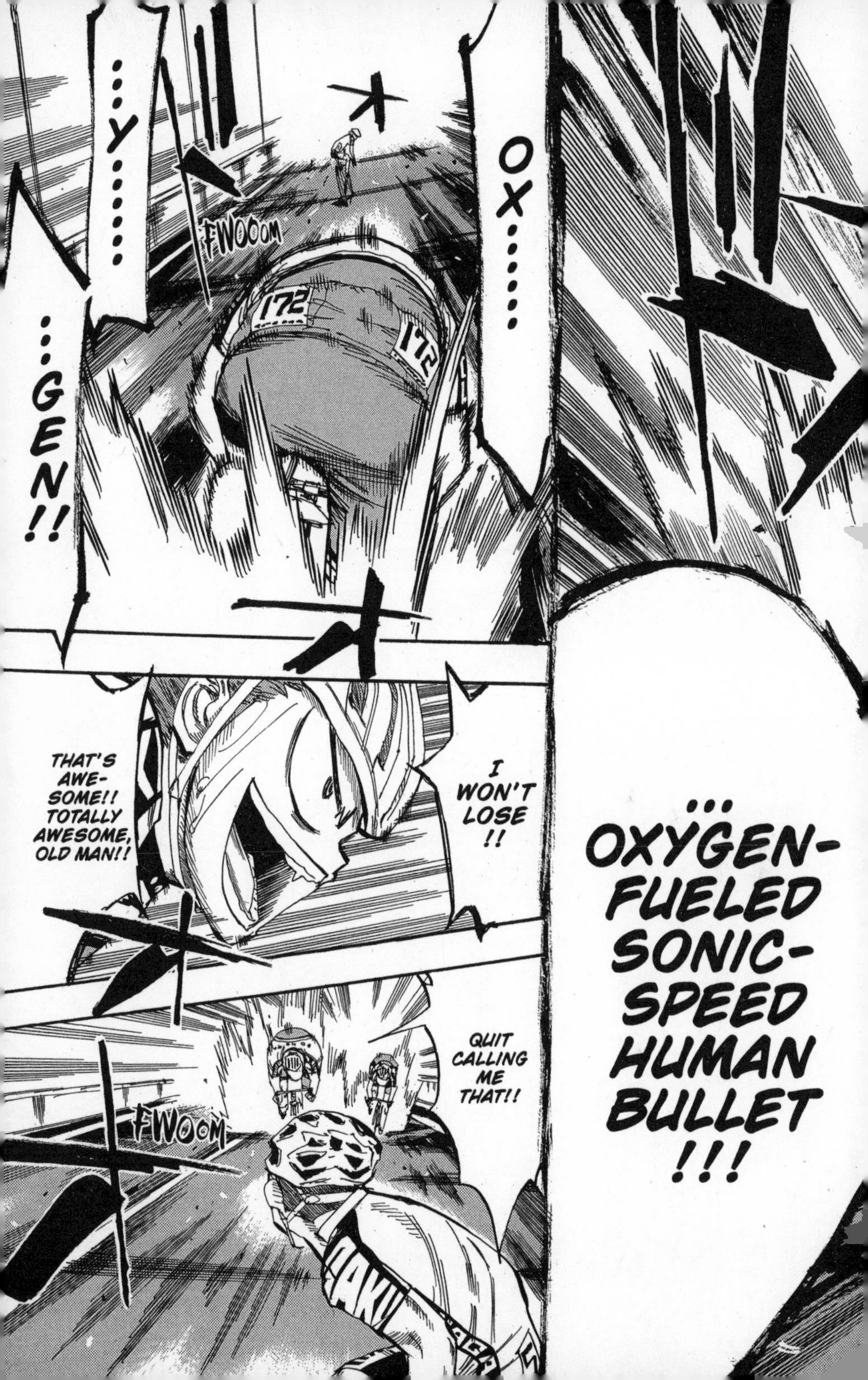
OX......
...Y.....
FWOOOM
...GEN!!
I WON'T LOSE!!
THAT'S AWESOME!! TOTALLY AWESOME, OLD MAN!!
QUIT CALLING ME THAT!!
FWOOM
...OXYGEN-FUELED SONIC-SPEED HUMAN BULLET!!!

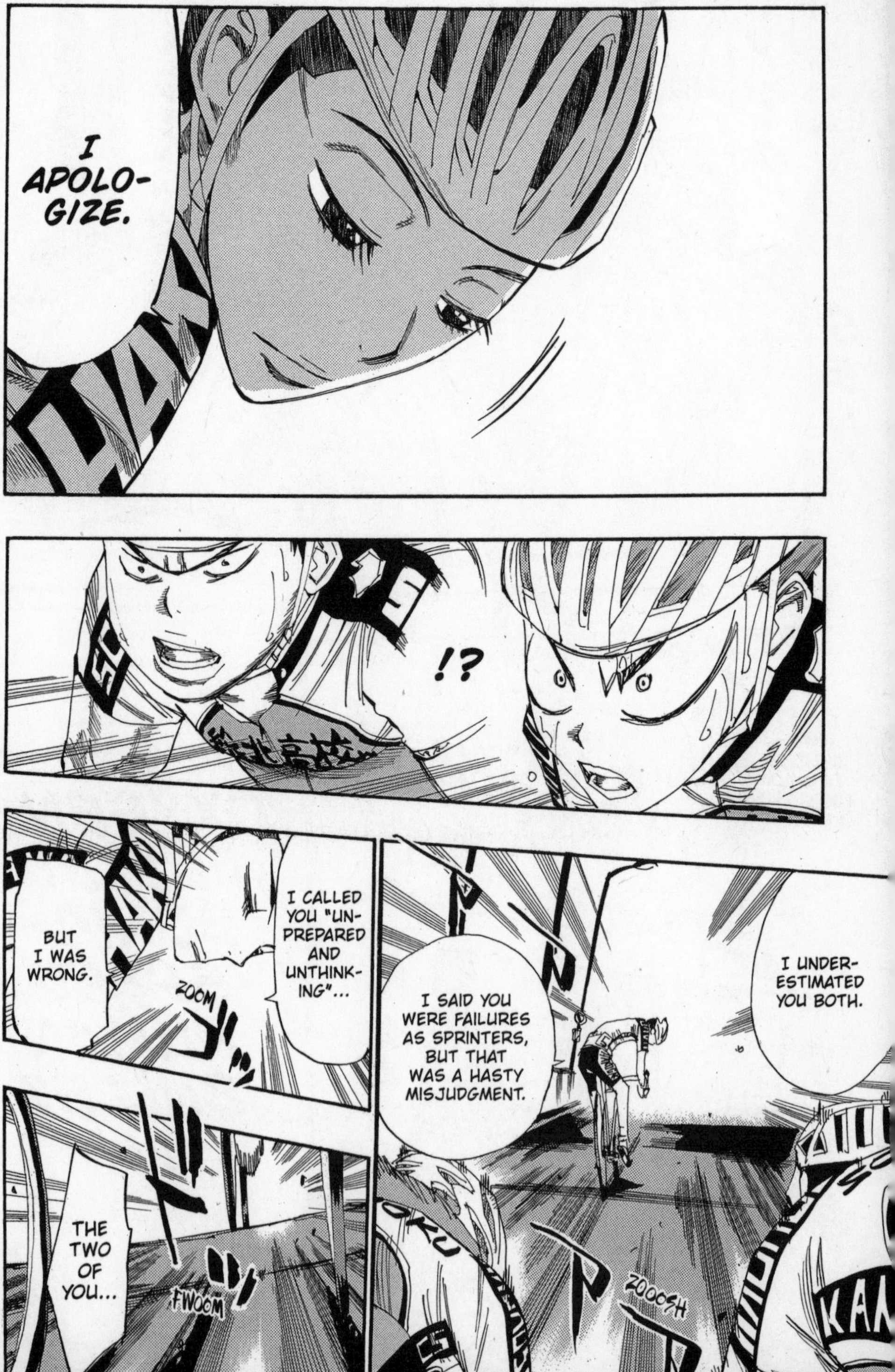
I APOLOGIZE.
!?
I UNDERESTIMATED YOU BOTH.
I SAID YOU WERE FAILURES AS SPRINTERS, BUT THAT WAS A HASTY MISJUDGMENT.
ZOOOSH
I CALLED YOU "UNPREPARED AND UNTHINKING"...
BUT I WAS WRONG.
ZOOM
THE TWO OF YOU...
FWOOM

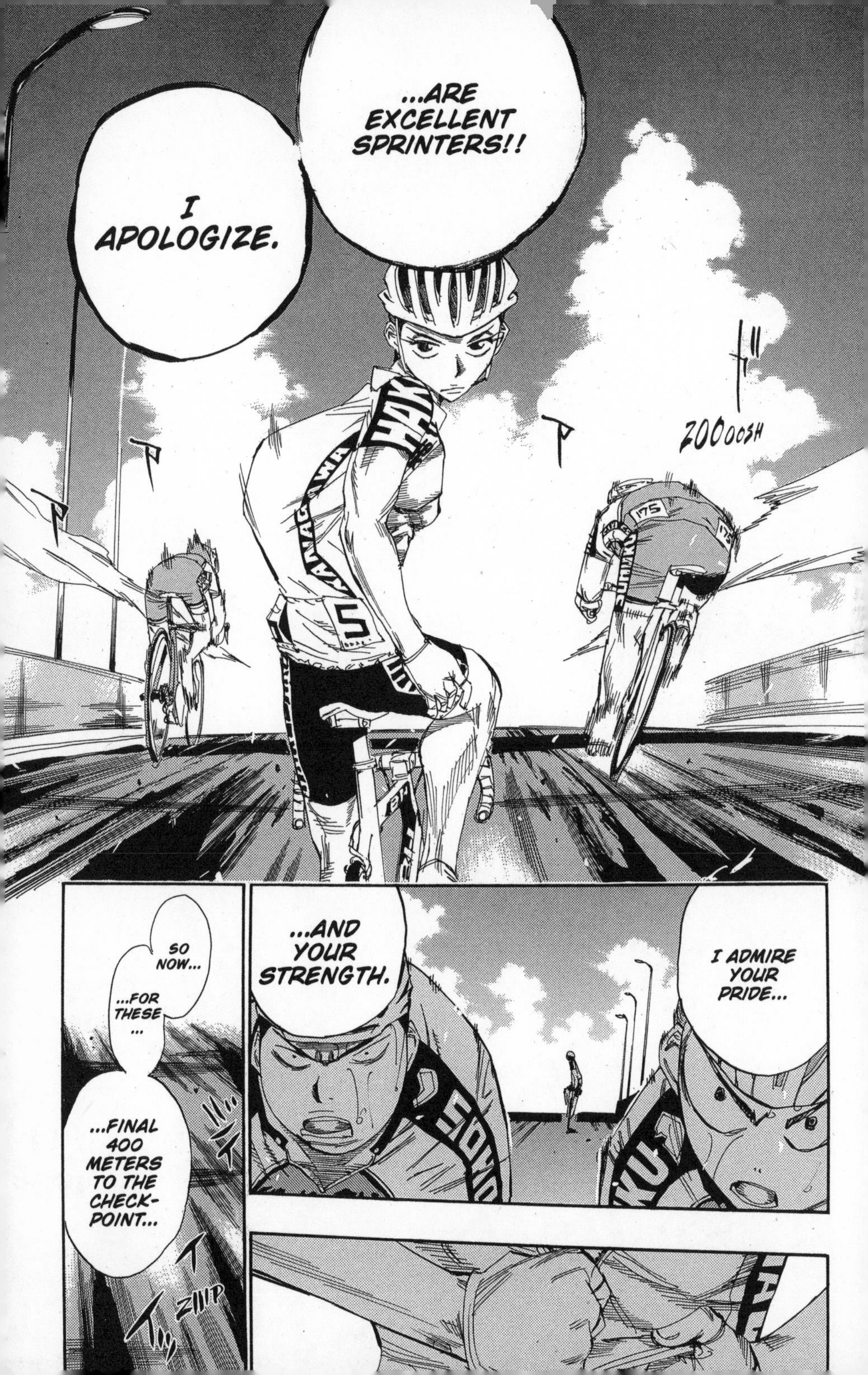
...ARE EXCELLENT SPRINTERS!!
I APOLOGIZE.
ZOOOOSH
I ADMIRE YOUR PRIDE...
...AND YOUR STRENGTH.
SO NOW...
...FOR THESE...
...FINAL 400 METERS TO THE CHECK-POINT...
ZIIIP

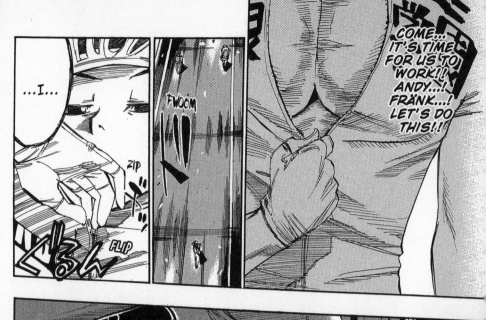

...I...

ZIP

FLIP

FWOOM

COME...!
IT'S TIME
FOR US TO
WORK!!
ANDY...!
FRANK...!
LET'S DO
THIS!!

THOOM

...WILL
RACE
ALL-OUT
AGAINST
YOU!!

RIDE.82 AWAKENING

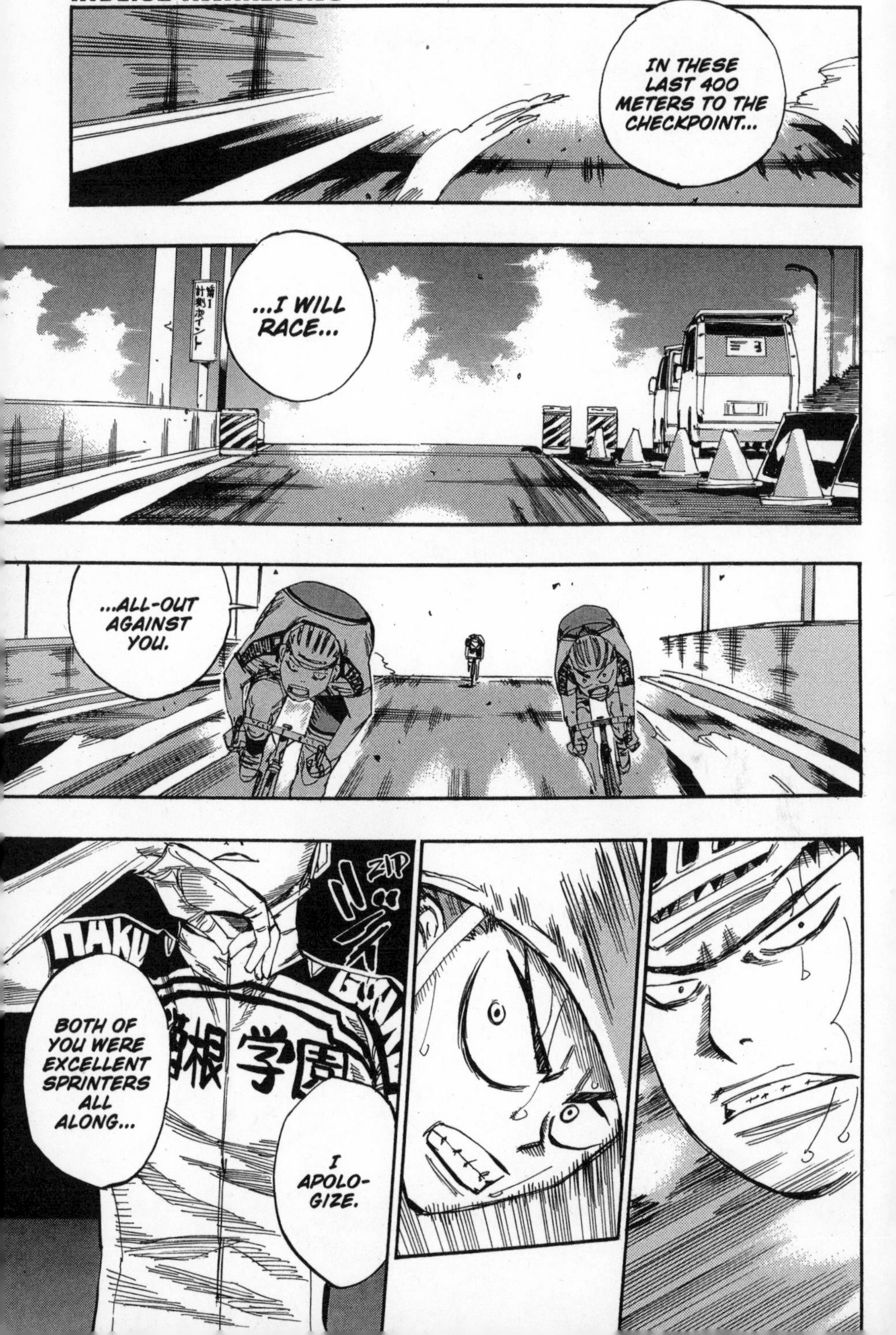
IN THESE LAST 400 METERS TO THE CHECKPOINT...
...I WILL RACE...
...ALL-OUT AGAINST YOU.
ZIP
BOTH OF YOU WERE EXCELLENT SPRINTERS ALL ALONG...
I APOLO-GIZE.

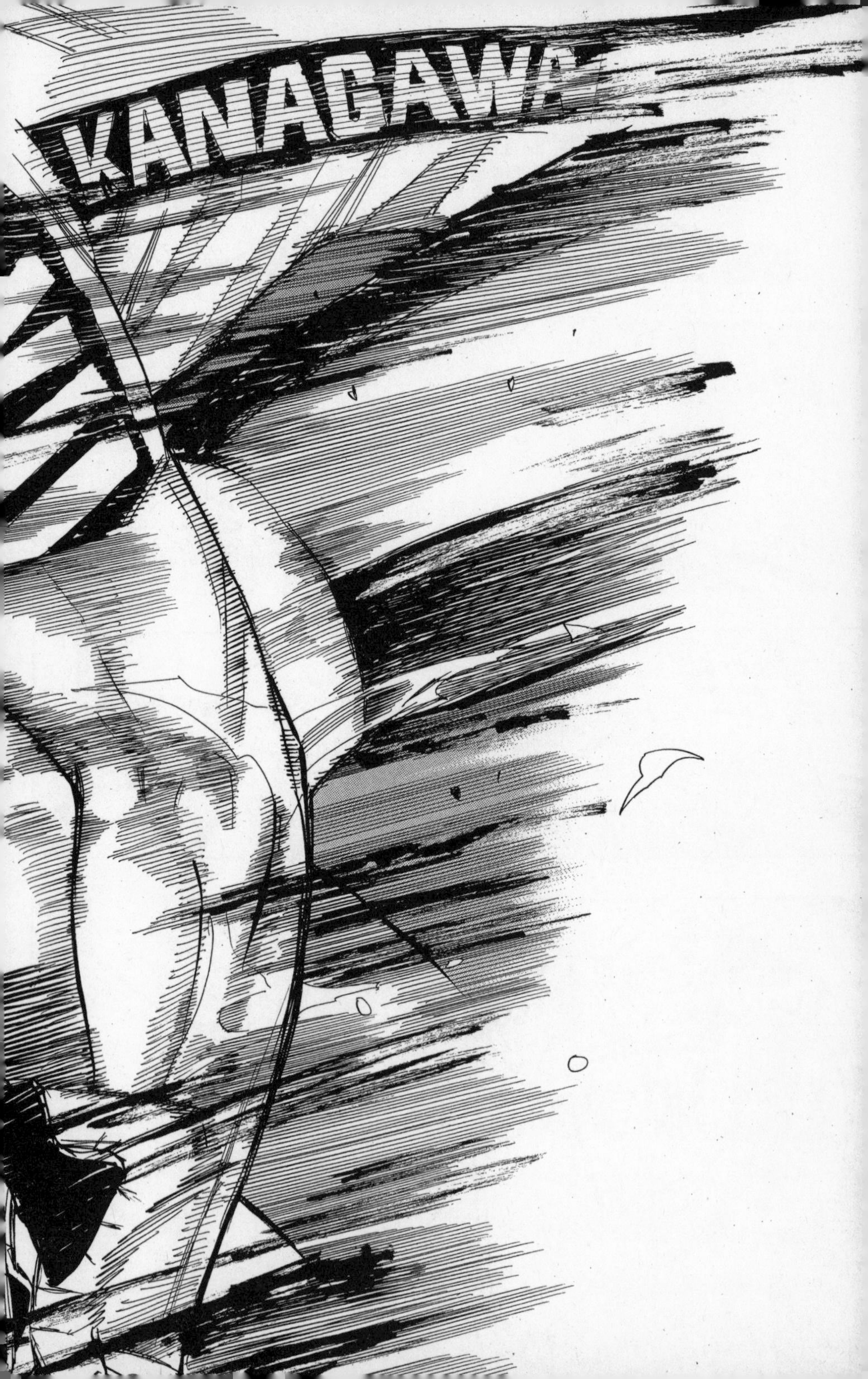
KANAGAWA

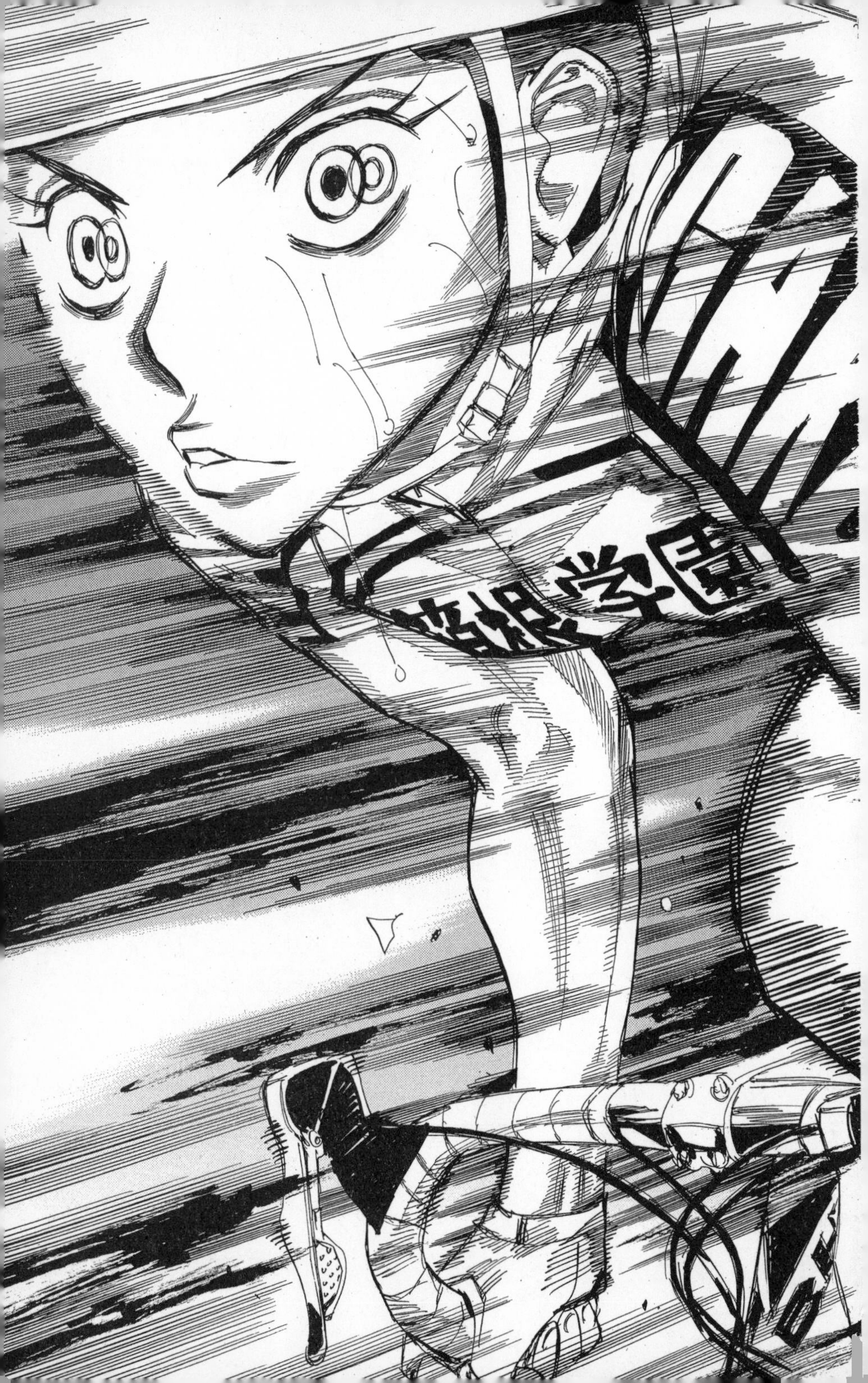
箱根学園

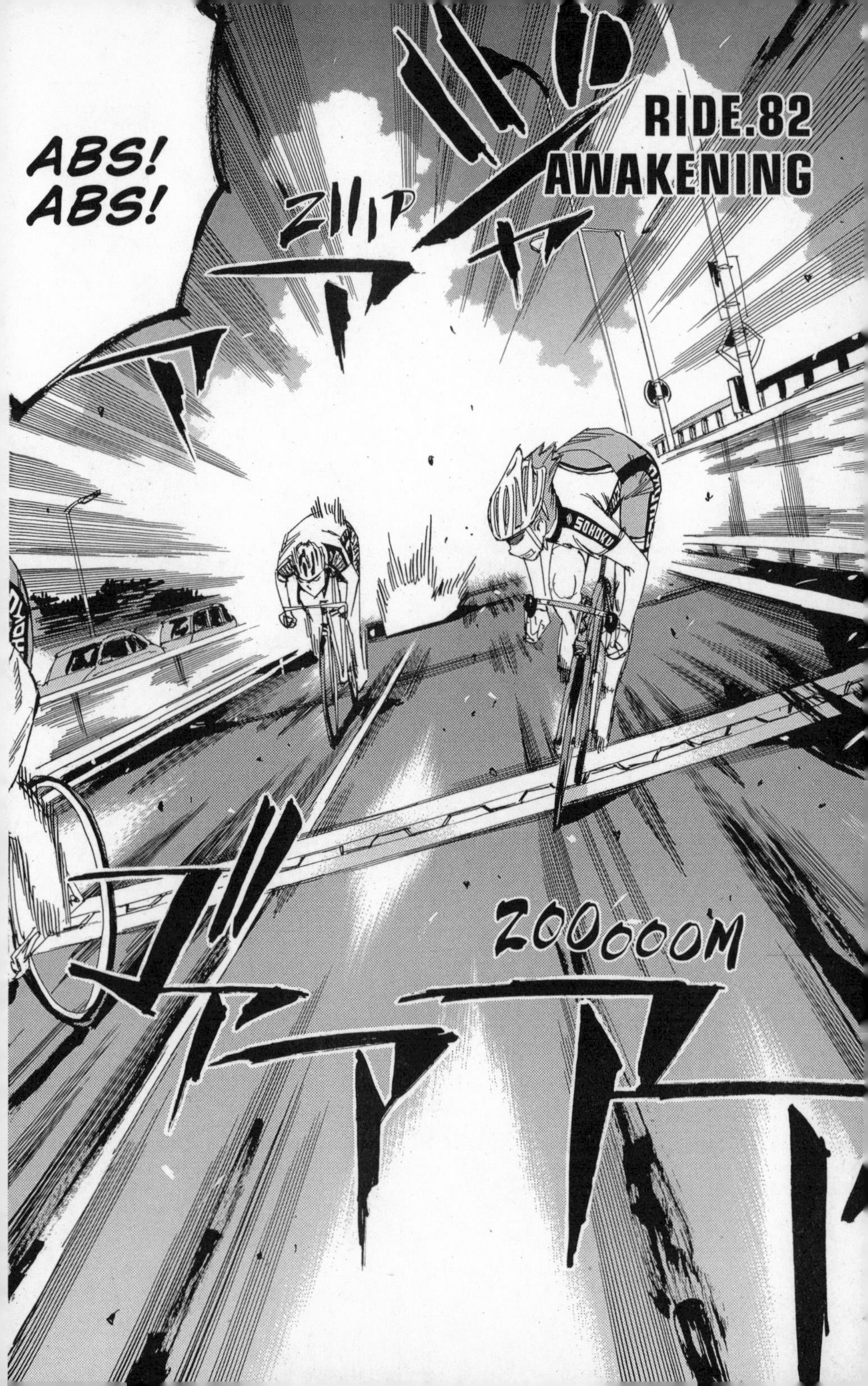
RIDE.82
AWAKENING
ABS!
ABS!
ZIIIP
ZOOOOOM

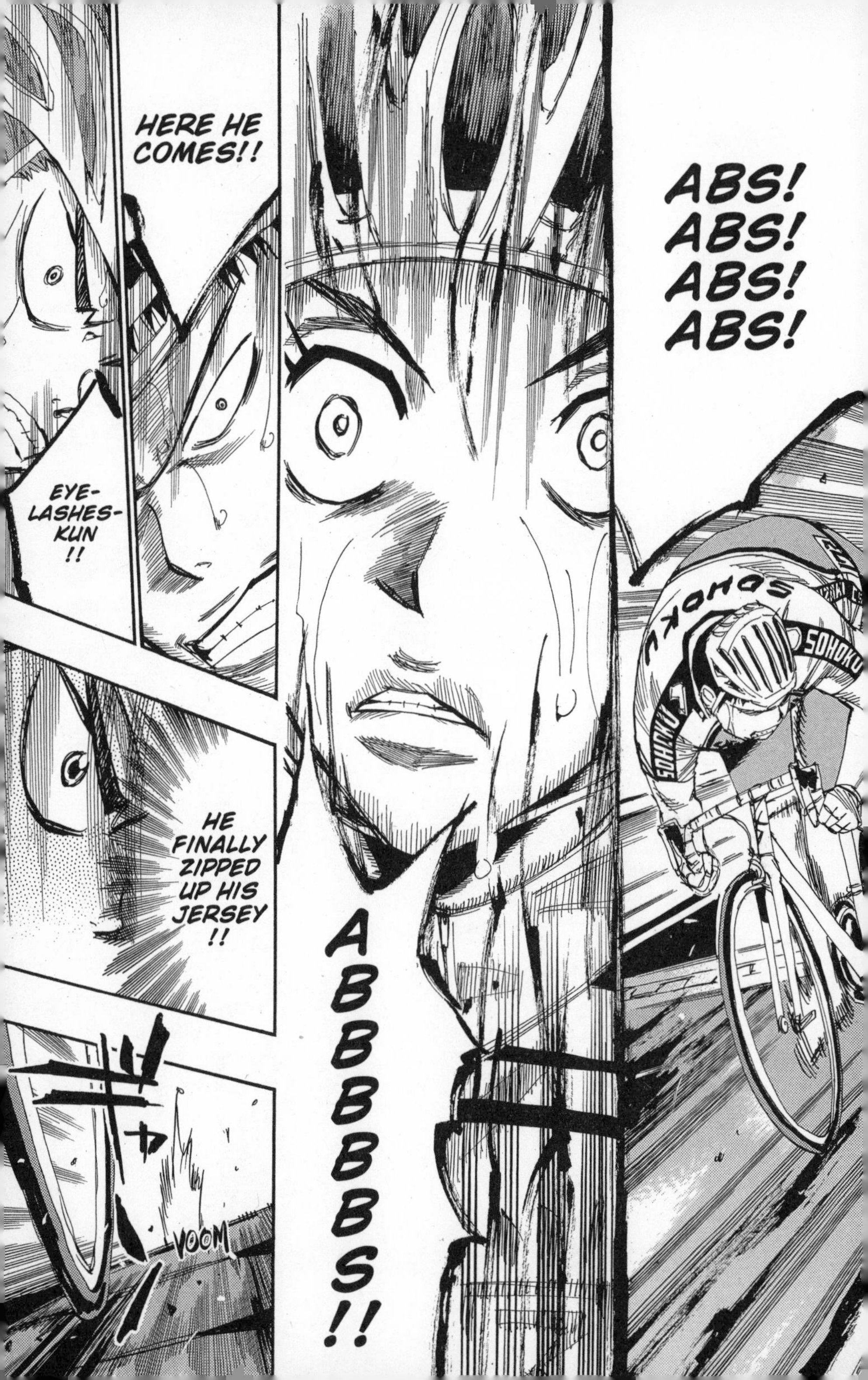
ABS!
ABS!
ABS!
ABS!
SOHOKU
ABBBBBBS!!
HERE HE COMES!!
EYE-LASHES-KUN!!
HE FINALLY ZIPPED UP HIS JERSEY!!
VOOM

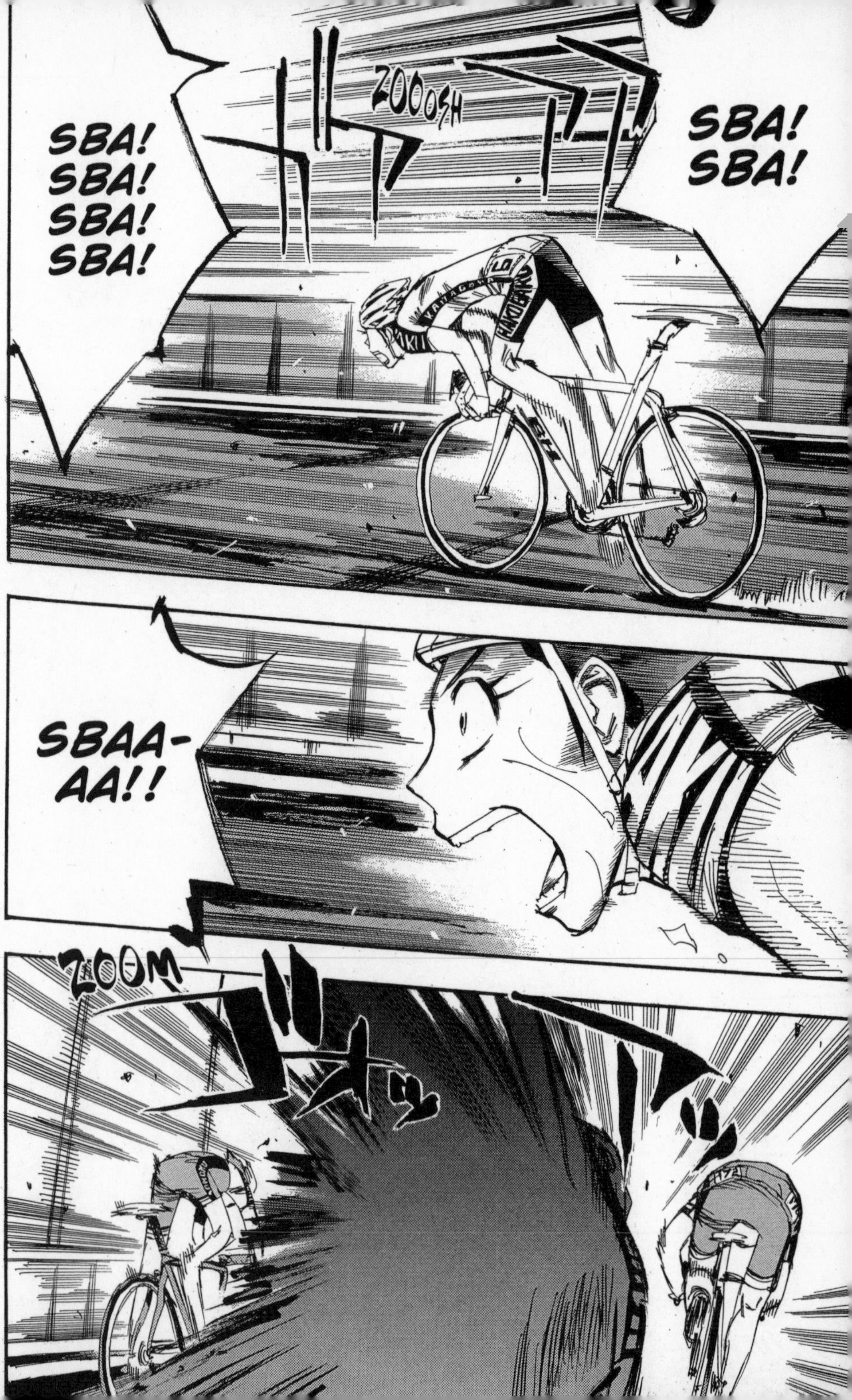
SBA!
SBA!
ZOOOSH
SBA!
SBA!
SBA!
SBA!
SBAA-
AA!!
ZOOM

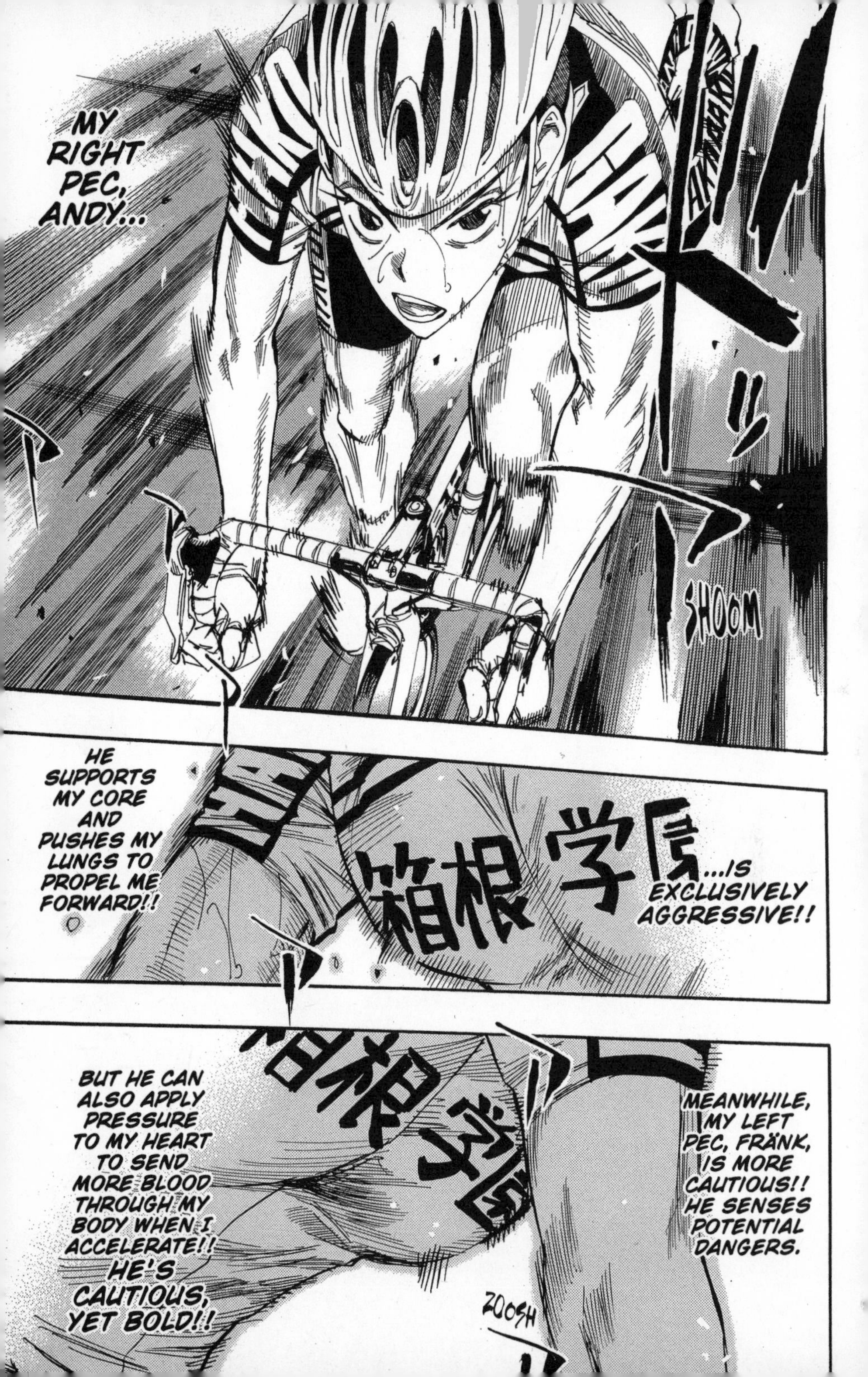

MY RIGHT PEC, ANDY...
SHOOM
箱根学园...IS EXCLUSIVELY AGGRESSIVE!!
HE SUPPORTS MY CORE AND PUSHES MY LUNGS TO PROPEL ME FORWARD!!
MEANWHILE, MY LEFT PEC, FRÄNK, IS MORE CAUTIOUS!! HE SENSES POTENTIAL DANGERS.
BUT HE CAN ALSO APPLY PRESSURE TO MY HEART TO SEND MORE BLOOD THROUGH MY BODY WHEN I ACCELERATE!! HE'S CAUTIOUS, YET BOLD!!
ZOOSH

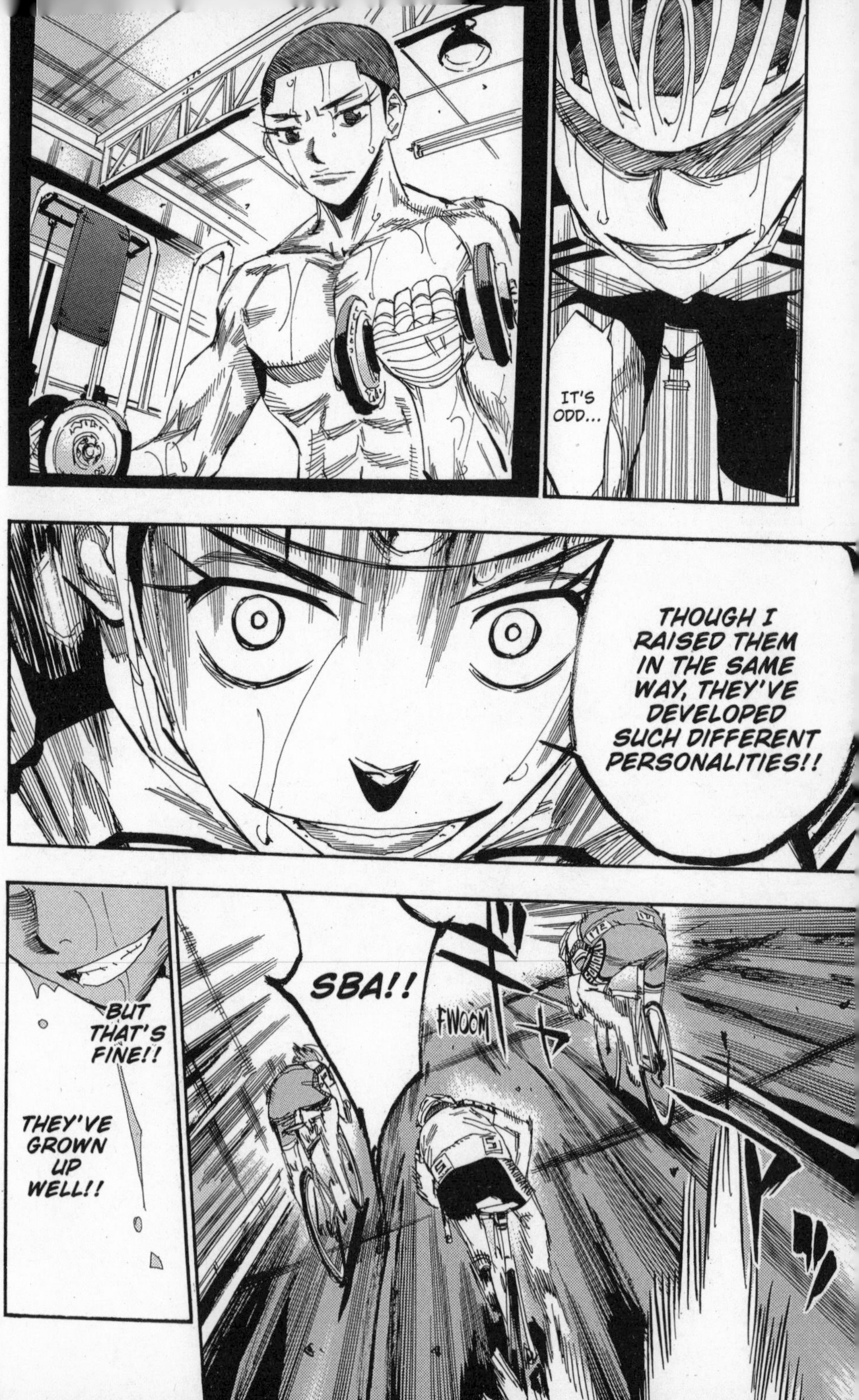
IT'S ODD...
THOUGH I RAISED THEM IN THE SAME WAY, THEY'VE DEVELOPED SUCH DIFFERENT PERSONALITIES!!
SBA!!
FWOOM
BUT THAT'S FINE!!
THEY'VE GROWN UP WELL!!

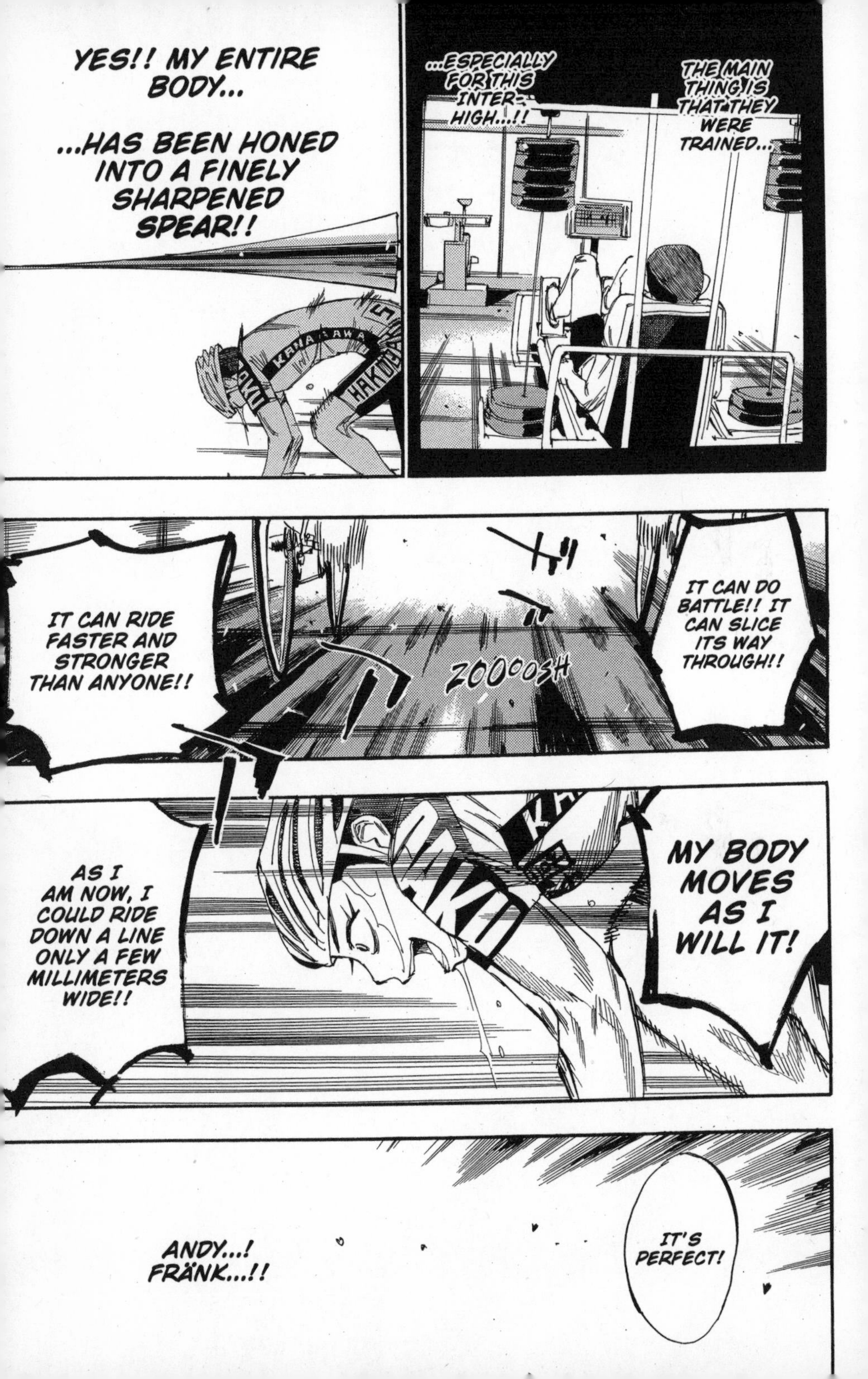
THE MAIN THING IS THAT THEY WERE TRAINED...
...ESPECIALLY FOR THIS INTER-HIGH...!!
YES!! MY ENTIRE BODY...
...HAS BEEN HONED INTO A FINELY SHARPENED SPEAR!!
IT CAN DO BATTLE!! IT CAN SLICE ITS WAY THROUGH!!
ZOOOOSH
IT CAN RIDE FASTER AND STRONGER THAN ANYONE!!
MY BODY MOVES AS I WILL IT!
AS I AM NOW, I COULD RIDE DOWN A LINE ONLY A FEW MILLIMETERS WIDE!!
IT'S PERFECT!
ANDY...! FRÄNK...!!

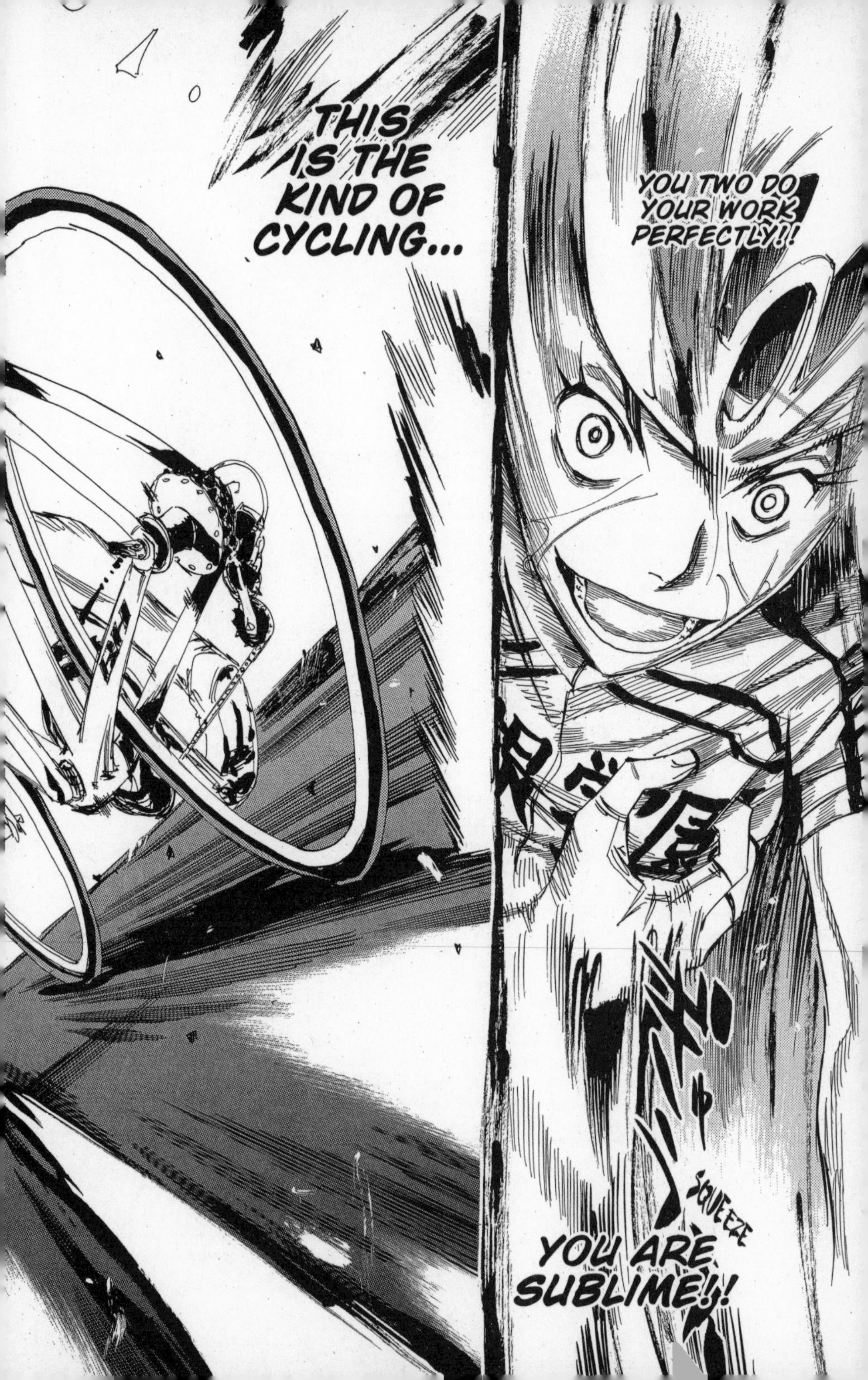
YOU TWO DO YOUR WORK PERFECTLY!!
SQUEEZE
YOU ARE SUBLIME!!
THIS IS THE KIND OF CYCLING...

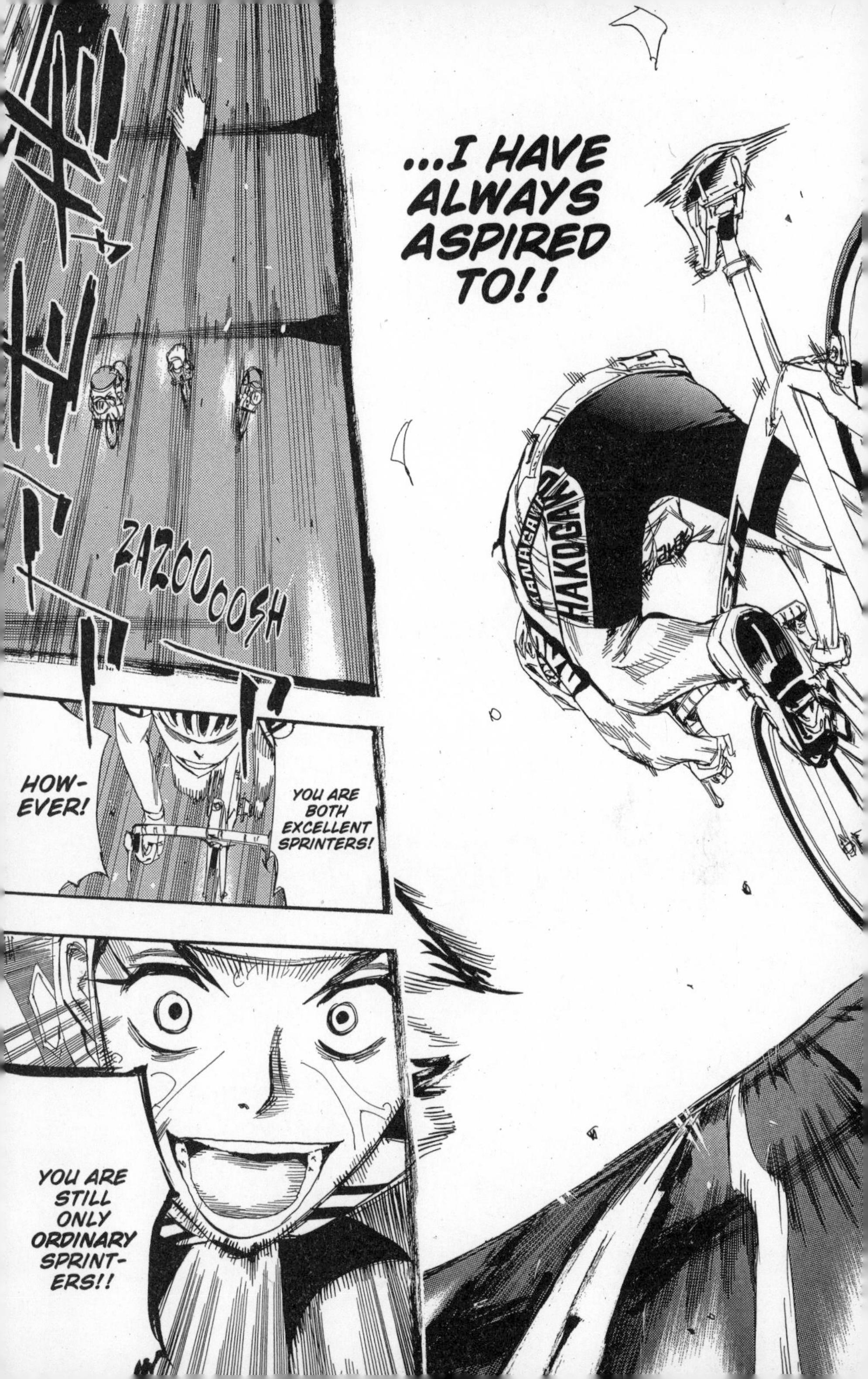
...I HAVE ALWAYS ASPIRED TO!!
HAKOGAKU
ZAZOOOOSH
YOU ARE BOTH EXCELLENT SPRINTERS!
HOW-EVER!
YOU ARE STILL ONLY ORDINARY SPRINT-ERS!!

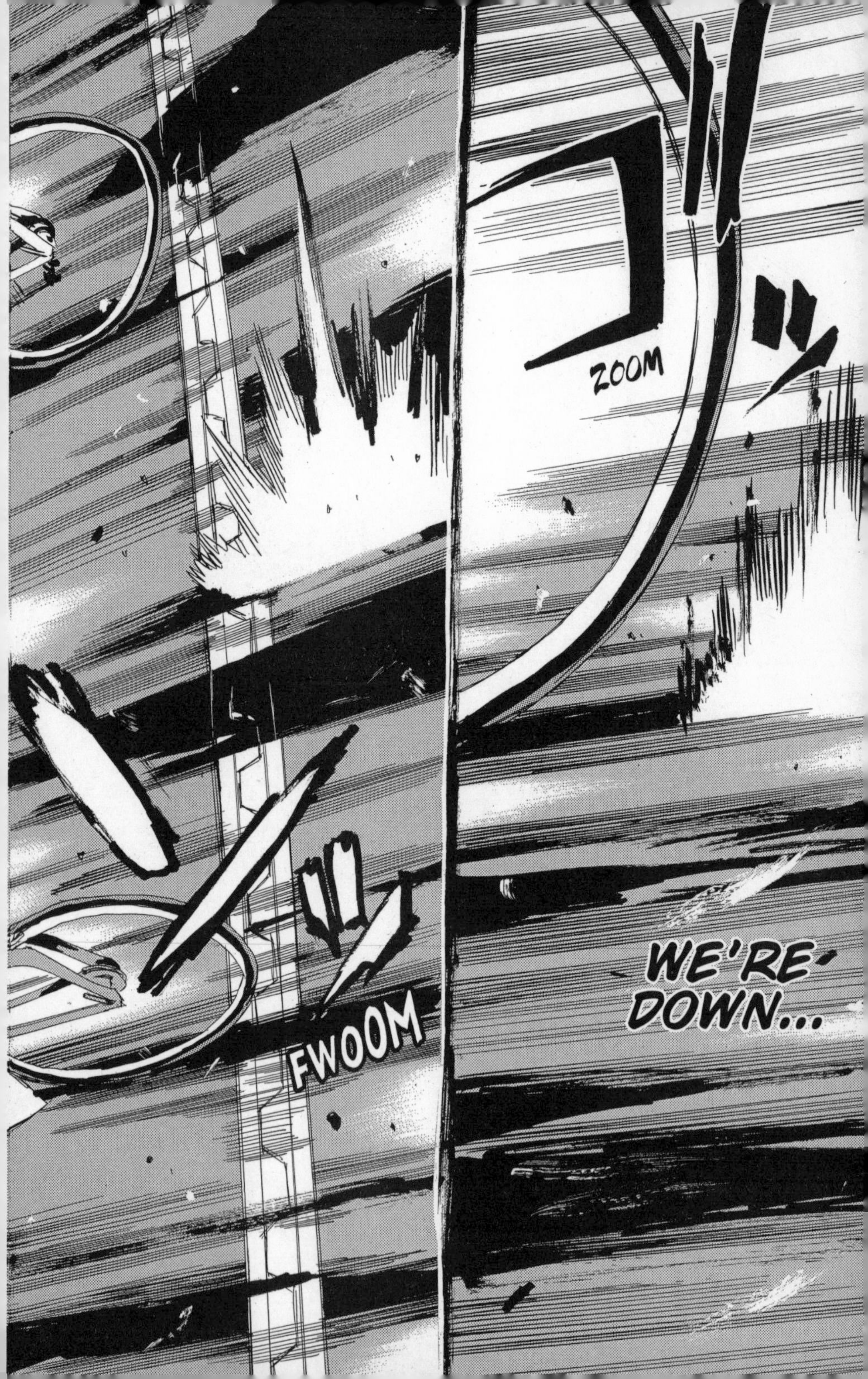
ZOOM
WE'RE-
DOWN...
FWOOM

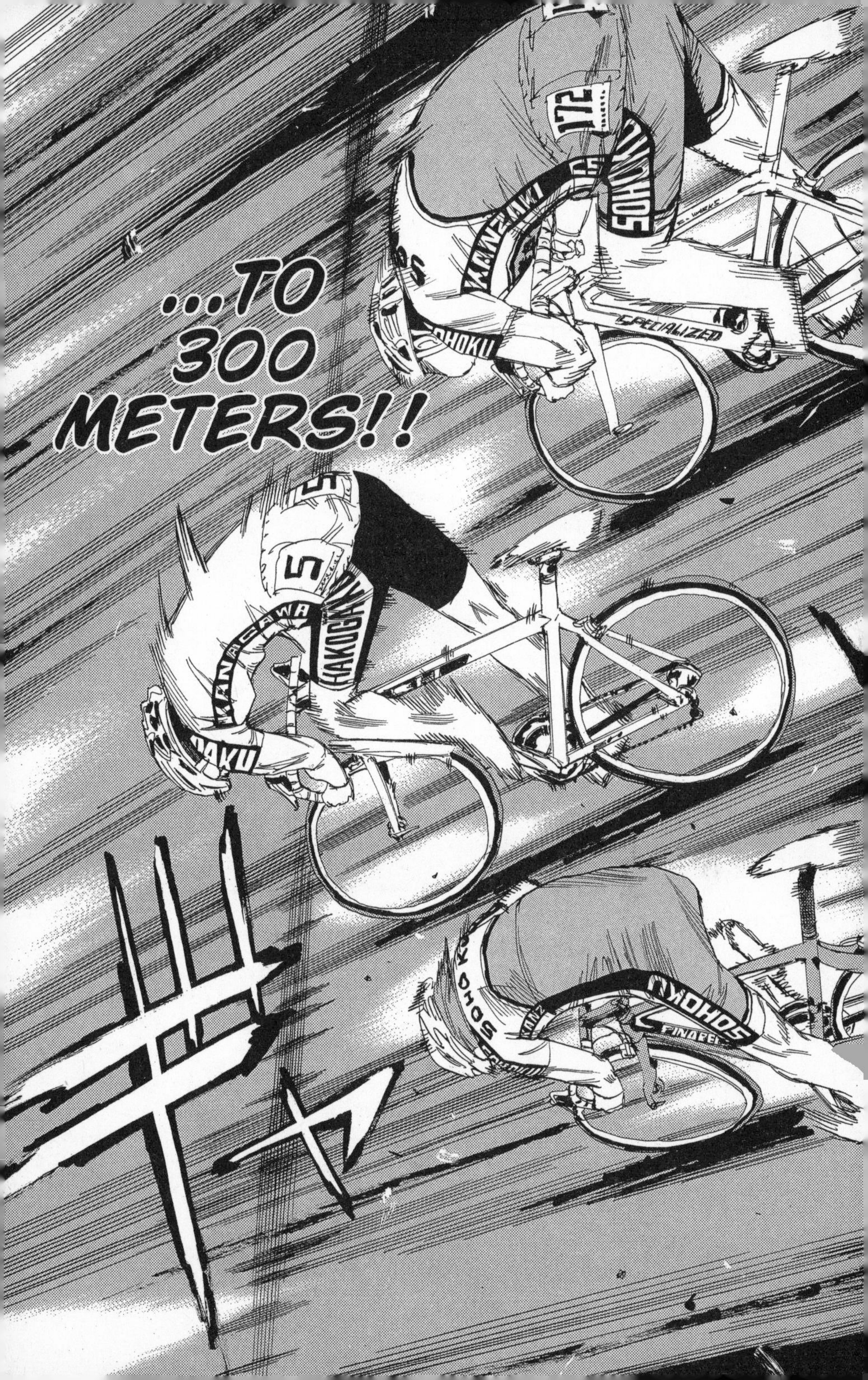
...TO 300 METERS!!

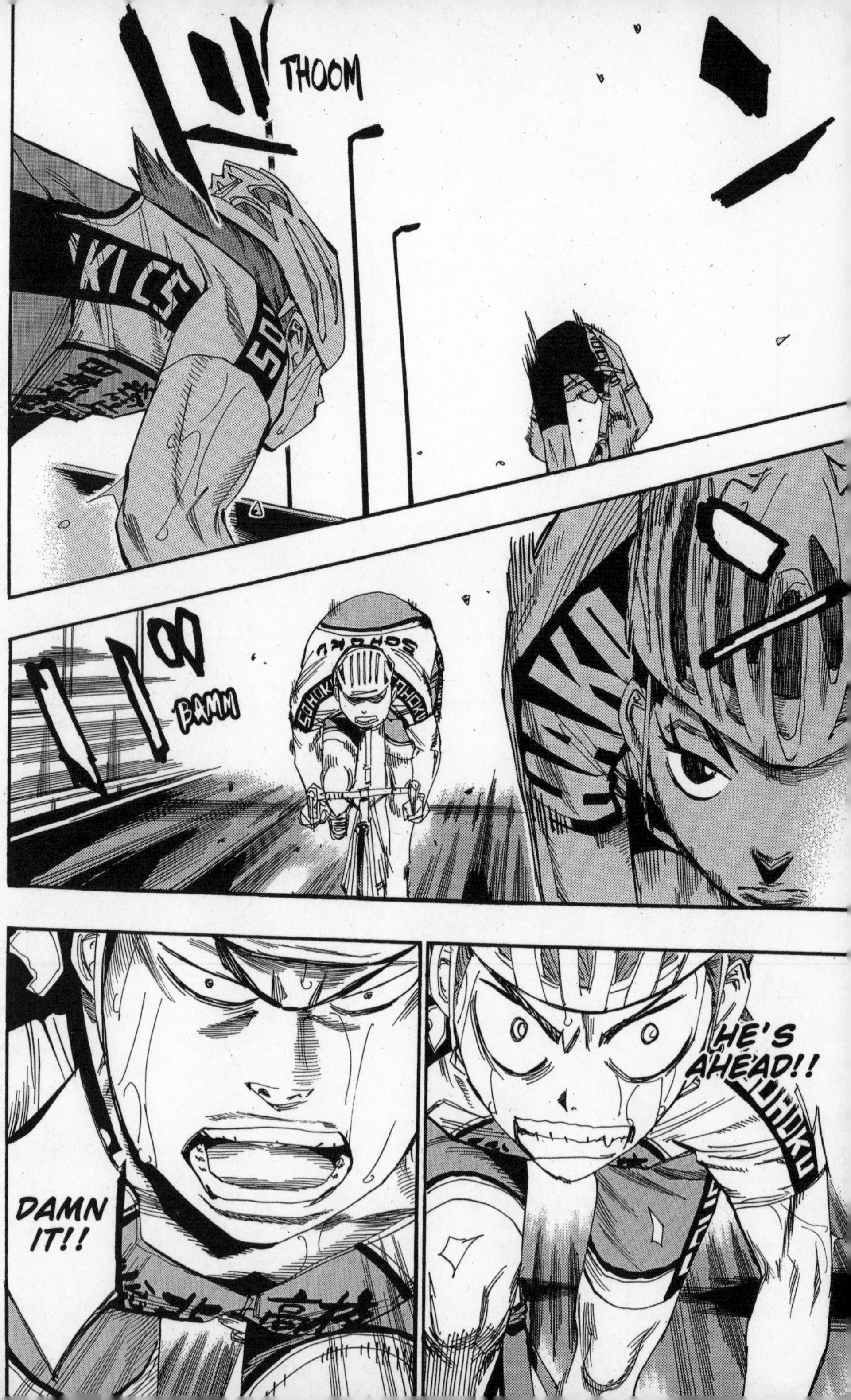
THOOM
BAMM
HE'S AHEAD!!
DAMN IT!!

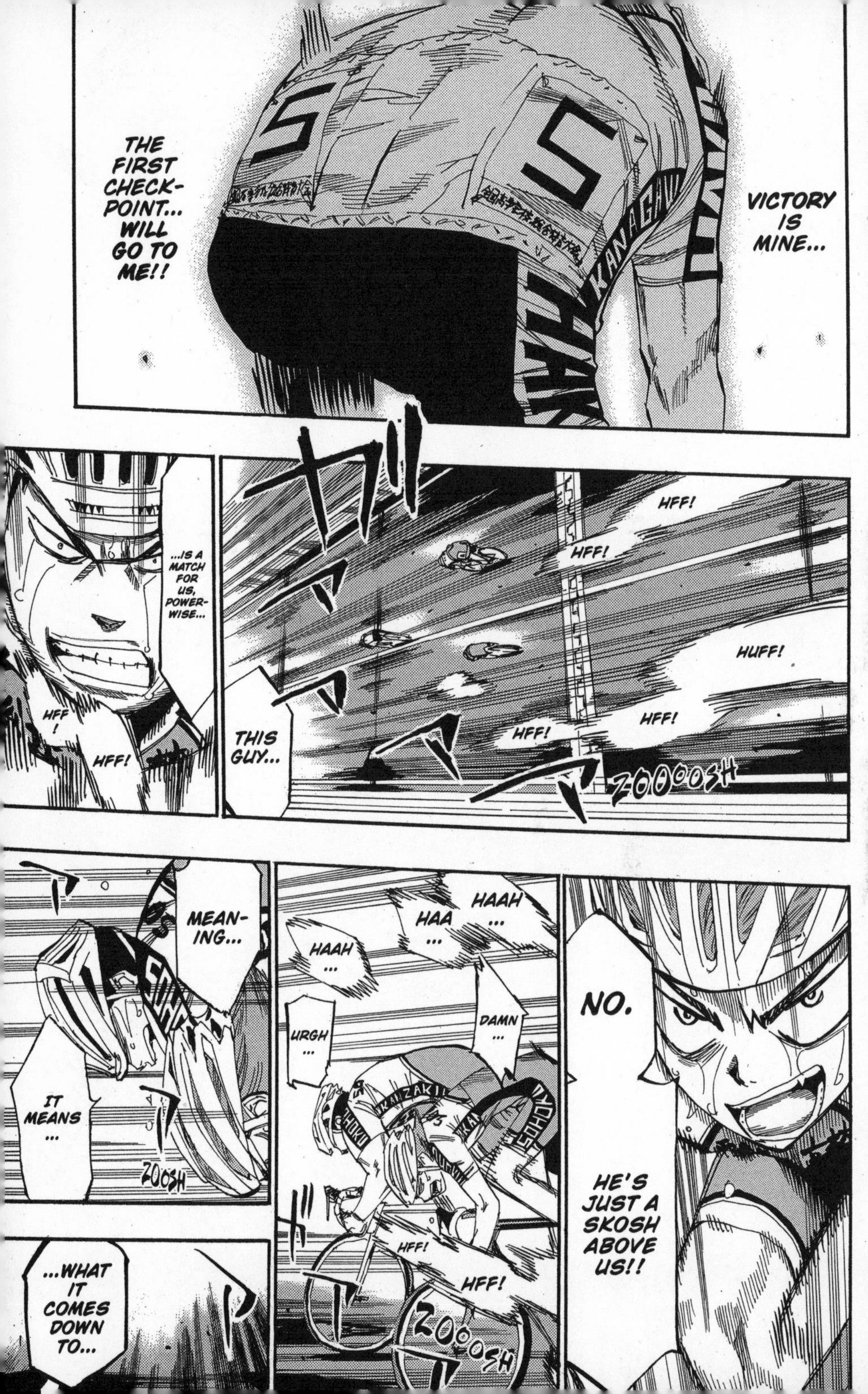
VICTORY IS MINE...
THE FIRST CHECK-POINT... WILL GO TO ME!!
HFF!
HFF!
HUFF!
HFF!
HFF!
ZOOOOSH
THIS GUY...
...IS A MATCH FOR US, POWER-WISE...
HFF!
HFF!
NO.
HE'S JUST A SKOSH ABOVE US!!
HAAH...
HAA...
HAAH...
DAMN...
URGH...
HFF!
HFF!
ZOOOSH
MEAN-ING...
IT MEANS...
ZOOSH
...WHAT IT COMES DOWN TO...

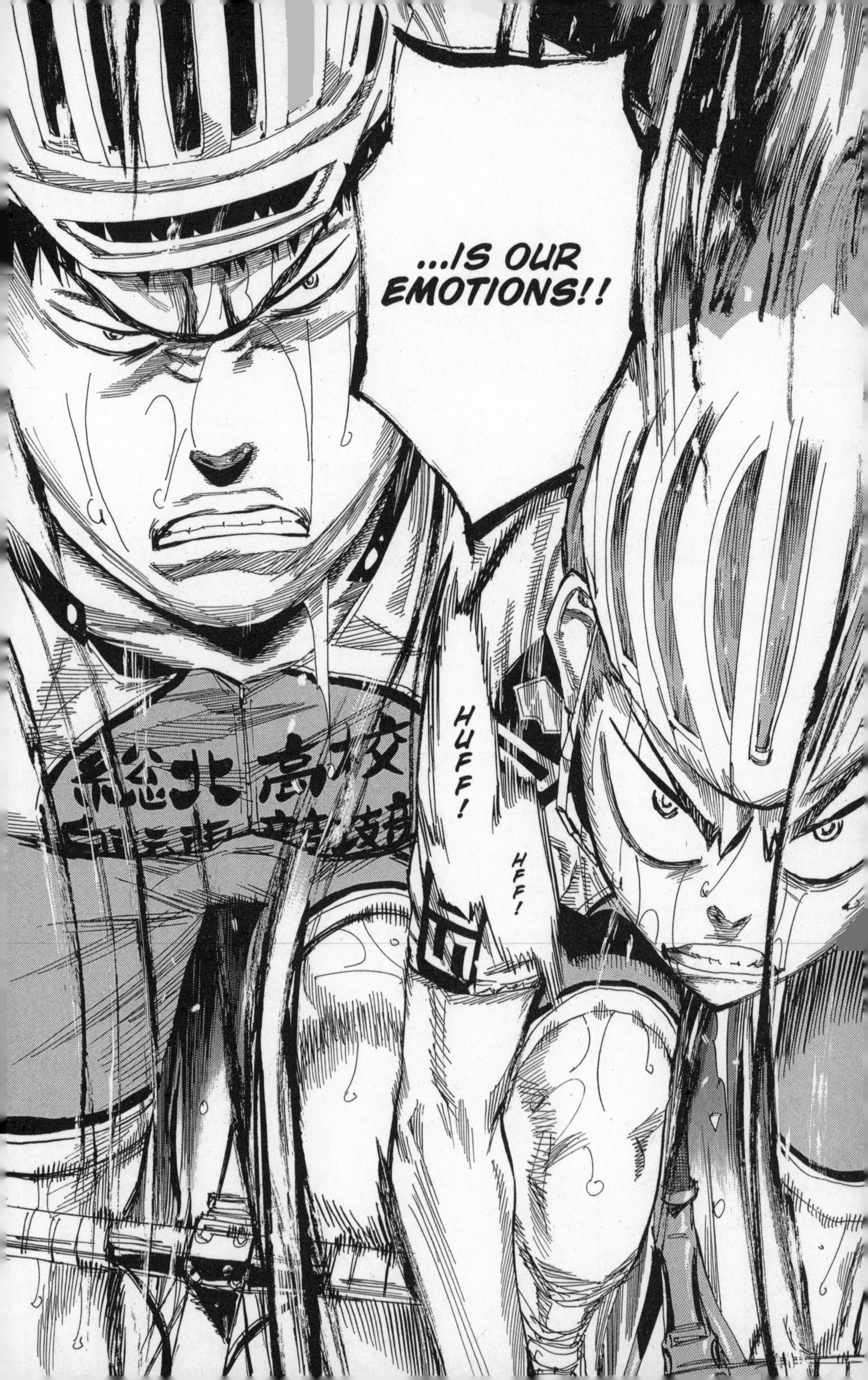
...IS OUR EMOTIONS!!
HUFF!
HFF!

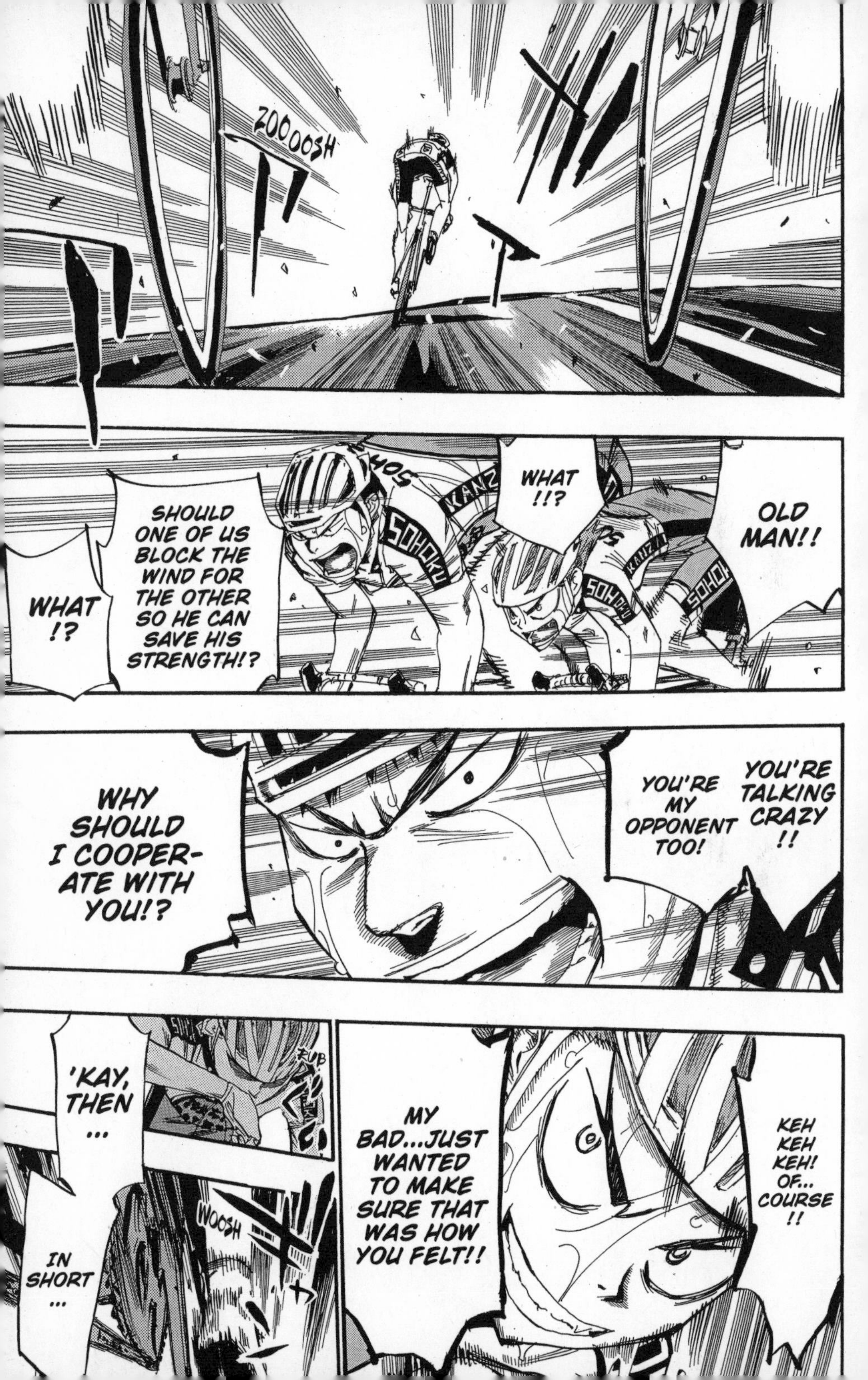
ZOOOOSH
OLD MAN!!
WHAT !!?
SHOULD ONE OF US BLOCK THE WIND FOR THE OTHER SO HE CAN SAVE HIS STRENGTH!?
WHAT !?
YOU'RE TALKING CRAZY !!
YOU'RE MY OPPONENT TOO!
WHY SHOULD I COOPER-ATE WITH YOU!?
KEH KEH KEH! OF... COURSE !!
MY BAD...JUST WANTED TO MAKE SURE THAT WAS HOW YOU FELT!!
RUB
'KAY, THEN ...
WOOSH
IN SHORT ...

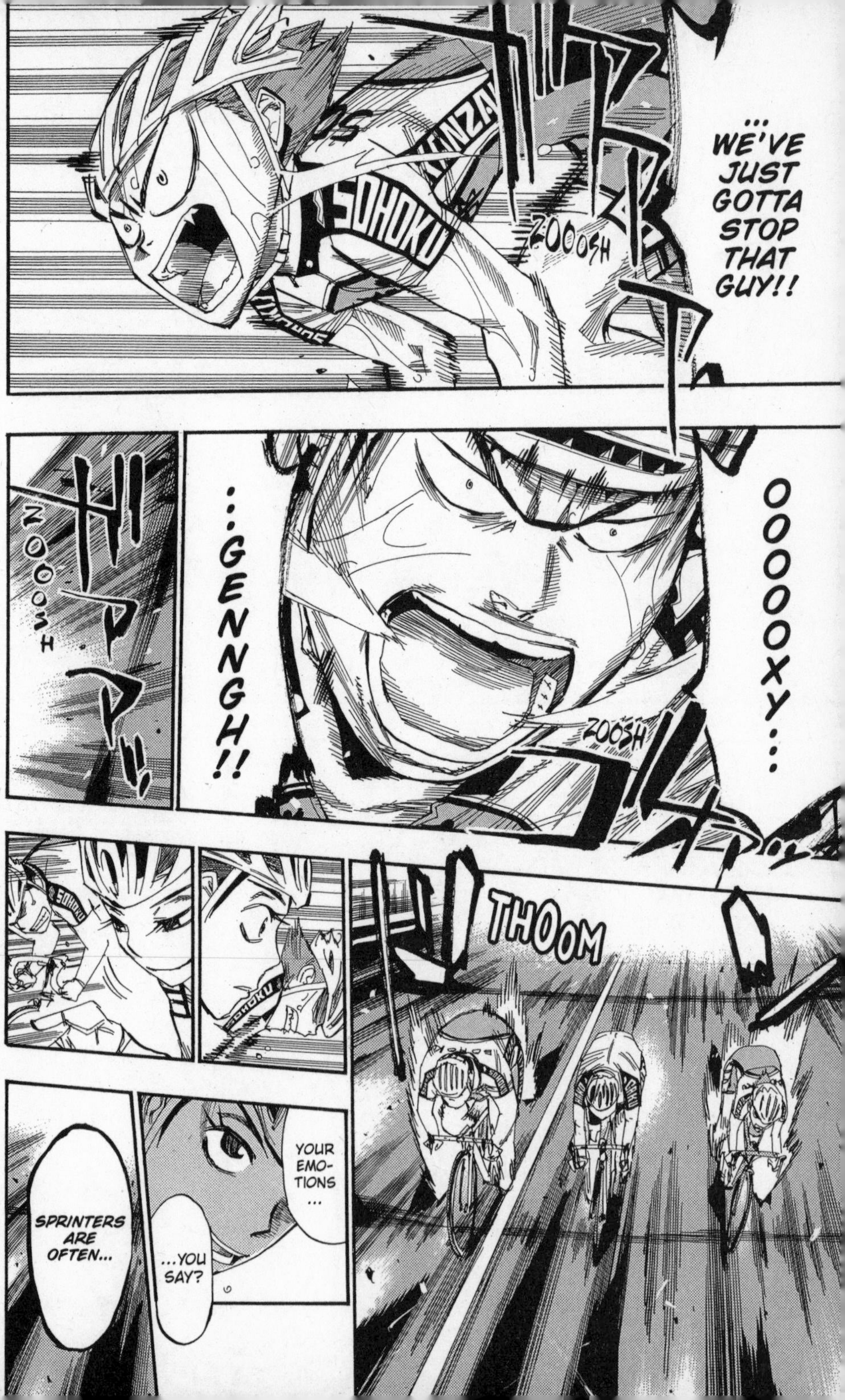
...WE'VE JUST GOTTA STOP THAT GUY!!
ZOOOSH
OOOOOOXY...
ZOOSH
...GENNGH!!
ZOOOSH
THOOM
YOUR EMO-TIONS...
...YOU SAY?
SPRINTERS ARE OFTEN...

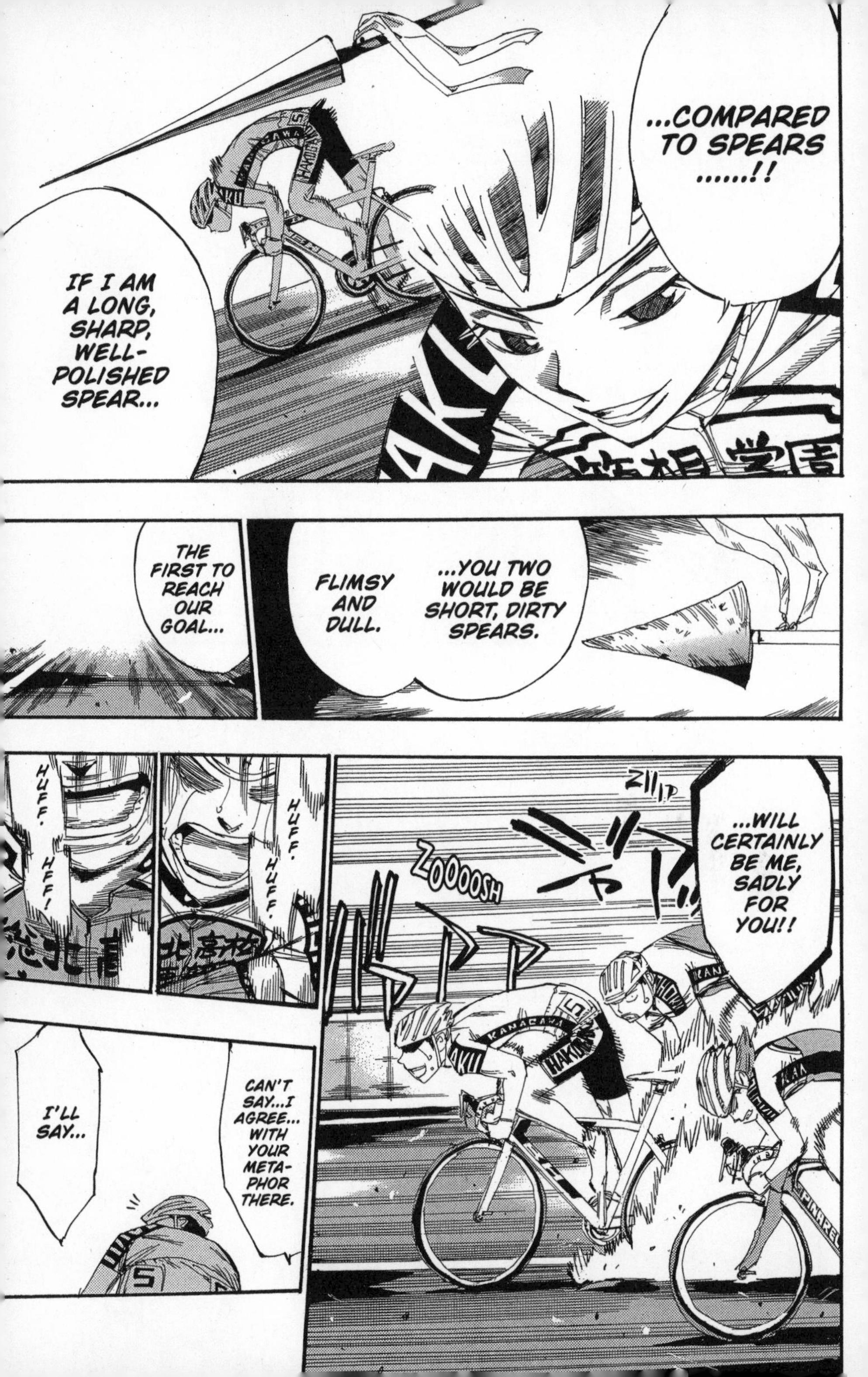
...COMPARED TO SPEARS ......!!
IF I AM A LONG, SHARP, WELL-POLISHED SPEAR...
...YOU TWO WOULD BE SHORT, DIRTY SPEARS.
FLIMSY AND DULL.
THE FIRST TO REACH OUR GOAL...
ZIIIP
...WILL CERTAINLY BE ME, SADLY FOR YOU!!
ZOOOOSH
HUFF. HUFF.
HUFF. HFF!
CAN'T SAY...I AGREE... WITH YOUR METAPHOR THERE.
I'LL SAY...

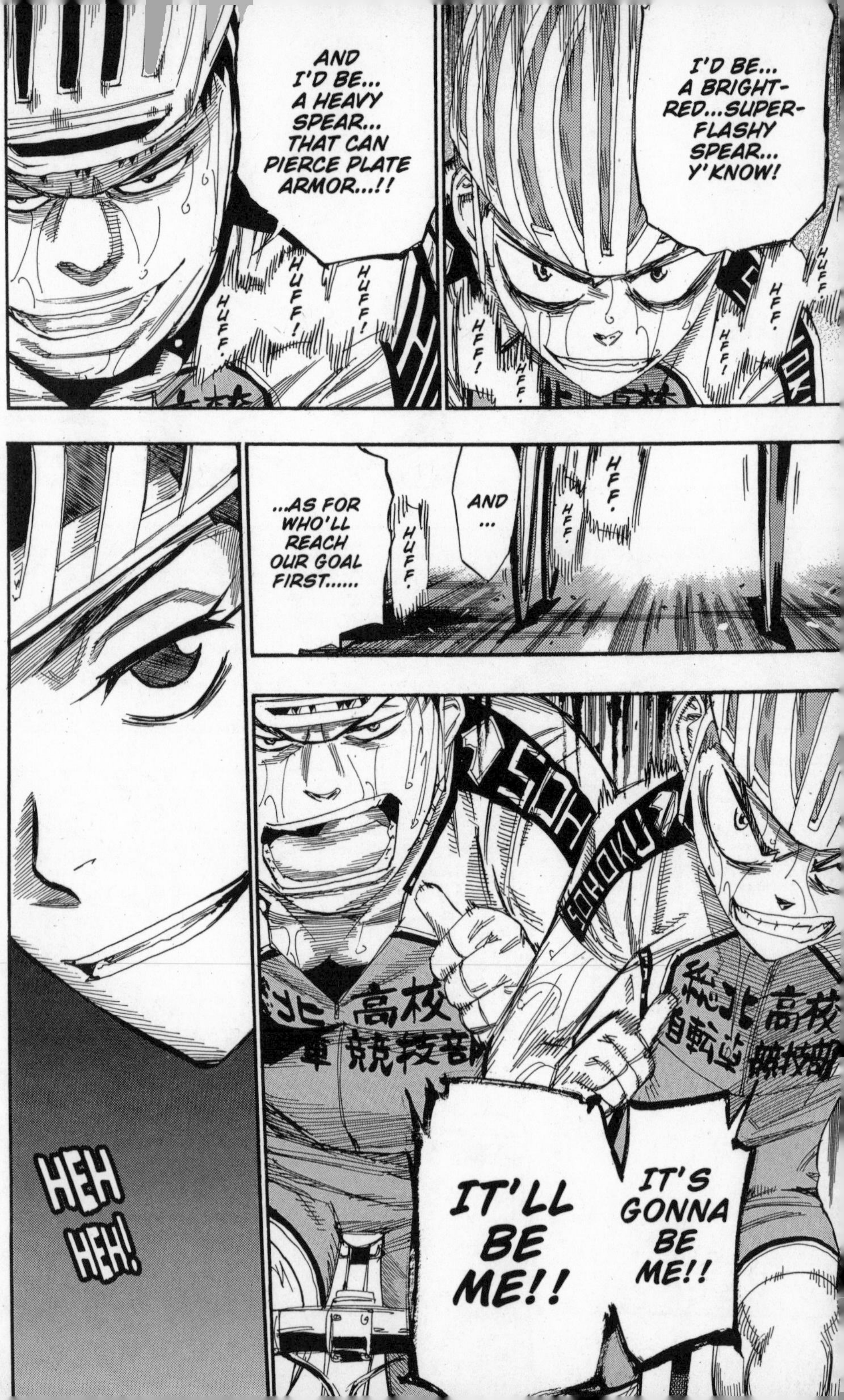
I'D BE... A BRIGHT-RED...SUPER-FLASHY SPEAR... Y'KNOW!
HUFF.
HFF.
HFF!
HFF!
HFF.
AND I'D BE... A HEAVY SPEAR... THAT CAN PIERCE PLATE ARMOR...!!
HUFF!
HUFF!
HUFF.
HFF.
HFF.
AND ...
HUFF.
...AS FOR WHO'LL REACH OUR GOAL FIRST......
IT'S GONNA BE ME!!
IT'LL BE ME!!
HEH HEH!

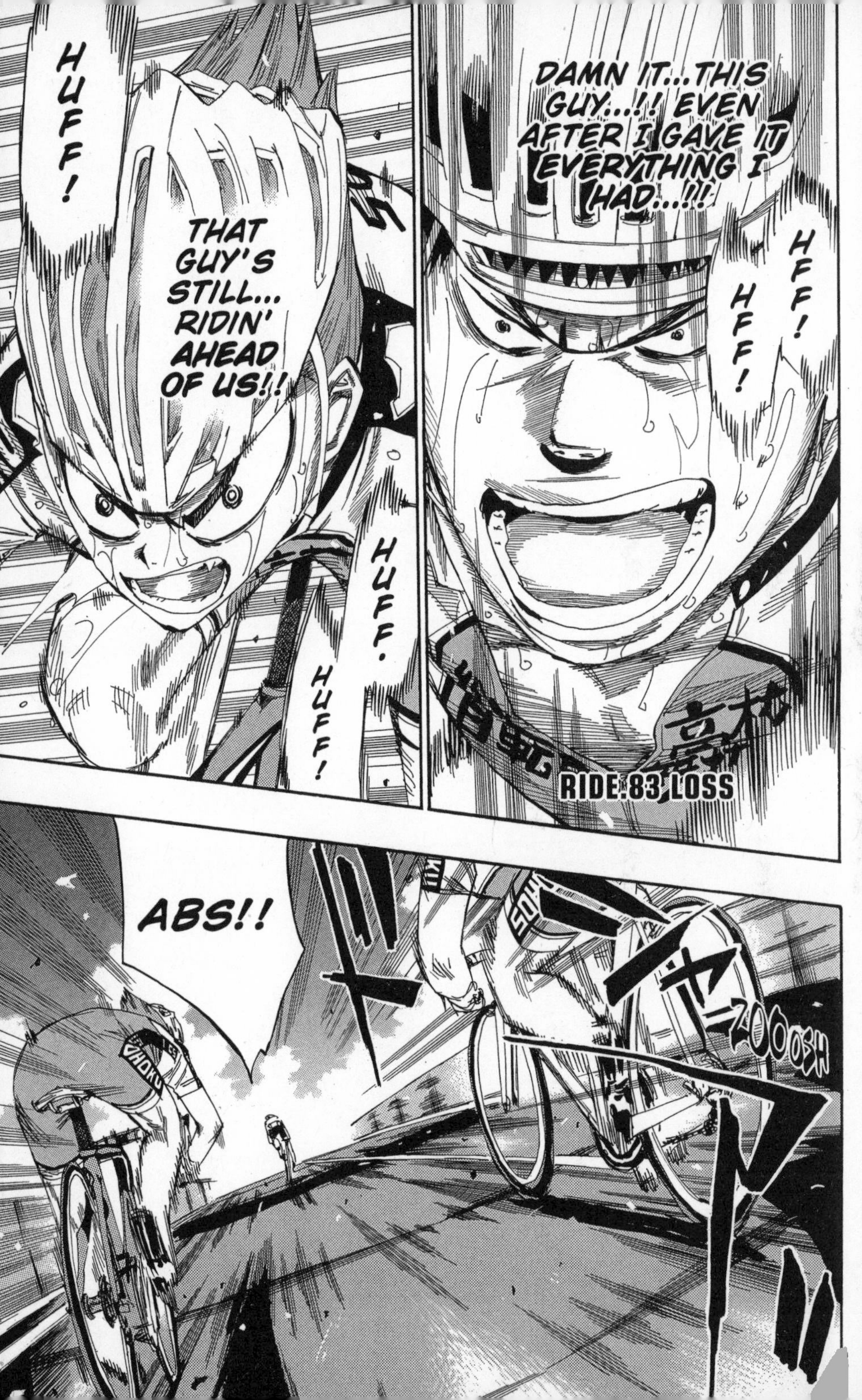
DAMN IT...THIS GUY...!! EVEN AFTER I GAVE IT EVERYTHING I HAD...!!
HFF!
HFF!
RIDE.83 LOSS
HUFF!
THAT GUY'S STILL... RIDIN' AHEAD OF US!!
HUFF.
HUFF!
ZOOOSH
ABS!!

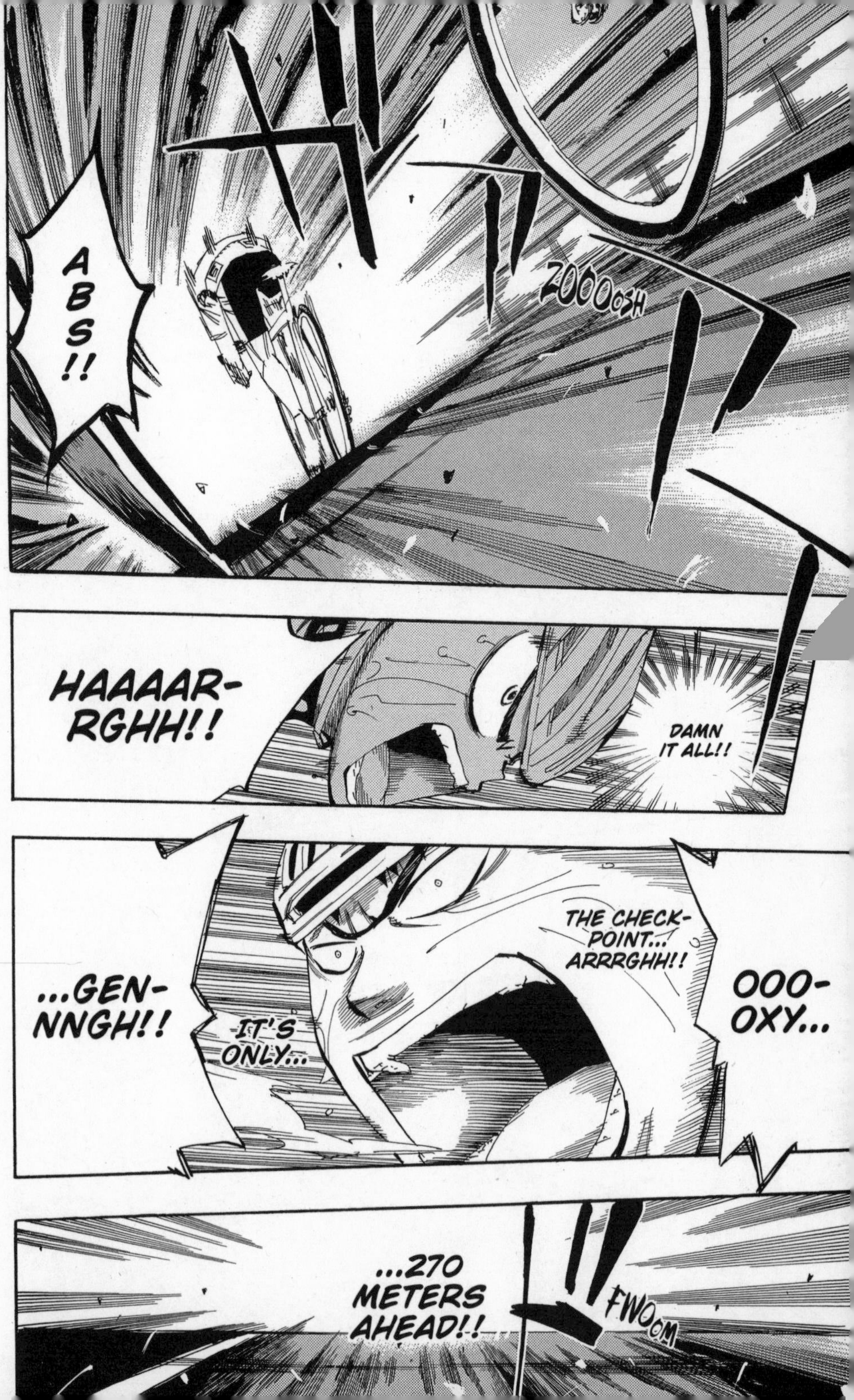
ZOOOOSH
ABS!!
DAMN IT ALL!!
HAAAAR-RGHH!!
OOO-OXY...
THE CHECK-POINT... ARRRGHH!!
IT'S ONLY...
...GEN-NNGH!!
FWOOM
...270 METERS AHEAD!!

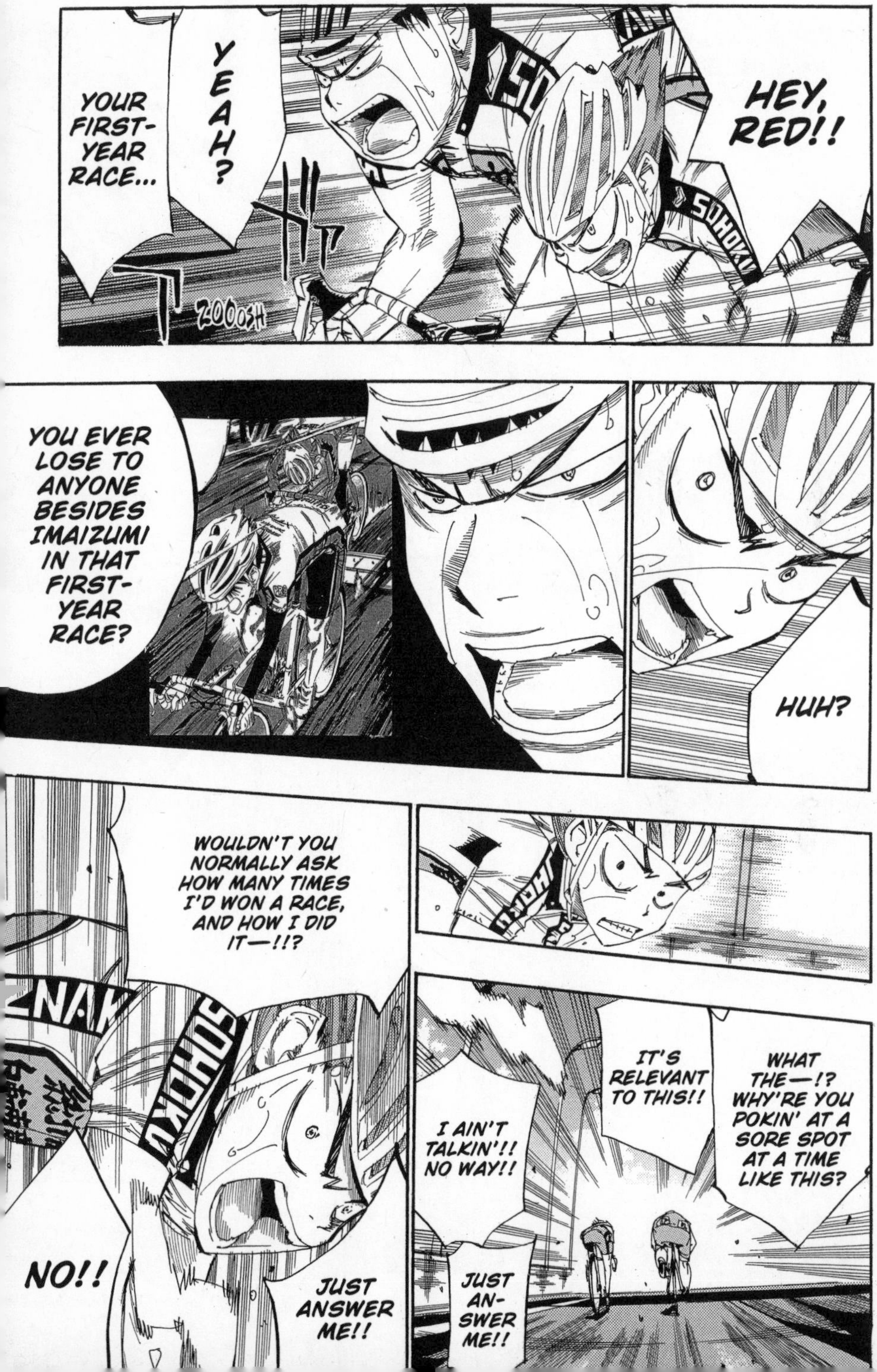
HEY, RED!!
YEAH?
YOUR FIRST-YEAR RACE...
ZOOOSH
HUH?
YOU EVER LOSE TO ANYONE BESIDES IMAIZUMI IN THAT FIRST-YEAR RACE?
WHAT THE—!? WHY'RE YOU POKIN' AT A SORE SPOT AT A TIME LIKE THIS?
IT'S RELEVANT TO THIS!!
I AIN'T TALKIN'!! NO WAY!!
JUST AN-SWER ME!!
WOULDN'T YOU NORMALLY ASK HOW MANY TIMES I'D WON A RACE, AND HOW I DID IT—!!?
JUST ANSWER ME!!
NO!!

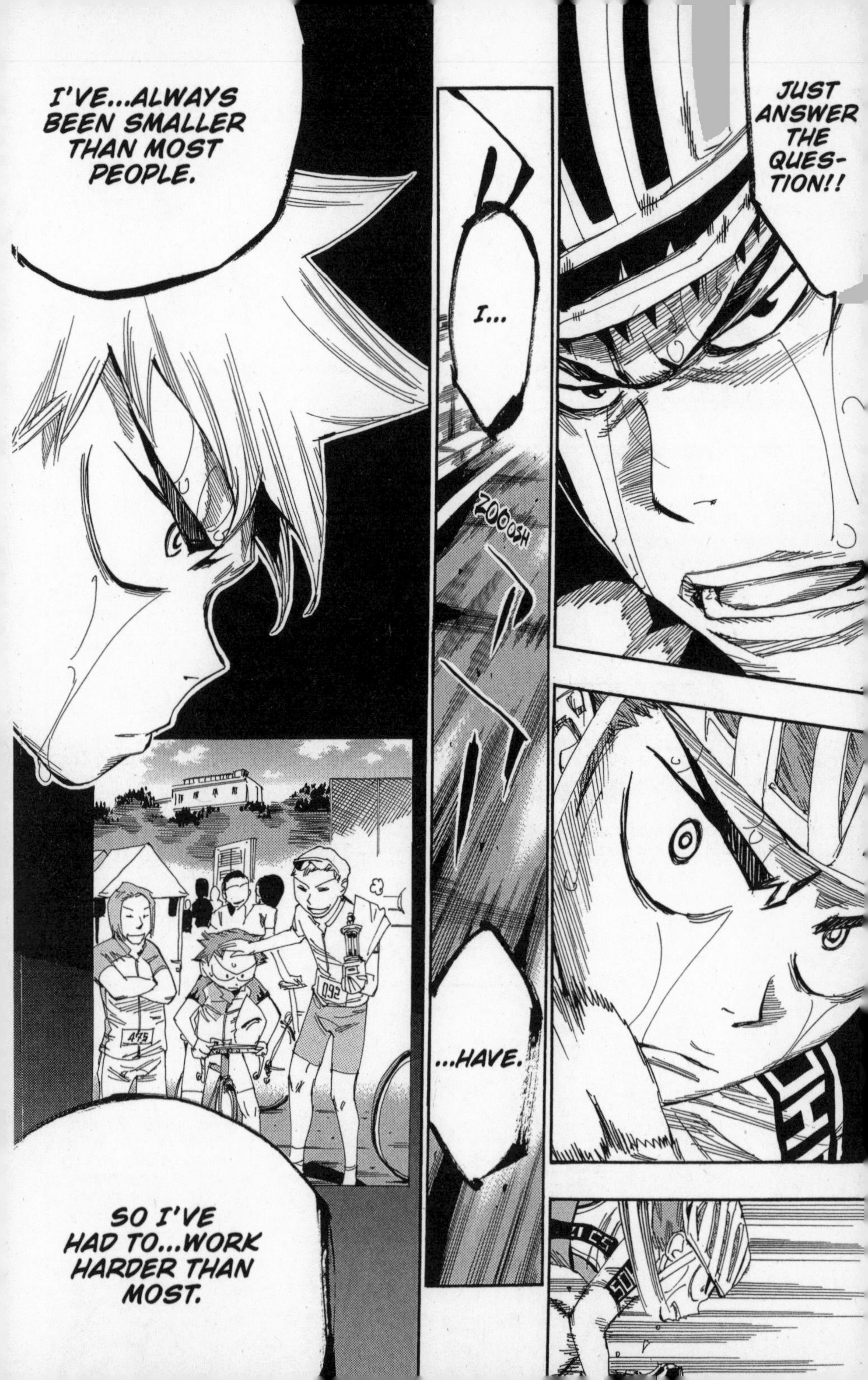
JUST ANSWER THE QUES-TION!!
I...
ZOOOSH
...HAVE.
I'VE...ALWAYS BEEN SMALLER THAN MOST PEOPLE.
SO I'VE HAD TO...WORK HARDER THAN MOST.

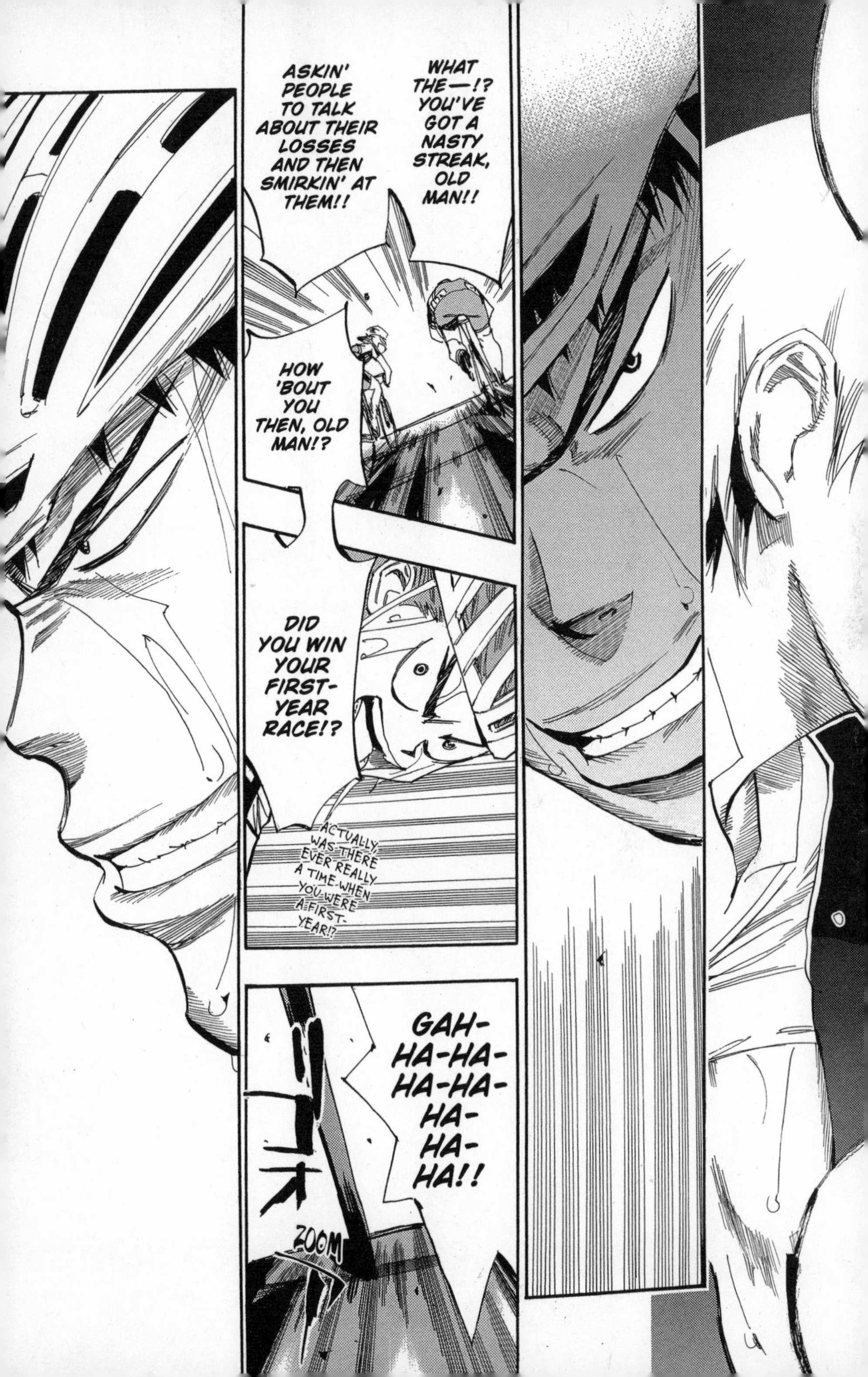
WHAT THE—!? YOU'VE GOT A NASTY STREAK, OLD MAN!!
ASKIN' PEOPLE TO TALK ABOUT THEIR LOSSES AND THEN SMIRKIN' AT THEM!!
HOW 'BOUT YOU THEN, OLD MAN!?
DID YOU WIN YOUR FIRST-YEAR RACE!?
ACTUALLY, WAS THERE EVER REALLY A TIME WHEN YOU WERE A FIRST-YEAR!?
GAH-HA-HA-HA-HA-HA-HA-HA!!
ZOOM

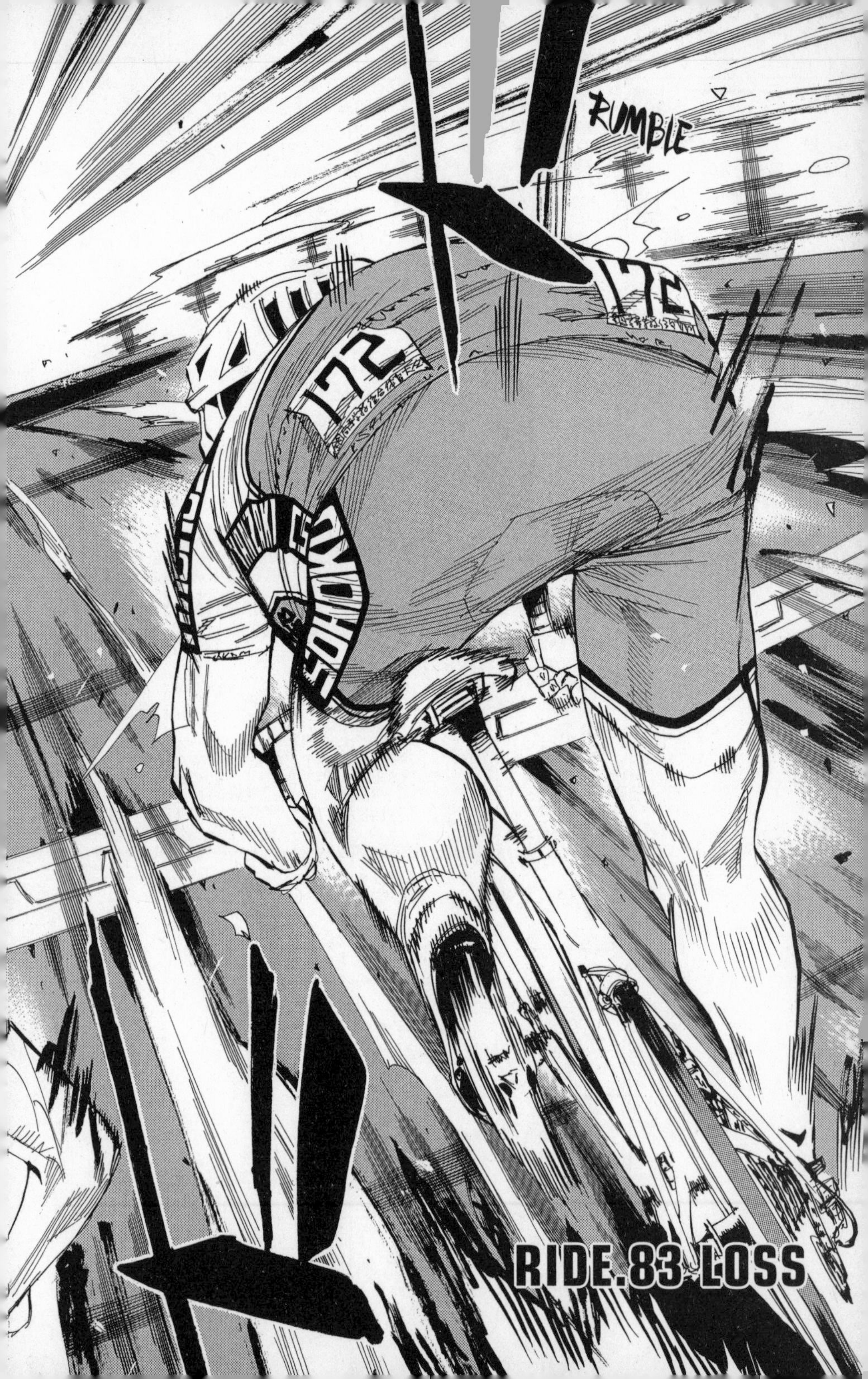
RUMBLE
RIDE.83 LOSS

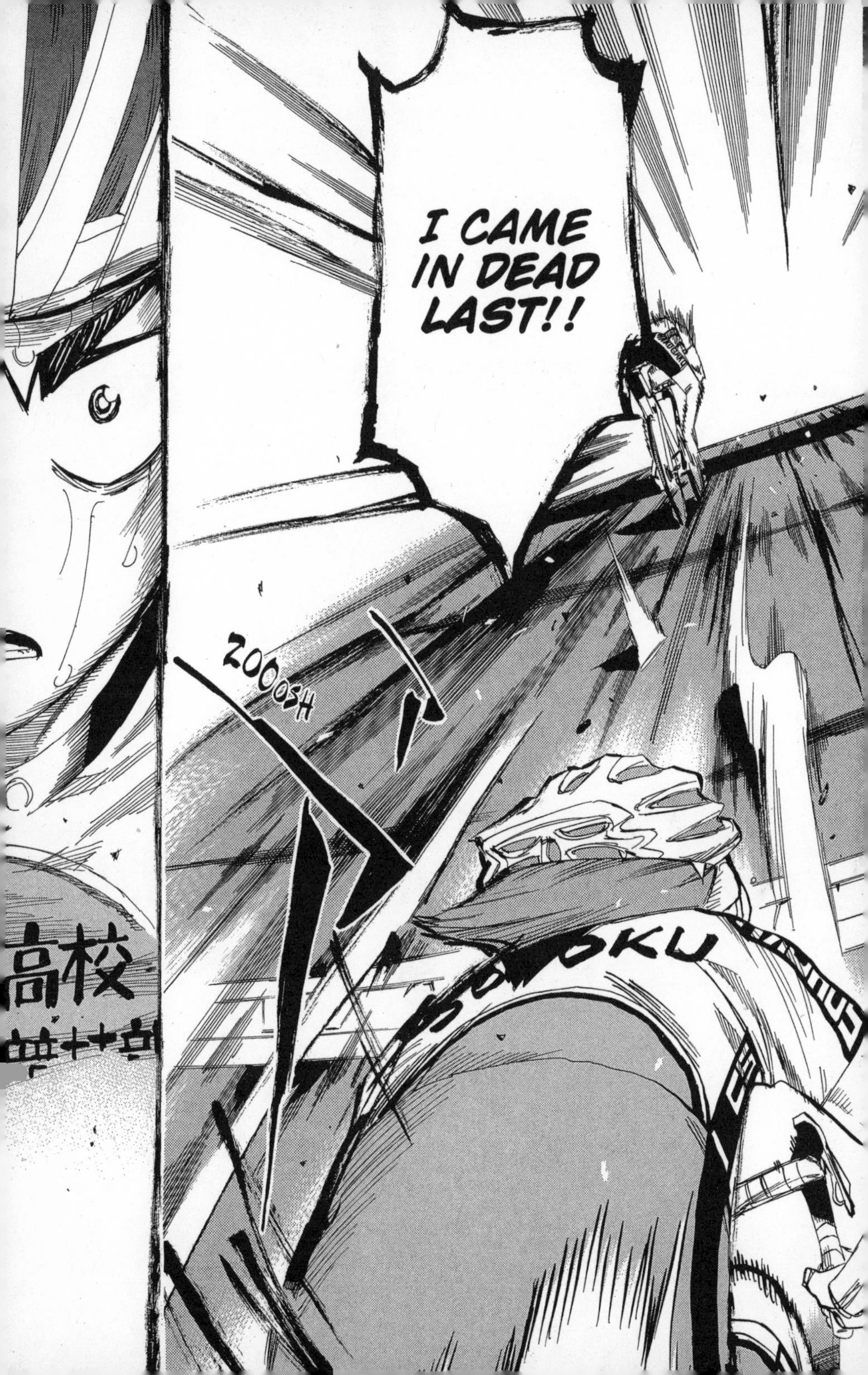
I CAME IN DEAD LAST!!
ZOOOSH
高校

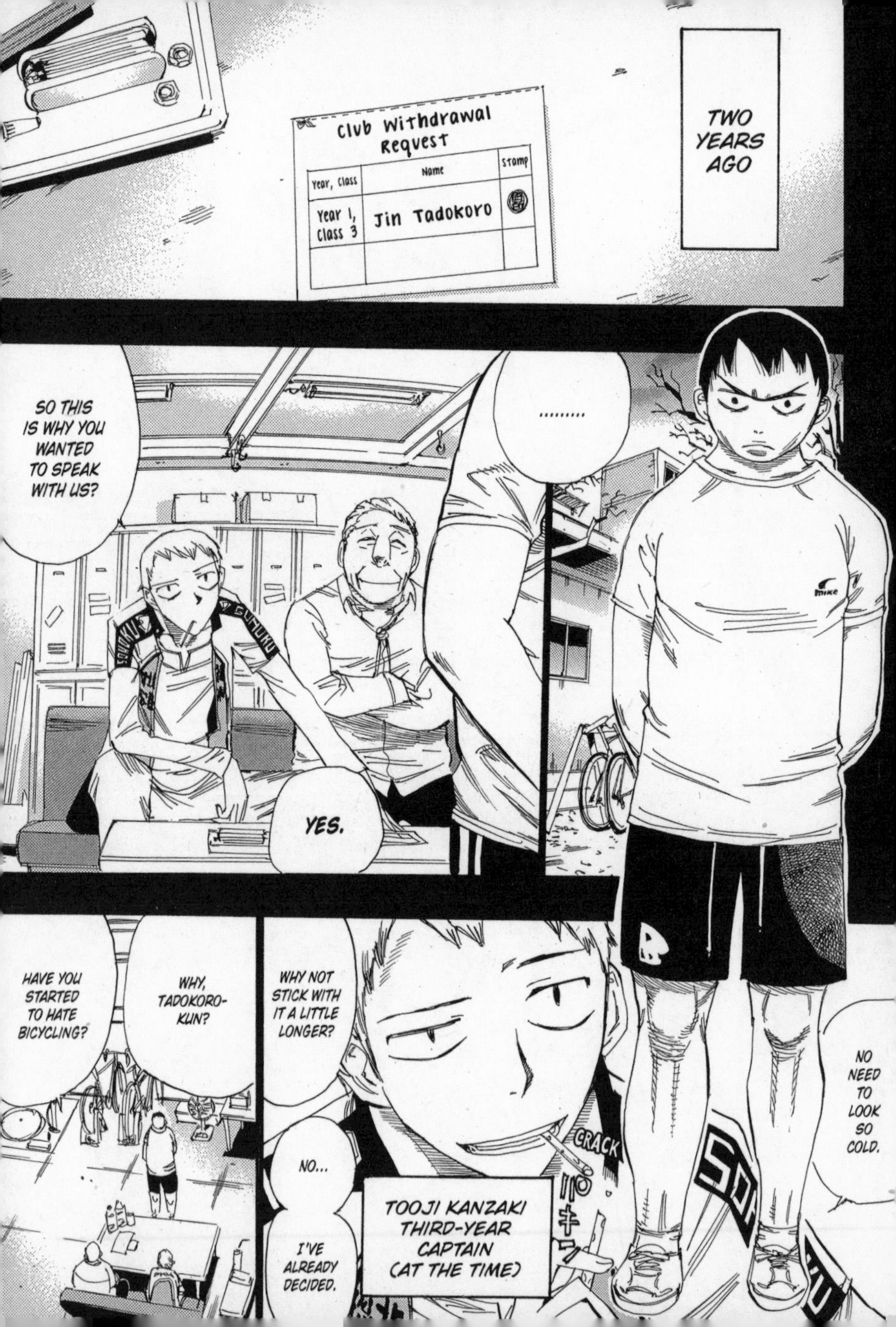
TWO YEARS AGO
Club Withdrawal Request
Year, Class
Name
Stamp
Year 1, Class 3
Jin Tadokoro
NO NEED TO LOOK SO COLD.
....
SO THIS IS WHY YOU WANTED TO SPEAK WITH US?
YES.
WHY NOT STICK WITH IT A LITTLE LONGER?
CRACK
TOOJI KANZAKI THIRD-YEAR CAPTAIN (AT THE TIME)
NO...
I'VE ALREADY DECIDED.
WHY, TADOKORO-KUN?
HAVE YOU STARTED TO HATE BICYCLING?

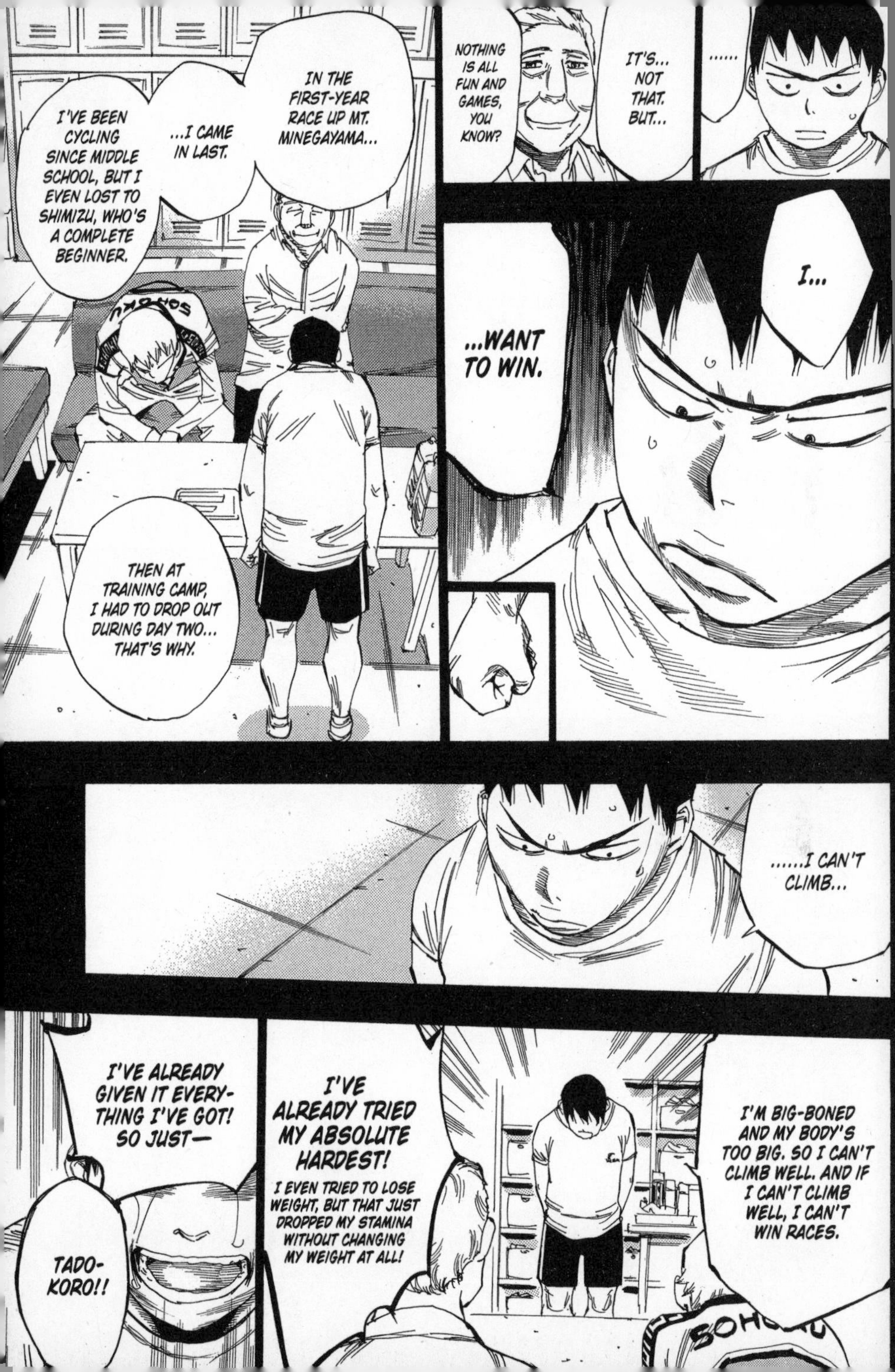
......
NOTHING IS ALL FUN AND GAMES, YOU KNOW?
IT'S... NOT THAT. BUT...
I...
...WANT TO WIN.
IN THE FIRST-YEAR RACE UP MT. MINEGAYAMA...
...I CAME IN LAST.
I'VE BEEN CYCLING SINCE MIDDLE SCHOOL, BUT I EVEN LOST TO SHIMIZU, WHO'S A COMPLETE BEGINNER.
THEN AT TRAINING CAMP, I HAD TO DROP OUT DURING DAY TWO... THAT'S WHY.
......I CAN'T CLIMB...
I'M BIG-BONED AND MY BODY'S TOO BIG. SO I CAN'T CLIMB WELL. AND IF I CAN'T CLIMB WELL, I CAN'T WIN RACES.
I'VE ALREADY TRIED MY ABSOLUTE HARDEST!
I EVEN TRIED TO LOSE WEIGHT, BUT THAT JUST DROPPED MY STAMINA WITHOUT CHANGING MY WEIGHT AT ALL!
I'VE ALREADY GIVEN IT EVERY-THING I'VE GOT! SO JUST—
TADO-KORO!!

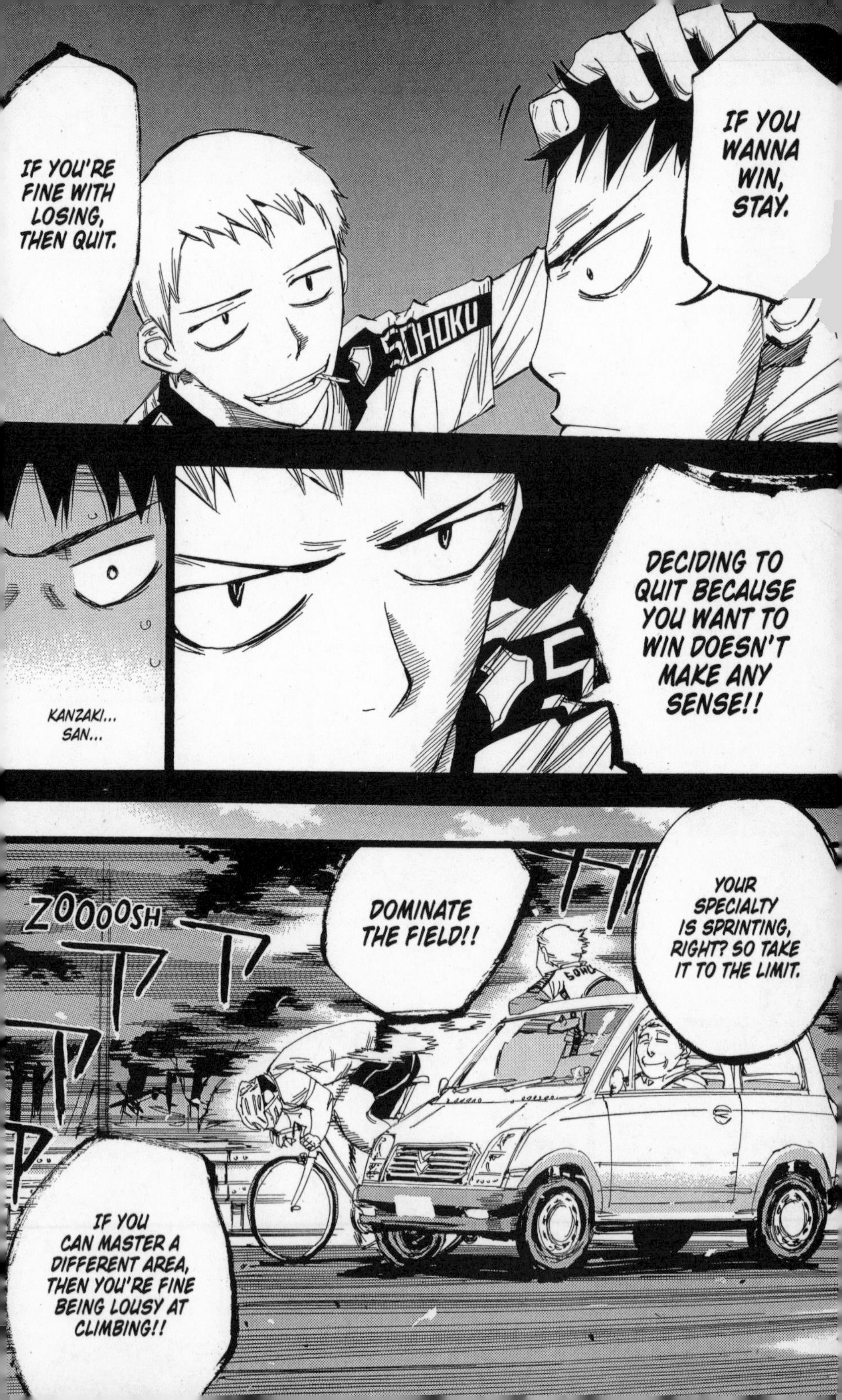
IF YOU WANNA WIN, STAY.
IF YOU'RE FINE WITH LOSING, THEN QUIT.
DECIDING TO QUIT BECAUSE YOU WANT TO WIN DOESN'T MAKE ANY SENSE!!
KANZAKI... SAN...
YOUR SPECIALTY IS SPRINTING, RIGHT? SO TAKE IT TO THE LIMIT.
DOMINATE THE FIELD!!
ZOOOOSH
IF YOU CAN MASTER A DIFFERENT AREA, THEN YOU'RE FINE BEING LOUSY AT CLIMBING!!

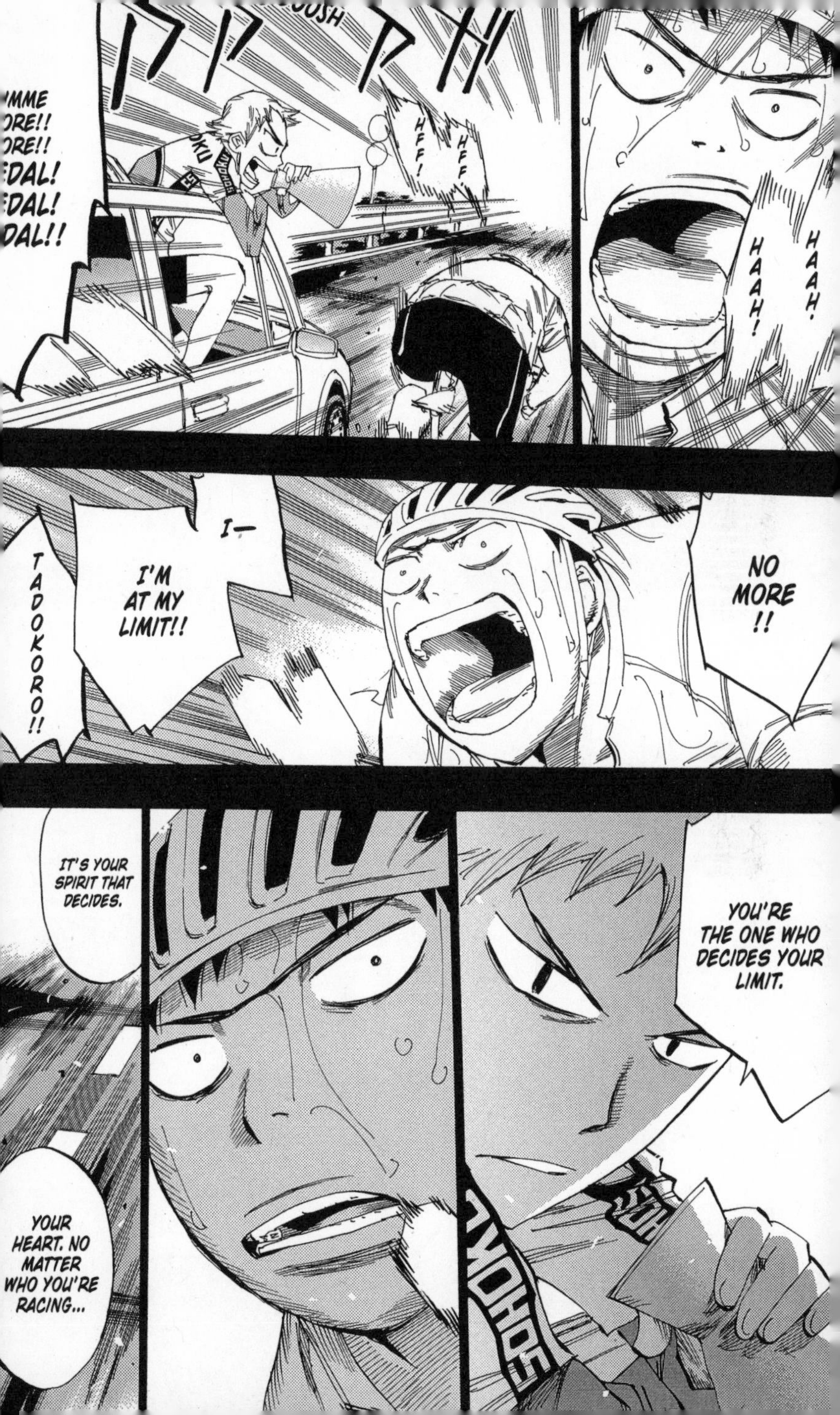
HAAAH!
HAAAH!
OUSH
IMME
ORE!!
ORE!!
EDAL!
EDAL!
EDAL!!
HFF!
HFF!
NO MORE!!
I'M AT MY LIMIT!!
I—
TADOKORO!!
YOU'RE THE ONE WHO DECIDES YOUR LIMIT.
IT'S YOUR SPIRIT THAT DECIDES.
YOUR HEART. NO MATTER WHO YOU'RE RACING...

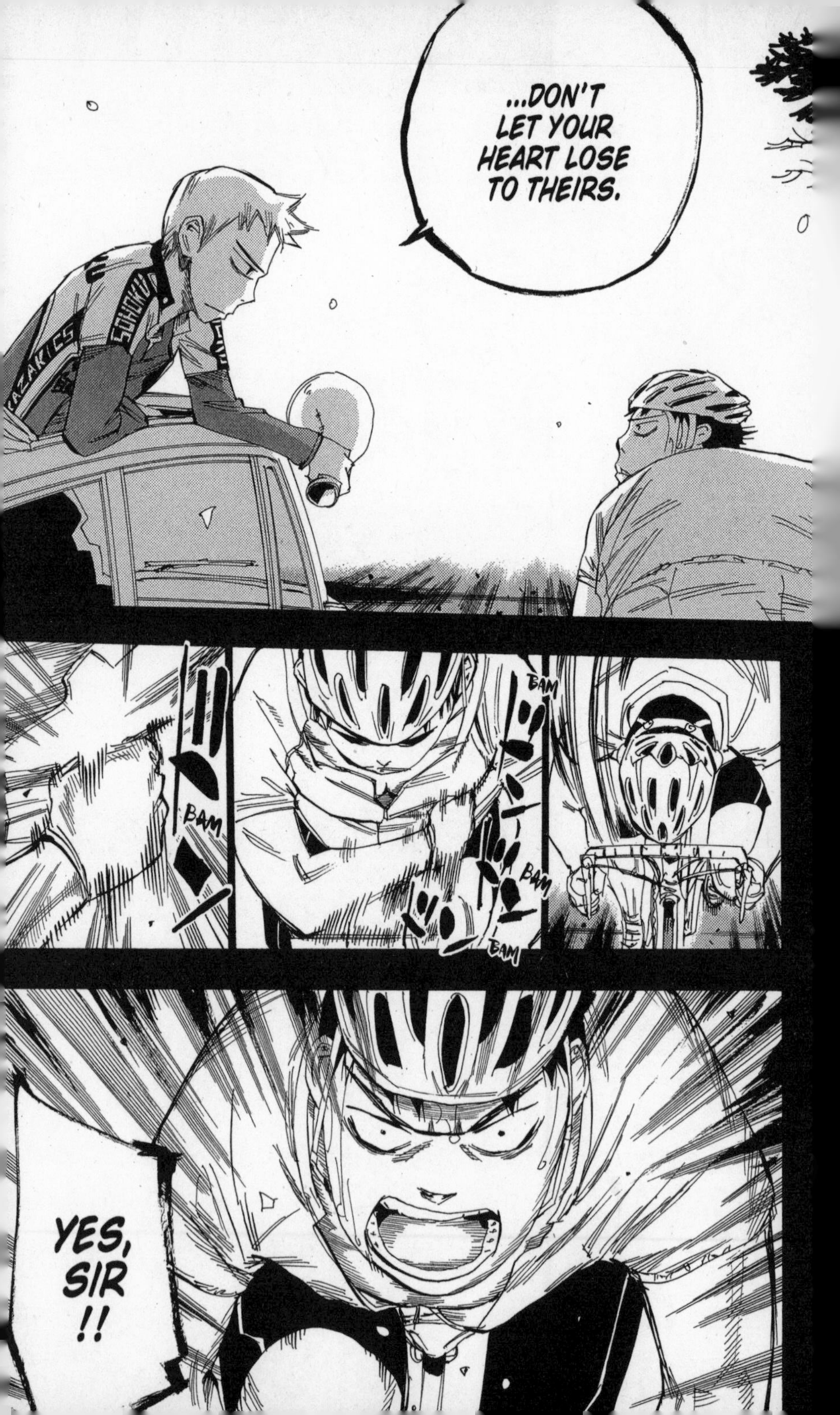
...DON'T LET YOUR HEART LOSE TO THEIRS.
BAM
BAM
BAM
BAM
YES, SIR !!

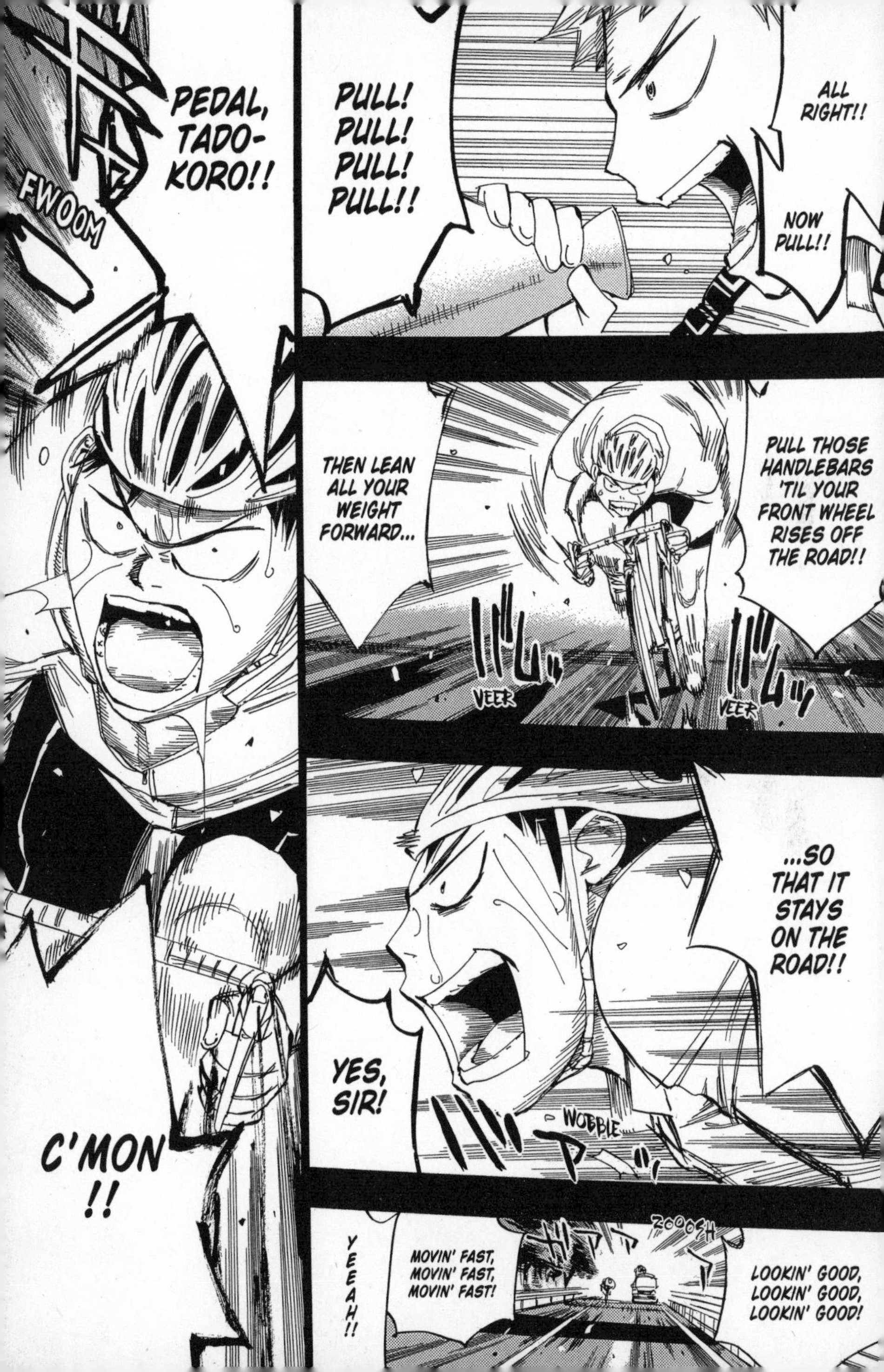
ALL RIGHT!!
NOW PULL!!
PULL! PULL! PULL! PULL!!
PULL THOSE HANDLEBARS 'TIL YOUR FRONT WHEEL RISES OFF THE ROAD!!
THEN LEAN ALL YOUR WEIGHT FORWARD...
VEER
VEER
...SO THAT IT STAYS ON THE ROAD!!
YES, SIR!
WOBBLE
ZOOOSH
LOOKIN' GOOD, LOOKIN' GOOD, LOOKIN' GOOD!
MOVIN' FAST, MOVIN' FAST, MOVIN' FAST!
YEEEAH!!
PEDAL, TADOKORO!!
FWOOM
C'MON!!

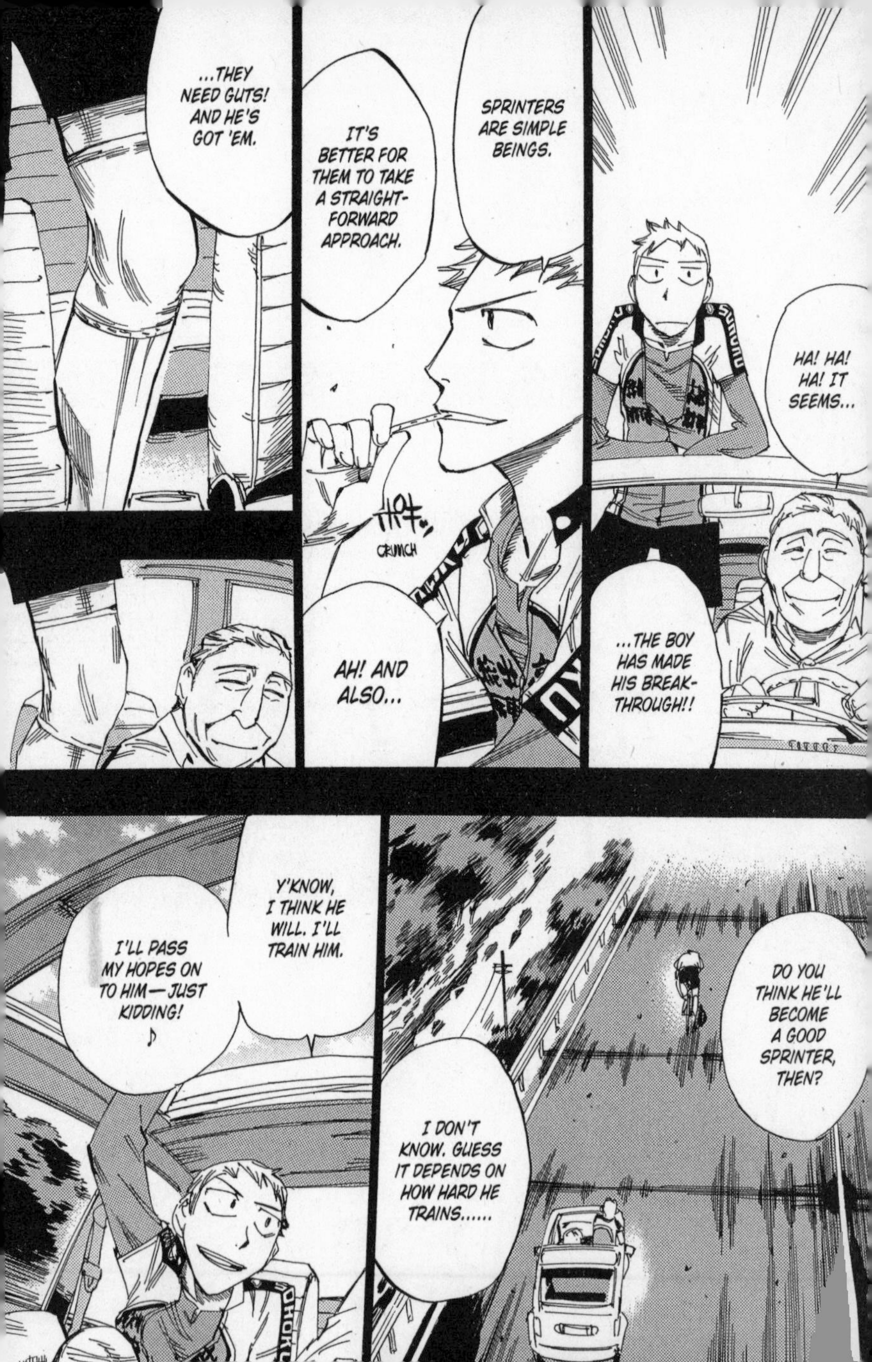
HA! HA! HA! IT SEEMS...
...THE BOY HAS MADE HIS BREAK-THROUGH!!
SPRINTERS ARE SIMPLE BEINGS.
IT'S BETTER FOR THEM TO TAKE A STRAIGHT-FORWARD APPROACH.
CRUNCH
AH! AND ALSO...
...THEY NEED GUTS! AND HE'S GOT 'EM.
DO YOU THINK HE'LL BECOME A GOOD SPRINTER, THEN?
I DON'T KNOW. GUESS IT DEPENDS ON HOW HARD HE TRAINS......
Y'KNOW, I THINK HE WILL. I'LL TRAIN HIM.
I'LL PASS MY HOPES ON TO HIM—JUST KIDDING! ♪

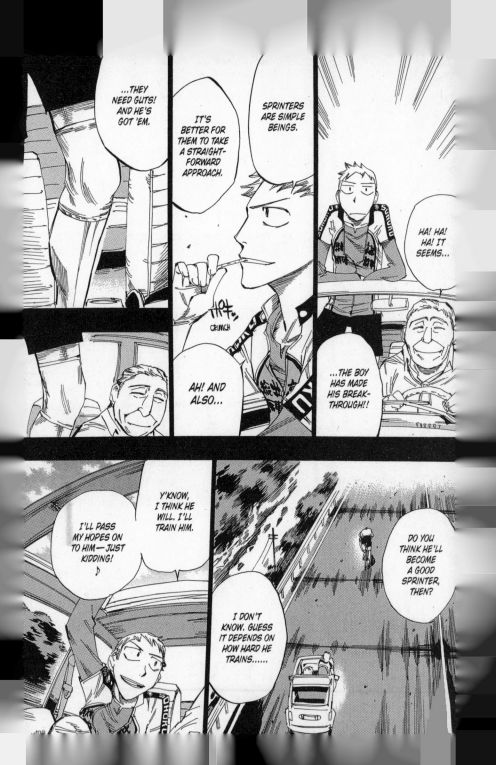

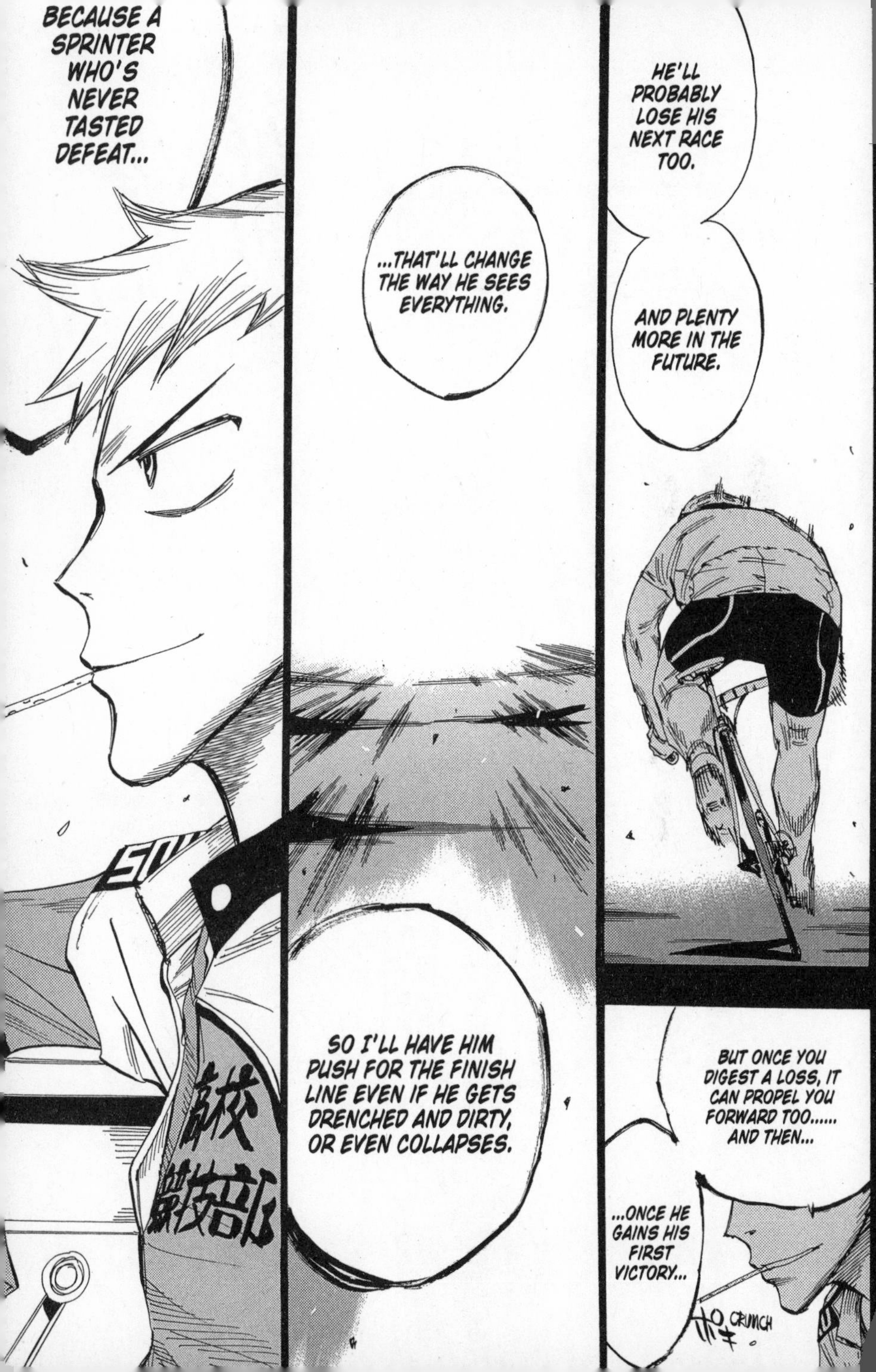
BECAUSE A SPRINTER WHO'S NEVER TASTED DEFEAT...
...THAT'LL CHANGE THE WAY HE SEES EVERYTHING.
SO I'LL HAVE HIM PUSH FOR THE FINISH LINE EVEN IF HE GETS DRENCHED AND DIRTY, OR EVEN COLLAPSES.
HE'LL PROBABLY LOSE HIS NEXT RACE TOO.
AND PLENTY MORE IN THE FUTURE.
BUT ONCE YOU DIGEST A LOSS, IT CAN PROPEL YOU FORWARD TOO...... AND THEN...
...ONCE HE GAINS HIS FIRST VICTORY...
CRUNCH

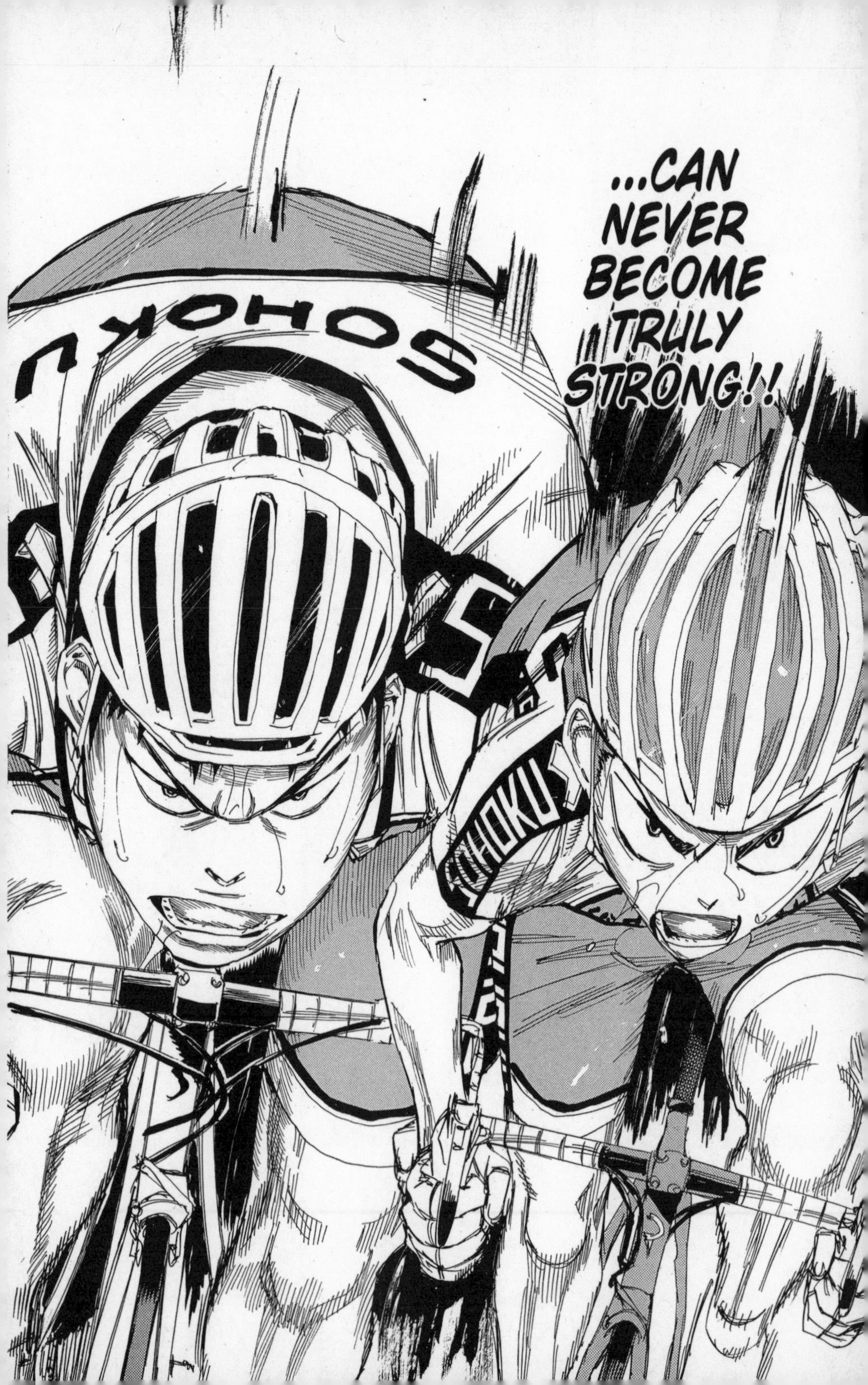
...CAN NEVER BECOME TRULY STRONG!!

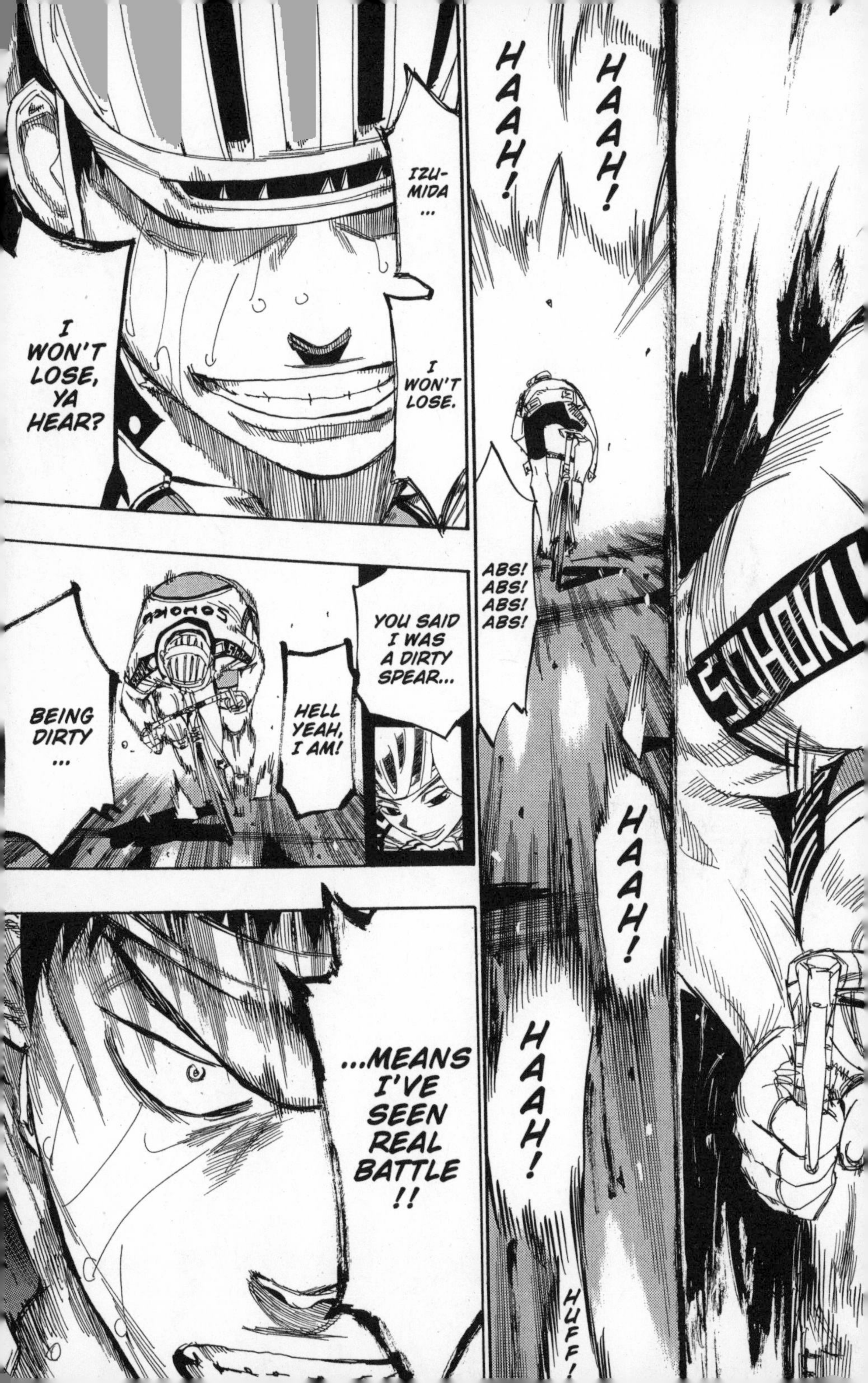
HAAAH!
HAAAH!
ABS! ABS! ABS! ABS!
HAAAH!
HAAAH!
HUFF!
IZUMIDA...
I WON'T LOSE.
I WON'T LOSE, YA HEAR?
YOU SAID I WAS A DIRTY SPEAR...
HELL YEAH, I AM!
BEING DIRTY...
...MEANS I'VE SEEN REAL BATTLE!!

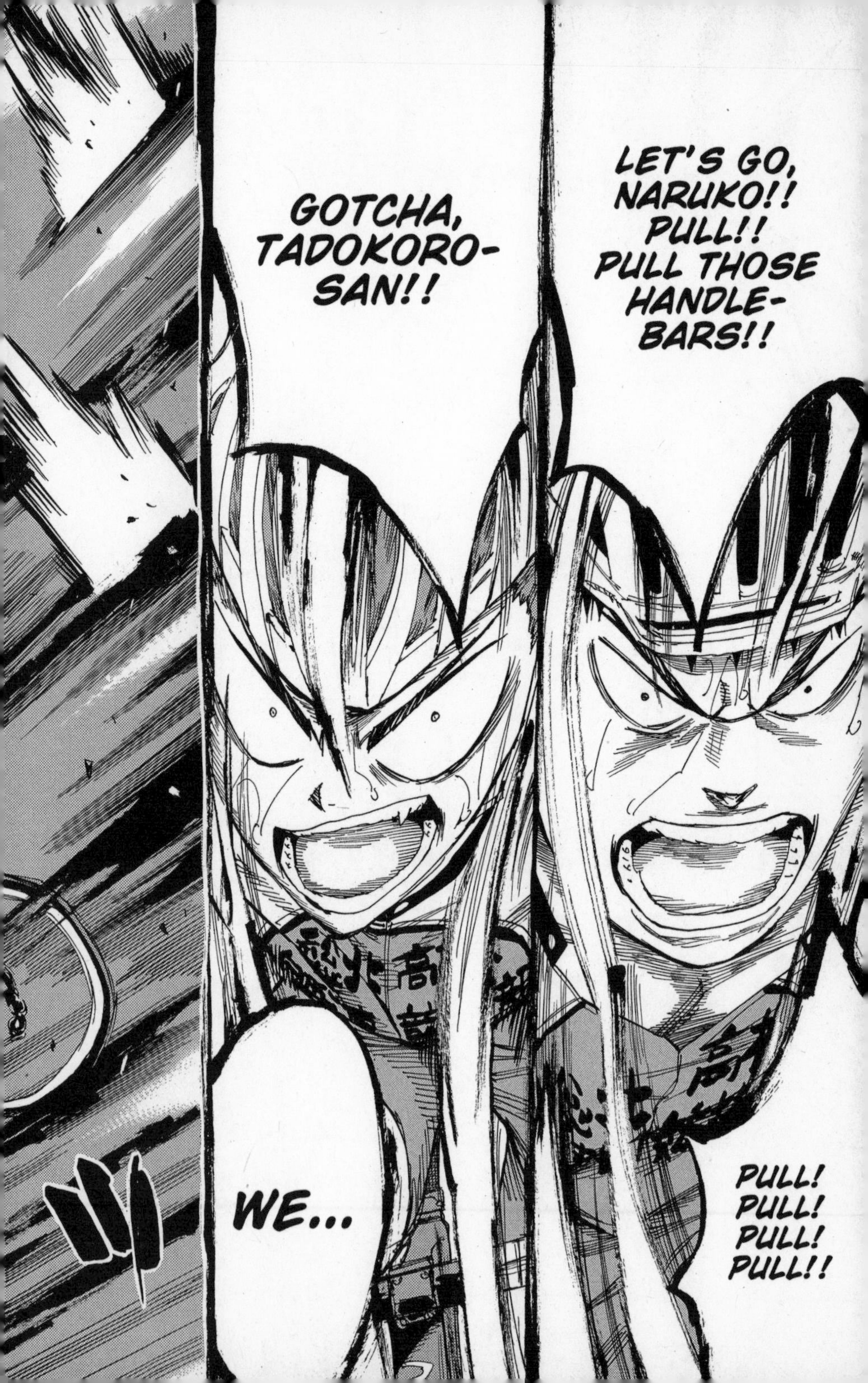
LET'S GO, NARUKO!! PULL!! PULL THOSE HANDLE-BARS!!
PULL! PULL! PULL! PULL!!
GOTCHA, TADOKORO-SAN!!
WE...

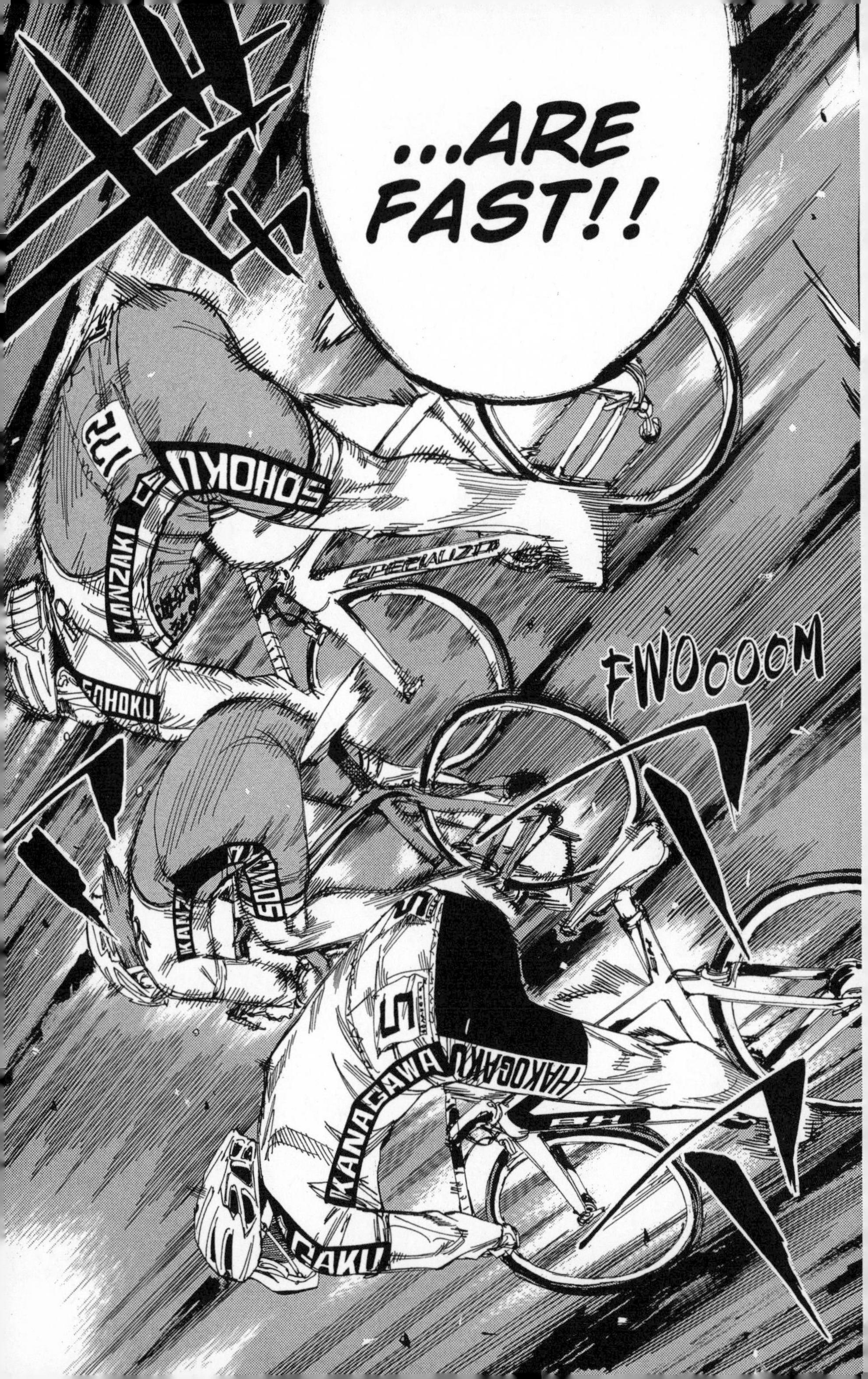
...ARE FAST!!
FWOOOOM

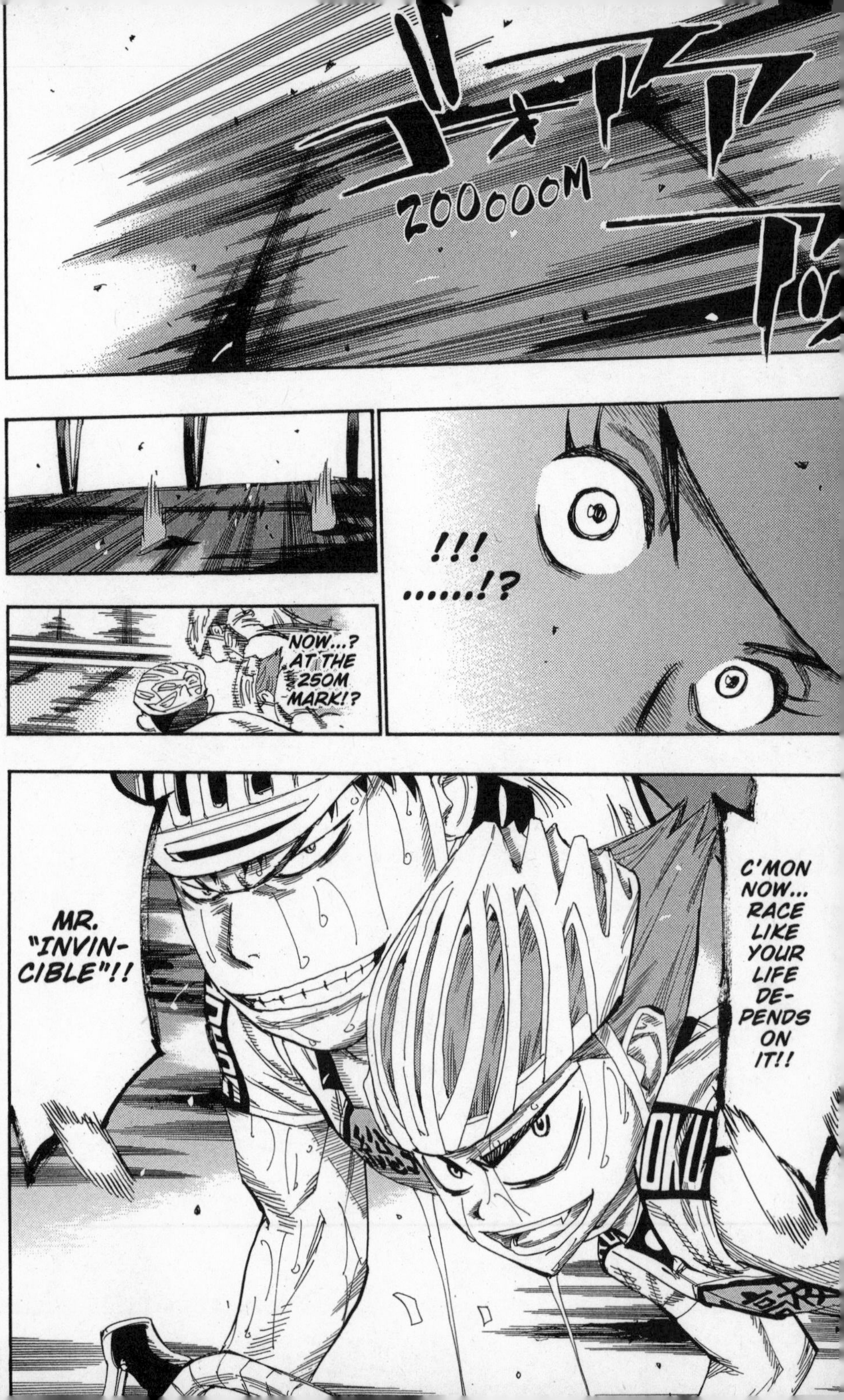
ZOOOOOM
!!!
......!?
NOW...? AT THE 250M MARK!?
C'MON NOW... RACE LIKE YOUR LIFE DE-PENDS ON IT!!
MR. "INVIN-CIBLE"!!

RIDE.84 THREE-WAY BATTLE

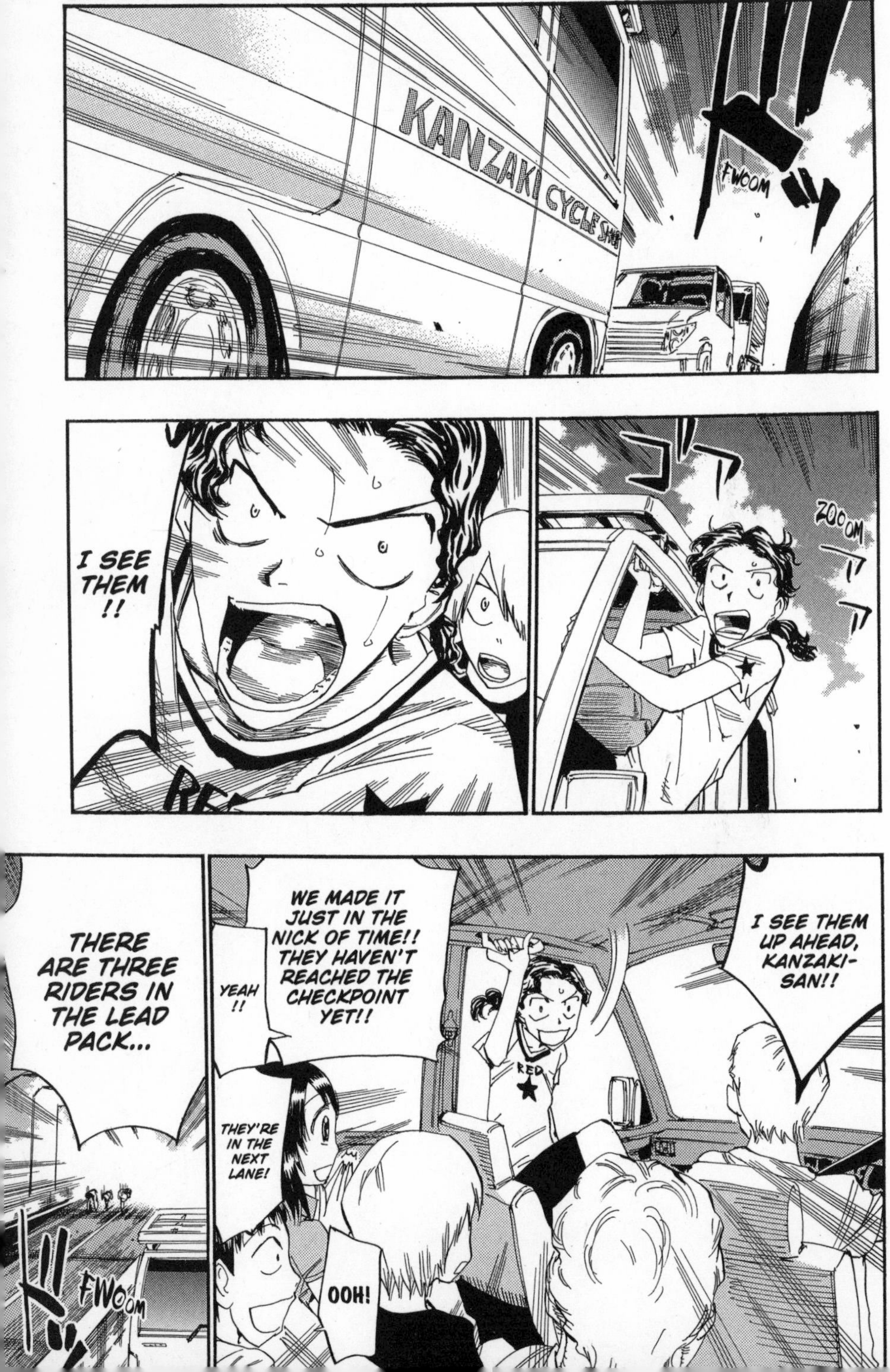
KANZAKI CYCLE SHOP
FWOOM
ZOOOM
I SEE THEM!!
I SEE THEM UP AHEAD, KANZAKI-SAN!!
WE MADE IT JUST IN THE NICK OF TIME!! THEY HAVEN'T REACHED THE CHECKPOINT YET!!
YEAH!!
RED
THEY'RE IN THE NEXT LANE!
OOH!
THERE ARE THREE RIDERS IN THE LEAD PACK...
FWOOM

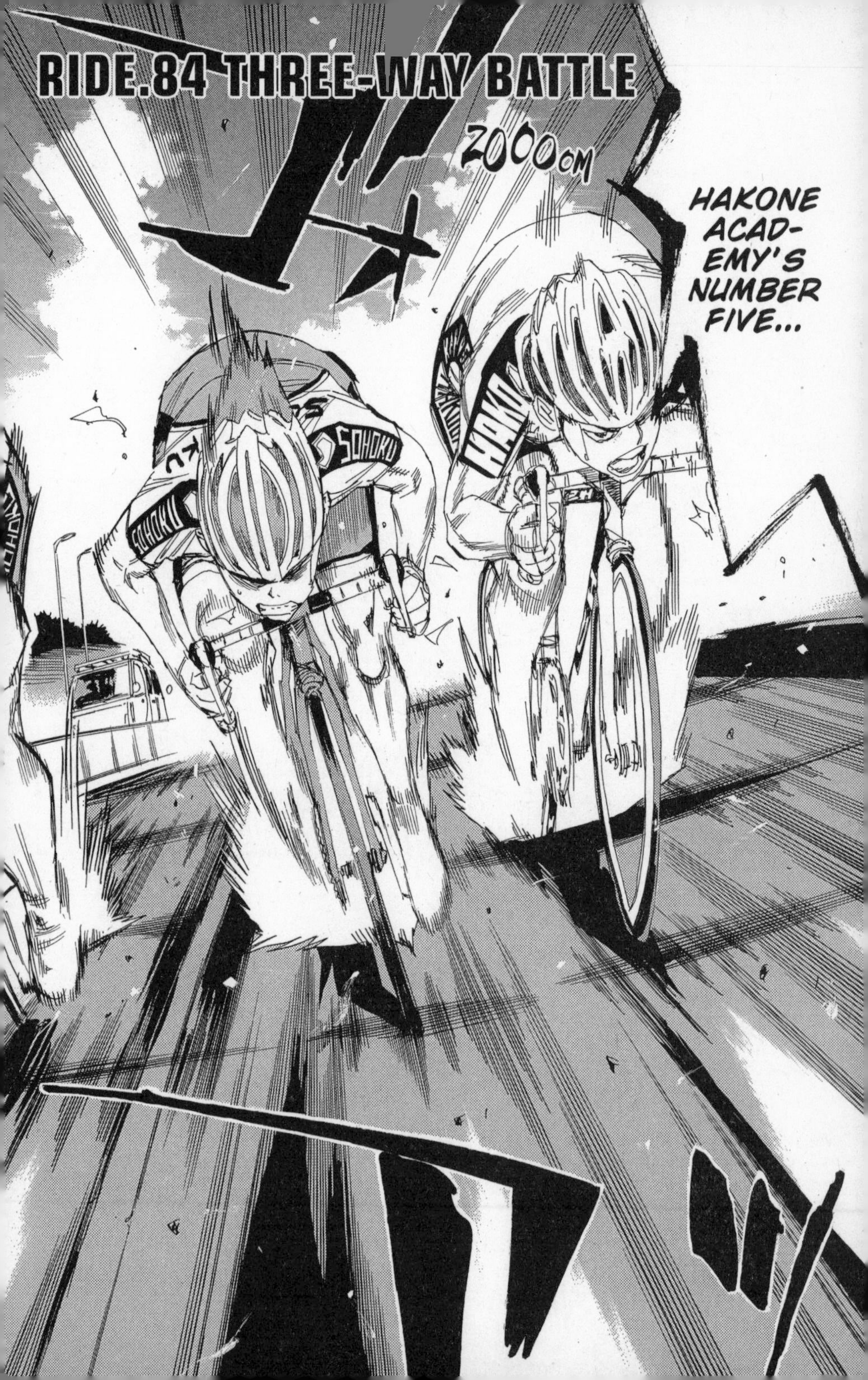
RIDE.84 THREE-WAY BATTLE
ZOOOOM
HAKONE ACAD-EMY'S NUMBER FIVE...
SOHOKU

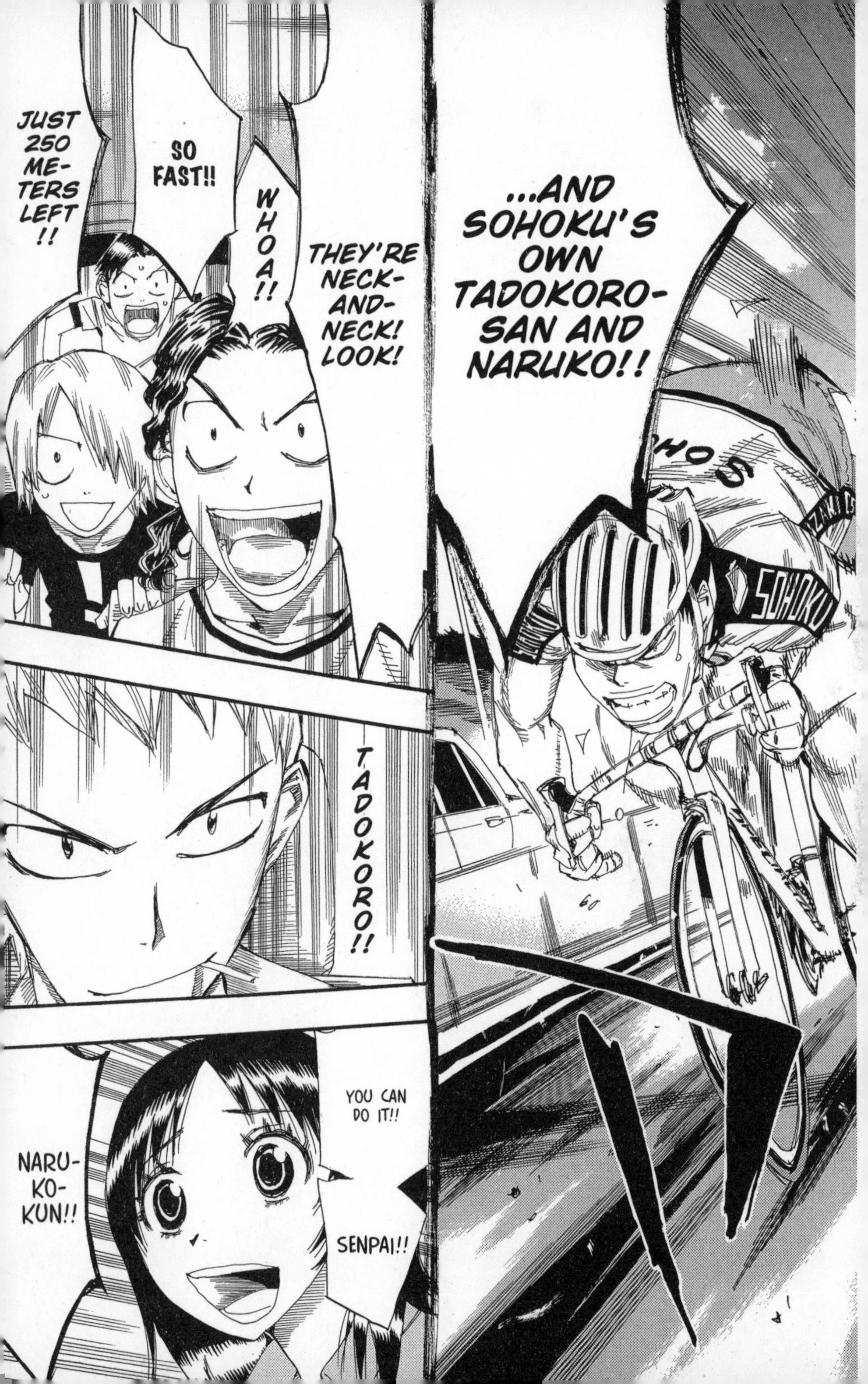
...AND SOHOKU'S OWN TADOKORO-SAN AND NARUKO!!
THEY'RE NECK-AND-NECK! LOOK!
WHOA!!
SO FAST!!
JUST 250 METERS LEFT!!
TADOKORO!!
YOU CAN DO IT!!
SENPAI!!
NARUKO-KUN!!

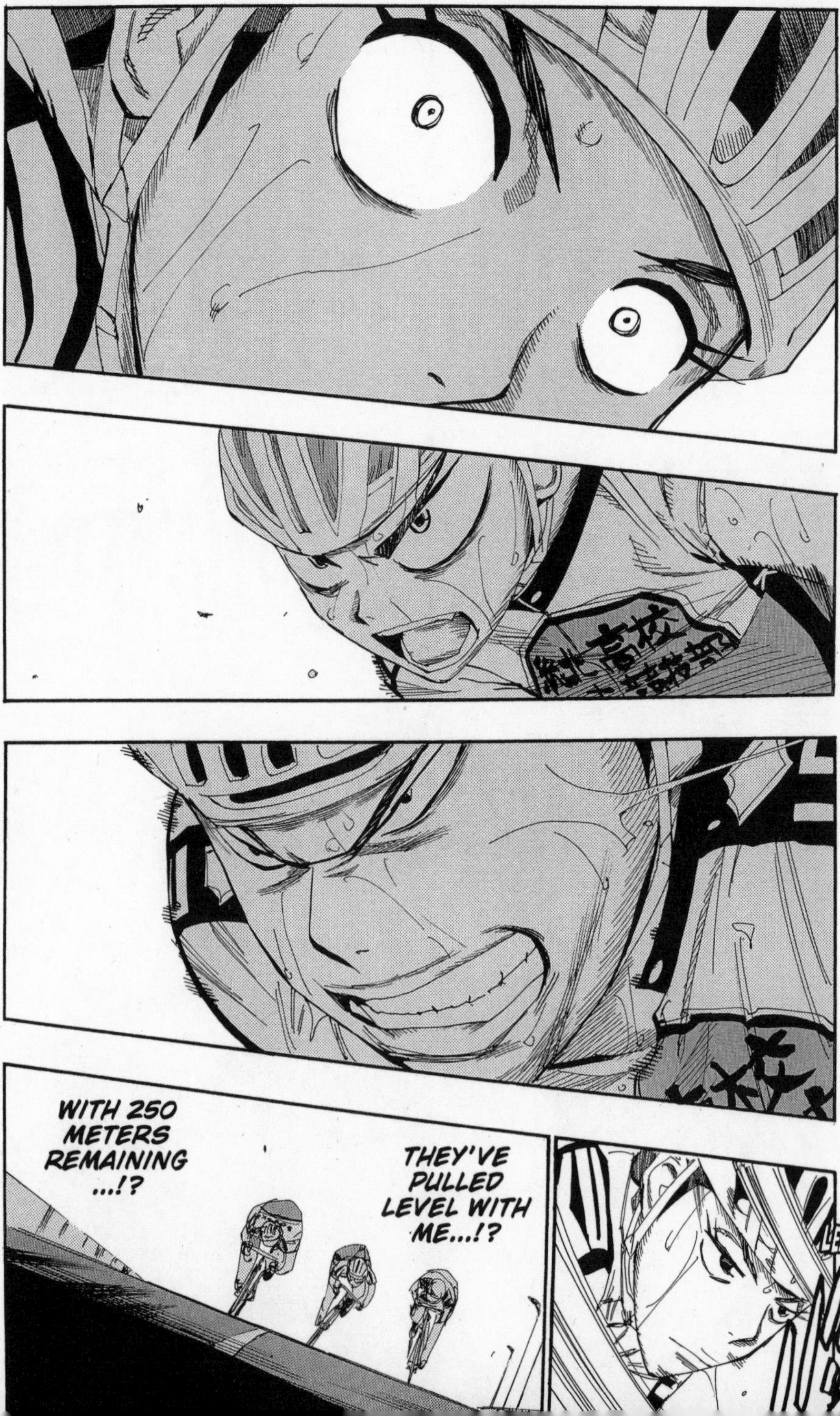
LEAN
WITH 250 METERS REMAINING ...!?
THEY'VE PULLED LEVEL WITH ME...!?

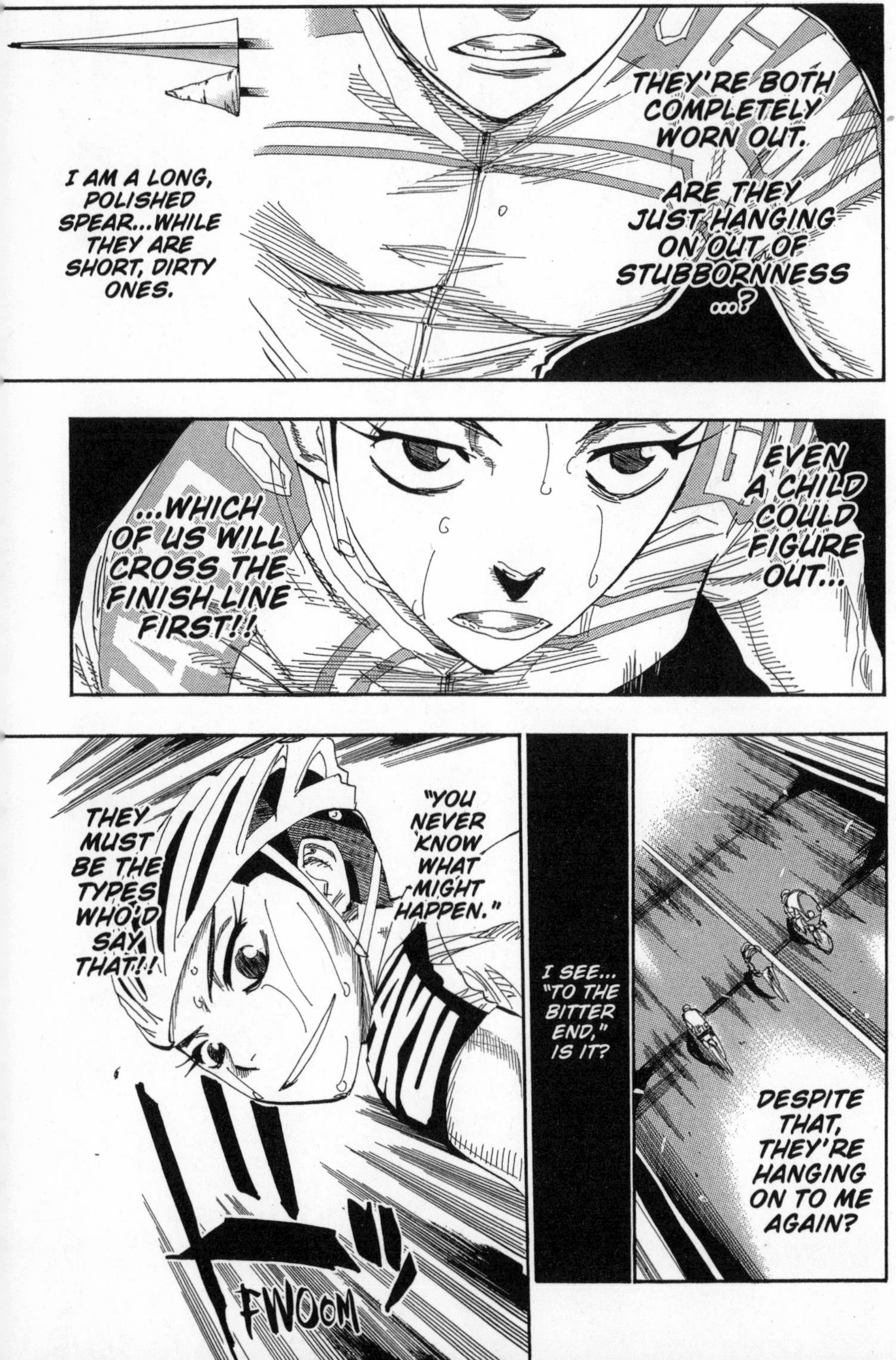
THEY'RE BOTH COMPLETELY WORN OUT.
ARE THEY JUST HANGING ON OUT OF STUBBORNNESS ...?
I AM A LONG, POLISHED SPEAR...WHILE THEY ARE SHORT, DIRTY ONES.
EVEN A CHILD COULD FIGURE OUT...
...WHICH OF US WILL CROSS THE FINISH LINE FIRST!!
DESPITE THAT, THEY'RE HANGING ON TO ME AGAIN?
I SEE... "TO THE BITTER END," IS IT?
"YOU NEVER KNOW WHAT MIGHT HAPPEN."
THEY MUST BE THE TYPES WHO'D SAY THAT!!
FWOOM

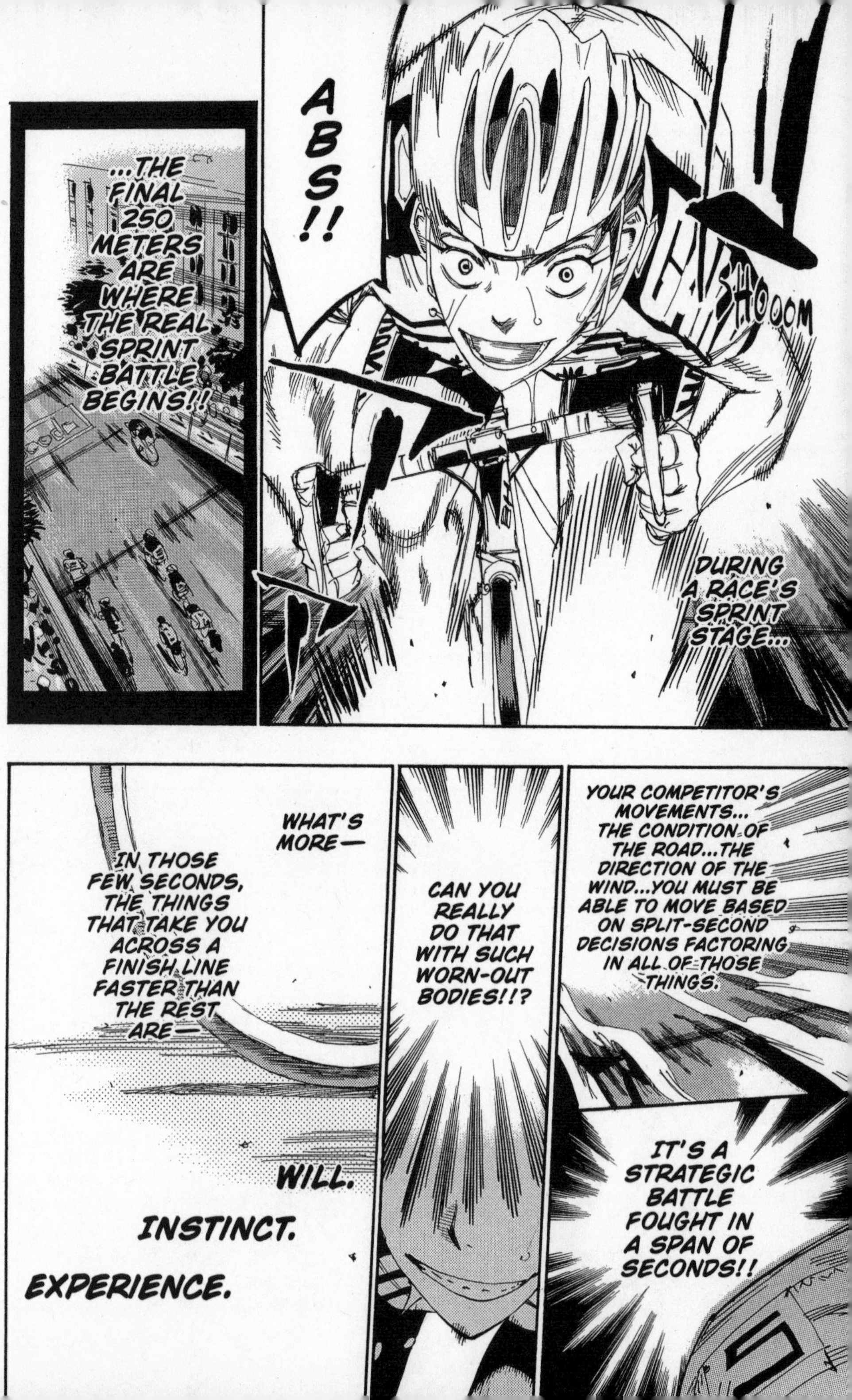
SHOOOM
ABS!!
DURING A RACE'S SPRINT STAGE...
...THE FINAL 250 METERS ARE WHERE THE REAL SPRINT BATTLE BEGINS!!
YOUR COMPETITOR'S MOVEMENTS... THE CONDITION OF THE ROAD...THE DIRECTION OF THE WIND...YOU MUST BE ABLE TO MOVE BASED ON SPLIT-SECOND DECISIONS FACTORING IN ALL OF THOSE THINGS.
IT'S A STRATEGIC BATTLE FOUGHT IN A SPAN OF SECONDS!!
CAN YOU REALLY DO THAT WITH SUCH WORN-OUT BODIES!!?
WHAT'S MORE—
IN THOSE FEW SECONDS, THE THINGS THAT TAKE YOU ACROSS A FINISH LINE FASTER THAN THE REST ARE—
WILL.
INSTINCT.
EXPERIENCE.

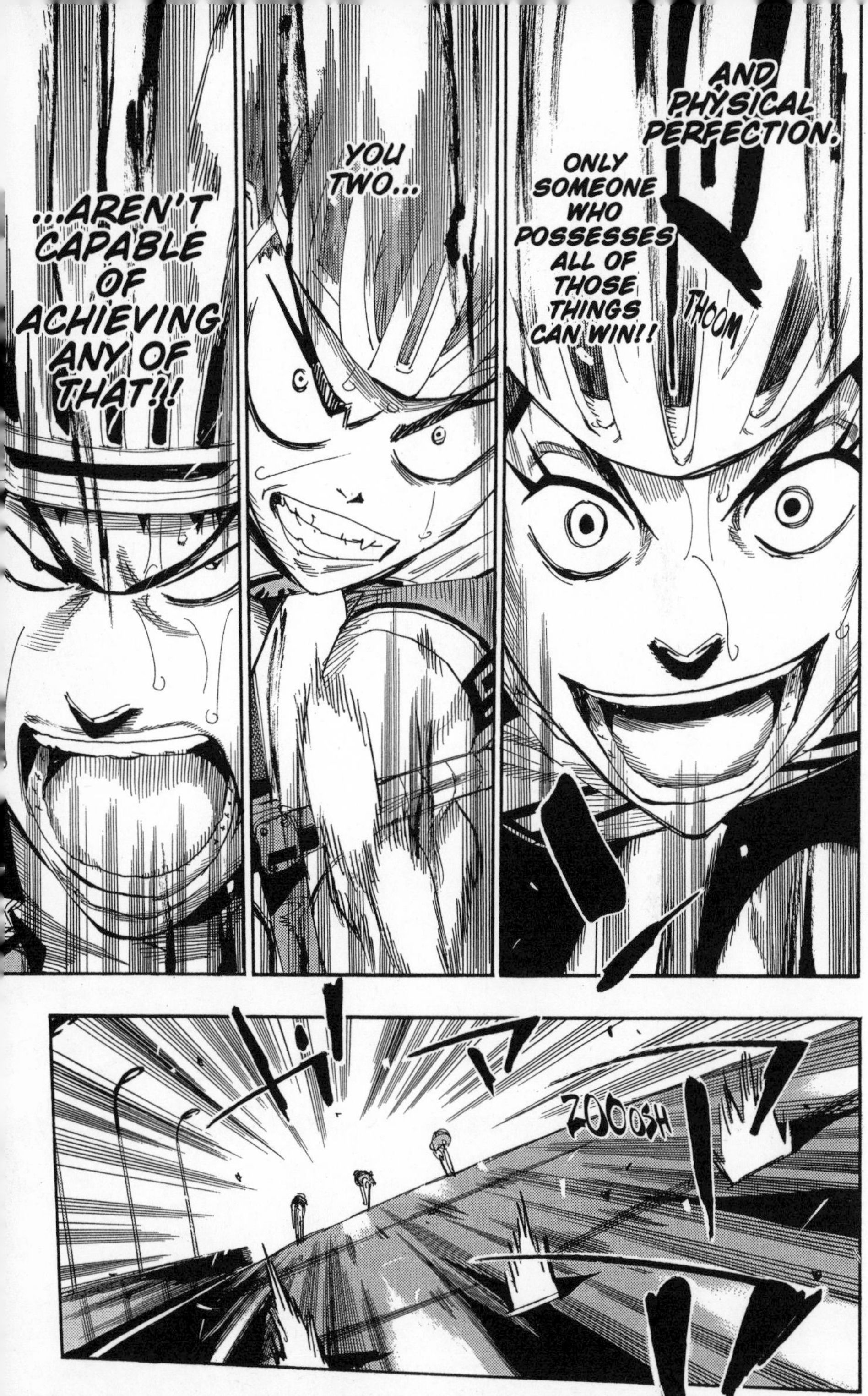
AND PHYSICAL PERFECTION.
ONLY SOMEONE WHO POSSESSES ALL OF THOSE THINGS CAN WIN!!
THOOM
YOU TWO...
...AREN'T CAPABLE OF ACHIEVING ANY OF THAT!!
ZOOOSH

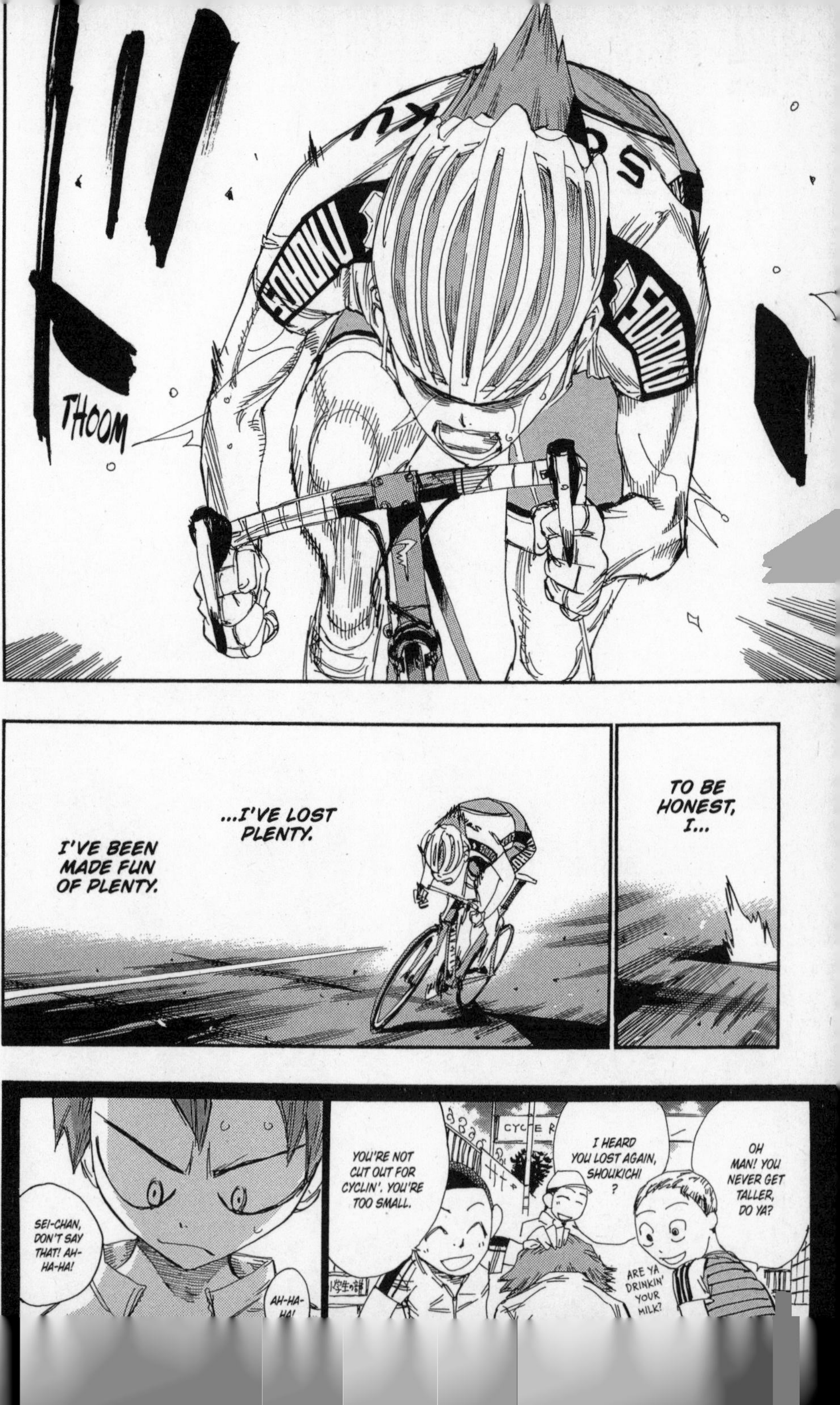
THOOM
TO BE HONEST, I...
...I'VE LOST PLENTY.
I'VE BEEN MADE FUN OF PLENTY.
OH MAN! YOU NEVER GET TALLER, DO YA?
I HEARD YOU LOST AGAIN, SHOUKICHI?
YOU'RE NOT CUT OUT FOR CYCLIN'. YOU'RE TOO SMALL.
ARE YA DRINKIN' YOUR MILK?
SEI-CHAN, DON'T SAY THAT! AH-HA-HA!
AH-HA-HA!

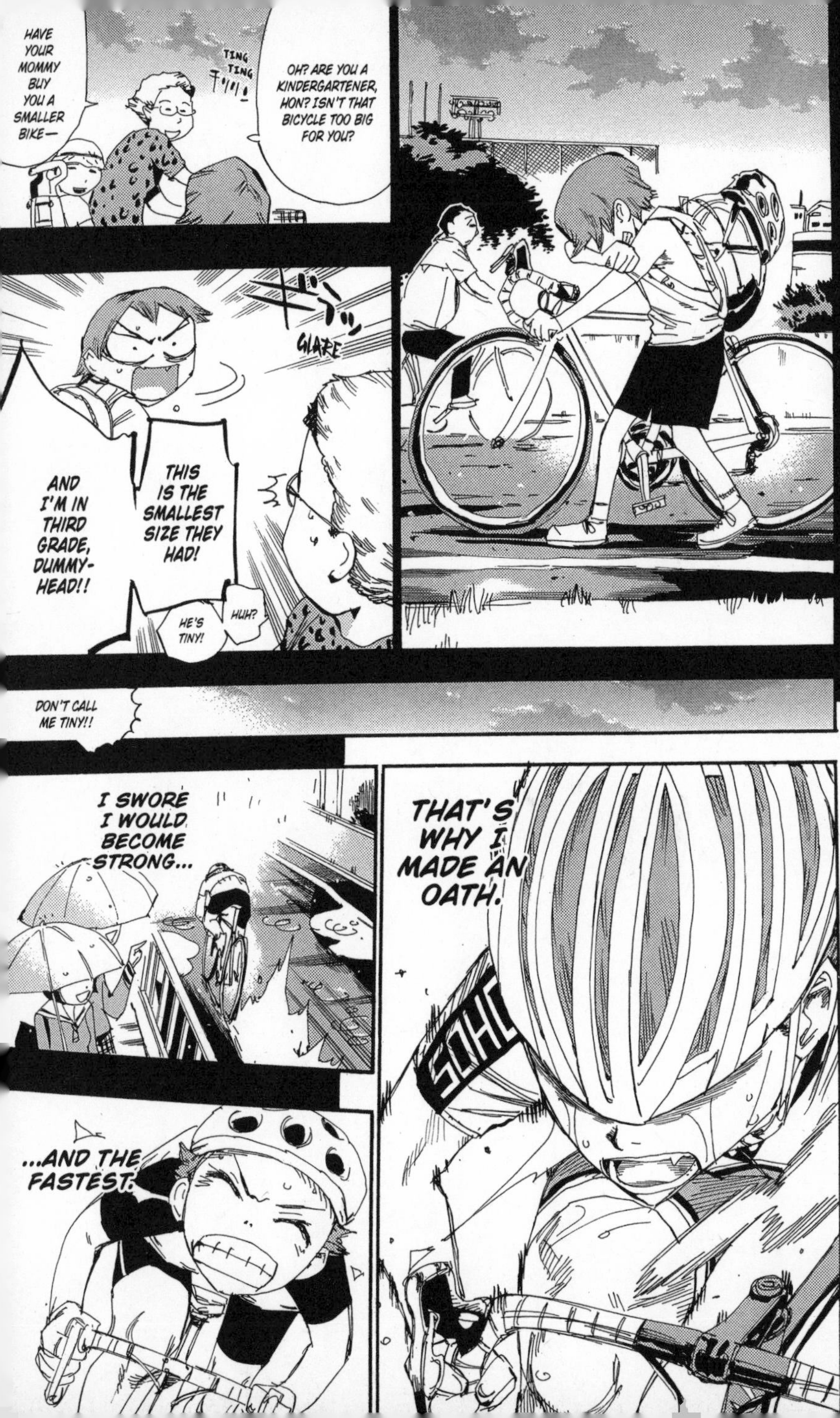
OH? ARE YOU A KINDERGARTENER, HON? ISN'T THAT BICYCLE TOO BIG FOR YOU?
TING TING
HAVE YOUR MOMMY BUY YOU A SMALLER BIKE—
GLARE
THIS IS THE SMALLEST SIZE THEY HAD!
AND I'M IN THIRD GRADE, DUMMY-HEAD!!
HUH?
HE'S TINY!
DON'T CALL ME TINY!!
THAT'S WHY I MADE AN OATH.
I SWORE I WOULD BECOME STRONG...
...AND THE FASTEST.

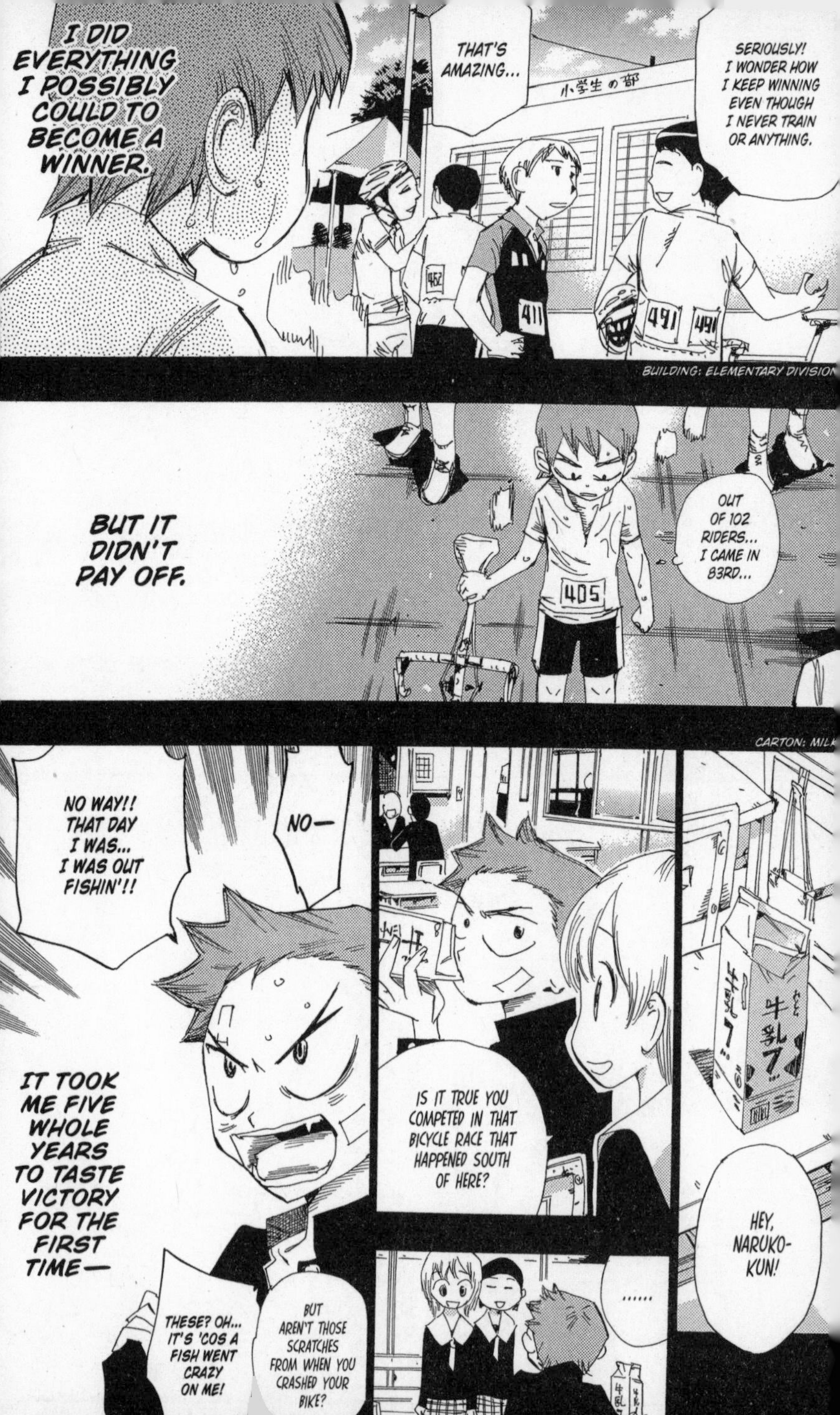
SERIOUSLY! I WONDER HOW I KEEP WINNING EVEN THOUGH I NEVER TRAIN OR ANYTHING.
THAT'S AMAZING...
I DID EVERYTHING I POSSIBLY COULD TO BECOME A WINNER.
BUILDING: ELEMENTARY DIVISION
OUT OF 102 RIDERS... I CAME IN 83RD...
BUT IT DIDN'T PAY OFF.
CARTON: MILK
HEY, NARUKO-KUN!
IS IT TRUE YOU COMPETED IN THAT BICYCLE RACE THAT HAPPENED SOUTH OF HERE?
......
BUT AREN'T THOSE SCRATCHES FROM WHEN YOU CRASHED YOUR BIKE?
NO—
NO WAY!! THAT DAY I WAS... I WAS OUT FISHIN'!!
IT TOOK ME FIVE WHOLE YEARS TO TASTE VICTORY FOR THE FIRST TIME—
THESE? OH... IT'S 'COS A FISH WENT CRAZY ON ME!

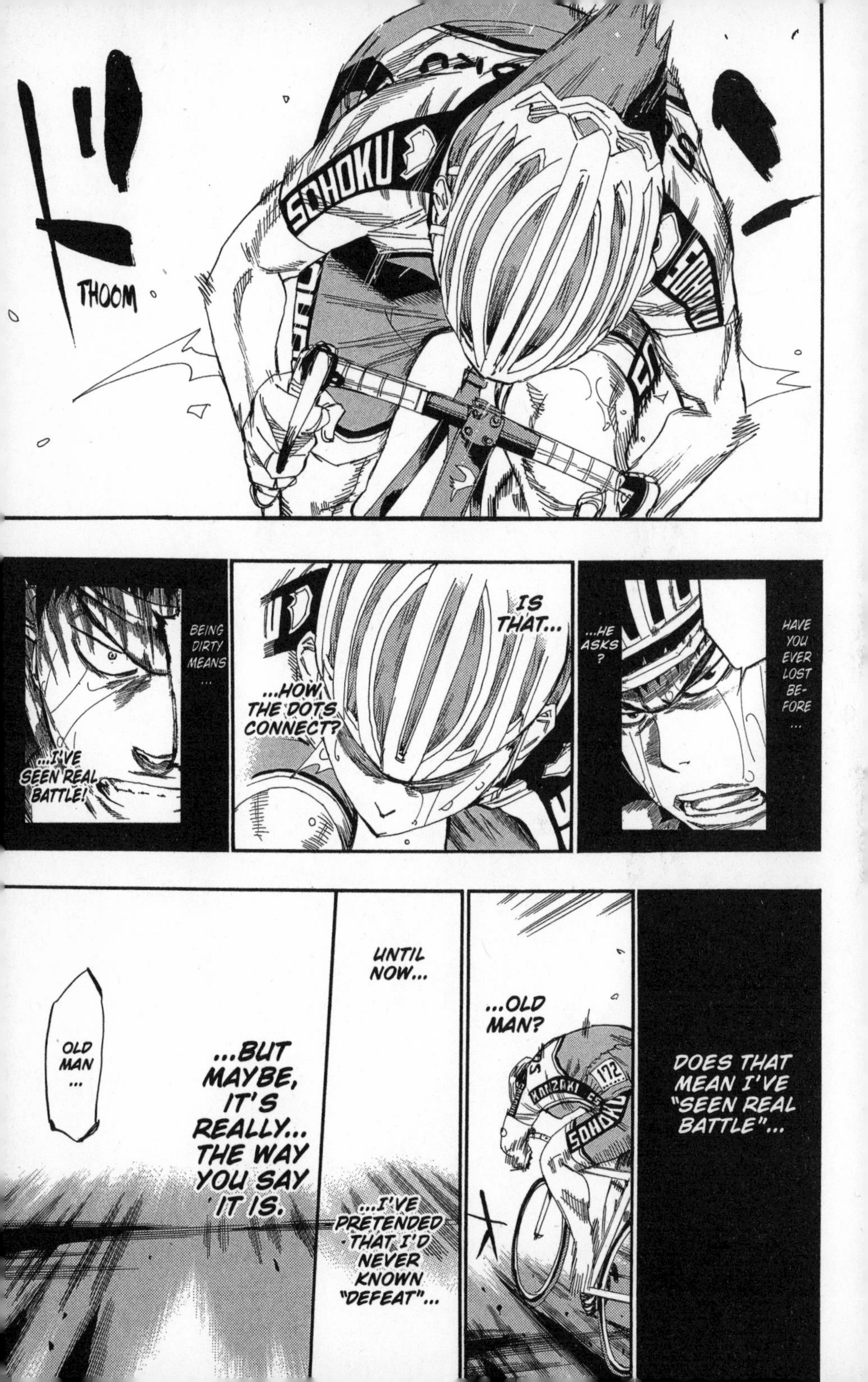
THOOM
HAVE YOU EVER LOST BEFORE ...
...HE ASKS ?
IS THAT...
...HOW THE DOTS CONNECT?
BEING DIRTY MEANS ...
...I'VE SEEN REAL BATTLE!
DOES THAT MEAN I'VE "SEEN REAL BATTLE"...
...OLD MAN?
UNTIL NOW...
...I'VE PRETENDED THAT I'D NEVER KNOWN "DEFEAT"...
OLD MAN ...
...BUT MAYBE, IT'S REALLY... THE WAY YOU SAY IT IS.

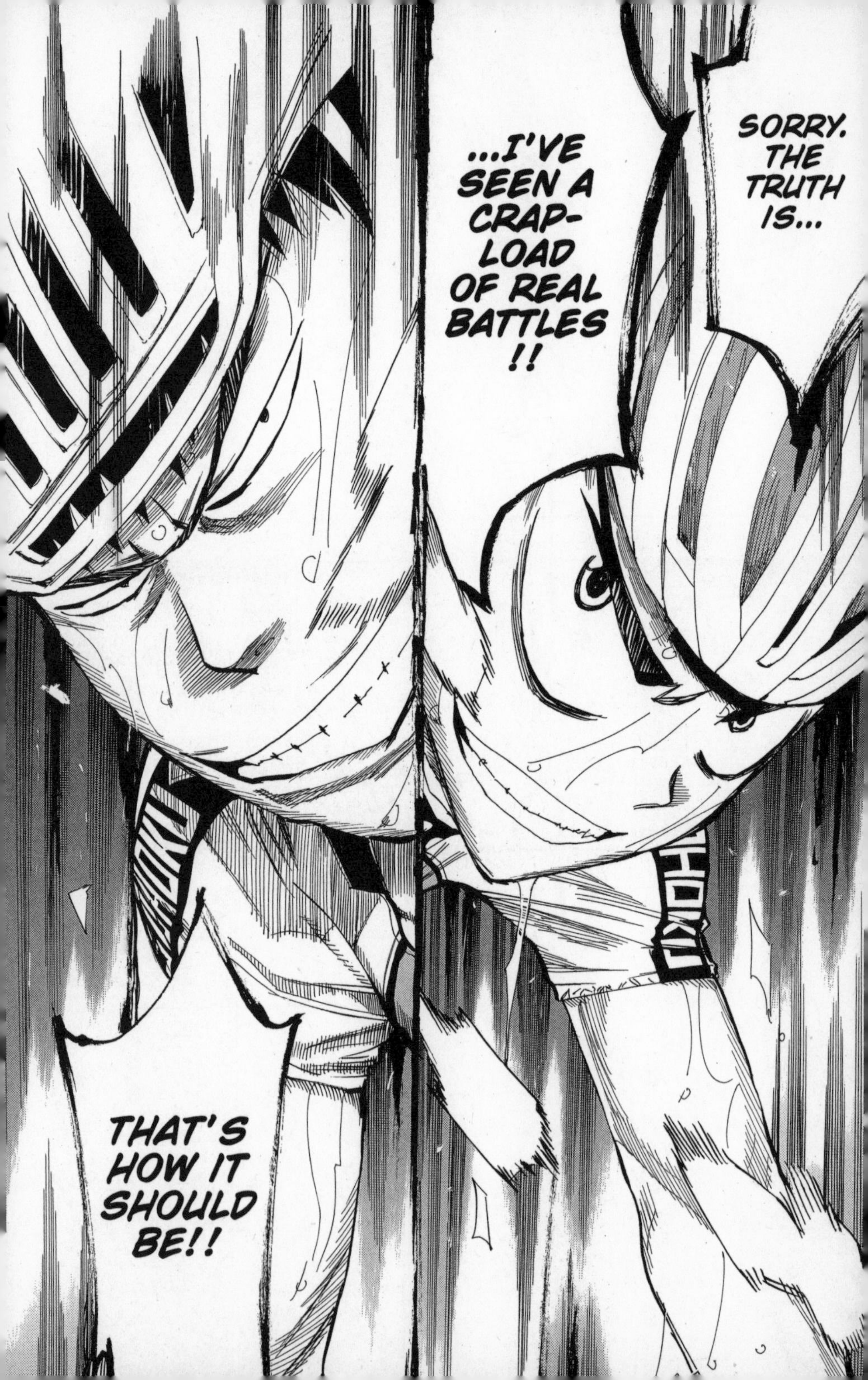
SORRY. THE TRUTH IS...
...I'VE SEEN A CRAP-LOAD OF REAL BATTLES!!
THAT'S HOW IT SHOULD BE!!

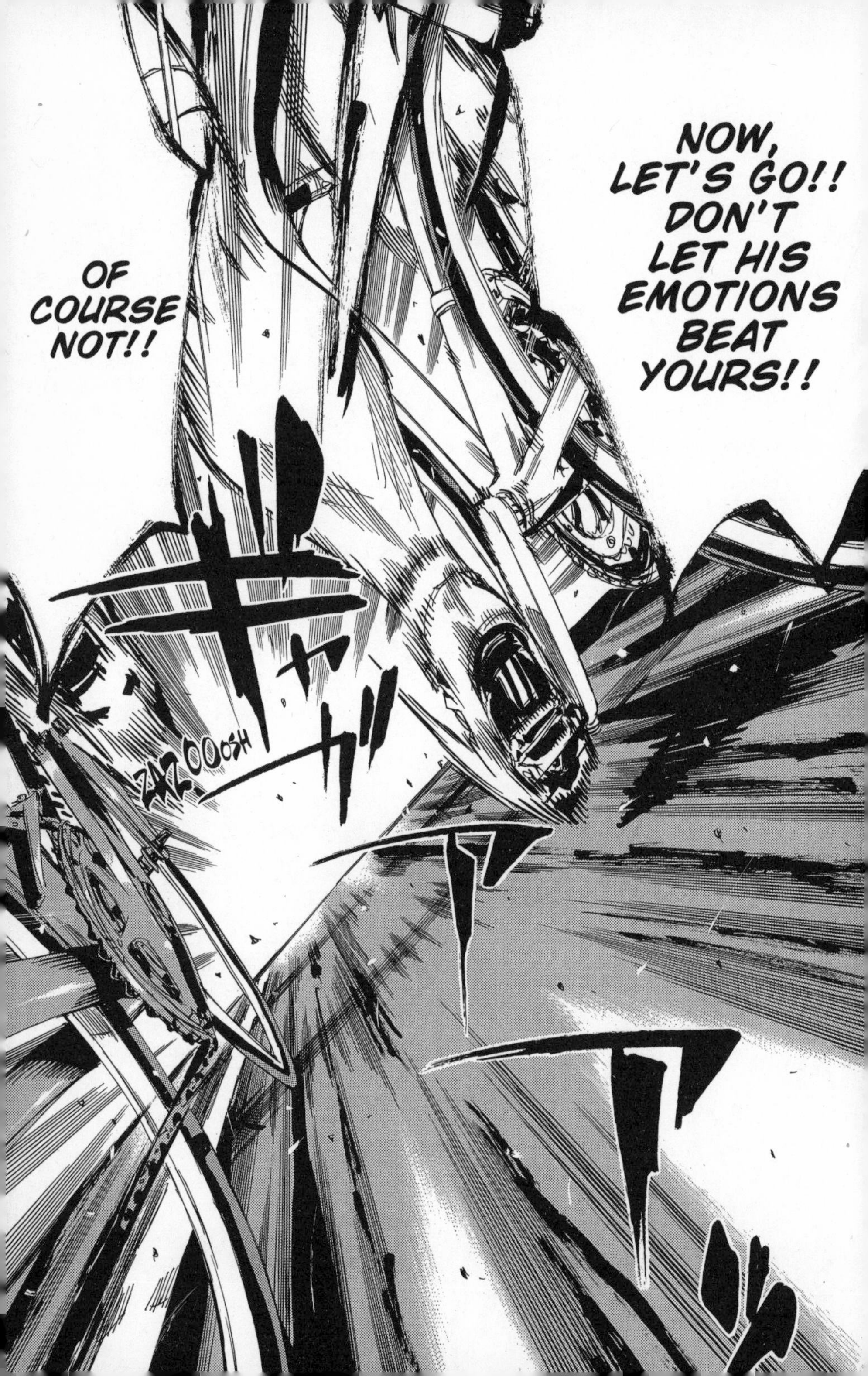
NOW, LET'S GO!! DON'T LET HIS EMOTIONS BEAT YOURS!!
OF COURSE NOT!!
ZAZOOOSH

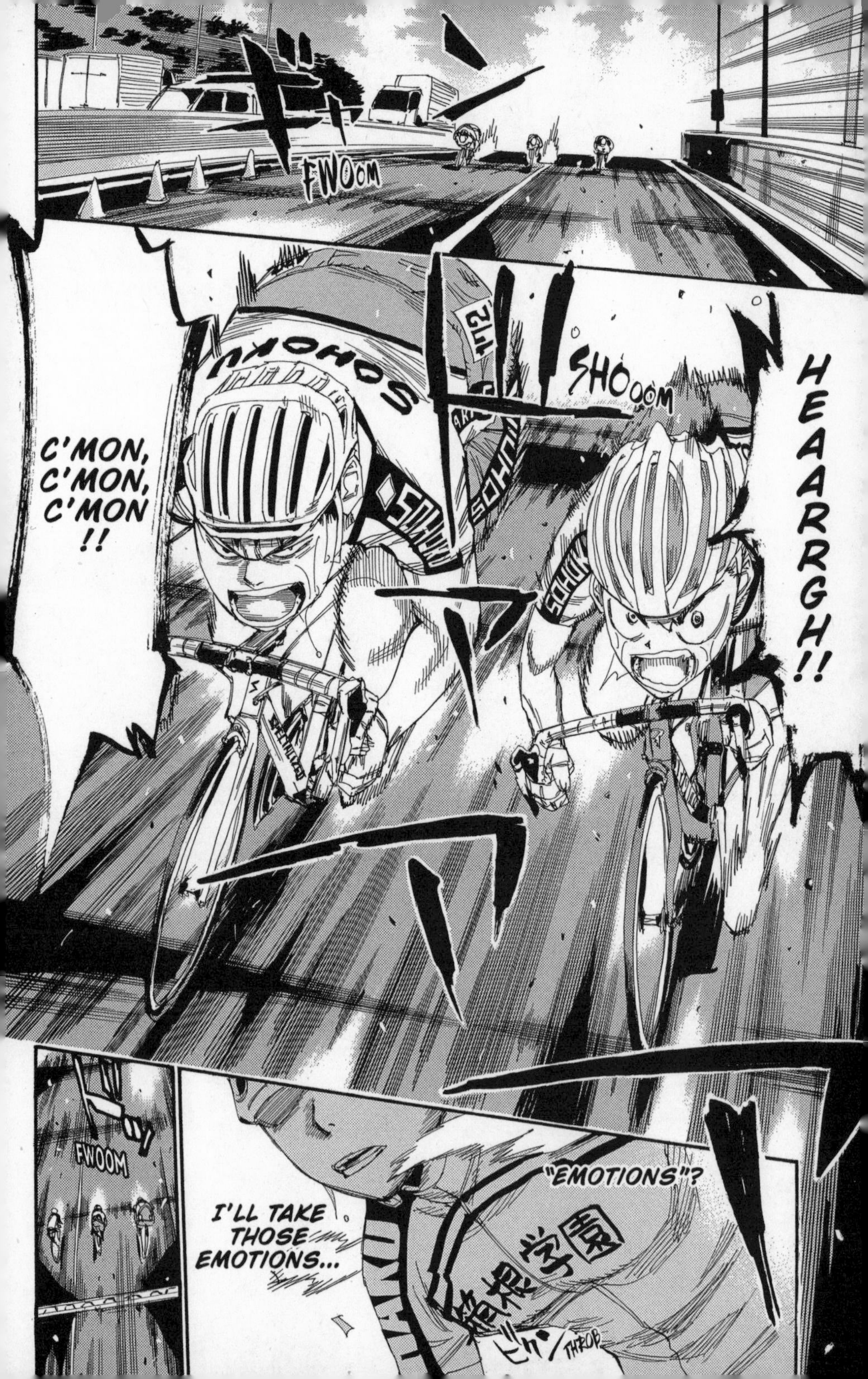
FWOOM
HEAARRGH!!
SHOOoOM
C'MON, C'MON, C'MON!!
"EMOTIONS"?
I'LL TAKE THOSE EMOTIONS...
THROB
FWOOM

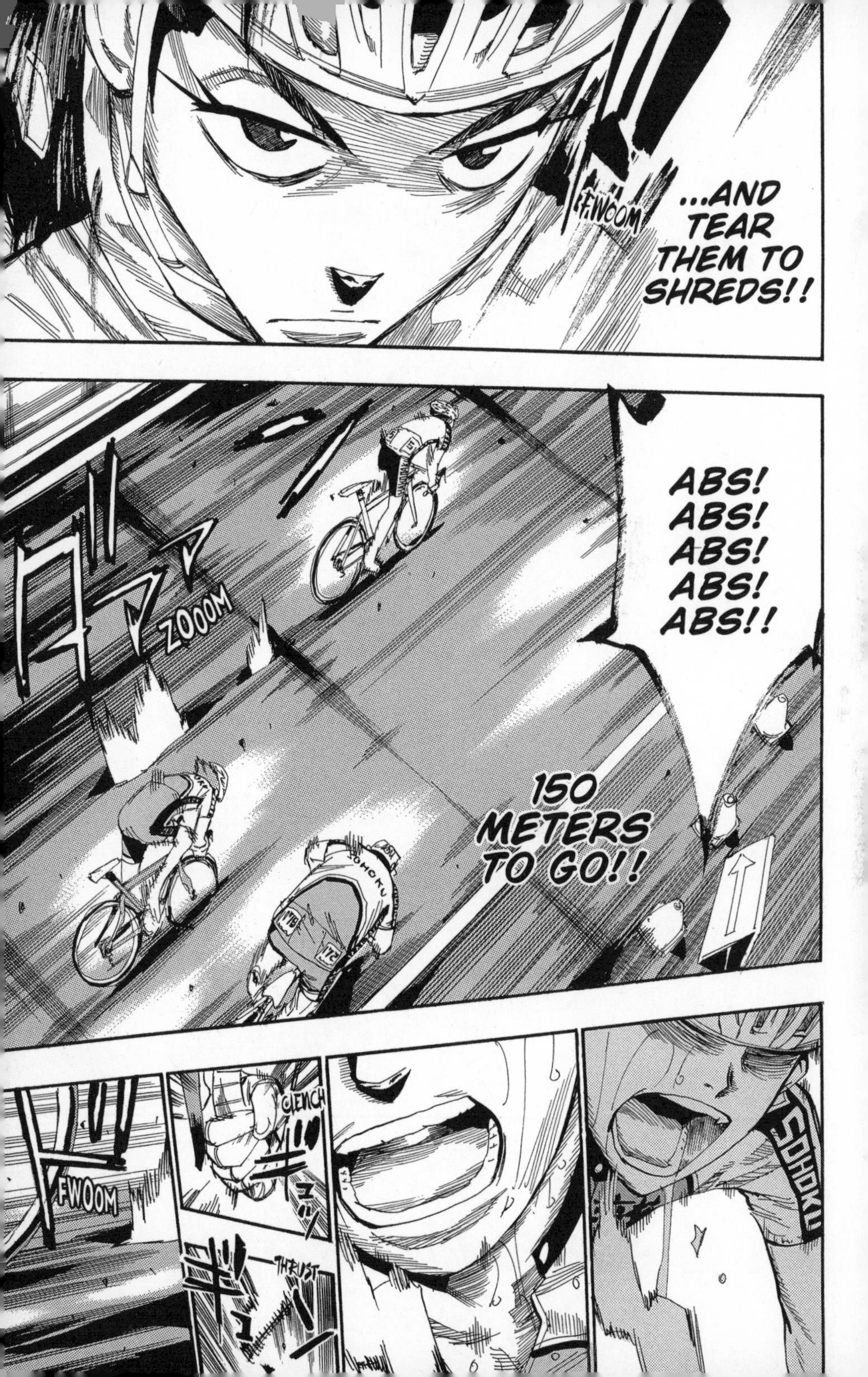
...AND TEAR THEM TO SHREDS!!
FWOOM
ABS! ABS! ABS! ABS! ABS!!
ZOOOM
150 METERS TO GO!!
CLENCH
THRUST
FWOOM

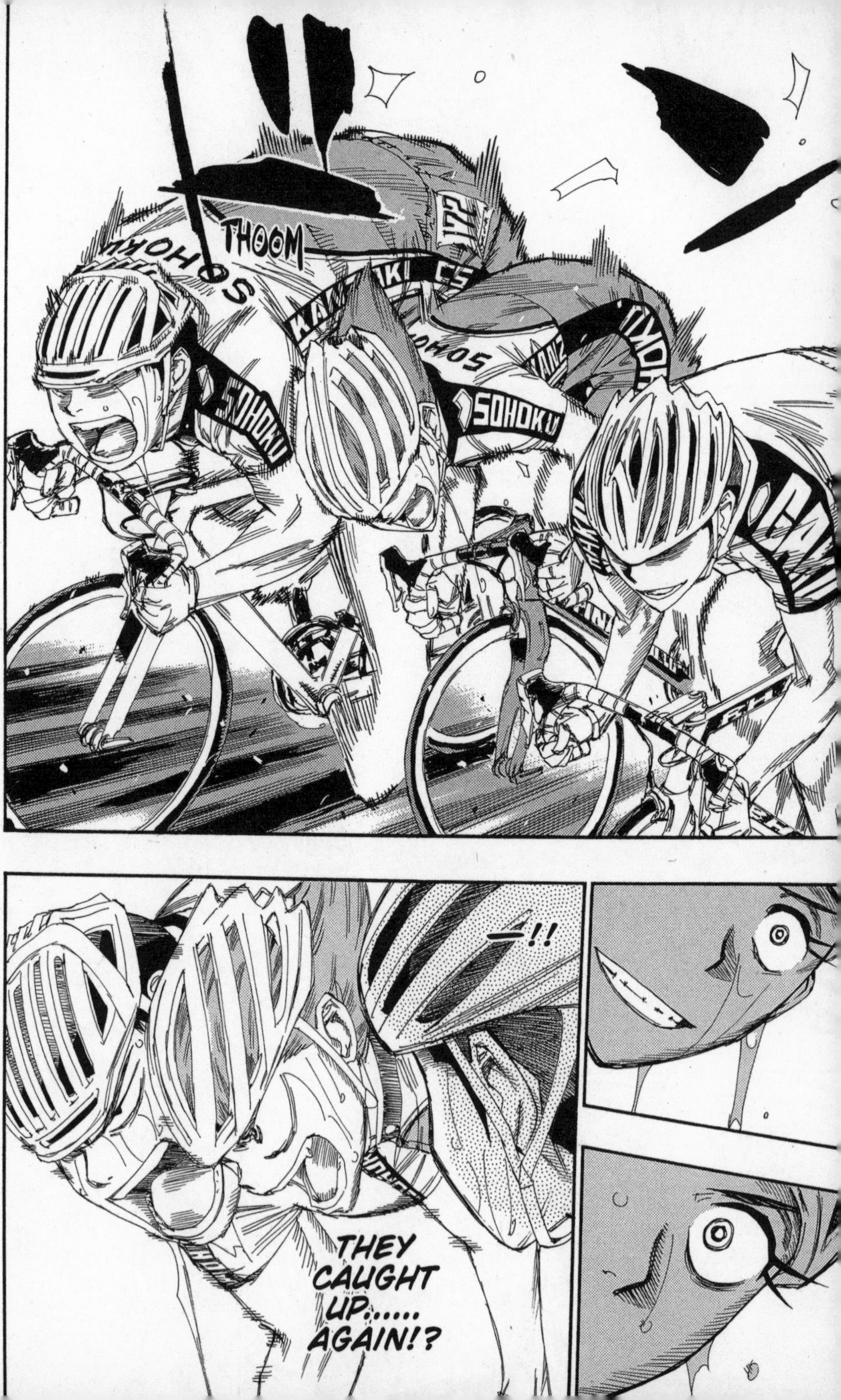
THOOM
—!!
THEY CAUGHT UP...... AGAIN!?

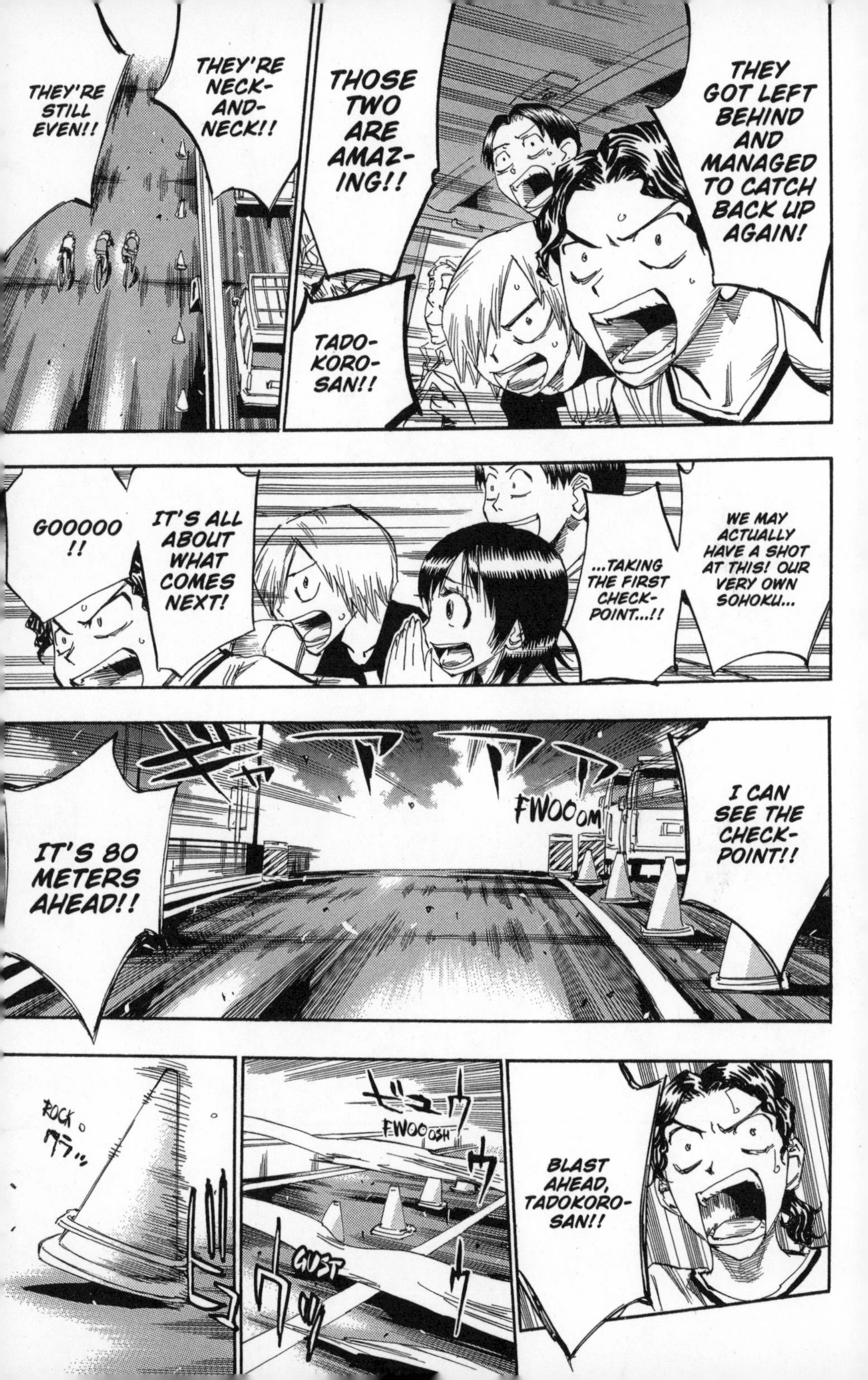
THEY GOT LEFT BEHIND AND MANAGED TO CATCH BACK UP AGAIN!
TADOKORO-SAN!!
THOSE TWO ARE AMAZING!!
THEY'RE NECK-AND-NECK!!
THEY'RE STILL EVEN!!
WE MAY ACTUALLY HAVE A SHOT AT THIS! OUR VERY OWN SOHOKU...
...TAKING THE FIRST CHECKPOINT...!!
IT'S ALL ABOUT WHAT COMES NEXT!
GOOOOO!!
I CAN SEE THE CHECKPOINT!!
FWOOOM
IT'S 80 METERS AHEAD!!
BLAST AHEAD, TADOKORO-SAN!!
FWOOOSH
GUST
ROCK

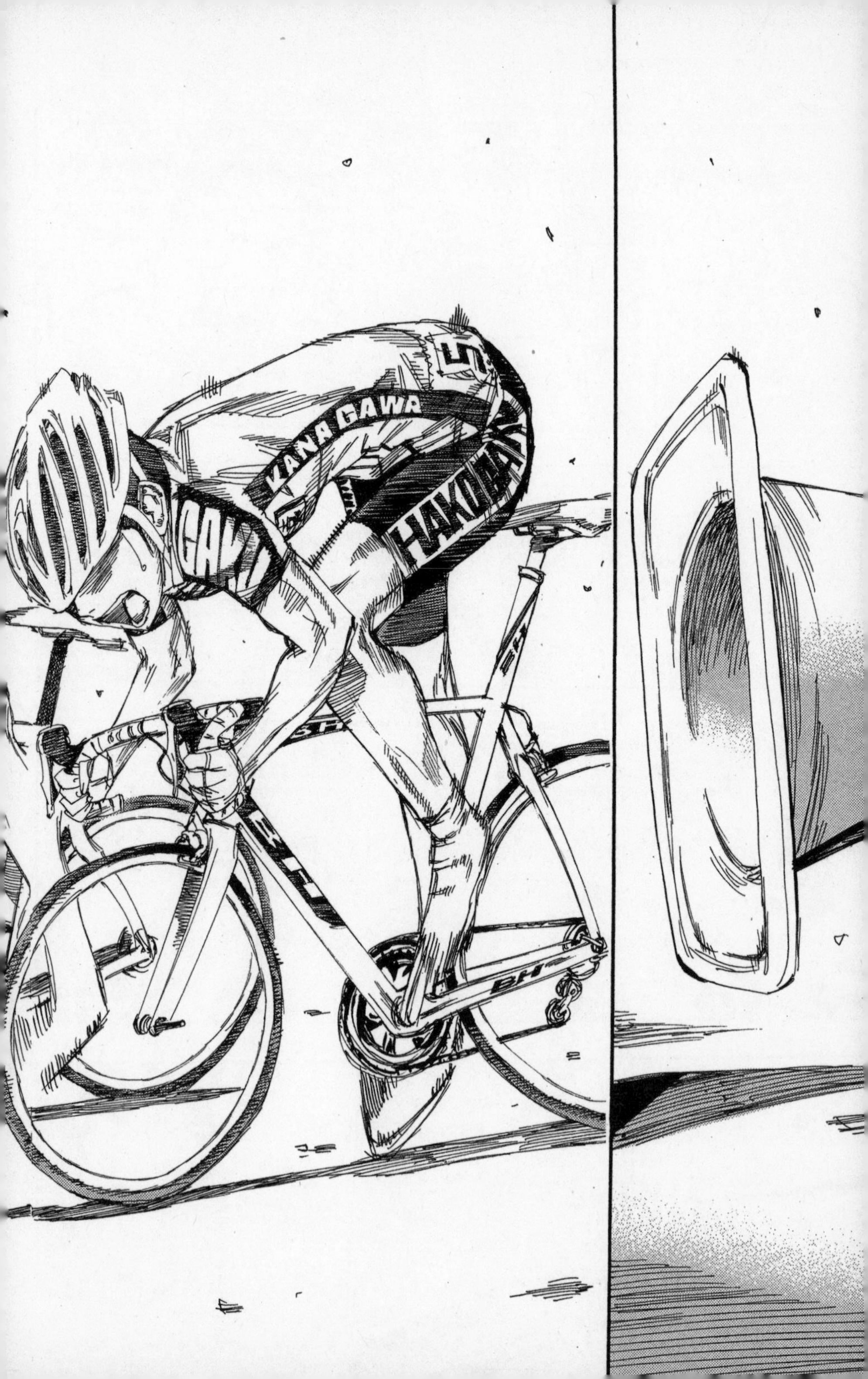
KANA GAWA

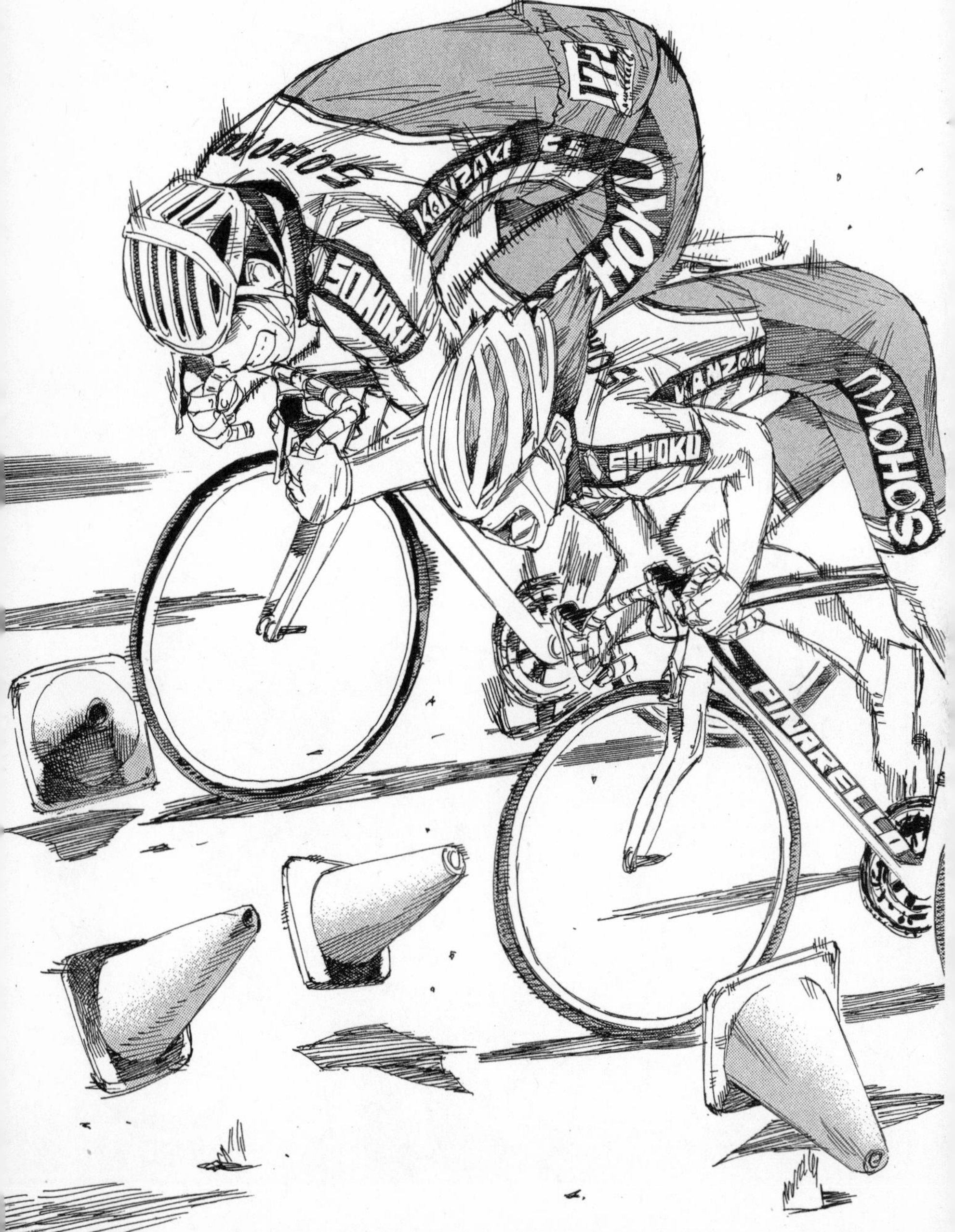
SOHOKU

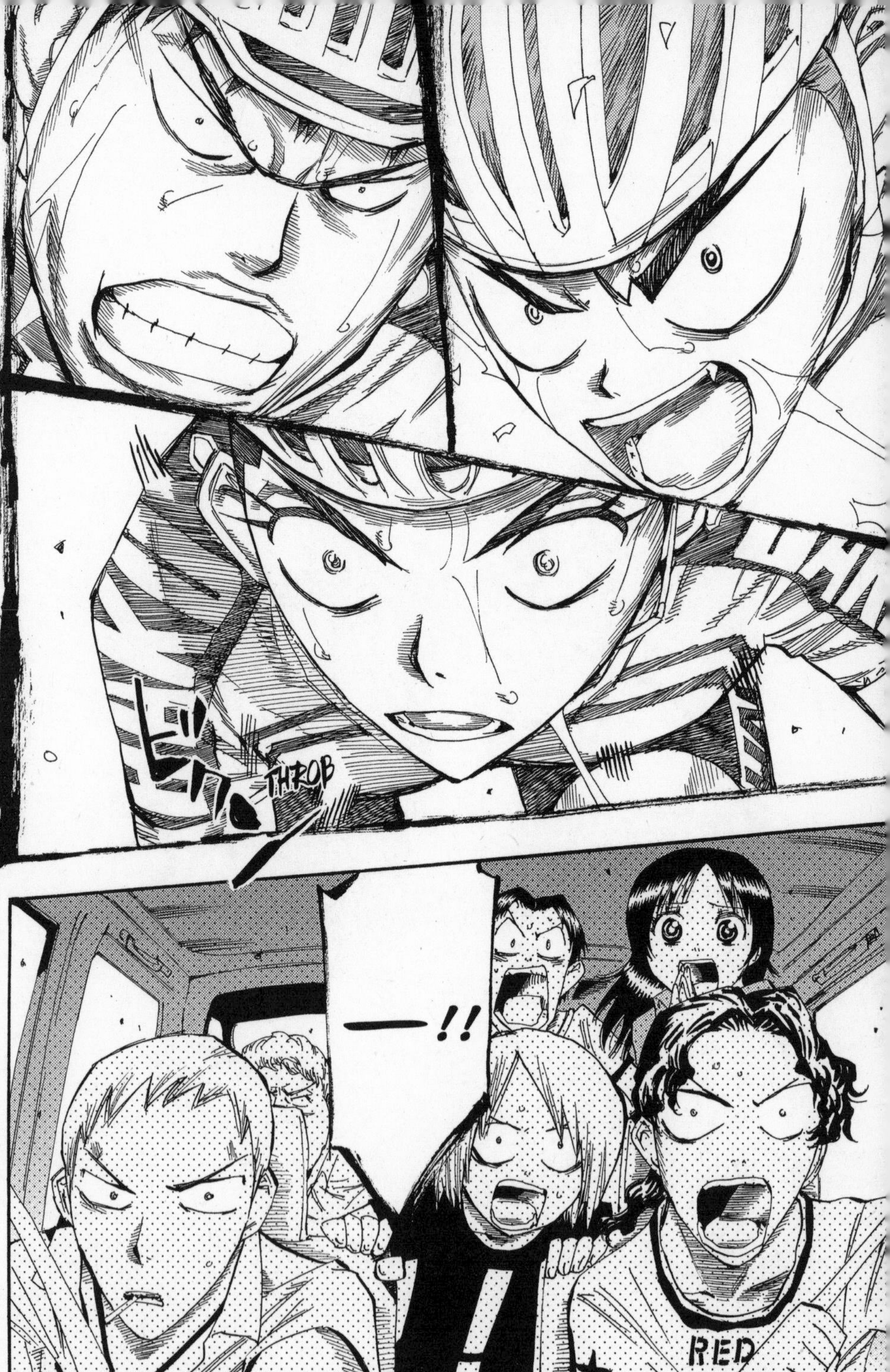
THROB
—!!
RED

RIDE.85 FAST SPRINTER

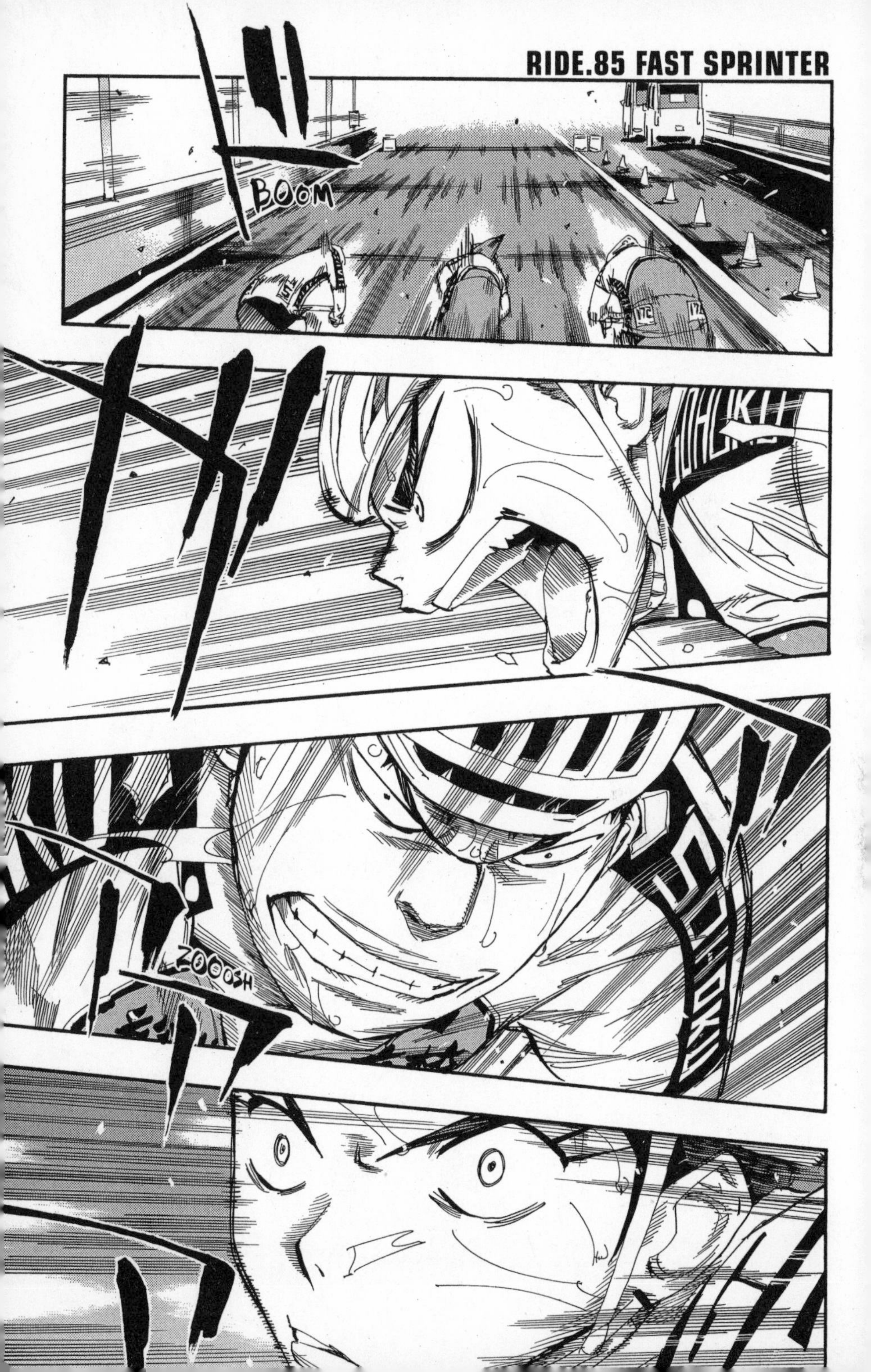
BOOM
ZOOOSH

RIDE.85 FAST SPRINTER

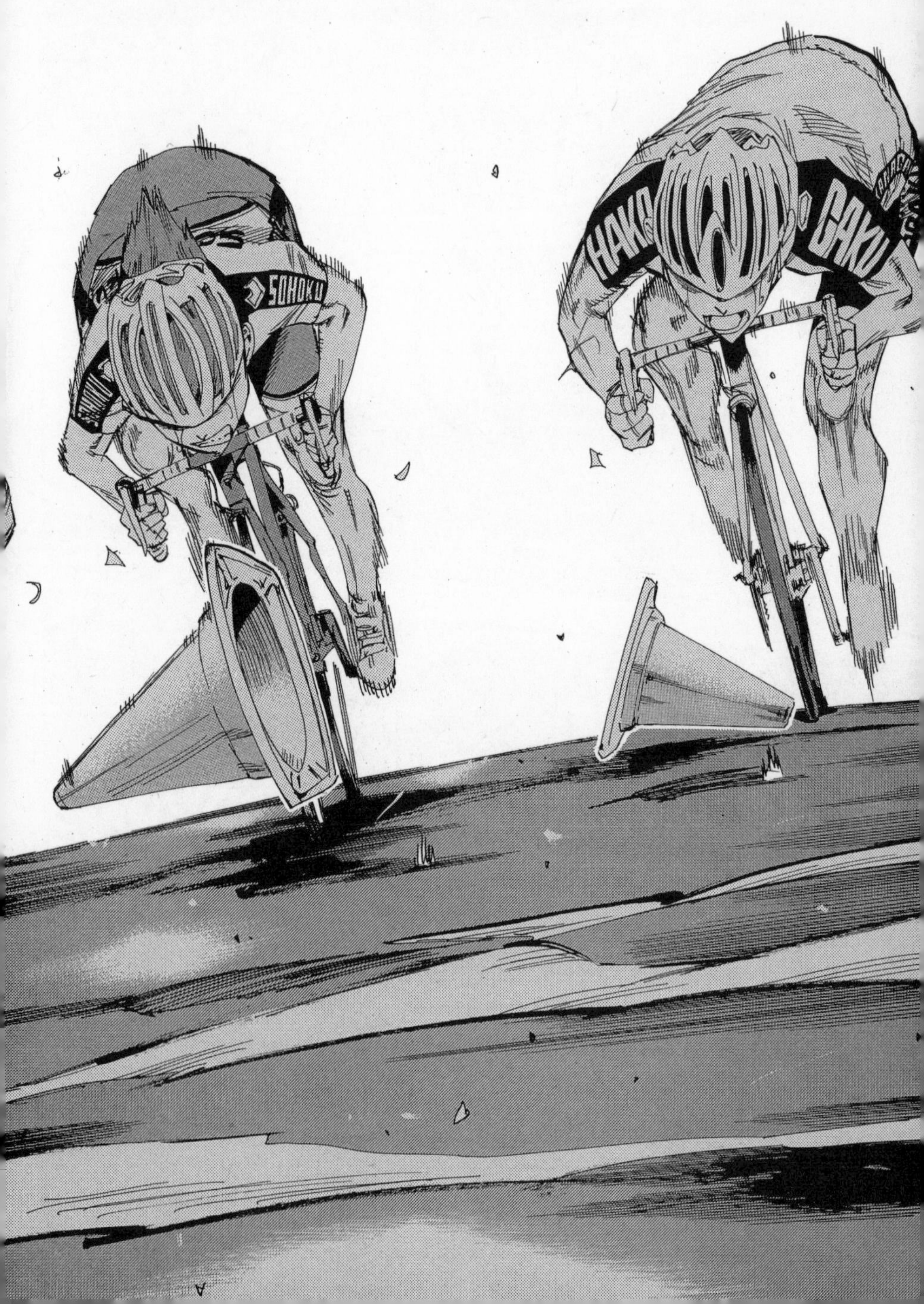
SOHOKU
HAKO
GAKU

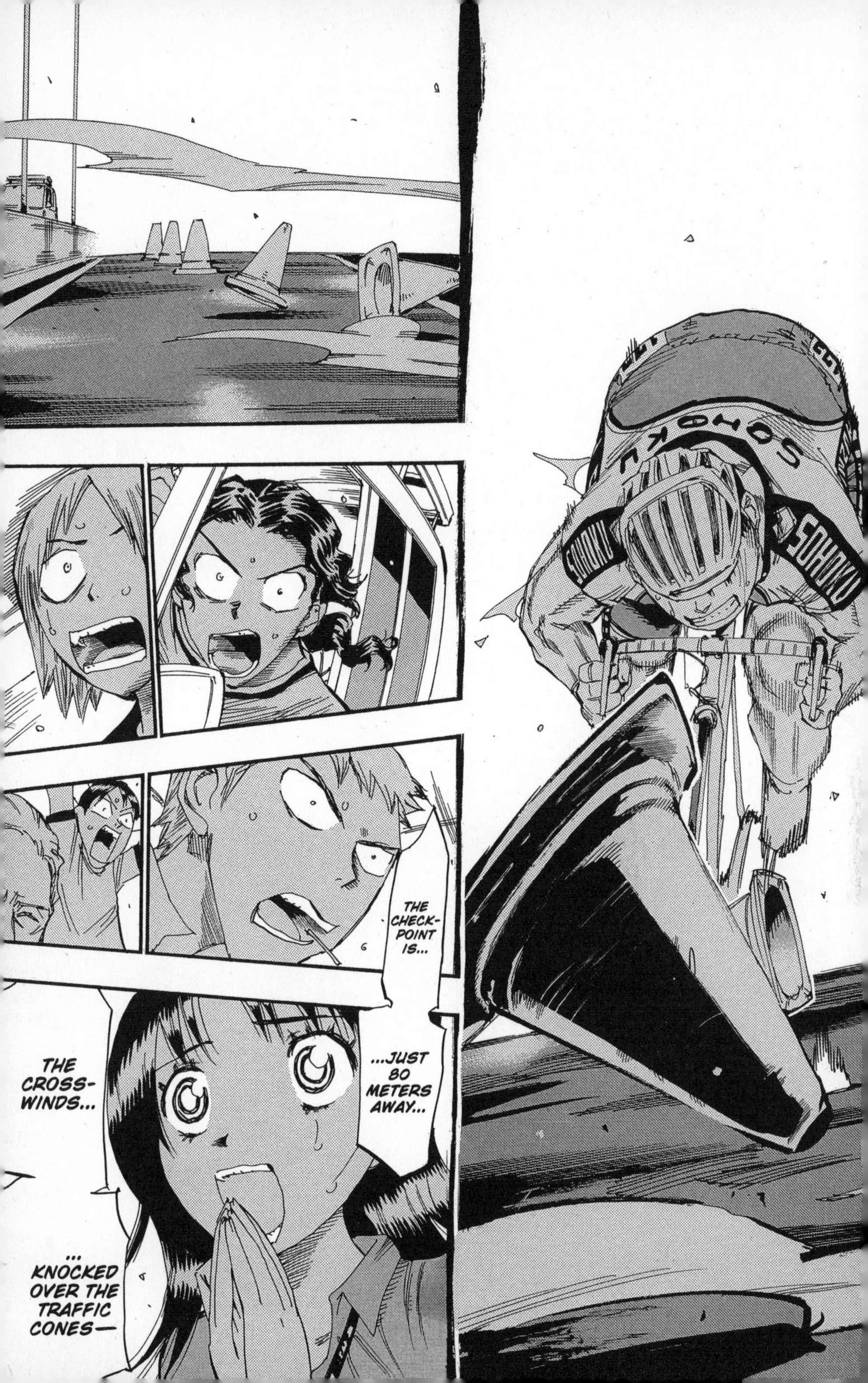
THE CHECK-POINT IS...
...JUST 80 METERS AWAY...
THE CROSS-WINDS...
...KNOCKED OVER THE TRAFFIC CONES—

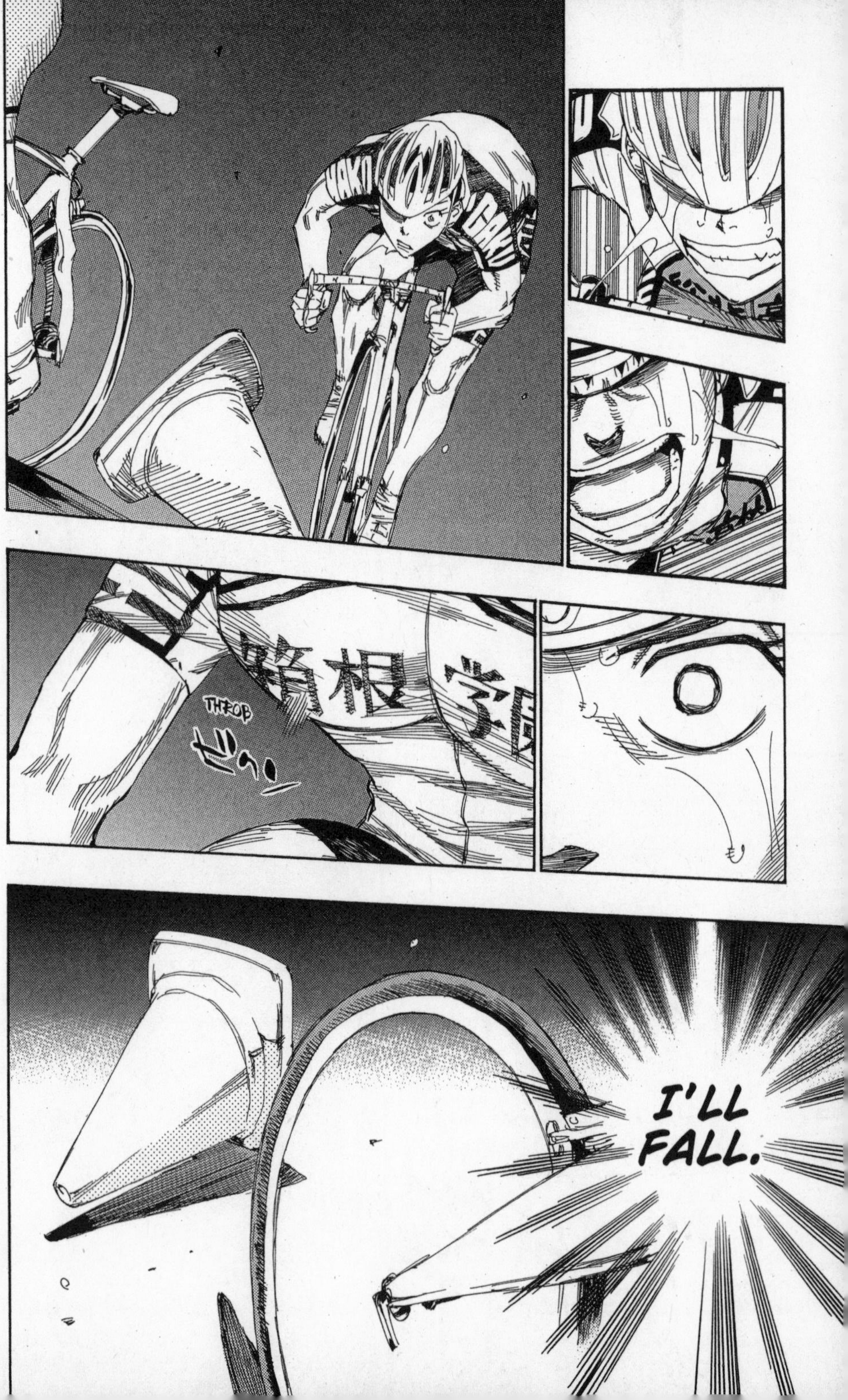
THROB
I'LL FALL.

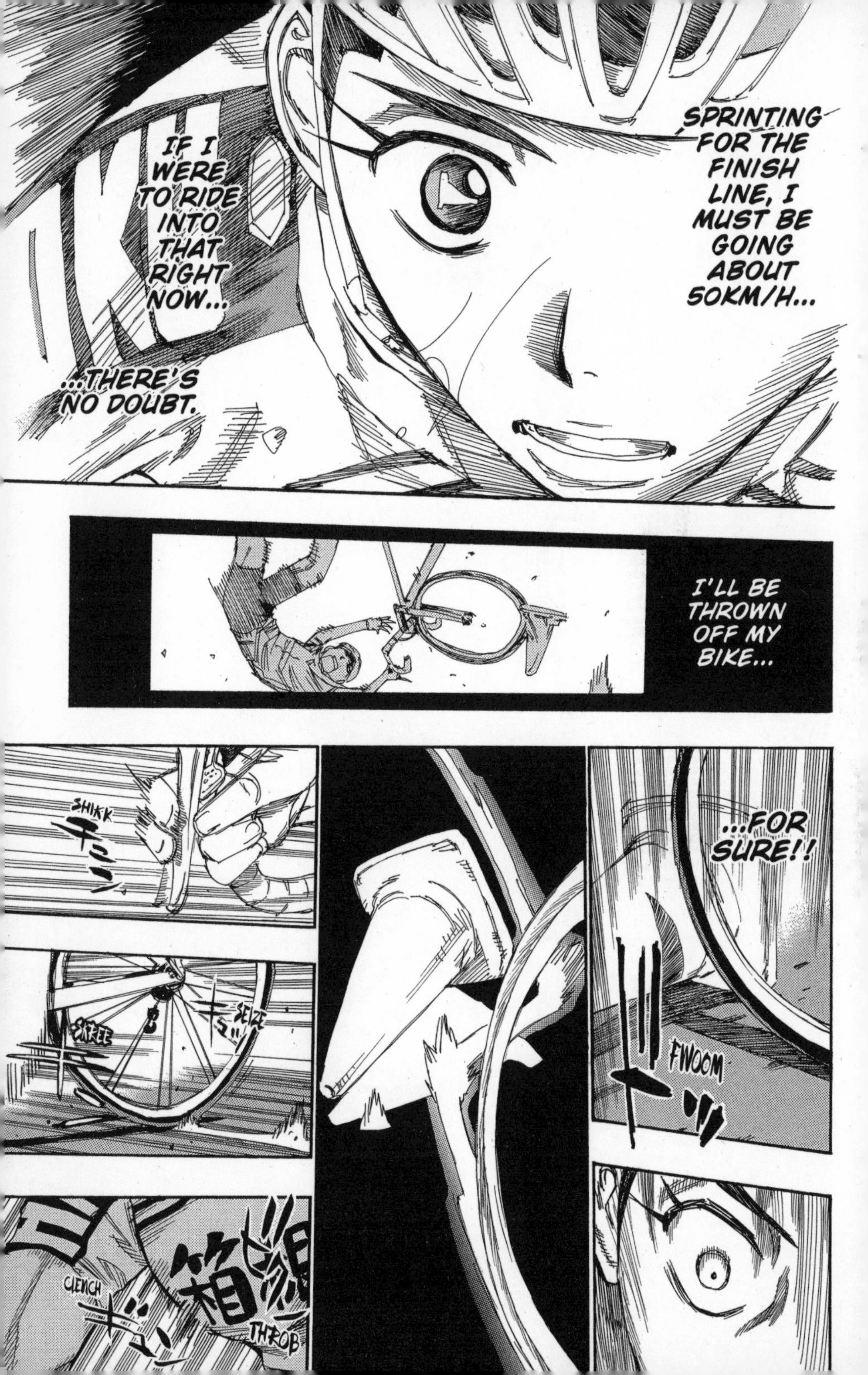
SPRINTING FOR THE FINISH LINE, I MUST BE GOING ABOUT 50KM/H...
IF I WERE TO RIDE INTO THAT RIGHT NOW...
...THERE'S NO DOUBT.
I'LL BE THROWN OFF MY BIKE...
...FOR SURE!!
FWOOM
SHIKK
SEIZE
SKREE
CLENCH
THROB

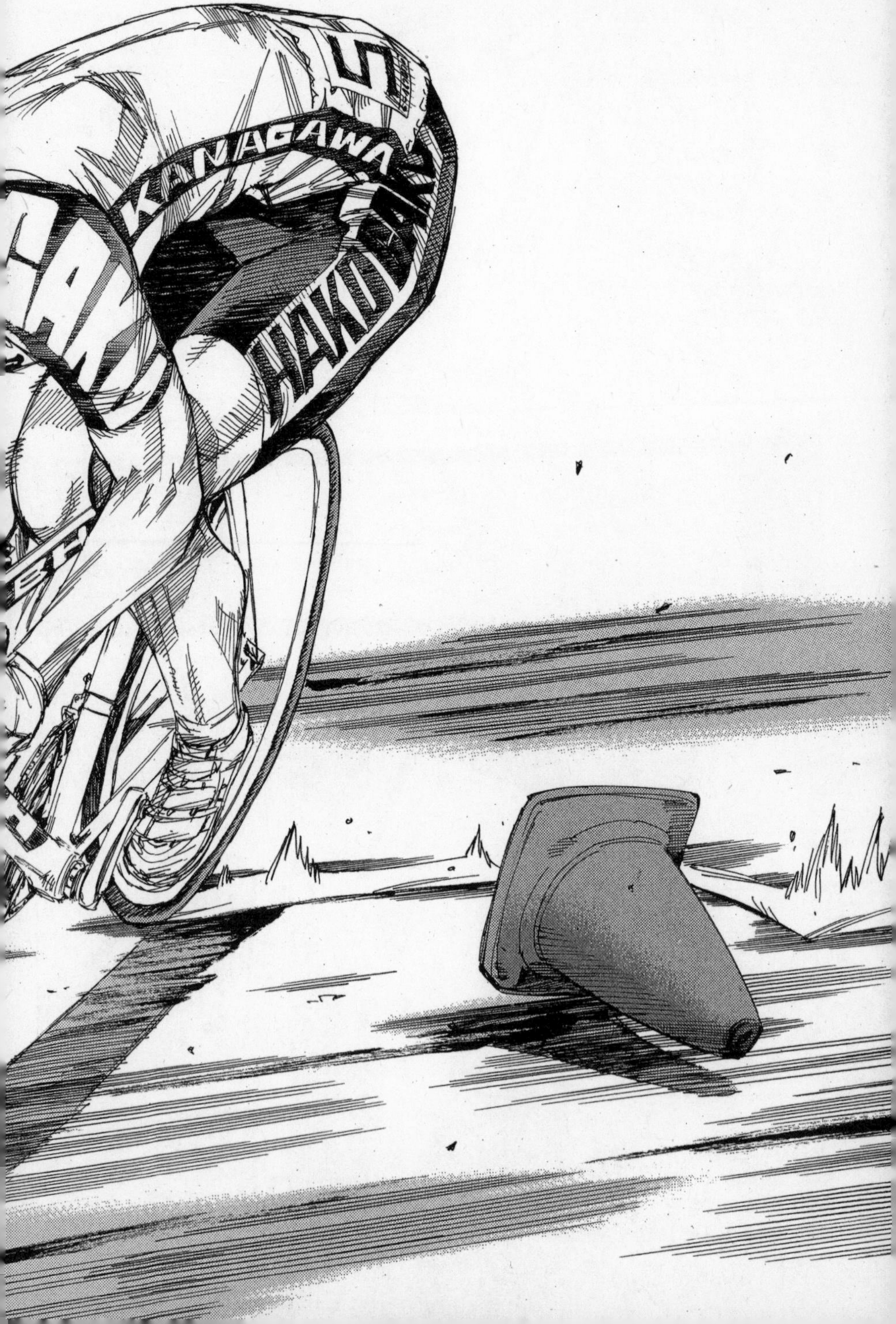
KANAGAWA

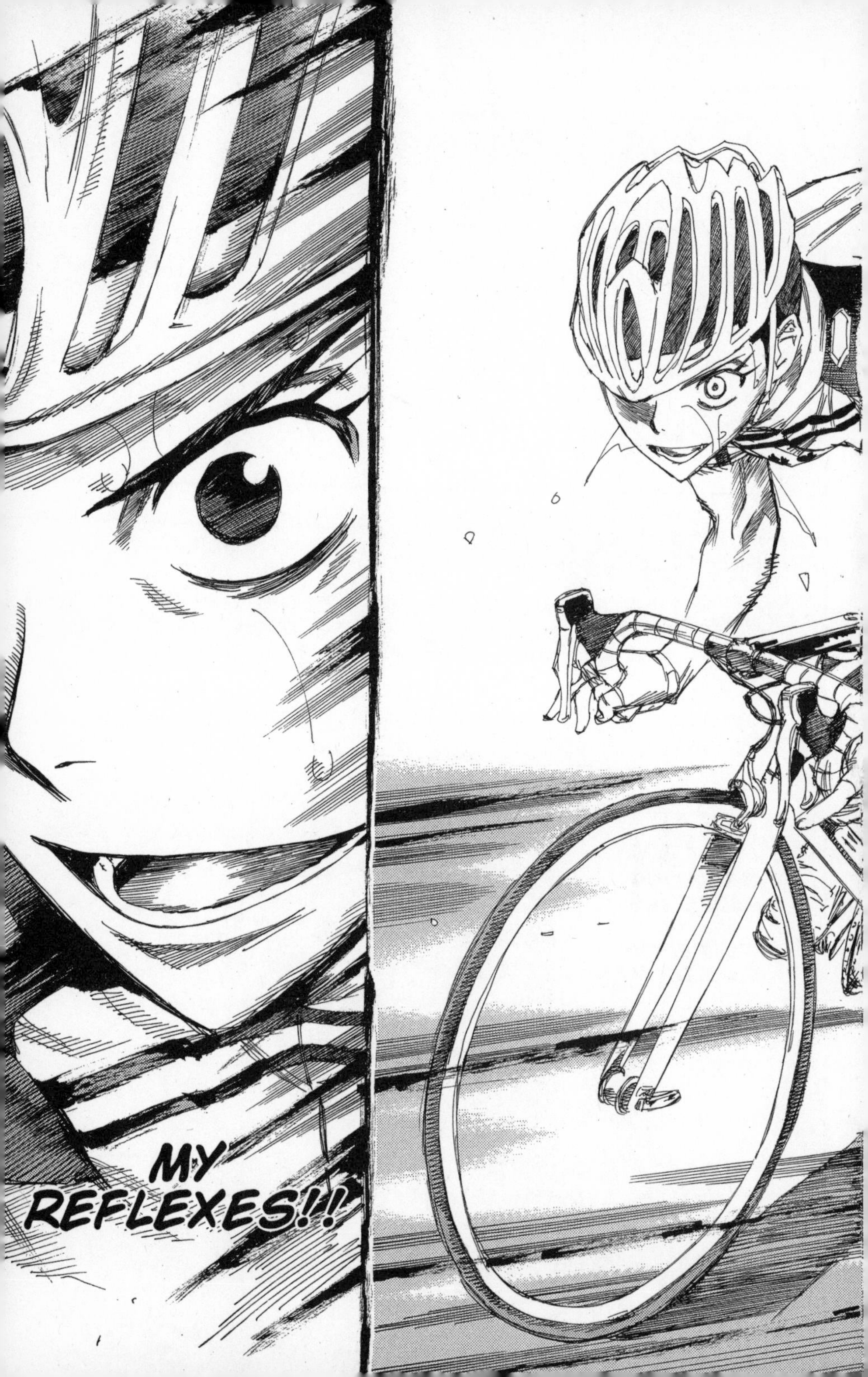
MY REFLEXES!!

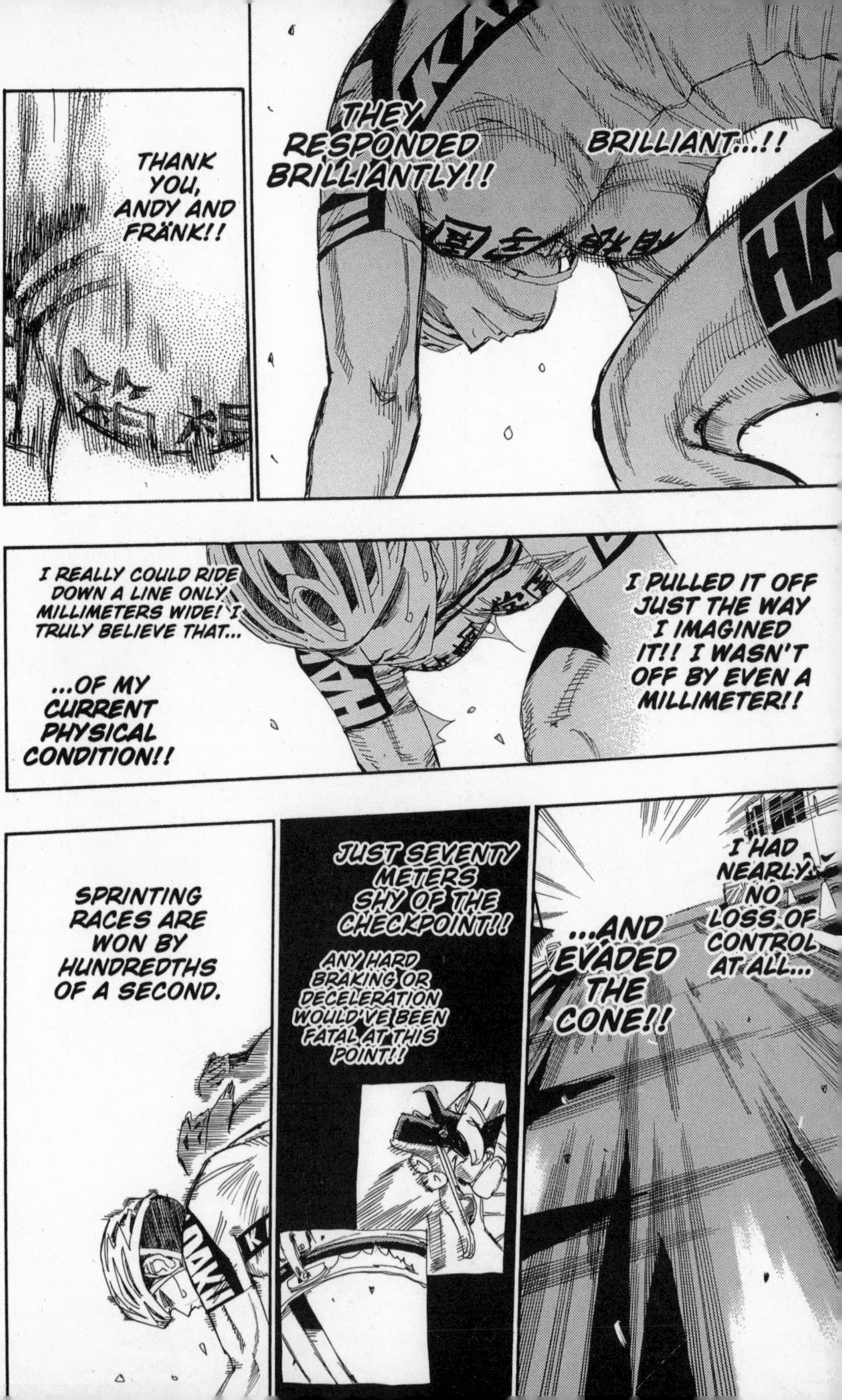
THEY RESPONDED BRILLIANTLY!!
BRILLIANT...!!
THANK YOU, ANDY AND FRÄNK!!
I PULLED IT OFF JUST THE WAY I IMAGINED IT!! I WASN'T OFF BY EVEN A MILLIMETER!!
I REALLY COULD RIDE DOWN A LINE ONLY MILLIMETERS WIDE! I TRULY BELIEVE THAT...
...OF MY CURRENT PHYSICAL CONDITION!!
I HAD NEARLY NO LOSS OF CONTROL AT ALL...
...AND EVADED THE CONE!!
JUST SEVENTY METERS SHY OF THE CHECKPOINT!!
ANY HARD BRAKING OR DECELERATION WOULD'VE BEEN FATAL AT THIS POINT!!
SPRINTING RACES ARE WON BY HUNDREDTHS OF A SECOND.

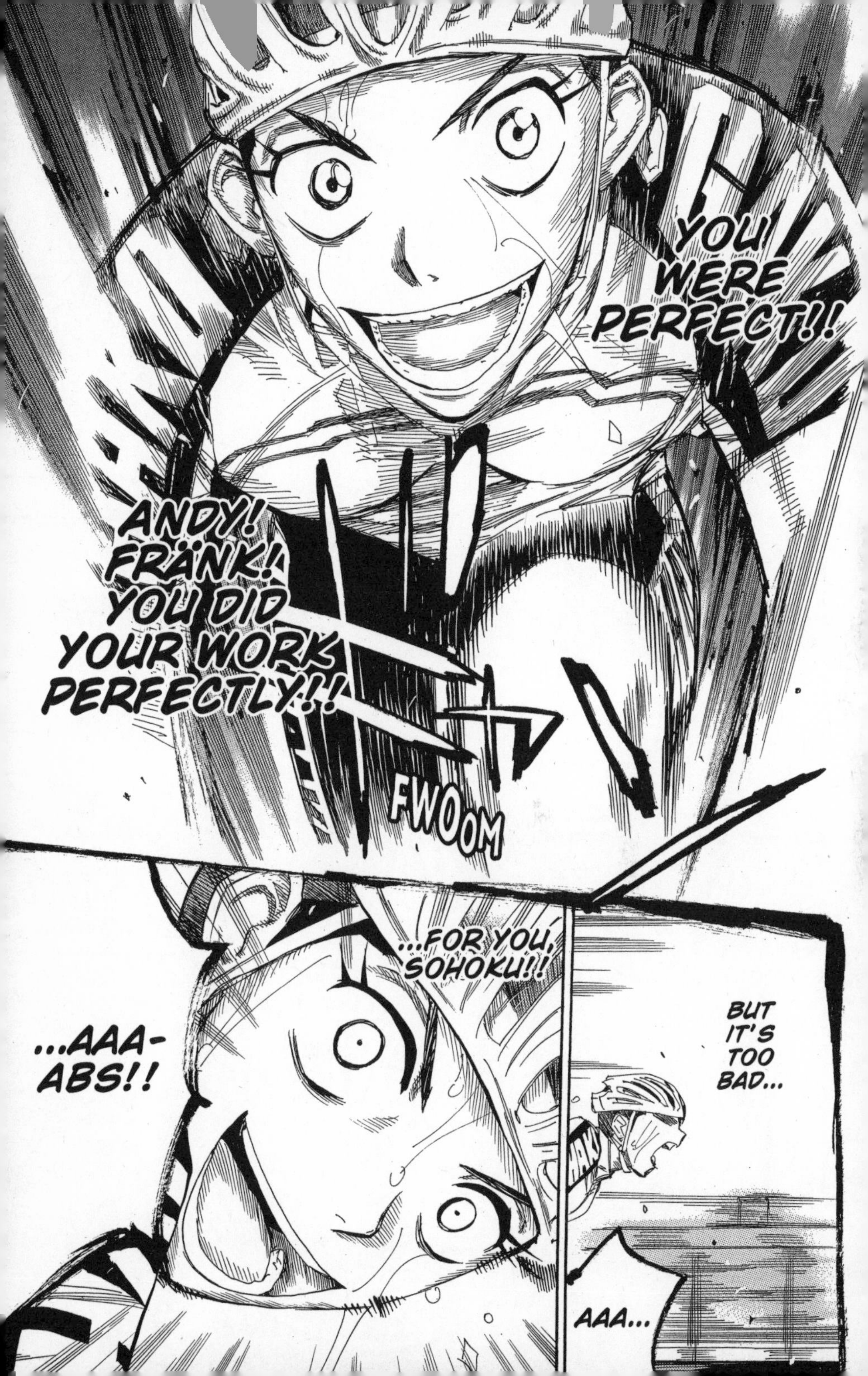
YOU WERE PERFECT!!
ANDY! FRÄNK! YOU DID YOUR WORK PERFECTLY!!
FWOOM
BUT IT'S TOO BAD...
AAA...
...FOR YOU, SOHOKU!!
...AAA-ABS!!

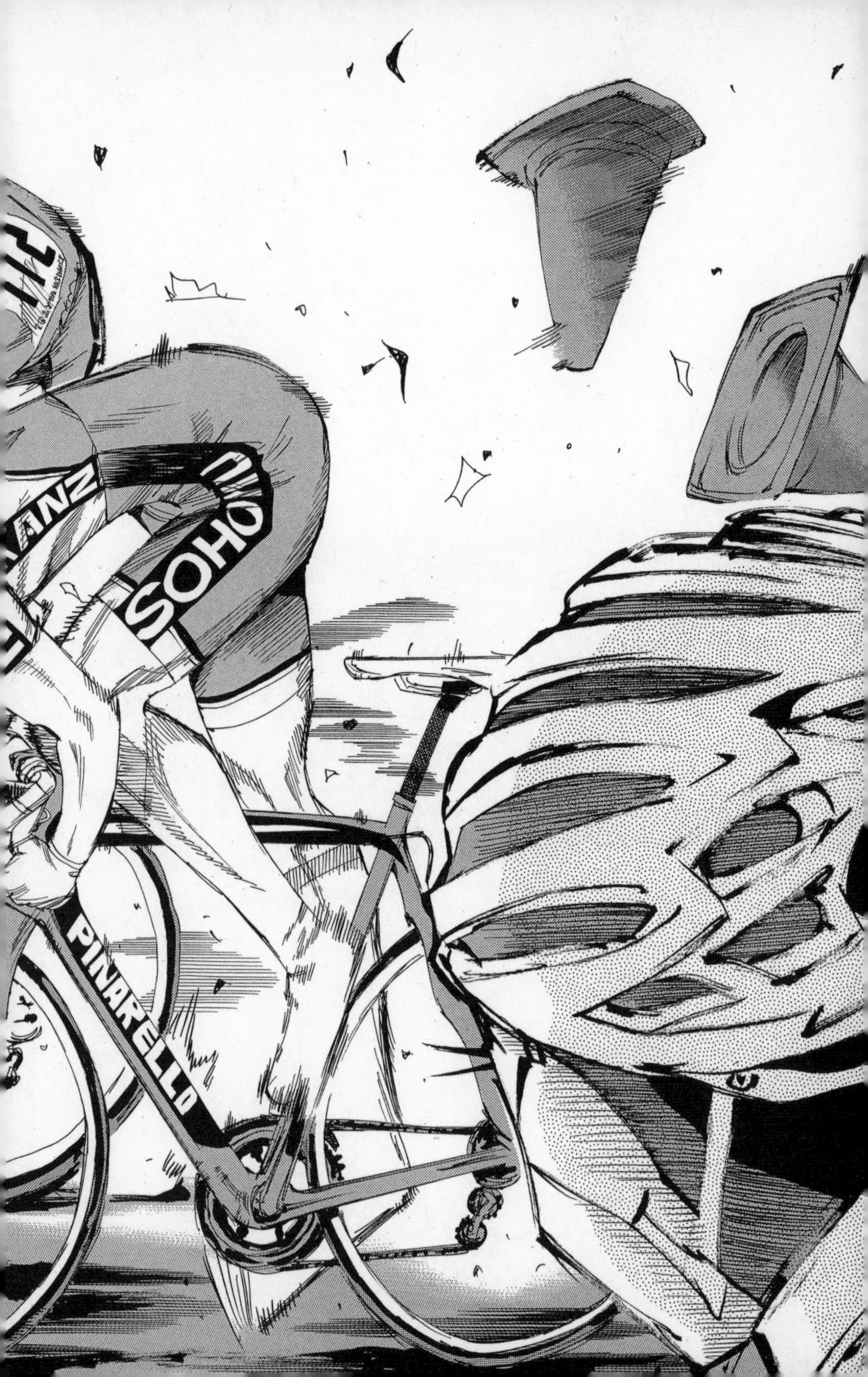
SOHO
PINARELLO

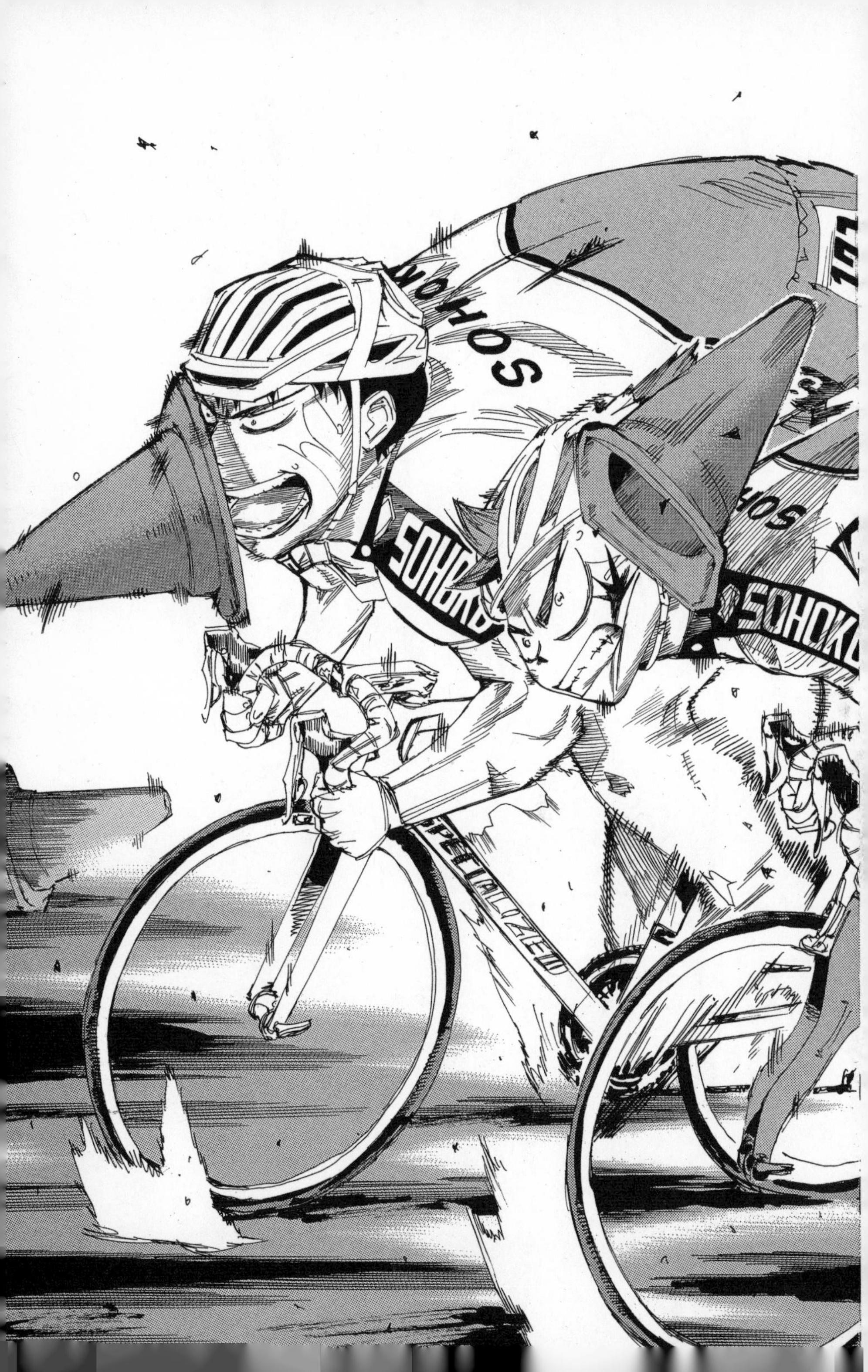
SOHOKU
SPECIALIZED

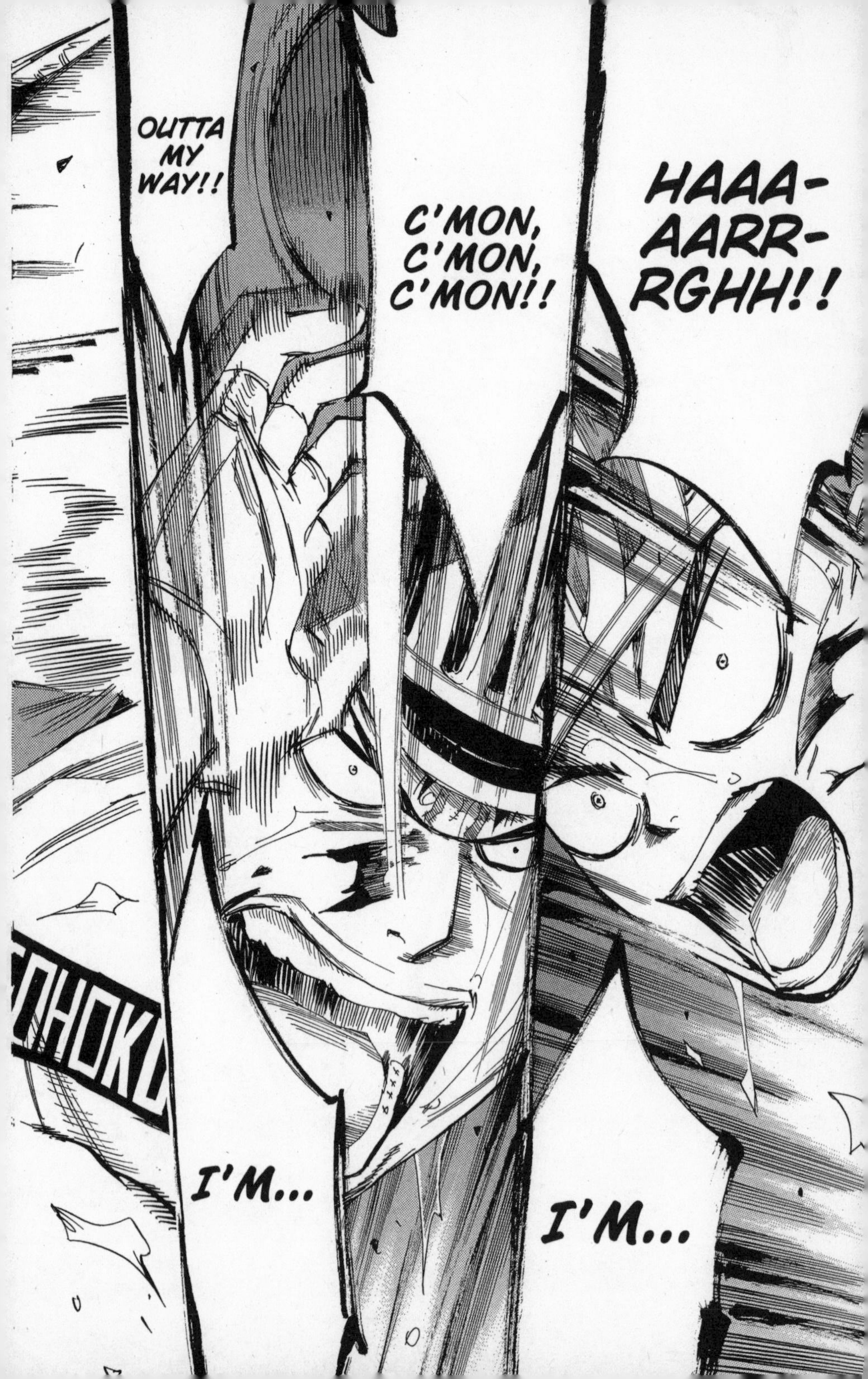
HAAAA-AARR-RGHH!!
I'M...
C'MON, C'MON, C'MON!!
I'M...
OUTTA MY WAY!!
OHOKU

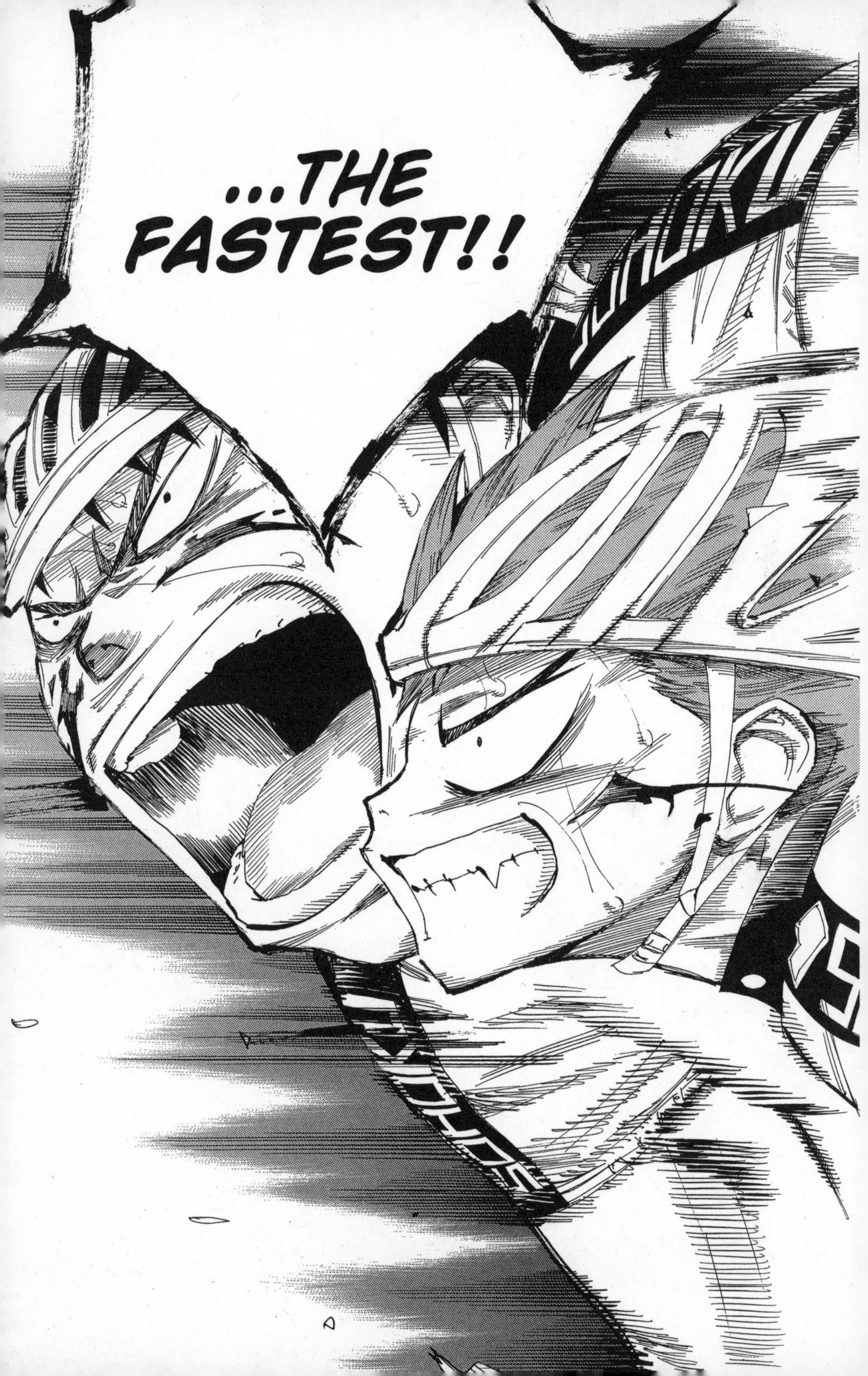
...THE FASTEST!!

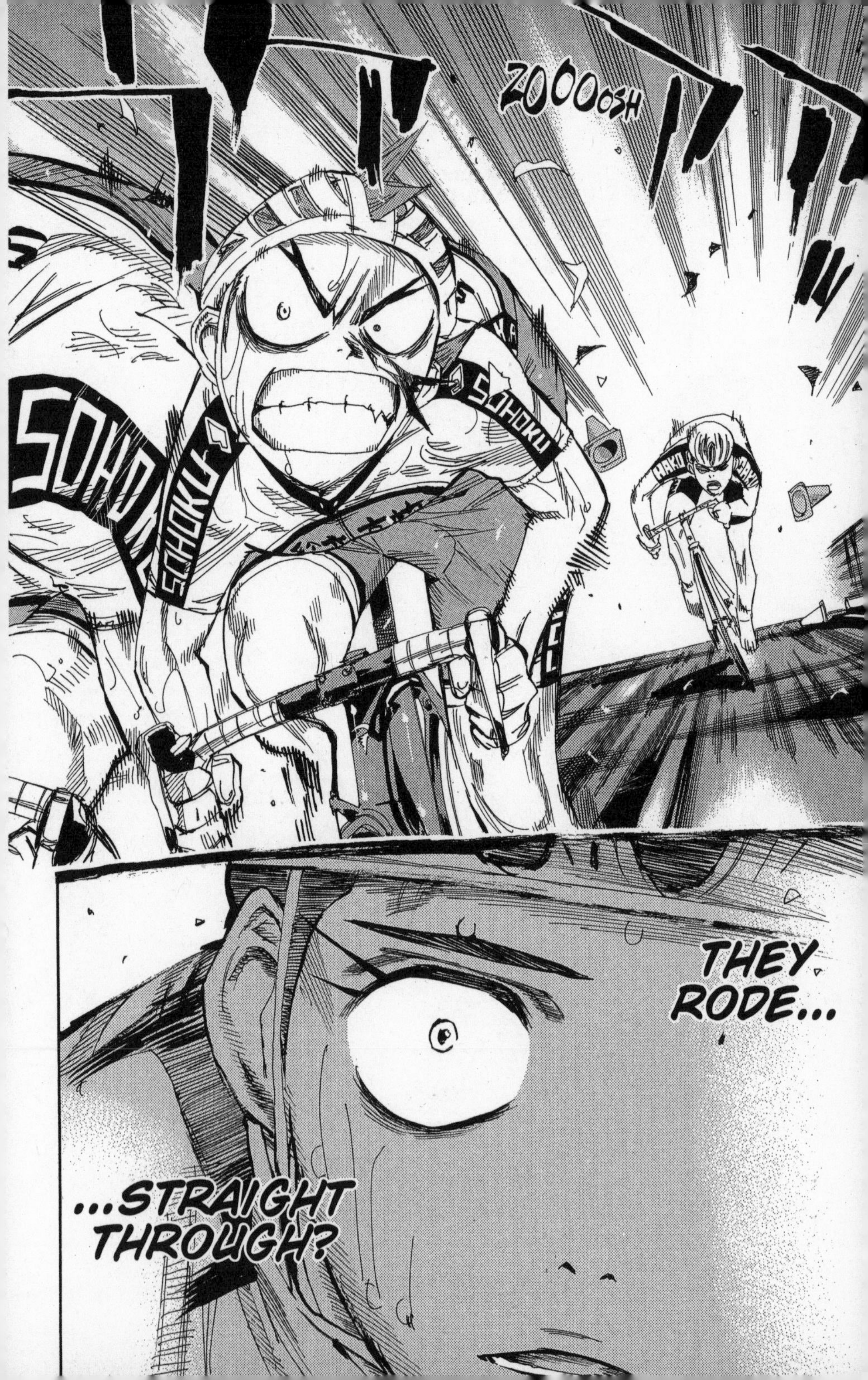
ZOOOOSH
THEY RODE...
...STRAIGHT THROUGH?

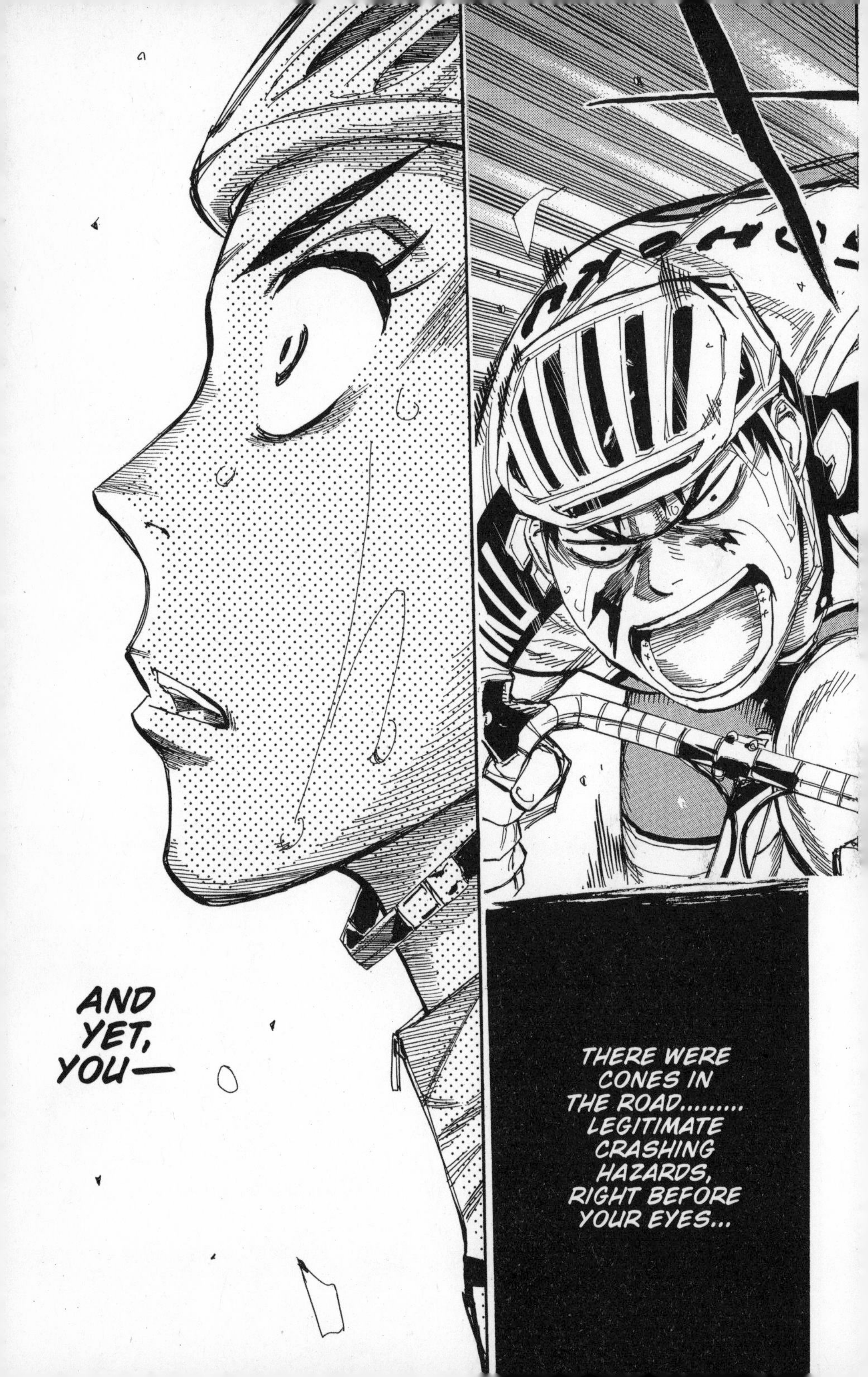
THERE WERE CONES IN THE ROAD......... LEGITIMATE CRASHING HAZARDS, RIGHT BEFORE YOUR EYES...
AND YET, YOU—

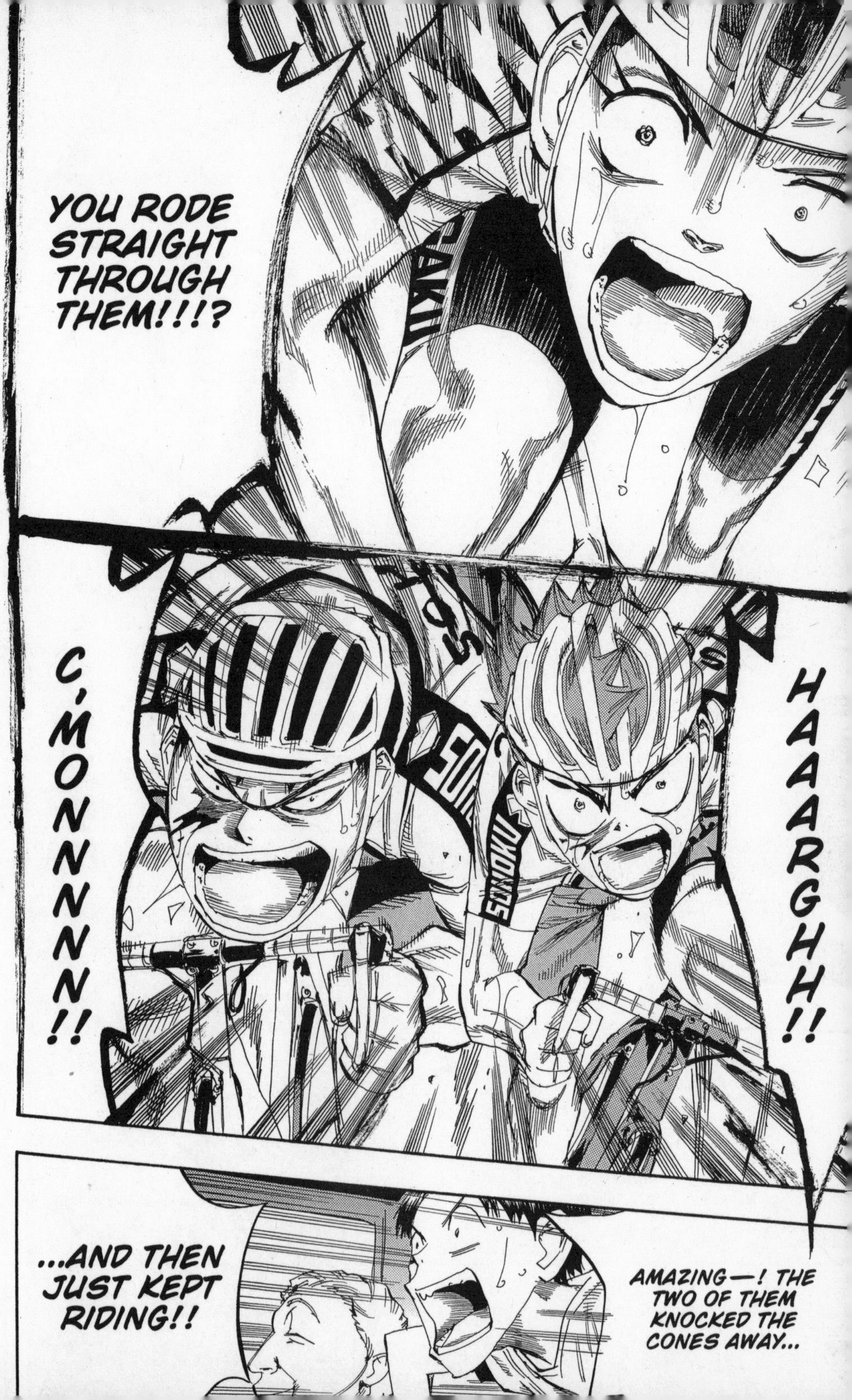
YOU RODE STRAIGHT THROUGH THEM!!!?
HAAARGHH!!
C'MONNNNNN!!
AMAZING—! THE TWO OF THEM KNOCKED THE CONES AWAY...
...AND THEN JUST KEPT RIDING!!

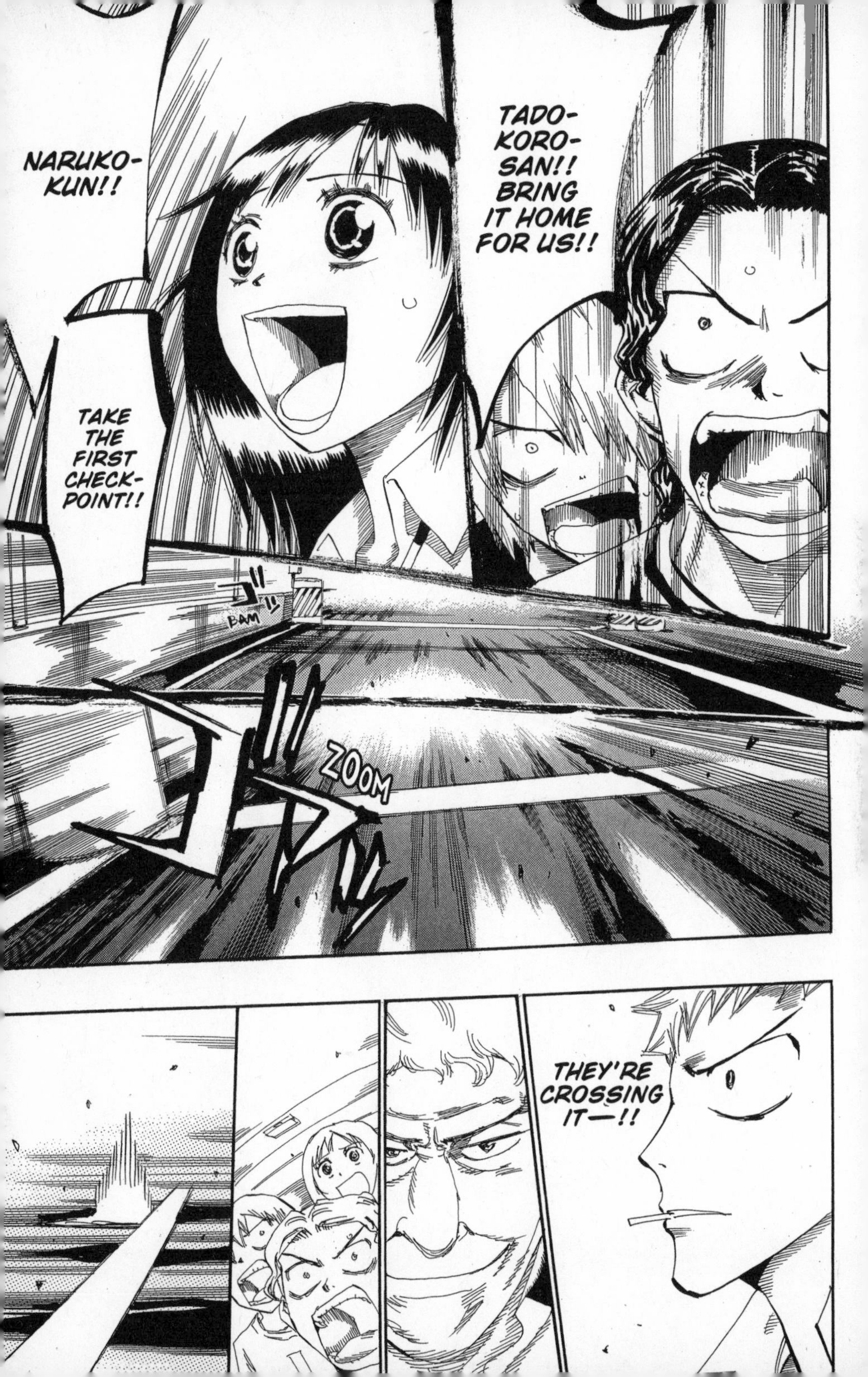
TADO-KORO-SAN!! BRING IT HOME FOR US!!
NARUKO-KUN!!
TAKE THE FIRST CHECK-POINT!!
BAM
ZOOM
THEY'RE CROSSING IT—!!

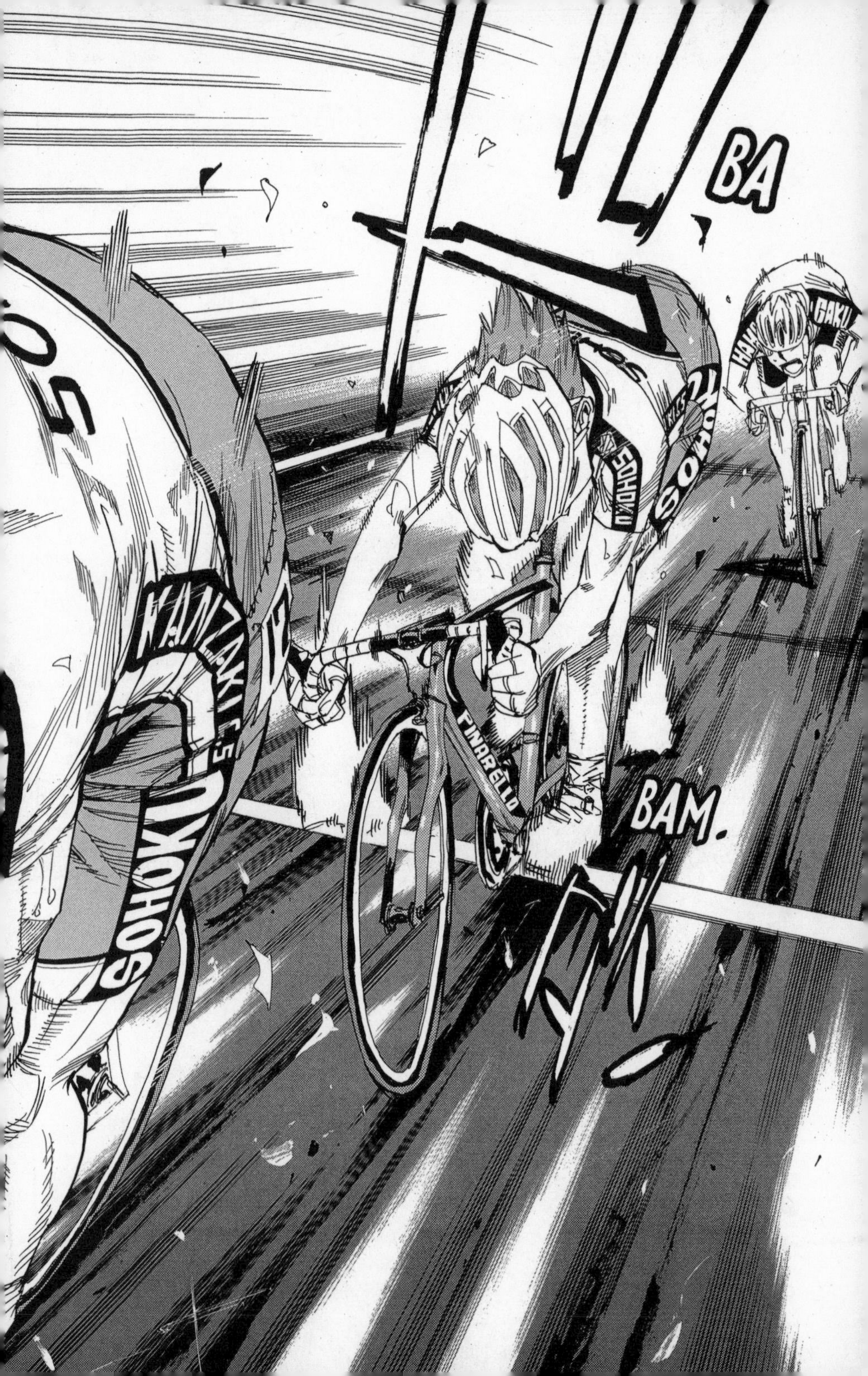
BA
BAM.

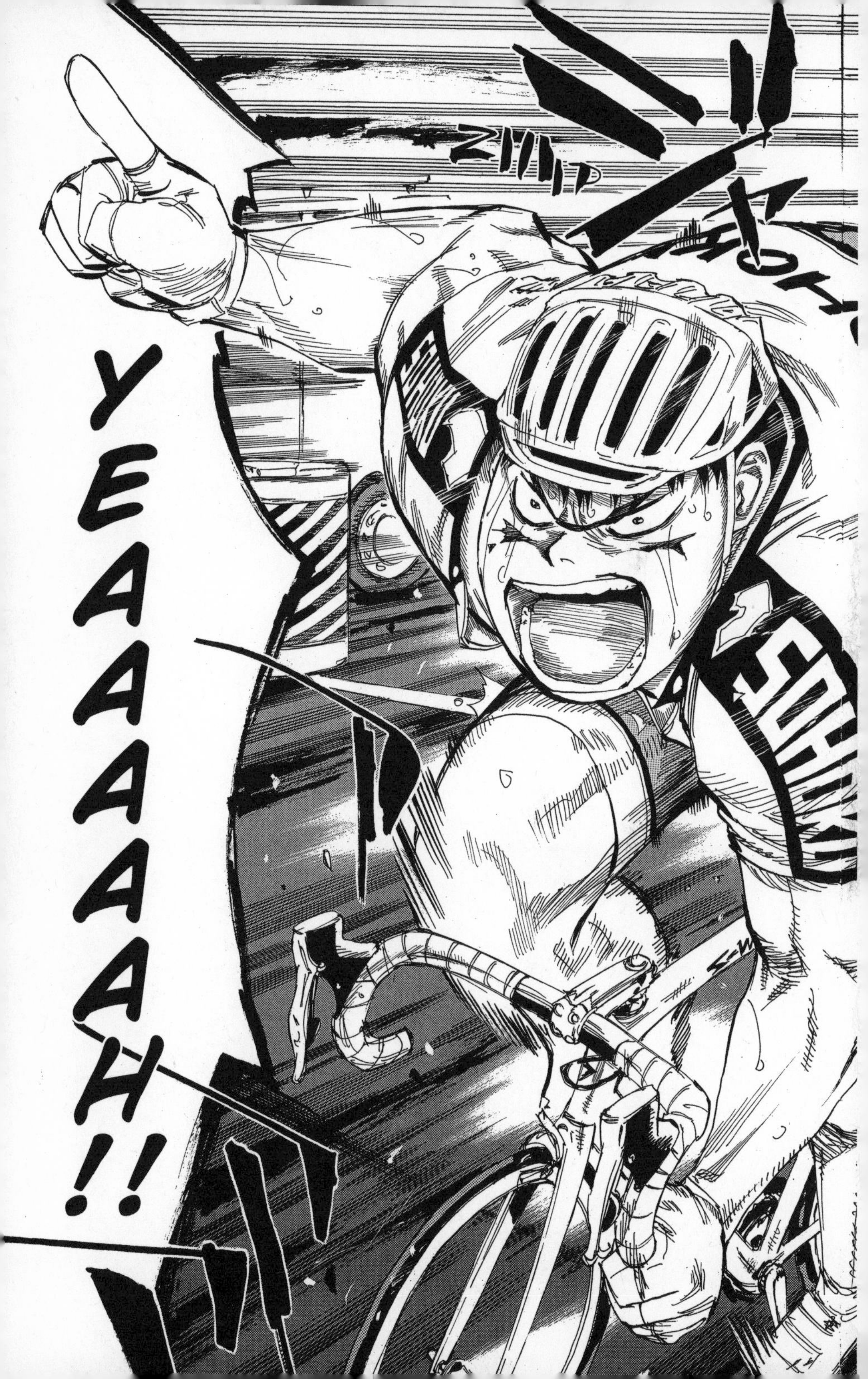
ZIIIP
YEAAAAAH!!

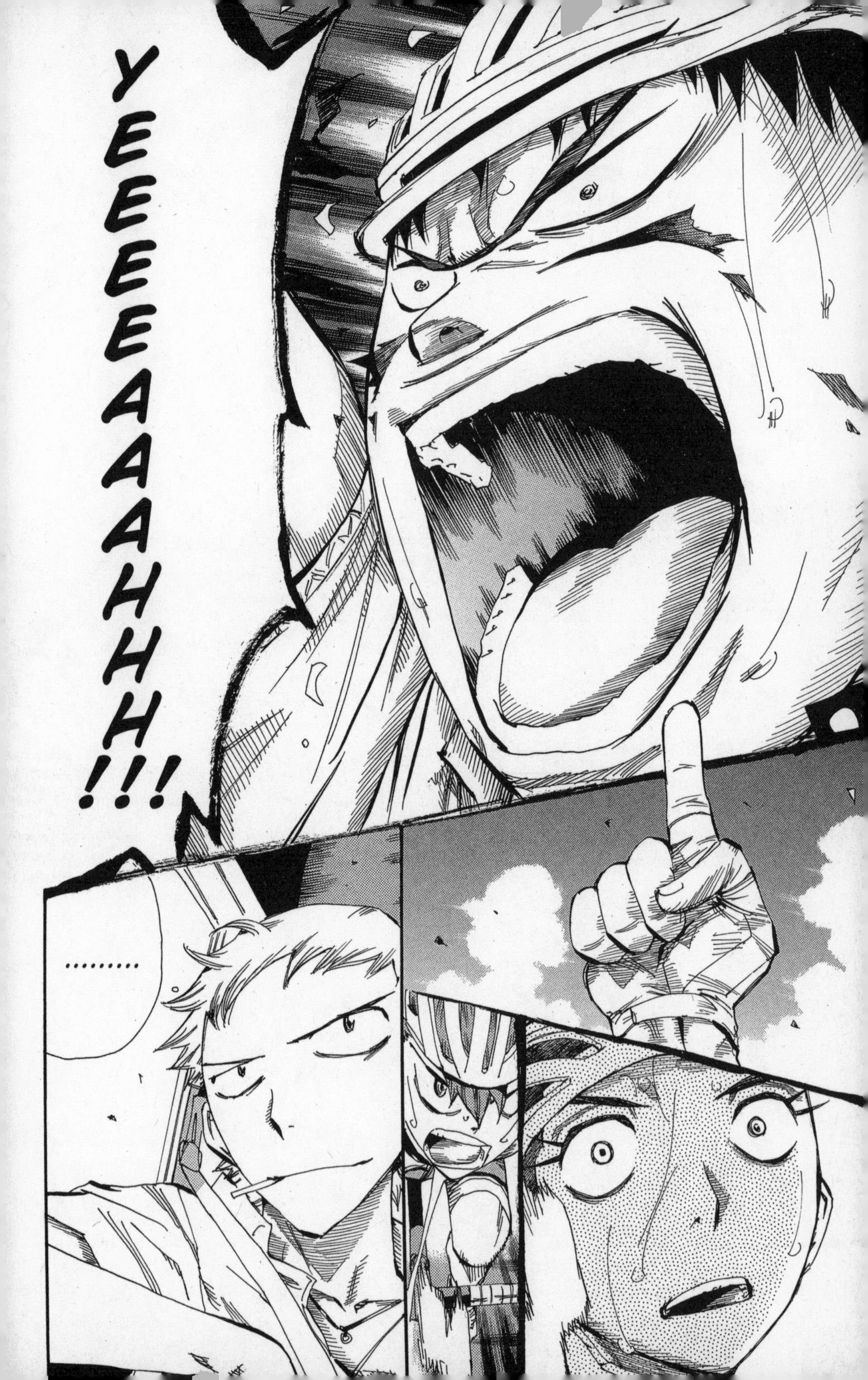
YEEEEEAAAAHHHH!!!
....

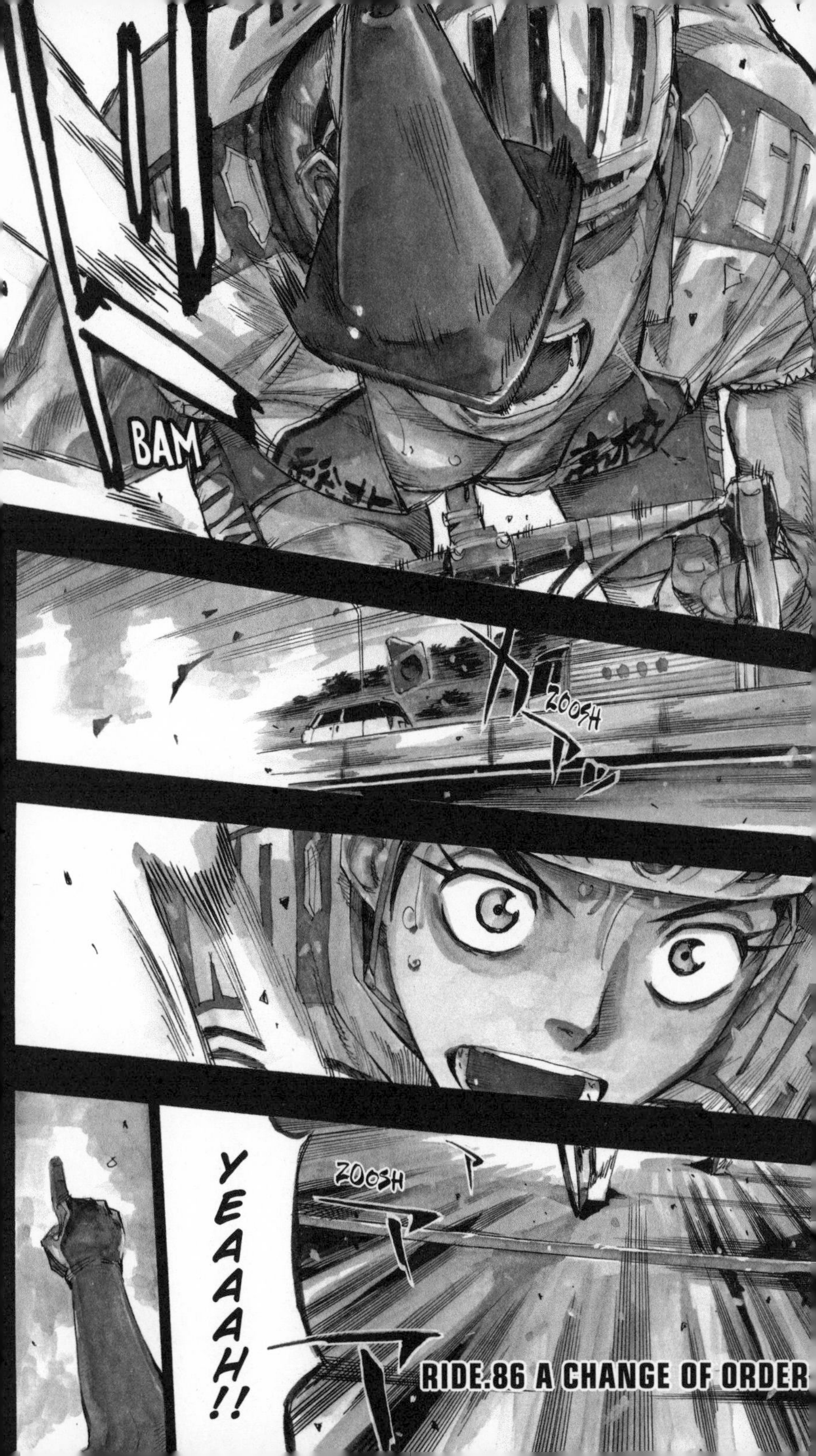
BAM
ZOOSH
YEAAAAH!!
ZOOSH
RIDE.86 A CHANGE OF ORDER

RIDE.86 A CHANGE OF ORDER

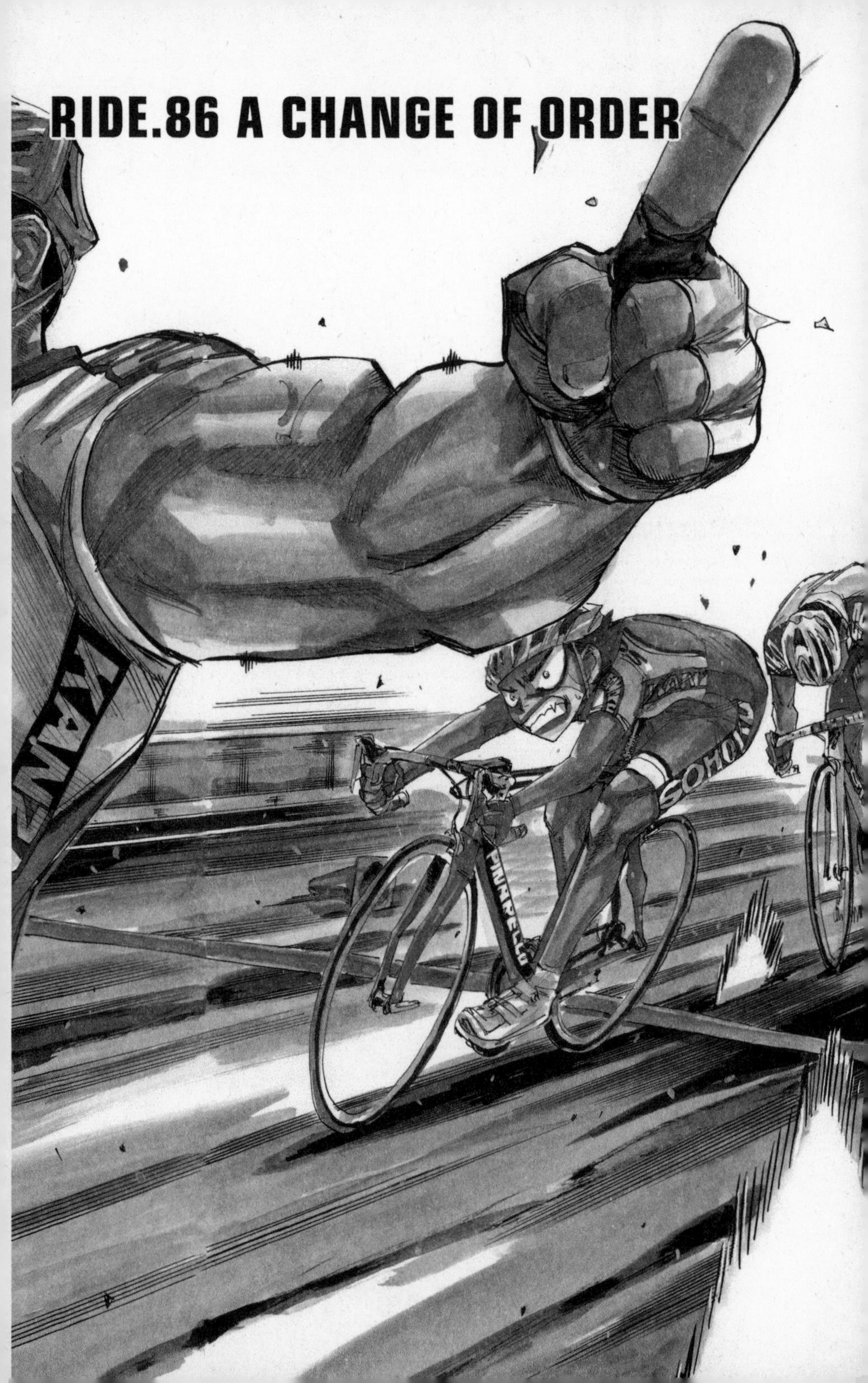

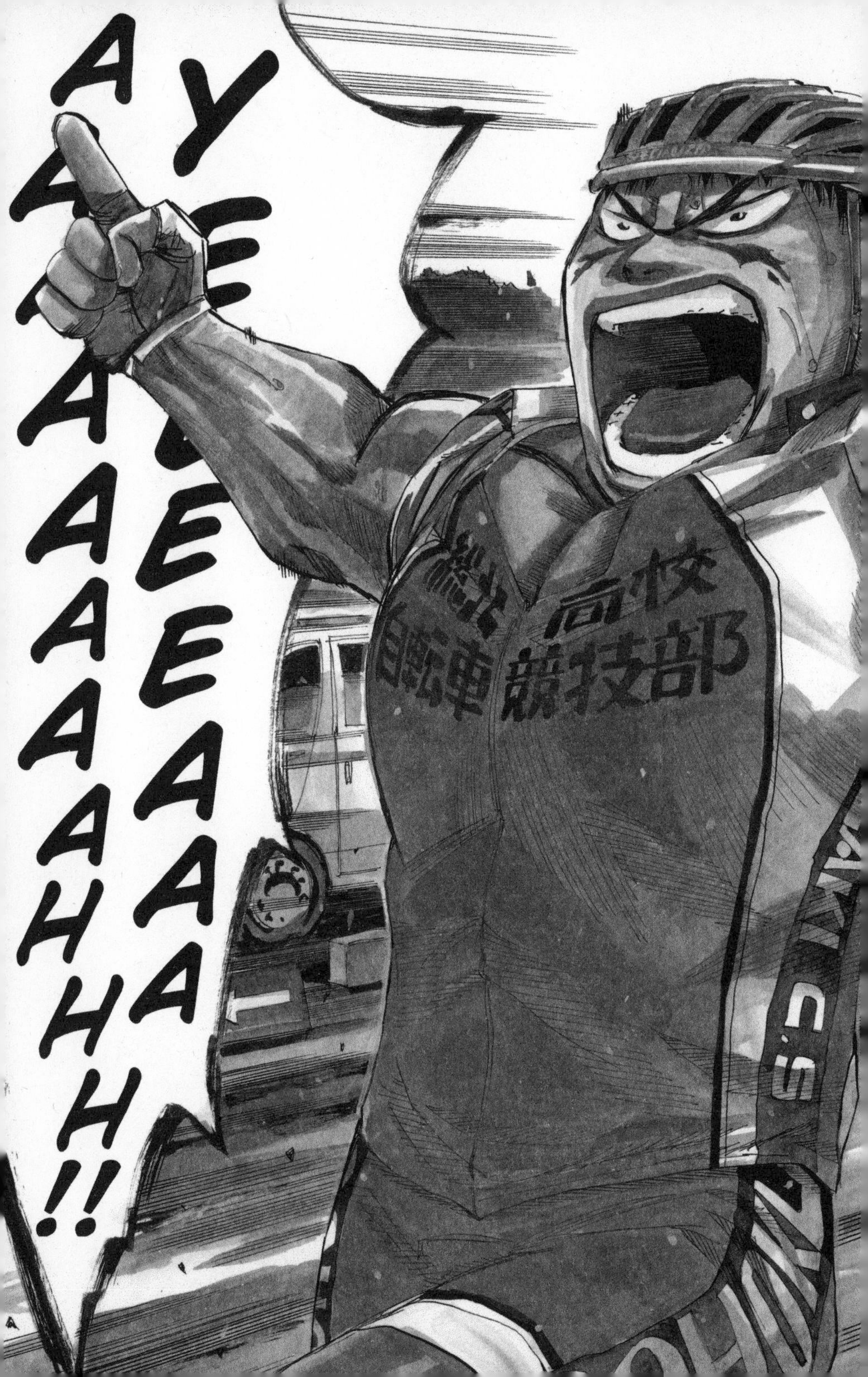
AAAAAAAAHHHH!!
YEEEEEAAAA
総北高校
自転車競技部

TADOKORO

YOWAMUSHI PEDAL

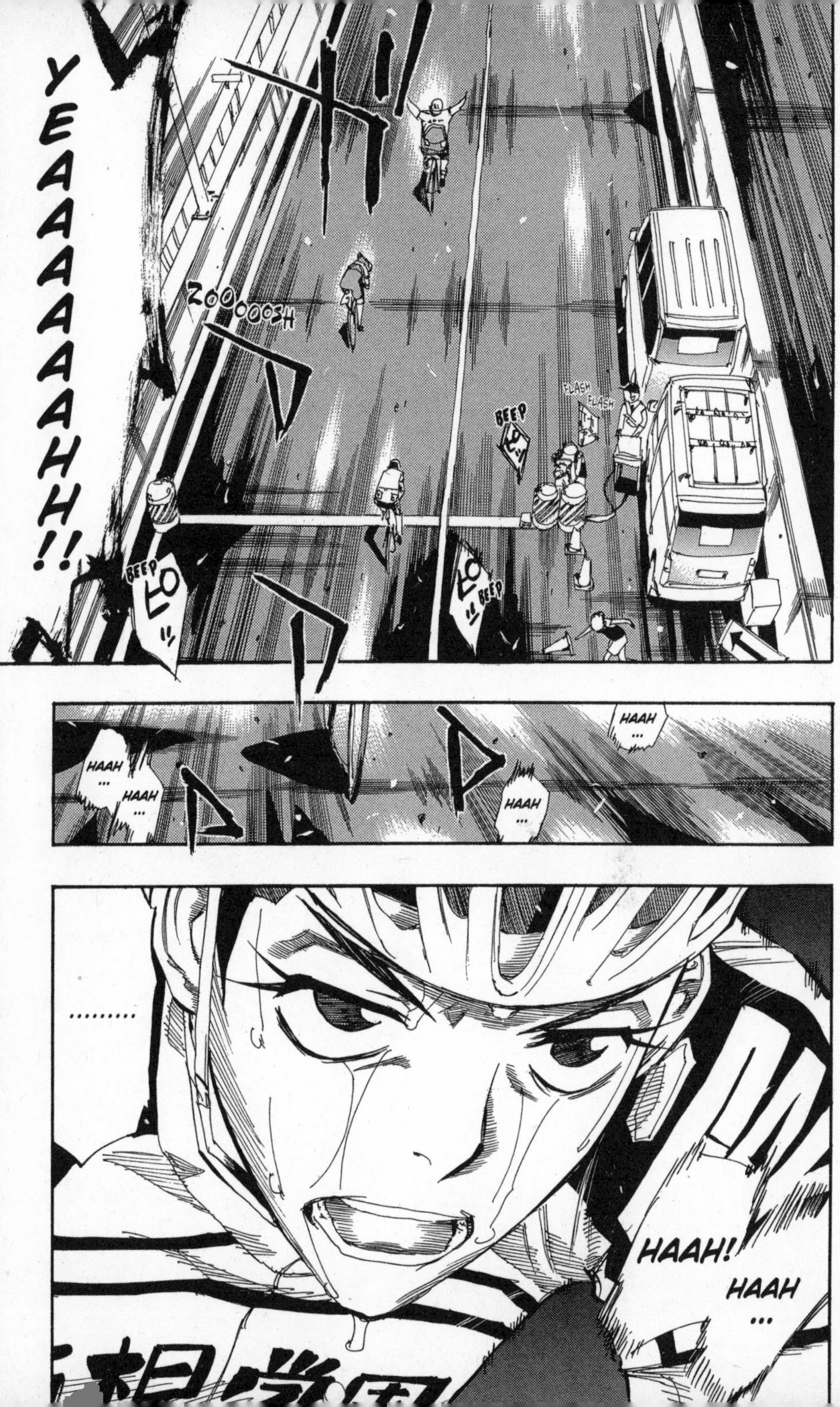
FLASH
FLASH
BEEP
ZOOOOOSH
BEEP
BEEP
YEAAAAAAAAHH!!
HAAH ...
HAAH ...
HAAH ...
HAAH ...
HAAH!
HAAH ...
....

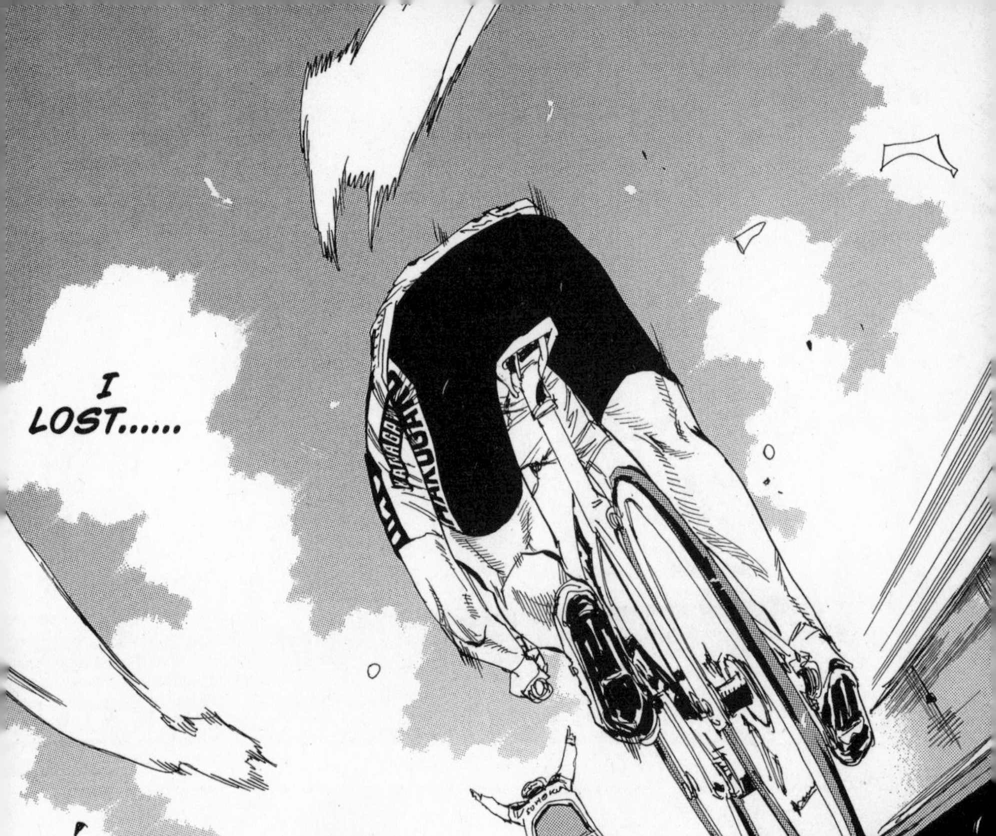
I LOST......
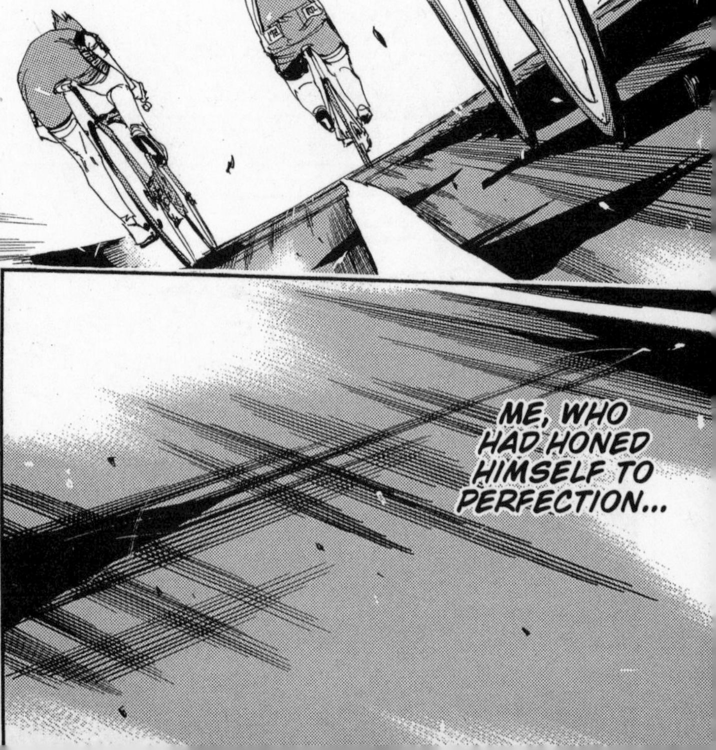
ME, WHO HAD HONED HIMSELF TO PERFECTION...
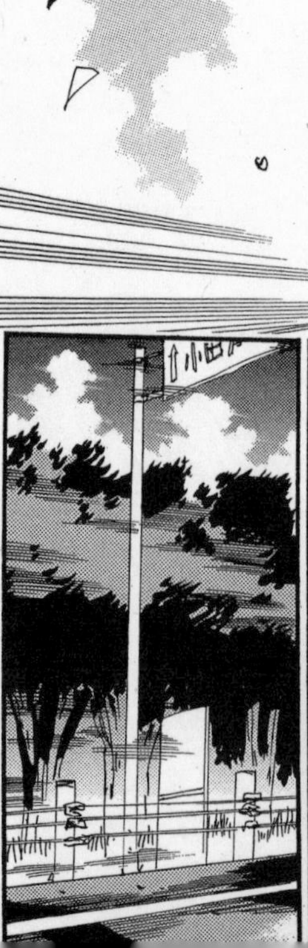

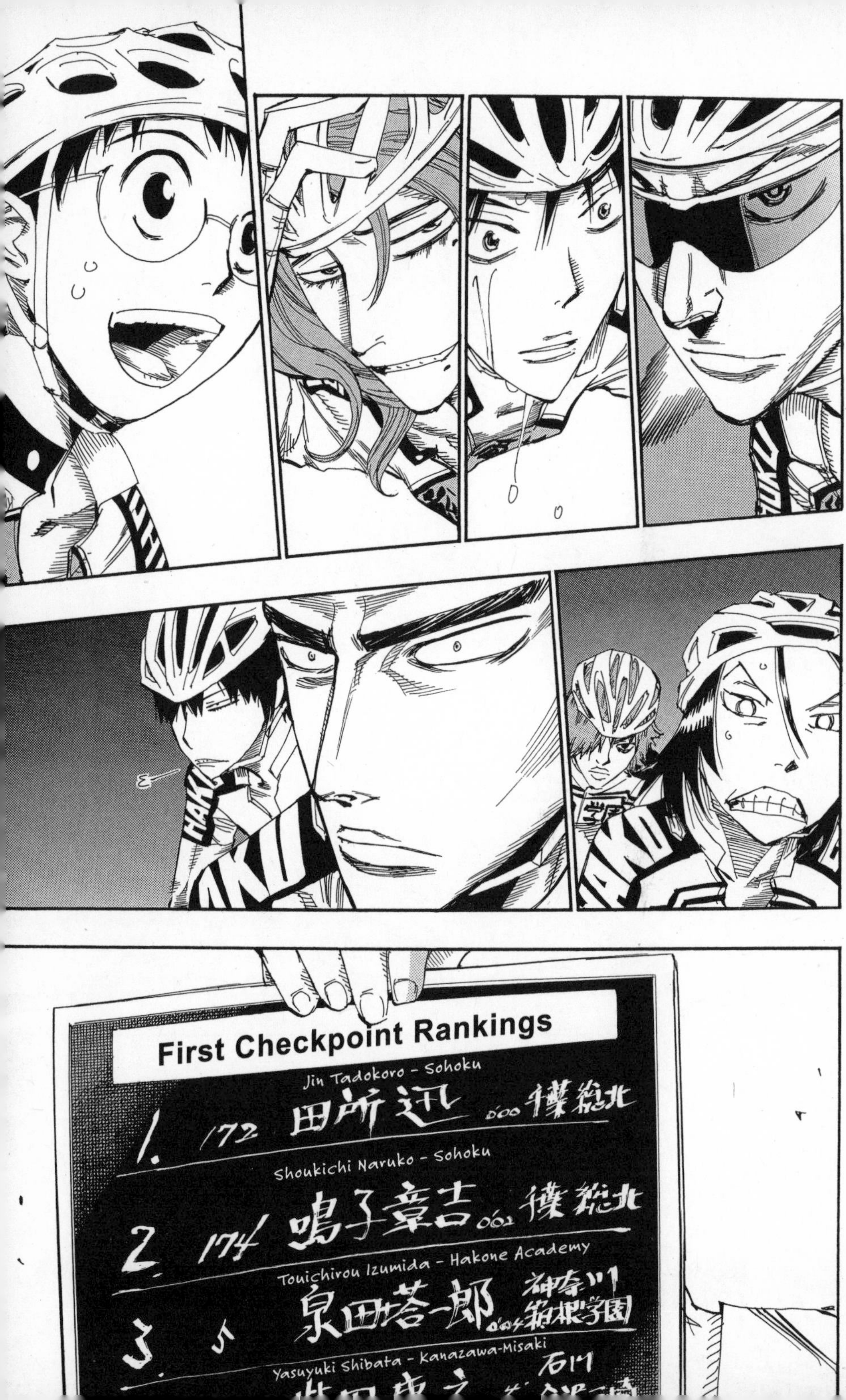
First Checkpoint Rankings
Jin Tadokoro - Sohoku
1. 172 田所迅 千葉総北
Shoukichi Naruko - Sohoku
2. 174 鳴子章吉 千葉総北
Touichirou Izumida - Hakone Academy
3. 5 泉田塔一郎 神奈川 箱根学園
Yasuyuki Shibata - Kanazawa-Misaki
石川

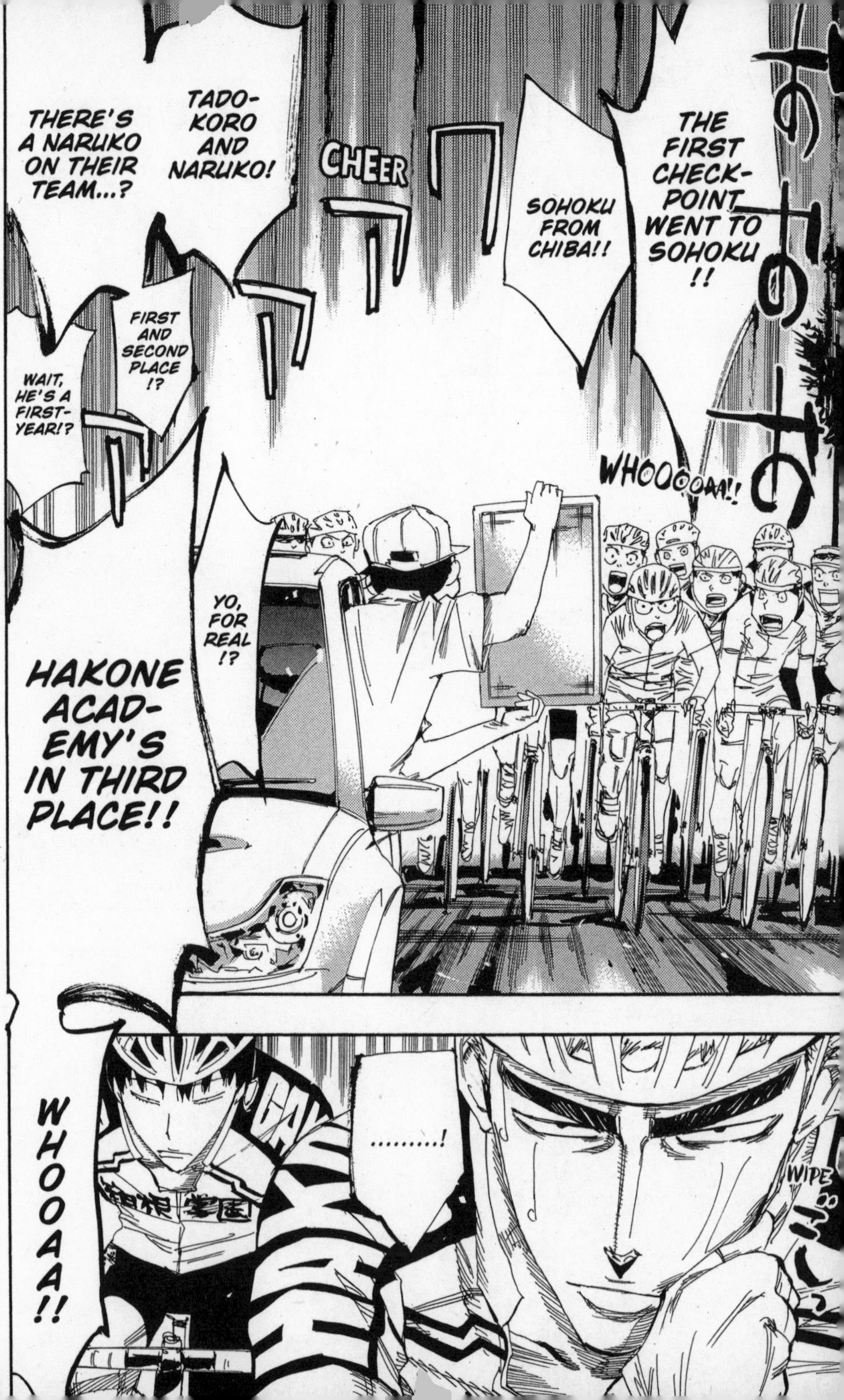
THE FIRST CHECKPOINT WENT TO SOHOKU!!
SOHOKU FROM CHIBA!!
TADOKORO AND NARUKO!
CHEER
THERE'S A NARUKO ON THEIR TEAM...?
FIRST AND SECOND PLACE!?
WAIT, HE'S A FIRST-YEAR!?
WHOOOOAA!!
YO, FOR REAL!?
HAKONE ACADEMY'S IN THIRD PLACE!!
WIPE
..........!
WHOOOAA!!

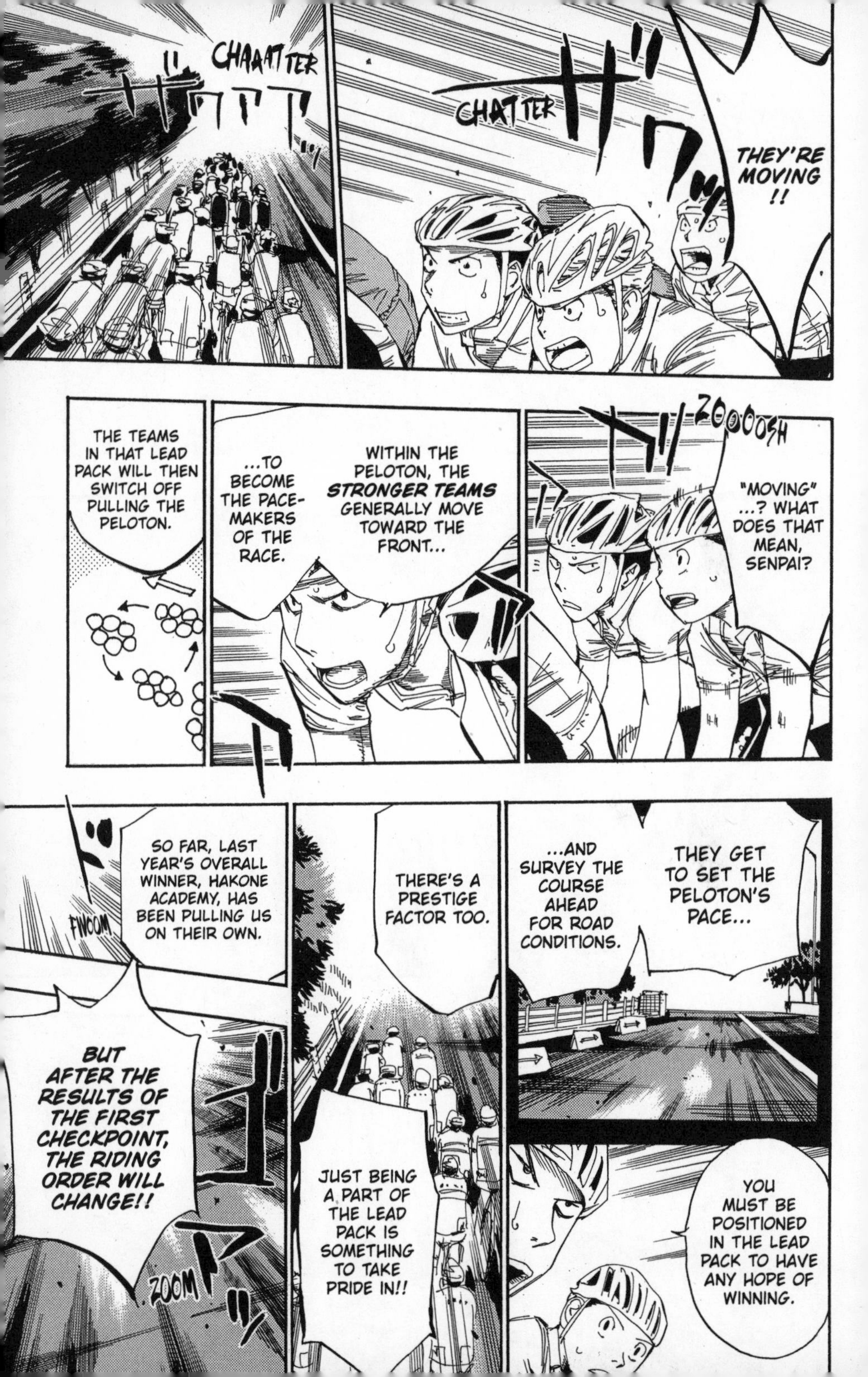
CHATTER
THEY'RE MOVING!!
CHAAATTER
ZOOOOSH
"MOVING"...? WHAT DOES THAT MEAN, SENPAI?
WITHIN THE PELOTON, THE STRONGER TEAMS GENERALLY MOVE TOWARD THE FRONT...
...TO BECOME THE PACE-MAKERS OF THE RACE.
THE TEAMS IN THAT LEAD PACK WILL THEN SWITCH OFF PULLING THE PELOTON.
THEY GET TO SET THE PELOTON'S PACE...
...AND SURVEY THE COURSE AHEAD FOR ROAD CONDITIONS.
YOU MUST BE POSITIONED IN THE LEAD PACK TO HAVE ANY HOPE OF WINNING.
THERE'S A PRESTIGE FACTOR TOO.
JUST BEING A PART OF THE LEAD PACK IS SOMETHING TO TAKE PRIDE IN!!
SO FAR, LAST YEAR'S OVERALL WINNER, HAKONE ACADEMY, HAS BEEN PULLING US ON THEIR OWN.
FWOOM
BUT AFTER THE RESULTS OF THE FIRST CHECKPOINT, THE RIDING ORDER WILL CHANGE!!
ZOOM

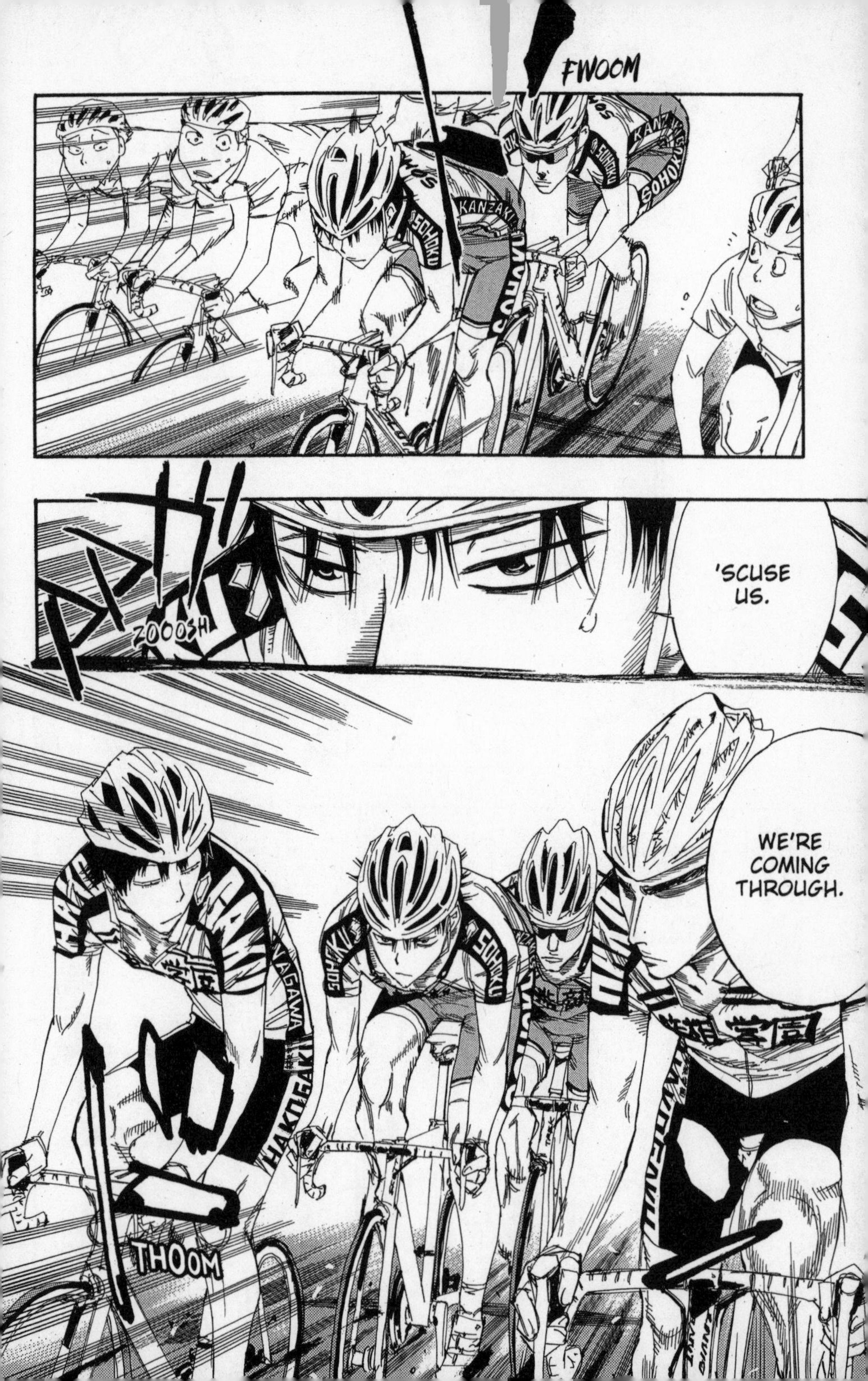
FWOOM
'SCUSE US.
ZOOOSH
WE'RE COMING THROUGH.
THOOM

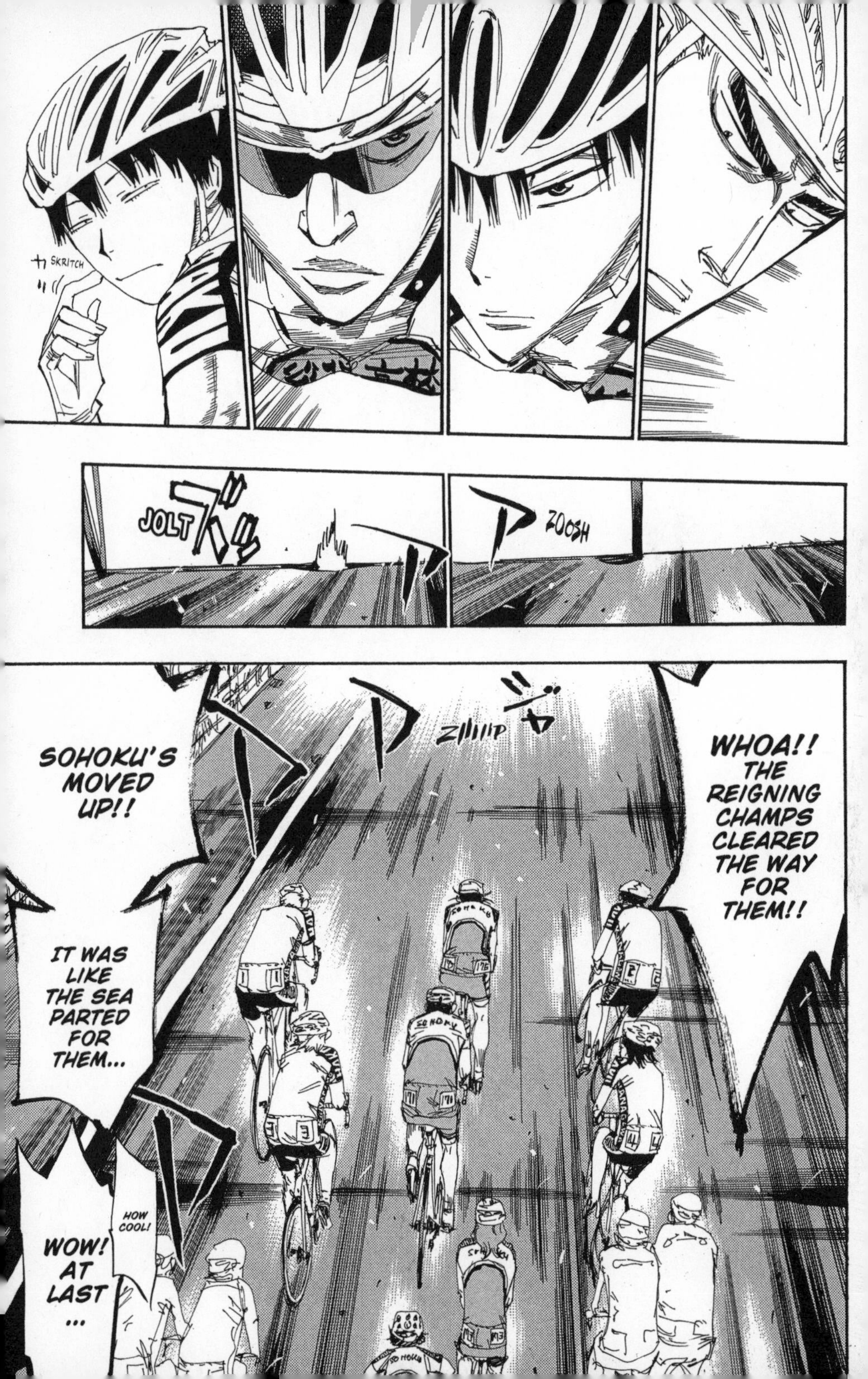
SKRITCH
ZOOSH
JOLT
WHOA!! THE REIGNING CHAMPS CLEARED THE WAY FOR THEM!!
ZIIIIP
SOHOKU'S MOVED UP!!
IT WAS LIKE THE SEA PARTED FOR THEM...
HOW COOL!
WOW! AT LAST ...

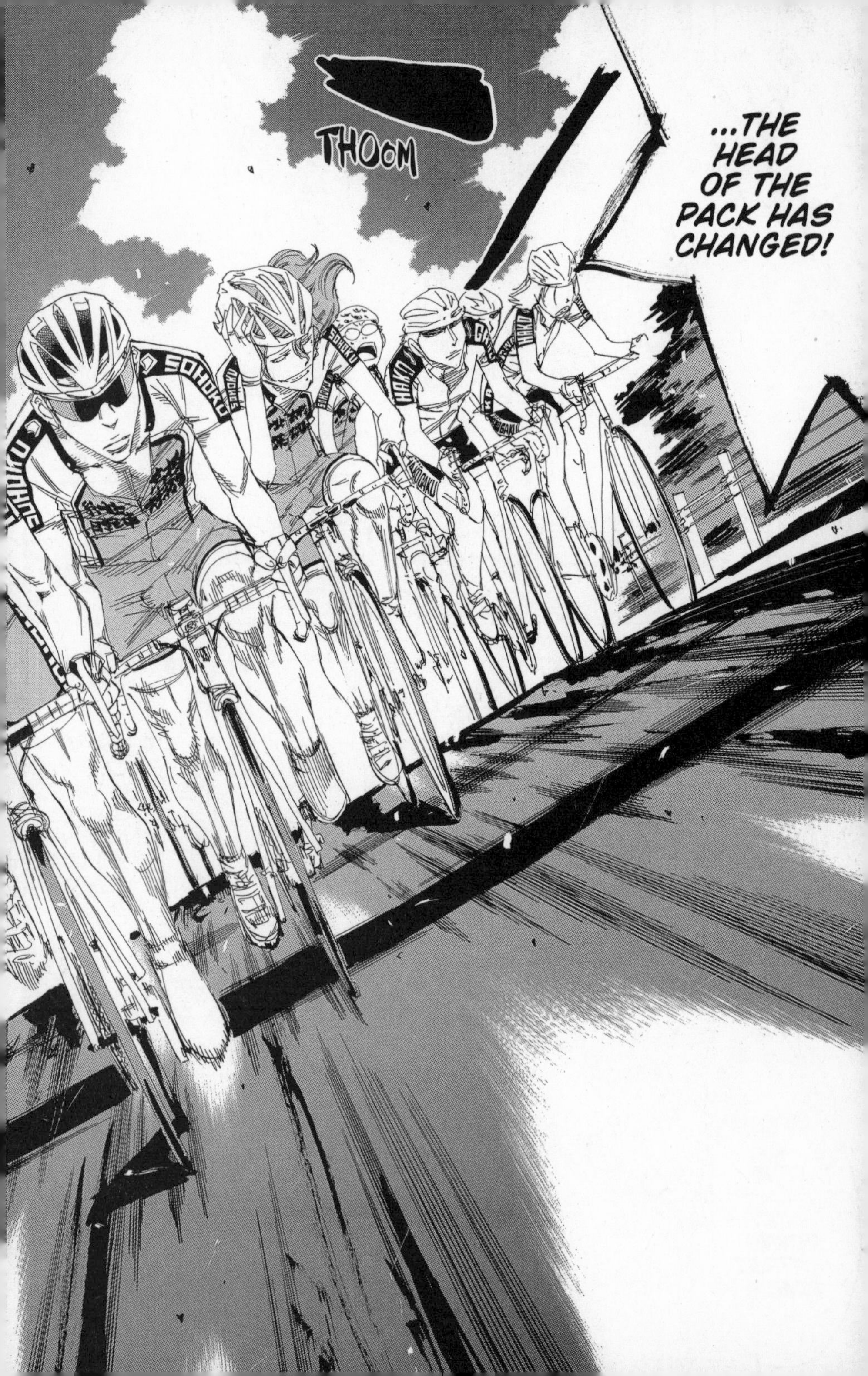
...THE HEAD OF THE PACK HAS CHANGED!
THOOM

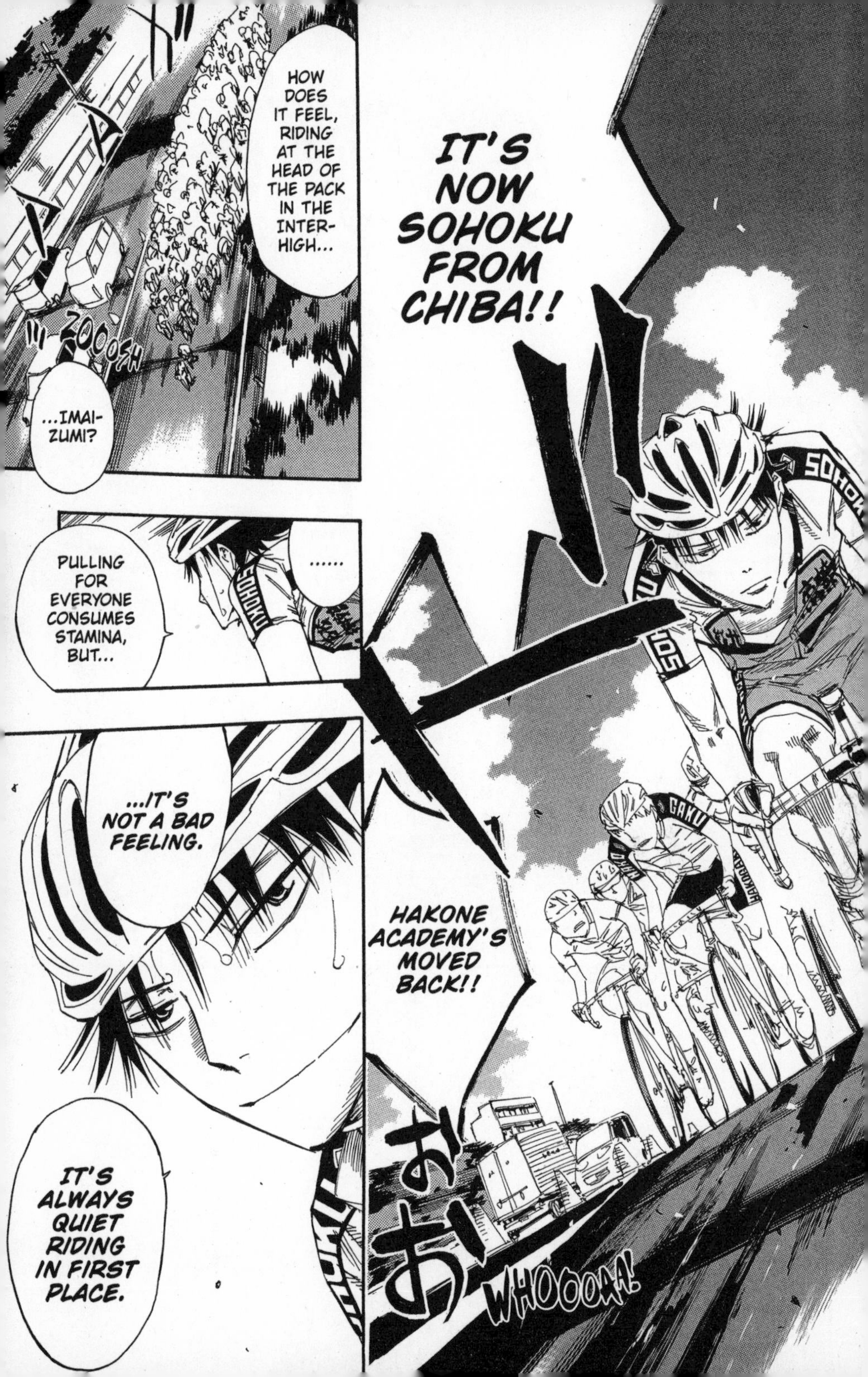
IT'S NOW SOHOKU FROM CHIBA!!
HAKONE ACADEMY'S MOVED BACK!!
WHOOOOA!
HOW DOES IT FEEL, RIDING AT THE HEAD OF THE PACK IN THE INTER-HIGH...
ZOOOSH
...IMAI-ZUMI?
......
PULLING FOR EVERYONE CONSUMES STAMINA, BUT...
...IT'S NOT A BAD FEELING.
IT'S ALWAYS QUIET RIDING IN FIRST PLACE.

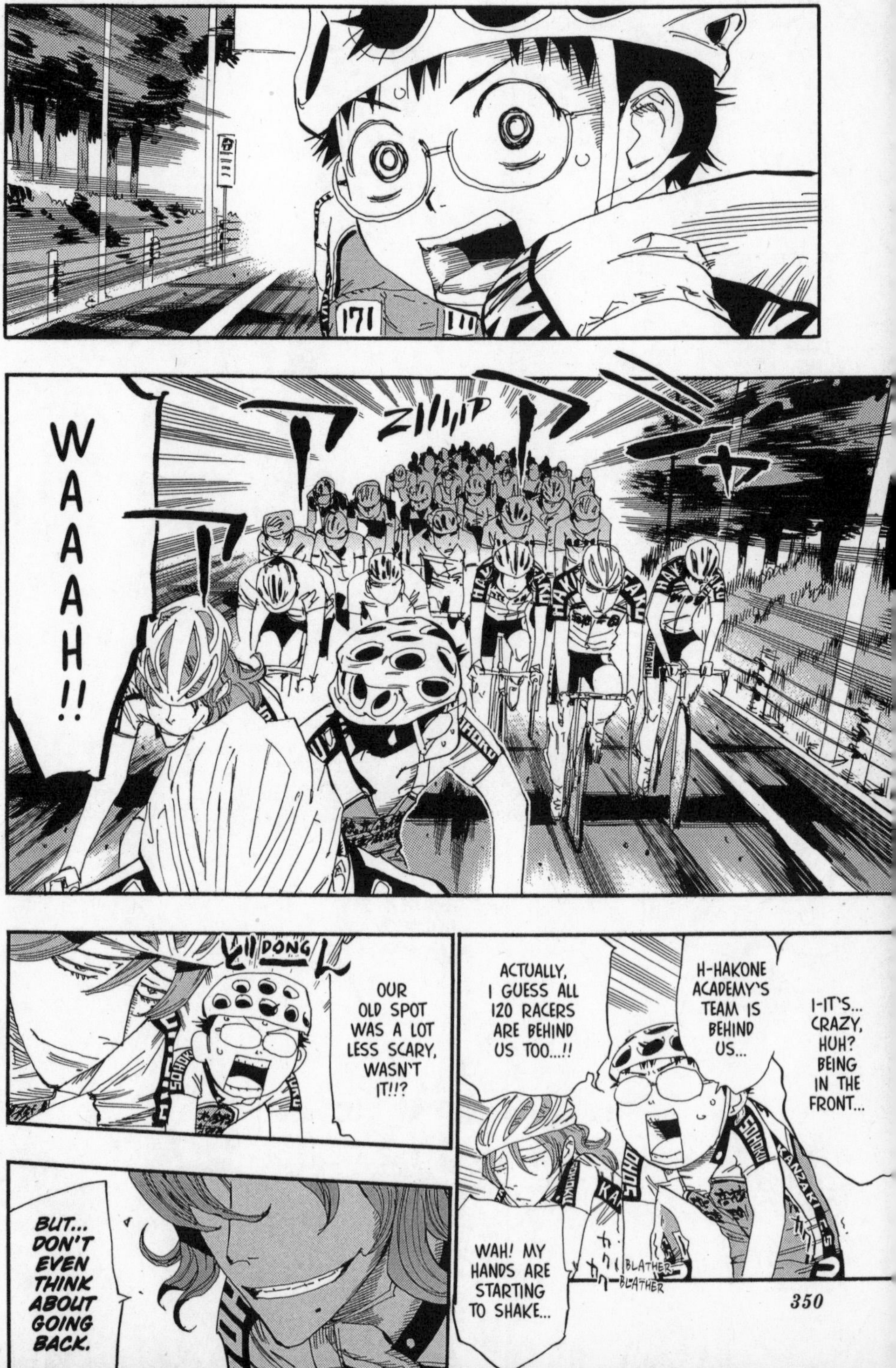
WAAAAH!!
ZIIIIIP
I-IT'S... CRAZY, HUH? BEING IN THE FRONT...
H-HAKONE ACADEMY'S TEAM IS BEHIND US...
ACTUALLY, I GUESS ALL 120 RACERS ARE BEHIND US TOO...!!
WAH! MY HANDS ARE STARTING TO SHAKE...
BLATHER BLATHER
DONG
OUR OLD SPOT WAS A LOT LESS SCARY, WASN'T IT!!?
BUT... DON'T EVEN THINK ABOUT GOING BACK.

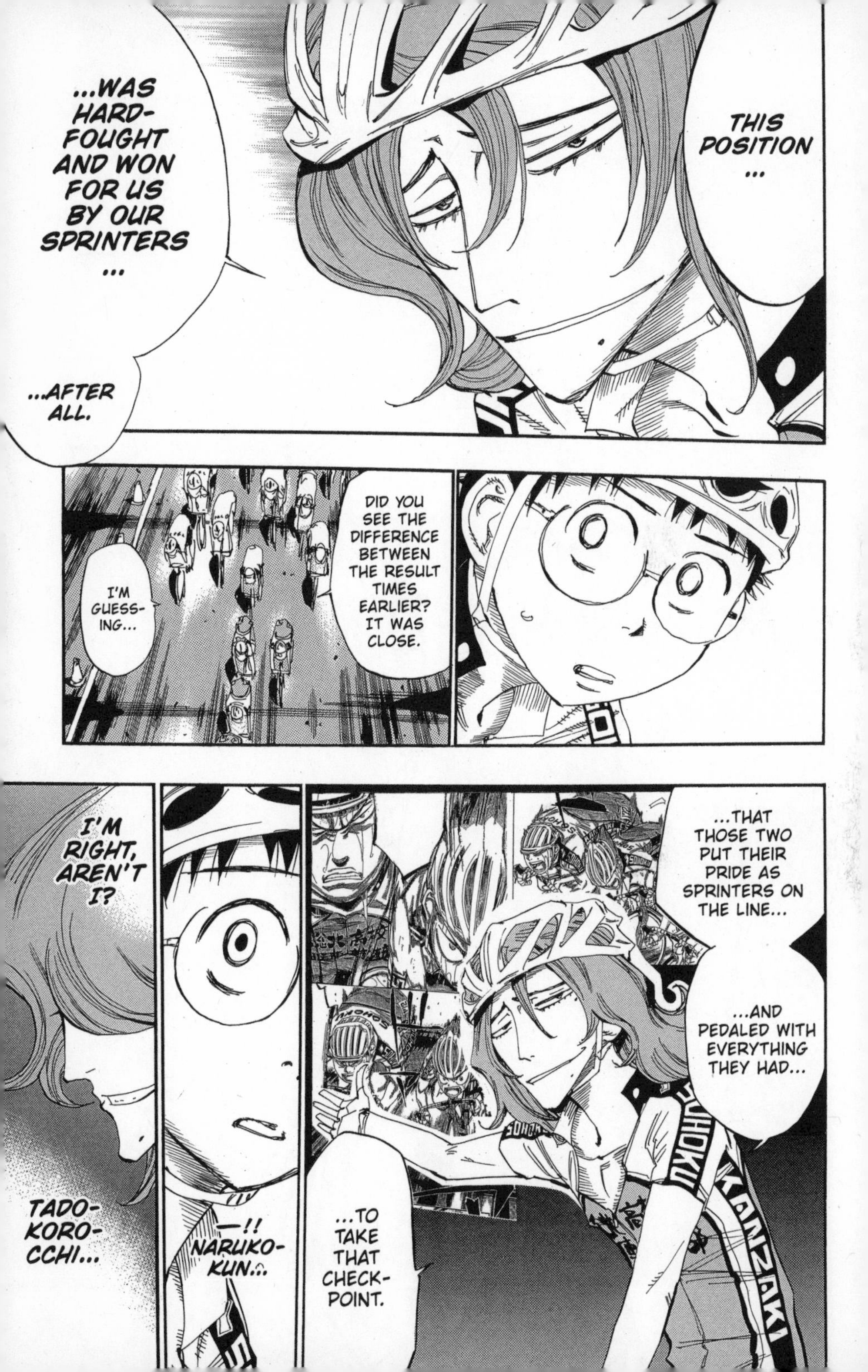
THIS POSITION ...
...WAS HARD-FOUGHT AND WON FOR US BY OUR SPRINTERS ...
...AFTER ALL.
DID YOU SEE THE DIFFERENCE BETWEEN THE RESULT TIMES EARLIER? IT WAS CLOSE.
I'M GUESSING...
...THAT THOSE TWO PUT THEIR PRIDE AS SPRINTERS ON THE LINE...
...AND PEDALED WITH EVERYTHING THEY HAD...
...TO TAKE THAT CHECKPOINT.
—!! NARUKO-KUN...
I'M RIGHT, AREN'T I?
TADO-KORO-CCHI...

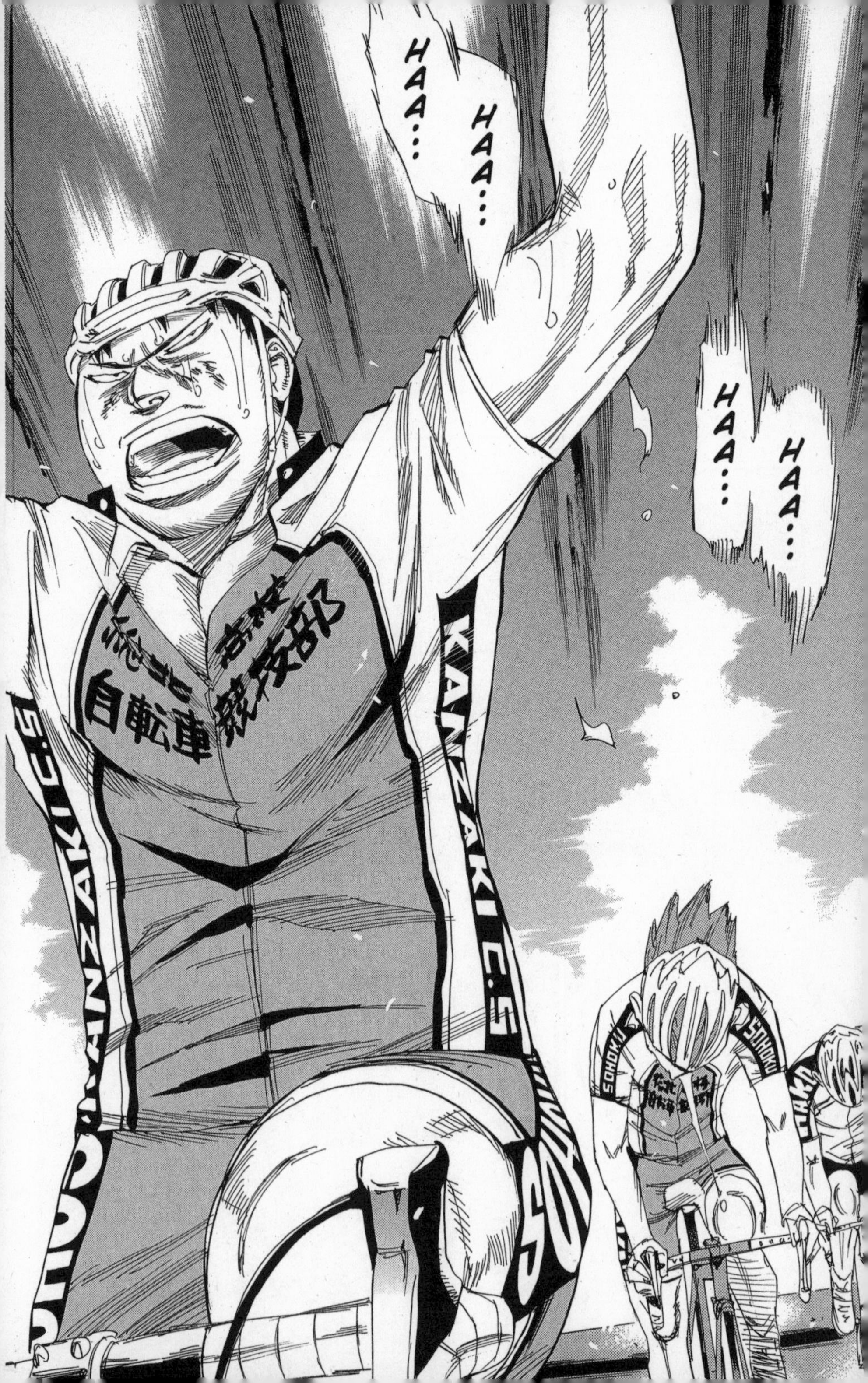
HAA...
HAA...
HAA...
HAA...

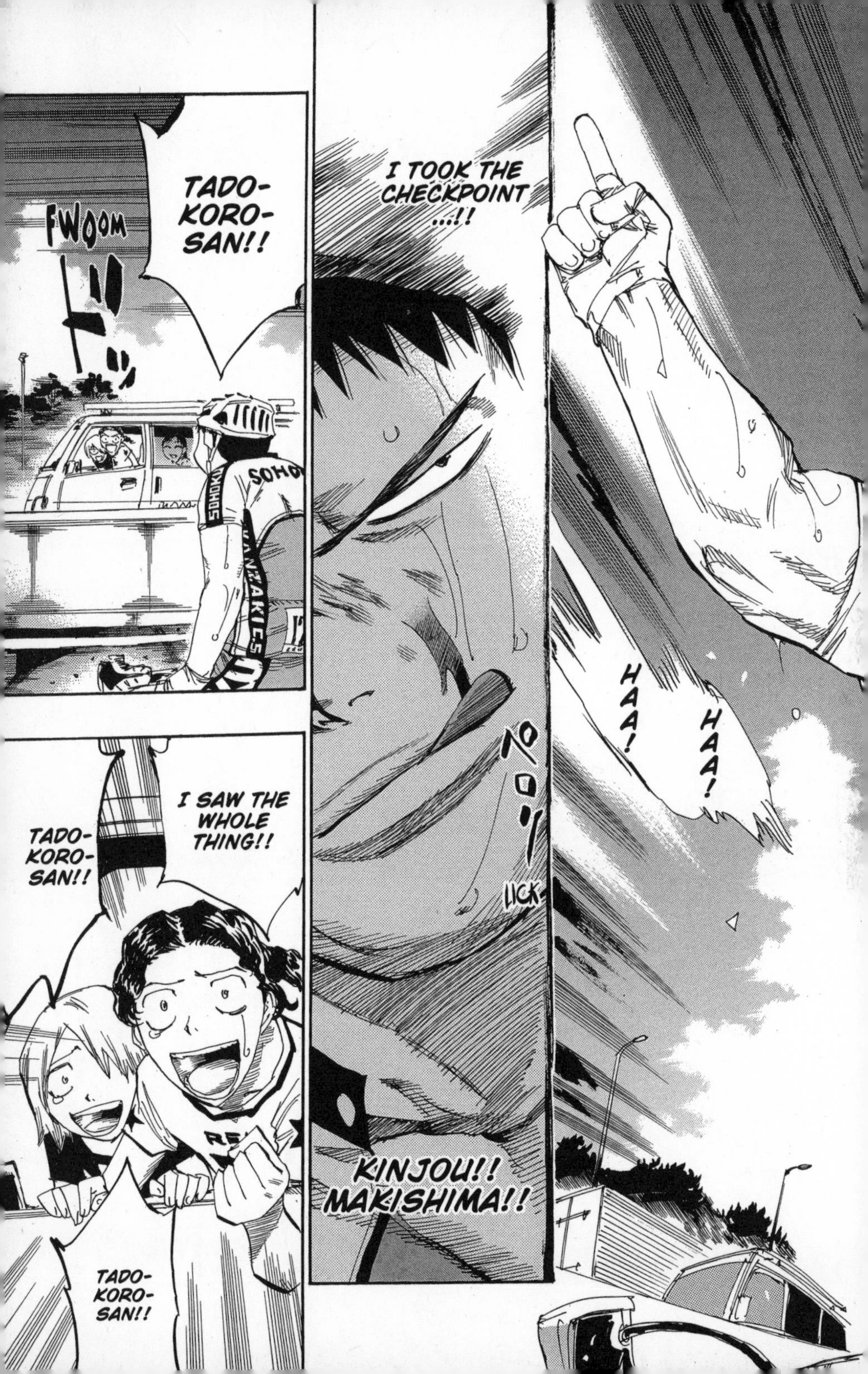
HAA!
HAA!
I TOOK THE CHECKPOINT ...!!
LICK
KINJOU!! MAKISHIMA!!
TADO-KORO-SAN!!
FWOOM
I SAW THE WHOLE THING!!
TADO-KORO-SAN!!
TADO-KORO-SAN!!

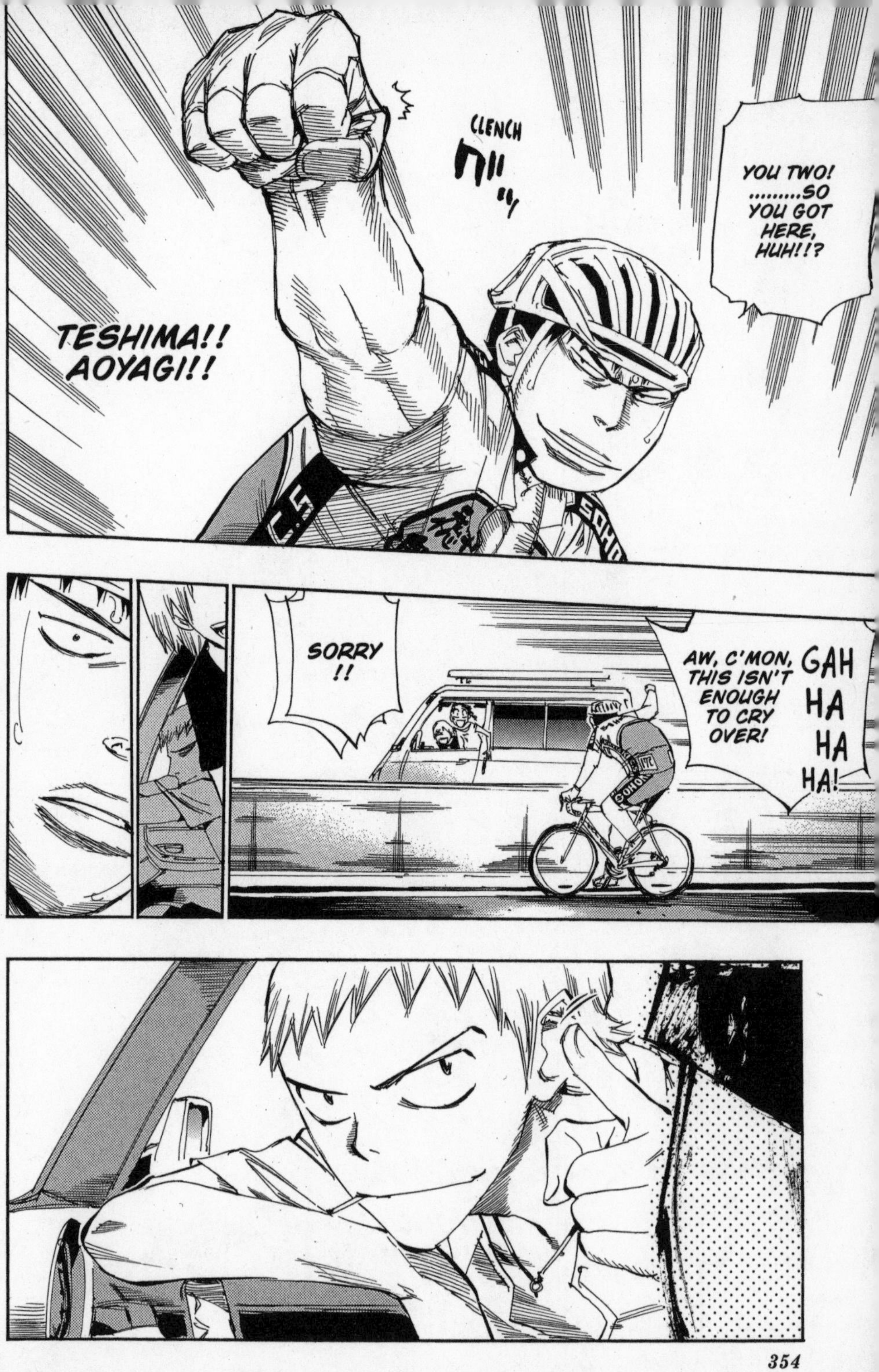
YOU TWO! ....SO YOU GOT HERE, HUH!!?
CLENCH
TESHIMA!! AOYAGI!!
GAH HA HA HA!
AW, C'MON, THIS ISN'T ENOUGH TO CRY OVER!
SORRY !!

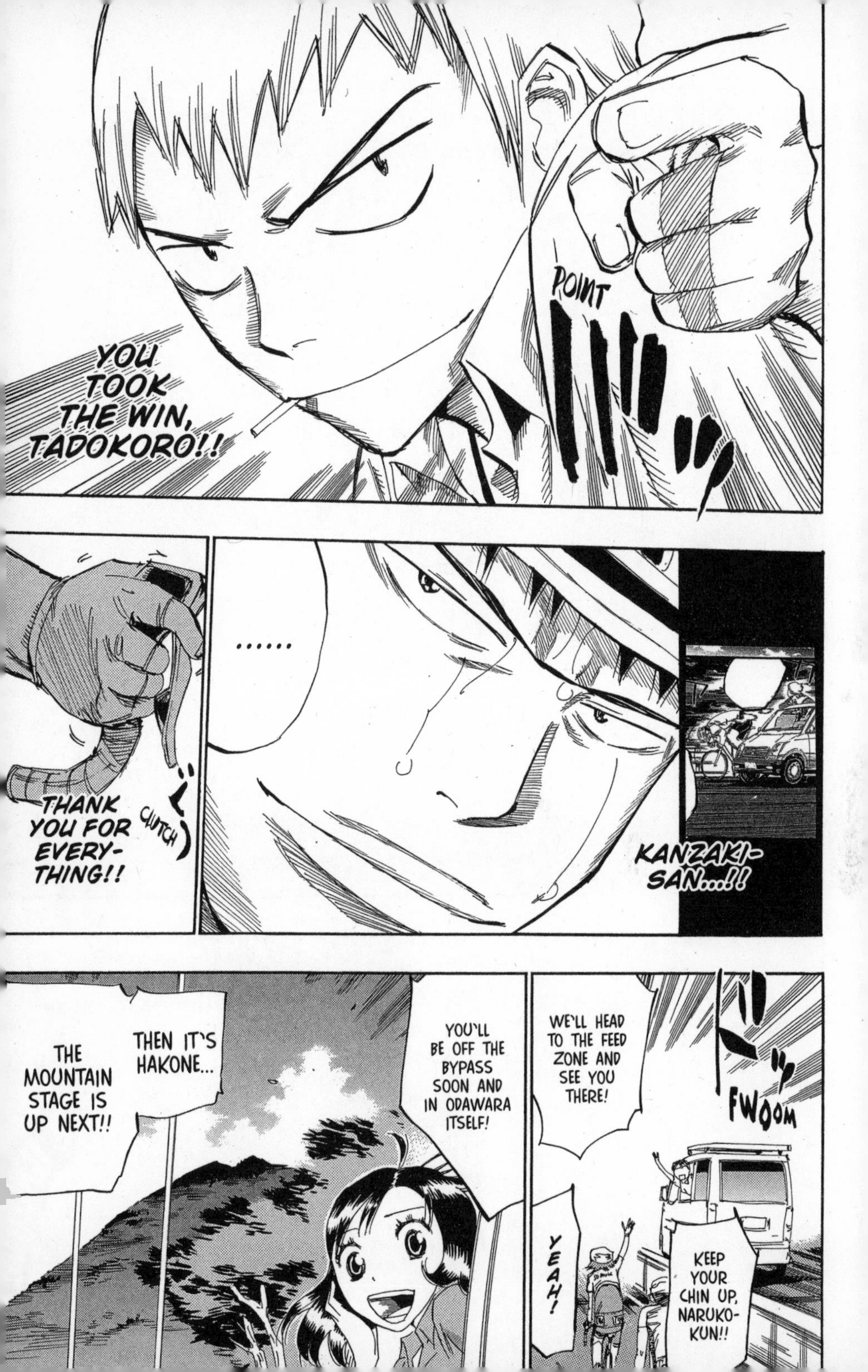
POINT
YOU TOOK THE WIN, TADOKORO!!
KANZAKI-SAN...!!
......
CLUTCH
THANK YOU FOR EVERY-THING!!
FWOOM
WE'LL HEAD TO THE FEED ZONE AND SEE YOU THERE!
YEAH!
KEEP YOUR CHIN UP, NARUKO-KUN!!
YOU'LL BE OFF THE BYPASS SOON AND IN ODAWARA ITSELF!
THEN IT'S HAKONE...
THE MOUNTAIN STAGE IS UP NEXT!!

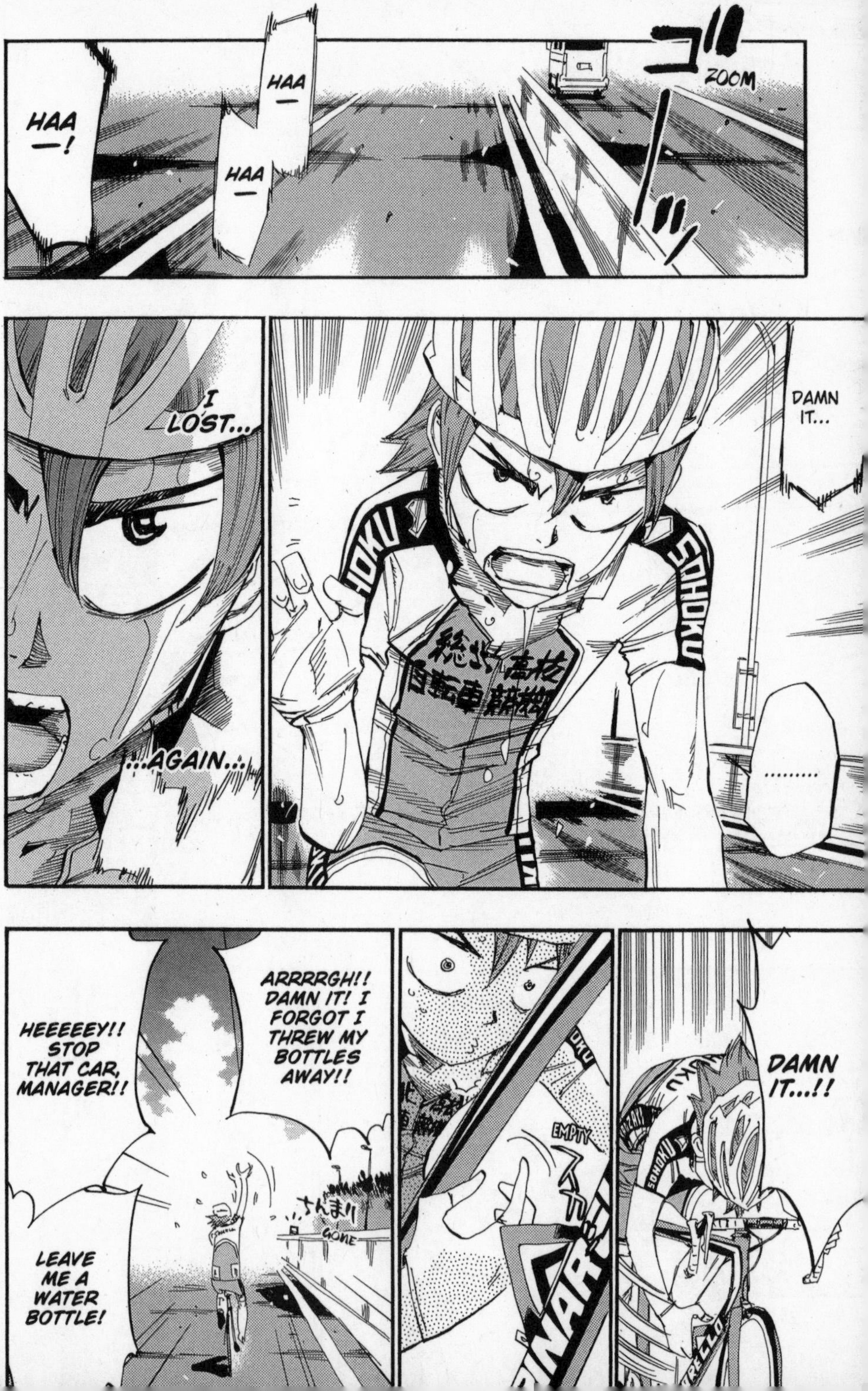
ZOOM
HAA—
HAA—
HAA—!
DAMN IT...
....
I LOST...
...AGAIN...
DAMN IT..!!
EMPTY
ARRRRGH!! DAMN IT! I FORGOT I THREW MY BOTTLES AWAY!!
HEEEEEY!! STOP THAT CAR, MANAGER!!
ちんまり
GONE
LEAVE ME A WATER BOTTLE!

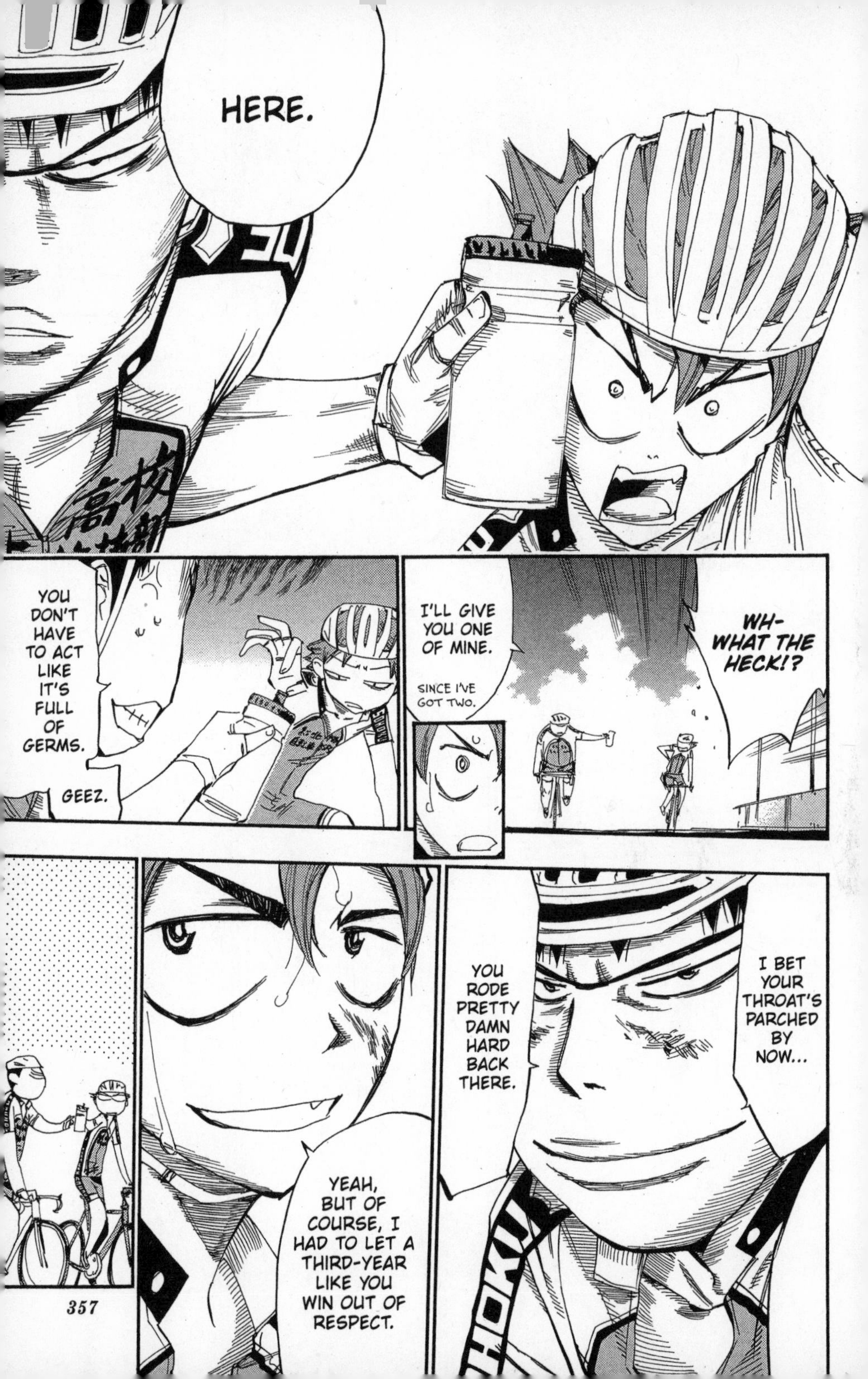
HERE.
WH- WHAT THE HECK!?
I'LL GIVE YOU ONE OF MINE.
SINCE I'VE GOT TWO.
YOU DON'T HAVE TO ACT LIKE IT'S FULL OF GERMS.
GEEZ.
I BET YOUR THROAT'S PARCHED BY NOW...
YOU RODE PRETTY DAMN HARD BACK THERE.
YEAH, BUT OF COURSE, I HAD TO LET A THIRD-YEAR LIKE YOU WIN OUT OF RESPECT.

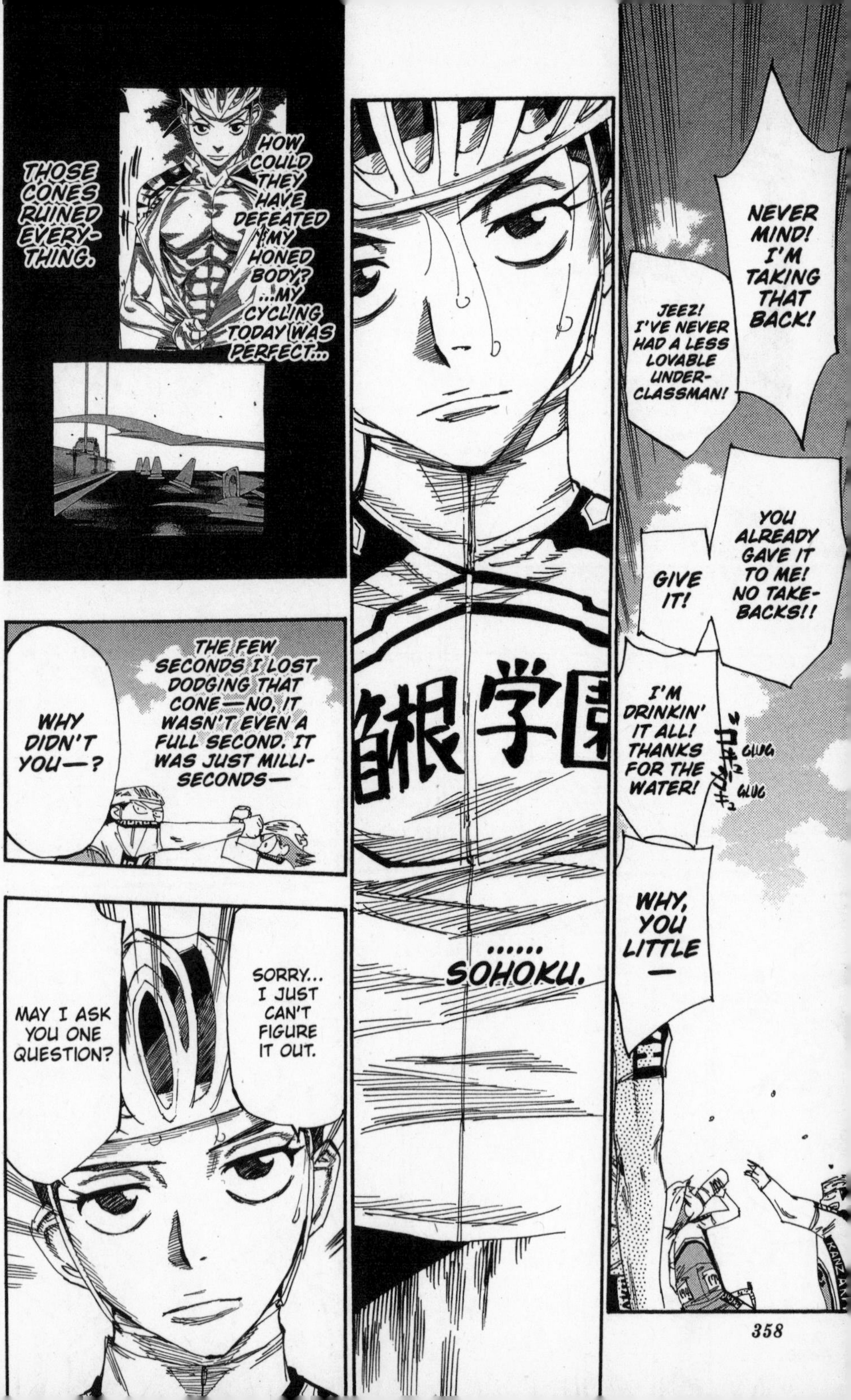
NEVER MIND! I'M TAKING THAT BACK!
JEEZ! I'VE NEVER HAD A LESS LOVABLE UNDER-CLASSMAN!
YOU ALREADY GAVE IT TO ME! NO TAKE-BACKS!!
GIVE IT!
I'M DRINKIN' IT ALL! THANKS FOR THE WATER!
GLUG
GLUG
WHY, YOU LITTLE—
...... SOHOKU.
HOW COULD THEY HAVE DEFEATED MY HONED BODY? ...MY CYCLING TODAY WAS PERFECT...
THOSE CONES RUINED EVERY-THING.
THE FEW SECONDS I LOST DODGING THAT CONE—NO, IT WASN'T EVEN A FULL SECOND. IT WAS JUST MILLI-SECONDS—
WHY DIDN'T YOU—?
SORRY... I JUST CAN'T FIGURE IT OUT.
MAY I ASK YOU ONE QUESTION?

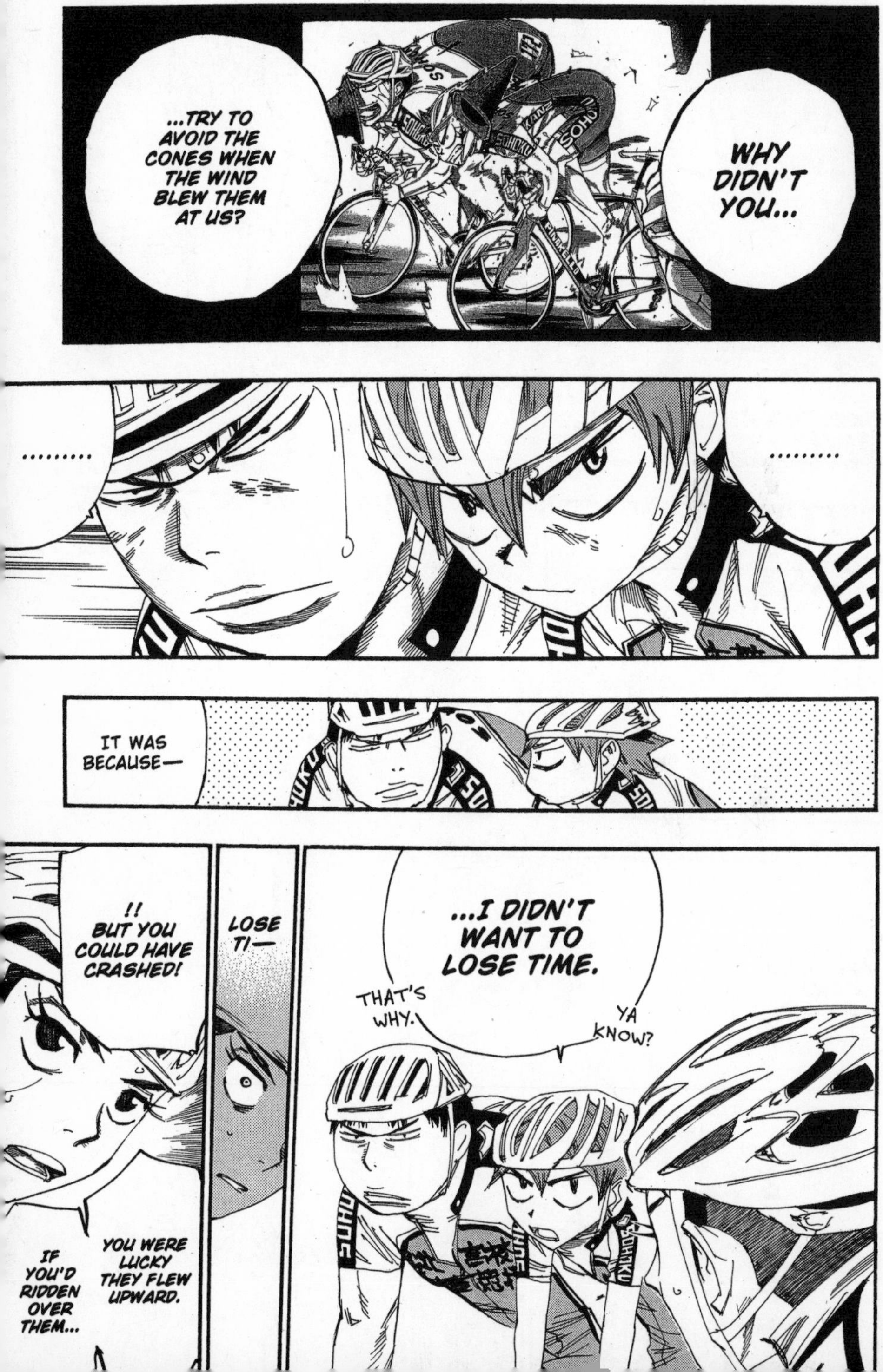
WHY DIDN'T YOU...
...TRY TO AVOID THE CONES WHEN THE WIND BLEW THEM AT US?
....
....
IT WAS BECAUSE—
...I DIDN'T WANT TO LOSE TIME.
THAT'S WHY.
YA KNOW?
LOSE TI—
!! BUT YOU COULD HAVE CRASHED!
YOU WERE LUCKY THEY FLEW UPWARD.
IF YOU'D RIDDEN OVER THEM...

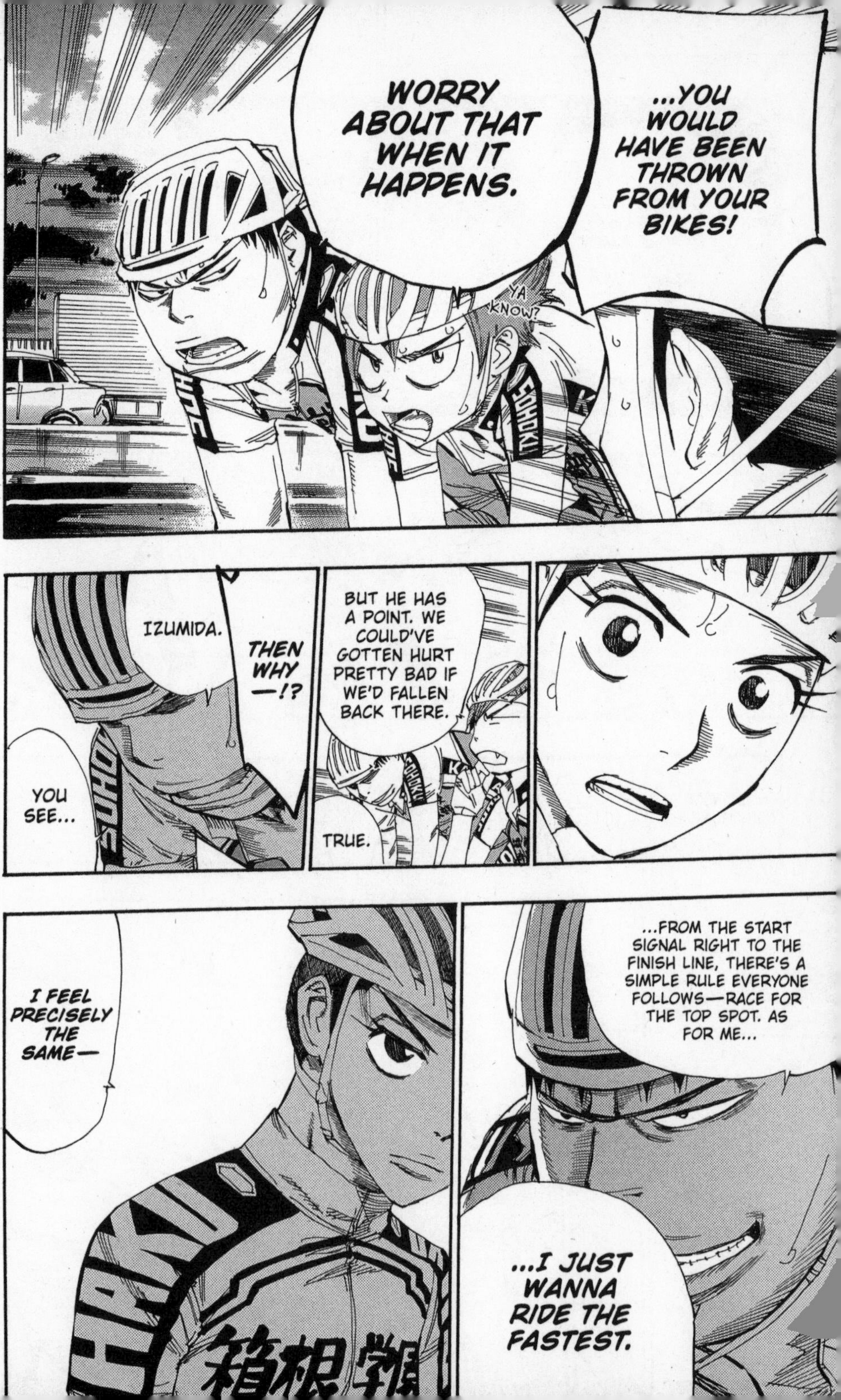
...YOU WOULD HAVE BEEN THROWN FROM YOUR BIKES!
YA KNOW?
WORRY ABOUT THAT WHEN IT HAPPENS.
BUT HE HAS A POINT. WE COULD'VE GOTTEN HURT PRETTY BAD IF WE'D FALLEN BACK THERE.
TRUE.
THEN WHY—!?
IZUMIDA.
YOU SEE...
...FROM THE START SIGNAL RIGHT TO THE FINISH LINE, THERE'S A SIMPLE RULE EVERYONE FOLLOWS—RACE FOR THE TOP SPOT. AS FOR ME...
...I JUST WANNA RIDE THE FASTEST.
I FEEL PRECISELY THE SAME—

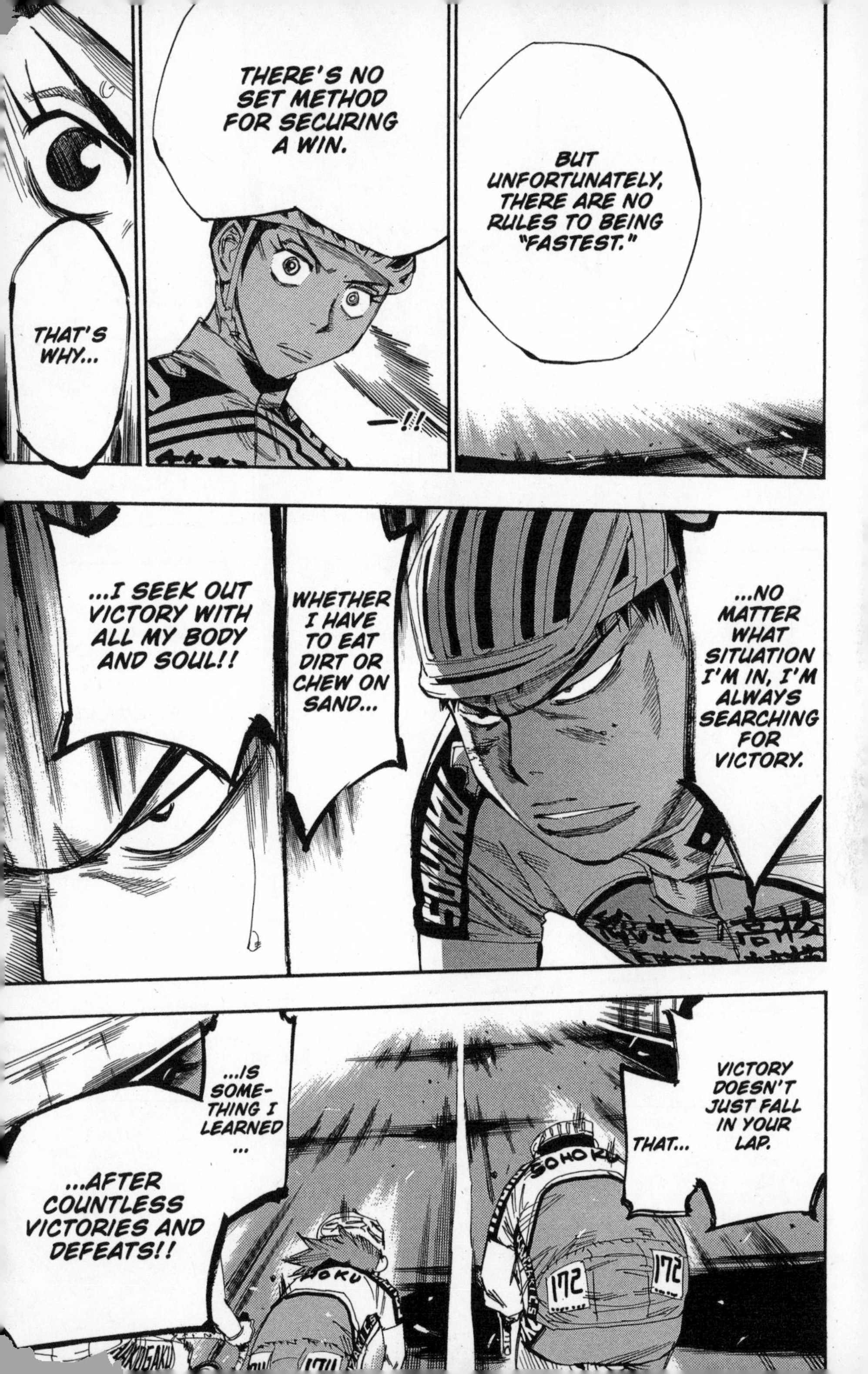
BUT UNFORTUNATELY, THERE ARE NO RULES TO BEING "FASTEST."
THERE'S NO SET METHOD FOR SECURING A WIN.
—!!
THAT'S WHY...
...NO MATTER WHAT SITUATION I'M IN, I'M ALWAYS SEARCHING FOR VICTORY.
WHETHER I HAVE TO EAT DIRT OR CHEW ON SAND...
...I SEEK OUT VICTORY WITH ALL MY BODY AND SOUL!!
VICTORY DOESN'T JUST FALL IN YOUR LAP.
THAT...
...IS SOME-THING I LEARNED ...
...AFTER COUNTLESS VICTORIES AND DEFEATS!!

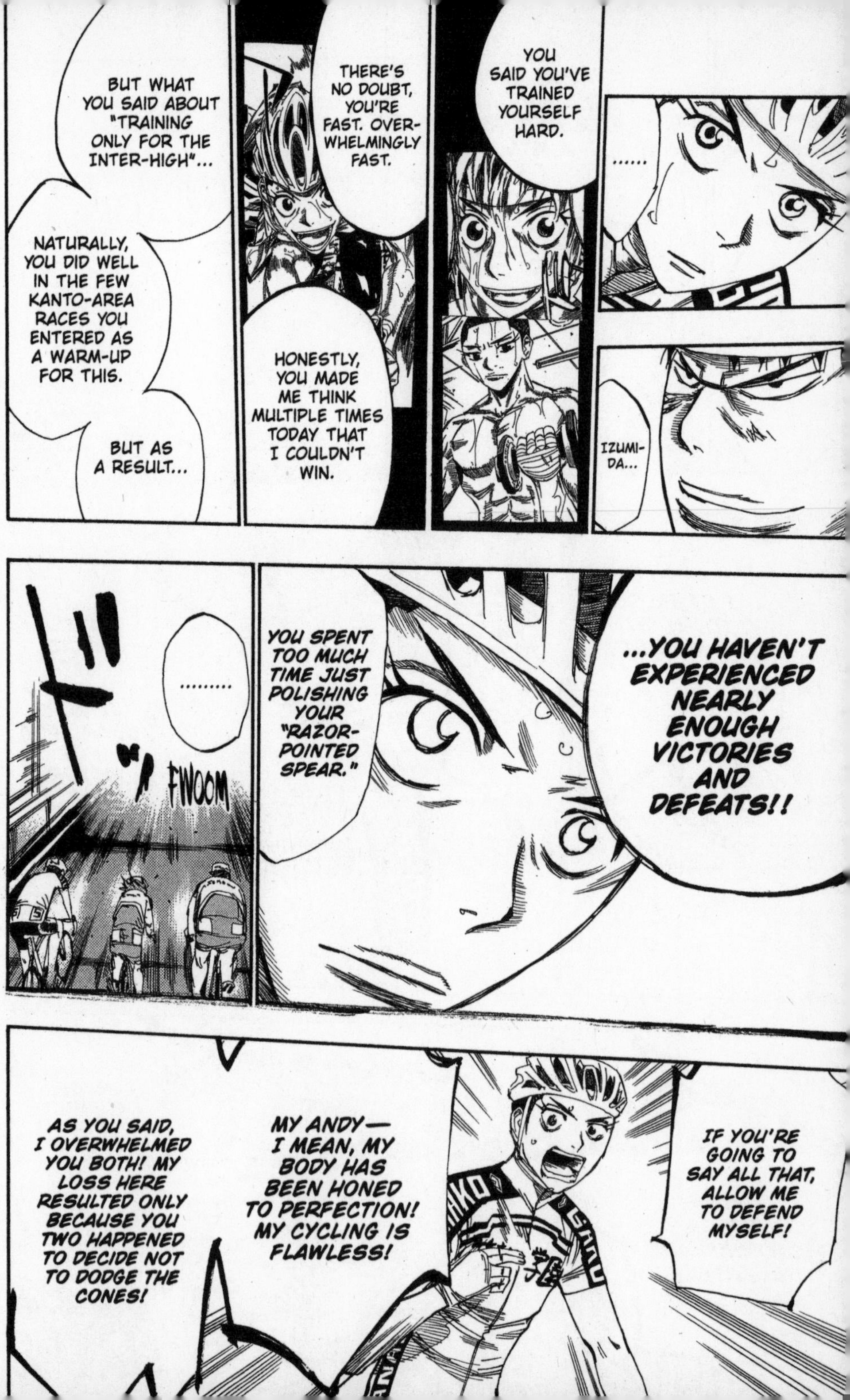
......
IZUMI-DA...
YOU SAID YOU'VE TRAINED YOURSELF HARD.
THERE'S NO DOUBT, YOU'RE FAST. OVER-WHELMINGLY FAST.
HONESTLY, YOU MADE ME THINK MULTIPLE TIMES TODAY THAT I COULDN'T WIN.
BUT WHAT YOU SAID ABOUT "TRAINING ONLY FOR THE INTER-HIGH"...
NATURALLY, YOU DID WELL IN THE FEW KANTO-AREA RACES YOU ENTERED AS A WARM-UP FOR THIS.
BUT AS A RESULT...
...YOU HAVEN'T EXPERIENCED NEARLY ENOUGH VICTORIES AND DEFEATS!!
YOU SPENT TOO MUCH TIME JUST POLISHING YOUR "RAZOR-POINTED SPEAR."
....
FWOOM
IF YOU'RE GOING TO SAY ALL THAT, ALLOW ME TO DEFEND MYSELF!
MY ANDY— I MEAN, MY BODY HAS BEEN HONED TO PERFECTION! MY CYCLING IS FLAWLESS!
AS YOU SAID, I OVERWHELMED YOU BOTH! MY LOSS HERE RESULTED ONLY BECAUSE YOU TWO HAPPENED TO DECIDE NOT TO DODGE THE CONES!

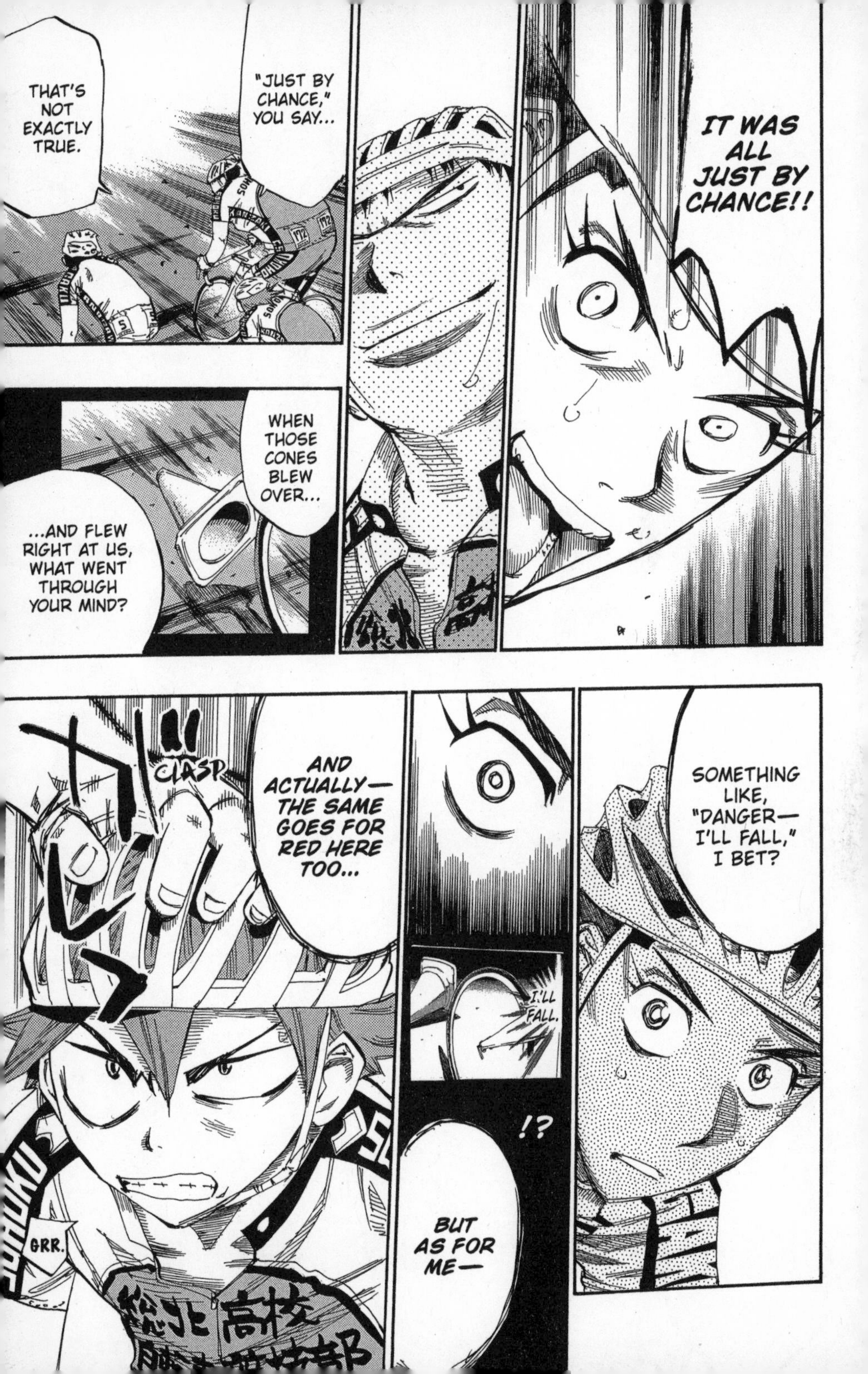
IT WAS ALL JUST BY CHANCE!!
"JUST BY CHANCE," YOU SAY...
THAT'S NOT EXACTLY TRUE.
WHEN THOSE CONES BLEW OVER...
...AND FLEW RIGHT AT US, WHAT WENT THROUGH YOUR MIND?
SOMETHING LIKE, "DANGER— I'LL FALL," I BET?
I'LL FALL.
!?
BUT AS FOR ME—
AND ACTUALLY— THE SAME GOES FOR RED HERE TOO...
CLASP
GRR.

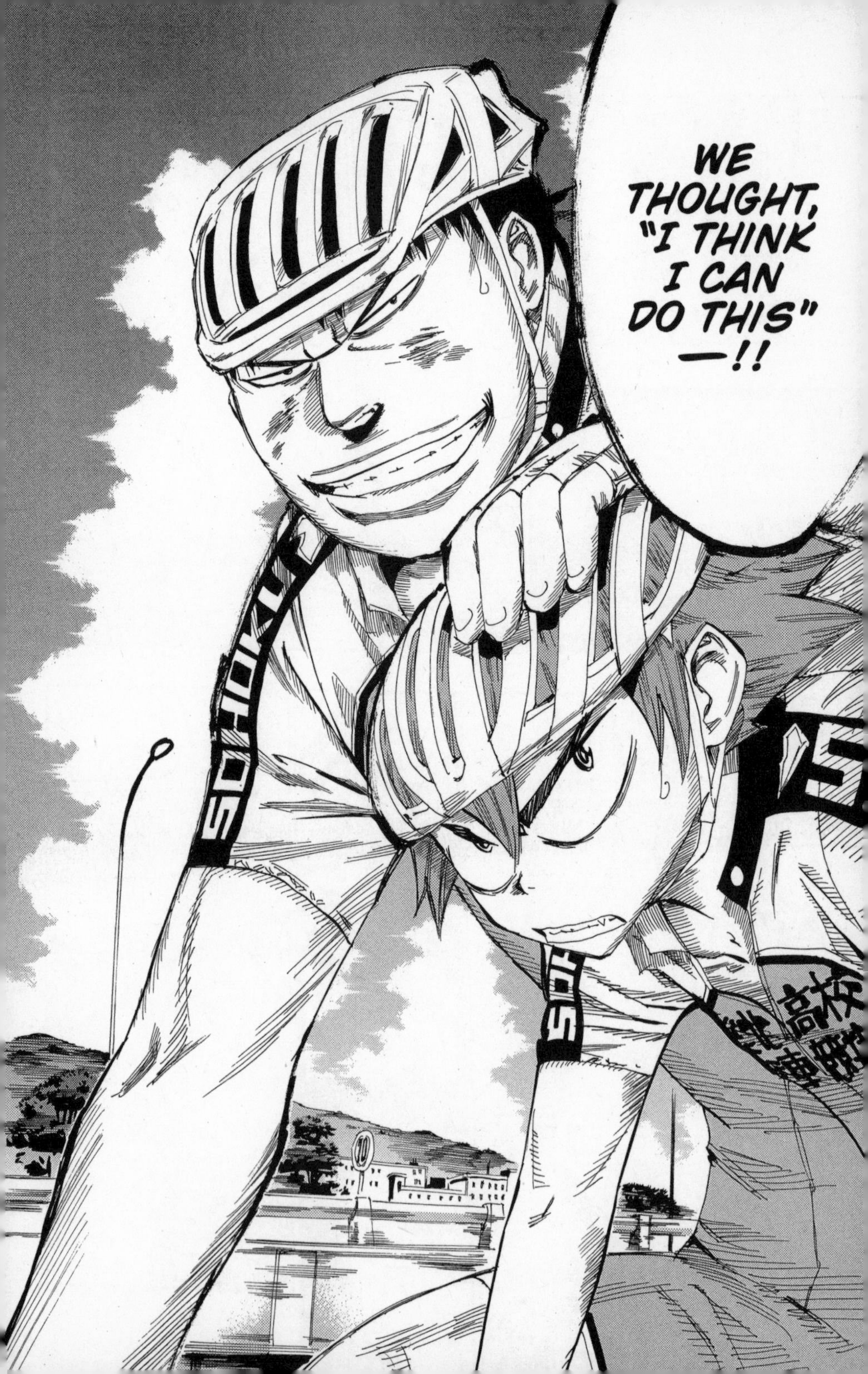
WE THOUGHT, "I THINK I CAN DO THIS"—!!

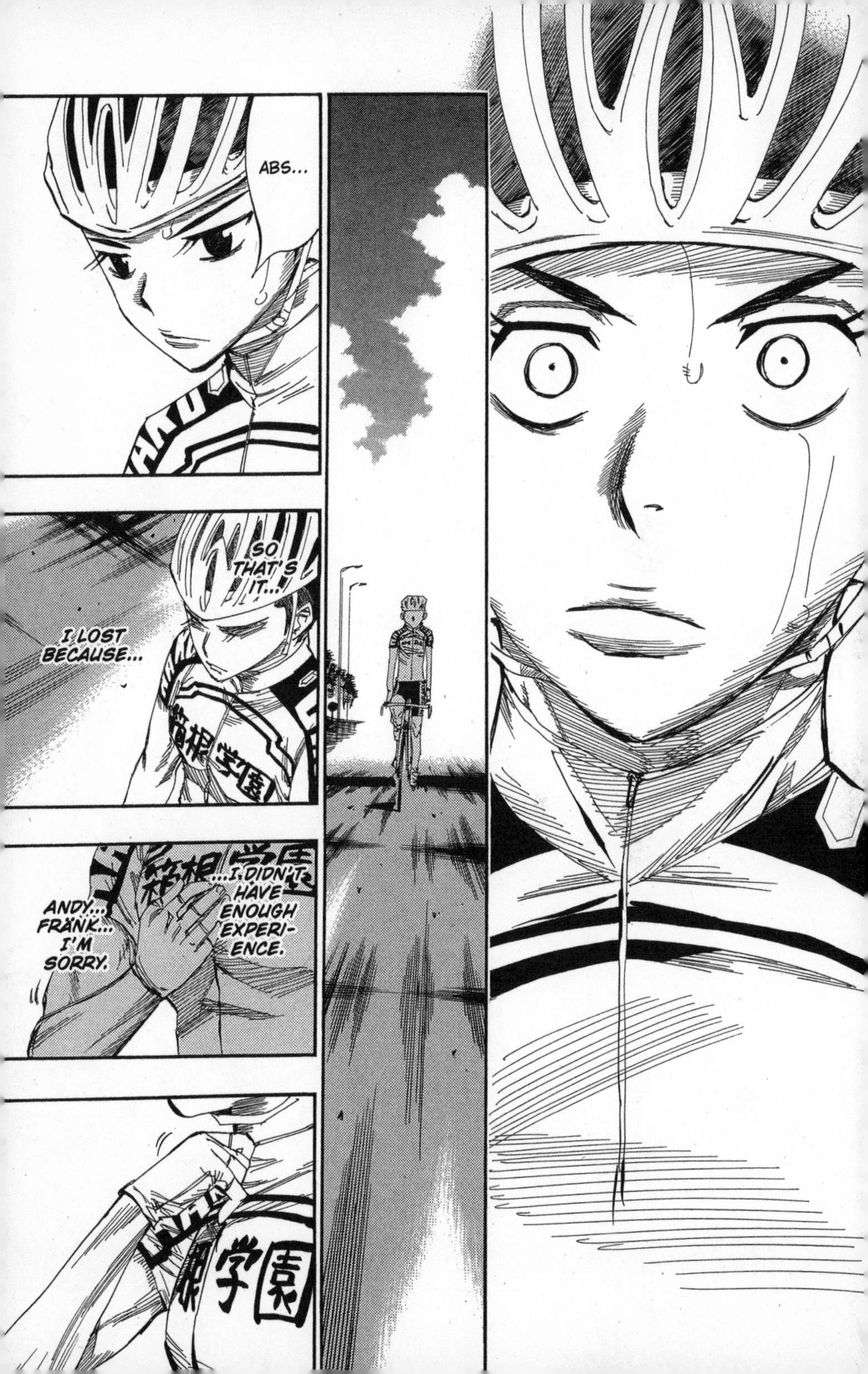
ABS...
SO THAT'S IT...
I LOST BECAUSE...
...I DIDN'T HAVE ENOUGH EXPERIENCE.
ANDY... FRÄNK... I'M SORRY.

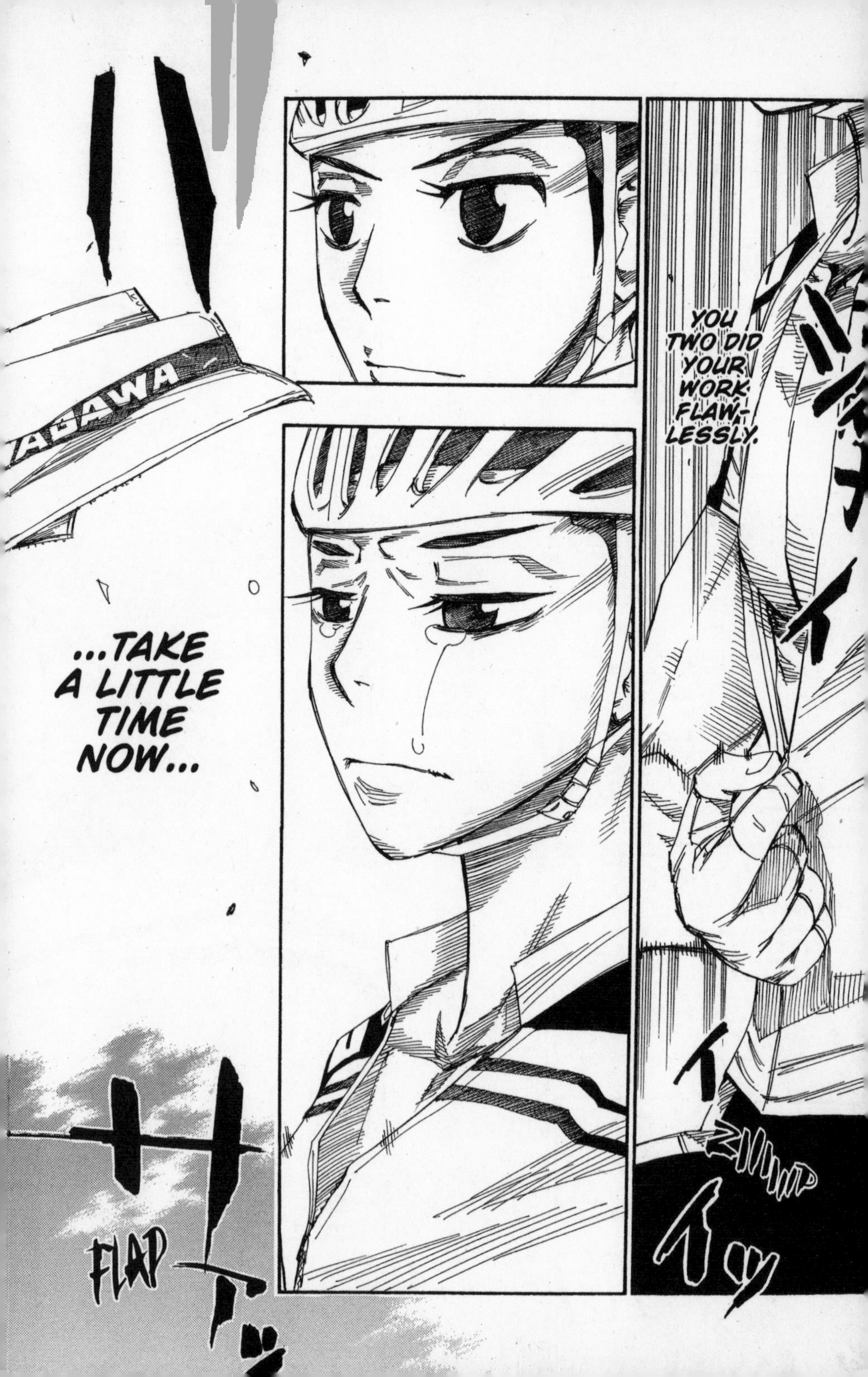
YOU TWO DID YOUR WORK FLAW-LESSLY.
ZIIIIIP
...TAKE A LITTLE TIME NOW...
FLAP

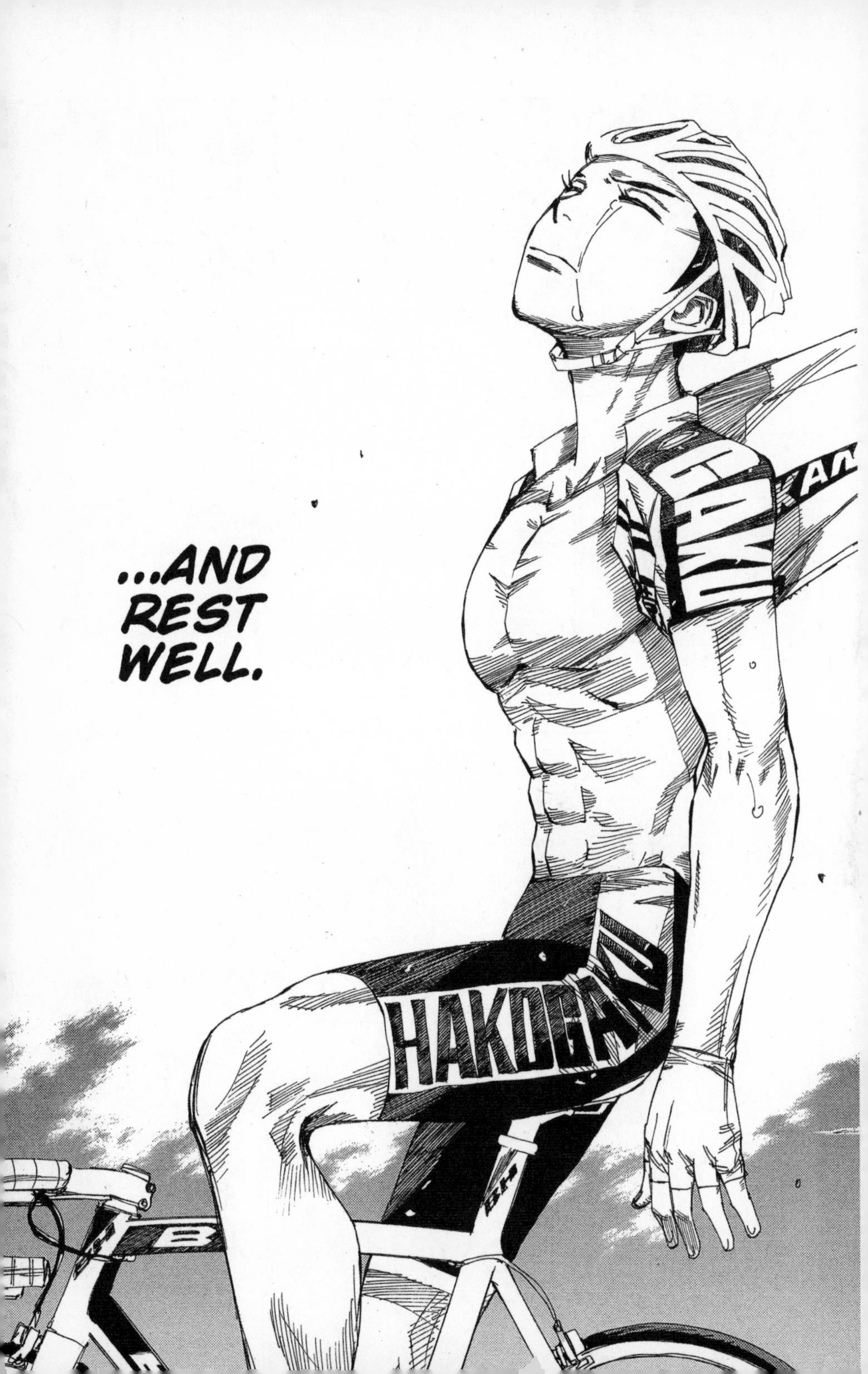
...AND REST WELL.
HAKOGAKU

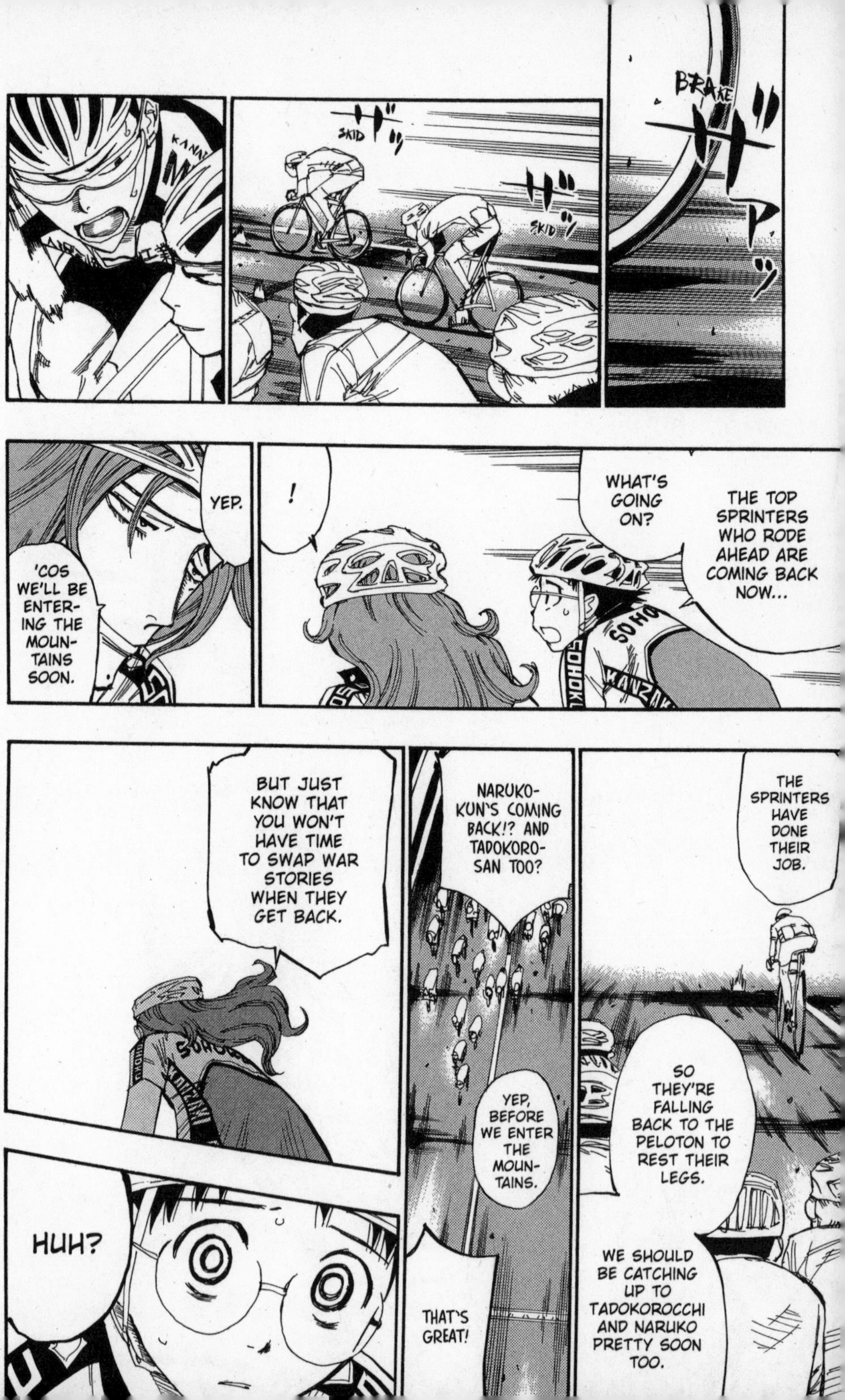
BRAKE
SKID
SKID
WHAT'S GOING ON?
THE TOP SPRINTERS WHO RODE AHEAD ARE COMING BACK NOW...
!
YEP.
'COS WE'LL BE ENTERING THE MOUNTAINS SOON.
THE SPRINTERS HAVE DONE THEIR JOB.
SO THEY'RE FALLING BACK TO THE PELOTON TO REST THEIR LEGS.
WE SHOULD BE CATCHING UP TO TADOKOROCCHI AND NARUKO PRETTY SOON TOO.
NARUKO-KUN'S COMING BACK!? AND TADOKORO-SAN TOO?
YEP, BEFORE WE ENTER THE MOUNTAINS.
THAT'S GREAT!
BUT JUST KNOW THAT YOU WON'T HAVE TIME TO SWAP WAR STORIES WHEN THEY GET BACK.
HUH?

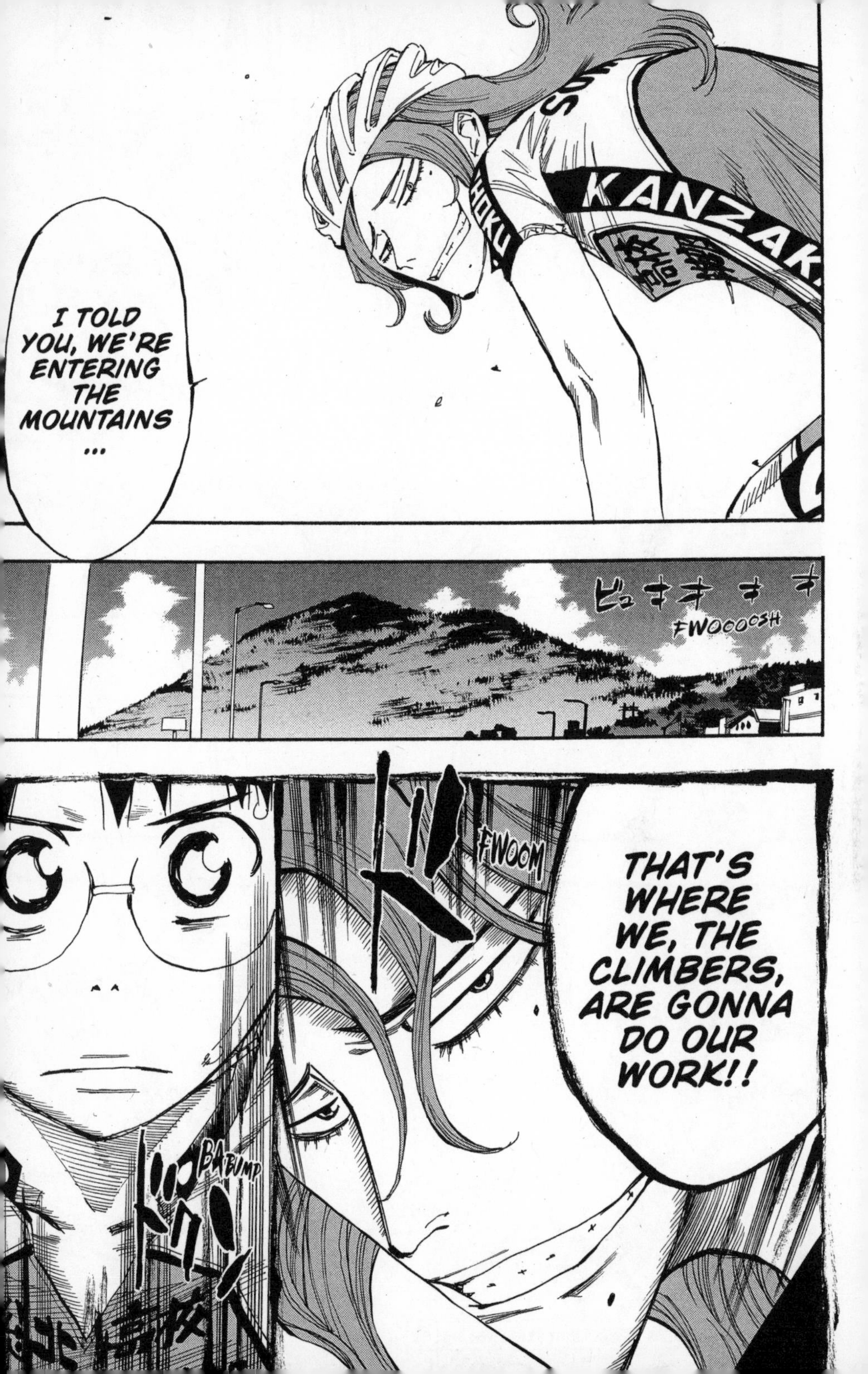
I TOLD YOU, WE'RE ENTERING THE MOUNTAINS ...
KANZAKI
FWOOOOSH
THAT'S WHERE WE, THE CLIMBERS, ARE GONNA DO OUR WORK!!
FWOOM
BA-BUMP

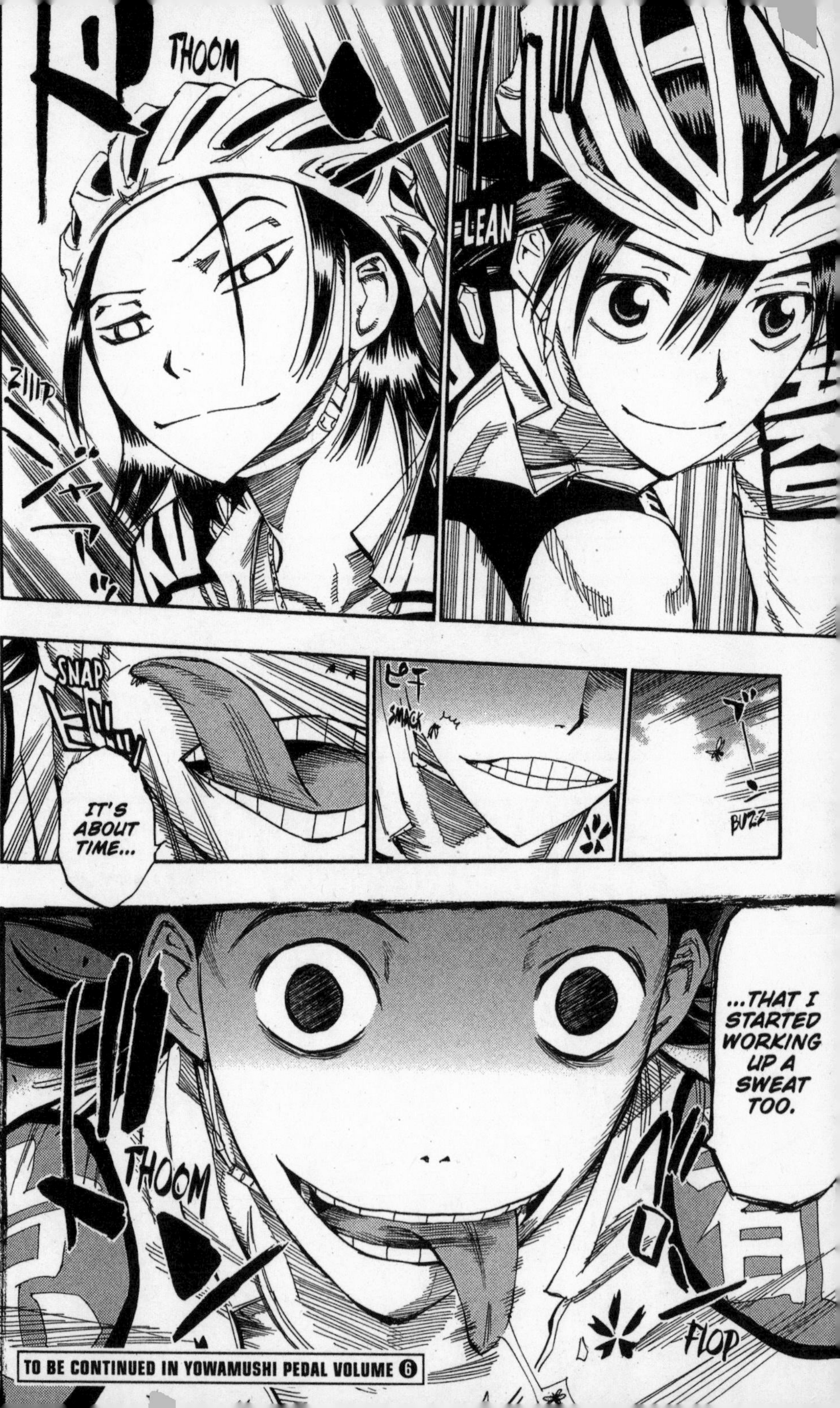
LEAN
THOOM
ZIIIP
BUZZ
SMACK
SNAP
IT'S ABOUT TIME...
...THAT I STARTED WORKING UP A SWEAT TOO.
THOOM
FLOP

TO BE CONTINUED IN YOWAMUSHI PEDAL VOLUME 6

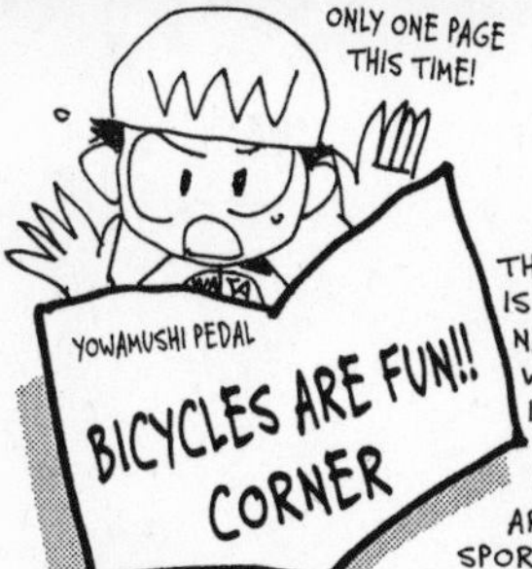
ONLY ONE PAGE THIS TIME!
YOWAMUSHI PEDAL
BICYCLES ARE FUN!! CORNER

ABOUT THE 2009 TOUR DE FRANCE

THE FIRST THING THAT COMES TO MIND WHEN SOMEONE SAYS "BICYCLE RACE" IS PROBABLY THE TOUR DE FRANCE. I'M SURE ALL OF YOU HAVE HEARD THE NAME, RIGHT? IN JAPANESE, WE PRONOUNCE IT "TSUURU," BUT IN ENGLISH, IT WOULD BE THE WORD "TOUR," AS IN "A JOURNEY." BUT TO CUT TO THE CHASE, IT'S BASICALLY A CIRCUIT AROUND FRANCE COMPLETED ENTIRELY ON BICYCLE, AND HAS BEEN GOING ON FOR ABOUT A HUNDRED YEARS NOW. IT APPARENTLY STARTED OUT WITH THE IDEA OF "WHO CAN COMPLETE A BICYCLE TOUR AROUND FRANCE THE FASTEST?" AND IS NOW THE MOST BRUTAL AND FAMOUS SPORTING EVENT IN THE WORLD. (AND JUST IMAGINE—A HUNDRED YEARS AGO, THEY DIDN'T HAVE THE BENEFIT OF SAG [SUPPORT AND GEAR] WAGONS TO SUPPLY MECHANICAL ASSISTANCE IF YOU BROKE DOWN, SO YOU WERE REALLY ON YOUR OWN OUT THERE!) (INCIDENTALLY, BICYCLES BACK THEN DIDN'T HAVE GEAR-SHIFTING CAPABILITIES YET...YIKES!!)

THAT'S THE KIND OF RICHLY HISTORIED SPORT CYCLING IS. THE TOUR DE FRANCE IS STILL EXTREMELY POPULAR, AND EVEN IF YOU'VE TRAINED PRETTY HARD, YOU CAN'T JUST GO AND ENTER IT. IN THE ENTIRE WORLD, ONLY TWENTY TEAMS OF NINE PEOPLE + A FEW WILDCARD TEAMS—A TOTAL OF JUST 200 PEOPLE—CAN PARTICIPATE EACH YEAR!! IT'S AN EVENT PACKED FULL OF THE TOP CYCLISTS IN THE WORLD—A RACE ANY PROFESSIONAL CYCLIST WOULD YEARN TO ENTER AT LEAST ONCE IN THEIR LIVES!!

AND IN **2009**, TEAM SKIL-SHIMANO'S **FUMIYUKI BEPPU** AND TEAM BBOX BOUYGUES TELECOM'S **YUKIYA ARASHIRO...**

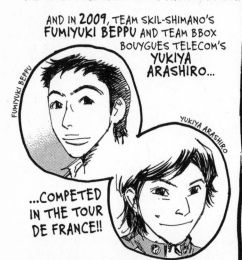

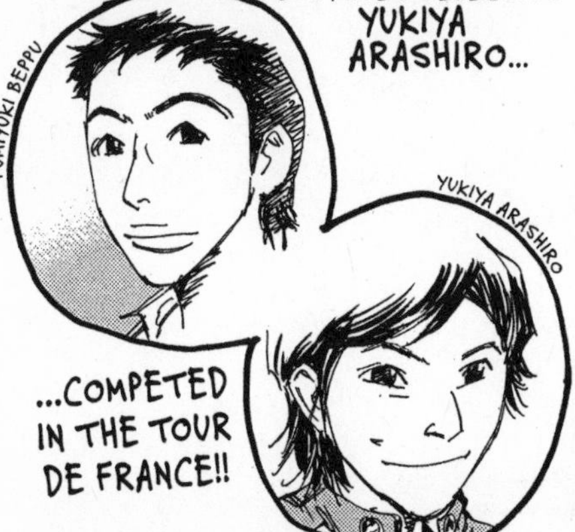
FUMIYUKI BEPPU
YUKIYA ARASHIRO

...COMPETED IN THE TOUR DE FRANCE!!

SIMPLY COMPETING IN THE TOUR IS DIFFICULT, AND MANY WONDERED IF THEY WOULD BE ABLE TO COMPLETE THE COURSE. DURING STAGE 2 (EACH DAY OF THE TOUR IS CALLED "STAGE" + THE DAY NUMBER), ARASHIRO-SAN ACTUALLY FINISHED IN 5TH PLACE!! IN STAGE 3 AND STAGE 19, BEPPU-SAN FINISHED IN 8TH AND 7TH PLACE, RESPECTIVELY—AND IN THE FINAL STAGE, HE WAS AWARDED THE COMBATIVITY AWARD!! TALK ABOUT AN IMPRESSIVE SET OF RESULTS TO LEAVE BEHIND!!

FOR ME (AND ALL OF JAPAN), IT WAS THRILLING TO SEE JAPANESE ATHLETES PARTICIPATING IN AN EVENT LIKE THAT AND GETTING WRITTEN ABOUT IN EUROPEAN NEWSPAPERS, AND FEATURED ON EUROPEAN TV!! AND OF COURSE, BOTH BEPPU-SAN AND ARASHIRO-SAN COMPLETED THE TOUR SUCCESSFULLY!!

IT WAS ACTUALLY THE FIRST TIME IN HISTORY THAT A JAPANESE CYCLIST MADE IT ALL THE WAY TO PARIS IN THE TOUR...!! ARASHIRO-SAN!! BEPPU-SAN!! **THANK YOU SO MUCH** FOR ACCOMPLISHING THIS DEEPLY EMOTIONAL FEAT!! I REALLY LOOK FORWARD TO SEEING WHAT YOU GO ON TO ACCOMPLISH IN THE FUTURE.

T O U R

INCIDENTALLY, THE FULL COURSE IS RACED OVER A 23-DAY PERIOD (21 STAGES WITH TWO REST DAYS INTERSPERSED). THE COURSE CHANGES EVERY YEAR. THIS MEANS THERE ARE BIDDING WARS TO HAVE THE TOUR PASS THROUGH VARIOUS CITIES EVERY YEAR TOO!

IT TAKES PLACE IN JULY ANNUALLY.

SINCE IT TAKES PLACE DURING SUMMER VACATION, LOTS OF PEOPLE COME TO WATCH THE TOUR. EVERY SPECTATOR SEEMS TO BE WATCHING THE RACE WITH A BEER OR GLASS OF WINE IN THEIR HAND, SO IT MAKES FOR A VERY LIVELY ATMOSPHERE. IT'S LIKE A SUPER-LONG FESTIVAL!

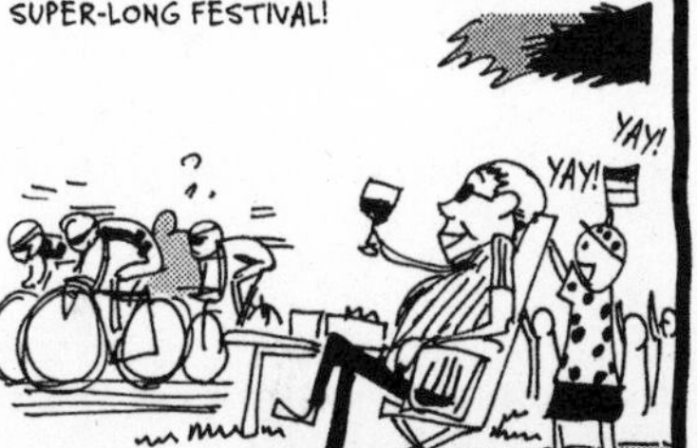
YAY!
YAY!

THE CYCLISTS RIDE A TOTAL OF 3,500KM (WHICH WOULD BE LIKE GOING FROM AOMORI TO TOKYO THEN ACROSS TO YAMAGUCHI AND BACK!) DURING A FLAT STAGE, THE CYCLISTS RIDE OVER 120KM IN A SINGLE DAY, SO FIRST AND FOREMOST, YOU NEED TO BE IN REALLY GOOD SHAPE OR YOU'LL END UP HAVING TO WITHDRAW PARTWAY THROUGH THE RACE (QUITE A FEW CYCLISTS DROP OUT EVERY YEAR). IT'S ACTUALLY PRETTY TOUGH MAKING IT THROUGH THE TWENTY-THREE-DAY RACE AND CROSSING THE FINISH LINE IN PARIS. (THE TOUR ALWAYS ENDS IN PARIS, BY THE WAY.) JUST COMPLETING THE TOUR IS QUITE AN ACHIEVEMENT.

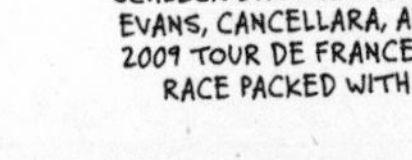

THE FINISH LINE IS ALWAYS ON THE CHAMPS-ÉLYSÉES.

THE EXCITING SUMMER OF THE 2009 TOUR DE FRANCE!

(IT REALLY WAS!)

← CONTADOR, THE LEGENDARY LANCE ARMSTRONG'S RETURN TO RACING, THE SCHLECK BROTHERS ANDY AND FRÄNK, EVANS, CANCELLARA, AND SO ON. THE 2009 TOUR DE FRANCE WAS REALLY A RACE PACKED WITH ALL-STARS.

Translation Notes

Common Honorifics
-*san*: The Japanese equivalent of Mr./Mrs./Miss. If a situation calls for politeness, this is the fail-safe honorific.
-*kun*: Used most often when referring to boys, this indicates affection or familiarity. Occasionally used by older men among their peers, but it may also be used by anyone referring to a person of lower standing.
-*chan*: An affectionate honorific indicating familiarity used mostly in reference to girls; also used in reference to cute persons or animals of either gender.
-*senpai*: A suffix used to address upperclassmen or more experienced co-workers
no honorific: Indicates familiarity or closeness; if used without permission or reason, addressing someone in this manner would constitute an insult.

A kilometer is approximately .6 of a mile.

PAGE 9
Hakogaku: This phrase, present on all Hakone Academy uniforms, is a shortened version of the school's name in Japanese (*Hakone Gakuen*).

PAGE 13
Hakone: A town located in a mountainous area of Kanagawa Prefecture, it's popular among tourists for its scenic views and hot springs.

Peloton: A cycling term for the "pack," or the main group of riders in a race.

PAGE 14
Shimane: A prefecture in the Chuugoku region of Japan; it has no relation to China, which is also called *Chuugoku* in Japanese. Shimane is located along the sea of Japan, and is home to the country's oldest shrine, Iwami Ginzan.

PAGE 57
Uphill roads: *Sakamichi* means "hilly road."

PAGE 61
Kyoto: Former capital of Japan located in the Kansai region. It's known for its plethora of traditional Japanese architecture, having come out of World War II relatively unscathed.

PAGE 68
Wussyzumi: In the Japanese version, Midousuji calls Imaizumi "Yowaizumi," playing off of the Japanese word for weak (*yowai*).

PAGE 77
Naive-zumi: This time, in the Japanese version, Midousuji refers to Imaizumi as "Amaizumi." *Amai* means soft or naive.

PAGE 79
Goofs: Midousuji uses the term *zaku* in the Japanese version, which means "assorted vegetables for *sukiyaki* hot pot." It refers to the rest of Kyoto-Fushimi being there to serve Midousuji.

PAGE 124
Tour: The Tour de France, the most famous bicycle racing event in the world.

Giro: The Giro d'Italia. Located in Italy, it is one of the three most prestigious, largest bicycle racing events in the world along with the Tour de France and the Velta a España.

PAGE 163
Kanazawa: Located in the Hokuriku region in the northwestern part of Japan's main island. Like Kyoto, Kanazawa preserved most of its traditional architecture by avoiding heavy damage during World War II.

PAGE 206
Chiba: A prefecture in the Kantou region of Japan. Chiba has both long stretches of mountains and large areas of flat plains, and is known for having mild summers and winters.

PAGE 371
Fumiyuki Beppu: A Japanese professional bicycle racer who was on Team Skil Shimano from 2008–2009. Since 2014, he has been on Team Trek Factory Racing.

Team Skil Shimano: A professional German cycling team. Its name has changed numerous times. As of 2017, it is known as Team Sunweb.

Yukiya Arashiro: Two-time winner of the Japanese National Road Race Championships. Arashiro was on Team BBox Bouygues Telecom from 2009–2015, and as of 2017 is on Team Bahrain-Merida.

Team BBox Bouygues Telecom: Originally named Bonjour, this particular name was used from 2009–2010. The team is currently known as Team Direct Énergie.

Contador: Alberto Contador, a Spanish professional cyclist who was the fifth person to ever win cycling's triple crown—the Tour de France (2007), the Giro d'Italia (2008), and the Velta a España (2008).

Andy and Fränk Schleck: Brothers and former professional cyclists from Luxembourg.

Evans: Cadel Evans, an Australian former professional cyclist and winner of the 2011 Tour de France.

Cancellara: Fabian Cancellara, a former Swiss road bicycle racer who won the opening stage of the Tour de France five times.

YOWAMUSHI PEDAL VOLUME 6

Read on for a sneak
peek of Volume 6,
available August 2017!

RIDE.87 HAKONE

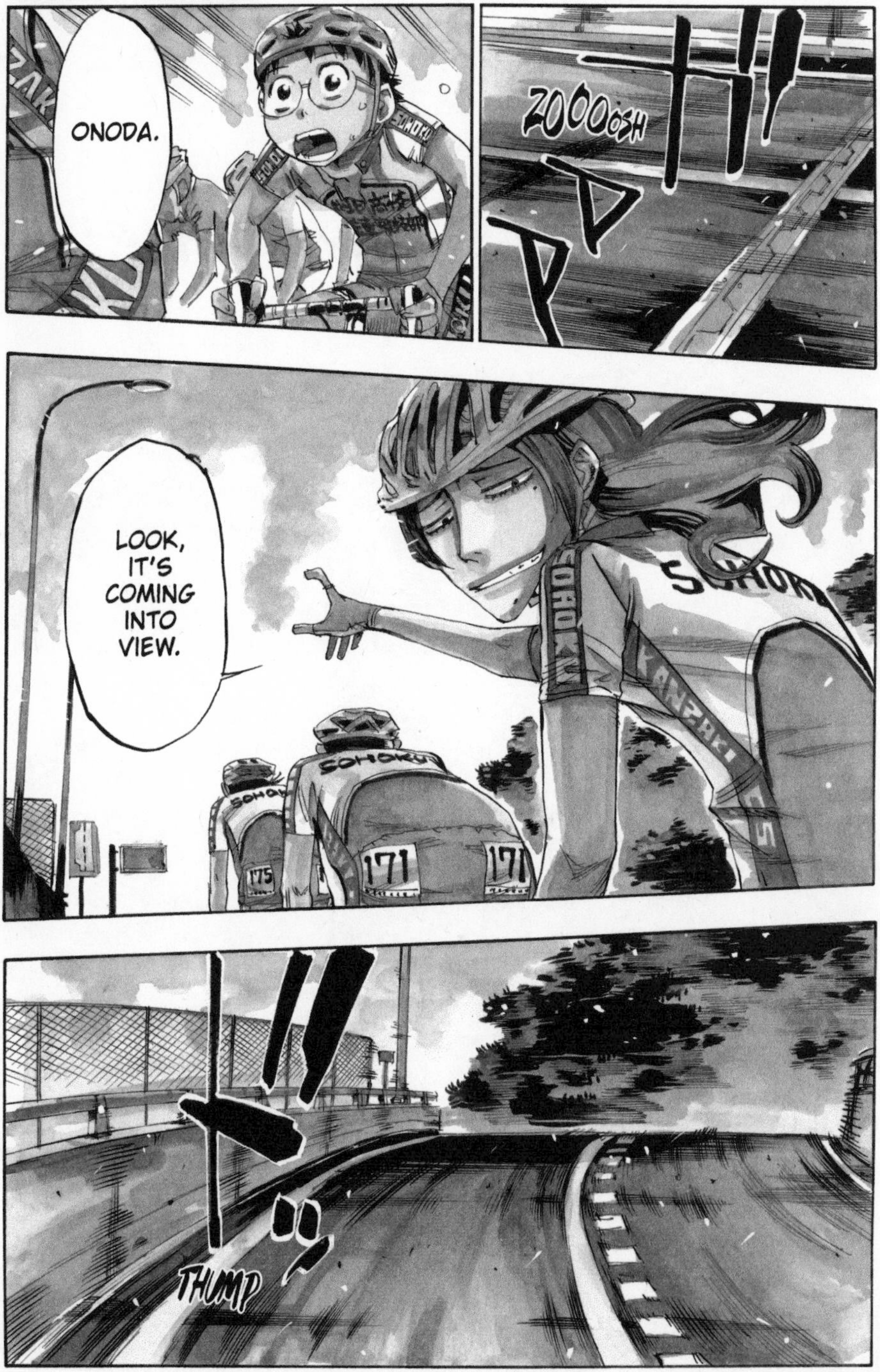
ZOOOOSH
ONODA.
LOOK, IT'S COMING INTO VIEW.
THUMP

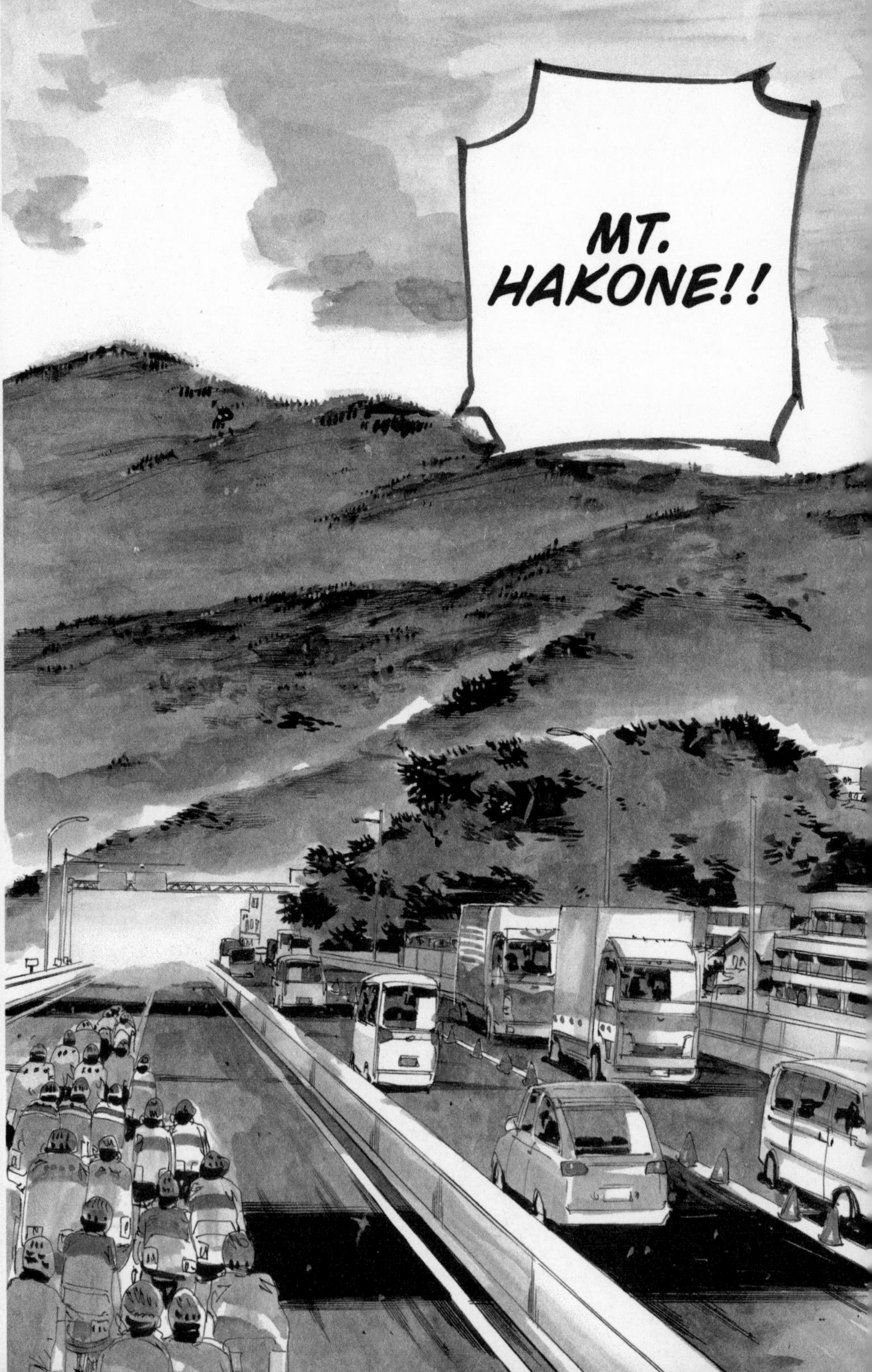
MT. HAKONE!!

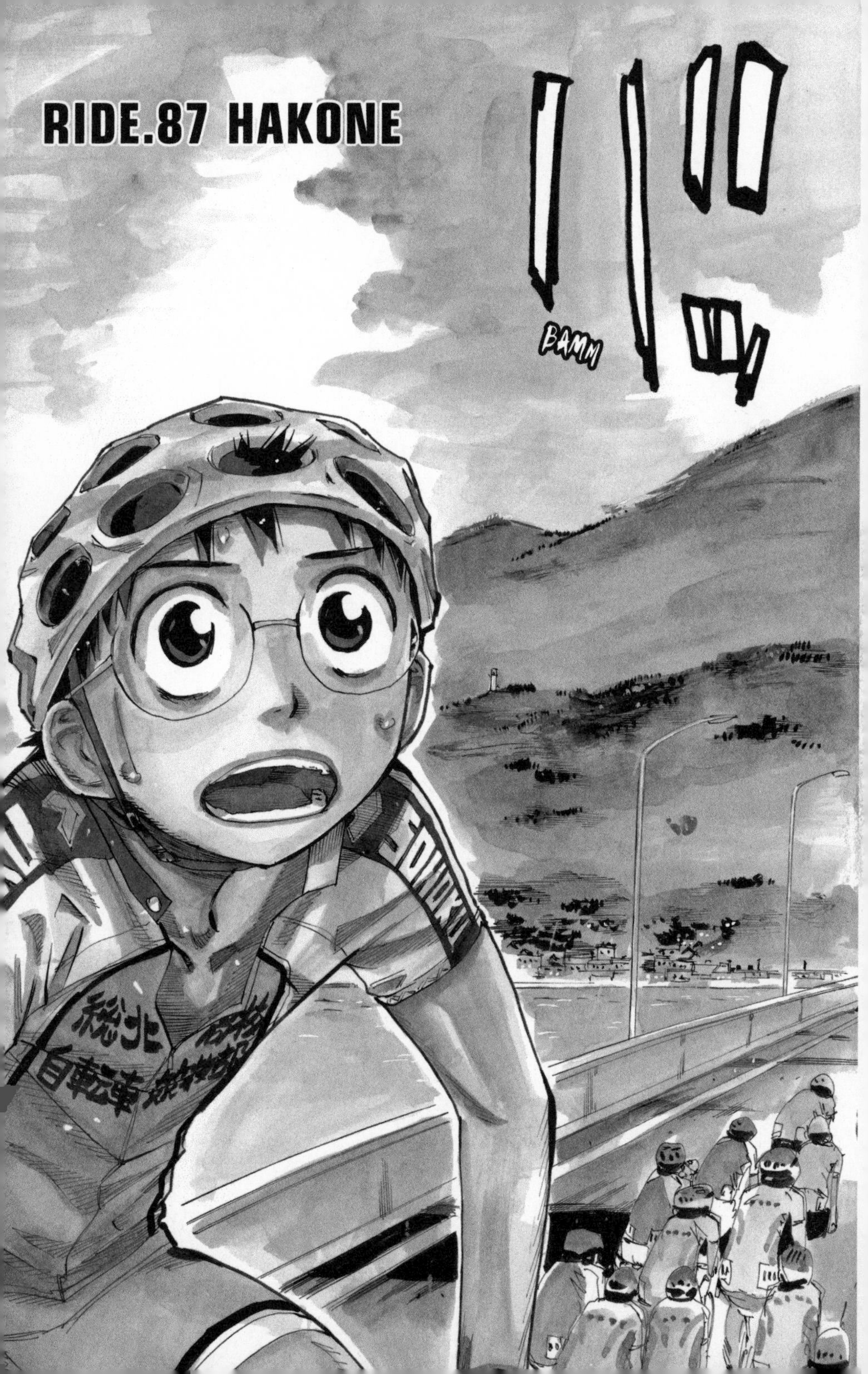
RIDE.87 HAKONE
BAMM

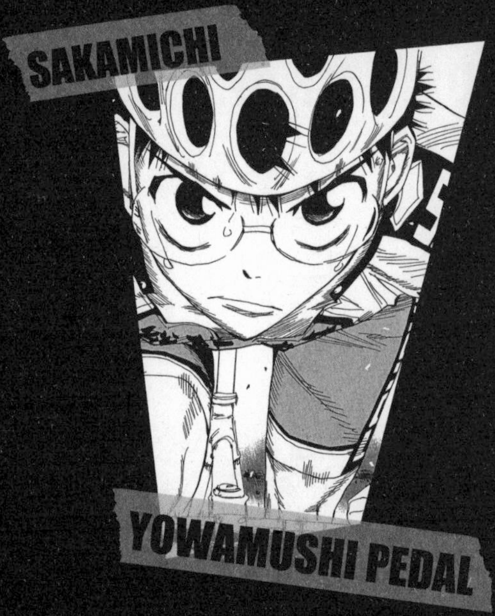
SAKAMICHI
YOWAMUSHI PEDAL

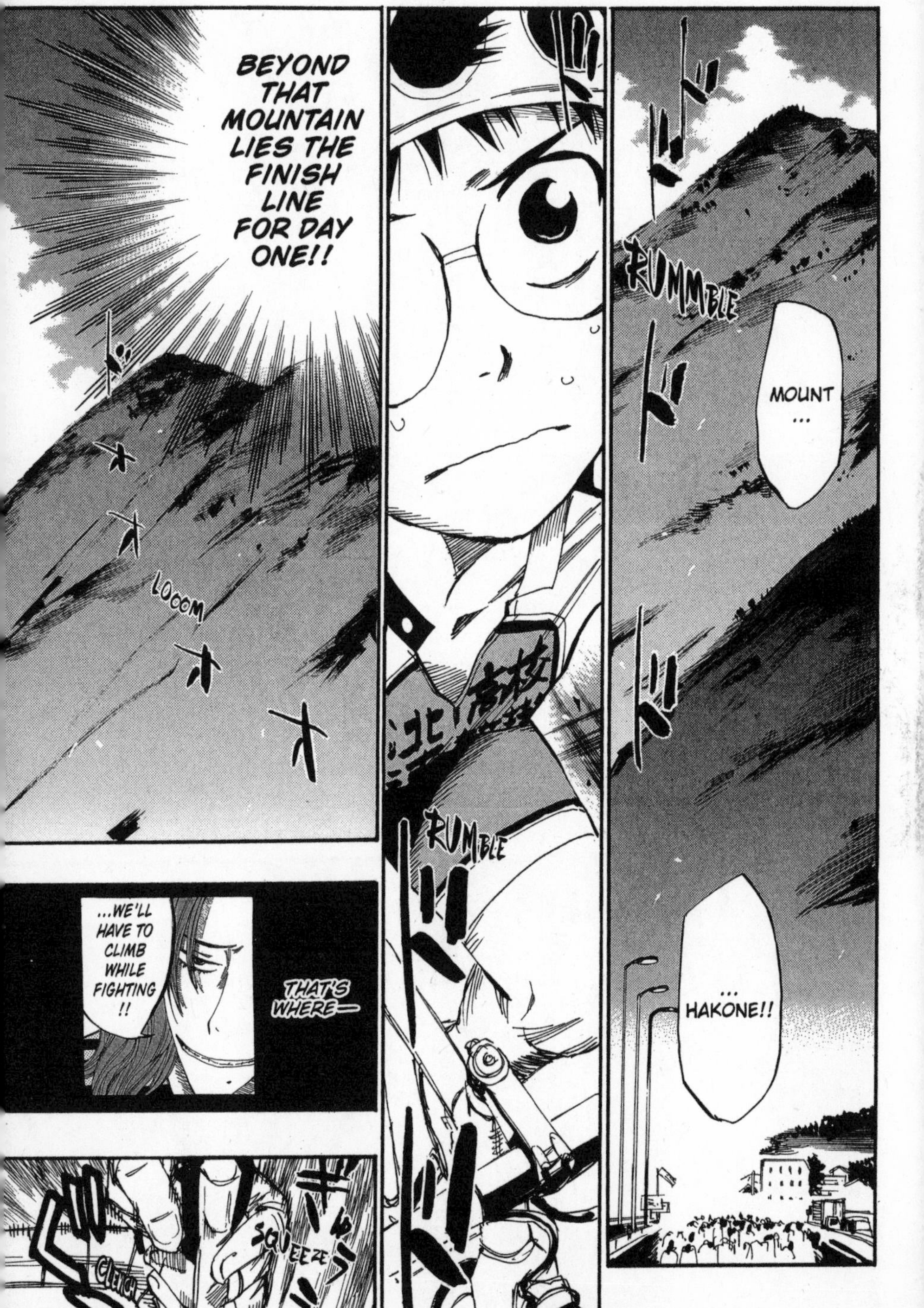
RUMMMBLE
MOUNT ...
... HAKONE!!
RUMBLE
BEYOND THAT MOUNTAIN LIES THE FINISH LINE FOR DAY ONE!!
LOOOM
THAT'S WHERE—
...WE'LL HAVE TO CLIMB WHILE FIGHTING!!
SQUEEZE
CLENCH

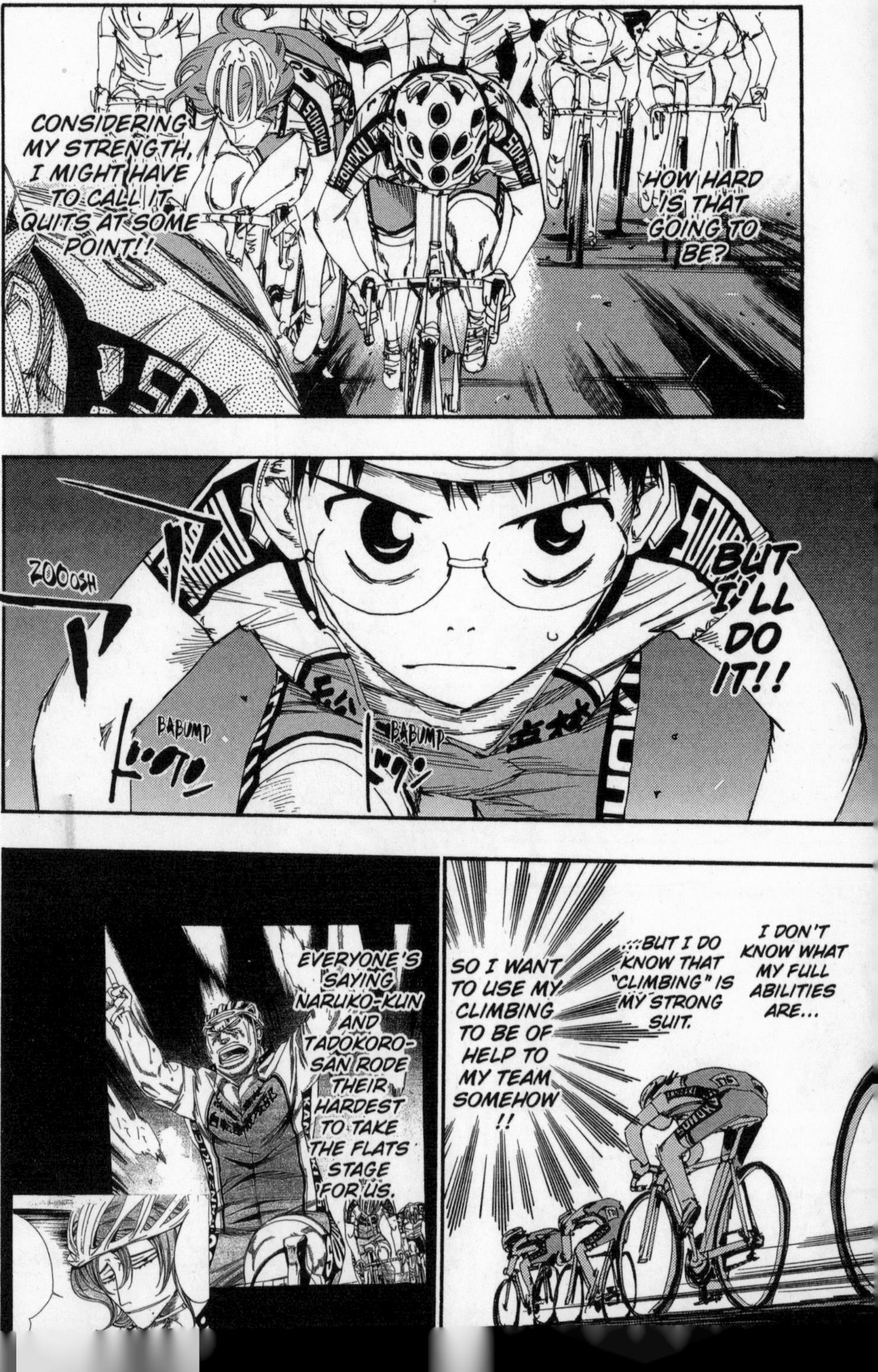

HOW HARD IS THAT GOING TO BE?
CONSIDERING MY STRENGTH, I MIGHT HAVE TO CALL IT QUITS AT SOME POINT!!
BUT I'LL DO IT!!
BABUMP
ZOOOSH
BABUMP
I DON'T KNOW WHAT MY FULL ABILITIES ARE...
...BUT I DO KNOW THAT "CLIMBING" IS MY STRONG SUIT.
SO I WANT TO USE MY CLIMBING TO BE OF HELP TO MY TEAM SOMEHOW!!
EVERYONE'S SAYING NARUKO-KUN AND TADOKORO-SAN RODE THEIR HARDEST TO TAKE THE FLATS STAGE FOR US.

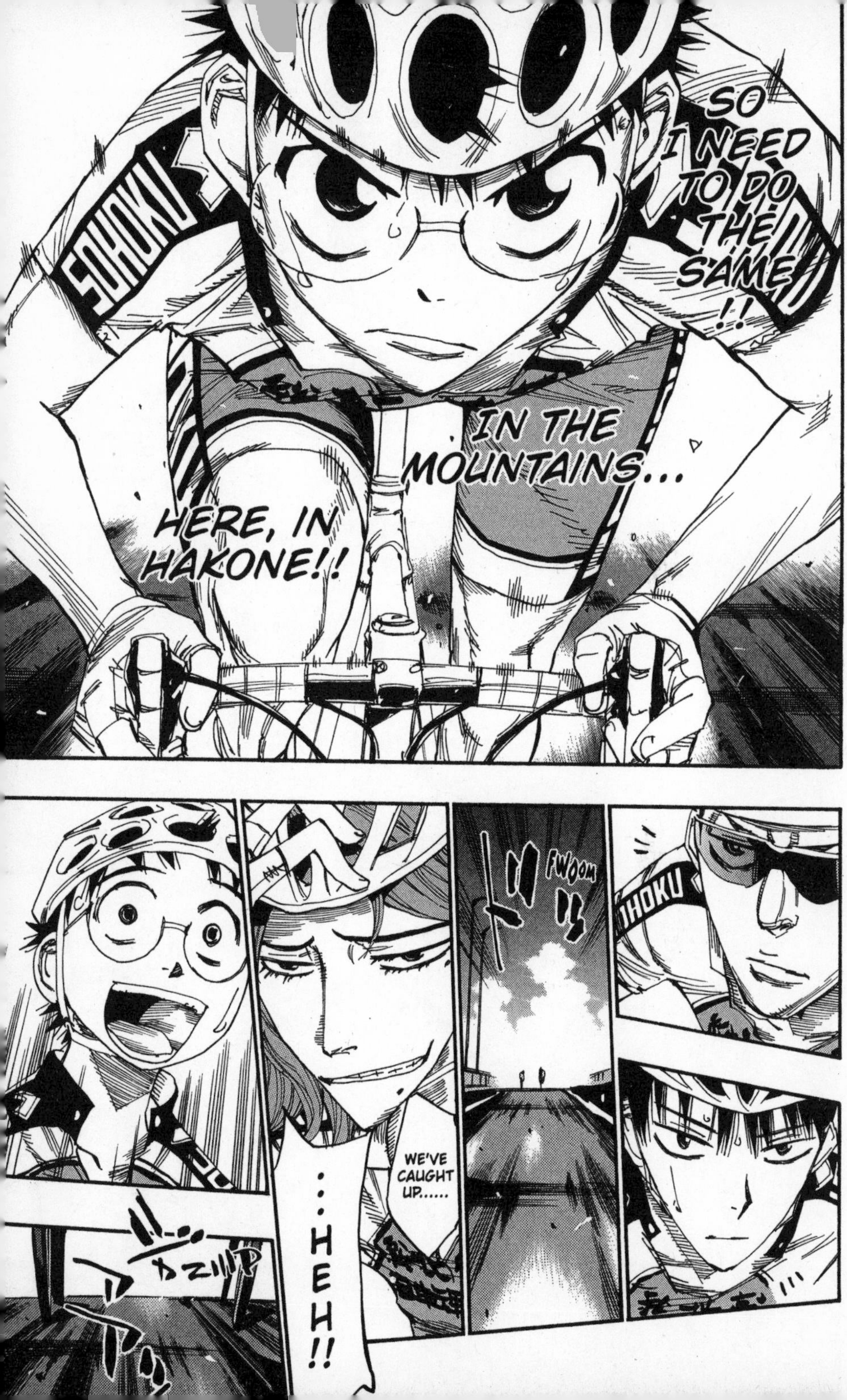
SO I NEED TO DO THE SAME!!
IN THE MOUNTAINS...
HERE, IN HAKONE!!
FWOOM
WE'VE CAUGHT UP......
...HEH!!
DZIIIP

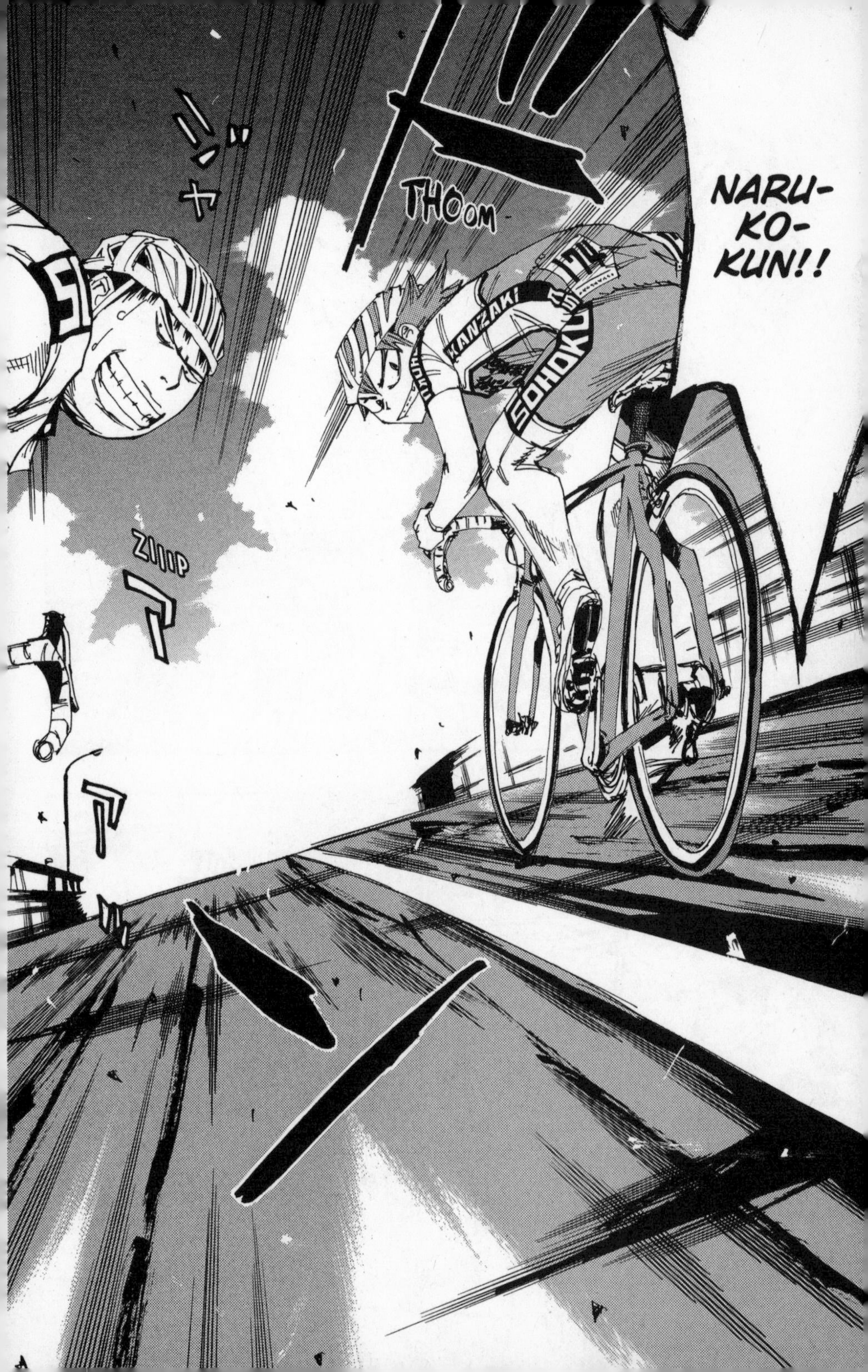
NARU-KO-KUN!!
THOOM
ZIIIP

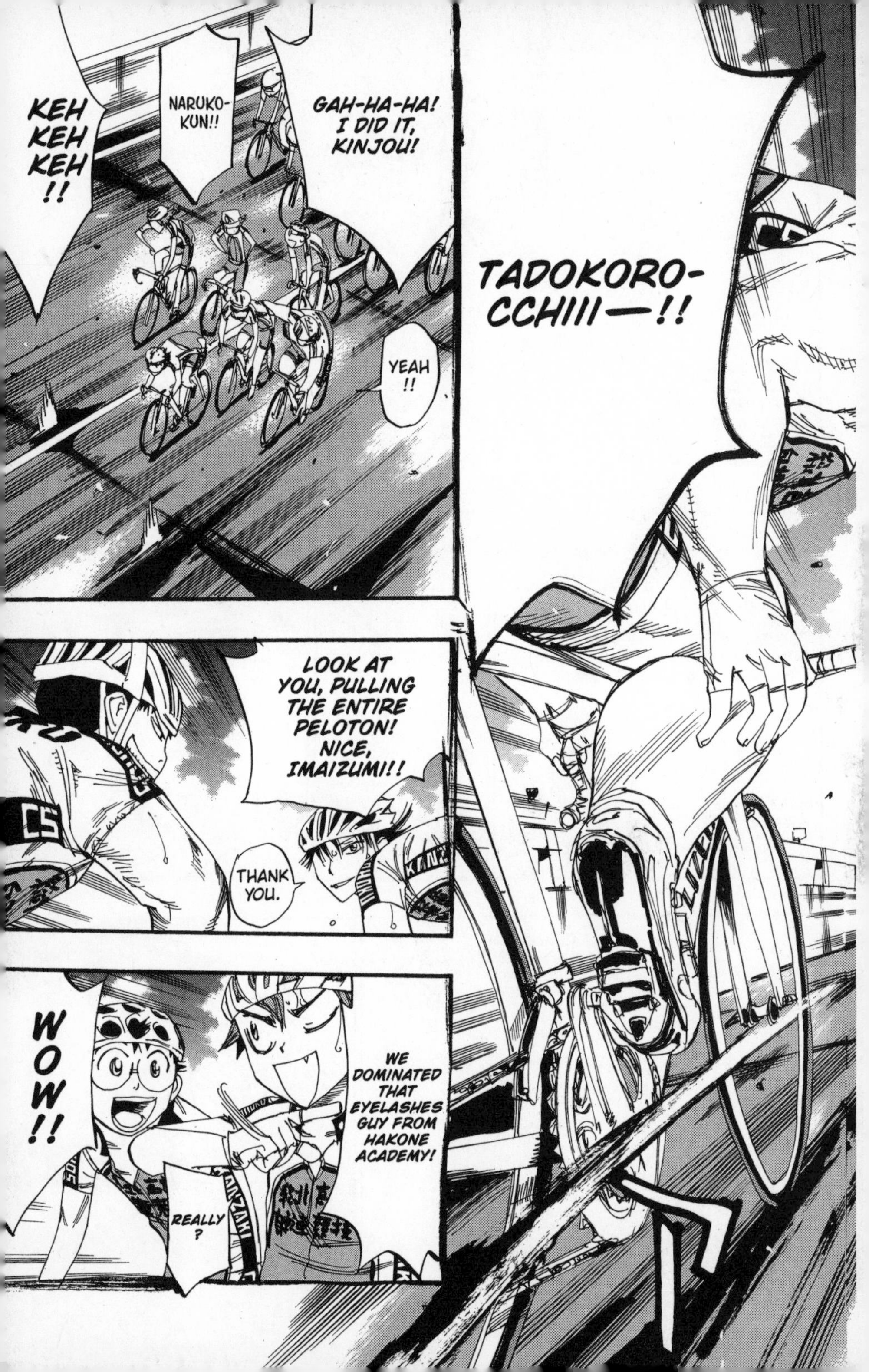
TADOKORO-CCHIII—!!
GAH-HA-HA! I DID IT, KINJOU!
NARUKO-KUN!!
KEH KEH KEH!!
YEAH!!
LOOK AT YOU, PULLING THE ENTIRE PELOTON! NICE, IMAIZUMI!!
THANK YOU.
WE DOMINATED THAT EYELASHES GUY FROM HAKONE ACADEMY!
WOW!!
REALLY?

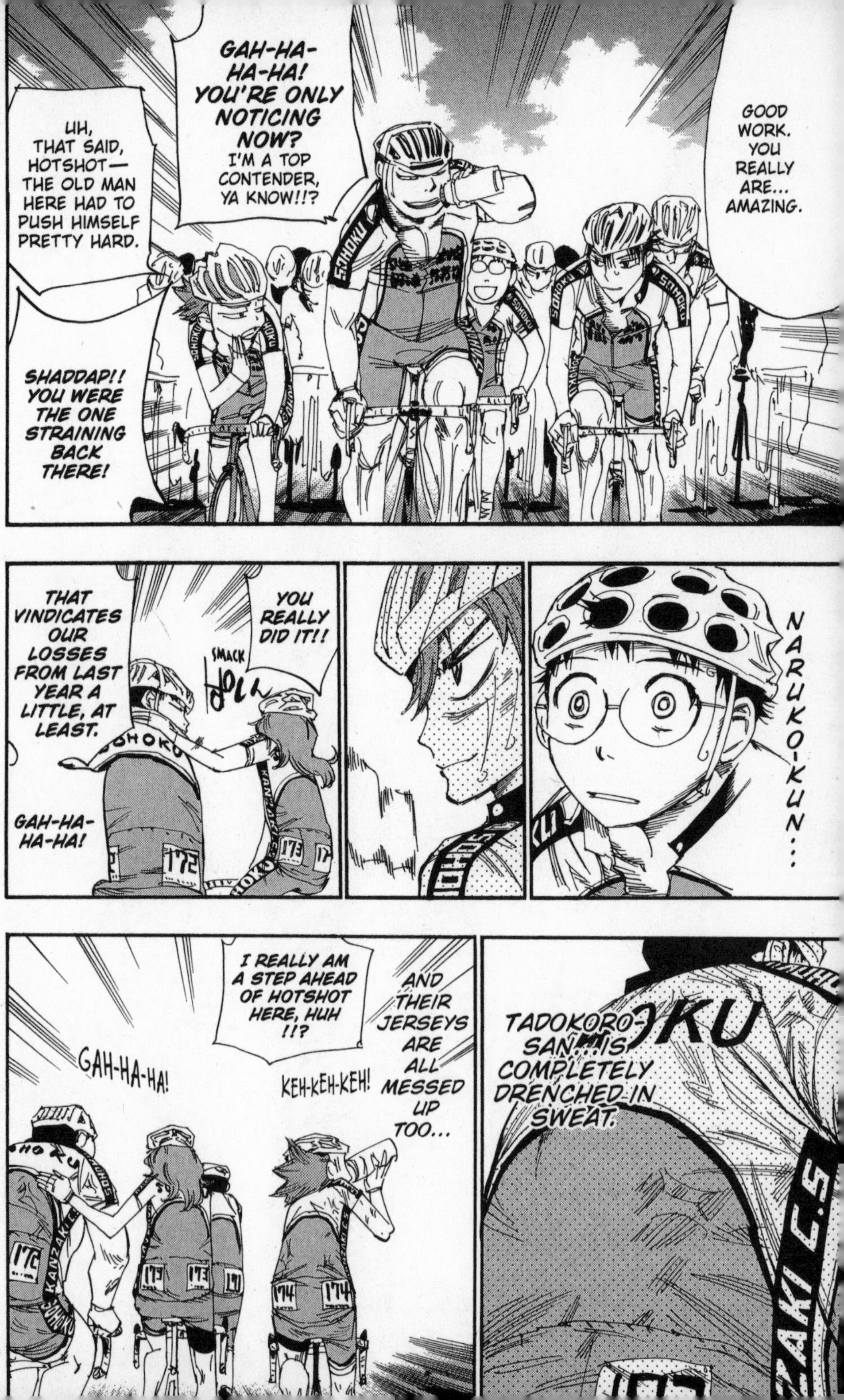
GOOD WORK. YOU REALLY ARE... AMAZING.
GAH-HA-HA-HA! YOU'RE ONLY NOTICING NOW? I'M A TOP CONTENDER, YA KNOW!!?
UH, THAT SAID, HOTSHOT— THE OLD MAN HERE HAD TO PUSH HIMSELF PRETTY HARD.
SHADDAP!! YOU WERE THE ONE STRAINING BACK THERE!
NARUKO-KUN...
YOU REALLY DID IT!!
SMACK
THAT VINDICATES OUR LOSSES FROM LAST YEAR A LITTLE, AT LEAST.
GAH-HA-HA-HA!
TADOKORO-SAN... IS COMPLETELY DRENCHED IN SWEAT.
AND THEIR JERSEYS ARE ALL MESSED UP TOO...
I REALLY AM A STEP AHEAD OF HOTSHOT HERE, HUH!!?
KEH-KEH-KEH!
GAH-HA-HA!

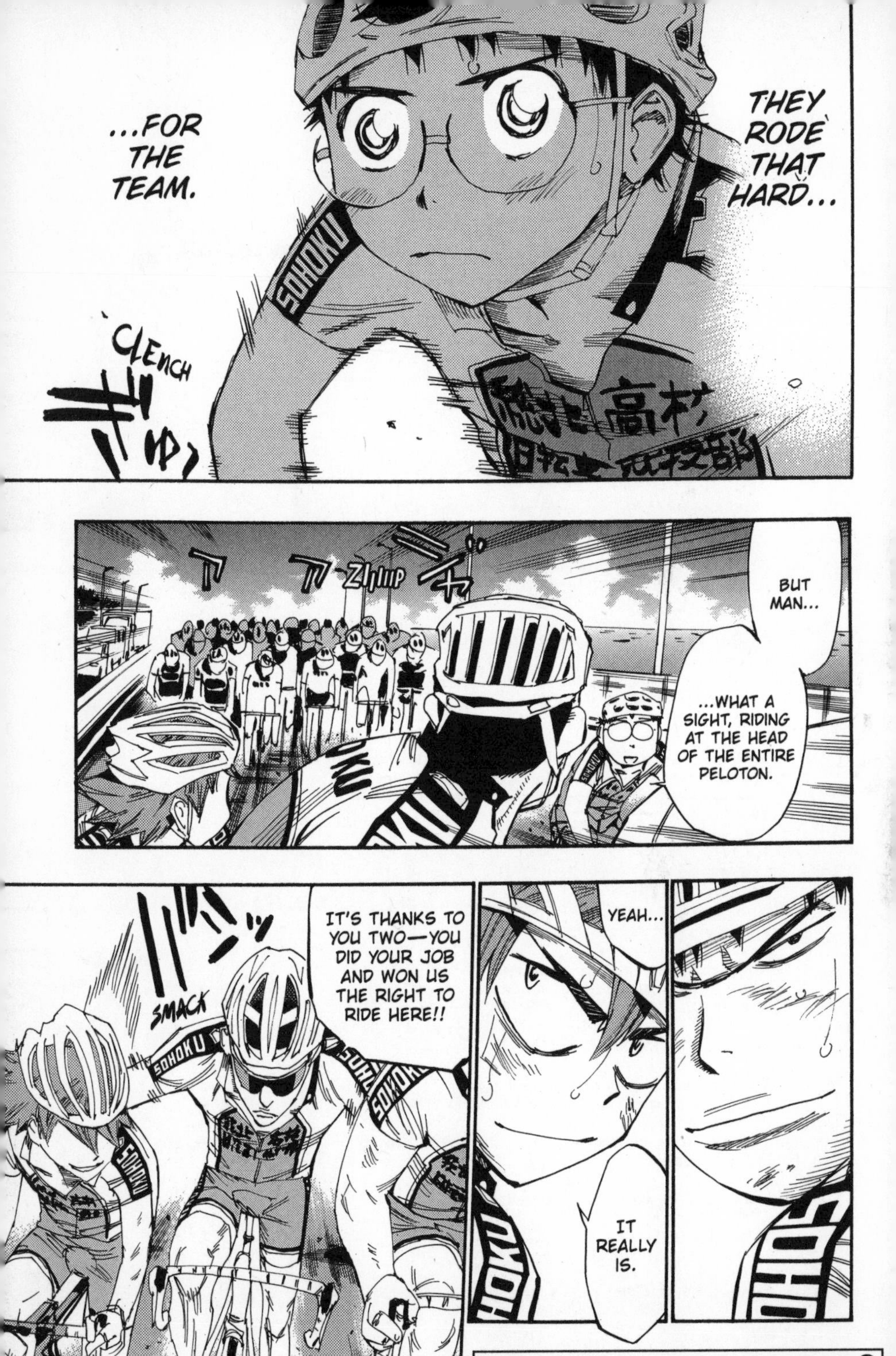
THEY RODE THAT HARD...
...FOR THE TEAM.
CLENCH
ZHUUP
BUT MAN...
...WHAT A SIGHT, RIDING AT THE HEAD OF THE ENTIRE PELOTON.
YEAH...
IT REALLY IS.
IT'S THANKS TO YOU TWO—YOU DID YOUR JOB AND WON US THE RIGHT TO RIDE HERE!!
SMACK

TO BE CONTINUED IN YOWAMUSHI PEDAL VOLUME 6

YOWAMUSHI PEDAL ⑤

WATARU WATANABE

Translation: Su Mon Han

Lettering: Lys Blakeslee, Brndn Blakeslee

This book is a work of fiction. Names, characters, places, and incidents are the product of the author's imagination or are used fictitiously. Any resemblance to actual events, locales, or persons, living or dead, is coincidental.

YOWAMUSHI PEDAL Volume 9, 10
© 2009, 2010 Wataru Watanabe
All rights reserved.
First published in Japan in 2009, 2010 by Akita Publishing Co., Ltd., Tokyo.
English translation rights arranged with Akita Publishing CO., Ltd. through Tuttle-Mori Agency, Inc., Tokyo.

English translation © 2017 by Yen Press, LLC

Yen Press
1290 Avenue of the Americas
New York, NY 10104

Visit us at yenpress.com
facebook.com/yenpress
twitter.com/yenpress
yenpress.tumblr.com
instagram.com/yenpress

First Yen Press Edition: April 2017

Yen Press is an imprint of Yen Press, LLC.
The Yen Press name and logo are trademarks of Yen Press, LLC.

The publisher is not responsible for websites (or their content) that are not owned by the publisher.

Library of Congress Control Number: 2015960124

ISBNs: 978-0-316-39367-6 (paperback)
       978-0-316-47132-9 (ebook)

10 9 8 7 6 5 4 3 2 1

BVG

Printed in the United States of America